Alyson A. Grine and Emily Coward

Raising Issues of Race in North Carolina Criminal Cases

2014

UNC SCHOOL OF GOVERNMENT

Printed in the United States of America

21 20 19 18 17 2 3 4 5 6

ISBN 978-1-56011-759-9

Z. Smith Reynolds
FOUNDATION

This publication was made possible by the support of the Z. Smith Reynolds Foundation. The views expressed in this publication do not necessarily reflect the views of the Foundation.

Contents

Note: Each chapter includes a detailed table of contents.

Preface

When we began considering this project in 2011, we had a broad sense of what we wanted to cover. We believed it important to provide North Carolina court actors with a comprehensive, reliable, and accessible resource on the ways in which issues of race may arise in criminal proceedings, from the beginning of a case to its conclusion, and how best to address them. Little did we realize the depth, breadth, and complexity of the issues, legal and social, that we had undertaken to address. After nearly three years of work, we are excited to release this first-ever reference manual, in North Carolina or elsewhere, devoted to these issues. We hope that the manual will aid defenders, court officials, law enforcement officers, and others who work so hard to uphold the integrity of our criminal justice system and keep it free from improper influences.

This manual would not have been possible without the support and assistance of many people. First and foremost, we wish to express gratitude to the Z. Smith Reynolds Foundation for its generous financial support of this project. Thanks go to the members of the manual's Advisory Board: Tye Hunter, former Executive Director of the Center for Death Penalty Litigation; Breana Smith Jeter, Attorney with Moore & Van Allen and former Assistant Public Defender for Mecklenburg County; Mary Pollard, Executive Director of North Carolina Prisoner Legal Services, Inc.; Richard Rosen, UNC School of Law Professor Emeritus; and James E. Williams Jr., Public Defender for Orange and Chatham Counties. They volunteered their time to review each chapter, offered their insights into the theory and practice of criminal defense, and endured long meetings to see this project to its conclusion. John Rubin, Albert Coates Professor of Public Law and Government at the UNC School of Government, supported the development of this manual, reviewing multiple drafts of each chapter and providing input on the content and presentation. Christopher Tyner, a research attorney at the School of Government, made important contributions to the research and writing of this manual. We also want to thank the many attorneys who responded to our questions and shared their insights and experiences with us as we wrote this manual. Special recognition also goes to the Office of Indigent Defense Services and the School of Government for supporting this manual. Their collaboration on this and other education projects has enhanced the resources available to indigent defense attorneys and the service they are able to provide their clients. Finally, thanks go to the members of the Publications, Marketing and Communications, and Information Technology Divisions of the School of Government for their assistance in designing and producing the manual.

A word about terminology: When it comes to descriptions of an individual's race or ethnicity, a myriad of viewpoints exists regarding language usage. For example, the terms "Latino" and "Hispanic" are often used interchangeably, but research suggests that these terms are not widely embraced by those they aim to describe.[1] While both terms receive their fair share of criticism, this manual will use the term "Latino" instead of "Hispanic" whenever

---

[1] *See, e.g.*, PAUL TAYLOR ET AL., PEW HISPANIC CENTER, WHEN LABELS DON'T FIT: HISPANICS AND THEIR VIEWS OF IDENTITY (2012) (finding that a majority of Hispanics or Latinos identify with their family's country of origin rather than with pan-ethnic labels).

possible. This choice reflects both our sense that the term "Latino" is generally viewed as a more inclusive term than "Hispanic" and our understanding that the term "Hispanic" was coined by the U.S. Census Bureau and did not originate from within the culture.[2] When discussing studies, the terms for racial and ethnic categories conform to the terms used in the studies described. So, for example, if a researcher refers to "Hispanics" rather than "Latinos," this manual will do the same. The terms "White" and "Black" are capitalized, as they refer to cultural groups and therefore will be treated as proper nouns.[3] The terms "Black" and "African American" will be used interchangeably, though "Black" is the preferred term as it is more inclusive.[4] "African American" will not be hyphenated to avoid any derogatory implications associated with "hyphenated Americans."[5]

This manual, current through September 2014, is a reference in the School's Indigent Defense Manual Series, available at http://defendermanuals.sog.unc.edu. Although the manuals are aimed at helping indigent defenders do their jobs effectively, we also hope they provide a useful, reliable review of the law for everyone working in the court system.

Any errors in the manual are our own. Comments and suggestions are welcome. They may be sent to Alyson Grine at the School of Government, CB #3330, Knapp-Sanders Building, The University of North Carolina at Chapel Hill, Chapel Hill, North Carolina 27599-3330. She can also be reached by telephone at (919) 966-4248 or by e-mail at agrine@sog.unc.edu.

Alyson Grine
Emily Coward
Fall 2014

---

[2] "Latino" refers to people of Latin American descent, while "Hispanic" refers to people of Spanish-speaking origin.

[3] *See, e.g.*, Kimberlé Williams Crenshaw, *Race, Reform, and Retrenchment: Transformation and Legitimation in Antidiscrimination Law*, 101 HARV. L. REV. 1331, 1332 n.2 (1988) (arguing that "Blacks, like Asians [and] Latinos, . . . constitute a specific cultural group and, as such, require denotation as a proper noun").

[4] Alex M. Johnson, Jr., *Defending the Use of Quotas in Affirmative Action: Attacking Racism in the Nineties*, 1992 U. ILL. L. REV. 1043, 1044 n.4 (1992) ("It is more convenient to invoke the terminological differentiation between black and white than say, between African-American and Northern European-American, which would be necessary to maintain semantic symmetry . . . .").

[5] *See* Patricia T. O'Conner & Stewart Kellerman, *Hyphenated Americans*, GRAMMARPHOBIA (Jan..27, 2012) (blog post explaining that dictionaries and style guides differ on the question of hyphenating terms such as African American and cautioning that hyphenation has been suggestive of bias).

About the North Carolina Indigent Defense Manual Series

The North Carolina Indigent Defense Manual Series is a collection of reference manuals addressing law and practice in areas in which indigent defendants and respondents are entitled to the representation of counsel at state expense. The series was created to address the need for comprehensive, up-to-date reference materials for public defenders and appointed counsel, who devote their time, skill, and effort to representing poor people. In addition to assisting indigent defenders with their responsibilities, the manuals may be useful to others who work in the court system and who need a reference source on the law. In keeping with the School of Government's commitment to practical scholarship, the manuals are written by authors with subject-matter expertise in their respective fields, experience in developing effective educational materials, and knowledge of how things work in practice. The editor of the series is John Rubin, a member of the School of Government faculty who specializes in indigent defense education. View the manuals in the series at http://defendermanuals.sog.unc.edu. Production of the series is made possible by funding from the North Carolina Office of Indigent Defense Services, which is responsible for overseeing and enhancing the provision of indigent defense representation in North Carolina.

About the Authors of Raising Issues of Race in North Carolina Criminal Cases

Alyson A. Grine has served as the Defender Educator at the School of Government since 2006, focusing on criminal law and procedure and indigent defense education. Prior to 2006, she worked for five years as an assistant public defender in Orange and Chatham counties. She served as a judicial clerk for Chief Justice Henry Frye of the North Carolina Supreme Court in 2000 and for Justice (then Judge) Patricia Timmons-Goodson of the North Carolina Court of Appeals in 1999. Ms. Grine earned a B.A. with distinction from UNC-Chapel Hill, an M.A. in Spanish from the University of Virginia, and a J.D. with honors from UNC-Chapel Hill. In 2012 she was honored with the School of Government's Albert and Gladys Hall Coates Teaching Excellence award. She is co-author of the North Carolina Juvenile Defender Manual and the North Carolina Defender Manual, Volume I (Pretrial).

Emily Coward has worked as a research attorney with the School of Government's Indigent Defense Education Group since 2012. She earned a B.A. from Oberlin College and a J.D. magna cum laude from Duke University School of Law. At Duke Law School, she served as lead articles editor for *Law and Contemporary Problems* and received the faculty award for outstanding achievement in criminal law and procedure in 2006. Ms. Coward served as a law clerk for Judge James Robertson of the United States District Court for the District of Columbia from 2006 to 2008, and for Justice Thembile Skweyiya of the Constitutional Court of South Africa in 2009. From 2009 to 2011, she represented clients in civil and post-conviction matters as a staff attorney with North Carolina Prisoner Legal Services.

Chapter 1
Recognizing and Addressing Issues of Race in Criminal Cases

1.1 Purpose of Manual

This practice manual aims to assist criminal defense attorneys and other court personnel in recognizing and addressing issues of race in criminal cases at the trial level in North Carolina. In particular, the manual seeks to help attorneys identify and respond to improper considerations of race in criminal cases in accordance with their duty of zealous advocacy and obligation to ensure that their clients get a fair and impartial trial.

Racial disparities in criminal cases raise numerous concerns, including the possibility that race could affect particular stages within a case, the ultimate outcome of a case, and the actual or perceived fairness of the criminal justice system. For example, concerns about fairness may arise if the jury pool does not reflect the makeup of the community or if a defendant of one race is released on bond while a similarly situated defendant of another race remains in jail pretrial.

The following explanation of racial disparity is a useful guide:

> Racial disparity in the criminal justice system exists when the proportion of a racial or ethnic group within the control of the system is greater than the proportion of such groups in the general population. . . . *Illegitimate or unwarranted* racial disparity in the criminal justice system results from the dissimilar treatment of similarly situated people based on race.[1]

Racial disparities may be produced not only by intentional discrimination; seemingly race-neutral policies may result in disparities because of the influence of implicit bias or structural factors, discussed further below. Regardless of their cause, racial disparities may not only affect case outcomes but also may undermine confidence in the criminal justice system and harm communities.[2] The manual examines the contexts in which racial disparities may arise and the ways that defense attorneys may address those disparities and their causes.

In an effort to provide concrete tools for court actors, the bulk of the manual is comprised of legal analyses, practice tips, and tools such as sample motions. Throughout the manual, we have incorporated anecdotes in which North Carolina practitioners share their experiences in recognizing issues of race in a particular defendant's case. For example, a defense attorney may describe the procedures he or she used to raise the issue in court, the response or outcome that followed, and what the attorney might have done differently in retrospect. Where relevant, chapters include suggestions for systemic changes and provide examples of collaborations between court actors, such as defense attorneys, prosecutors, and judges, to address concerns about racial disparities in their jurisdictions.

Several issues are beyond the scope of this manual. This manual focuses primarily on noncapital cases and does not examine the role that race may play in the imposition of the death penalty. The manual also does not address possible questions of race in the appellate process, commutation, parole, and the treatment of prison inmates and jail detainees. The manual explores the ways in which law enforcement misconduct may be challenged in criminal cases, but does not address law enforcement misconduct claims in civil cases.

We recognize that African Americans are not the only ones who may experience bias in the criminal justice system. North Carolina is a diverse state, and other racial or ethnic groups, such as Latinos, Native Americans, and Asians, may be subject to discriminatory treatment. This manual addresses bias that pertains to race, skin color, and ethnicity, such as in vehicle stops resulting from "profiling" or targeting of individuals based on their actual or perceived association with a racial or ethnic group. This manual does not cover in depth issues relating to immigration law or language access. When appropriate, this manual includes cross-references to other resources on those topics.[3]

Finally, we recognize that the topic of race is challenging, emotionally charged, and often controversial. The term "race" itself is complex and subject to different interpretations.[4] This manual does not try to resolve debates about the meaning of race. We are primarily concerned with differential treatment that people may receive in the criminal justice system based on perceptions of their race. When we refer to race and ethnicity in this manual, we are referring to "groups of people loosely bound together by history, ancestry, and socially significant elements of their physical appearance"; these categories, in turn, "are given meaning by society . . . [and are] self-reinforcing processes rooted in the daily decisions we make as individuals and institutions."[5]

While race may not be an easy subject to address, it cannot be ignored. Defense attorneys have an obligation to identify and challenge disparate treatment of their clients based on race. Doing so may help to protect clients' rights, foster a trusting attorney-client relationship, encourage scrutiny of possible unwarranted racial disparities in the criminal process, and promote fairness in the administration of criminal justice.

1.2 Scope of Chapter

This chapter is intended to provide a foundation for the discussion that follows, and addresses key concepts, such as: What is bias? What are its potential sources? What factors other than bias may contribute to racial disparities in the criminal justice system? What role does a defense lawyer have with regard to raising bias and these other factors during the course of representation? Many scholarly works examine the existence and causes of racial disparities in the criminal justice system, and some of these works are in conflict. This chapter is not intended to resolve those debates, but instead to distill major principles from the scholarly work and to provide a context, working vocabulary, and framework for considering issues of race in the criminal justice system.

1.3 Potential Factors Relevant to Racial Disparities in the Criminal Justice System

This section identifies factors that may contribute to racial disparities in the criminal justice system, including structural racialization, implicit and explicit bias, crime rates, and legislation. This discussion is not intended to quantify the extent to which these factors may be the cause of racial disparities in the criminal justice system. Instead, the aim of the discussion is to introduce concepts relevant to the consideration of racial bias, provide an overview of current research into racial disparities in the justice system, and suggest steps to take in addressing these issues.

A. Structural Racialization

The term "structural racialization," also referred to as "structural racism," stands for the principle that structures, such as neighborhoods and schools, shape opportunities in racially uneven ways. One scholar explains that "the structural model helps us analyze how housing, education, employment, transportation, health care, and other systems interact to produce racialized outcomes . . . and how structures shape life chances."[6] Some scholars think that this framework helps to explain racial disparities in the criminal justice system because it accounts for factors such as poverty, culture, and history.[7]

Structural racialization does not depend on a bad actor or even a bad act, but instead describes the interrelated forces that contribute to inequality.[8] "[R]ather than understanding racism as an isolated or individual phenomenon, a structural racism approach understands it as an outcome and suggests that different societal institutions work together to distribute or limit opportunity along racial lines."[9] Unlike other formulations of racism that rely on individual acts of prejudice, "[s]tructural racism operates automatically and thus is perpetuated simply by doing nothing about it."[10]

Lawyers can use this framework to think beyond the confines of the courtroom when analyzing a case. For example, some pretrial release programs utilize electronic monitoring devices that require a telephone in the home. If a defendant is homeless or living in a home without a phone, this option is not available. Because people of color are overrepresented in impoverished communities, a policy of releasing only those people who can be monitored telephonically will have a disproportionate impact on minorities, and a lawyer may be able to challenge it on that basis.[11] A lawyer who recognizes the potential impact of structural racialization on his or her client may discover opportunities for advocacy where another lawyer would simply see insurmountable poverty issues.

Additionally, a structural analysis may help attorneys relay their clients' experiences in a more detailed—and therefore more compelling—way to prosecutors, judges, and others. For example, in plea negotiations, a lawyer could explain to a prosecutor that her client was expelled from the Wake County school system as a result of a zero-tolerance policy that was applied overwhelmingly to youth of color.[12] This framework might also be useful in explaining to a judge the influence of racial profiling on a client's criminal record. In *U.S. v. Leviner*, 31 F. Supp. 2d 23 (D. Mass. 1998), for example, a federal judge imposed a reduced sentence on a Black defendant based on a finding that most of his prior convictions arose out of traffic stops conducted by the Boston police, and that the unlawful practice of racial profiling may have contributed to his prior record.

An understanding of structural racialization may facilitate collaboration among actors in the criminal justice system.[13] Through this lens, criminal defense attorneys, judges, prosecutors, probation officers, law enforcement officers, and community leaders can address racial disparities without battles over causation or fault, and ask critical questions, such as: Is there a practice or policy in effect that is producing racial inequality in our jurisdiction? If so, what steps can we take to remedy the harm?

B. Overview of Bias

Unlike structural racialization, which describes a socio-cultural phenomenon, bias describes a mental state. Racial bias refers to positive or negative racial preferences, either conscious (explicit) or unconscious (implicit).[14] As one scholar observes:

> [A] typical trial courtroom setting mixes together many people, often strangers, from different social backgrounds, in intense, stressful, emotional, and sometimes hostile contexts. In such environments, a complex jumble of implicit and explicit biases will inevitably be at play. It is the primary responsibility of the judge and other court staff

> to manage this complex and bias-rich social situation to the end that fairness and justice be done—and be seen to be done.[15]

The possible impact of these forms of bias on the criminal justice system is discussed below.

C. Explicit Bias

Of the two broad formulations of bias, explicit bias is easier to recognize. "Explicit bias is a conscious preference (positive or negative) for a social category," and a person who expresses explicit bias does so knowingly.[16] Explicit bias may not be readily observable, however. "If no social norm against these biases exists within a given context, a person will freely broadcast them to others. But if such a norm exists, then explicit biases can be concealed to manage the impressions that others have of us."[17] One example of explicit bias in the criminal justice system is former Los Angeles detective Mark Fuhrman's use of over 40 racial slurs recorded on a series of audiotapes, portions of which were introduced into evidence in the O.J. Simpson murder trial.[18] In a more recent example, Justice Sotomayor criticized a prosecutor's cross-examination as racially biased and unconstitutional when the prosecutor challenged a defendant's testimony by asking, "You've got African-Americans, you've got Hispanics, you've got a bag full of money. Does that tell you—a light bulb doesn't go off in your head and say This is a drug deal?"[19]

Manifestations of explicit bias are evident in North Carolina history. For example, in the early 1800's, North Carolina laws imposed harsher punishment on Black offenders than White offenders: the rape of a white woman was a capital offense when committed by enslaved or free Blacks but not when committed by Whites.[20] After ratification of the Thirteenth Amendment officially abolishing slavery in 1865, explicit bias continued in North Carolina by means of a "Black Code" preventing freed African Americans from voting, serving on juries, bearing arms, and exercising other rights. North Carolina's Black Code was intended to replicate the controls of slavery. According to historian Laura F. Edwards, the Code's purpose was to ensure that newly free African Americans would not "be confused with citizens . . . acquir[ing] only the duties and obligations, not the rights of freedom."[21] The explicit bias in North Carolina's Black Code was followed by other manifestations of overt discrimination, such as the ban on miscegenation, and—beginning in the last quarter of the nineteenth century and persisting through much of the twentieth century—the establishment of Jim Crow laws denying African Americans access to public spaces, opportunities, and resources.

A recent example of explicit bias in the criminal justice context is illustrated by *Miller-El v. Dretke*, 545 U.S. 231 (2005), in which the court recognized that a particular prosecutor's office had intentionally excluded minorities from jury service for many years. The court observed:

> [T]he District Attorney's Office had adopted a formal policy to exclude minorities from jury service. . . . A manual entitled 'Jury

> Selection in a Criminal Case' . . . [had been] distributed to prosecutors. It contained an article authored by a former prosecutor (and later a judge) under the direction of his superiors in the District Attorney's Office, outlining the reasoning for excluding minorities from jury service. Although the manual was written in 1968, i t remained in circulation until 1976, if not later[.][22]

Similarly, at a national prosecutors' training, participants were given cheat sheets identifying race-neutral peremptory strike justifications to use when responding to claims that a prosecutor's peremptory strike was based on race.[23]

Many criminal justice reforms have been enacted since the time of North Carolina's Black Code, and overt racial bias is no longer codified in North Carolina's laws. However, bias may still influence North Carolina criminal justice processes and may creep into individual cases via decision-making of individual actors. For example, in a 2002 hearing on a motion to dismiss, a North Carolina defense attorney testified that a highway trooper had justified pulling over his client in a previous case as follows: "[I]f they're Hispanic and they're driving, they're probably drunk."[24] In the case in which that testimony was offered, the N.C. Court of Appeals conducted an extensive review of evidence that the same trooper's stop of a Latino driver was racially motivated. Ultimately, the court upheld the trial judge's finding that the driver's seat belt, which the trooper had claimed was not buckled, was not actually visible to the trooper and therefore the stop was unlawful.

D. Implicit Bias

History and definition. Implicit biases are attitudes and stereotypes that people are not aware of, but that can influence their thoughts and behavior. These biases result from the brain's natural tendency to categorize stimuli into various categories or "schemas.".[25] All people rely on schemas to help sort the vast amount of information facing them each day, and schemas often involve stereotypes.[26] As scholar john powell puts it, "[w]e cannot live without schemas. Having biases and stereotypes does not make us racist, it makes us human."[27]

Research suggests that people may not be aware of their own biases. In fact, an implicit bias may conflict with a consciously held belief.[28] For example, an employer may believe in equal opportunity hiring, but pass over a Black applicant for a job based on lack of relevant experience without realizing that White applicants with similar experience levels have not been eliminated.[29] In the criminal justice context, Justice Marshall recognized that "[a] prosecutor's own [possibly] . . . unconscious racism may lead him easily to the conclusion that a prospective black juror is 'sullen,' or 'distant,' a characterization that would not have come to his mind if a white juror had acted identically."[30] As the examples suggest, while implicit biases may arise from our natural tendency to associate categories, they may result in disparate treatment when they go unexamined.

Researchers have been interested in the brain's tendency to link racial categories with positive or negative attributes for some time. Many will be familiar with Kenneth and Mamie Clark's famous "doll test" conducted in the 1940's, which demonstrated that Black children preferred White dolls to Black dolls and were more likely to describe Black dolls as "bad" and White dolls as "nice."[31] This study was recreated by filmmaker Kiri Davis in 2007 with similar results.[32] The "doll test" was cited by the U.S. Supreme Court when it declared school segregation unconstitutional in 1954.[33] Today, implicit bias researchers address the same types of questions with more sophisticated techniques to measure unconscious attitudes and prejudices. In one example, an implicit bias study in the criminal justice context discovered that participants held implicit associations between "Black" and "guilty" and that these associations predicted the ways in which participants evaluated ambiguous evidence.[34]

In recent years, social scientists have gained significant insights into the operation of implicit biases. The largest study of implicit bias is the Implicit Association Test (IAT), an electronically administered test that "revolutionized the way the world looked at and understood implicit bias."[35] The IAT emerged in the 1990s and has been administered over six million times.[36] In administering the IAT, researchers discovered that "the majority of tested Americans harbor negative implicit attitudes and stereotypes toward blacks [and] dark-skinned people . . . among others. . . . [P]eople consistently implicitly associate black with negative attitudes such as *bad* and *unpleasant*, and with negative stereotypes such as *aggressive* and *lazy*."[37] Scholar Jerry Kang illustrates how implicit biases may play out in the courtroom through this example: "Do we associate aggressiveness with Black men, such that we see them as more likely to have started the fight than to have responded in self-defense?"[38]

Studies specific to the criminal justice system raise concerns about the potential impact of implicit biases. Two studies found that criminal defendants with a relatively greater degree of what one study termed "Afrocentric" and what another study termed "stereotypically Black" facial features received more severe criminal punishment in some contexts.[39] Implicit racial biases have also been detected among judges and capital defense attorneys.[40] In another study, participants with implicit stereotypes of White lawyers as better litigators judged the performance of White litigators as superior, in accordance with their stereotypes.[41]

Litigating implicit bias. Awareness of implicit bias may empower criminal defense attorneys to neutralize or mitigate it in the courtroom. Research shows that implicit biases are malleable.[42] When the subject of race is addressed explicitly, people tend to correct for their implicit biases and act in accordance with more objective standards. For example, jury studies show that when racial considerations are relevant and are explicitly brought to the attention of the jury, White jurors tend to treat Black and White defendants similarly. Thus, the act of addressing race during voir dire may counteract its influence in jury deliberations. "However, when race is present as a factor but not highlighted, White jurors tend to treat Black defendants more harshly."[43] Further, "suppressing or denying prejudiced thoughts can actually increase prejudice rather than eradicate it."[44] These studies suggest that raising relevant issues of race in criminal trials may cause implicit biases to recede. Conversely, failing to raise issues of race may exacerbate bias or at least leave it in place.

Unexamined implicit bias may influence law enforcement practices. For example, disparities in drug arrests can result from police policies and practices in which "race shapes perceptions of who and what constitutes [the] drug problem, as well as the organizational response to that problem."[45] As a result of the police department's definition of the drug problem in Seattle, for example, police officers focused almost exclusively on crack cocaine sales.[46] Due in large part to this focus, 64.2 percent of drug arrestees were Black even though the majority of those who delivered serious drugs were White.[47] Closer to home, the Winston-Salem Police Department recently announced changes to its driver's license checkpoint policy after the North Carolina ACLU's Racial Justice Project reported the policy's disparate impact on minority drivers. While there was no evidence that the policy was designed to target people of color, "85 percent of the 244 traffic checkpoints set up by Winston-Salem police in an 11-month period were in predominantly minority areas."[48] Awareness of implicit bias research can help attorneys identify and challenge law enforcement policies and practices that have a disparate impact on minorities.

In addition, a defense attorney's awareness of his or her own implicit bias can improve client representation. Unexamined implicit biases may prevent an attorney from understanding the circumstances of a client's life or may cause the attorney to make inaccurate race-based assumptions about potential jurors or other court actors. For example, a lawyer may presume that Black people favor lenient sentencing and consequently fail to probe a prospective juror's opinions on punishment as well as experiences bearing on the case. As defense attorney Andrea Lyon argued, it is important for defense attorneys to "recognize our own biases and ensure that they do not inhibit our ability to represent our clients."[49]

Implicit bias studies may be introduced into evidence in individual cases when relevant. Consider, for example, *Brown v. Board of Education*,[50] in which the Supreme Court referred to seven different social science studies in holding that "separate but equal" violated the Equal Protection Clause.[51] More recently, courts have taken notice of the "growing body of social science recogniz[ing] the pervasiveness of unconscious racial and ethnic stereotyping and group bias," in contexts such as the alleged exclusion of certain ethnic minorities from jury service.[52] In one case, a federal judge relied in part on studies concerning implicit stereotypes of Asian Americans as passive in finding "a sizable risk that perceptions and decisions made here may have been affected by unconscious bias."[53]

Case study: A judge reflects on implicit bias. In the passage below, Judge Louis A. Trosch, Jr., District Court Judge for North Carolina District 26, reflects on the problem of implicit bias, including his own. His personal account captures, in ways that legal analyses may not fully convey, the importance of understanding and combating implicit bias in the criminal justice system.

I have been a District Court Judge for the past 13 years and have spent much of my time hearing juvenile court cases. About five years ago I found myself presiding over juvenile first appearance and detention hearings. One of the first cases that I called involved a newly filed armed robbery from a local fast food restaurant. Two young men were accused of attempting to rob the restaurant while wearing "Scream" masks and carrying handguns. They were not very accomplished robbers and were quickly apprehended.

When I called the first co-defendant's, who I'll refer to as Joe, case into the courtroom he entered from a holding cell wearing shackles and accompanied by two deputies. This was to be expected given the serious nature of the allegations and danger to the community. In addition, Joe's parents, grandparents, relatives, and pastor also came into the courtroom. I heard a short rendition of the facts and then heard from the attorneys and Juvenile Court Counselor (JCC) regarding Joe's detention status. As is typical in such serious cases, I ordered that Joe remain detained, but that the JCC investigate less restrictive alternatives, such as electronic monitoring or pre-trial supervision through our Alternatives to Detention (ATD) program. A detention review hearing was scheduled for the next week and the matter was adjourned. It was a pretty routine hearing really, except for the fact that Joe had no delinquent history of any kind. First offenders don't typically start off with such serious charges.

Thinking that a bit odd, I called in the co-defendant's, who I'll call Sam, case. The deputies didn't stir towards the holding cell. In fact, I was getting ready to remind them to retrieve the juvenile, when Sam walked into court with his family. He was dressed in khaki pants, a button down shirt and loafers rather than a jumpsuit and shackles. Like Joe, he also had a number of family members present to support him, along with his Coach. Everyone sat down and I proceeded with the first appearance. No one acknowledged the striking difference in circumstances between the two juveniles. I assumed there must be some difference between them that explained Joe being locked in detention while Sam was freed to live at home, so I began asking questions. Maybe Joe had been the one with the gun. No, they both had guns according to the police report. Maybe Joe was the mastermind or forced Sam into participating or was more threatening to the victims. Again the answer was no. As I asked more and more questions it became clear that Joe and Sam were alike in almost every way. They had been friends since childhood, they lived one street from one another, they both came from 2 parent families with tons of family support, both were average students with no history of suspensions, and both were involved in extracurricular activities, Joe in his church and Sam as a high school athlete. I couldn't come up with a significant difference in these two young men that explained their detention status, save one.

The fact that most readers of this account know implicitly what that difference was along with the race of each of these juveniles says much about how deeply race impacts all of us and the decisions we make. Just to be clear, Joe was Black and Sam was White. I do not believe that anyone explicitly decided to lock up the Black juvenile and release the White juvenile, but implicit bias powerfully influenced the decisions made by the police, the JCCs, and the attorneys in this case. After putting Sam into detention and ordering that the JCC look into alternatives to detention, I left the courtroom and sat down to think. How many times have less egregious disparities for children of color gone right by me, unnoticed and uncorrected. How many times had my own implicit biases affected my decisions. These are daunting questions for all of us who work in the justice system. The good news is that there are many, many steps that one can take to mitigate implicit bias, both individually and systemically. As a judge, it is critical that I learn as much as I can about implicit bias and take steps to overcome my own bias. It is a constant struggle, but it is essential to reach just decisions.

E. Discretionary Decision-Making and the Cumulative Nature of Disparities

Subjective decisions may be particularly vulnerable to the types of bias described in the preceding sections. One recent study of millions of school and juvenile justice records in Texas illustrates the cumulative effect of discretionary decision-making. The researchers found, for example, that students of all races were removed from school for mandatory disciplinary violations at comparable rates, but Black and Latino students were far more likely than White students to be disciplined for discretionary reasons.[54]

The exercise of discretion is an essential part of the criminal justice system. "It is neither desirable nor possible to eliminate discretion throughout the criminal justice system; professional judgment is a core component of making day-to-day operations manageable."[55] Nevertheless, criminal defense attorneys and other court actors must be alert to the risk of bias creeping in at the numerous junctures in a criminal case that involve subjective decision-making. Discretionary decisions in the criminal justice system—made by law enforcement officers, magistrates, judges, prosecutors, and defense attorneys—include:

- Where checkpoints should be set up
- Which vehicles should be stopped on a busy highway
- When a brief investigatory detention or "Terry stop" should be initiated
- Who should be asked for consent to search
- Who should be arrested
- Who should be charged and with what offense
- Whether to seek a transfer to superior court for a juvenile
- When a plea to a lesser charge should be offered
- Who should be indicted as a habitual felon
- Who should be released before trial and what conditions of pretrial release should be imposed
- Who should be advised to accept a guilty plea
- Which prospective jurors to strike peremptorily
- Who should be sentenced to active time and who should be sentenced to probation

Any one of these decisions can affect the direction and outcome of a case. For example, defendants who are denied pretrial release are less able to assist their attorneys, more likely to plead guilty, more likely to be found guilty if they go to trial, and more likely to receive a sentence of imprisonment if convicted.[56] Recent publications highlight that disparities at early stages of criminal proceedings may be compounded at successive stages and affect criminal case outcomes.[57]

Subjective decision-making may operate in tandem with other factors, such as structural racialization. One researcher concluded that outcomes in criminal cases are influenced not only by disparate treatment at certain key decision points, but also by structural factors such as a defendant's economic resources and networks of support, which may come into play at various stages in the criminal justice process.[58]

In drug cases in particular, the cumulative effect of subjective decision-making may have a racially disparate impact. For example, racial disparities in drug convictions are more pronounced than racial disparities in drug arrests.[59] Drug cases are discussed further in subsection F., below.

F. Crime Rates

Any discussion of racial disparities in the criminal justice system must address the question of whether minority overrepresentation in the justice system is simply a reflection of racially disparate crime rates. "The primary debate has been between those who argue that there are problematic racial disparities and those who argue or imply that observed differences in rates of imprisonment are for the most part 'warranted' by differential criminal involvement by the races."[60] This brief discussion does not attempt to resolve this issue; instead, it identifies key considerations and additional resources.

In the context of drug offenses, data indicate that racially disparate arrest, conviction, and incarceration rates do not reflect actual offense rates. In 2006, African Americans represented 35% of those arrested for drug offenses and 53% of drug convictions, but that same year, according to the U.S. Department of Health and Human Services, African Americans made up only 14% of drug users.[61] In other words, although Blacks and Whites use drugs at roughly the same rates, African Americans are substantially more likely to be arrested and convicted for drug offenses. In North Carolina, Black inmates accounted for 84% of those admitted to prison for drug offenses in 1996, although only 22% of the State's population was Black.[62] Beyond the drug offense context, the data is less clear. Unlike the rate of drug use, which is tracked by health departments, crime commission rates in other contexts are generally extrapolated from other criminal justice statistics.[63]

Some criminologists have relied on arrest rate statistics as a proxy for offense rates.[64] The Uniform Crime Reports (UCR) published by the Federal Bureau of Investigation is one commonly cited source of national arrest rate data.[65] In 2006, for example, the UCR indicated that African Americans accounted for 39% of people arrested for violent crime and 31% of all people arrested for property crime.[66] These arrest statistics, however, do not necessarily reflect offense rates by African Americans. Experts increasingly recognize that arrest and offense rates cannot be equated.[67] Arrest rates are influenced by factors such as discretionary decisions by officers, distribution of police in low-income neighborhoods, and policies and priorities of various police departments. In other words, if "criminal investigations focus on African Americans, more African Americans necessarily will be arrested and convicted of crimes, thereby creating a self-fulfilling prophesy."[68] Some research suggests that minority suspects are more likely to be arrested than White suspects.[69] Additionally, arrest rates do not capture crimes that are *not* reported to the police, which account for more than half of all violent crimes and over 60% of all property crimes.[70]

Another method employed by criminologists when estimating offense rates is to use "victimization survey data in which victims identify the perceived race of their assailant," such as the National Crime Victimization Survey (NCVS).[71] Data collected by the NCVS can be viewed on the website of the U.S. Bureau of Justice Statistics.[72] However, there are some concerns about the reliability of data collected from victims about the race of offenders, as "perception bias on the part of victims with respect to offender race presents an intractable problem with NCVS race and crime data."[73] The data collected by the NCVS is also incomplete: "information about victim perceptions of perpetrators' race is available for only a few violent offenses," so "crime victimization survey data present an incomplete picture of crime commission rates by race."[74]

Racially disparate arrest and victimization rates also do not explain racial disparities in imprisonment rates. One criminologist concludes, "[a]lthough violent crime arrest rates for Blacks are higher than for Whites, the differential has long been declining. Group differences in violent crime do not explain racial disparities in prison."[75]

G. Legislation

Laws passed by local, state, and federal legislatures can significantly affect the racial composition of the population that is involved with the criminal justice system. In one of the most well-known examples of this phenomenon, the Anti-Drug Abuse Act of 1986 employed a 100:1 crack/cocaine sentencing differential in federal criminal sentencing. Thus, the Act created harsher penalties for drug offenses involving crack (disproportionately used by African American cocaine users) than for offenses involving powder cocaine (used more by White cocaine users). For example, a person convicted of possessing only 5 grams of crack cocaine was subject to the same mandatory prison sentence (5 years) as a person convicted of possessing 500 grams of powder cocaine. This sentencing scheme had a remarkably disproportionate impact on African Americans and, in the words of one court, had no "penological or scientific justification."[76]

At the time the law was passed, the media portrayed "crack-user horror stories" in which "[i]mages of young black men [involved in the drug trade] . . . saturated the screens of our televisions . . . . [and] branded onto the public mind and the minds of legislators that young black men were solely responsible for the drug crisis in America."[77] Congress considered these media accounts in concluding that crack cocaine caused violence and crack users posed a greater threat to society than cocaine users.[78] Scientific evidence, however, refuted the notion that crack was more addictive and caused users to be more violent, and showed that the effects of powder cocaine and crack cocaine on the body are essentially identical.[79]

Lawyers, scientists, the U.S. Sentencing Commission, judges and others all called for the repeal of the 100:1 crack/cocaine federal sentencing ratio. Although the ratio remained law for 24 years, in 2010 Congress modified the ratio to 18:1.[80] Data from this period shows the racially disparate impact of the crack/cocaine distinction. During the period in which the 100:1 ratio was in effect, the average time African American drug offenders served in federal prison increased by 77%, compared to an increase of 33% for Caucasian offenders.[81] The average federal drug sentence for African Americans was 11% higher than the average federal drug sentence for Whites when the Anti-Drug Abuse Act was passed in 1986; four years later that disparity had grown to 49%.[82] In 2010, the year the law was changed, almost 80% of those sentenced under federal crack cocaine laws were African Americans, and less than 8% were White.[83] Changes in drug laws and sentencing for drug offenses have been identified as playing a role in the decreasing incarceration rate for African Americans; however, while the rate has declined over the last decade, it still exceeds the incarceration rate of Whites and Latinos.[84]

Racial disparities related to legislation can be found at the state level as well. Three strike schemes and other habitual offender laws have been adopted by many states. By the mid-1990s, "'repeat offender' laws [had been] passed in forty-one states as well as in the federal system, and twenty-four states [had] enacted 'three strikes' laws."[85] North Carolina's habitual felon law imposes a significant sentencing enhancement for a defendant who, having already been convicted of three felonies, commits a fourth.[86] This enhancement does not attach automatically on conviction of a fourth felony; rather, prosecutors have discretion whether to indict a person as a habitual felon. Statistics suggest that the law has had disparate results. The NCAJ Task Force on Racial and Ethnic Bias reports that "African Americans are 2.46 times as likely to be incarcerated as habitual felons than Caucasians" and represent "70% of all incarcerated habitual felons."[87]

Because of concerns about the potential impact of sentencing legislation, Minnesota, Iowa, Oregon, and Connecticut now require the preparation of racial impact statements during the legislative process to prevent unwarranted racial disparities in the criminal justice system.[88] In Florida, Mississippi, Wisconsin, and Arkansas, racial impact statement legislation has been introduced.[89] A racial impact statement serves as "a predictive report summarizing the effects that legislation may have on minority groups. The goal of these statements is to force lawmakers to confront the potential racial consequences of criminal sentencing policies prior to enacting new legislation."[90] North Carolina does not currently have such a procedure, but attorneys, other court actors, and community members can play a role in informing legislators about the potential racially disparate impact that may result from existing or proposed legislation.

1.4 Sources of Law

Below is a brief summary of the sources of law for addressing racial disparities in North Carolina criminal cases. These sources are discussed in greater detail in the applicable chapters of this manual.

Equal Protection. As long ago as 1891, the U.S Supreme Court recognized that under the Fourteenth Amendment, "no state can deprive particular persons or classes of persons of equal and impartial justice under the law."[91] The Equal Protection Clause has been the subject of numerous interpretations in the intervening years. As one scholar observed, however, it was "[n]ot until the last decade of the Warren Court," when heightened scrutiny became law, "[that] the equal protection clause evolve[d] from a largely moribund constitutional provision to a potent egalitarian instrument."[92]

Today, the Equal Protection Clause of the Fourteenth Amendment is an important source of rights for defendants challenging unequal treatment in the criminal justice system. It may be relied on by defendants challenging practices such as selective policing based on race,[93] selective prosecution based on race,[94] discrimination in the pretrial release setting,[95] racially biased jury selection procedures,[96] racially biased grand jury foreperson selection procedures,[97] race-based use of peremptory challenges,[98] and considerations of race at sentencing.[99]

Due Process. The Due Process Clause of the Fourteenth Amendment to the U.S. Constitution prevents states from depriving "any person of life, liberty, or property without due process of law." This right includes protections against racial bias in criminal cases. For example, the Due Process Clause is an important source of rights for defendants challenging an unreliably suggestive cross-racial identification.[100]

Fourth Amendment. The Fourth Amendment to the U.S. Constitution protects "[t]he right of the people to be secure in their persons, houses, papers, and effects, against unreasonable searches and seizures." Generally, evidence of a law enforcement officer's racially-motivated purpose cannot be considered in a Fourth Amendment challenge to a pedestrian or traffic stop. This is because "the constitutional basis for objecting to intentionally discriminatory application of laws is the Equal Protection Clause, not the Fourth Amendment. Subjective intentions play no role in ordinary, probable-cause Fourth Amendment analysis."[101]

However, a Fourth Amendment claim may succeed where reasonable suspicion is lacking or evidence of racially biased intent undermines the credibility of the officer's stated reason for a stop.[102] Additionally, a defendant may challenge as pretextual a license or other checkpoint where the real purpose of the stop was impermissible under the Fourth Amendment.[103]

Sixth Amendment. The Sixth Amendment to the U.S. Constitution requires that trial juries be drawn from a "fair cross-section" of the community.[104] Unlike an equal protection challenge, in which a defendant must show intentional discrimination in the composition of the jury venire, a fair cross-section challenge requires a defendant to demonstrate that the exclusion of a distinctive class of people was "systematic" or an inevitable result of the selection procedure.[105]

North Carolina Constitution. The North Carolina Constitution is a significant and sometimes overlooked source of protections against racial bias in criminal cases. Article I, section 19 provides:

> No person shall be taken, imprisoned, or disseized of his freehold, liberties, or privileges, or outlawed, or exiled, or in any manner deprived of his life, liberty, or property, but by the law of the land. No

> person shall be denied the equal protection of the laws; nor shall any person be subjected to discrimination by the State because of race, color, religion, or national origin.

The Equal Protection and Law of the Land Clauses in this section of the state constitution provide protections analogous to those in the Equal Protection and Due Process Clauses of the Fourteenth Amendment to the U.S. Constitution. The North Carolina Supreme Court has held generally that "[t]he law of the land and due process of law are interchangeable terms."[106] In general, "law of the land" and state equal protection challenges should be raised whenever parallel federal challenges, such as federal due process violations, are raised.

The North Carolina Constitution is a particularly important source of rights in the jury context. Article I, section 26 prohibits exclusion "from jury service on account of sex, race, color, religion, or national origin." This section, along with the "law of the land" clause in article I, section 19, may be relied on to challenge discrimination in the selection of a grand jury,[107] or in the selection of a grand jury foreperson.[108] Article I, section 24 of the N.C. Constitution guarantees the right to a trial by jury, providing that "[n]o person shall be convicted of any crime but by the unanimous verdict of a jury in open court. The General Assembly may, however, provide for other means of trial for misdemeanors, with the right of appeal for trial de novo." Defendants raising fair cross-section challenges may rely on this section as well as on article 1, section 26 of the N.C. Constitution.[109]

Outside of the jury context, article 1, section 27 of the North Carolina Constitution contains a provision prohibiting excessive bail, which may be useful to defendants raising challenges in the pretrial release context. It states: "Excessive bail shall not be required, nor excessive fines imposed, nor cruel or unusual punishments inflicted."

North Carolina statutes. Last, North Carolina statutes are a source of rights for criminal defendants challenging racial bias in a criminal case. Several statutes address law enforcement investigations.

To help address potential racial profiling, North Carolina law requires the Division of Criminal Information of the Department of Justice to collect statistics on traffic stops by state troopers and other state law enforcement officers.[110] This statute also requires the Division to collect statistics on many local law enforcement agencies.[111]

North Carolina statutes also provide rights relating to interrogation and eyewitness identification, such as the right to have counsel present during a nontestimonial identification procedure,[112] and the right to have live identification procedures videotaped whenever practical.[113] Such rights may be important in ensuring that race does not play an improper role in criminal cases. Nationwide, in over one third of wrongful convictions overturned by DNA testing, cross-racial eyewitness identification was used as evidence to convict the defendant.[114]

In the context of police interrogations, protections against coerced statements may be important for populations that are potentially susceptible to improper law-enforcement pressure. Recently enacted legislation expands interrogation recording requirements to include all custodial interrogations of juveniles conducted at a place of detention, along with all custodial interrogations conducted at a place of detention related to a "Class A, B1, or B2 felony, and any Class C felony of rape, sex offense, or assault with a deadly weapon with intent to kill inflicting serious injury."[115]

Requirements for motor vehicle checkpoints are also addressed by North Carolina law. Under G.S. 20-16.3A(d), the "placement of checkpoints should be random or statistically indicated, and agencies shall avoid placing checkpoints repeatedly in the same location or proximity."[116] Under G.S. 20-16.3A(2a), "no individual officer may be given discretion as to which vehicle is stopped or, of the vehicles stopped, which driver is requested to produce drivers license, registration, or insurance information."[117] Under G.S. 20-16.3A(a1), the pattern designated for stopping vehicles "shall not be based on a particular vehicle type" (other than commercial vehicles).[118] These statutes limit potential discrimination in checkpoint operations.

North Carolina statutes set forth procedures for invoking the exclusionary rule and suppressing evidence for a violation of a suspect's constitutional or statutory rights.[119] These provisions may warrant suppression of racially discriminatory actions.[120]

North Carolina statutes bearing on the trial and other aspects of a criminal case—such as G.S. 15A-1214(a), which provides that the selection of jurors from the jury pool for questioning must be random—are discussed where applicable in this manual.

1.5 Overcoming Concerns About Raising Race

Addressing issues of race in the criminal justice system is no easy task.

> The one thing that is absolutely certain about the American experience is that never in our history as a people have any of us, black or white, been "neutral" on the matter of race. It has been, and remains, the great overriding issue throughout all our history, in all our law, in all our institutions.[121]

Criminal defense attorneys face considerable obstacles when raising claims of racial bias. One writer notes that "enormous systemic, financial, and other pressures . . . make it extremely difficult . . . to raise and vindicate" such claims.[122] Large caseloads and limited resources magnify these challenges. However, public defenders and appointed counsel must remain alert to the issues discussed in this manual, since racial and ethnic minorities are more likely to live in poverty and therefore more likely to be represented by assigned counsel. African Americans are nearly five times as likely as Whites to rely on appointed counsel.[123]

Criminal defense attorneys have an obligation to advocate for their clients, including raising issues of race in appropriate cases. The North Carolina State Bar Rules of Professional Conduct (RPC) provide that attorneys must "act with commitment and dedication to the interests of the client and with zeal in advocacy upon the client's behalf."[124] The RPC state that a lawyer is "an officer of the legal system, and a public citizen having special responsibility for the quality of justice," who "should be mindful of deficiencies in the administration of justice."[125]

Why might some attorneys not raise issues of race when race may be adversely affecting a client's case? Some factors that might cause a lawyer to refrain from raising racial issues include:

- lack of awareness that race is an issue in the case,
- concern that a judge may reject the argument,
- unfamiliarity with supporting law, required factual showing, and strategies,
- reluctance to step outside of one's comfort zone,
- concern that this strategy may affect the case in unpredictable ways, and
- the existence of contrary legal precedent or the fear of creating bad precedent

This manual is intended to equip attorneys and other court actors with the information and tools they need to address issues of race effectively and overcome concerns such as those above. The chapters that follow identify ways in which racial considerations may unlawfully affect criminal cases and provide legal support and practical strategies for addressing those issues. Some concerns, such as the potential of weakening relationships with other court actors or creating bad precedent, are outweighed by the obligation an attorney owes to an individual client. In appropriate cases, the attorney has an ethical obligation to advance all arguments that would assist the client. Failing to do so may leave constitutional and other violations unaddressed, result in an incomplete record for appellate review, constitute ineffective assistance of counsel, and deprive the client of a fair trial.

Raising issues of race where appropriate in individual cases may have an aggregate positive effect even if the claims do not always succeed. Doing so may create an environment in which "race discrimination and bias issues are openly joined on the record instead of relegated to the background."[126] Everyone involved in the criminal justice system has a role in helping to stem racial discrimination, but defense attorneys have a particularly important voice. As recognized by the Equal Justice Initiative's report on racial discrimination in jury selection, "[t]he entire community—including prosecutors, judges, court administrators, civil rights and community groups, and elected officials—has a role to play in addressing this issue, but racial bias in the courtroom cannot be confronted effectively without vigilance and advocacy by defense lawyers."[127] We hope this manual helps North Carolina criminal defense attorneys recognize and raise issues of race in an informed and effective manner.

---

[1] ASHLEY NELLIS ET AL., THE SENTENCING PROJECT, REDUCING RACIAL DISPARITY IN THE CRIMINAL JUSTICE SYSTEM: A MANUAL FOR PRACTITIONERS AND POLICYMAKERS 1 (2d ed. 2008) (emphasis in original), *available at* www.sentencingproject.org/doc/publications/rd_reducingracialdisparity.pdf.

[2] Robert M.A. Johnson, *Chair's Counsel: Racial Bias in the Criminal Justice System and Why We Should Care*, ABA CRIMINAL JUSTICE, Winter 2007 (observing that we should care about racial disparities in the criminal justice system, whatever their cause, because "lack of trust severely impacts the criminal justice system's ability to serve and protect society").

[3] *See, e.g.*, SEJAL ZOTA & JOHN RUBIN, IMMIGRATION CONSEQUENCES OF A CRIMINAL CONVICTION IN NORTH CAROLINA (UNC School of Government 2008), *available at* http://defendermanuals.sog.unc.edu.

[4] *See, e.g.,* American Anthropological Association, *AAA Statement on Race*, 100 AMERICAN ANTHROPOLOGIST 712, 712 (1998) (observing that scientists have discovered greater genetic variation within racial groups than between them), *reproduction of statement available at* www.aaanet.org/stmts/racepp.htm; Natalie Angier, *Do Races Differ? Not Really, DNA Shows*, N.Y. TIMES, August 22, 2000 (reporting that researchers involved in sequencing human DNA declared that "there is only one race—the human race"), *available at* www.nytimes.com/library/national/science/082200sci-genetics-race.html; Ian F. Haney Lopez, *The Social Construction of Race: Some Observations on Illusion, Fabrication, and Choice*, 29 HARV. C.R.-C.L. L. REV. 1, 13 (1994) (concluding that "[t]he notion that humankind can be divided along White, Black, and Yellow lines reveals the social rather than the scientific origin of race"); JACQUELINE JONES, A DREADFUL DECEIT: THE MYTH OF RACE FROM THE COLONIAL ERA TO OBAMA'S AMERICA, xvii (2013) (stating that "[i]n the early twenty-first century, the words 'race,' 'racism,' and 'race relations,' are widely used as shorthand for specific historical legacies that have nothing to do with biological determinism and everything to do with power relations").

[5] Research Working Group & Task Force on Race and the Criminal Justice System, *Preliminary Report on Race and Washington's Criminal Justice System*, 47 GONZ. L. REV. 251, 258–59 (2012).

[6] john a. powell, *Structural Racism: Building Upon the Insights of John Calmore*, 86 N.C. L. REV. 791, 793 (2008); *see also* john a. powell, *How Implicit Bias and Structural Racialization Can Move Us Toward Social and Personal Healing, in* PATHWAYS TO RACIAL HEALING AND EQUITY IN THE AMERICAN SOUTH: A COMMUNITY PHILANTHROPY STRATEGY (U. of Ark. Clinton School of Public Service 2013), *available at* http://clintonschool.uasys.edu/wp-content/uploads/2013/12/Clinton-School-Compendium-2013.pdf.

---

[7] *See, e.g.*, William M. Wiecek, *Structural Racism and the Law in America Today: An Introduction*, 100 KY. L. J. 1 (2011); Jamie Fellner, *Race, Drugs, and Law Enforcement in the United States*, 20 STAN. L. & POL'Y REV. 257, 285–89 (2009).

[8] powell (2008), *supra* note 6, 86 N.C. L. REV. at 795–800.

[9] Kirwan Institute at Ohio State University, *Bibliographic Guide to Structural Racism*, *available at* http://www.scribd.com/doc/49092126/Kirwan-Institute-Structural-Racism-Bibliography.

[10] Wiecek, *supra* note 7, at 6–7 (listing eight characteristics that distinguish structural racism from more traditional formulations of racism).

[11] NELLIS ET AL., *supra* note 1, at 7.

[12] JASON LANGBERG ET AL., ADVOCATES FOR CHILDREN'S SERVICES, LAW ENFORCEMENT OFFICERS IN WAKE COUNTY SCHOOLS: THE HUMAN, EDUCATIONAL, AND FINANCIAL COSTS (2011), *available at* www.law.unc.edu/documents/faculty/sroreportv2.pdf.

[13] powell (2008), *supra* note 6, at 86 N.C. L. REV. 809 (noting the success of collaboration in other contexts).

[14] Shawn C. Marsh, *The Lens of Implicit Bias*, 18 JUVENILE AND FAMILY JUSTICE TODAY 16, 16–19 (Summer 2009), *available at* www.ncjfcj.org/sites/default/files/the%20lens%20of%20implicit%20bias.pdf.

[15] JERRY KANG, IMPLICIT BIAS: A PRIMER FOR COURTS 6 (National Center for State Courts 2009), *available at* www.ncsc.org/~/media/Files/PDF/Topics/Gender%20and%20Racial%20Fairness/kangIBprimer.ashx.

[16] Marsh, *supra* note 14, at 17.

[17] Jerry Kang et al., *Implicit Bias in the Courtroom*, 59 UCLA L. REV. 1124, 1132 (2012).

[18] Roger C. Park, *Character Evidence Issues in the O.J. Simpson Case—Or, Rationales of the Character Evidence Ban, with Illustrations from the Simpson Case*, 67 U. COLO. L. REV. 747, 758 (1996).

[19] *Calhoun v. United States*, 568 U.S. ___, 133 S.Ct. 1136, 1136 (2013) (Sotomayor, J., concurring in denial of cert.).

---

[20] Seth Kotch & Robert P. Mosteller, *The Racial Justice Act and the Long Struggle with Race and the Death Penalty in North Carolina*, 88 N.C. L. REV. 2031, 2046 (2010) (citing laws to this effect).

[21] Laura F. Edwards, *"The Marriage Covenant is at the Foundation of all Our Rights": The Politics of Slave Marriages in North Carolina after Emancipation*, 14 LAW & HIST. REV. 81, 96 n.30 (1996) (citing laws to this effect).

[22] *Miller-El v. Dretke*, 545 U.S. 231, 263–64 (2005) (citing *Miller-El v. Cockrell*, 537 U.S. 322, 334–35 (2003)).

[23] *See Top Gun II Batson Justifications: Articulating Juror Negatives* in the Race Materials Bank at www.ncids.org (select "Training & Resources").

[24] *State v. Villeda*, 165 N.C. App. 431, 432 (2004) (reviewing at length evidence that trooper's stop of Latino driver was racially motivated and upholding trial court's finding that trooper was not able to observe whether driver was wearing seat belt, in spite of trooper's testimony to the contrary).

[25] john powell & Rachel Godsil, *Implicit Bias Insights as Preconditions to Structural Change*, 20 POVERTY & RACE, no. 5 (Poverty & Race Research Action Council), 2011, at 4, *available at* http://prrac.org/newsletters/sepoct2011.pdf.

[26] Kang, *supra* note 15, at 1.

[27] PowerPoint Slides of john powell, *Exploring the Unconscious: The Dynamics of Race and Reconciliation* at 22 (2011 Dinner of Reconciliation, John Hope Franklin Center for Reconciliation), *available at* www.jhfcenter.org/wp-content/uploads/2009/09/john-powell.pdf.

[28] Jerry Kang, *Implicit Bias and Pushback from the Left*, 54 ST. LOUIS L.J. 1139, 1139 (2010).

[29] Marianne Bertrand & Sendhil Mullainathan, *Are Emily and Greg More Employable than Lakisha and Jamal? A Field Experiment on Labor Market Discrimination*, 94 THE AMERICAN ECONOMIC REVIEW 991, 991–1013 (2004).

[30] *Batson v. Kentucky,* 476 U.S. 79, 106 (1986) (Marshall, J., concurring).

[31] Kenneth B. Clark & Mamie P. Clark, *Racial Identification and Preference in Negro Children, in* READINGS IN SOCIAL PSYCHOLOGY 602, 602–11 (Eleanor E. Maccoby et al. eds., 3d ed. 1958); *see also* Film Documentary: A GIRL LIKE ME (Kiri Davis, Director, Reel Works Teen Filmmaking, 2006), (recreating the Clarks' doll experiment in 2007 with similar results), *available at* www.mediathatmattersfest.org/films/a_girl_like_me/.

[32] *See* Film Documentary: A GIRL LIKE ME, *supra* note 31.

[33] *Brown v. Board of Education*, 347 U.S. 483, 494 n.11 (1954).

[34] Justin D. Levinson et al., *Guilty by Implicit Racial Bias: The Guilty/Not Guilty Implicit Association Test*, 8 OHIO ST. J. CRIM. L. 187, 207 (2010).

[35] Robert J. Smith & Justin D. Levinson, *The Impact of Implicit Racial Bias on the Exercise of Prosecutorial Discretion*, 35 SEATTLE U. L. REV. 795, 801 (2012).

[36] Anna Roberts, *(Re)forming the Jury: Detection and Disinfection of Implicit Juror Bias*, 44 CONN. L. REV. 827, 847–49 (2012).

[37] Smith & Levinson, *supra* note 35, at 802 (emphasis in original) (citing published research).

[38] Kang, *supra* note 15, at 2.

[39] *See* Irene V. Blair et al., *The Influence of Afrocentric Facial Features in Criminal Sentencing*, 15 PSYCHOL. SCI. 674 (2004); Jennifer L. Eberhardt et al., *Looking Deathworthy: Perceived Stereotypicality of Black Defendants Predicts Capital-Sentencing Outcomes*, 17 PSYCHOL. SCI. 383 (2006).

[40] *See* Theodore Eisenberg & Sheri Lynn Johnson, *Implicit Racial Attitudes of Death Penalty Lawyers*, 53 DEPAUL L. REV. 1539, 1542 (2004); Jeffrey J. Rachlinski et al., *Does Unconscious Racial Bias Affect Trial Judges?*, 84 NOTRE DAME L. REV. 1195, 1195–96 (2009).

[41] Jerry Kang et al., *Are Ideal Litigators White? Measuring the Myth of Colorblindness*, 7 J. EMPIRICAL LEGAL STUD. 886 (2010).

[42] Kang, *supra* note 15, at 4–5.

[43] powell & Godsil, *supra* note 25, at 6.

[44] powell, *supra* note 27, at 23.

[45] Katherine Beckett et al., *Race, Drugs, and Policing: Understanding Disparities in Drug Delivery Arrests*, 44 CRIMINOLOGY 105, 105 (2006); *see also* KATHERINE BECKETT, RACE AND DRUG LAW ENFORCEMENT IN SEATTLE (2008), *available at* http://faculty.washington.edu/kbeckett/Race%20and%20Drug%20Law%20Enforcement%20in%20Seattle_2008.pdf.

[46] BECKETT (2008), *supra* note 45, at 15, 59–98 (concluding that, while the racial composition of those who deliver serious drugs in Seattle, the enforcement focus on outdoor drug activity, and the enforcement focus on the downtown drug trade all contributed modestly to racial disparities in Seattle drug arrests, the focus on crack-cocaine sales constituted the largest factor contributing to disparities).

[47] BECKETT (2008), *supra* note 45, at 11.

[48] John Hinton, *Police Will Use New Methods to Set Up Traffic Checkpoints*, WINSTON-SALEM JOURNAL, Sep. 10, 2012, *available at* www.journalnow.com/news/local/police-will-use-new-methods-to-set-up-traffic-checkpoints/article_08f0139a-26e2-520e-9756-239a3f23950a.html.

[49] Andrea D. Lyon, *Race Bias and the Importance of Consciousness for Criminal Defense Attorneys*, 35 SEATTLE U. L. REV. 755, 758 (2012).

[50] 347 U.S. 483, 494 n.11 (1954).

[51] Eva Paterson, *Litigating Implicit Bias*, 20 POVERTY & RACE, no. 5 (Poverty & Race Research Action Council) 2011, at 8, *available at* http://prrac.org/newsletters/sepoct2011.pdf.

[52] *Chin v. Runnels*, 343 F. Supp. 2d 891, 906 (N.D. Cal. 2004) (citing and considering such studies in ruling on a challenge to the alleged exclusion of certain ethnic minorities from service as foreperson on indicting grand jury), *aff'd sub nom. Chin v. Carey*, 160 F. App'x 633 (9th Cir. 2005) (unpublished).

[53] *Chin*, 343 F. Supp. 2d at 905–908.

[54] TONY FABELO, ET. AL., BREAKING SCHOOLS' RULES: A STATEWIDE SURVEY OF HOW SCHOOL DISCIPLINE RELATES TO STUDENTS' SUCCESS AND JUVENILE JUSTICE INVOLVEMENT (Council for State Gov'ts Justice Ctr. 2011), *available at* http://knowledgecenter.csg.org/kc/system/files/Breaking_School_Rules.pdf.

[55] NELLIS ET AL., *supra* note 1, at 11.

[56] Cynthia E. Jones, *"Give Us Free": Addressing Racial Disparities in Bail Determinations*, 16 N.Y.U. J. LEGIS. & PUB. POL'Y 919, 936–37 (2013) (citing various studies and scholarly articles to this effect).

[57] *See, e.g.*, Traci Schlesinger, *The Cumulative Effects of Racial Disparity in Criminal Processing*, THE ADVOCATE, May 2008, at 22, 27–32, *available at* http://apps.dpa.ky.gov/library/advocate/pdf/2008/adv050108.pdf; Meghan Sacks & Alissa R. Ackerman, *Bail and Sentencing: Does Pretrial Detention Lead to Harsher Punishment?*, 25 CRIM. JUST. POL'Y REV. 59, 59, 71 (2014) (noting that "[d]ecisions at the beginning of the criminal case process, such as bail decisions, can affect the entire course of the case and the ultimate punishment handed down in sentencing"; finding that "[d]efendants who were detained prior to trial received longer sentences than defendants who were released on bail").

[58] Schlesinger, *supra* note 57, at 24.

[59] NELLIS ET AL., *supra* note 1, at 6 (reporting that African Americans account for 35% of those arrested for drug offenses but 53% of drug convictions).

[60] Robert D. Crutchfield, *Warranted Disparity? Questioning the Justification of Racial Disparity in Criminal Justice Processing*, 36 COLUM. HUMAN RIGHTS L. REV. 15, 16–22 (2004). *Compare* David A. Harris, *The Reality of Racial Disparity In Criminal Justice: The Significance of Data Collection*, 66 L. & CONTEMP. PROB. 71 (2003), *with* Heather Mac Donald, *High Incarceration Rate Of Blacks Is Function Of Crime, Not Racism*, INVESTOR'S BUSINESS DAILY, Apr. 29, 2008, *available at* http://news.investors.com/042908-445638-high-incarceration-rate-of-blacks-is-function-of-crime-not-racism.htm?Ntt=incarceration&p=4.

[61] NELLIS ET AL., *supra* note 1, at 6. *See also*, Michael Tonry & Matthew Melewski, *The Malign Effects of Drugs and Crime Control Policies on Black Americans*, 37 CRIME AND JUSTICE, 1, 33–34 (2008).

[62] Human Rights Watch, *Punishment and Prejudice: Racial Disparities in the War on Drugs*, Vol. 12, No. 2 at Table 13 (May 2000), HRW.ORG, www.hrw.org/legacy/reports/2000/usa/Table13.pdf.

[63] *See, e.g.*, Research Working Group & Task Force on Race and the Criminal Justice System, *supra* note 5, at 269 (noting that "crime commission rates cannot be known directly and can only be estimated").

[64] *See, e.g.*, Alfred Blumstein, *On the Racial Disproportionality of the U.S. States' Prison Populations*, 73 J. CRIM. L. & CRIMINOLOGY 1259 (1982).

[65] *Uniform Crime Reports*, FEDERAL BUREAU OF INVESTIGATION, www.fbi.gov/about-us/cjis/ucr/ucr (last visited Apr. 7, 2014).

[66] *Crime in the United States, 2006*, FEDERAL BUREAU OF INVESTIGATION, http://www2.fbi.gov/ucr/cius2006/ (last visited Apr. 9, 2014).

[67] *See, e.g.*, Crutchfield, *supra* note 60, at 16–22.

[68] Kevin R. Johnson, *The Case Against Race Profiling in Immigration Enforcement*, 78 WASH. U. L. Q. 675, 684 (2000).

[69] Tammy Rinehart Kochel et al., *Effect of Suspect Race on Officers' Arrest Decisions*, 49 CRIMINOLOGY 473, 475 (2011); FRANK R. BAUMGARTNER & DEREK EPP, NORTH CAROLINA TRAFFIC STOP STATISTICS ANALYSIS 5 (2012) (North Carolina traffic stop data indicates that racial minorities are more likely to be searched and arrested following a traffic stop than White drivers who are pulled over on the same basis), *available at* https://www.ncaj.com/index.cfm?pg=NCCREDPublications.

[70] Jennifer L. Truman & Michael R. Rand, *Criminal Victimization, 2009*, BUREAU OF JUSTICE STATISTICS, U.S. DEP'T OF JUSTICE, SER. NO. NCJ 231327, 2010, at 9 Table 12, *available at* http://bjs.ojp.usdoj.gov/content/pub/pdf/cv09.pdf.

[71] Research Working Group & Task Force on Race and the Criminal Justice System, *supra* note 5, at 269.

[72] *See Data Collection: National Crime Victimization Survey (NCVS)*, BUREAU OF JUSTICE STATISTICS, www.bjs.gov/index.cfm?ty=dcdetail&iid=245.

[73] *See, e.g.*, Paul Knepper, *Race, Racism, and Crime Statistics*, 24 S.U. L. REV. 71, 96–98 (1996).

[74] Research Working Group & Task Force on Race and the Criminal Justice System, *supra* note 5, at 269.

[75] Michael Tonry, *The Social, Psychological, and Political Causes of Racial Disparities in the American Criminal Justice System*, 39 CRIME & JUST. 273, 274 (2010).

[76] *United States v. Smith*, 359 F. Supp. 2d 771, 777 (E.D. Wis. 2005).

[77] *United States v. Clary*, 846 F. Supp. 768, 783 (E.D. Mo. 1994), *rev'd* 34 F.3d 709 (8th Cir.1994).

[78] *Clary,* 846 F. Supp. at 783–84.

[79] Dorothy K. Hatsukami & Marian W. Fischman, *Crack Cocaine And Cocaine Hydrochloride: Are The Differences Myth Or Reality?*, 276 JOURNAL OF AM. MED. ASS'N 1580 (1996).

[80] *See* Fair Sentencing Act of 2010, Pub. L. No. 111–220, 124 Stat. 2372 (2010).

[81] BUREAU OF JUSTICE STATISTICS, COMPENDIUM OF FEDERAL JUSTICE STATISTICS, 1994 85 Table 6.11; BUREAU OF JUSTICE STATISTICS, COMPENDIUM OF FEDERAL JUSTICE STATISTICS, 2003 112 Table 7.16.

[82] BARBARA S. MEIERHOEFER, THE GENERAL EFFECT OF MANDATORY MINIMUM PRISON TERMS: A LONGITUDINAL STUDY OF FEDERAL SENTENCES IMPOSED 20 (1992), *available at* www.fjc.gov/public/pdf.nsf/lookup/geneffmm.pdf/$file/geneffmm.pdf.

[83] U.S. Sentencing Comm'n, 2010 Sourcebook of Federal Sentencing Statistics, Table 34 (2010), UNITED STATES SENTENCING COMMISSION, www.ussc.gov/Research_and_Statistics/Annual_Reports_and_Sourcebooks/2010/sbtoc10.htm.

---

[84] Erica Goode, *Incarceration Rates for Blacks Have Fallen Sharply, Report Shows*, N.Y. TIMES, Feb. 27, 2013, *available at* www.nytimes.com/2013/02/28/us/incarceration-rates-for-blacks-dropped-report-shows.html?_r=0.

[85] Craig Haney, *Politicizing Crime and Punishment: Redefining "Justice" to Fight the "War on Prisoners,"* 114 W. VA. L. REV. 373, 391–392 (2012).

[86] *See* Jeffrey B. Welty, *North Carolina's Habitual Felon, Violent Habitual Felon, and Habitual Breaking and Entering Laws*, ADMINISTRATION OF JUSTICE BULLETIN NO. 2013/07 (UNC School of Government, Aug. 2013), *available at* http://sogpubs.unc.edu/electronicversions/pdfs/aojb1307.pdf; *see also* Jamie Markham, *Changes to the Habitual Felon Law*, N.C. CRIM. L., UNC SCH. OF GOV'T BLOG (Nov. 10, 2011), http://nccriminallaw.sog.unc.edu/?p=3042; *see also* G.S. 14-7.25 through G.S. 14-7.31 (providing that, in the case of felony breaking and entering, the habitual status may attach upon the commission of a second breaking and entering offense).

[87] North Carolina Advocates for Justice (NCAJ) Task Force on Racial and Ethnic Bias Executive Summary, *available at* www.ncaj.com/index.cfm?pg=NCCREDPublications.

[88] Catherine London, *Racial Impact Statements: A Proactive Approach to Addressing Racial Disparities in Prison Populations*, 29 LAW & INEQ. 211 (2011) (discussing racial impact statement requirements in Minnesota, Iowa, and Connecticut); 2013 Or. Laws, Ch. 600, *available at* https://www.oregonlegislature.gov/bills_laws/lawsstatutes/2013orLaw0600.pdf.

[89] *See, e.g.*, John Lyon, *Arkansas Legislature: Proposal Would Require Racial Impact Statements For Some Bills*, TIMES RECORD ONLINE EDITION, March 4, 2013, *available at* http://swtimes.com/sections/news/politics/arkansas-legislature-proposal-would-require-racial-impact-statements-some.

[90] London, *supra* note 88, at 212.

[91] *Caldwell v. Texas*, 137 U.S. 692, 697 (1891).

[92] J. Harvey Wilkinson, III, *The Supreme Court, the Equal Protection Clause, and the Three Faces of Constitutional Equality*, 61 VA. L. REV. 945, 945 (1975).

[93] *Whren v. United States*, 517 U.S. 806 (1996).

[94] *United States v. Armstrong*, 517 U.S. 456 (1996).

[95] *Pugh v. Rainwater*, 572 F.2d 1053 (5th Cir. 1978) (en banc).

[96] *Peters v. Kiff*, 407 U.S. 493 (1972).

---

[97] *State v. Cofield*, 320 N.C. 297 (1987).

[98] *Batson v. Kentucky*, 476 U.S. 79 (1986).

[99] *United States v. Smart*, 518 F.3d 800, 804 n.1 (10th Cir. 2008).

[100] *See Manson v. Brathwaite*, 432 U.S. 98 (1977); *Neil v. Biggers*, 409 U.S. 188 (1972); *State v. Harris*, 308 N.C. 159 (1983).

[101] *Whren v. United States*, 517 U.S. 806, 813 (1996); *see also State v. McClendon*, 350 N.C. 630 (1999) (adopting *Whren* under state constitution).

[102] *See infra* § 2.3A, Equal Protection Claims May Strengthen Fourth Amendment Challenges.

[103] *See infra* § 2.6C, Challenging Checkpoints as Racially Discriminatory.

[104] *See Taylor v. Louisiana*, 419 U.S. 522 (1975); *State v. McNeill*, 326 N.C. 712 (1990).

[105] *See Duren v. Missouri*, 439 U.S. 357 (1979).

[106] *Eason v. Spence*, 232 N.C. 579, 584 (1950).

[107] *See State v. Wright*, 274 N.C. 380 (1968).

[108] *See State v. Cofield*, 320 N.C. 297 (1987).

[109] *McNeill*, 326 N.C. 712.

[110] *See* G.S. 114-10.01.

[111] *Id.*; *see also infra* § 2.6I, Collecting Traffic Stop Data to Support Equal Protection Claims.

[112] *See* G.S. 15A-279(d); G.S. 7A-451(b)(2).

[113] *See* G.S. 15A-284.52(b)(14)

[114] The Innocence Project, *The Role of Race in Misidentification*, INNOCENCE BLOG (Aug. 11, 2008), www.innocenceproject.org/Content/The_role_of_race_in_misidentification.php.

[115] G.S. 15A-211(d) (effective for offenses committed on or after December 1, 2011).

[116] G.S. 20-16.3A(d).

[117] G.S. 20-16.3A(2a).

[118] G.S. 20-16.3A(a1).

---

[119] *See* G.S. 15A-971 through G.S. 15A-980.

[120] *See, e.g.*, *State v. Cooper,* 186 N.C. App. 100 (2007) (evidence from warrantless search should have been suppressed where officer's knowledge that a Black male had committed armed robbery did not, without more, constitute reasonable suspicion of criminal activity justifying a "Terry" stop).

[121] Norman C. Amaker, *The Haunting Presence of the Opinion in* Brown v. Board of Education, 20 S. ILL. U. L.J. 3, 6–7 (1995).

[122] Robin Walker Sterling, *Raising Race*, THE CHAMPION, April 2011, at 24, 26.

[123] *See* CHRISTOPHER HARTNEY & LINH VUONG, NATIONAL COUNCIL ON CRIME AND DELINQUENCY, CREATED EQUAL: RACIAL AND ETHNIC DISPARITIES IN THE U.S. CRIMINAL JUSTICE SYSTEM 14 (2009).

[124] NORTH CAROLINA RULES OF PROF'L CONDUCT R. 1.3.1 (Diligence), *available at* www.ncbar.com/rules/rpcsearch.asp.

[125] NORTH CAROLINA RULES OF PROF'L CONDUCT R. 0.1.1, 0.1.6 (Preamble).

[126] Sterling, *supra* note 122, at 26.

[127] EQUAL JUSTICE INITIATIVE, ILLEGAL RACIAL DISCRIMINATION IN JURY SELECTION: A CONTINUING LEGACY (2010), *available at* www.eji.org/files/EJI%20Race%20and%20Jury%20Report.pdf.

Chapter 2
Police Investigation: Stops, Searches, and Arrests

2.1 Scope of Chapter

This chapter explains how a person's race (as well as proxies for race, such as the geographic area where a person lives) may affect initial encounters with police. The focus of this chapter is on race-based challenges to police action based on the Equal Protection Clause of the Fourteenth Amendment to the U.S. Constitution, the prohibition against unreasonable searches and seizures in the Fourth Amendment to the U.S. Constitution, and parallel provisions in the N.C. Constitution. The focus of the chapter is on warrantless police encounters, by consent or seizure, which for many people are the initial point of contact with the criminal justice system. Race may play a role in other aspects of police encounters not addressed in this chapter.

Most of this chapter is organized according to the type of encounter between law enforcement officers and individuals, such as traffic stops or arrests. However, for several reasons the chapter begins with a discussion of the law on equal protection challenges to selective enforcement. First, claims based on the Equal Protection Clause may be raised in response to all encounters covered in this chapter; readers may therefore find it useful to have a basic understanding of equal protection claims before examining issues unique to particular police encounters. Second, criminal defense attorneys tend to be more familiar with Fourth Amendment claims and less familiar with equal protection claims, the development of which has occurred largely in the civil context. Where appropriate, equal protection principles articulated in the civil context have been incorporated into this section.

This chapter does not repeat all of the applicable Fourth Amendment principles. For this reason, the discussion should be read in conjunction with Chapter 15 of Volume 1 of the North Carolina Defender Manual, which lays out the law on warrantless seizures and searches in greater detail; Chapter 14 of the same manual, which contains guidance on making motions to suppress evidence; and other reference sources on search and seizure law.

2.2 Overview of Racial Profiling Concerns

The U.S. Department of Justice defines the unlawful practice of racial profiling as decisions by law enforcement that "rest[] on the erroneous assumption that any particular individual of one race or ethnicity is more likely to engage in misconduct than any particular individual of other races or ethnicities." U.S. DEP'T OF JUSTICE, RACIAL PROFILING FACT SHEET 1 (2003). Studies in various jurisdictions indicate that racial profiling may have an impact on decisions made during initial encounters by law enforcement officers. In Maryland, an analysis of traffic stop data concluded that, while 74.7% of those violating traffic laws on Maryland highways were White and 17.5% were Black, Black drivers constituted 79.2% of the drivers searched. DEBORAH RAMIREZ ET AL., U.S. DEP'T OF JUSTICE, A RESOURCE GUIDE ON RACIAL PROFILING DATA COLLECTION SYSTEMS: PROMISING PRACTICES AND LESSONS LEARNED 6–7 (2000). In New York City, a federal judge found that the New York Police Department's "stop and frisk" program, pursuant to which police officers were instructed to target young Black and Latino men for *Terry* stops, was influenced by racial bias and was unconstitutional. *Floyd v. City of New York*, 959 F.Supp.2d 540, 662–64 (S.D.N.Y. 2013).

In North Carolina, most law enforcement agencies are required by statute to collect traffic stop data encompassing, among other information, the "[i]dentifying characteristics of the drivers stopped, including the race or ethnicity" and "the race or ethnicity . . . of each person searched." *See* G.S. 114-10.01; *see also infra* § 2.6I, Collecting Traffic Stop Data to Support Equal Protection Claims. A 2012 study of data from approximately 13 million North Carolina traffic stops concluded that, compared to White motorists, Black and Latino motorists and passengers in North Carolina are almost twice as likely to be searched and twice as likely to be arrested following a traffic stop. North Carolina Advocates for Justice (NCAJ) Task Force on Racial and Ethnic Bias, Executive Summary. The same study concluded that these racial and ethnic disparities appear most pronounced when officer discretion is greatest, as in the case of stops based on seat belt, vehicle equipment, and vehicle regulatory violations. *See* FRANK R. BAUMGARTNER & DEREK EPP, NORTH CAROLINA TRAFFIC STOP STATISTICS ANALYSIS: FINAL REPORT TO THE NORTH CAROLINA ADVOCATES FOR JUSTICE TASK FORCE ON RACIAL AND ETHNIC BIAS 5 (2012) [hereinafter "Baumgartner Study"].

In Alamance County, following a two-year investigation, the United States Department of Justice filed a complaint alleging that Latino drivers are between four and ten times more likely to be stopped by Sheriff's deputies than non-Latino drivers, and that some deputies had been specifically directed by the Sheriff to "go out there and catch [] some Mexicans." Anne Blythe, *U.S. Justice Department Sues Alamance County Sheriff, Accusing Him of Discriminating Against Latinos*, NEWS & OBSERVER (Raleigh), Dec. 20, 2012. In support of its claims, the Department of Justice submitted a report in which racial profiling expert Dr. John Lamberth stated that, on three different highways in Alamance County, Latino motorists are between 6 and 7.13 times more likely than non-Latino drivers to be cited for traffic violations, and that these observed disparities are the largest he had ever measured in the United States. *See* United States' Reply in Support of its Motion to Modify the Expert Disclosure Deadline as to a Single Expert, Exhibit C at 2–3, *United States v. Terry Johnson*, No. 12-cv-1349 (2012).

Initial encounters with police represent the entry point into the criminal justice system. Stop, search, and arrest practices, where discriminatory, risk introducing racial disparities at the outset of the case that may be compounded at later stages and affect outcomes. *See supra* § 1.3E, Discretionary Decision-Making and the Cumulative Nature of Disparities. Criminal defense attorneys should therefore seek to identify and raise challenges to law enforcement conduct where it appears that race played an improper role in the investigation.

2.3 Equal Protection Challenges to Police Action

This section covers general considerations relevant to all equal protection challenges to police action. For application of these principles to specific investigative actions, such as stops or arrests, see the relevant sections below.

A. Equal Protection Claims May Strengthen Fourth Amendment Challenges

Equal protection challenges to racially-motivated police action and challenges under the Fourth Amendment to the State's assertion of reasonable suspicion or probable cause are often mutually reinforcing, and defense attorneys may benefit by raising them in tandem. Generally, evidence of an officer's racially-motivated purpose cannot be considered in the Fourth Amendment context. *See Whren v. United States*, 517 U.S. 806, 813 (1996) ("[T]he constitutional basis for objecting to intentionally discriminatory application of laws is the Equal Protection Clause, not the Fourth Amendment. Subjective intentions play no role in ordinary, probable-cause Fourth Amendment analysis."). However, such evidence is appropriate and even necessary to an equal protection claim. A defendant raising an equal protection violation may introduce evidence such as:

- an officer's racially derogatory statements;
- statistical evidence of an officer's pattern of targeting minorities for traffic stops; and
- results from internal police investigations of the officer in question.

Such evidence, when introduced in connection with an equal protection claim, may cast doubt on whether the officer had the necessary legal justification to make a seizure under the Fourth Amendment. In particular, a judge who is faced with compelling evidence of discriminatory intent by an officer may be inclined to find that the officer's purported reason for a traffic stop is not credible. For example, in *State v. Villeda*, 165 N.C. App. 431, 434 (2004), a Latino defendant charged with impaired driving presented extensive evidence in support of his equal protection claim—including the trooper's statement that "Hispanics are more prone than other races to get in a car after they have been drinking"—casting doubt on the trooper's race-neutral explanations for the traffic stop. The defendant's equal protection and Fourth Amendment claims succeeded in the trial court. The N.C. Court of Appeals reviewed the evidence of racial profiling before upholding the trial court's finding that the stop was not supported by reasonable suspicion because the trooper could not have observed whether the driver was wearing his seat belt, as the trooper had claimed. Even though the appellate court did not reach the equal protection claim, evidence of the trooper's subjective motivations for traffic stops undermined his credibility and strengthened the defendant's Fourth Amendment claim.

In an opinion discussing both equal protection and Fourth Amendment protections, the N.C. Supreme Court concluded that, while it could not determine whether the stop of a car driven by a black male was "selective enforcement of the law based upon race," which would violate the defendant's right to equal protection, the officer lacked justification for the stop because there were no grounds to stop the defendant for failure to use a turn signal. *State v. Ivey*, 360 N.C. 562, 564 (2006), *abrogated in part on other grounds by State v. Styles*, 362 N.C. 412 (2008). Noting concerns over stops for "driving while black," the court declared that it "will not tolerate discriminatory application of the law" based on race. *Id.* While the court found that it could not determine whether the stop constituted selective enforcement based on race, those concerns appeared to influence the Court's approach to the case.

These cases suggest that, even when a defendant does not prevail on an equal protection claim, litigating it may be instrumental in getting evidence suppressed on Fourth Amendment grounds.

B. State and Federal Constitutions Guarantee Equal Protection of the Law

The Equal Protection Clause of the Fourteenth Amendment to the U.S. Constitution and article I, section 19 of the N.C. Constitution recognize the right to equal protection under the law. Both provisions prohibit "selective enforcement of the law based on considerations such as race." *State v. Ivey,* 360 N.C. 562, 564 (2006) (quoting *Whren v. United States*, 517 U.S. 806, 813 (1996)), *abrogated in part on other grounds by State v. Styles*, 362 N.C. 412 (2008). In *State v. Ivey*, the North Carolina Supreme Court stated that it "will not tolerate discriminatory application of the law based upon a citizen's race." *Ivey,* 360 N.C. at 564. Our Supreme Court has recognized that the principle of the equal protection of the law was "inherent in the Constitution of this State" even before its express incorporation in article I, section 19, which became effective on July 1, 1971. *S. S. Kresge Co. v. Davis*, 277 N.C. 654, 660 (1971). Interpretations of the Equal Protection Clause by federal courts, while persuasive, do not control the North Carolina Supreme Court's construction of rights guaranteed by the N.C. Constitution's Equal Protection Clause. *See McNeill v. Harnett County*, 327 N.C. 552 (1990).

An equal protection challenge to police action "does not fit neatly into the various stages of Fourth Amendment search and seizure analysis," as "the central intention behind the Equal Protection Clause is the prevention of official conduct discriminating on the basis of race." *United States v. Avery*, 137 F.3d 343, 353 (6th Cir. 1997) ("A citizen's right to equal protection of the laws, however, does not magically materialize when he is approached by the police. Citizens are cloaked at all times with the right to have the laws applied to them in an equal fashion—undeniably, the right not to be exposed to the unfair application of the laws based on their race."). If law enforcement officers engage in racial discrimination at any point in the criminal process, including during the adoption of a policy or the development of an informal police practice, a challenge may be brought on equal protection grounds. *Id.* at 355.

C. Elements of a Selective Enforcement Claim

A defendant claiming that a law enforcement officer violated his or her right to equal protection of the law must show either that:

1. A law or policy contains an express racial classification that singles out members of the person's race for disfavored treatment, *see Wayte v. United States*, 470 U.S. 598, 610 n.10 (1985); or
2. A facially neutral law or policy was selectively enforced against members of the defendant's race in an intentionally discriminatory manner, *see Yick Wo v. Hopkins*, 118 U.S. 356, 373–74 (1886). This is referred to as a "selective enforcement" claim.

The first type of claim, based on express racial classifications, will rarely arise because express racial classifications have been removed from our criminal laws. Such classifications may occasionally be found in official policies, however. *See, e.g.*, *Miller-El v. Dretke*, 545 U.S. 231, 263–64 (2005) (describing prosecutor's manual containing reasons for excluding minorities from jury service).

Defendants are more likely to pursue the second type of claim, based on selective enforcement. The U.S. Supreme Court summed up selective enforcement claims in *Yick Wo v. Hopkins*:

> Though the law itself be fair on its face and impartial in appearance, yet, if it is applied and administered by public authority with an evil eye and an unequal hand, so as practically to make unjust and illegal discriminations between persons in similar circumstances, material to their rights, the denial of equal justice is still within the prohibition of the Constitution.

118 U.S. 356, 373–74 (1886). *See also State v. Howard*, 78 N.C. App. 262, 266 (1985) (quoting *Yick Wo*). To succeed on a claim of racially selective enforcement, a defendant must show that the challenged police action:

- was motivated by a *discriminatory purpose*; and
- had a *discriminatory effect* on a racial group to which the defendant belongs.

S. S. Kresge Co. v. Davis, 277 N.C. 654 (1971) (reversing motion to dismiss suit alleging that the City of High Point selectively enforced a law regarding the sale of certain products on Sundays, holding that the facts alleged, if true, would constitute a denial of equal protection of the law). The discussion below addresses these elements of a selective enforcement claim.

Discriminatory purpose. To show that the officer at issue acted with a discriminatory purpose or intent, the defendant must show that the officer selected a particular course of action because of its effect on an identifiable group. *See Wayte v. United States*, 470 U.S. 598, 610 (1985). In other words, a defendant must show "that in the exercise of . . . discretion there has been intentional or deliberate discrimination by design." *In re Register*, 84 N.C. App. 336, 341, 346 (1987) (prosecutor engaged in selective prosecution in violation of the Equal Protection Clause by making the ability of a juvenile to pay compensation the "determinative factor in the decision of whether to file a complaint as a juvenile petition"). The discriminatory purpose requirement does not require defendants to prove that race was "the sole, predominant, or determinative factor in a police enforcement action." *Floyd v. City of New York*, 959 F. Supp. 2d 540, 662 (S.D.N.Y. 2013). Nor must the defendant show that the discrimination was based on "ill will, enmity, or hostility." *Id.* (quotation omitted) (citing *Ferrill v. Parker Grp., Inc.,* 168 F.3d 468, 473 & n.7 (11th Cir. 1999)). To establish this prong of an equal protection claim, it is sufficient to show that "a discriminatory purpose has been *a* motivating factor" in the challenged action. *Village of Arlington Heights v. Metropolitan Hous. Dev. Corp.*, 429 U.S. 252, 265–66 (1977) (emphasis added).

Generally, evidence of unequal treatment alone, without at least circumstantial evidence of discriminatory purpose, will not be sufficient to establish an equal protection violation. *In re Register*, 84 N.C. App. 336, 341 (1987). The failure of police to avoid or avert unequal treatment is not sufficient to establish discriminatory purpose. *See Wayte v. United States*, 470 U.S. 598, 610 (1985) ("Discriminatory purpose . . . implies more than . . . intent as awareness of consequences. It implies that the decisionmaker . . . selected or reaffirmed a particular course of action at least in part because of, not merely in spite of, its adverse effects upon an identifiable group." (internal quotations omitted)); *S. S. Kresge Co. v. Davis*, 277 N.C. 654, 661 (1971) ("Mere laxity, delay or inefficiency of the police department . . . in the enforcement of a statute or ordinance, otherwise valid, does not destroy the law or render it invalid and unenforceable."). Additionally, when based on considerations other than race, ethnicity, or other impermissible factors, selectivity in enforcement is not unlawful. *S. S. Kresge Co.,* 277 N.C. 654, 661.

A showing of discriminatory intent is sometimes made with direct evidence that law enforcement decisions were based on the defendant's race, such as an officer's admission that he approached the defendant because he was a young black male on a street corner who fit the profile of a drug dealer. More typically, however, discriminatory intent is shown through circumstantial evidence. *See United States v. Avery*, 137 F.3d 343, 355 (6th Cir. 1997) ("[o]ften it is difficult to prove directly the invidious use of race," so "'an invidious discriminatory purpose may often be inferred from the totality of the relevant facts'" (quoting *Washington v. Davis*, 426 U.S. 229, 242 (1976))); *United States v. Alcaraz-Arellano*, 441 F.3d 1252, 1264 (10th Cir. 2006) ("Discriminatory intent can be shown by either direct or circumstantial evidence.").

In some cases, "stark" statistical evidence of a racially disparate impact may be sufficient to prove the discriminatory intent element of an equal protection claim. *See, e.g., Village of Arlington Heights v. Metro. Hous. Dev. Corp.*, 429 U.S. 252, 266 (1977) ("Sometimes a clear pattern, unexplainable on grounds other than race, emerges from the effect of the state action even when the governing legislation appears neutral on its face."). For example, in *Yick Wo v. Hopkins*, 118 U.S. 356, 373 (1886), when the City of San Francisco granted no laundry permits to the over 200 Chinese applicants while granting permits to all but one white applicant, the statistical disparity was so extreme as to "warrant and require" a conclusion of purposeful discrimination. Even when not definitive, statistical evidence of disparate impact is highly relevant and will strengthen a claim of intentional discrimination. "Statistics showing racial or ethnic imbalance are probative . . . because such imbalance is often a telltale sign of purposeful discrimination." *Int'l Bhd. of Teamsters v. United States*, 431 U.S. 324, 339 n.20 (1977). Generally, evidence that law enforcement action "bears more heavily on one race than another," provides "an important starting point" in an equal protection inquiry. *Village of Arlington Heights v. Metro. Hous. Dev. Corp.*, 429 U.S. 252, 266 (1977) (internal quotations omitted).

In *McCleskey v. Kemp*, 481 U.S. 279, 293 (1987), the U.S. Supreme Court observed that "statistical proof normally must present a 'stark' pattern to be accepted as the sole proof of discriminatory intent under the Constitution." The *McCleskey* Court's refusal to treat a death penalty study reflecting racial disparities in capital sentencing as evidence of discriminatory purpose has led some courts to conclude that statistics alone are typically insufficient to prove discriminatory intent. *See, e.g., United States v. Barlow*, 310 F.3d 1007, 1011 (7th Cir. 2002) (statistics alone are rarely sufficient to prove an equal protection violation); *Chavez v. Illinois State Police*, 251 F.3d 612, 647–48 (7th Cir. 2001) (statistics may not serve as sole proof of discriminatory intent in a racial profiling case). This reading of *McCleskey* may be overbroad, however, and narrowly tailored statistical evidence may be distinguishable from the statewide study that was offered in *McCleskey*. *See, e.g.,* Michael R. Smith, *Depoliticizing Racial Profiling: Suggestions for the Limited Use and Management of Race in Police Decision-Making*, 15 GEO. MASON U. CIV. RTS. L.J. 219, 247 (2005) (while the "*McCleskey* Court believed that the Baldus study was insufficient to support an inference of discrimination, a properly conducted analysis of an individual officer's traffic stop patterns can produce exceptionally clear evidence of purposeful discrimination" (quotation omitted)). The data in *McCleskey* encompassed statewide statistics from over 2,000 Georgia death penalty cases involving multiple decision-makers; in contrast, a selective enforcement claim typically names only a single police officer, unit, or department. In more tailored selective enforcement claims, the court is not confronted with the difficult task of "deducing purposeful discrimination . . . based on the aggregate analysis of decisions made by many other entities." *Id.* at 246.

Police officers exercise broad discretion in making stops and arrests. In other contexts involving the broad exercise of discretion, discriminatory intent has been inferred from statistical proof presenting a stark pattern of racial disparities. *See Batson v. Kentucky*, 476 U.S. 79, 97 (1986) (a "pattern of strikes against black jurors" may give rise to an inference of discrimination, as may a "prosecutor's questions and statements during voir dire"); *Int'l Bhd. of Teamsters v. United States*, 431 U.S. 324, 339 n.20 (1977) (courts have frequently relied on statistical evidence to prove employment discrimination, which in many cases is "the only available avenue of proof . . . to uncover clandestine and covert discrimination by the employer or union involved" (quoting *United States v. Ironworkers Local 86*, 443 F.2d 544, 551 (1971))); *Castaneda v. Partida*, 430 U.S. 482, 494–95 (1977); *see also* David Rudovsky, *Litigating Civil Rights Cases to Reform Racially Biased Criminal Justice Practices,* 39 COLUM. HUM. RTS. L. REV. 97, 111 (2007).

While statistical evidence showing that an officer stops, searches, or arrests a disproportionate number of minorities may not suffice alone to show discriminatory intent, discriminatory purpose may be demonstrated with some combination of the following direct, statistical, and circumstantial evidence:

- data demonstrating a significant disparity between the overall population and the population targeted by the officer;
- data demonstrating a significant disparity between the population of violators and the population targeted by the officer;
- data demonstrating a significant disparity between the population targeted by the officer and the population targeted by similarly situated officers;
- an officer's failure to comply with department training and supervisory polices;
- an officer's failure to comply with state law mandating reporting of traffic stop data;
- an officer's questions or statements to the defendant or others related to race during the encounter;
- an officer's history of racially motivated behavior, as evidenced by interviews with community members or internal affairs investigations;
- a police department's history of racially motivated behavior, as reflected in reports, investigations, or complaints;
- data demonstrating that when the suspect is a racial minority, an officer more frequently conducts *Terry* stops, consent searches, discretionary stops (for reasons such as seat belt or vehicle regulatory violations), or canine searches; and
- any other relevant evidence supporting an inference of discriminatory purpose.

Practice note: *Washington v. Davis*, 426 U.S. 229 (1976), in which the U.S. Supreme Court announced the requirement of proving "discriminatory intent" in equal protection claims, was decided long before social scientists studying implicit bias recognized the influence of race on decision-making. In light of empirical studies on the subject, *see supra* § 1.3.D, Implicit Bias, defendants should incorporate into their equal protection claims the impact of implicit racial bias.

For example, Professors Ralph Richard Banks and Richard Thompson Ford argue that existing equal protection jurisprudence prohibits state action prompted by either implicit or explicit racial motivation, and contend that evidence of either will satisfy the "discriminatory purpose" prong of an equal protection claim. Ralph Richard Banks & Richard Thompson Ford, *(How) Does Unconscious Bias Matter?: Law, Politics, and Racial Inequality*, 58 EMORY L. J. 1053, 1089–1100 (2009) ("One might conclude that the [claimant] need not prove bias at all, but instead simply that the decision would have been different but for the races of the parties"); *see also* Sheila Foster, *Intent and Incoherence*, 72 TUL. L. REV. 1065, 1094–97 (1998) (explaining that, in the peremptory challenge context, strikes motivated by race may be challenged successfully without proof of conscious intent to discriminate).

While it is still relatively rare for courts to consider implicit bias in criminal cases, some judges reviewing equal protection claims raised by criminal defendants have acknowledged the possible problems caused by unconscious bias. *See, e,g.*, *Chin v. Runnels*, 343 F. Supp. 2d 891, 906 (N.D. Cal. 2004) (in reviewing equal protection claim, court noted that grand jury foreperson selection involves "subjective judgments entail[ing] subtle and unconscious mental processes susceptible to bias"); *Gonzalez-Rivera v. INS*, 22 F.3d 1441, 1450 (9th Cir. 1994) ("[A]s we have recognized in prior cases, racial stereotypes often infect our decision-making processes only subconsciously. . . . Thus, Border Patrol officers may use racial stereotypes as a proxy for illegal conduct without being subjectively aware of doing so."); *Georgia v. McCollum*, 505 U.S. 42, 68 (1992) (O'Connor, J. dissenting) ("It is by now clear that conscious and unconscious racism can affect the way white jurors perceive minority defendants and the facts presented at their trials, perhaps determining the verdict of guilt or innocence.").

Introducing social science evidence concerning implicit bias in support of your equal protection claim may help inform the court, present a more complete picture of discrimination faced by your client, and develop jurisprudence that takes into account racial bias as it is understood today. For more information on introducing evidence of implicit bias when litigating equal protection claims, see the Equal Justice Society Scholar Packet, EQUAL JUSTICE SOCIETY (last visited June 24, 2014) (downloadable packet of materials including scholarship and jurisprudence addressing implicit bias and the intent doctrine).

Discriminatory effect. Police action has a "racially discriminatory effect when members of a protected racial group . . . receive less favorable treatment than nonmembers." *United States v. Barlow*, 310 F.3d 1007, 1010 (7th Cir. 2002). The U.S. Supreme Court has "repeatedly relied on statistics" to prove discriminatory effect. *Chavez v. Illinois State Police,* 251 F.3d 612, 638 (7th Cir. 2001) (citing *Hunter v. Underwood*, 471 U.S. 222, 227 (1985)). Statistical evidence of discriminatory effect may be found in court files, State Bureau of Investigation (SBI) files, surveys or analyses conducted by statisticians or other academic researchers, and other public records such as traffic stop data. *See infra* § 2.3D, Gathering Evidence to Support a Claim of Selective Enforcement; § 2.6I, Collecting Traffic Stop Data to Support Equal Protection Claims. For example, in *Floyd v. City of New York*, 959 F. Supp. 2d 540 (S.D.N.Y. 2013), discriminatory effect was demonstrated with evidence that the New York Police Department (1) carries out more stops in areas where there are more Black and Latino residents, even when other variables are constant; (2) is more likely to stop Blacks and Latinos than Whites, even controlling for other relevant factors; (3) is more likely to use force against Blacks and Latinos, even controlling for other relevant factors; and (4) stops Blacks and Latinos with less justification than Whites. Anecdotal evidence also supported a finding of discriminatory effect in *Floyd.*

At least one court has found that discriminatory effect can be presumed where there is proof of discriminatory purpose. *Doe v. Village of Mamaroneck*, 462 F. Supp. 2d 520, 543 (S.D.N.Y. 2006) ("Once racially discriminatory intent infects the application of a neutral law or policy, the group that is singled out for discriminatory treatment is no longer similarly situated to any other in the eyes of the law, so adverse effects can be presumed.").

Discriminatory effect and the "similarly situated" requirement. In *United States v. Armstrong*, 517 U.S. 456, 465 (1996), the Court held that plaintiffs claiming *selective prosecution* based on race must demonstrate that "similarly situated individuals of a different race were not prosecuted." Courts have differed in their application of this holding to claims of *selective enforcement*, the focus of the discussion in this chapter. Within the Second Circuit, the similarly situated requirement only applies to claims of selective prosecution, not to other equal protection claims such as claims of selective enforcement. The Second Circuit Court of Appeals has held that, unless the plaintiff or defendant complains of selective prosecution, he or she is not "obligated to show a better treated, similarly situated group of individuals of a different race in order to establish a claim of denial of equal protection." *Pyke v. Cuomo*, 258 F.3d 107, 109–10 (2d Cir. 2001) (to prevail on a claim of selective prosecution, plaintiffs must "establish the existence of similarly situated individuals who were not prosecuted; that is because courts grant special deference to the executive branch in the performance of the 'core' executive function of deciding whether to prosecute"). In an unpublished opinion, the Fourth Circuit Court of Appeals, citing *Armstrong*, stated that defendants pursuing selective enforcement claims must "show that the law enforcement practice was not enforced against similarly situated individuals of a different race." *United States v. Suarez*, 321 F. App'x 302, 305 (4th Cir. 2009) (unpublished). In jurisdictions that apply the "similarly situated" requirement to selective enforcement claims, this requirement is generally treated as an aspect of the "discriminatory effect" element. *See, e.g.*, *United States v. Barlow*, 310 F.3d 1007, 1012 (7th Cir. 2002); *Chavez v. Illinois State Police,* 251 F.3d 612, 638 (7th Cir. 2001).

North Carolina appellate courts have not addressed this question conclusively. In an early case, the North Carolina Court of Appeals stated that "to establish a prima facie case of selective enforcement or selective prosecution defendant was required at least to show that others similarly situated have not been proceeded against," but that observation was dicta with regard to selective enforcement because the claim before the court was for selective prosecution. *State v. Ward*, 66 N.C. App. 352, 354 (1984) (quotation omitted). In a recent unpublished decision analyzing a claim of selective enforcement, the North Carolina Court of Appeals acknowledged the "similarly situated" requirement articulated in *Armstrong*, but did not apply that requirement to the facts before the court. *State v. Mendez*, 216 N.C. App. 587 (2011) (unpublished) (quoting *Armstrong*, 517 U.S. 456,

465). In a claim of selective enforcement, the defendant's obligation to identify similarly situated individuals of other races who were not subjected to the challenged law enforcement action therefore appears to be an open question in North Carolina. When arguing that no such requirement exists, defendants should advance the logic articulated in *Pyke v. Cuomo*, 258 F.3d 107, 110 (2d Cir. 2001), and argue that it is only in cases of selective prosecution, where separation of powers concerns are most pronounced, that this requirement should apply.

If the trial court requires the defendant to identify similarly situated individuals of another race who were not subjected to the challenged enforcement action, the defendant should be prepared to identify such individuals or articulate a definition of the class of similarly situated individuals. *See Washington v. Johnson*, 125 Wash. App. 1040 (Wash. Ct. App. 2005) (unpublished) (holding that the trial court's decision to adopt defendants' definition of the class of similarly situated individuals in a case alleging racially selective enforcement of drug laws was not reversible error); *Chavez v. Illinois State Police,* 251 F.3d 612, 636 (7th Cir. 2001) (no "magic formula" for determining who is similarly situated for purposes of selective enforcement cases; the inquiry is a common sense one and the class should not be defined too narrowly; this requirement may be satisfied by identifying a similarly situated individual of a different race who received more favorable treatment). For example, in *Chavez*, 251 F.3d 612, 636, a white female driver following a Latino motorist was similarly situated for purposes of establishing the discriminatory effect prong of the Latino motorist's selective enforcement claim, where both motorists drove the same stretch of highway at the same time, both were visible to the officer who stopped the Latino driver, and neither committed a traffic violation.

D. Gathering Evidence to Support a Claim of Selective Enforcement

Attorney's investigation. An attorney pursuing a selective enforcement claim should conduct an investigation to determine whether evidence exists that the client was targeted by police for a racially motivated reason. Sources of evidence include:

- interviews with your client regarding officers' statements, demeanor, and questions;
- interviews with your client's family members regarding the client's early account of the encounter;
- interviews with community members in the area where the encounter took place about officers' habits and law enforcement patterns;
- interviews with other defense attorneys and court personnel regarding officers' attitudes and practices;
- information concerning the unit responsible for your client's arrest (for example, evidence that your client was pulled over by a unit that specifically targets drug trafficking even though the stated purpose of the stop was a vehicle regulatory issue or seatbelt violation);
- data available in court files, SBI records, and the Automated Criminal Infraction System (ACIS), *see infra* § 2.6I, Collecting Traffic Stop Data to Support Equal Protection Claims;

- studies and statistical analyses performed by academic researchers, *see, e.g.*, Katherine Beckett, *Race, Drugs, and Law Enforcement: Toward Equitable Policing*, 11 CRIMINOLOGY & PUB. POL'Y 641 (2012); KATHERINE BECKETT, RACE AND DRUG LAW ENFORCEMENT IN SEATTLE (2008).

Discovery. Sometimes evidence obtained through an attorney's independent investigation will not be enough to make out a prima facie claim of selective enforcement; often it will be necessary for an attorney to obtain discovery from the State. Through discovery, an attorney may obtain evidence such as:

- videotapes of traffic stops, along with information identifying the date, time, location and person stopped;
- information about the patrol area of the officers in question;
- results of internal affairs investigations, including responses to citizen complaints of racial profiling, *see* Sample Letters Sustaining Complaints from the Durham Police Department's Professional Standards Division in the Race Materials Bank at www.ncids.org (select "Training & Resources"). To obtain an officer's personnel records, the defense will need to make a showing to the court that the information is necessary to the defense and outweighs any confidentiality interest in the information. *See* 1 NORTH CAROLINA DEFENDER MANUAL Ch.4 (Discovery) (2d ed. 2013); *see also Maryland Dep't of State Police v. Maryland State Conference of NAACP Branches*, 59 A.3d 1037 (Md. 2013) (upholding order requiring State Police to disclose redacted copies of internal affairs investigation records in an action filed under Maryland Public Information Act for purpose of determining whether the Maryland State Police were in compliance with a consent decree entered in an earlier racial profiling lawsuit);
- the law enforcement agency's standard operating procedures, e.g., for setting up vehicle checkpoints, using audio or video recording equipment, conducting surveillance, or requesting consent to search;
- the names and races of all individuals stopped by the officer in question during the time period of the defendant's arrest, including the date and time of stop; length of stop; reason for stop; location of stop; outcome of stop and names of all other law enforcement officers involved in the stop.

See Discovery Order in Selective Enforcement Case in the Race Materials Bank at www.ncids.org (select "Training & Resources"). For a general discussion of the defendant's right to discovery in criminal cases, see 1 NORTH CAROLINA DEFENDER MANUAL Ch. 4. (Discovery) (2d ed. 2013).

Some defenders have sought court-ordered depositions of police officers where evidence of discriminatory effect is strong but evidence of discriminatory purpose is not as strong. For example, public defenders litigating claims of selective enforcement in Seattle, after presenting statistical evidence of racially disparate enforcement of drug laws, successfully moved for an extensive discovery order. That discovery order, affirmed by a state court of appeals, permitted the attorneys to depose numerous police commanders about the department's drug enforcement priorities, policies, and resource allocation. *See* Public Defender Association: Racial Disparity Project, *Past Projects*, RDP.DEFENDER.ORG (last visited Sept. 25, 2014).

In *United States v. Armstrong*, 517 U.S. 456, 458–60 (1996), the U.S. Supreme Court held that a defendant must make a threshold showing "that the Government declined to prosecute similarly situated suspects of other races" before the court may order discovery of the prosecutor's charging practices in a *selective prosecution* claim. In reliance on federal rules governing discovery, the Court stated that discovery will only be ordered on a "credible showing of different treatment of similarly situated persons." *Id.* at 470 (holding that the requisite showing had not been made when defendants presented evidence that all 24 crack cocaine possession or conspiracy cases prosecuted in one court in a single year involved black defendants, because defendant failed to show that similarly situated offenders of other races were treated more favorably). It is unclear whether North Carolina courts would require such a showing before ordering broad-ranging discovery on a claim of *selective enforcement* based on state rules of discovery. *See supra* "Discriminatory effect and the 'similarly situated' requirement" in § 2.3C, Elements of a Selective Enforcement Claim; *infra* "Discovery related to selective prosecution claims in North Carolina courts" in § 5.4A, Obtaining Discovery Relating to a Selective Prosecution Claim.

Case study: Pursing public records requests alongside discovery. In addition to requests for discovery in support of selective enforcement claims, defense attorneys may file a public records request seeking the same materials. In the following anecdote, Shelby attorney Calvin Coleman reflects on a selective enforcement case in which he employed this strategy after his motions to obtain discovery were denied. The motions and orders described in the case study are listed at the end of the discussion and are available in the Race Materials Bank at www.ncids.org (select "Training and Resources").

In a recent case, I became concerned that my Latino client may have been subjected to unlawful selective enforcement based on both the facts of his case and evidence from a prior case showing that the Highway 85 traffic stop patterns of at least one deputy sheriff involved in my client's case disproportionately impacted Latinos. In the earlier case, the deputy sheriff had testified that (1) he had been involved in 29 stops where seizures were made since the creation of the Cleveland County Sheriff's Department Immigrations and Customs Enforcement team in 2004; (2) all but one of these stops involved a person of color; and (3) the vast majority involved Latinos. I filed a motion to suppress and several discovery motions relating to the selective enforcement claim.

Soon thereafter, the State decided to pursue federal charges concerning the same conduct against my client, and the case was pending in both forums for months. In federal court, I filed a motion to stay proceedings until the proper forum could be determined and for the federal court to maintain jurisdiction. I sought to keep the case in federal court because, under the circumstances, my client would face less time under federal criminal law. I also filed a Freedom of Information Act (FOIA) request in federal court, which the magistrate judge stated he intended to grant. The government subsequently dropped the federal case, and the State prosecuted the case in Cleveland County Superior Court only.

When the case was again in superior court, I filed additional discovery motions relating to the defendant's claim of selective enforcement. When the court denied our discovery motions, I filed a request for public records pursuant to G.S. 132.1 with the Sheriff, seeking documentation of the citations and warning tickets written by the officers involved in the case over a two-and-a-half year period (concluding at the end of the month in which the defendant was pulled over) and where the initial observations of the people receiving citations or warning tickets were made on Highway 85.

After consulting with the county attorney, the Sheriff released several documents we had not been able to obtain through discovery. These documents helped the defendant prevail on his claim of selective enforcement. Ultimately, the trial court found that "[t]he ICE team wrote a disproportionate number of citations and/or warning tickets to Hispanic persons as compared to other races. This evidence circumstantially shows that the ICE team stopped more Hispanic drivers than any other race, that the ICE team targets Hispanics, and that the ICE team selectively enforced the law based on race." *See* Order Allowing Motion to Suppress in the Race Materials Bank at www.ncids.org (select "Training and Resources"); *see also* Rebecca Clark, *Judge says sheriff's deputy used racial profiling in I-85 stops*, THE SHELBY STAR, May 15, 2013. The State did not appeal the court's dismissal of the charges against my client and his co-defendant. *See* Motion to Suppress Illegal Stop and Illegal Search and Motion to Disclose Officer's ID Number; Affidavit in Support of Motion to Suppress Illegal Stop and Illegal Search; Motion to Suppress; Motion to Stay Proceedings; Motion for Additional Discovery; Request for Public Records; Order Allowing Motion to Suppress; and Dismissal; all in the Race Materials Bank at www.ncids.org (select "Training and Resources").

Practice note: If the law enforcement agency responds to your motion to suppress and/or motion to dismiss by initiating an investigation of the officer in question, it may be in your client's interest for you to provide the results of your investigation to the agency and agree to allow the client to be interviewed. Be sure to obtain client consent before disclosing any confidential information. In addition to addressing possible discrimination within the law enforcement agency, the results of the agency's internal investigation may be available to you in discovery in the criminal case. For example, in *State v. Villeda*, 165 N.C. App. 431 (2004), following the defendant's motion to suppress, the State Highway Patrol initiated an internal affairs investigation of the trooper. The defense obtained information about the investigation through discovery. *See* Order for Production and Review of Evidence in the Race Materials Bank at www.ncids.org (select "Training & Resources") (ordering production of, among other materials, "Copies of all materials, memoranda, notes, reports, interview, and findings that have been collected, produced and generated pursuant to the Highway Patrol Internal affairs investigation of Trooper XXX" for *in camera* review); Order Producing and Disclosing Material Information to Defendant in the Race Materials Bank www.ncids.org (select "Training & Resources") (concluding that the materials reviewed *in camera* were relevant to defendant's constitutional claims and ordering their production to the Office of the Public Defender).

Additionally, some law enforcement agencies have a specific process for investigating citizen complaints about law enforcement actions, the results of which either may be available through discovery or be provided directly to the complainant. If your client believes he or she was the target of racial profiling, you may want to inform your client of this procedure where available. *See* Sample Letters Sustaining Complaints from the Durham Police Department's Professional Standards Division in the Race Materials Bank at www.ncids.org (select "Training & Resources").

E. Burden of Proof and Burden Shifting

Burden of proof. In a selective enforcement claim, the defendant bears the burden of proving, by a preponderance of the evidence, that the challenged police action violates the Equal Protection Clause of the Fourteenth Amendment and article I, section 19 of the North Carolina Constitution. *State v. Howard*, 78 N.C. App. 262, 266 (1985). That burden is met when a prima facie case of selective enforcement is established and the State fails to rebut the defendant's evidence of discriminatory purpose and discriminatory effect. *See, e.g., State v. Segars*, 799 A.2d 541 (N.J. 2002).

Selective enforcement distinguished from selective prosecution. A defendant's burden of proof may be lighter when challenging selective police enforcement than when challenging selective prosecution. This is so because the two claims involve different considerations. *See supra* "Discriminatory effect and the 'similarly situated' requirement" in § 2.3C, Elements of a Selective Enforcement Claim (discussing possible difference in obligation to show similarly situated individuals receiving more favorable treatment for the two types of claims). Courts reviewing selective enforcement claims have often applied the standards articulated by the Supreme Court in *United States v. Armstrong*, 517 U.S. 456, 465 (1996), but *Armstrong* was a selective prosecution case and therefore arguably involved a heightened standard of deference. *See, e.g., Johnson v. Crooks*, 326 F.3d 995, 1000 (8th Cir. 2003); *Bradley v. United States*, 299 F.3d 197, 205–06 (3d Cir. 2002). The *Armstrong* court emphasized that the standard of review it employed turned on the principle of deference to prosecutorial discretion; the court described the standard for making out a claim of selective prosecution as a "demanding one," since the claim "asks a court to exercise judicial power over a 'special province' of the Executive." *Armstrong*, 517 U.S. 456, 464 (citation omitted).

In contrast, police discretion typically is more circumscribed than prosecutorial discretion. In selective enforcement challenges to police action, separation of powers considerations are not present to the same extent, and challenges to racially biased police practices do not have to overcome the presumption of prosecutorial correctness. *See, e.g., City of Chicago v. Morales*, 527 U.S. 41, 60 (1999) (holding that a city ordinance was void for vagueness when it permitted police to break up loitering "criminal street gang members" in public places, in part because the ordinance encouraged arbitrary, discriminatory enforcement).

Several cases in which North Carolina appellate courts have rejected criminal defendants' equal protection claims have involved concerns specific to selective prosecution. *See, e.g., State v. Spicer*, 299 N.C. 309, 314 (1980); *State v. Howard*, 78 N.C. App. 262 (1985), *State v. Garner*, 340 N.C. 573 (1995). Defense attorneys raising selective enforcement claims should distinguish challenges to police action from those involving the exercise of prosecutorial discretion. *See generally* David Rudovsky, *Litigating Civil Rights Cases to Reform Racially Biased Criminal Justice Practices,* 39 COLUM. HUM. RTS. L. REV. 97, 112 (2007).

Burden shifting. If you file a motion to suppress evidence or a motion to dismiss charges on equal protection grounds, once you have made out a prima facie case of selective enforcement, "the burden of proof shifts to the State to rebut the presumption of unconstitutional action" by demonstrating that the racially disparate impact was not the result of racially motivated state action. *Alexander v. Louisiana*, 405 U.S. 625, 631–32 (1972); *see also Floyd v. City of New York*, 959 F. Supp. 2d 540 (S.D.N.Y. 2013) (internal quotations omitted) ("Once it is shown that a decision was motivated at least in part by a racially discriminatory purpose, the burden shifts to the [government] to show that the same result would have been reached even without consideration of race. If the [government] comes forward with no such proof or if the trier of fact is unpersuaded that race did not contribute to the outcome of the decision, the equal protection claim is established."); *Marshall v. Columbia Lea Regional Hospital*, 345 F.3d 1157 (10th Cir. 2003) (in a § 1983 claim involving allegations of racial profiling by a police officer, court applied a burden shifting test and reversed trial court's entry of summary judgment against plaintiffs on racial profiling claims). Essentially, the State must show that the same law enforcement decision or practice would have occurred had race not been a factor. *Sylvia Dev. Corp. v. Calvert County, Md.*, 48 F.3d 810, 819 n.2 (4th Cir. 1995). Alternatively, the State must demonstrate a compelling State interest in the racial classification that is narrowly tailored to the accomplishment of that legitimate purpose. *Palmore v. Sidoti*, 466 U.S. 429, 432–33 (1984).

When proffering race-neutral explanations for disparities, "mere denials or reliance on the good faith of the officers [will not] suffice." *State v. Soto*, 734 A.2d 350, 360 (N.J. Super. Ct. Law Div. 1996) (citing *Castaneda v. Partida*, 430 U.S. 482, 498 n.19 (1977)). As the Supreme Court has recognized in a related context, if mere assertions of good faith and denials of discriminatory intent were enough to defeat a claim of discrimination, "the Equal Protection Clause would be but a vain and illusory requirement." *Batson v. Kentucky*, 476 U.S. 79, 98 (U.S. 1986) (internal quotation omitted). In other words, it is the court's job, in evaluating an equal protection claim, to look behind alleged race-neutral reasons to determine whether official action was undertaken for a racially discriminatory reason.

Additionally, if the defendant makes out a prima facie case of selective enforcement, the State generally cannot rebut the defendant's evidence by simply pointing out unmeasured variables in the defendant's statistics. Instead, the State must introduce evidence demonstrating specific flaws in the defendant's evidentiary showing or by proffering convincing explanations of reasons for the disparities. *Bazemore v. Friday*, 478 U.S. 385 (1986). For example, if a defendant presents evidence demonstrating that the percentage of black people arrested for drug crimes is significantly higher than the percentage of black people in the population at issue, the State may rebut this evidence with evidence that the drug arrest rates reflect the racial makeup of the population of offenders, if such evidence exists.

F. Remedy for an Equal Protection Violation

When raising equal protection claims of selective enforcement, defense attorneys should seek both suppression of evidence seized in violation of the state and federal guarantees of equal protection, as well as dismissal of all charges arising out of the equal protection violation.

Suppression. If the State has obtained evidence by violating a suspect's constitutional rights, the usual remedy is exclusion of the evidence at trial. *See Mapp v. Ohio*, 367 U.S. 643 (1961); G.S. 15A-974; *State v. Carter*, 322 N.C. 709 (1988). The procedure for invoking the exclusionary rule is to file a motion to suppress the illegally obtained evidence, pursuant to G.S. 15A-971 through 15A-980. The exclusionary rule is frequently applied to unreasonable searches and seizures in violation of the Fourth Amendment. In North Carolina, the exclusionary rule also applies to equal protection claims, as G.S. 15A-974(a)(1) requires suppression of all evidence obtained in violation of the United States or the North Carolina Constitution. Additionally, our Supreme Court has held that, "[u]nder the judicial integrity theory, our constitution demands the exclusion of illegally seized evidence." *Carter*, 322 N.C. 709, 722–23 (explaining that North Carolina, justifies the exclusionary rule, in part, on "the preservation of the integrity of the judicial branch," rejecting good faith exception to exclusionary rule, and holding that "our constitution demands the exclusion of illegally seized evidence"); *see also State v. Villeda*, 165 N.C. App. 431, 435 (2004) (noting that the trial court suppressed all evidence seized as a result of a traffic stop after finding that the stop amounted to "intentional racially discriminatory law enforcement conduct" in violation of the Equal Protection Clause of the Fourteenth Amendment, and an unlawful detention in violation of the Fourth Amendment).

Some states have differed over application of the exclusionary rule to equal protection violations. *Compare, e.g., Commonwealth v. Lora*, 886 N.E.2d 688, 699 (Mass. 2008) (concluding that "the application of the exclusionary rule to evidence obtained in violation of the constitutional right to the equal protection of the laws is entirely consistent with the policy underlying the exclusionary rule"), *with People v. Fredericks,* 829 N.Y.S.2d 78, 78 (N.Y. App. Div. 2007) ("Suppression of evidence is not a recognized remedy for [an equal protection violation] . . . ."). However, North Carolina law, cited above, clearly supports exclusion for an equal protection violation. The exclusionary rule also has served as a remedy for violations of other constitutional rights beyond those guaranteed by the Fourth Amendment, including confessions in violation of the right against compelled self-incrimination, as protected by the Fifth Amendment to the United States Constitution, *see, e.g., Dickerson v. United States*, 530 U.S. 428, 432, (2000), and evidence obtained from government interrogations in violation of the Sixth Amendment to the United States Constitution, *see, e.g., Maine v. Moulton*, 474 U.S. 159, 179–80 (1985). The following articles may prove useful should attorneys find it necessary to argue that the exclusionary rule applies to evidence obtained in violation of the Equal Protection Clause and N.C. Constitution article I, section 19: Brooks Holland, *Race and Ambivalent Criminal Procedure Remedies*, 47 GONZ. L. REV. 341 (2012);

Brooks Holland, *Safeguarding Equal Protection Rights: The Search for an Exclusionary Rule under the Equal Protection Clause*, 37 AM. CRIM. L. REV. 1107 (2000).

Dismissal. Defendants raising claims of selective enforcement also should seek dismissal of all charges. In North Carolina, when a criminal defendant raising a selective enforcement claim "sustains his heavy burden [of proving discrimination by a clear preponderance of the evidence] he is entitled to dismissal." *State v. Howard*, 78 N.C. App. 262, 266 (1985); *see also State v. Villeda*, 165 N.C. App. 431, 435 (2004) (noting that the trial court dismissed all charges arising out of a traffic stop after finding that the stop amounted to "intentional racially discriminatory law enforcement conduct" in violation of the Equal Protection Clause of the Fourteenth Amendment, and an unlawful detention in violation of the Fourth Amendment). In cases of flagrant violations of constitutional rights, North Carolina law provides that dismissal is the appropriate remedy. G.S. 15A-954(a)(4) (providing that when "defendant's constitutional rights have been flagrantly violated and there is such irreparable prejudice to the defendant's preparation of his case . . . there is no remedy but to dismiss the prosecution").

2.4 Overview of Protections Against Unreasonable Searches and Seizures

The Fourth Amendment to the U.S. Constitution protects "the right of the people to be secure in their persons, houses, papers, and effects, against unreasonable searches and seizures." U.S. CONST. amend. IV. The parallel state constitutional provision provides that "[g]eneral warrants, whereby any officer or other person may be commanded to search suspected places without evidence of the act committed, or to seize any person or persons not named, whose offense is not particularly described and supported by evidence, are dangerous to liberty and shall not be granted." N.C. CONST. art. I, § 20. Both constitutional provisions "require[] the exclusion of evidence obtained by unreasonable search and seizure." *State v. Carter*, 322 N.C. 709, 712 (1988).

Attorneys should raise challenges to unreasonable searches and seizures under both state and federal constitutional provisions and argue specifically that the protections afforded by the state constitution are broader than those guaranteed by the federal constitution. North Carolina appellate courts have ordinarily construed search and seizure provisions in the North Carolina and federal constitutions as protecting the same rights, but state courts may interpret their state constitutions as providing greater protections. *See, e.g., Virmani v. Presbyterian Health Servs. Corp.*, 350 N.C. 449, 475 (1999) (stating that "the United States Constitution provides a constitutional floor of fundamental rights guaranteed all citizens of the United States, while the state constitutions frequently give citizens of individual states basic rights in addition to those guaranteed by the United States Constitution"); *Jones v. Graham Cnty. Bd. of Educ.*, 197 N.C. App. 279, 289–93, (2009) (noting that "[i]f we determine that the policy does not violate the Fourth Amendment, we may then proceed to determine whether Article I, Section 20 provides basic rights in addition to those guaranteed by the [Fourth Amendment]" (quotation omitted)).

2.5 Consensual Encounters

A. Overview

The protections of the Fourth Amendment do not come into play during consensual encounters in which no seizure has taken place. As a general rule, a person is seized when, in view of all of the circumstances, a reasonable person would have believed that he or she was not "free to leave." *U.S. v. Mendenhall,* 446 U.S. 544, 554 (1980). *See also Florida v. Bostick,* 501 U.S. 429 (1991) (when a person's freedom of movement is restricted for reasons independent of police conduct, such as when a person is a passenger on a bus, the test is whether a reasonable person would have felt free to decline the officer's requests or terminate the encounter). For a further discussion on how to distinguish between a consensual encounter and a seizure, *see* 1 NORTH CAROLINA DEFENDER MANUAL § 15.2A (Did the Officer Seize the Defendant?) (2d ed. 2013).

B. Relevance of Race to "Free to Leave" Test

Courts consider the totality of the circumstances in evaluating whether a reasonable person would have felt free to leave an allegedly consensual encounter. *See INS v. Delgado*, 466 U.S. 210, 215 (1984); *United States v. Analla*, 975 F.2d 119, 124 (4th Cir. 1992). In some cases, a defendant's race may be a factor in the totality of relevant circumstances. The U.S. Supreme Court has held that the individual's responses to police actions are not relevant to whether a reasonable person would have felt free to leave, which is an objective determination. *See Michigan v. Chesternut*, 486 U.S. 567, 574 (1988) (holding that the reasonable person standard "ensures that the scope of Fourth Amendment protection does not vary with the state of mind of the particular individual being approached"). Nevertheless, some courts have indicated that a defendant's characteristics—such as race or immigration status—may play a role in determining whether a reasonable person in the defendant's position would have felt free to leave.

For example, the Ninth Circuit Court of Appeals held that an encounter between two White police officers and an African American defendant was not consensual, as a reasonable person in the defendant's circumstances would not have felt free to leave. *U.S. v. Washington,* 490 F.3d 765 (9th Cir. 2007). In that case, the court relied on, among other things, the strained relations between police and the African American community and the reputation of police among African Americans. *Id. See also* DONALD HAIDER-MARKEL ET AL., CONSTRUCTING DISTRUST: THE CONSEQUENCES OF AFRICAN AMERICAN ENCOUNTERS WITH POLICE (2012) (finding, for example that Black people are far more likely than White people to agree with the statement "the police are out to get me"); NATIONAL INSTITUTE OF JUSTICE, MEASURING WHAT MATTERS: PROCEEDINGS FROM THE POLICING RESEARCH INSTITUTE MEETINGS 135 (Robert H. Langworthy ed., 1999) (reporting that only 32% of African Americans hold a great deal or quite a lot of confidence in the police, as opposed to 66% of whites).

In the context of police encounters in airports, the Fourth Circuit Court of Appeals included "the characteristics of the particular defendant" as one of three main factors to consider when determining whether an encounter was consensual. *United States v. Gray*, 883 F.2d 320, 322 (4th Cir. 1989) (citing *United States v. Black*, 675 F.2d 129, 134–35 (7th Cir. 1982), in which the Seventh Circuit noted in "free to leave" analysis, that defendant was an articulate, intelligent college graduate and therefore "not so naive or vulnerable to coercion that special protection from police contacts was required by the Fourth Amendment"). *But see Monroe v. City of Charlottesville*, 579 F.3d 380, 386–87 (4th Cir. 2009) ("[t]o agree that [the defendant's] subjective belief that he was not free to terminate the encounter was objectively reasonable because relations between police and minorities are poor would result in a rule that all encounters between police and minorities are seizures. Such a rule should be rejected."). One federal district court within the Fourth Circuit discussed without deciding whether a defendant's particular attributes—including limited English proficiency, limited formal education, and unfamiliarity with American police procedure—may be relevant to determining whether the defendant's encounter with a police officer constituted a seizure. *Santos v. Frederick County Bd. of Comm'rs*, 884 F. Supp. 2d 420, 427 n.5 (D. Md. 2012) (unpublished), *aff'd in part, vacated in part by* 725 F.3d 451 (2013) (recognizing that defendant's limited English proficiency "may have added to the coerciveness of the situation" but finding that "the language barrier, on its own, [was] insufficient to turn the otherwise consensual encounter into a seizure"). The U.S. Supreme Court has held analogously that a child's age is a relevant factor to consider in determining whether the child was in custody for *Miranda* purposes, even though whether a suspect is in custody is an objective inquiry. *See J.D.B. v. North Carolina*, __ U.S. __, 131 S. Ct. 2394, 2399 (2011).

C. Consensual Encounters Between Officers and Pedestrians

Race-based "consensual" encounters. Even if an encounter is consensual and therefore not subject to Fourth Amendment protections, an officer may violate the Equal Protection Clause of the Fourteenth Amendment and article I, section 19 of the N.C. Constitution if the defendant is selected for such an encounter because of the defendant's race. *See Whren v. U.S.*, 517 U.S. 806, 813 (1996) ("the Constitution prohibits selective enforcement of the law based on considerations such as race[;] [b]ut the constitutional basis for objecting to intentionally discriminatory application of laws is the Equal Protection Clause, not the Fourth Amendment"); *U.S. v. Avery,* 137 F.3d 343 (6th Cir. 1997); *U.S. v. Travis*, 62 F.3d 170 (6th Cir. 1995); *U.S. v. Taylor,* 956 F.2d 572 (6th Cir. 1992); *see also supra* § 2.3, Equal Protection Challenges to Police Action.

If you suspect that "Officer Jones" singled out your client for a consensual encounter on the basis of race, you may want to review court files in which Officer Jones was the arresting officer for evidence of racially discriminatory practices. By recording data such as the race of the person charged for a relevant time period, e.g., a one-year period before your client's encounter, you may be able to discern a pattern of enforcement decisions. If the charges initiated by the officer in question appear to be racially skewed, they may be compared to (1) census data reflecting the demographics of the area patrolled by the officer, and/or (2) the enforcement patterns of other officers responsible for patrolling the same area during approximately the same hours. *See* Michael R. Smith, *Depoliticizing Racial Profiling: Suggestions for the Limited Use and Management of Race in Police*

Decision-Making, 15 GEO. MASON U. CIV. RTS. L.J. 219, 247 (2005) ("A promising technique for assessing potential discrimination in the traffic stop practices of a particular officer is to compare the racial composition of the officer's stops to the racial composition of stops made by other officers who work the same assignment in the same general area and at approximately the same time of day."). This sort of information may be obtained by pulling court files in which other officers were the arresting officers. If you see a disparity in enforcement, you may have grounds for obtaining additional discovery about departmental practices. *See supra* "Discovery" in § 2.3D, Gathering Evidence to Support a Claim of Selective Enforcement. Ultimately, an equal protection claim of selective enforcement arising out of a consensual encounter must be supported by evidence demonstrating that the officer's consensual encounters were driven by racial motivations and resulted in racially disparate effects. *See supra* § 2.3D, Gathering Evidence to Support a Claim of Selective Enforcement.

D. Consensual Encounters at Home: The "Knock and Talk" Technique

Race-based "knock and talks." The "knock and talk" practice is one in which law enforcement officers, acting without a warrant and often without probable cause, knock on the door of a dwelling in order to question its inhabitants and often ask for consent to search their home. This practice has been criticized as one that allows targeting of minorities or other vulnerable populations. *See* Brian J. Foley, *Policing From the Gut: Anti-Intellectualism in American Criminal Procedure*, 69 MD. L. REV. 261, 340 (2010) (observing that "when police do not have to give reasons for discretionary searches or seizures, conscious and unconscious racism may prevail"). Attorneys may raise Equal Protection Clause challenges to race-based decisions to initiate "knock and talks." Such challenges might be considered, for example, if it appears that police officers are targeting predominantly minority neighborhoods for "knock and talks." These challenges should also be raised under article I, section 19 of the N.C. Constitution. *See supra* § 2.5C, Consensual Encounters Between Officers and Pedestrians and *supra* § 2.3, Equal Protection Challenges to Police Action.

Consent to search following a "knock and talk." Searches following "knock and talks" are permissible when the occupant freely, voluntarily, and unequivocally consents to the search. *U.S. v. Miller*, 933 F. Supp. 501, 505 (M.D.N.C. 1996). In *U.S. v. Johnson*, 333 U.S. 10 (1948), the Supreme Court characterized a defendant's alleged permission to search following a "knock and talk" as a "submission to authority rather than as an understanding and intentional waiver of a constitutional right" and rejected it as non-consensual. The burden is on the State to demonstrate that the defendant's consent was voluntary. *See, e.g., United States v. Morrow*, 731 F.2d 233, 236 (4th Cir. 1984) (where the State argues that defendant consented to a search of his or her home, it must prove that the defendant "freely and intelligently [gave his or her] unequivocal and specific consent to the search, uncontaminated by any duress or coercion, actual or implied" (internal quotation omitted)).

In *Schneckloth v. Bustamonte*, 412 U.S. 218, 226 (1973), the Supreme Court recognized that characteristics of the accused are relevant in the determination of whether consent to search was voluntarily given. "[A]ccount must be taken of subtly coercive police questions, as well as the possibly vulnerable subjective state of the person who consents"). *Id.* at 229. Based on this authority, defense counsel could argue that a defendant's race, ethnicity, age, limited education, or limited English proficiency should be taken into consideration in determining whether consent was freely given. Challenges to the validity of consent should be raised under the Fourth Amendment as well as article I, sections 19, 20, and 23 of the N.C. Constitution.

For a fuller discussion of the "knock and talk" technique, *see* 1 NORTH CAROLINA DEFENDER MANUAL § 14.2E (Knock and Talk) (2d ed. 2013).

E. Practice Tips: Challenges to Alleged Consensual Encounters

If your client is facing charges arising out of an allegedly consensual encounter with an officer and you believe race may have played a role in the encounter, the following questions may help you identify viable Fourth Amendment or Equal Protection challenges on which to base a motion to suppress evidence or dismiss charges:

- Is there evidence, direct or circumstantial, that your client may have been approached for a consensual encounter because of his or her race? For example, is there a pattern of police officers engaging in such encounters more often in predominantly minority neighborhoods? If so, the encounter may have violated your client's right to equal protection guaranteed by the N.C. Constitution and U.S. Constitution, even if the encounter did not constitute a seizure.
- Was there a show of force or other coercive action by the officer? If so, the court will be more likely to find that the encounter was a seizure requiring reasonable suspicion or an arrest requiring probable cause.
- Was your client in a particularly vulnerable state when approached by the officer, or was your client subjected to police pressure, making his or her consent involuntary and therefore invalid?
- Is there evidence that your client is a member of a minority community with a particularly strained relationship with the police? If so, those attributes may be relevant in determining whether, given the totality of the circumstances, a reasonable person would have perceived the encounter as consensual.
- Does your client have a history of traumatic interactions with police officers? For example, has your client ever been tasered or treated in any fashion that may have rendered him or her more likely to have his or her will overborne?

2.6 Traffic and Pedestrian Stops

A. Traffic Stops

The majority of police-civilian interactions in the United States occur during traffic stops. *See* CHRISTINE EITH & MATTHEW R. DUROSE, BUREAU OF JUSTICE STATISTICS, U.S.

DEP'T OF JUSTICE, CONTACTS BETWEEN POLICE AND THE PUBLIC, 2008 3 (2011) (finding that more than half of all civilian-police contacts occur in the traffic context). Generally, law enforcement officers may stop a vehicle and initiate a brief investigative detention if they have reasonable suspicion of a criminal or traffic violation. *Delaware v. Prouse*, 440 U.S. 648 (1979); *State v. Styles*, 362 N.C. 412 (2008). *See generally* 1 NORTH CAROLINA DEFENDER MANUAL Ch. 15 (Stops and Warrantless Searches) (2d ed. 2013).

Given the prevalence of traffic violations, police officers may lawfully stop nearly any motorist on the road. Thus, "racial profiling," or targeting drivers who are racial minorities, has been identified as a potential concern. *See White v. Williams*, 179 F. Supp. 2d 405, 410 (D. N.J. 2002) (defining racial profiling as "any action taken by a state trooper during a traffic stop that is based upon racial or ethnic stereotypes and that has the effect of treating minority motorists differently than non-minority motorists" (citation omitted)); David Rudovsky, *Litigating Civil Rights Cases to Reform Racially Biased Criminal Justice Practices,* 39 COLUM. HUM. RTS. L. REV. 97, 107 (2007) ("Since violations of the traffic laws are commonplace, police have enormous discretion to effectuate stops of a very high number of cars. This discretion provides the opportunity for pretextual stops and searches" based on race, ethnicity, or national origin.).

B. The Fourth Amendment and Pretextual Traffic Stops

The impact of *Whren v. United States*. Historically, many challenges to racially motivated pretextual stops were raised under the Fourth Amendment. *See, e.g., United States v. Harvey*, 24 F.3d 795, 799 (6th Cir. 1994). However, in 1996, the United States Supreme Court held that an officer's actual motivation in making a stop (for example, to investigate for drugs) is generally irrelevant for Fourth Amendment purposes if the officer has legal justification for the stop and could have stopped the person for a permissible reason (for example, speeding):

> [T]he Constitution prohibits selective enforcement of the law based on considerations such as race. But the constitutional basis for objecting to intentionally discriminatory application of laws is the Equal Protection Clause, not the Fourth Amendment. Subjective intentions play no role in ordinary, probable-cause Fourth Amendment analysis.

Whren v. United States, 517 U.S. 806, 813 (1996). The Supreme Court's holding in *Whren* effectively ended consideration of Fourth Amendment challenges to stops on the basis of pretext. *Accord State v. McClendon*, 350 N.C. 630 (1999) (adopting *Whren* under state constitution); *State v. Hamilton*, 125 N.C. App. 396 (1997) (court recognizes effect of *Whren* under U.S. Constitution).

There are some notable limitations to the *Whren* doctrine, however. First, the defendant may prevail on a Fourth Amendment claim where reasonable suspicion is lacking or evidence of racially biased intent undermines the credibility of the officer's stated reason for the stop. *See supra* § 2.3A, Equal Protection Claims May Strengthen Fourth Amendment Challenges. Second, if an officer stops a defendant because of his or her race, the stop may violate the Equal Protection Clause regardless of whether probable cause or reasonable suspicion exists. *See supra* § 2.3, Equal Protection Challenges to Police Action. Third, a defendant may challenge as pretextual a license or other checkpoint when the real purpose is impermissible under the Fourth Amendment. *See infra* § 2.6C, Challenging Checkpoints as Racially Discriminatory. These three theories are discussed further below.

Officer's "hunch" is not reasonable suspicion, especially where informed by race. North Carolina courts have consistently held that reasonable suspicion may not be based on an "unparticularized suspicion or hunch." *State v. Murray*, 192 N.C. App. 684, 687 (2008) (internal quotations omitted); *see also, State v. Chlopek*, 209 N.C. App. 358 (2011) (same). An officer's "hunch" may be viewed with particular skepticism when it is informed by a defendant's race. In *State v. Cooper*, 186 N.C. App. 100 (2007), the N.C. Court of Appeals determined that an officer did not have reasonable suspicion to stop the defendant, a black male, simply because he was in the vicinity of a crime scene in which the suspect was also described as a black male. Similarly, in *In re J.L.B.M.*, 176 N.C. App. 613 (2006), the N.C. Court of Appeals found that reasonable suspicion did not exist where the officer received a dispatch about a suspicious Hispanic male at a gas station, and the officer saw a Hispanic male in baggy clothes who spoke to someone in another car and then walked away from the officer's patrol car. In that case, the Court stated that "the rule is clear under both federal and state law that an officer must have a reasonable and articulable suspicion of 'criminal activity,' not merely suspicious activity." *In re J.L.B.M*, 176 N.C. App. 613, 621; *see also infra* "Innocent behavior cannot support reasonable suspicion" in § 2.6D, The Fourth Amendment and Terry Stops; § 2.6F, Seizures in Reliance on Descriptions of Suspect's Race.

Investigation tips: Pretextual stops. If your client is facing charges arising out of a potentially pretextual traffic stop, the following questions may help you identify Fourth Amendment challenges:

- Were the factors giving rise to reasonable suspicion known to the officer at the time of the seizure or could they be characterized as a post-hoc justification? *See, e.g., Devenpeck v. Alford*, 543 U.S. 146, 152 (2004) ("Whether probable cause exists depends upon the reasonable conclusion to be drawn from the *facts known to the arresting officer at the time of the arrest.*" (emphasis added)).
- Does the officer have a pattern of stopping minority drivers or targeting minority neighborhoods or locations? *See infra* § 2.6I, Collecting Traffic Stop Data to Support Equal Protection Claims.
- Were the alleged race-neutral grounds for reasonable suspicion not credible, given the totality of the circumstances? *State v. Villeda*, 165 N.C. App. 431 (2004).
- Did the officer asserting reasonable suspicion characterize innocent behavior as suspicious? *See infra* "Innocent behavior cannot support reasonable suspicion" in § 2.6.D, The Fourth Amendment and *Terry* Stops.

- Did the officer's asserted reasonable suspicion rely too heavily on a description of the suspect's race? *See infra* § 2.6F, Seizures in Reliance on Descriptions of Suspect's Race.
- Did the officer's alleged reasonable suspicion rely on proxies for race, such as presence in a predominantly minority neighborhood or age of car? *See infra* § 2.6E, Challenging Proxies for Race Used to Support Reasonable Suspicion.

Case study: Pretextual traffic stops. The following account was provided by an Assistant Public Defender in North Carolina who uncovered evidence that her client was stopped on the basis of his ethnicity.

When a deputy sheriff testified in a probable cause hearing in a cocaine trafficking case that he had stopped the truck for following too close, and that he stopped cars almost daily for following too close, I had a gut sense that he was not telling the truth. In my years of experience in court, I had rarely seen a ticket for following too close unless it was part of a traffic accident case. I checked the deputy's arrest history through the Automated Criminal Infraction System (ACIS) and learned that he had issued only one ticket in nine years for following too close. My suspicions grew. I wanted to get a look at the officer's warning tickets to see if I could uncover impeachment evidence. I was lucky enough to find a judge who was willing to sign an order giving me copies of the last five years of the deputy's warning tickets.

When the copies arrived, I charted them out. Of the 265 warning tickets issued by the deputy over the past four years, 148 of the drivers appeared to be Hispanic based on their surnames. Thus, Hispanics received 55% of the warning tickets in a geographic area in which Hispanics made up only about 8% of the population.

I then focused on the warning tickets for following too close. Of the 265 total, 130 warning tickets were for following too close. It appeared that the officer really was making regular stops for following too close, as he had testified. Of the 130 recipients, 77 appeared to be Hispanic. Thus, Hispanics received 59% of the deputy's warning tickets for following too close. I then uncovered a figure that was even more surprising: of the 130 warning tickets for following too close, 124 of the cars had out of state tags! I studied the warning tickets for charges other than following too close and saw that they also involved a disproportionate number of Hispanic drivers.

The overall pattern revealed that the deputy was targeting non-white people of obvious ethnicity who primarily were driving out of state cars. I surmised that he was making traffic stops in an effort to uncover drug couriers but achieving this goal in only a small percentage of cases. Meanwhile, he was inconveniencing and in all likelihood violating the constitutional rights of a large number of innocent people. I learned that although discriminatory behavior may be occurring, it is rarely uncovered because of obstacles, such as warning tickets not being readily accessible. To his credit, the prosecutor dismissed the case when confronted with these figures, which was a great result for this client, but on a less positive note, prevented the evidence of this officer's bias from coming to light in a public forum.

See Ex Parte Motion and Order to Require Sheriff's Department to Provide Records of Officer's Warning Tickets in the Race Materials Bank at www.ncids.org (select "Training & Resources").

C. Challenging Checkpoints

Constitutional requirements for checkpoints. In *Delaware v. Prouse,* 440 U.S. 648 (1979), the Supreme Court held that officers may not randomly stop motorists to check their driver's license or vehicle registration. The Court indicated, however, that checkpoints at which drivers' licenses and registrations are systematically checked may be permissible. *See also State v. Veazey*, 201 N.C. App. 398 (2009). A defendant who is stopped at a checkpoint has standing to challenge the constitutionality of the checkpoint. *See State v. Haislip,* 186 N.C. App. 275 (2007), *vacated and remanded,* 362 N.C. 499 (2008) (remanded to trial court for written findings of fact and conclusions of law). For further discussion of constitutional challenges to checkpoints, including challenges when a person turns away from a checkpoint and is thereafter stopped, see 1 NORTH CAROLINA DEFENDER MANUAL § 15.3J (Motor Vehicle Checkpoints) and § 15.3K (Drug and Other Checkpoints) (2d ed. 2013); *see also* Jeffrey B. Welty, *Motor Vehicle Checkpoints*, ADMINISTRATION OF JUSTICE BULLETIN NO. 2010/04 (UNC School of Government, Sept. 2010).

Equal protection challenges to checkpoints. In *State v. Burroughs*, 196 N.C. App. 178 (2009) (unpublished), the Court considered an equal protection challenge to the execution of a checkpoint. In that case, two drivers, one black and one white, had been drinking together at a local tavern before each approached the same checkpoint at about the same time. The black driver was subjected to all four screening tests allowed by the checkpoint plan while the white driver was not asked any questions or subjected to any screening tests. The court found that evidence demonstrating that the white male was treated more favorably than the similarly situated black male failed to establish a discriminatory purpose and was therefore insufficient to establish an equal protection violation. The court noted that the "findings may be sufficient to raise a suspicion about the manner in which the checkpoint was conducted," but that "the evidence presented at the hearing was not sufficient to establish intentional racial discrimination." *Id.* at *4. While the N.C. Court of Appeals found that the evidence did not show discriminatory intent, the case provides an example of how the claim may be raised and the potential availability of relief.

Pretextual checkpoints. A license or impaired-driving checkpoint is subject to challenge as pretextual under the Fourth Amendment. *See City of Indianapolis v. Edmond,* 531 U.S. 32 (2000) (checkpoint is unconstitutional if primary purpose is unlawful; checkpoint was unlawful in this case because primary purpose was to investigate for drugs).

Drug checkpoints. The U.S. Supreme Court has refused to uphold drug checkpoints. *See City of Indianapolis v. Edmond,* 531 U.S. 32 (2000); *see also U.S. v. Huguenin,* 154 F.3d 547 (6th Cir. 1998) (drug checkpoint unconstitutional); *Wilson v. Commonwealth,* 509 S.E.2d 540 (Va. Ct. App. 1999) (drug checkpoint inside entrance to public housing project unconstitutional); *Commonwealth v. Rodriguez,* 722 N.E.2d 429 (Mass. 2000) (drug checkpoint violated state constitution).

Public housing checkpoints. While there is no North Carolina decision addressing this issue, courts in other jurisdictions have found unconstitutional public housing checkpoints aimed at general crime control. *See, e.g., State v. Hayes,* 188 S.W.3d 505 (Tenn. 2006) (identification checkpoint at entrance to public housing development violated Fourth Amendment where goal was to reduce crime, exclude trespassers, and enforce lease agreement provisions to decrease crime and drug use; checkpoint was aimed at general crime control).

Location of checkpoints. The location of a vehicle checkpoint plays a large role in determining the racial composition of the population that is stopped. *See* Press Release, Civil Rights Division of the U.S. Dep't of Justice, Justice Department Releases Investigative Findings on the Alamance County, N.C., Sheriff's Office: Findings Show Pattern or Practice of Discriminatory Policing Against Latinos (Sept. 18, 2012) (finding that Sheriff's Deputies in Alamance County routinely located checkpoints near Latino neighborhoods). *See also* Letter to Raul Pinto, Racial Justice Fellow, American Civil Liberties Union of North Carolina, from Scott Cunningham, Chief of Police, Winston-Salem Police Department (Oct. 27, 2011) (defending location of checkpoints by department in response to ACLU's claim that department did not locate license checkpoints in areas with lower concentrations of Latinos and African Americans; letter acknowledges that 15% of the checkpoints were in areas with Caucasian populations from 44% to 100%). If you believe the location of checkpoints in your community is not race-neutral, consider providing the information to the ACLU of North Carolina. Forms to report possible checkpoint violations can be found at www.acluofnc.org.

D. The Fourth Amendment and *Terry* Stops

In *Terry v. Ohio*, 392 U.S. 1 (1968), the U.S. Supreme Court held that a law enforcement officer may initiate a brief investigatory detention of a pedestrian if the officer has reasonable suspicion that criminal activity is afoot, and may pat down the person's outer garments to check for weapons if the officer has reasonable suspicion that the person is armed and dangerous. These stops are typically referred to as "*Terry* stops" or "stop and frisks."

Both defense lawyers and prosecutors have suggested that, in some localities, minorities are more likely than whites to be subjected to "stop and frisk" tactics. *See, e.g.,* Joseph Goldstein, *Prosecutor Deals Blow to Stop-and-Frisk Tactic*, N.Y. TIMES, September 25, 2012. In New York City, the practice produced dramatic racial disparities. For example, a 2009 study found that 87 percent of people stopped were Black and Latino. CENTER FOR CONSTITUTIONAL RIGHTS, STOP-AND-FRISK: FAGAN REPORT SUMMARY (2010). In response to these practices, a class action lawsuit, *Floyd v. City of New York*, was filed challenging the city's "stop and frisk" practices as violations of the Fourth and Fourteenth Amendments. *Id.* In August, 2013, Federal District Judge Shira Scheindlin found that the department engaged in a "practice of making stops that lack individualized reasonable suspicion," and let racial bias guide police decision making. Judge Scheindlin ruled that the city's stop and frisk program was unconstitutionally applied, and appointed an independent monitor to oversee changes to the program. *See Floyd v. City of New*

York, 959 F. Supp. 2d 540 (S.D.N.Y 2013). On January 30, 2014, the City agreed to drop its appeal of that ruling and begin the joint remedial process ordered by the district court. *See* Press Release, Center for Constitutional Rights, City of New York and Center for Constitutional Rights Announce Agreement in Landmark Stop and Frisk Case (January 30, 2014).

Generally, the concerns arising in the *Terry* stop context resemble those arising in the traffic stop context. As in the traffic stop context, an officer's asserted grounds of reasonable suspicion may be insufficient to support an investigative detention of a pedestrian. *See supra* § 2.6B, The Fourth Amendment and Pretextual Traffic Stops. Obtaining comprehensive records of an officer's *Terry* stops of pedestrians may be more difficult than obtaining those relating to traffic stops, as there is no statutory requirement for law enforcement agencies to document and report to the State Bureau of Investigation all *Terry* stops. In other words, it is likely that in many cases, there may be records of only those *Terry* stops that resulted in an arrest or the issuance of a citation or warning citation. Where an attorney has concerns that an officer is influenced by race or ethnicity in determining when to initiate a *Terry* stop, she may submit a public records request to the relevant officer's law enforcement agency for all arrests, citations, warning citations, and other records of stops involving pedestrians during a specific period of time that includes the time of the client's *Terry* stop. Agencies may not currently maintain such information, however. *See, e.g.*, Center for Constitutional Rights, *Synopsis of Daniels, et al. v. City of New York*, CCRJUSTICE.ORG (last visited Jun. 24, 2014) (settlement of class action lawsuit alleging selective enforcement required NYPD, among other things, to maintain and audit stop-and-frisk records, and to maintain a written, binding, and constitutionally compliant anti-racial profiling policy).

Innocent behavior cannot support reasonable suspicion. In several recent *Terry* stop cases, the Fourth Circuit Court of Appeals admonished the Government for mischaracterizing "innocent facts as indicia of suspicious activity," especially when the police appeared to be targeting African Americans. *United States v. Black*, 707 F.3d 531 (4th Cir. 2013) (citing *United States v. Powell*, 666 F.3d 180 (4th Cir. 2011); *United States v. Massenburg*, 654 F.3d 480 (4th Cir. 2011); *United States v. Digiovanni*, 650 F.3d 498 (4th Cir. 2011); and *United States v. Foster*, 634 F.3d 243 (4th Cir. 2011)). In *Foster*, a police officer noticed the African American defendant rise from the passenger seat of a parked SUV in a low crime area and make sudden arm movements. Officers blocked the SUV with two vehicles, approached the SUV with a gun drawn, ordered the occupants to show their hands, and conducted a pat-down search of the driver. The *Foster* court found that the stop was not supported by reasonable suspicion and criticized official descriptions of innocent behavior as suspicious:

> We also note our concern about the inclination of the Government toward using whatever facts are present, no matter how innocent, as indicia of suspicious activity . . . . [A]n officer and the Government must do more than simply label a behavior as "suspicious" to make it so . . . Moreover, we are deeply troubled by the way in which the Government attempts to spin these largely mundane facts into a web of

> deception. . . . [T]he Government cannot rely upon post hoc rationalizations to validate those seizures that happened to turn up contraband.

634 F.3d 243, 248–49 (4th Cir. 2011). In *United States v. Massenburg*, also involving an African American defendant, the court rejected the State's assertion that looking down while refusing to grant consent to search gave rise to reasonable suspicion. 654 F.3d 480 (4th Cir. 2011); *see also United States v. Powell*, 666 F.3d 180 (4th Cir. 2011) (an individual's prior record, standing alone, is insufficient to support reasonable suspicion).

In *United States v. Black*, the Fourth Circuit clarified that the recurring failure to provide facts sufficient to support claims of individualized reasonable suspicion raised concerns about the presence of racial bias. 707 F.3d 531 (4th Cir. 2013). In that case, the court found that characterizing innocent behavior in an allegedly "high crime area" at night as suspicious puts minorities at greater risk of police intrusion:

> To conclude that mere presence in a high crime area at night is sufficient justification for detention by law enforcement is to accept carte blanche the implicit assertion that Fourth Amendment protections are reserved only for a certain race or class of people. We denounce such an assertion. . . . The facts of this case give us cause to pause and ponder the slow systematic erosion of Fourth Amendment protections for a certain demographic.

Id. at 542. In light of these concerns, the Court reversed the denial of the defendant's motion to suppress evidence.

In *Black*, the officers made several judgments that may have been influenced by the defendant's race or the race of his acquaintances. First, officers became suspicious about possible drug activity simply based on an individual's presence at a gas station; the Court found that this characterization "borders on absurd." *Id.* at 539. Second, the officers seized the gun of one of the defendant's acquaintances because, though legally possessed and displayed, the officers assumed its possessor was in violation of laws preventing felons from possessing guns, raising concerns that officers were relying on a racial profile. The Court recognized that this assumption was impermissible, as "[b]eing a felon in possession of a firearm is not the default status." *Id.* at 540. Third, the officers attempted to rely on the lawful possession of a handgun by the defendant's acquaintance to support reasonable suspicion that the defendant was engaged in criminal activity. The Court "refuse[d] to find reasonable suspicion merely by association." *Id.* Finally, the officers characterized the defendant's "overly cooperative behavior" as suspicious. *Id.* at 541. The Court observed that if reasonable suspicion can be based on cooperation with the police, individuals belonging to vulnerable minority populations may face a quandary:

> In certain communities that have been subject to overbearing or harassing police conduct, cautious parents may counsel their children

> to be respective, compliant, and accommodating to police officers, to do everything officers instruct them to do. If police officers can justify unreasonable seizures on a citizen's acquiescence, individuals would have no Fourth Amendment protections unless they interact with officers with the perfect amount of graceful disdain.

Id.

E. Challenging Proxies for Race Used to Support Reasonable Suspicion

"High-crime area" or "high-drug area" as a proxy for race. A defendant's presence in a "high crime area" is closely correlated with both socioeconomic status and race. *See United States v. Black*, 707 F.3d 531, 542 (4th Cir. 2013) ("In our present society, the demographics of those who reside in high crime neighborhoods often consist of racial minorities and individuals disadvantaged by their social and economic circumstances."). For this reason, concerns arise when a defendant's presence in a "high crime area" is cited as the sole or primary basis for an officer's reasonable suspicion of criminal activity. "The citing of an area as 'high-crime' requires careful examination by the court, because such a description, unless properly limited and factually based, can easily serve as a proxy for race or ethnicity." *United States v. Montero-Camargo*, 208 F.3d 1122, 1138 (9th Cir. 2000); *see also* David A. Harris, *Factors for Reasonable Suspicion: When Black and Poor Means Stopped and Frisked*, 69 IND. L.J. 659, 677–78 (1994) ("African Americans and Hispanic Americans make up almost all of the population in most of the neighborhoods the police regard as high crime areas."). As one commentator notes,

> '[H]igh crime area' becomes a centerpiece of the *Terry* analysis, serving almost as a talismanic signal justifying investigative stops. Location in America, in this context, is a proxy for race or ethnicity. By sanctioning investigative stops on little more than the area in which the stop takes place, the phrase 'high crime area' has the effect of criminalizing race.

Lewis R. Katz, *Terry v. Ohio at Thirty Five: A Revisionist's View*, 74 MISS. L.J. 423, 493–94 (2004).

In *United States v. Massenburg,* the Fourth Circuit Court of Appeals condemned this practice, stating that the government's generalized justification for stopping and frisking the defendant would effectively sanction "a regime of general searches of virtually any individual residing in or found in high-crime neighborhoods." 654 F.3d 480, 488 (4th Cir. 2011). The court observed that "general searches" had been decried as "'instruments of slavery . . . and villainy,' which 'place the liberty of every man in the hands of the petty officer.'" *Id.* The court concluded that the officer "lacked the reasonable suspicion needed to conduct a lawful nonconsensual frisk." *Id.* at 496.

Presence in a "high-crime area", in the absence of other suspicious factors, does not constitute reasonable suspicion. *See, e.g., Brown v. Texas,* 443 U.S. 47 (1979); *State v.*

Butler, 331 N.C. 227, 234–35 (1992) (defendant's presence with others on a corner known for drug-related activity would not, standing alone, justify investigatory stop); *State v. Blackstock*, 165 N.C. App. 50, 58 (2004) (defendant's presence in a high-crime area is a factor that may support reasonable suspicion, but is not sufficient to support a claim of reasonable suspicion on its own). The North Carolina Court of Appeals has also held that running in a "high-crime area" does not give rise to reasonable suspicion when it is not clear that the defendant is fleeing from officers: "To conclude the officers were justified in effectuating an investigatory stop, on these facts, would render any person who is unfortunate enough to live in a high-crime area subject to an investigatory stop merely for the act of running." *State v. White*, 214 N.C. App. 471, 480 (2011). *Cf. Illinois v. Wardlow*, 528 U.S. 119, 124 (2000) (presence in "area of heavy narcotics trafficking," along with headlong, unprovoked flight upon noticing the police provided reasonable suspicion of criminal activity). Recently, the North Carolina Court of Appeals held that walking away from one's companion twice after observing law enforcement officers in an area known for drug activity does not create reasonable suspicion. *State v. Jackson*, __ N.C. App. __, 758 S.E.2d 39 (2014) (distinguishing *Butler*, 331 N.C. 227, 234 (defendant's flight after making eye contact with officers gave rise to reasonable suspicion)), *temporary stay allowed*, __ N.C. __, __ S.E.2d __ (Jun. 6, 2014).

Courts have struggled with the question of how to evaluate testimony that an area is "high-crime" or "high-drug." The North Carolina Court of Appeals has held that trial courts may not take judicial notice of an area's status as a "high-crime area" since that determination is "no doubt a matter of debate within the community." *Hinkle v. Hartsell*, 131 N.C. App. 833, 837 (1998) (suggesting that the trial court could have determined that the area in question was "high crime" on the basis of testimony to that effect). The U.S. Supreme Court in *Wardlow*, 528 U.S. 119, did not clarify whether an officer's subjective impressions are sufficient to establish the "high-crime area" factor, or whether it must be substantiated with objective proof. As Judge Kozinski explained, "the question is not *whether* the characteristics of the area may be taken into account, but *how* these characteristics are established." *United States v. Montero-Camargo*, 208 F.3d 1122, 1143 (9th Cir. 2000) (Kozinski, J., concurring) (emphasis in original). Considerations include: "(1) what type of evidence should courts require to determine if an area is a high-crime area; (2) what standard of proof should courts adopt to evaluate that metric of crime; and (3) how should courts cabin the 'area' so designated to make it a meaningful and relevant description for Fourth Amendment purposes." Andrew Guthrie Ferguson & Damien Bernache, *The "High-Crime Area" Question: Requiring Verifiable And Quantifiable Evidence For Fourth Amendment Reasonable Suspicion Analysis*, 57 AM. U. L. REV. 1587, 1607 (2008).

Some courts have adopted fairly exacting tests for assessing officers' testimony about "high crime areas." For example, the First Circuit Court of Appeals held that, when considering an officer's testimony that a stop occurred in a "high crime area," a court must identify the relationship between the charged offense and the type of crime the area is known for, the geographic boundaries of the allegedly "high crime area," and the temporal proximity between the evidence of criminal activity and the observations allegedly giving rise to reasonable suspicion. *United States v. Wright*, 485 F.3d 45 (1st

Cir. 2007) (cited with approval in *United States v. Swain*, 324 Fed. Appx. 219, 222 (4th Cir. 2009) (unpublished) (observing that "'the high-crime-area' factor, like most [other factors pertaining to reasonable suspicion], can be implicated to varying degrees . . . an open-air drug market location presents a different situation than a parking lot where an occasional drug deal might occur")). *But see State v. Morgan*, 539 N.W.2d 887 (Wis. 1995) (holding that courts should defer to officers' perceptions of "high crime" areas).

Practice note: At present, officers' contentions that a stop occurred in a "high crime area" appear to be escaping careful scrutiny. Counsel should inform the court about approaches taken by courts such as the First Circuit Court of Appeals, and argue that requiring objective proof under articulable standards may discourage unjustified stops and frisks.

If the reasonable suspicion supporting the seizure of your client relates to your client's presence in a "high-crime" or "high-drug" area, you should consider developing evidence that the "high crime area" label is a proxy for "Black neighborhood" or "Latino neighborhood." You may want to seek discovery on, and consider investigating, the following questions:

- Was your client's presence in a "high-crime area" the only or primary factor supporting the officer's alleged reasonable suspicion?
- How strong are the other factors supporting the officer's alleged reasonable suspicion?
- What facts support the officer's characterization of the area in question as a "high crime area"? How recent are those facts?
- What is the relationship between the grounds for reasonable suspicion supporting the officer's stop of your client and the criminal activity for which the area is allegedly known?
- What are the geographic boundaries of the allegedly "high crime area"?
- What is the demographic composition of the allegedly "high crime area"?
- Does the investigating officer know of any Black or Latino neighborhoods in the county/city that would not be considered "high crime areas"?
- How familiar with the area is the officer in question? How long has he or she worked in or around that area?

Other proxies for race. Vehicle age may act as a proxy for race or ethnicity. *See, e.g.*, *United States v. Harvey*, 16 F.3d 109, 110–12 (6th Cir. 1994) (police officer testified that he stopped the car because three young Black males were occupants in an old vehicle). For example, police officers may target older model cars in order to investigate low-income Latinos for drinking or immigration offenses. *See* Memorandum of Law Racial Profiling – Motion to Dismiss and Motion to Suppress in the Race Materials Bank at www.ncids.org (select "Training & Resources"). Similarly, vehicles with after-market extras such as large rims, tinted windows, and loud audio systems may be targeted based on a perception that these features fit the profile of Black or Latino drivers and so are more likely to contain contraband. *See, e.g., United States v. Ferguson*, 130 F. Supp. 2d 560, 563 (S.D.N.Y. 2001) (evidence suppressed where officers stopped an African American male because they believed him to be driving a car with "excessively tinted windows"); *see also* Michael L. Birzer, RACIAL PROFILING: THEY STOPPED ME BECAUSE I'M ----------- 97–130 (2012). A prior criminal record could also be seen as a proxy for race, considering that Black people are overrepresented in the population of people with criminal records. *United States v. Powell*, 666 F.3d 180 (4th Cir. 2011) (an individual's prior record, standing alone, is insufficient to support reasonable suspicion).

Defense attorneys concerned that one or more of these vehicle features may have been used as a proxy for race should investigate the types of vehicles the officer has targeted over a representative time period (such as one year before the client's stop) and any departmental training materials on spotting suspicious vehicles. This sort of allegation could be supported by statistics showing the percentage of older model cars on the road in a certain area compared to the percentage of older model cars stopped by a particular officer. *See* Memorandum of Law Racial Profiling – Motion to Dismiss and Motion to Suppress in the Race Materials Bank at www.ncids.org (select "Training & Resources") (where, during an 18-month time period including defendant's stop, 60.9% of an officer's 905 traffic citations were issued to Latinos and 72.5% were issued to drivers of cars over 10 years old, defendant argued that this data, along with data showing that only 35.4% of cars on the road are over 10 years old, supported his argument that the officer unlawfully used vehicle age as a proxy for low-income, Latino drivers). Counsel can develop cross-examination questions to elicit any pattern of using proxies, and present social science research (such as the articles cited in this section) or expert testimony to link reliance on proxies to racial bias. *See, e.g.,* John Knowles et al., *Racial Bias in Motor Vehicle Searches: Theory and Evidence*, 109 J. POL. ECON. 203, 204 n.2 (2001) (describing Illinois Police training manual informing officers that "tinted windows . . . leased vehicles, [and] religious paraphernalia used to divert suspicion," should arouse officer suspicion).

F. Seizures in Reliance on Descriptions of Suspect's Race

A Fourth Amendment claim may arise when a seizure is based on a description of the suspect that relies primarily or entirely on race. The U.S. Supreme Court has held that race alone does not justify a stop or an arrest. In *United States v. Brignoni-Ponce*, 422 U.S. 873, 887 (1975), the Court declared that "standing alone [Mexican ancestry] does not justify stopping all Mexican-Americans to ask if they are aliens." *See also Brown v. Oneonta*, 221 F.3d 329, 334 (2d Cir. 2000) ("a description of race and gender alone will rarely provide reasonable suspicion justifying a police search or seizure"); *Buffkins v. City of Omaha*, 922 F.2d 465, 467, 470 (8th Cir. 1990) (holding that a tip that a black person or persons arriving on a flight from Denver would be importing cocaine to the Omaha, Nebraska, area before 5:00 p.m. on March 17, 1987, was not sufficient to justify *Terry* stop of a Black woman carrying toy animal); *Orhorhaghe v. INS*, 38 F.3d 488, 497 (9th Cir. 1994) (no reasonable suspicion justified seizure where sole basis was racial background or national origin, assumed from defendant's "foreign-sounding" surname); *Brown v. United States*, 590 A.2d 1008, 1019 (D.C. 1991) (no reasonable suspicion supported *Terry* stop; general race-based description of suspect could have matched many neighborhood residents and "no meaningful similarities had been positively established except that Brown . . . is a black male"); *see also* Dov Fox, *The Second Generation of Racial Profiling*, 38 AM. J. CRIM. L. 49 (2010) (arguing that, while judges and scholars generally view reliance on race-based suspect descriptions as legitimate, they will become harder to defend as advances in forensic technology allow more reliable identifiers of an offender's appearance).

G. Equal Protection Challenges to Seizures

North Carolina defendants have relied on the rights guaranteed by the Equal Protection Clause and article I, section 19 of the N.C. Constitution to challenge practices such as stopping motorists for "driving while black," *State v. Ivey*, 360 N.C. 562, 564 (2006), *abrogated in part on other grounds by State v. Styles*, 362 N.C. 412 (2008), and targeting Hispanic drivers for traffic stops, *State v. Mendez*, 216 N.C. App. 587 (2011) (unpublished); *see also* Order Allowing Motion to Suppress in the Race Materials Bank at www.ncids.org (select "Training and Resources"). Claims based on the state and federal guarantees of equal protection must show that the challenged police action was motivated by a discriminatory intent and produced a discriminatory effect. *See supra* § 2.3, Equal Protection Challenges to Police Action. This subsection addresses procedures for raising equal protection challenges to the use of racial profiling in traffic and pedestrian stops, along with considerations that arise in these contexts.

Direct evidence of discriminatory intent. Defendants are in the best position to demonstrate discriminatory intent when they possess direct evidence that an officer's action was racially motivated. Such evidence is often hard to uncover. *U.S. v. Avery*, 137 F.3d 343, 355 (6th Cir. 1997) (noting that "discrimination can be proved through direct evidence, which seldom exists"). However, there are times when officers candidly acknowledge that a defendant's race played a role in the officer's decision to initiate a stop. *See United States v. Weaver*, 966 F.2d 391 (8th Cir. 1992) (officers testified that they stopped defendant at least in part because he was a young black male who fit the racial profile of a drug trafficker); *United States v. Condelee*, 915 F.2d 1206 (8th Cir. 1990) (same); *Chavez v. Illinois State Police*, 251 F.3d 612, 625 (7th Cir. 2001) (officer "asked if he could search [African American defendant's] car, twice stating that one can never tell with 'you people'"); *State v. Villeda*, 165 N.C. App. 431 (2004) (trooper at issue stated personal opinion that "Hispanics are more prone than other races to get in a car after they have been drinking").

While such evidence may not immediately be evident, it sometimes can be uncovered through investigation. The first place to start is with the client. Counsel should seek a detailed narrative of the stop to learn the nature of the interaction. In addition to the usual considerations, including the length of the stop, questions unrelated to the initial purpose of the stop, the use of drug dogs on a routine traffic stop, calls for backup, requests to step out of the car, rough treatment, requests to search, or roadside searches, be alert to whether the officer:

- questioned the client about matters such as gang membership or immigration status not relevant to the asserted ground for the stop;
- questioned the client about his reason for being in the present location, or suggested that the client should not have been in the area (if predominantly white);
- stopped the client in an area frequented primarily by members of the defendant's race, for example, near the Mercado Latino; or
- made reference to minorities or a minority group.

Statistical evidence of discriminatory intent. In addition to direct evidence of discriminatory intent, attorneys may use statistical evidence, typically along with other circumstantial evidence, to support claims of discriminatory intent. *See Washington v. Davis*, 426 U.S. 229, 242 (1976) ("[A]n invidious discriminatory purpose may often be inferred from the totality of the relevant facts, including the fact, if it is true, that the [practice] bears more heavily on one race than another"); *State v. Soto*, 734 A.2d 350, 360 (N.J. Super. Ct. Law Div. 1996) ("While defendants have the burden of proving 'the existence of purposeful discrimination,' discriminatory intent may be inferred from statistical proof presenting a stark pattern or an even less extreme pattern in certain limited contexts" (quoting *McCleskey v. Kemp*, 481 U.S. 279 (1987))). *See supra* "Discriminatory purpose" in § 2.3C, Elements of a Selective Enforcement Claim; *infra* § 2.6H, Types of Statistical Evidence Supporting Equal Protection Claims.

Statistical evidence of discriminatory effect. Defendants raising selective enforcement claims in the context of pretextual stops will almost always need to support their motions with statistical evidence of a discriminatory effect. In most cases, statistical evidence will be required to show that the challenged practice had a discriminatory effect on a discrete racial group to which the defendant belongs. *Chavez v. Illinois State Police*, 251 F.3d 612, 638 (2001). Factors to consider when assembling statistical evidence are discussed in greater detail below.

H. Types of Statistical Evidence Supporting Equal Protection Claims

Not all statistical evidence carries the same weight. "[S]tatistics are not irrefutable; they come in infinite variety and, like any other kind of evidence, they may be rebutted. In short, their usefulness depends on all of the surrounding facts and circumstances." *International Bhd. of Teamsters v. United States*, 431 U.S. 324, 340 (1977). In claims of selective enforcement, "[t]he statistics proffered must address the crucial question of whether one class is being treated differently from another class that is otherwise similarly situated." *Chavez v. Illinois State Police*, 251 F.3d 612, 638 (7th Cir. 2001). Defendants have attempted to make this statistical showing in a number of different ways; there is no one approach.

Surveys of traffic law violators compared to traffic stop data supported claim of selective enforcement. In *State v. Soto*, 734 A.2d 350, 360 (N.J. Super. Ct. Law Div. 1996), the court considered comprehensive surveys covering both the racial composition of motorists on a particular stretch of the New Jersey Turnpike (the "traffic survey") and the racial composition of motorists observed violating speeding and other moving violation laws along the same stretch of the interstate (the "violation survey"). These surveys indicated that the motorist population was 13.5% black and the violator population was 15% black, while the traffic stop data indicated that 46.2% of motorists stopped on this particular stretch of highway were black. Black motorists were thus 4.85 times more likely than white motorists to be stopped on this particular stretch of interstate. The judge found that the unrebutted surveys were well designed and statistically reliable and that they supported a finding that the state troopers engaged in a "de facto policy" of targeting black motorists in violation of the Equal Protection Clause. The judge therefore granted the defendants' motion to suppress evidence obtained through traffic stops of black motorists on this stretch of highway. *See also State v. Kennedy*, 588 A.2d 834 (N.J. Super. App. Div. 1991); *Wilkins v. Maryland State Police*, No. MJG-93-468 (D. Md. 2003) (lawsuit that concluded in a Consent Decree outlining a new Maryland State Police policy to prevent racial profiling); *United States' Reply in Support of its Motion to Modify the Expert Disclosure Deadline as to a Single Expert*, Exhibit C at 2–3, *United States v. Terry Johnson*, No. 12-cv-1349.

In cases where a comparison of bare traffic stop data to census data reflects racial disparities in traffic stops, you may be able to petition the court for funds for an expert to conduct the type of study described above. For sources of basic statistical information that may be part of a claim or support a request for funds for further study, see *infra* "Data sources relevant to North Carolina traffic stops" in § 2.6I, Collecting Traffic Stop Data to Support Equal Protection Claims. For a discussion of obtaining an expert for an indigent defendant, see 1 NORTH CAROLINA DEFENDER MANUAL Ch. 5 (Experts and Other Assistance) (2d ed. 2013).

Comprehensive statistics of stops may be enough to satisfy both effect and intent prongs of equal protection claim. *See State v. Soto*, 734 A.2d 350, 360 (N.J. Super. Ct. Law Div. 1996) ("While defendants have the burden of proving the existence of purposeful discrimination, discriminatory intent may be inferred from statistical proof presenting a stark pattern or an even less extreme pattern in certain limited contexts. . . . [D]iscriminatory intent may be inferred from statistical proof in a traffic stop context probably because only uniform variables [violations of New Jersey motor vehicle statutes] are relevant to the challenged stops and the State has an opportunity to explain the statistical disparity.") (internal quotation and citation omitted).

Comparisons of officers' patterns more significant when officers conduct similar work. *See United States v. Hare*, 308 F.Supp.2d 955, 966 (D. Neb. 2004) (defendants' general statistics comparing all troopers within a troop area rather than similarly situated troopers with similar patrols "prove almost nothing") (citing *United States v. Alcaraz-Arellano*, 302 F.Supp.2d 1217 (D. Kan. 2004) (evidence that a deputy stopped more Latinos than others in the sheriff's department was not meaningful because deputy in question patrolled I-70 almost exclusively while other deputies did not)); *see also* Michael R. Smith, *Depoliticizing Racial Profiling: Suggestions for the Limited Use and Management of Race in Police Decision-Making*, 15 GEO. MASON U. CIV. RTS. L.J. 219, 247 (2005) ("A promising technique for assessing potential discrimination in the traffic stop practices of a particular officer is to compare the racial composition of the officer's stops to the racial composition of stops make by other officers who work the same assignment in the same general area and at approximately the same time of day."). When collecting data about officers conducting similar work, "sound methodological practice requires comparing officers' stops to a cohort of other officers by similar job assignment, geographic location, and time of day." *Id.* at 250–56 (providing an example of a study that accounted for such variables). This approach has been referred to as "internal benchmarking," and it has been accepted by at least one federal court as partial evidence of selective enforcement. *Id.*; *United States v. Mesa-Roche*, 288 F. Supp. 2d 1172, 1190 (D. Kan. 2003).

Statewide census data not a proxy for the racial composition of motorists on a particular stretch of highway. *See Chavez v. Illinois State Police*, 251 F.3d 612, 644 (7th Cir. 2001) (no prima facie case of selective enforcement because benchmark data used for comparison with traffic stop data were statewide census figures, which "tell us very little about the number of Hispanics and African Americans driving on [the] Illinois interstate highways [at issue in this case], which is crucial to determining the population of motorists encountered by the . . . officers"). Tailored benchmarks, such as census data regarding the population in a specific area within a city or survey data reflecting the demographic composition of motorists on a particular stretch of road, will be more persuasive than generalized statewide census data. For further discussion of traffic-specific data available in North Carolina, see *infra* § 2.6I, Collecting Traffic Stop Data to Support Equal Protection Claims.

Defendant's statistical evidence should be from a relevant time period including the defendant's case, or as contemporaneous as possible. *See United States v. Barlow*, 310 F.3d 1007, 1011–12 (7th Cir. 2002) (citing with approval surveys conducted in *Soto*, which were conducted two years after the end of the time period relevant to the selective enforcement claims, but were relevant for comparative purposes because "there was no evidence that traffic patterns had changed between 1991 and 1993").

I. Collecting Traffic Stop Data to Support Equal Protection Claims

North Carolina requirements for collection of traffic stop data. North Carolina lawmakers responded to concerns over possible racial profiling in traffic stops by passing legislation mandating the collection of traffic stop data encompassing, among other statistics, the "[i]dentifying characteristics of the drivers stopped, including the race or ethnicity" and "the race or ethnicity . . . of each person searched." *See* G.S. 114-10.01. Pursuant to this law, the Division of Criminal Information of the North Carolina Department of Justice must collect statistics on traffic stops by state troopers and other state law enforcement officers. *Id.* This statute also requires the Division to collect statistics on many local law enforcement agencies. *Id.* In 2009, the law was amended by "An Act . . . to Prevent Racial Profiling and to Provide for the Care of Minor Children When Present at the Arrest of Certain Adults." S.L. 2009-544. As a result of this amendment, agencies that fail to submit traffic stop statistics to the Division of Criminal Statistics in compliance with the data collection law shall be penalized and ineligible to receive any state law enforcement grants until the required data is submitted. G.S. 114-10.01(d1).

Data sources relevant to North Carolina traffic stops. Defense attorneys seeking data relevant to North Carolina traffic stops may consult a number of relevant sources. Traffic stop reports reflecting traffic stop data collected pursuant to G.S. 114-10, including reports identifying the race and ethnicity of drivers or passengers stopped and/or searched, may be accessed on the North Carolina Traffic Stop Statistics section of the department's website. This web-based tool allows users to create reports reflecting stops, searches, and enforcement actions taken by various law enforcement agencies during time periods designated by the user. The Baumgartner study, analyzing approximately thirteen million North Carolina traffic stops made between January 1, 2000 and June 14, 2011, may be accessed on the website of the North Carolina Commission on Racial and Ethnic Disparities in the Criminal Justice System, which also contains additional publications and resources potentially relevant to North Carolina traffic stops. Traffic stop data collected by the U.S. Bureau of Justice Statistics is available on the Traffic Stops section of the Bureau of Justice Statistics website. U.S. Census Data, which in some circumstances may be relevant to selective enforcement claims, may be found on the U.S. Census Bureau's website. *See* Michael R. Smith, *Depoliticizing Racial Profiling: Suggestions for the Limited Use and Management of Race in Police Decision-Making*, 15 GEO. MASON U. CIV. RTS. L.J. 219, 251–56 (2005) (describing study in which traffic stops were mapped and aggregated by census area, allowing for comparison with census data).

An additional resource for lawyers seeking North Carolina traffic stop data is currently under development by the Southern Coalition for Social Justice ("SCSJ"). SCSJ is developing a website to help users analyze possible racial disparities in traffic stops, searches, and arrests conducted by North Carolina law enforcement officers. The website will allow users to:

- generate statistical reports, drawn from the aggregate data reported to the SBI pursuant to G.S. 114-10.01, detailing the relative probability of Black, White, and Latino motorists being searched when stopped by a particular department for a given offense;
- access statewide averages for comparative purposes;
- generate reports on contraband discovery rates, broken down by race, age, and gender;
- identify any departments in North Carolina that are not in compliance with the requirements imposed by the data collection statute;
- use the website as a management tool within law enforcement agencies to identify officers generating the largest racial disparities.

The website, which will be available beginning in late 2014 or early 2015 and updated regularly, will include all reported traffic stops that have occurred in the state of North Carolina since January 1, 2000—currently an estimated 14 million. Questions about the website may be directed to SCSJ attorney and Soros Justice Fellow Ian A. Mance at ianmance@southerncoalition.org, who, at the time of publication, was available to assist attorneys in analyzing traffic stop data as necessary.

In some cases, attorneys may be able to enlist academics, researchers, consultants, or graduate students to assist with statistical analyses. *See, e.g.*, Lamberth Consulting, LAMBERTHCONSULTING.COM (consulting firm providing racial profiling assessment, training, and communication services to a range of clients). Traffic stop data study author Frank Baumgartner may be able to either assist attorneys in analyzing traffic stop data or direct attorneys to someone else who can do so. For a list of other relevant data sources, see *infra* Chapter 10, Sources of Information about Matters of Race.

Gathering, interpreting, and analyzing traffic stop data. Data collected pursuant to the traffic data collection law is an important source for attorneys litigating equal protection challenges to traffic stops. In addition to accessing traffic stop data and data analysis through the NC DOJ website and, eventually, SCSJ's website, attorneys may obtain the underlying information used to create the reports required under G.S. 114-10.01 by submitting a request to the SBI Traffic Stop Unit for the information collected on SBI-122 forms. *See* SBI-122 Traffic Stop Form in the Race Materials Bank at www.ncids.org (select "Training & Resources"). The SBI-122 forms contain data entered by the officer and forwarded electronically to the SBI Traffic Stops Unit by the officer's agency. This data is likely to be more extensive than the data contained in court files for cases arising out of traffic stops. A subpoena or court order should not be necessary to obtain these records. Unless a specific statutory exception exists, records maintained by state and local government agencies are public records. *See generally News and Observer Publishing Co. v. Poole,* 330 N.C. 465 (1992). Counsel may tailor the request by asking for data for all stops made by the law enforcement agency in question during the time period and in the geographic location in which the client was stopped. *See* Sample Request for SBI-122 Records in the Race Materials Bank at www.ncids.org (select "Training & Resources"). Alternatively, counsel may submit a public records request to the relevant law enforcement agency for the traffic stop data sought. *See* Request for Public Records and Affidavit in Support of Motion to Suppress Illegal Stop and Illegal Search (noting that the contents of the affidavit were based in part on materials provided by the sheriff's department in response to a public records request) in the Race Materials Bank at www.ncids.org (select "Training and Resources").

In recent years, officers have begun to use additional numeric codes when entering the required data on the SBI-122 forms. For example, a motorist's race may be recorded as "3" and sex may be identified as "1". Thus, attorneys must use a glossary of codes to decipher the recent forms. A glossary may be found in the Race Materials Bank at www.ncids.org (select "Training & Resources").

The officer's name is not included on the SBI-122 forms. In place of a name, the officer enters a number that is assigned by the officer's employing agency. G.S. 114-10.01(d) states that the "correlation between the identification numbers and the names of the officers shall not be a public record." Although this information is not available to the public generally, the statute allows the officer's employing agency to disclose this information when required by a court order to resolve a claim or defense before the court. Motions for disclosure of an officer's identification number may be made before or alongside motions to suppress evidence arising out of a stop or search. See Motion to Suppress Illegal Stop and Search and Motion to Disclose Officer's ID Number in the Race Materials Bank at www.ncids.org (select "Training & Resources"). In addition to seeking disclosure of such information through a court order, some North Carolina attorneys have determined the identity of individual stopping officers associated with the SBI-122 numbers by comparing public court files with the data in the SBI-122 forms. For example, Durham attorney Kerstin Walker Sutton of Sutton & Lindsay, PLLC, has compared data from SBI forms, ACIS, and court files to determine an officer's SBI-122 number and analyze whether the evidence supported a claim of selective enforcement. *See* Attorney Kerstin Walker Sutton's Method for Analyzing Traffic Stop Data and Example from Litigated Case in the Race Materials Bank at www.ncids.org (select "Training & Resources"). In these cases, identifying the officer listed on the SBI-122 forms allowed her to examine possible enforcement patterns across all traffic stops by the officer, not just those that resulted in the filing of formal charges. *See id.*

Examples of traffic stop data collection using ACIS. In a case that was eventually heard in the North Carolina Court of Appeals, defense attorneys overheard a trooper discussing racially profiling Latino drivers for vehicle stops. An attorney who represented a Latino man who had been stopped by this trooper used ACIS to obtain the numbers of all of the citations issued by the trooper. Still using ACIS, she learned the race of the individuals who had received the citations. Based on this data, the attorney concluded that over a 14-month period, 71% of DWI citations issued by the trooper in question were issued to Latinos. In contrast, 2000 Census data revealed that Latinos made up approximately 32% of the population in one of the concentrated areas of the trooper's stops. This data, along with the statements heard by defense attorneys, formed the basis of a successful motion to suppress in the trial court based on the Equal Protection Clause of the Fourteenth Amendment and Article I, Sec. 19 of the North Carolina Constitution. Although the North Carolina Court of Appeals did not reach the equal protection claim, it concluded that the trooper had no reasonable suspicion of criminal activity because, contrary to his testimony, he was not able to observe the defendant's seat belt. *State v. Villeda*, 165 N.C. App. 431 (2004); *see also supra* § 2.3A, Equal Protection Claims May Strengthen Fourth Amendment Challenges. For materials about ACIS data, see Discovery Order in Selective Enforcement Case; Order for Production and Review of Evidence; and AOC Computer Instructions in the Race Materials Bank at www.ncids.org (select "Training & Resources").

Case study: Using traffic stop data as a management tool. In the following anecdote, Chapel Hill Police Chief Christopher Blue explains how his office uses the traffic stop data collected on SBI-122 forms as a management tool. *See supra* "Gathering, interpreting, and analyzing traffic stop data" in this subsection I (explaining contents of SBI-122 forms).

In 2012, the Chapel Hill Police Department developed a process to conduct reviews of our officers' traffic stops to identify any irregularities or patterns in them. At the time, some law enforcement agencies were beginning to think about how to address the problem of disproportionate minority contact, and we wanted to get a clearer picture of our own officers' encounters with citizens. We also wanted to raise awareness with our officers about the possible influence of bias on their decisions because concerns about the possible influence of bias on law enforcement decision-making were being raised around the country in the media and in studies.

The process we created involves quarterly reviews of each officer's stops by his/her supervisor to review data from the officer's traffic stops. Supervisors review the SBI-122 traffic stop forms that the officer has submitted and, if those forms suggest some irregularity, the supervisors may consult other documents, such as incident reports. The supervisor compares demographic information from the officer's encounters (vehicle stops, searches, and arrests) with the demographics of the community as a whole. Supervisors also have the option of comparing an officer's data with data submitted by other officers under their supervision. Following the reviews, and any subsequent meetings as needed, the supervisors must certify that the audits are complete. They must identify any irregularities or trends, and detail any resulting actions. Thankfully, as of this writing, this review process has not resulted in any disciplinary actions.

This process has helped us ensure that our officers are submitting their traffic stop forms in a timely manner and it has afforded us excellent opportunities to have important conversations with our officers about how we interact with our community. Personally, I think it is healthy for organizations to build systems that require periodic reviews of all processes, particularly those involving the potential for bias, whether intentional or not. Finally, the review process reinforces two of our most important departmental values, Mutual Respect and Accountability.

J. Information about Personal Impact of Equal Protection Violation

When raising an equal protection violation, attorneys should consider including information about the personal impact of unwarranted traffic stops. While not an element of an equal protection claim, such information may reinforce to the court the deleterious effect of racial profiling. Usually, "only those on whom contraband is found are charged with crimes, and those charged with crimes have the strongest incentive to challenge the stop." *U.S. v. Mubdi*, 691 F.3d 334, 345 (2012) (Davis, J., concurring in part), *judgment vacated*, __ U.S. __, 133 S.Ct. 2851 (2013). But, legal literature, including case law, has noted the wider impact of racial profiling on minorities. *Mubdi*, 691 F.3d 334, 347 n.4 (collecting sampling of recent literature). *See also* Ian Mance, *Racial Profiling in North Carolina: Racial Disparities in Traffic Stops*, 2000–2011, NCAJ TRIAL BRIEFS, June 2012, at 23 (describing humiliation and trauma experienced by African American male who was stopped); Kami Chavis Simmons, *Beginning to End Racial Profiling: Definitive Solutions to an Elusive Problem*, 18 WASH. & LEE J. CIVIL RTS. & SOC. JUST. 25, 27 n.7 (2011) (citing compilations of stories about impact of stops on minorities); Michael L. Birzer, RACIAL PROFILING: THEY STOPPED ME BECAUSE I'M ------------ 97–130 (2012) (discussing interviews with 87 minority citizens who believed they were racially profiled by law enforcement officers and reporting that the subjects (1) perceived that stereotypes influenced an officer's decision to stop them for a pretextual reason, (2) reported experiencing accusatory or demeaning treatment from officers, and (3) described emotional distress resulting from the interaction).

Jay-Z's song "99 Problems," which expresses the perception of many Black men that they are targeted by law enforcement officers on account of their race and youth, has even made it into the legal literature:

> So I . . . pull over to the side of the road
> And I heard 'Son do you know what I'm stopping you for?'
> 'Cause I'm young and I'm black and my hat's real low?'
> Do I look like a mind reader sir, I don't know
> Am I under arrest or should I guess some mo'?

See Caleb Mason, *Jay-Z's 99 Problems, Verse 2: A Close Reading With Fourth Amendment Guidance For Cops And Perps*, 56 ST. LOUIS U. L.J. 567 (cited in *Davis v. City of New York*, 902 F. Supp. 2d 405, 411 n.22 (S.D.N.Y. 2012); *United States v. Schuett*, 2012 WL 3109394 (E.D. Mich. July 31, 2012) (unpublished)).

2.7 Other Selected Aspects of Warrantless Stops

A. Questioning

To comply with the Fourth Amendment, an investigative detention must be temporary and last no longer than necessary to effectuate the purpose of the stop. The U.S. Supreme Court has held that an officer may inquire into "matters unrelated to the justification for the traffic stop . . . [without] convert[ing] the encounter into something other than a lawful seizure, so long as those inquiries do not measurably extend the duration of the stop." *Arizona v. Johnson*, 555 U.S. 323, 333 (2009). Some North Carolina cases have held that officers need additional reasonable suspicion to extend a stop once the original purpose of the stop has been addressed. *See, e.g.*, *State v. Jackson*, 199 N.C. App. 236 (2009). However, recent cases have found that the Fourth Amendment is not implicated if the delay is de minimis. *See, e.g.*, *State v. Sellars,* __ N.C. App. __, 730 S.E.2d 208 (2012) (finding delay of four minutes and 37 seconds de minimis). The length of any delay caused by questions or investigation unrelated to the purpose of the stop is an important factor in determining whether officers acted within the lawful scope of the stop. *See State v. Branch*, 194 N.C. App. 173 (2008) (ten minute delay unlawful); *United States v. Peralez*, 526 F.3d 1115, 1119–20 (8th Cir. 2008) (thirteen minute delay for questions unrelated to justification for stop unconstitutionally extended the detention). Also, the reason for the delay may be a significant factor. *See also State v. Cottrell*, __ N.C. App. __, 760 S.E.2d 274 (2014) (officer violated the defendant's Fourth Amendment rights by detaining the defendant after the purpose of the traffic stop was met, without having developed reasonable suspicion of criminal activity).

The Fourth Circuit Court of Appeals has adopted a potentially fruitful way to assess questioning and other investigative actions unrelated to the purpose of the stop. The court has held that an officer exceeds the limits of a lawful traffic stop when, without reasonable suspicion, he drops the investigation of the originally suspected traffic offense and "embark[s] on another sustained course of investigation." *United States v. Guijon-*

Ortiz, 660 F.3d 757, 766 (4th Cir. 2011) (quotation omitted). Under this approach, the reasonableness of prolonging a traffic stop is judged not merely on the duration of the stop but also on whether the officer diligently pursued the purpose of the stop, during which time it was necessary to detain the defendant. *Id.* at 770 ("Possessing probable cause that a driver has committed a traffic infraction does not give an officer free rein to keep the vehicle and its passengers on the side of the road while the officer investigates any hunch, whether through questioning or other methods, so long as the stop is shorter than the time it would have taken to conduct the ordinary incidents of a traffic stop.")

These principles provide some Fourth Amendment protections to motorists against pretextual stops because they limit an officer's actions following the stop. A lengthy detention following an otherwise routine traffic stop also may raise concerns that the stated reason for the stop masks an actual purpose of generalized criminal investigation in reliance on a criminal profile. For example, a trooper in one case "testified that he began to follow [the defendant] to '*see if I could find a violation*,' and admitted 'in an attempt to find a violation on [defendant's] vehicle . . . *I was going to conduct a pretextual stop*, stop him for a traffic violation, conduct a brief interview of him, [and] see if I observed any indicators of other criminal activity.'" *United States v. Foreman*, 369 F.3d 776, 786–87 (4th Cir. 2004) (Gregory, J. concurring in part and dissenting in part) (emphasis in original) (internal citation omitted). Admissions such as these will be rare, since, as Judge Davis of the Fourth Circuit Court of Appeals observed, "[a]t an earlier time, some law enforcement officers freely employed the term 'pretextual stop' although, with increased sensitivity over racial profiling, the terms seems to have fallen from favor." *United States v. Mubdi*, 691 F.3d 334, 347 n.3 (4th Cir. 2012) (Davis, J., concurring in part), *rev'd on other grounds*, 133 S. Ct. 2851 (2013). Even with such admissions, the defendant must ultimately show that the stopping officer did not have an objective ground for the stop in order to make out a Fourth Amendment violation (in both *Foreman* and *Mubdi*, the majority found a basis for the stop) and will have to show discriminatory intent and effect to make out an equal protection violation.

Attorneys may want to review police policies regarding traffic stops, if any, to determine the extent to which they permit employing drug-sniffing dogs on traffic stops, asking that vehicle occupants step out of their cars, requesting permission to search, and other techniques that may extend traffic stops and increase their potential consequences. Such a review may reveal areas in which officers are exceeding their authority or treating similarly situated drivers differently, or areas in which officer discretion is unregulated. For example, in a recent Cleveland County case, testimony revealed that the arresting law enforcement officers had followed an informal practice—directly contradicting the Sheriff's written policy—by which deputy sheriffs would turn off the audio recording equipment during a search in order to prevent defense attorneys from discovering the techniques used in executing a search. This and other evidence led the court to discredit the arresting officer's asserted reason for the stop. Order Allowing Motion to Suppress in the Race Materials Bank at www.ncids.org (select "Training & Resources").

Arguments that a delay exceeded the scope of the stop. In arguing that questioning was beyond the scope of the stop, and that information discovered as a result must be suppressed pursuant to the Fourth Amendment and article I, sections 19, 20, and 23 of the N.C. Constitution, the defendant is in the strongest position if the following factors are present:

- The original purpose for the stop was a discrete matter that would not require additional investigation following the stop, e.g., failure to signal.
- The original purpose for the stop was met before the additional questioning began—for example, the officer issued a citation or warning and returned the defendant's driver's license.
- A reasonable person would not have felt free to leave at the time of the questioning, e.g., because officers blocked the defendant's car, maintained possession of the defendant's license or other documents, or instructed him not to leave, *see* 1 NORTH CAROLINA DEFENDER MANUAL § 15.2A (Consensual Encounters) (2d ed. 2013).
- The questions were not related to the basis for the stop and instead constituted a new criminal investigation, e.g., for drug possession.
- The amount of time spent questioning the defendant on matters unrelated to the basis for the stop was not de minimis.
- The amount of time spent questioning the defendant on matters unrelated to the basis for the stop exceeded the amount of time spent questioning the defendant on matters related to the basis of the stop.
- The officer had not developed reasonable suspicion of additional criminal activity.
- The officer detained the defendant after the purpose of the stop was met to summon a drug-sniffing dog to the scene. *See State v. Cottrell*, __ N.C. App. __, 760 S.E.2d 274 (2014).

See generally State v. Hernandez, 170 N.C. App. 299 (2005) (trooper expanded scope of stop for seat belt violation by asking defendant about contraband and weapons, but reasonable suspicion of criminal activity supported further detention); *State v. Sutton*, 167 N.C. App. 242 (2004) (questioning of defendant during stop was permissible; questions were brief and directly related to suspicion that gave rise to stop); *United States v. Digiovanni*, 650 F.3d 498 (4th Cir. 2011) (unreasonable to spend ten minutes of a fifteen minute traffic stop asking drug-related questions); *United States v. Everett*, 601 F.3d 484 (6th Cir. 2010) (holding that whether delay is de minimis turns on totality of circumstances, including whether officer is diligently moving toward completion of stop and ratio of stop-related to non-stop-related questions).

Involuntary confessions. Police questioning following a traffic stop may result in confessions, which are admissible only when made voluntarily. *See, e.g.*, *State v. Campbell*, 133 N.C. App. 531, 537–38 (1999) ("Incriminating statements obtained by the influence of hope or fear are involuntary and thus inadmissible."). In some cases, North Carolina defendants have claimed that a law enforcement officer's exploitation of race during questioning rendered their confessions involuntary and therefore inadmissible. *See State v. Graham*, ___ N.C. App. ___, ___ 733 S.E.2d 100, 104 (2012) (where a detective asked the defendant, "brother to brother," to tell the truth, the court rejected the defendant's argument that the detective's reliance on their shared racial background constituted evidence of coercion); *State v. Campbell*, 133 N.C. App. 531, 538 (1999) (while it may have been "manipulative" to select a detective to interrogate the defendant based on his shared race and sex, the defendant did not demonstrate that this choice raised defendant's hopes or fears so as to make defendant's confession involuntary); *State v. White*, 68 N.C. App. 671, 675 (1984) (court rejected Black defendant's argument that his confession was involuntary where he was arrested by four White officers and was alone with one of the officers in an interrogation room at the time of the confession). *See also State v. Wilson*, 322 N.C. 91, 95 (1988) (explaining that in *State v. Whitfield*, 70 N.C. 356 (1874), the defendant's confession "was held involuntary . . . because of the coercive circumstances resulting from racial tension manifest in the confrontation").

Confessions secured following suggestions that, because of a suspect's race, he or she will not be treated fairly by the criminal justice system, may be ruled involuntary and inadmissible. Recently, the Indiana Supreme Court considered a case in which a detective interrogating a Black suspect warned him:

> Don't let twelve people who are from Schererville, Crown Point—white people, Hispanic people, other people that aren't from Gary, from your part of the hood—judge you. Because they're not gonna put people on there who are from your neck of the woods. You know that. They're not gonna be the ones to decide what happens to you. You know that. I know that. Everybody knows that. All they're gonna see is, oh, look at this, another young motherf***** who didn't give a f***.

Bond v. State, 9 N.E.3d 134, 136–37 (Ind. 2014). The court unanimously held that, because the detective suggested that the defendant "might not receive a fair trial because of his race and the likely [racial and ethnic] composition of a prospective jury," the defendant's subsequent confession was involuntary and inadmissible. *Id.* at 138. The *Bond* court found that the detective's statement constituted "an intentional misrepresentation of rights ensconced in the very fabric of our nation's justice system—the rights to a fair trial and an impartial jury, and the right not to be judged by or for the color of your skin—carried out as leverage to convince a suspect in a criminal case that his only recourse was to forego his claim of innocence and confess." *Id.* While the court acknowledged that, in the past, it had allowed the admission of confessions secured in spite of an officer's misleading or deceptive tactics during questioning, it held that such tactics were impermissible where a suspect is "intentionally deceived as to the fairness of the criminal justice system itself because of the color of [the defendant's] skin." *Id.* at 140.

For additional considerations regarding coerced confessions, see 1 NORTH CAROLINA DEFENDER MANUAL § 14.3 (Illegal Confessions or Admissions) (2d ed. 2013).

B. Pretextual Inventory Searches

In certain instances, searches may be challenged as pretextual in violation of the Fourth Amendment's prohibition on unreasonable searches. For example, in *Florida v. Wells*, 495 U.S. 1, 4 (1990), the Court stated that warrantless inventory searches "must not be a ruse for a general rummaging in order to discover incriminating evidence." The Court indicated that inventory searches should be "designed to produce an inventory" and must not be "turned into a purposeful and general means of discovering evidence of crime." *Id.* (internal quotation omitted). *See also Whren v. United States*, 517 U.S. 806, 813 (1996) (noting the Court's disapproval of pretextual inventory searches and administrative inspections); *Fair v. State*, 627 N.E.2d 427 (Ind. 1993) (inventory search violated Fourth Amendment where vehicle presented only a "marginal threat," and "several indicia of pretext" raised a question about whether search was conducted in good faith); *United States v. Matthews*, 591 F.3d 230, 235 (4th Cir. 2009) (inventory searches must be "performed in good faith"). Allegations that an inventory search violates the Fourth Amendment will be stronger where the law enforcement agency responsible for the search has no written policy on impoundment or inventory searches, the State is unable to produce evidence that the officer employed a standardized procedure, and the State fails to identify a legitimate rationale for impoundment. *See United States v. Duguay*, 93 F.3d 346, 352 (7th Cir. 1996) ("An impoundment must either be supported by probable cause, or be consistent with the police role as 'caretaker' of the streets and completely unrelated to an ongoing criminal investigation.").

C. Vehicle Consent Searches

In recent years, "consent searches" during traffic stops have become increasingly commonplace. *See* Ric Simmons, *Not "Voluntary" but Still Reasonable: A New Paradigm for Understanding the Consent Searches Doctrine*, 80 IND. L.J. 773 (2005) (reporting that "[o]ver 90% of warrantless police searches are accomplished through the use of the consent exception to the Fourth Amendment"). In a case reviewed by the Fourth Circuit Court of Appeals concerning the voluntariness of a defendant's consent to search, a state trooper testified that he searches 97% of the cars he pulls over, suggesting to one judge that the trooper "rarely takes no for an answer." *U.S. v. Lattimore*, 87 F.3d 647, 653 n.1 (4th Cir. 1996) (en banc) (Hall, J., dissenting). "Consent searches are no longer an occasional event" in which people suspected of a crime may inform the police of their willingness to be searched; they are "now a wholesale activity accompanying a great many traffic stops." 3 WAYNE R. LAFAVE ET AL., CRIMINAL PROCEDURE § 9.3, at 397 (3d ed. 2007).

In deciding when to ask for consent to search, law enforcement officers have broad discretion. Some drivers have raised challenges in racial profiling lawsuits to the alleged misuse of this discretion. *See Maryland State Conference of NAACP Branches v. Maryland State Police*, 454 F. Supp. 2d 339, 353–54 (D. Md. 2006) (rejecting state troopers' motions for summary judgment on plaintiffs' claims that (1) trooper stopped African-American motorist in violation of Fourteenth and Fourth Amendments and (2) trooper coerced African-American motorist's consent to search in violation of the Fourth

Amendment). Concerns about misuse of this discretion have prompted some states to pass legislation banning the use of consent searches; and the California Highway Patrol voluntarily adopted a policy prohibiting its officers from requesting consent to search from drivers. Note, *The Fourth Amendment and Antidilution: Confronting the Overlooked Function of the Consent Search Doctrine*, 119 HARV. L. REV. 2187, 2187–88 (2006). In North Carolina, the Fayetteville City Council issued a moratorium on consent searches amid concerns about racial profiling. Following a court order temporarily halting the ban, the Mayor announced that police officers would begin using consent forms requiring a driver's signature when seeking consent to search. *See, e.g.*, Andrew Barksdale, *City Manager Dale Iman's reversal on Fayetteville police consent searches stirs criticism*, FAYETTEVILLE OBSERVER, March 3, 2012 (reporting concerns that 75% of motorists whose vehicles were searched by police in Fayetteville in 2011 were minorities). In Durham, the City's Human Relation Commission (HRC), charged by Durham Mayor Bill Bell with investigating allegations of racial profiling by the Durham Police Department, voted to recommend that the city implement a mandatory written consent to search policy for all vehicle consent searches by Durham Police. Jim Wise, *Durham panel urges additional training for Durham police*, NEWS AND OBSERVER (Raleigh), March 11, 2014. After this proposal received support from the City Council, City Manager Tom Bonfield ordered the implementation of a new policy, effective October 1, 2014, requiring officers to receive written consent before conducting consent searches of a vehicle or building. Ray Gronberg, *City adopts written-consent policy for searches*, THE HERALD SUN (Durham), September 16, 2014.

Practice note: The North Carolina Department of Justice makes traffic stop data available to the public, as required by G.S. 114-10.01. If you are developing a claim that an officer's request for consent to search your client's vehicle constituted a denial of his or her right to equal protection, you will want to discover data concerning the use of consent searches by the officer or police department responsible for the search. You may obtain data on the race and ethnicity of motorists and passengers searched by particular law enforcement agencies during specific time periods by running reports on the NC DOJ's website. The search data on the NC DOJ's website currently is disaggregated by basis for search (for example, consent, probable cause, or search incident to arrest), but currently "basis for search" data is not disaggregated by race and ethnicity (although this information may be obtained by requesting SBI-122 forms directly from the State Bureau of Investigation). The web tool currently under development by the Southern Coalition for Social Justice will eventually allow users to determine the race and ethnicity of motorists and passengers asked for consent to search. *See supra* "Data sources relevant to North Carolina traffic stops" in § 2.6I, Collecting Traffic Stop Data to Support Equal Protection Claims.

North Carolina appellate decisions may impose an important limitation on an officer's ability to ask for consent to search. In *State v. Parker,* 183 N.C. App. 1, 9 (2007), the North Carolina Court of Appeals stated that "[i]f the officer's request for consent to search is unrelated to the initial purpose for the stop, then the request must be supported by reasonable articulable suspicion of additional criminal activity." In that case, the court determined that, because the request for consent to search was "based on reasonable articulable suspicion that [the officer] would find additional contraband . . . his request did not exceed the scope of the traffic stop and continuation of the detention to complete the search did not violate the Fourth Amendment." *Id.* at 13. *See also State v. Myles*, 188 N.C. App. 42 (2008) (nervousness of defendant and other passenger did not justify continued detention, questioning, and request for consent to search after officer considered traffic stop complete), *aff'd per curiam*, 362 N.C. 344 (2008). *Parker* suggests that requests for consent to search may differ from other types of questioning, which are not impermissible if they do not unduly prolong the stop. *See supra* § 2.7A, Questioning; "Requests for consent and questioning" *in* 1 NORTH CAROLINA DEFENDER MANUAL § 15.4E (Nature, Length, and Purpose of Detention) (2d ed. 2013); *see also State v. Cottrell*, __ N.C. App. __, 760 S.E.2d 274 (2014) (consent to search vehicle was not valid where officer had addressed original purpose of stop and obtained defendant's consent by threatening to conduct dog sniff that officer did not have legal right to conduct; intrusion was not justified as "de minimis"). Other decisions indicate that the issue is in dispute in North Carolina. *See, e.g.*, *State v. Jacobs*, 162 N.C. App. 251 (2004) (holding that, despite defendant's contention that reasonable suspicion is required to request defendant's consent to search, "[n]o such showing is required"). The U.S. Supreme Court has not specifically addressed the question.

Other states have specifically recognized that reasonable suspicion of additional criminal activity is required if the request for consent to search is not related to the initial purpose of the stop. *See, e.g.*, *State v. Estabillio*, 218 P.3d 749, 757–61 (Haw. 2009); *Commonwealth v. Torres*, 674 N.E.2d 638, 641-43 (Mass. 1997); *State v. Fort*, 660 N.W.2d 415, 418–19 (Minn. 2003); *State v. Elders*, 192 N.J. 224, 927 A.2d 1250, 1260–61 (N.J. 2007). A smaller number of states have held that consent searches in the context of traffic stops are valid unless the duration of the seizure is unduly extended. *See, e.g.*, *State v. Jenkins*, 3 A.3d 806, 826 (Conn. 2010).

For additional considerations regarding consent to search, such as factors bearing on the voluntariness or withdrawal of consent, *see* 1 NORTH CAROLINA DEFENDER MANUAL § 15.4E (Nature, Length, and Purpose of Detention) and 15.5D (Consent) (2d ed. 2013).

D. Roadside Searches of Individuals

The decision to conduct roadside searches or strip-searches represents a discretionary determination that may, at times, be influenced by race. *See* Baumgartner Study at 5 (concluding that Black and Hispanic individuals are more likely to be searched following a traffic stop). In determining whether the decision to search your client may have been influenced by race, consider:

- Was the search conducted in accordance with the law enforcement agency's policies concerning roadside searches?
- Do any of the facts of the client's case suggest that race may have been a factor in the search? For example, was your client asked to step out of the car for a search while another passenger of a different race was not?

- Was the officer's unit tasked with using routine traffic stops to search for indicators of criminal activity?
- How frequently do officers from the arresting law enforcement agency conduct roadside searches of drivers and passengers stopped? This information may be obtained by running a report of "Drivers and Passengers Searched by Sex, Race, and Ethnicity" by the relevant law enforcement agency on the NC Department of Justice's Traffic Stop Statistics website. In addition to accessing data about searches through the NC DOJ website, attorneys may obtain the underlying information used to create the reports required under G.S. 114-10.01 by submitting a request to the SBI Traffic Stop Unit for the information collected on SBI-122 forms. *See* SBI-122 Traffic Stop Form in the Race Materials Bank at www.ncids.org (select "Training & Resources"). The information on the forms extends beyond what is currently accessible through generating a report on the NC DOJ website, and includes (1) the type of search; (2) the basis for the search; (3) the person/s or vehicle searched; and (4) the sex, race, and ethnicity of each person searched. This sort of information will eventually be available on the website under construction by the Southern Center for Social Justice. *See supra* "Data sources relevant to North Carolina traffic stops" in § 2.6I, Collecting Traffic Stop Data to Support Equal Protection Claims.

Interviews with clients and witnesses, discovery requests, and public records requests may prove useful in obtaining the information identified above. For a discussion of legal restrictions on roadside searches of individuals, *see* "Warrant requirement and exceptions" *in* 1 NORTH CAROLINA DEFENDER MANUAL § 14.2B (Search Warrants) (2d ed. 2013); "Strip search during search incident to arrest" *in* 1 NORTH CAROLINA DEFENDER MANUAL § 15.6C (Other Limits on Searches Incident to Arrest) (2d ed. 2013); "Strip searches based on probable cause" *in* 1 NORTH CAROLINA DEFENDER MANUAL § 15.6D (Probable Cause to Search Person) (2d ed. 2013).

E. Arrests

Equal protection claims based on arrest patterns. If an individual officer or law enforcement agency engages in a discriminatory pattern of arresting drivers following traffic stops, this action may be challenged under the Equal Protection Clause and article I, section 19 of the North Carolina Constitution as an unconstitutional selective enforcement of the law. A recent study of data made available as a result of G.S. 114-10.01, which reviewed 13 million traffic stops conducted between January 1, 2000 and June 14, 2011, indicated that minorities are more likely to be arrested, and correspondingly less likely to be issued a warning, for the same offenses as whites. According to the study, "disparities appear greatest when the level of officer discretion is highest—seat belts, vehicle equipment, and vehicle regulatory issues." Baumgartner Study at 2. Arrest data disaggregated by race and ethnicity may be accessed by running a report of "Enforcement Action Take by Driver's Sex, Race, and Ethnicity" concerning the relevant law enforcement agency on the NC Department of Justice's Traffic Stop Statistics website. For data reflecting arrests of passengers as well as drivers, attorneys may submit a request to the SBI Traffic Stop Unit for the information collected on SBI-122 forms. *See* SBI-122 Traffic Stop Form in the Race Materials Bank at www.ncids.org

(select "Training & Resources"). This sort of information will eventually be available on the website under construction by the Southern Center for Social Justice. *See supra* "Data sources relevant to North Carolina traffic stops" in § 2.6I, Collecting Traffic Stop Data to Support Equal Protection Claims. Additional arrest statistics reflecting the number of arrestees by race, age, sex, law enforcement agency, year, and offense type is collected by the U.S. Bureau of Justice Statistics and is searchable on the Bureau's website.

To establish a Fourth Amendment or equal protection violation, counsel will need additional supporting information. The courts have found that the Fourth Amendment does not prohibit a pretextual arrest if objective grounds exist for the arrest. In *Arkansas v. Sullivan*, 532 U.S. 769 (2001), the Court held that an officer's decision to arrest a person for a traffic violation, if supported by probable cause, is not invalid even though the arrest is a pretext for a narcotics search incident to arrest. (On remand, the Arkansas Supreme Court held that a pretextual arrest violates the state constitution. *See State v. Sullivan*, 74 S.W.3d 215 (Ark. 2002)). Therefore, consistent with the approach discussed previously for stops (*see supra* § 2.6, Traffic and Pedestrian Stops), counsel will need to show either that grounds did not exist for the arrest or that the officer engaged in selective enforcement within the meaning of equal protection law.

Arrests in reliance on descriptions of suspect's race. A description of a suspect that is based on race alone is not sufficient to justify a seizure. *See supra* "Officer's 'hunch' is not reasonable suspicion, especially where informed by race" in § 2.6B, The Fourth Amendment and Pretextual Traffic Stops; § 2.6F, Seizures in Reliance on Descriptions of Suspect's Race; *see also Washington v. Lambert*, 98 F.3d 1181, 1183–84 (9th Cir. 1996) (invalidating arrest of two Black individuals whose only resemblance to wanted robbery suspects was their race, noting that the descriptions were "exceedingly vague and general" and that such general descriptions could lead to demeaning treatment of African Americans). An arrest requires probable cause, a higher level of justification than the reasonable suspicion required for a stop. *See State v. Joe,* ___ N.C. App. ___, 730 S.E.2d 779 (2012) (rejecting State's argument that suppression was erroneous because officer had reasonable suspicion to conduct an investigatory stop and finding that an arrest, not an investigatory stop, had occurred, and that no probable cause supported the arrest). Thus, even more meaningful similarities between a suspect and a description, beyond a general race-based description, may be required to justify an arrest.

2.8 Beyond Litigation

Police departments, along with individual police officers, enjoy significant discretion in deciding how to monitor and enforce compliance with the law. Law enforcement "polices regarding geographic deployment, enforcement priority, and enforcement tactics determine how the benefits and burdens of policing are distributed." Nirej S. Sekhon, *Criminal Law: Redistributive Policing*, 101 J. CRIM. L. & CRIMINOLOGY 1171, 1225 (2011). For example, before a patrol officer decides who to approach, police department administrators determine that it is appropriate for that officer to be in that particular location at that particular time. Departmental decisions may play a significant role in determining where to deploy law-enforcement resources.

Responses to police practices that have a racially disparate impact may involve not only challenges in individual cases, but also efforts outside of the courtroom. Examples of different approaches, by community groups, law enforcement officials, and elected leaders, are described here.

In Fayetteville, the Fayetteville City Council issued a moratorium on consent searches in response to complaints from citizens, including a minority lawyer association and the NAACP, that police were using racial profiling to stop and search black drivers three times more often than white drivers. A superior court judge lifted the moratorium, but the Fayetteville Police Department changed its consent search procedure in response to the public's concerns, requiring officers to use written forms when requesting consent. A driver must affirmatively represent on the form that he or she voluntarily agreed to the search and was not intimidated or coerced into making the decision.

In Durham, the FADE ("Fostering Alternatives to Drug Enforcement") coalition of residents has organized to address "the interrelated issues of racial profiling, selective enforcement, excessive force, and police harassment in our city." *See* FADE Coalition Policy Recommendations to the Durham Human Relations Commission in the Race Materials Bank at www.ncids.org (select "Training & Resources"). FADE members appeared several times before the Durham Human Relations Commission (HRC), in which they presented their views on the Durham Police Department's policing practices. For example, FADE presented information that black men comprise 17.4% of the city's population but account for 65.2% of all people searched during traffic stops; and that Durham police conduct "consent searches" of black motorists at twice the rate of white motorists. *Id.*; *see also* Durham Police Department Stop-and-Search Data compiled by the Southern Coalition for Social Justice (SCSJ) in the Race Materials Bank at www.ncids.org (select "Training & Resources"). In light of this data, FADE recommended the following policy proposals:

> (1) mandate that written consent be sought and obtained before any and all consent searches undertaken by DPD officers; (2) openly repudiate the department's current practice of racial profiling and selective enforcement in the context of both traffic stops and drug law enforcement; (3) make marijuana enforcement Durham's lowest law enforcement priority (LLEP) and increase the availability of pre-trial diversion programs; (4) mandate racial equity training for DPD leadership and rank-and-file officers alike; and (5) create an inclusive task force—one including HRC members, FADE members, PAC [Partners Against Crime] chairs, representatives of the DPD, as well as persons directly affected by police misconduct—to investigate and make formal recommendations regarding best practices for the Durham Civilian Review Board."

See FADE Coalition Policy Recommendations to the Durham Human Relations Commission in the Race Materials Bank at www.ncids.org (select "Training and Resources"). In response to information presented by the FADE Coalition and others concerning allegations of racial profiling, the Human Relations Commission voted to recommend the adoption of over 50 measures to the City Council, including requiring officers to document and make public the reasons for each traffic stop and each search, requiring officers to obtain written consent for searches, and creating an independent entity to regularly review traffic-stop data to identify unusual trends. Jim Wise, *Durham panel urges additional training for Durham police*, NEWS AND OBSERVER (Raleigh), March 11, 2014. With the support of the City Council, City Manager Tom Bonfield ordered the implementation of a new policy, effective October 1, 2014, requiring Durham police officers to receive written consent before conducting consent searches of a vehicle or building. Ray Gronberg, *City adopts written-consent policy for searches*, THE HERALD SUN (Durham), September 16, 2014. Updates on the efforts of the FADE Coalition can be found at http://www.southerncoalition.org/.

Local police civilian review boards provide an avenue for community oversight of and feedback about policing practices. In North Carolina, four cities have civilian police review boards: Charlotte, Durham, Greensboro, and Winston-Salem. Some state lawmakers, including Charlotte-based Representative Rodney Moore, have expressed interest in sponsoring legislation to grant additional authority to police civilian review boards. Trish Williford, *Lawmaker wants to take action after officer-involved fatal shooting*, WSOCTV.COM, (Jan. 30, 2014) (reporting that Representative Moore plans to sponsor such reform as part of a comprehensive legislative response to concerns over racial profiling). Charlotte recently went through a process of reforming their civilian police review board. *See* Charlotte Police Complaint Review Program, CHARMECK.ORG (last visited Sept. 25, 2014). In Durham, the Civilian Police Review Board sometimes holds public hearings to consider suggestions for improvement of the board's mission, duties, responsibilities, processes, and jurisdiction. *See* Email Listserv Announcement-Civilian Police Review Board to Hold Public Information and Feedback Session in the Race Materials Bank at www.ncids.org (select "Training & Resources"); *see also* Ray Gronberg, *Police review board not seeking additional powers*, THE HERALD SUN (Durham), April 7, 2014. Civilian review boards, because of their potential to facilitate resolution of complaints, increase trust, and improve police practices, are not only of interest to civilians, but may be welcomed by law enforcement organizations as well. When Durham's Civilian Police Review Board was formed in 1998, former Durham police officer and former N.C. Police Benevolent Association President Andy Miller supported the formation of the board, stating that "[w]e think that it brings an air of transparency that you often don't get within the normal channels of the city." Samiha Khanna, *From the INDY Archives: Durham Civilian Police Review Board*, INDYWEEK (Jan. 8, 2014). For more information about national efforts to establish and strengthen civilian review of police departments, see National Association for Civilian Oversight of Law Enforcement, NACOLE.ORG (last visited Sept. 25, 2014).

In North Carolina, organizations to address racial disparities in the criminal justice system have been formed both within and beyond the indigent defense community. The recently formed North Carolina Public Defender Committee on Racial Equity (NC PDCORE) is a state-wide organization of defenders focused on the public defender's unique role in creating a fair, just, and racially-equitable criminal justice system. Public defenders may join NC PDCORE and review weekly updates by visiting the organization's website. The North Carolina Commission on Racial and Ethnic Disparities in the Criminal Justice System, a collaborative research-based organization whose mission is to identify, document, and address racial and ethnic disparities in the criminal justice system, is comprised of an array of criminal justice system stakeholders, including prosecutors, judges, defense attorneys, and community members. Its current areas of focus include implicit bias training, pretrial release, and juvenile justice.

Collaborative efforts to address concerns over racial profiling have been undertaken in other parts of the country. In 1999, attorneys from the Defender Association in Seattle, Washington founded the Racial Disparity Project (RDP) to address racial bias in the criminal justice system. *See* Racial Disparity Project Website, *Mission, History, Funding*, RACIAL DISPARITY PROJECT (last visited July 8, 2014). While the RDP originally focused on selective enforcement litigation addressing racial disparities in street-level drug law enforcement, it eventually developed a community-based, collaborative pre-booking diversion pilot project to steer people accused of low-level drug and prostitution crimes out of the criminal justice system and into treatment. *See* Racial Disparity Project Website, *Projects*, RACIAL DISPARITY PROJECT (last visited July 8, 2014). This project aims to reduce the harm caused by drug use, the drug trade, and drug law enforcement practices that produce racial disparities in criminal processing. *Id.* The Law Enforcement Assisted Diversion Program (LEAD) is supported by the RDP, the Seattle City Mayor, the King County Executive, the King County Prosecuting Attorney's Office, the Seattle City Attorney, the King County Sheriff's Office, the Seattle Police Department, the Washington State Department of Corrections, Community Advisory Boards representing members of the communities served, and the ACLU of Washington. The program authorizes police officers to exercise their discretion in a manner that may reduce (1) disparities in arrest and incarceration rates, (2) reliance on incarceration for low-level offenses, and (3) barriers to accessing community-based treatment programs. *See* Law Enforcement Assisted Diversion Website, Law Enforcement Assisted Diversion, LEADKINGCOUNTY.ORG (last visited July 8, 2014). The program, which began in 2011, has been established through the support of foundation grants at no cost to the public; evaluation of its impact will begin shortly. *Id.*

In New York City, stop and frisk litigation by the Center for Constitutional Rights (discussed *supra* in § 2.6D, The Fourth Amendment and *Terry* Stops) led to the formation of Communities United for Police Reform, a group focused on non-litigation strategies to reduce racial profiling in the city. One of the efforts supported by the coalition was the passage of two pieces of legislation aimed at addressing racial profiling: the End Discriminatory Profiling Act and the NYPD Oversight Act. Two additional proposed bills that may be considered by New York's City Council in the future would (1) impose limitations and regulations on consent searches, and (2) require officers to identify and explain their identity and the purpose of their law enforcement activity to all individuals approached. Communities United for Police Reform reports that similar laws governing consent searches exist in Colorado and West Virginia, and that similar laws requiring officers to identify themselves and the purpose of their law enforcement activity exist in Arkansas, Minnesota, and Colorado. *See* Communities United for Police Reform Website, *About the Community Safety Act*, COMMUNITIES UNITED FOR POLICE REFORM (last visited July 8, 2014); *see supra* § 2.7C, Vehicle Consent Searches.

Community groups and individual community members often become aware of a problematic police practice before attorneys perceive its impact in individual criminal cases. For this reason, defense attorneys may wish to engage in an exchange of information and concerns with community-based groups and individuals in minority communities to learn more about police practices that may be of concern and develop strategies for addressing such practices inside and outside court. For example, the ACLU of North Carolina has asked community members to provide it with information about possible racial profiling practices and locations in North Carolina. Individuals who have information about racial profiling may provide the information to the ACLU using the following link: https://www.acluofnorthcarolina.org/index.php/English/racial-profiling-complaint-formhtml. More information, resources, and strategies regarding the potential for community engagement in defenders' efforts to address racial disparities in the criminal justice system can be found in the following resources: ASHLEY NELLIS ET AL., THE SENTENCING PROJECT, REDUCING RACIAL DISPARITY IN THE CRIMINAL JUSTICE SYSTEM: A MANUAL FOR PRACTITIONERS AND POLICYMAKERS 1 (2d ed. 2008); Communities United for Police Reform, CHANGETHENYPD.ORG (last visited Sept. 25, 2014); and the Racial Disparity Project, RDP.DEFENDER.ORG (last visited Sept. 25, 2014).

Chapter 3
Eyewitness Identifications

3.1 Scope of Chapter

This chapter guides attorneys in protecting their clients against misidentifications. Counsel should ensure that procedures used to identify a client are lawful and insulated from suggestibility. Chapter 3 reviews the standards on unduly suggestive and thus unreliable identifications based on the due process clauses in the Fourteenth Amendment to the U.S. Constitution and article I, section 19 of the North Carolina Constitution, as well as the additional protections found in the North Carolina Eyewitness Identification Reform Act, G.S. 15A-284.50 through G.S. 15A-284.53, which regulates live lineups and photo identification procedures. This chapter also addresses the procedures for raising claims of a violation, including the evidentiary showing required, the procedures for obtaining expert assistance when needed, and the type of relief available.

3.2 Overview of Risks of Misidentification

A. Nature of the Problem

Research and studies. Eyewitness identifications play a major role in the charging and conviction of criminal defendants, providing the basis for criminal charges against approximately 77,000 people each year. Gary L. Wells & Elizabeth A. Olson, *Eyewitness Identification: Information Gain from Incriminating and Exonerating Behaviors*, 8 J. EXPERIMENTAL PSYCHOL.: APPLIED 155 (2002).

Scientific research, academic literature, and overturned convictions, however, have raised concerns about the reliability of eyewitness identifications in general and cross-racial identifications in particular. *See also infra* "State guarantee of due process" in § 3.4A, Due Process (discussing recent cases from the U.S. Court of Appeals for the Fourth Circuit and state supreme courts reviewing research raising concerns about eyewitness identification evidence). The U.S. Supreme Court has observed that "the annals of criminal law are rife with instances of mistaken identification." *United States v. Wade*, 388 U.S. 218, 228 (1967); *see also Perry v. New Hampshire*, 565 U.S. __, 132 S.Ct. 716, 738–39 (2012) (Sotomayor, J., dissenting) ("[A] staggering 76% of the first 250 convictions overturned due to DNA evidence since 1989 involved eyewitness misidentification."). Experts believe that "eyewitness error is the leading contributing factor in wrongful convictions in the United States." *See* ELIZABETH F. LOFTUS ET AL., EYEWITNESS TESTIMONY: CIVIL AND CRIMINAL § 1-2 (5th ed. 2013) [hereinafter EYEWITNESS TESTIMONY]; *see also* EDWARD CONNORS ET AL., NATIONAL INSTITUTE OF JUSTICE, CONVICTED BY JURIES, EXONERATED BY SCIENCE: CASE STUDIES IN THE USE OF DNA EVIDENCE TO ESTABLISH INNOCENCE AFTER TRIAL (1996); C. Ronald Huff et al., *Guilty Until Proved Innocent*, 32 CRIME & DELINQUENCY 518 (1986); Innocence Project, Facts on Post-Conviction DNA Exonerations, INNOCENCEPROJECT.ORG (last visited Sept. 25, 2014).

A review of post-conviction DNA exonerations found that at least 40% of cases in which the defendant was exonerated as a result of DNA evidence involved cross-racial eyewitness identifications. Innocence Project, Facts on Post-Conviction DNA Exonerations, INNOCENCEPROJECT.ORG (last visited Sept. 25, 2014). As discussed in greater detail below, researchers have found that White eyewitnesses are more likely than Black eyewitnesses to make erroneous cross-racial identifications and that most cross-racial identification errors made by White eyewitnesses are false positives—that is, the erroneous identification of a person as the perpetrator. Christian A. Meissner & John C. Brigham, *Thirty Years of Investigating the Own-Race Bias in Memory for Faces: A Meta-Analytic Review*, 7 PSYCHOL. PUB. POL'Y & L. 3 (2001); *see infra* § 3.3, Cross-Racial Impairment.

Case study: The role of race in the Shawn Massey case. Below are the reflections of Duke University School of Law John S. Bradway Professor of Law and Wrongful Convictions Clinic Co-Director James E. Coleman on the Shawn Massey case:

Shawn Massey spent twelve years in prison for crimes he did not commit, and the hard truth is that race played a role in this miscarriage of justice. In 1999, a jury wrongfully convicted him of kidnapping, armed robbery, and breaking and entering based on allegations that in May 1998 he forced a woman and her children at gunpoint into their Charlotte apartment and took $60 from them. The adult victim in this case, a White woman, described the perpetrator of the crime as a 5-foot-9, 180-pound African American male who wore his hair "pulled back from his face and four braids on the back of his head." At trial, the victim clarified that she meant to describe cornrows. However, the White police officers and prosecutors handling the case did not understand the cornrow hairstyle, and this misunderstanding caused them to focus on the wrong suspect, create a photo lineup with inappropriate fillers, and prosecute an innocent man. If the police officers investigating the case had been familiar with the cornrow hairstyle or had focused on Mr. Massey's appearance before concluding that he was the assailant, they would have discovered that he was both shorter and slimmer than the perpetrator, did not wear his hair in cornrows, did not have enough hair for that hairstyle, and should have been excluded as a suspect.

At the time of the offense, Mr. Massey was 26 years-old, working a construction job, and living with his grandmother. He had been charged with petty offenses, but had never been to prison. I became involved with his case through my work in Duke Law School's Wrongful Conviction Clinic. We decided to investigate his claim of innocence because the only evidence in the case was the victim's eyewitness identification of Mr. Massey, and her identification was always conditioned on the assailant having the cornrow hairstyle. Because of the general unreliability of eyewitness identification evidence, we believe that any prosecution based entirely on eyewitness identification evidence merits an innocence investigation.

In this case, the misidentification problem arose when the victim was shown a photo lineup including Mr. Massey and a number of fillers. Neither Mr. Massey nor the fillers wore their hair in cornrows. In the photo shown to the victim, Mr. Massey's hair was very short. Asked if she saw the assailant in the six- photograph lineup, the victim told police that Mr. Massey looked most like the man, except that Mr. Massey did not have braids and the assailant's hair was longer. This kind of relative judgment is typical in cases of misidentification. Because Mr. Massey's hair was not in cornrows, however, the victim stated that she couldn't be sure of her identification unless she saw Mr. Massey in person.

The first time the victim saw Mr. Massey in person was in court. Just before the trial started, she told the prosecutor that she had doubts about her identification, both because the defendant's hair was not in cornrows and because he appeared smaller than her attacker. Mr. Massey's trial attorney was not informed of the victim's eleventh-hour doubts; we uncovered this *Brady* violation during our innocence investigation. The only person who consistently maintained that Mr. Massey was the perpetrator was the investigating officer, a White detective who relied exclusively upon an alleged statement by Mr. Massey's friend that Mr. Massey wore his hair "pulled back and 4 or 5 braids on the back of his head." At trial, however, this friend denied making such a statement, and denied that Mr. Massey wore braids or that his hair was long enough to braid. Mr. Massey's friends and family members uniformly testified that he had never worn his hair in cornrows or long enough to braid, but the statements did not persuade the jury.

While investigating the case, we discovered seven photographs of Mr. Massey in the District Attorney's files, one of which was taken in March 1998, nine weeks before the crime. The seven photographs were taken over a nine-year period. In all of the photos, including the one taken in March 1998, Mr. Massey's hair was very short. We showed these photographs to professional barbers familiar with African American hairstyles, who all agreed that Mr. Massey could not have grown his hair long enough to wear cornrows by the time of the offense. At the time of Mr. Massey's prosecution, police and prosecutors did not appreciate the significance of these photographs because they were not familiar with the cornrow hairstyle; as a result, they did not disclose the photographs to the defense. Until the victim testified at trial, the police and prosecutor assumed that cornrows were worn only on the back of the head and neck, and therefore concluded that photographs showing only the front of Mr. Massey's head did not exclude him as a suspect.

At the conclusion of our investigation, we sent a letter to the Mecklenburg County District Attorney laying out the evidentiary basis of Mr. Massey's claim of innocence, along with a description of the *Brady* violations we uncovered. We included the photograph of Mr. Massey with short hair taken in March 1998, prior to the offense, along with the opinions of professional barbers familiar with African American hairstyles. In response to this evidence, District Attorney Peter Gilchrist filed an ex parte motion to vacate the conviction and dismiss the charges, which was granted by a superior court judge. Mr. Massey was released in 2010, approximately two years before the expiration of his sentence.

This was a case of cross-racial identification, and race played an important role in the wrongful conviction of Shawn Massey, beginning with the police and prosecutor's misinterpretation of the witness's description of the perpetrator. This misinterpretation illustrates the importance of obtaining an accurate description of the assailant from the very outset and making sure one understands what is being described. Prompt investigation of identification procedures also provides counsel with an opportunity to clarify any confusion or misunderstanding on the part of the police or prosecutor, or to litigate pretrial the admissibility of a questionable identification. If the issue is not raised until trial, jurors likely will see the dispute as one involving only the credibility of witnesses, and, as some studies have shown, the race of a witness may affect jurors' perceptions of whether the witness is telling the truth. In Mr. Massey's case, the jurors chose to believe the White police officers and not the Black witnesses who all testified Mr. Massey did not wear braids and did not have hair long enough to braid.

When the introduction of a flawed identification can't be avoided, defenders should emphasize not only the problems with cross-racial identification, but also specific contextual factors that may make the witness identification less reliable. For example, in this case, opinions from professional barbers familiar with African American hairstyles could have been introduced as evidence supporting Mr. Massey's claim that his hair could not have been worn in cornrows at the time of the offense. Without such information, jurors are often misled by the common but mistaken belief that a victim never forgets the face of his or her attacker.

Mr. Massey's experience also underscores the recommendation of scholar Elizabeth Loftus, that whenever possible, officers of the same race as the suspect should be involved in identification procedures. If an African American police officer had constructed the lineup in this case or been part of the investigation, he or she probably would have been familiar with the cornrow hairstyle and Mr. Massey might never have been wrongfully convicted. If the White police officers or prosecutor had queried the victim about her description, Mr. Massey also might never have been convicted. These are flaws that can be fixed or, at a minimum, raised early in the case by the defense attorney.

B. Factors Affecting Eyewitness Identifications

Assuming that witnesses for the most part are earnestly trying to construct an accurate account of a past event, why do eyewitness errors occur and why do they lead to wrongful convictions? This section discusses the causes of eyewitness errors, while subsection C, below, discusses jury perceptions of eyewitness testimony.

Generally. Researchers have concluded that eyewitness mistakes generally result from the "normal and natural processes that occur whenever human beings attempt to acquire, retain, and retrieve information." EYEWITNESS TESTIMONY at § 2-1. Some studies suggest that because of these natural processes eyewitnesses make correct identifications only 50% of the time. BRIAN L. CUTLER & STEVEN D. PENROD, MISTAKEN IDENTIFICATION 218 (1995) [hereinafter MISTAKEN IDENTIFICATION].

Factors affecting the accuracy of eyewitness identification fall into three broad categories: problems of acquisition, problems of retention, and problems of retrieval. EYEWITNESS TESTIMONY at § 2-2. Familiarity with these factors may assist counsel in assessing the possibility of a misidentification and preparing for discussions with expert witnesses. *See infra* § 3.6D, Expert Testimony.

Acquisition stage. In the acquisition stage, when an eyewitness memory is formed, the accuracy of the witness's perception may be affected by factors such as lighting conditions, the duration of the event at issue, violence, stress, fear, age, sex, race, and expectations. EYEWITNESS TESTIMONY at § 2-2. Research has found that cross-racial eyewitness identifications are particularly susceptible to error at this stage. *See infra* § 3.3, Cross-Racial Impairment.

Retention stage. The retention stage encompasses the time between when the witness's memory was formed and when the witness describes the memory. Memory is malleable. The accuracy of a memory during the retention stage is influenced by the length of the retention interval and post-event experiences. For example, a suggestive pretrial identification procedure, especially one involving cross-racial identification, could distort an eyewitness's memory of the actual event. "An eyewitness who is told that it is very important for her to view a photoarray or lineup immediately is more likely to infer that the investigators have identified the perpetrator than is an eyewitness who is told that she could drop by the station whenever it is convenient for her to do so," and this inference may exert subtle pressure on the witness to provide a positive identification. MISTAKEN IDENTIFICATION at 113–14. Similarly, the memory of an eyewitness who is given positive feedback after participating in an identification procedure may be influenced by such feedback. *Id.* at 186–90. One study concluded that in the trials of offenders exonerated by DNA evidence between 1989 and 2010 that involved eyewitness testimony, 57% of the eyewitnesses were initially uncertain of their eyewitness identifications, an indicator of unreliability at the retention stage. BRANDON L. GARRETT, CONVICTING THE INNOCENT: WHERE CRIMINAL PROSECUTIONS GO WRONG 64 (2011).

Retrieval stage. In the context of a criminal trial, the retrieval stage refers to the moment when the witness testifies about the identification. When retrieving events from memory, eyewitnesses are susceptible to the manner in which information is solicited. Frequent review of the event, through questioning, identification procedures, and preparation to testify, may artificially increase witness confidence when retrieving the memory at trial. MISTAKEN IDENTIFICATION at 186–87. Witness confidence exerts a powerful influence on jurors, but researchers have found that "eyewitness confidence is not a great or consistent indicator of eyewitness accuracy." EYEWITNESS TESTIMONY at § 3-12; *see also* MISTAKEN IDENTIFICATION at 95; Siegfried Ludwig Sporer et al., *Choosing, Confidence, and Accuracy: A Meta-Analysis of the Confidence/Accuracy Relation in Eyewitness Identification Studies,* 118 PSYCHOL. BULL. 315 (1995); Neil Vidmar et al., *Rethinking Reliance on Eyewitness Confidence*, 94 JUDICATURE 16 (2010).

Illustration: The wrongful conviction of Ronald Cotton illustrates the problems that may arise with the acquisition, retention, and retrieval stages of eyewitness identifications. Ronald Cotton was convicted of the rape of Jennifer Thompson in Burlington, North Carolina and sentenced to life plus 54 years based on Thompson's eyewitness identification. Ronald Cotton served 10.5 years in prison before he was exonerated by DNA evidence. Jennifer Thompson, a White woman, made a cross-racial identification of Ronald Cotton, a Black man. Ms. Thompson later observed that she "studied every single detail on the rapist's face . . . [and] was going to make sure he was put in prison." Jennifer Thompson, *I Was Certain, But I Was Wrong*, N.Y. TIMES, June 18, 2000. In the time between the crime and the trial of Mr. Cotton, Ms. Thompson grew more and more confident in her mistaken identification. She reflected that, when she saw Ronald Cotton in a photo array, she was "completely confident" that he was the assailant; and when she picked him out of a lineup, she was "sure . . . [she] had picked the right guy." *Id.* However, her confidence did not correspond with accuracy. "From description, to creating an Identikit, to reviewing a photo array, to identifying the wrong man in a lineup and in court—each step unconsciously became a process of picking the individual most resembling the prior step, not most resembling the perpetrator." Joseph F. Savage Jr. & James P. Devendorf, *Conviction After Misidentification: Are Jury Instructions a Solution?*, THE CHAMPION, June 2011, at 30, n.7 (discussing factors contributing to Jennifer Thompson's misidentification of Ronald Cotton).

Estimator and system variables. Variables that affect eyewitness identifications can be categorized as either "estimator" or "system" variables. *See* Gary L. Wells, *Applied Eyewitness Testimony Research: System Variables and Estimator Variables*, 36 J. PERSONALITY & SOC. PSYCHOL. 1546 (1978) (using these categories for the first time). Familiarity with these variables may assist counsel in assessing the identification and discussing it with an expert. Additionally, counsel may use these variables to structure cross-examination in order to show how a given variable, such as the presence of a gun, affected the reliability of eyewitness testimony.

Some variables that bear on the accuracy of eyewitness identifications are within the control of the criminal justice system while others are not. Estimator variables occur before the case enters the criminal justice system and include factors such as: the lighting at the time of the event, the duration of the witness's exposure to the perpetrator, and the race of the witness and perpetrator. In contrast, system variables are or may be within the control of the criminal justice system, such as the construction of a lineup, the questioning of the eyewitness, and the method in which the lineup is presented. Examples of system and estimator variables are as follows. (The list is reproduced verbatim from Joseph F. Savage & James P. Devendorf, *Conviction After Misidentification: Are Jury Instructions a Solution?*, THE CHAMPION, June 2011, at 30, 31, except that examples of variables that have been added are set off in brackets.)

1. *Wording of questions:* The wording of questions posed to an eyewitness can affect the witness's testimony about an event. [For example, if an eyewitness is asked how many minutes she was able to observe the assailant, she may be more likely to estimate that the event took a matter of minutes, rather than seconds.]

2. *Lineup instructions:* The instructions given to the witness at a lineup can affect the witness's willingness to make an identification. [For example, studies have shown that instructions implying that the suspect is in fact in the photo array "increas[e] the likelihood that the eyewitness will make a positive—though not necessarily correct—identification." MISTAKEN IDENTIFICATION at 115–23.]

3. *Confidence malleability:* Factors unrelated to identification accuracy can influence a witness's confidence. [For example, a witness's confidence may rise when she is told that another witness has identified the same person. MISTAKEN IDENTIFICATION at 186–90.]

4. *Mugshot-induced bias:* Exposure to mugshots of a suspect increases the likelihood that the witness will later choose that suspect in a lineup.

5. *Post-event information:* Testimony of eyewitnesses about an event often reflects not only what they actually saw but information they obtained after the event.

6. *Child witness suggestibility:* Young children are more vulnerable than adults to interviewer suggestion, peer pressures, and other social influences.

7. *Attitudes and expectations:* A witness's perception and memory of an event may be affected by his or her attitudes and expectations. [For example, if a person is attacked in the dark in an area primarily frequented by Latinos, he or she may be more likely to believe that his or her attacker was Latino.]

8. *Hypnotic suggestibility:* Hypnosis increases suggestibility to leading and misleading questions.

9. *Alcohol intoxication:* Alcohol intoxication impairs an eyewitness's later ability to recall persons and events.

10. *Cross-race bias:* Eyewitnesses are more accurate when identifying members of their own race than members of other races.

11. *Weapon focus:* The presence of a weapon impairs an eyewitness's ability to accurately identify the perpetrator's face.

12. *Accuracy-confidence correlation:* A witness's confidence is not a good predictor of his or her identification accuracy.

13. *Forgetting curve:* The rate of memory loss for an event is greatest right after the event and then levels off over time.

14. *Exposure time:* The less time an eyewitness has to observe an event, the less well he or she will remember it.

15. *Presentation format:* Witnesses are more likely to misidentify someone by making a relative judgment when presented with a simultaneous (as opposed to sequential) lineup.

16. *Unconscious transference:* Eyewitnesses sometimes identify as a culprit someone they have seen in another situation or context.

Defense attorneys can attempt to mitigate the influence of system variables by, for example, ensuring that law enforcement officers present individuals or photographs to witnesses sequentially rather than simultaneously. *See infra* § 3.5, Eyewitness Identification Reform Act. Additionally, counsel can educate jurors about the impact of system and estimator variables on the reliability of eyewitness testimony through expert testimony, cross-examination of eyewitnesses, and jury instructions concerning factors influencing eyewitness reliability. *See infra* § 3.6, Procedures for Challenging Eyewitness Identification Evidence.

C. Jurors' Perceptions of Eyewitness Identification

Concerns about eyewitness identification, discussed in the preceding section, are compounded by the weight jurors may give such testimony. Studies have concluded that jurors tend to overestimate the reliability of eyewitness testimony. *See, e.g.*, Tanja Rapus Benton et al., *Eyewitness Memory is Still Not Common Sense: Comparing Jurors, Judges and Law Enforcement to Eyewitness Experts*, 20 APPLIED COGNITIVE PSYCHOL. 115 (2006); Richard S. Schmechel et al., *Beyond the Ken? Testing Jurors' Understanding of Eyewitness Reliability Evidence*, 46 JURIMETRICS 177 (2006); *Perry v. New Hampshire*, ___ U.S. ___, ___, 132 S. Ct. 716, 739 (2012) (Sotomayor, J., dissenting) (observing that "jurors routinely overestimate the accuracy of eyewitness identifications"). In 2004, the Public Defender Service for the District of Columbia surveyed nearly 1,000 potential jurors about eyewitness identification. The researchers concluded that the survey members often underestimated the difficulties eyewitnesses experience in making cross-racial identifications, the impact of stress on memory, and the ways in which police procedures may undermine eyewitness accuracy. Timothy P. O'Toole et al., *District of Columbia Public Defender Survey*, THE CHAMPION, Apr. 2005, at 28; *see also*, Richard S. Schmechel et al., *Beyond the Ken? Testing Jurors' Understanding of Eyewitness Reliability Evidence*, 46 JURIMETRICS 177 (2006); EYEWITNESS TESTIMONY at § 6-6.

One reason that lay people misunderstand the reliability of eyewitness identification is that much of what experts now know about memory and eyewitness testimony is counter-intuitive. For example, even though experts now recognize that eyewitness confidence is not reliably correlated with accuracy, "it would seem logical that a more certain witness would be a more accurate one, [and therefore] it would be surprising if jurors understood the relationship between confidence and accuracy as a matter of common sense." Timothy P. O'Toole et al., *District of Columbia Public Defender Survey*, THE CHAMPION, Apr. 2005, at 28, 29. As one court observed, "while science has firmly established the inherent unreliability of human perception and memory, this reality is outside the jury's common knowledge, and often contradicts jurors' commonsense understandings. To a jury, there is almost nothing more convincing than a live human being who takes the stand, points a finger at the defendant, and says, 'That's the one!'" *United States v. Brownlee*, 454 F.3d 131, 142 (3d Cir. 2006) (quotations and citations omitted). *See also Phillips v. Allen*, 668 F.3d 912, 916 (7th Cir. 2012) (stating that "nothing is obvious about the psychology of eyewitness identification" and "most people's intuitions on the subject of identification are wrong").

Practice note: Counsel may file a motion in limine requesting the court to preclude the prosecutor from drawing a correlation between witness confidence and witness accuracy. *See* Lisa Steele, *Trying Identification Cases: An Outline For Raising Eyewitness ID Issues*, THE CHAMPION, Nov. 2004, at 8.

3.3 Cross-Racial Impairment

A. Empirical Evidence of Cross-Racial Impairment

A cross-racial identification occurs when an eyewitness is asked to identify a person of another race. The effect of race on the accuracy of eyewitness identification was considered as early as 1914. *See* Gustave A. Feingold, *The Influence of Environment on Identification of Persons and Things*, 5. J. CRIM. L. & CRIMINOLOGY 39, 50 (1914) ("other things being equal, individuals of a given race are distinguishable from each other in proportion to our familiarity, to our contact with the race as a whole"). Researchers have since identified the phenomenon as own-race bias, cross-race effect, or other-race effect. Christian A. Meissner & John C. Brigham, *Thirty Years of Investigating the Own-Race Bias in Memory for Faces: A Meta-Analytic Review*, 7 PSYCHOL. PUB. POL'Y & L. 3, 4 (2001). Several studies have evaluated the difficulty of cross-racial identification and concluded that eyewitnesses are less likely to misidentify a person of their own race than a person of another race. Radha Natarajan, *Racialized Memory and Reliability: Due Process Applied to Cross-Racial Eyewitness Identifications*, 78 N.Y.U. L. REV. 1821, 1822–23 (2003) (concluding that "[w]hile all eyewitness identifications are prone to error, cross-racial eyewitness identifications are more often wrong than same-race identifications"); *see also* Gary L. Wells & Elizabeth A. Olson, *The Other-Race Effect in Eyewitness Identification: What Do We Do About It?*, 7 PSYCHOL. PUB. POL'Y & L. 230, 230 (2001). Some courts, in reliance on such studies, have recognized that cross-racial identifications raise particular concerns about reliability. *See, e.g.*, *State v. Henderson*, 27 A.3d 872 (N.J. 2011) (referencing a Report of the Special Master prepared for the case regarding eyewitness identification science and law, *available at* www.eyeID.org); *Gonzales v. Thaler*, 643 F.3d 425, 432 (5th Cir. 2011); *United States v. Jernigan*, 492 F.3d 1050, 1054 (9th Cir. 2007).

B. Impact of Cross-Racial Impairment

The cross-racial effect may be stronger when White witnesses attempt to identify Black subjects. Sheri Lynn Johnson, *Cross-Racial Identification Errors in Criminal Cases*, 69 CORNELL L. REV. 934, 938–39 (1984); MISTAKEN IDENTIFICATION at 104 (reviewing a set of studies and concluding that "the cross-racial effect appears to be stronger for whites than for blacks"). *But see* EYEWITNESS TESTIMONY at § 4-13 (noting that in studies concerning cross-racial impairment, "the cross-race effects were comparable for black witnesses and white witnesses"). Among White eyewitnesses, cross-racial impairment leads more often to false positives (the erroneous identification of a person as the perpetrator) than to false negatives (the erroneous failure to identify the perpetrator). James M. Doyle et al., *Discounting the Error Costs: Cross-Racial False Alarms in the Culture of Contemporary Criminal Justice*, 7 PSYCHOL. PUB. POL'Y & L. 253, 254 (2001). Studies have suggested that such false positives have risen over time. *Id.* (citing Christian A. Meissner & John C. Brigham, *Thirty Years of Investigating the Own-Race Bias in Memory for Faces: A Meta-Analytic Review*, 7 PSYCHOL. PUB. POL'Y & L. 3 (2001)).

Among wrongful convictions uncovered by DNA analysis, 36% occurred in cases where White witnesses mistakenly identified innocent Black defendants. James M. Doyle et al., *Discounting the Error Costs: Cross-Racial False Alarms in the Culture of Contemporary Criminal Justice*, 7 PSYCHOL. PUB. POL'Y & L. 253, 253 (2001); *see also* Innocence Project, Facts on Post-Conviction DNA Exonerations, INNOCENCEPROJECT.ORG (last visited Sept. 25, 2014) (at least 40% of cases in which the defendant was exonerated as a result of DNA evidence involved cross-racial eyewitness identifications). The impact of cross-racial impairment may be magnified by the relative representation of people of color in the criminal justice system compared to their representation on juries. Samuel R. Sommers & Phoebe C. Ellsworth, *White Juror Bias: An Investigation of Prejudice Against Black Defendants in the American Courtroom*, 7 PSYCHOL. PUB. POL'Y & L. 201 (2001).

Case study: *State v. Terence Garner*. Below are the reflections of attorney Mark Montgomery on the role of race in the wrongful conviction of Terence Garner. More information about the case can be found at PBS Frontline: An Ordinary Crime, PBS.ORG (last visited Sept. 25, 2014).

In State v. Terence Garner, cross-racial eyewitness identifications played a role in Garner's wrongful conviction for robbery, kidnapping, and attempted murder. The case involved two young Black men with similar names: Terence Garner, who in 1997 was 16 years old and living with his mother in Goldsboro; and Terrance DeLoach, a 24-year-old man from New Jersey who spent five years in prison in New York for robbery before moving to Goldsboro where his cousin, Richard Keith Riddick, lived.

On April 25, 1997, Riddick and his acquaintance, Kendrick Henderson, robbed the Quality Finance Company in Princeton, North Carolina, along with a third man. In the course of the robbery, the third man shot one of the company employees, Alice Wise, assaulted her boss, Charles Woodard, and robbed a customer, Bertha Miller. When police officers questioned Henderson, whose fingerprints were found at the scene, he said that he committed the robbery with Riddick and Riddick's cousin from New York, "Terrance," and provided the address of Terrance DeLoach. When officers were unable to locate DeLoach, they arrested Terence Garner at a different address. Henderson told them they had the wrong "Terrance."

Alice Wise, who lost an eye in the shooting, first identified Terence Garner as the shooter under suggestive circumstances: Terence Garner was in a jail uniform and shackled to co-defendant Henderson. At trial, the two White victims, Ms. Wise and Mr. Woodard, identified Terence Garner as the shooter. In contrast, the lone Black victim, Ms. Miller, testified that she knew Terence Garner from the community and did not see him at the robbery. Co-defendant Henderson testified that Terence Garner was not involved; he always maintained that the police had picked up the wrong "Terrance." Several of Garner's friends and relatives testified that Garner was with them at the time of the robbery. Co-defendant Riddick testified that Terence Garner was the third robber and received a reduced sentence. Riddick perjured himself at trial by denying that he had a cousin named "Terrance," and later recanted his testimony identifying Terence Garner as the shooter.

Terence Garner was found guilty on the basis of eyewitness identifications from Alice Wise and Charles Woodard and the later recanted testimony of Keith Riddick. He was sentenced to over 25 years in prison. Subsequently, police located Terrance DeLoach, who confessed to being the third robber and shooter, but later recanted his confession. Terence Garner served nearly four years in prison. After his case received national attention in a PBS Frontline documentary, prosecutor Tom Lock consented to a Motion for Appropriate Relief granting Terence Garner a new trial. He then took a voluntary dismissal and said publicly that he no longer thought Terence Garner was guilty.

C. Causes of Cross-Racial Impairment

Several researchers have sought explanations for cross-racial impairment. June E. Chance & Alvin G. Goldstein, *The Other-Race Effect and Eyewitness Identification*, *in* PSYCHOLOGICAL ISSUES IN EYEWITNESS IDENTIFICATION 153, 155–56 (1996). Studies have concluded that cross-racial impairment does not stem from conscious racial prejudice; witnesses who do not harbor conscious racial prejudice are as likely to make an erroneous cross-racial identification as those who harbor racial prejudice. Sheri Lynn Johnson, *Cross-Racial Identification Errors in Criminal Cases*, 69 CORNELL L. REV. 934, 943–44 (1984).

Some evidence suggests that the extent, frequency, and quality of a witness's contact with members of the subject's race may play a role in the witness's ability to make accurate cross-racial identifications. June E. Chance & Alvin G. Goldstein, *The Other-Race Effect and Eyewitness Identification*, *in* PSYCHOLOGICAL ISSUES IN EYEWITNESS

IDENTIFICATION 153, 158–68 (1996). However, the evidence also suggests that exposure to members of the other racial group, alone, does not necessarily improve the accuracy of identifications. *Id.* at 170–72.

Practice note: Some research indicates that frequent, quality contact with members of another race may improve cross-racial recognition. *See, e.g., id.* at 158–68. For example, a White witness who has Black family members, lives in a predominantly Black neighborhood, works with a large number of Black colleagues, or has numerous Black friends, may be more adept at making an eyewitness identification of a Black suspect than a White witness who has fewer cross-racial interactions. However, other studies indicate that contact with members of the defendant's race does not necessarily mitigate cross-racial impairment because implicit racial biases may be held even by those who encounter counterexamples to negative racial stereotypes in their daily lives. *See id.* at 170–72. Counsel therefore may raise the issue of cross-racial impairment in an appropriate case even if the eyewitness has had substantial interaction with members of the defendant's race. In such a case, counsel may want to employ an expert witness who can testify about the reliability of cross-racial identifications compared to same-race identifications. June E. Chance & Alvin G. Goldstein, *The Other-Race Effect and Eyewitness Identification*, *in* PSYCHOLOGICAL ISSUES IN EYEWITNESS IDENTIFICATION 153, 170–72 (1996).

3.4 Due Process, Right to Counsel, and Rules of Evidence

Because of concerns about the reliability of eyewitness identification in general, and cross-racial eyewitness identification in particular, it is important for counsel to be familiar with legal requirements relevant to the field of eyewitness identifications.

A. Due Process

State and federal guarantees of due process, under the Fourteenth Amendment to the U.S. Constitution and article I, section 19 of the North Carolina Constitution, protect defendants from suggestive eyewitness identification procedures that create a substantial likelihood of irreparable mistaken identification. *See Manson v. Brathwaite*, 432 U.S. 98 (1977); *Neil v. Biggers*, 409 U.S. 188 (1972); *State v. Harris*, 308 N.C. 159 (1983); *State v. Pigott*, 320 N.C. 96 (1987); *State v. McCraw*, 300 N.C. 610 (1980); *State v. Breeze*, 130 N.C. App. 344 (1998). In reviewing a due process challenge to suggestive procedures, our courts employ a two step process:

> First, the court must determine whether the identification procedures were impermissibly suggestive. Second, if the procedures were impermissibly suggestive, the Court must then determine whether the procedures created a substantial likelihood of irreparable misidentification.

State v. Fowler, 353 N.C. 599 (2001) (citations omitted). North Carolina cases use the terms “impermissibly suggestive” and “unnecessarily suggestive” interchangeably. *Compare State v. Stowes*, ___ N.C. App. ___, 727 S.E.2d 351, 356 (2012) (using “impermissibly suggestive” terminology), *with State v. Jones*, 216 N.C. App. 225, 231 (2011) (using “unnecessarily suggestive” terminology). Federal and state courts have concluded that suggestive pretrial identification procedures that do not result from government action do not violate a defendant’s due process rights. *Perry v. New Hampshire*, 565 U.S. ___, 132 S. Ct. 716 (2012); *State v. Fisher*, 321 N.C. 19, 24 (1987).

Impermissibly or unnecessarily suggestive. “A procedure is unnecessarily suggestive if a positive identification is likely to result from factors other than the witness’s own recollection of the crime.” *Satcher v. Pruett*, 126 F.3d 561, 566 (4th Cir. 1997). “To determine whether a pretrial identification procedure is suggestive, the court should consider: (1) whether the accused is somehow distinguished from others in the line-up or in a set of photographs; and (2) whether the witness is given some extraneous information by the police which leads her to identify the accused as the perpetrator of the offense.” *State v. Rainey*, 198 N.C. App. 427, 435 (2009) (internal quotations omitted).

A lineup or photo array is suggestive if the defendant improperly stands out from the fillers. *See, e.g.*, *State v. Pigott*, 320 N.C. 96 (1987) (photo array suggestive where 6 of 10 photos unclear and seventh photo showed deputy in uniform). A showup, in which “a suspect is shown singularly to a witness or witnesses for the purposes of identification,” is inherently suggestive. *State v. Harrison*, 169 N.C. App. 257, 262 (2005). This is because, when considering a suspect presented in a showup, “the witness would likely assume that the police have brought him to view persons whom they suspected might be the guilty parties.” *State v. Oliver*, 302 N.C. 28, 45 (1981) (quotation omitted). *See also State v. Flowers*, 318 N.C. 208, 220 (1986); *see infra* “Suppressing showups” in § 3.6A, Motions to Suppress Pretrial Identifications and Prevent In-Court Identifications. While inherently suggestive, courts will look at the totality of the relevant circumstances to determine whether a showup resulted in a substantial risk of irreparable misidentification and violated a defendant’s due process rights in an individual case. *State v. Turner*, 305 N.C. 356, 364 (1982) (“Pretrial show-up identifications . . . , even though suggestive and unnecessary, are not per se violative of a defendant’s due process rights”). In some cases, courts have found that a showup’s inherent suggestibility is outweighed by other indications of the identification’s reliability. *See, e.g.*, *State v. Jackson*, __ N.C. App. __, 748 S.E.2d 50 (2013).

Substantial likelihood of irreparable misidentification. If it determines that a procedure was impermissibly suggestive, “a court must look at several factors to determine if the identification testimony is nevertheless reliable.” *Satcher v. Pruett*, 126 F.3d 561, 566 (4th Cir. 1997). “Whether there is a substantial likelihood of misidentification depends upon the totality of the circumstances.” *State v. Pigott*, 320 N.C. 96, 99 (1987) (photo array unconstitutionally suggestive where over half of the photos were unclear and one photo showed deputy in uniform). In determining whether a suggestive procedure resulted in a substantial likelihood of misidentification, the court generally considers five factors (hereinafter “the *Harris* factors”):

- the opportunity to view the perpetrator at the time of the crime;
- the witness's degree of attention;
- the accuracy of the witness's prior description of the perpetrator;
- the certainty of the witness at the time of confrontation;
- the time elapsed between the crime and the confrontation.

State v. Harris, 308 N.C. 159 (1983) (citing *Neil v. Biggers*, 409 U.S. 188 (1972)); *see also State v. Pinchback*, 140 N.C. App. 512, 518 (2000) (granting new trial to defendant where pretrial identification was suggestive and resulted in a substantial likelihood of misidentification).

In-court identifications may be tainted by unconstitutional pretrial identification procedures. An impermissibly suggestive pretrial identification procedure may taint an in-court identification. *State v. Flowers*, 318 N.C. 208 (1986); *State v. Headen*, 295 N.C. 437 (1978). Generally, the standard for permitting an in-court identification in the wake of an unconstitutional pretrial identification is identical to the standard for admitting an out-of-court identification. "In both cases, the eyewitness testimony will be permitted unless the pretrial identification procedure was so unnecessarily suggestive as to give rise to such a substantial likelihood of irreparable misidentification that admitting the identification testimony would be a denial of due process." *United States v. Clausen*, 328 F.3d 708, 713 (3d Cir. 2003). Before allowing an in-court identification that has been challenged as tainted by an impermissibly suggestive pretrial procedure, the court should conduct a voir dire of the witness and determine by clear and convincing evidence that the in-court identification does not result from the pretrial identification, but rather is of independent origin, meaning that it is based on the witness's observations of the suspect at the time of the crime. *Flowers*, 318 N.C. 208, 216; *State v. Freeman*, 313 N.C. 539, 545 (1985); *State v. Thompson*, 303 N.C. 169, 172–73 (1981). A court determines whether an eyewitness identification is of independent origin by weighing the *Harris* factors, discussed above, against the corrupting influence of the suggestive pretrial identification procedure. *State v. Farmer*, 177 N.C. App. 710, 717 (2006) (quoting *Flowers*, 318 N.C. 208, 220); *State v. Pigott*, 320 N.C. 96, 100 (1987).

Practice note: According to some scholars, the standard employed by North Carolina courts to determine whether an identification is admissible despite a suggestive pretrial identification procedure is based on a misinterpretation of U.S. Supreme Court case law. Law professor Brandon L. Garrett observes that most states, including North Carolina, allow in-court identifications following impermissibly suggestive pretrial identification procedures if the identification has an "independent origin" or "independent source," terms that are used interchangeably to indicate that the identification stems from the witness's observations of the suspect at the time of the crime rather than from the suggestive pretrial procedure. *See Farmer*, 177 N.C. App. 710, 716; *State v. Jordan*, 49 N.C. App. 561, 565 (1980). Garrett argues that this interpretation conflicts with the one announced in *Manson v. Brathwaite*, 432 U.S. 98 (1977), and confuses two lines of U.S. Supreme Court cases addressing the admissibility of eyewitness identifications. *See* Brandon L. Garrett, *Eyewitnesses and Exclusion*, 65 VAND. L. REV. 451, 478–79 (2012).

Garrett posits that the applicable standard for evaluating an in-court identification should be the one articulated in *Brathwaite*, 388 U.S. 218—that is, whether the pretrial identification procedure was "unnecessarily suggestive" and, if so, whether the in-court identification is "nevertheless reliable." *See* Brandon L. Garrett, *Eyewitnesses and Exclusion*, 65 VAND. L. REV. 451, 468. According to Garrett, the U.S. Supreme Court's opinions in *Brathwaite*, 432 U.S. 98 and *United States v. Wade,* 388 U.S. 218 (1967), instruct that the "independent origin" test only applies to challenges based on the Sixth Amendment right to counsel—that is, where defense counsel was not present during a post-indictment lineup and the State nevertheless seeks to introduce an identification by the witness who participated in the uncounseled lineup. *United States v. Wade,* 388 U.S. 218 (1967); *State v. Hunt,* 339 N.C. 622, 646–47 (1994). *See infra* § 3.4B, Right to Counsel. The "independent origin" inquiry is more appropriate in the context of a Sixth Amendment challenge, where the constitutional violation is primarily procedural, not substantive as in a case in which the pretrial identification procedure was unnecessarily suggestive. *See* Brandon L. Garrett, *Eyewitnesses and Exclusion*, 65 VAND. L. REV. 451, 465 (2012) ("There are stronger arguments that an identification could have an 'independent origin' in court if the pretrial identification was not suggestive."). Garrett's view is bolstered by scientific evidence indicating the difficulty of determining how a witness's memory may have been affected by a suggestive pretrial identification procedure, which casts into doubt the ability of the court to determine whether a witness's in-court identification is based on observations of the suspect at the time of the crime, a pretrial identification procedure, or some combination of the two. BRANDON L. GARRETT, CONVICTING THE INNOCENT: WHERE CRIMINAL PROSECUTIONS GO WRONG (2011).

In light of the above, in resisting a ruling that a challenged in-court identification is of independent origin and therefore reliable, defenders should argue that the "independent origin" standard is inconsistent with U.S. Supreme Court decisions governing the interpretation of the Due Process Clause and with scientific evidence about the impact of suggestive pretrial identification procedures on witness memory.

State guarantee of due process. Although North Carolina appellate courts have not found that the state constitutional guarantee of due process exceeds the protections provided by the Fourteenth Amendment in the eyewitness identification context, attorneys should continue to assert the law of the land clause of article I, section 19 of the North Carolina Constitution. Recently, judges in other jurisdictions have questioned the U.S. Supreme Court's test for the admissibility of eyewitness testimony "based on the last 35 years of social science research into the reliability of eyewitness identifications." *United States v. Greene*, 704 F.3d 298, 305 n.3 (4th Cir. 2013) (discussing *New Jersey v. Henderson*, 27 A.3d 872 (N.J. 2011) and *Oregon v. Lawson*, 291 P.3d 673 (Or. 2012)).

In *Henderson*, the New Jersey Supreme Court held that state guarantees of due process provided greater protections than those afforded by the Fourteenth Amendment as interpreted by the U.S. Supreme Court in *Manson v. Brathwaite*, 432 U.S. 98 (1977). The court found that a defendant is entitled to a hearing to explore "all relevant system and estimator variables" related to an eyewitness identification if he meets an initial burden of showing some evidence of suggestiveness tied to a system variable (one that is a product of the criminal justice process) rather than an estimator variable (one that is not). *Henderson*, 27 A.3d 872, 919. (For a further discussion of system and estimator variables, see *supra* "Estimator and system variables" in § 3.2B, Factors Affecting Eyewitness Identifications.) On such a showing, the burden shifts to the State to offer proof that the eyewitness identification is reliable, considering both system and estimator variables. The identification must be suppressed if, under a totality of circumstances, the court determines that there is a very substantial likelihood of misidentification. If this standard is not met, the court still must provide tailored jury instructions concerning the problems with eyewitness identification.

The New Jersey Supreme Court determined that the governing test for evaluating the admissibility of identifications needed revision, since "[s]tudy after study revealed a troubling lack of reliability in eyewitness identifications." *Henderson*, 27 A.3d 872, 877. The court unanimously concluded that greater protections were needed to guard against suggestiveness caused by system variables, and warned that "the very integrity of the criminal justice system and the courts' ability to conduct fair trials" was at stake. *Id.* at 879. Similarly, the Oregon Supreme Court noted that in the past 33 years, over 2,000 empirical studies have attested to the unreliability of eyewitness identification, and that the court's existing method of evaluating the admissibility of eyewitness testimony was "incomplete and, at times, inconsistent with modern scientific findings." *Oregon v. Lawson*, 291 P.3d 673, 688 (Or. 2012). The Fourth Circuit Court of Appeals recently stated:

> The New Jersey and Oregon opinions represent a growing awareness that the continuing soundness of the *Manson* test has been undermined by a substantial body of peer-reviewed, highly reliable scientific research.

United States v. Greene, 704 F.3d 296, 305 n.3 (4th Cir. 2013) (citing Brandon L. Garrett, *Eyewitnesses and Exclusion*, 65 VAND. L. REV. 451, 453 (2012) (observing that *Manson* was decided before the bulk of the research that has "revolutionize[d] our understanding of human memory")). While no North Carolina opinions have undertaken a similar review to date, the passage of the Eyewitness Identification Reform Act reflects the State's recognition of the importance of social science in devising standards and procedures to guard against the risks of misidentification. *See infra* § 3.5, Eyewitness Identification Reform Act.

B. Right to Counsel

Sixth Amendment right to counsel at lineups and showups. The right to counsel at a lineup after the initiation of adversary proceedings (the holding of initial appearance or indictment, whichever occurs first) in which the accused is exhibited to an identifying witness is assured by the Sixth Amendment. U.S. CONST. amend. VI; *see Rothgery v. Gillespie County*, 554 U.S. 191 (2008); *United States v. Wade,* 388 U.S. 218 (1967); *Gilbert v. California*, 388 U.S. 263 (1967); *State v. Cherry*, 298 N.C. 86 (1979). The presence of counsel in such circumstances is intended to guard against the "dangers and variable factors which might seriously, even crucially, derogate from a fair trial." *Wade*, 388 U.S. 218, 228. In contrast, the Sixth Amendment does not guarantee the right to counsel where a lineup occurs before adversarial proceedings have commenced. *State v. Henderson,* 285 N.C. 1 (1974), *vacated on other grounds,* 428 U.S. 902 (1976). Nor does the Sixth Amendment guarantee the right to counsel at a photographic identification procedure. *United States v. Ash,* 413 U.S. 300 (1973).

If a violation occurs, the identification must be suppressed. Further, an in-court identification by a witness who took part in an invalid pretrial lineup must be excluded unless the State demonstrates by clear and convincing evidence that the in-court identification is of independent origin and not tainted by the illegal pretrial procedure. *See State v. Hunt,* 339 N.C. 622, 646–47 (1994); *see also supra* "In-court identifications may be tainted by unconstitutional pretrial identification procedures" and "Practice note" in § 3.4A, Due Process.

For a further discussion of the right to counsel generally and at lineups, see 1 NORTH CAROLINA DEFENDER MANUAL Ch. 12 (Right to Counsel) (2d ed. 2013).

Statutory right to counsel during nontestimonial identification procedures. A suspect has a right to have counsel present during a nontestimonial identification procedure. *See* G.S. 15A-279(d); G.S. 7A-451(b)(2); *State v. Satterfield*, 300 N.C. 621 (1980). Any statements made during the proceeding must be suppressed if the defendant does not have counsel present. G.S. 15A-279(d); *see also State v. Coplen*, 138 N.C. App. 48 (2000) (refusing to suppress results of identification procedure, as distinguished from statements of defendant, for violation of statutory right to counsel); 1 NORTH CAROLINA DEFENDER MANUAL § 14.4 (Illegal Identification Procedures) (2d ed. 2013).

C. North Carolina Rules of Evidence

A largely untested but potential avenue for excluding unreliable identifications is through reliance on the North Carolina Rules of Evidence. The evidence arguments are that an unreliable identification: (1) risks prejudicing or misleading the jury in violation of N.C. R. EVID. 403; (2) is not based on "personal knowledge" but is instead based on the influence of system variables (*see supra* "Estimator and system variables" in § 3.2B, Factors Affecting Eyewitness Identifications) that have interfered with the eyewitness's memory in violation of N.C. R. EVID. 602; and (3) is not "rationally based on the perception of the witness" but is instead a result of post-event factors that have distorted the original memory in violation of N.C. R. EVID. 701.

Support for these arguments can be found in a recent U.S. Supreme Court decision, in which the court observed that one of the "safeguards built into our adversary system" in the context of fallible eyewitness identifications is "[s]tate . . . rules of evidence . . . [that] permit trial judges to exclude relevant evidence if its probative value is substantially outweighed by its prejudicial impact or potential for misleading the jury." *Perry v. New Hampshire*, 565 U.S. ___, ___, 132 S.Ct. 716, 728–29 (2012). *See also Oregon v. Lawson*, 291 P.3d 673 (Or. 2012) (en banc) (analyzing admissibility of eyewitness identifications under Oregon Rules of Evidence 602, 701, and 403). Seeking exclusion of unreliable identifications on the basis of evidentiary rules offers the additional benefits of: (1) protecting against unreliable identifications regardless of their source (after *Perry*, 565 U.S. ___, ___, 132 S.Ct. 716, federal due process guarantees only apply to cases in which the suggestive identification procedures are orchestrated by the police); and (2) potentially shifting the initial burden of establishing the reliability of the identification to the State for purposes of Rule 602 and 701 analyses. *See Lawson*, 291 P.3d 673, 689 (ruling that the State bears the initial burden of establishing the admissibility of eyewitness identification evidence challenged on evidentiary grounds since, "[i]n evidentiary matters . . . the proponent of the evidence—in identification matters, usually the state, although not necessarily so—traditionally bears the initial burden of establishing the admissibility of the proffered evidence").

3.5 Eyewitness Identification Reform Act

North Carolina's Eyewitness Identification Reform Act (EIRA), G.S. 15A-284.50 through G.S. 15A-284.53, was passed in 2007. EIRA sets forth rules governing pretrial eyewitness identification lineups, whether live or by photo array. The law was passed after organizations such as the North Carolina Actual Innocence Commission, among others, found that certain identification procedures help prevent wrongful identifications and wrongful convictions. The opening section of the EIRA reflects this view: "The purpose of this Article is to help solve crime, convict the guilty, and exonerate the innocent in criminal proceedings by improving procedures for eyewitness identification of suspects." G.S. 15A-284.51. The law reflects best practices developed to prevent suggestive pretrial identification procedures, including a requirement that lineups must be "double-blind", i.e., conducted by someone who is not participating in the investigation and does not know which person is the suspect; that individuals or photographs should be presented to witnesses sequentially rather than simultaneously; and that lineups should include at least five fillers resembling the suspect at the time of the crime. G.S. 15A-284.52(b) and (c).

The specific statutory requirements go beyond the constitutional minimum in ensuring that lineups are conducted in a non-suggestive manner. Reliability is at the heart of whether an identification procedure is constitutional, however, and the EIRA requirements could be viewed as North Carolina's interpretation of what it takes to ensure that identification procedures are reliable.

In the case of an EIRA violation, the following remedies are available:

- Failure to comply with EIRA shall be considered by the court in adjudicating motions to suppress eyewitness identification.
- Failure to comply with the requirements of EIRA is admissible in support of claims of misidentification, so long as the evidence is otherwise admissible.

- When evidence of compliance or noncompliance with EIRA is presented at trial, the jury shall be instructed that it may consider credible evidence of compliance or noncompliance in determining the reliability of eyewitness identifications.

G.S. 15A-284.52(d).

3.6 Procedures for Challenging Eyewitness Identification Evidence

There are three main ways in which defense attorneys can seek to mitigate the problems associated with cross-racial identifications: by ensuring that identification practices are not suggestive, by suppressing unreliable eyewitness identifications, and by educating triers of fact about the hazards of cross-racial identifications. Sample motions to suppress eyewitness identifications can be found in the Race Materials Bank at www.ncids.org (select "Training & Resources").

A. Motions to Suppress Pretrial Identifications and Prevent In-Court Identifications

General considerations. In determining whether your client has a viable motion to suppress evidence of pretrial identification procedures and prevent in-court identifications, you should focus on the following questions:

- Does the case involve a cross-racial identification?
- Did a "suggestive" pretrial identification procedure take place?
- If so, did the suggestive procedure create a substantial risk of misidentification?
- Did the pretrial identification procedure comply with EIRA?
- Was there a lineup conducted outside of the presence of counsel after the initiation of adversary proceedings (the holding of initial appearance or issuance of indictment, whichever came first)?
- Would any improper pretrial identification procedure taint an in-court identification of the defendant?

Voir dire of the eyewitness. In challenging the admissibility of an eyewitness identification, you should request a hearing involving voir dire of the challenged witness. *See State v. Flowers*, 318 N.C. 208, 216 (1986) ("Before admitting challenged in-court identification testimony, the trial court should conduct a voir dire, find facts, and determine the admissibility of the testimony.").

Practice note: Even if you are ultimately unsuccessful with your pretrial motion to suppress an eyewitness identification, litigating the suppression motion may uncover useful information that will help you to prepare your cross-examination of the eyewitness. The ultimate issue concerning such a motion is whether, under the totality of the circumstances, the eyewitness identification is reliable. For this reason, the scope of the inquiry is broad. Moving to suppress an eyewitness identification may lead to useful discovery and allow you to avoid surprises when you cross-examine the eyewitness.

Implication of cross-racial impairment on lineup construction. In support of your motion to suppress an identification made by a witness who is of a different race than your client, consider whether the pretrial identification procedures may have exacerbated problems associated with cross-racial identifications. Lineups should include the suspect and several fillers who resemble the suspect and are consistent with the witness's description of the perpetrator. EIRA provides that lineups "shall be composed so that the fillers generally resemble the eyewitness's description of the perpetrator, while ensuring that the suspect does not unduly stand out from the fillers"; and that "[a]ll fillers selected shall resemble, as much as practicable, the eyewitness's description of the perpetrator in significant features, including any unique or unusual features." G.S. 15A-284.52(b)(5). Violations of EIRA must be considered by the court in ruling on motions to suppress evidence of eyewitness identification. G.S. 15A-284.52(d)(1).

To ensure that the fillers resemble the description of the perpetrator and the suspect reasonably resembles the fillers, it is important that the person selecting fillers for lineups is capable of identifying people who adequately resemble the suspect and witness's description of the perpetrator. Three studies found that lineup constructors are "more selective about which photos [go] into their own-race lineups than their other-race lineups. As a result, the fairness of other-race lineups [is] negatively affected." EYEWITNESS TESTIMONY § 4-13 (citing John C. Brigham & David J. Ready, *Own-Race Bias in Lineup Construction*, 9 LAW & HUM. BEHAV. 415 (1985); R. C. L. Lindsay et al., *Does Race Influence Measures of Lineup Fairness?*, 13 APPLIED COGNITIVE PSYCHOL. S109 (1999); John C. Brigham et al., *Standards for Evaluating the Fairness of Photograph Lineups*, 11 BASIC & APPLIED SOC. PSYCHOL. 149 (1990). Accordingly, experts recommend that lineups be created by law enforcement officers of the same race as the subjects pictured in the lineup whenever possible. *See, e.g.,* EYEWITNESS TESTIMONY at § 4-13; June E. Chance & Alvin G. Goldstein, *The Other-Race Effect and Eyewitness Identification, in* PSYCHOLOGICAL ISSUES IN EYEWITNESS IDENTIFICATION 153, 173 (1996).

Illustration: Defense motions to suppress in two North Carolina cases at the trial level illustrate the ways in which race may affect pretrial eyewitness identification procedures. The descriptions below are drawn from those motions, which are available in the Race Materials Bank at www.ncids.org (select "Training & Resources").

In a Cleveland County case involving cross-racial identification, a Black defendant was placed in a lineup after a robbery and kidnapping in which a witness identified the perpetrator as a Black male with short hair, parted down the middle. *See* Motion to Suppress, 2003 Cross-Racial ID Case in the Race Materials Bank at www.ncids.org (select "Training & Resources"). In the photo lineup shown to the White witnesses, only the suspect had his hair parted down the middle; the fillers did not. One witness identified the defendant by explicit reference to his middle part. The defendant filed a motion to suppress the pretrial identification and preclude in-court identification as irreparably tainted. In anticipation of the objection that it would have been difficult to find a photograph of a Black man with a middle part, counsel's affidavit in support of his motion to suppress the pretrial eyewitness identification procedures included information from an investigator who interviewed Cleveland County barbers reflecting that the middle part was a common hair style for Black men in Cleveland County. Right before jury selection, the eyewitnesses told the prosecutor they were unable to identify the defendant if asked to point him out in the courtroom, and the charges were dismissed. *See* Motion to Suppress, 2003 Cross-Racial ID Case; Motion to Prevent In-Court ID of Defendant, 2003 Cross-Racial ID Case; Suppression Affidavit, 2003 Cross-Racial ID Case; and Motion to Hire Eyewitness ID Expert, 2003 Cross Racial ID Case; all in the Race Materials Bank at www.ncids.org (select "Training & Resources").

In another case involving cross-racial eyewitness identification, a Black defendant was charged with robbery after a White witness identified him in a photo lineup in which he was the only subject with corn-rows or braids, while all the other subjects had hairstyles resembling one another. *See* Motion to Suppress, 2002 Cross-Racial ID Case in the Race Materials Bank at www.ncids.org (select "Training & Resources"). Further, the defendant was the only person in the lineup with a black hat, and witnesses had indicated that the robber was wearing a black hat. Before hearing the motion, the same White eyewitness who had identified him from the photo lineup saw the defendant in open court, observed that he was far shorter than the perpetrator, and said, "That's not him." The case was then dismissed.

These cases illustrate that officers constructing lineups may fail to take unique or unusual features into account, resulting in suggestive identification procedures.

Attorneys concerned that the filler photos in a lineup do not adequately resemble their client may want to determine the race of the police officer responsible for assembling the lineup. If the officer is of a different race than the subjects pictured in the lineup, defense counsel should consider using the above studies as part of a motion to suppress the pretrial identification procedure and prevent any subsequent in-court identification. If the motion to suppress is denied, counsel should consider presenting expert testimony about cross-racial lineup construction to educate the jury about the risk that the police officer's race may have affected his or her ability to construct a non-suggestive identification procedure. *See infra* § 3.6D, Expert Testimony.

Suppressing showups. A showup is a pretrial identification procedure in which a "suspect is shown singularly to a witness or witnesses for the purposes of identification." *State v. Harrison*, 169 N.C. App. 257, 262 (2005). Showups usually occur shortly after a crime's commission, when an officer arrests a suspect and seeks confirmation from a witness that he or she has apprehended the correct person.

The U.S. Supreme Court and North Carolina appellate courts disfavor showups. *See Stovall v. Denno*, 388 U.S. 293, 302 (1967) ("The practice of showing suspects singly to persons for the purpose of identification, and not as part of a lineup, has been widely condemned."); *State v. Lee*, 154 N.C. App. 410, 414 (2002) (showups are "strongly disfavored methods of identification"). Our Supreme Court has observed that "the use of a showup where other methods of identification are feasible has been widely condemned." *State v. Matthews,* 295 N.C. 265, 285–86 (1978) (noting that showups "may [be] inherently suggestive for the witnesses would likely assume that the police had brought them to view persons whom they suspected might be the guilty parties"). However, not all showups will violate a defendant's due process rights. *See State v. Lee*, 154 N.C. App. at 414 (noting that "this Court has approved the use of show-ups on numerous occasions"). As in the evaluation of any pretrial identification procedure, "[t]he trial court must employ the totality of the circumstances test to evaluate the reliability of a show-up identification and determine whether the procedures created a substantial likelihood of irreparable misidentification." *Id.* (quoting *State v. Fowler*, 353 N.C. 599, 617 (2001)) (internal quotations omitted); *see also* ROBERT L. FARB, ARREST, SEARCH, AND INVESTIGATION IN NORTH CAROLINA 558–59 (UNC School of Government, 4th ed. 2011) (noting that a showup "is a suggestive identification procedure that normally should be avoided" but that it may be permissible in an emergency or soon after a crime is committed).

While confirming that showups are "sometimes troubling," the North Carolina Court of Appeals has held that EIRA does not apply to showups. *State v. Rawls*, 207 N.C. App. 415, 423 (2010). (The *Rawls* court did not address the question of whether EIRA applies to "photo showups," in which an eyewitness is shown a single photograph of a suspect during a pretrial identification procedure.) *Rawls* should not be read to mean that officers may avoid EIRA lineup requirements by conducting showups when not warranted by legitimate law enforcement objectives. *Rawls* involved a situation in which officers decided to do a showup in light of the exigencies of the situation. Officers arrived on the scene within minutes after the victim's apartment had been broken into; they located the defendant and other suspects shortly thereafter, who were still in the area; and they drove the victim to where the suspects were being held, which took a mere 45 seconds. Other instances, when a showup is unnecessary or is employed to avoid EIRA procedures, may violate both statutory as well as constitutional requirements. Whether or not EIRA applies to a showup in a particular case, the statutory provisions may assist defenders in framing an argument that the showup was unconstitutionally suggestive. For example, the provision in EIRA mandating at least five fillers in all lineups reflects legislative concerns that, the fewer persons included in a lineup, the more likely it is to result in mistaken identification. G.S. 15A-284.52(b)(5).

Importance of raising issue pretrial in motion to suppress rather than in motion to dismiss. North Carolina appellate courts have held that an eyewitness's identification of the defendant as the perpetrator is generally sufficient to defeat a motion to dismiss on the basis of identity. *See State v. Carpenter*, __ N.C. App. __, 754 S.E.2d 478 (2014); *State v. Mobley*, 86 N.C. App. 528, 532 (1987). This standard underscores the importance of challenging identification evidence pretrial.

Practice note: While you must make a motion to suppress evidence of pretrial identifications and tainted in-court identifications before trial (subject to certain exceptions), if your motion is denied you also must object to the evidence of the pretrial identification procedure when it is introduced and to the in-court identification of the defendant when it is made to preserve those issues for appeal. *See State v. Hunt*, 324 N.C. 343, 355 (1989) ("Assuming arguendo that defendant's constitutional right of assistance of counsel at the lineup was violated, defendant waived that error by failing to object when the witness later identified him before the jury as the man he had picked out of the lineup."). If you fail to object, you will waive the objections and will have to meet the higher standard of plain error on appeal. *See State v. Hammond*, 307 N.C. 662, 666 (1983); *State v. Stowes*, ___ N.C. App. ___, 727 S.E.2d 351, 355 (2012).

B. Voir Dire

Voir dire is the defense's first opportunity to question the jurors about the eyewitness identification issues central to the defendant's theory of the case. It provides an important opportunity for eliciting information from prospective jurors about their experiences and views on cross-racial identification. Defense attorneys should consider integrating cross-racial eyewitness identification issues into their voir dire questions when it is at issue. For example, if your case involves a cross-racial identification, you may want to inform the potential jurors of this fact and explore their opinions and experiences regarding cross-racial identification. If your theory of the case involves cross-racial impairment, your goal in voir dire is to weed out jurors who may not be receptive to evidence of this phenomenon. For example, you may want to ask potential jurors:

- Tell me about the most memorable time when someone mistook you or someone you know for someone else. In your opinion, what factors played into that mistake?
- Tell me about your most memorable experience where you or someone you know jumped to a conclusion about a person because of that person's race.
- Do you have an opinion about whether White people find it more difficult to identify Black people than to identify other White people? Tell me about that opinion. Tell me your most memorable experience where you or someone you know had trouble identifying a person of another race.
- Do you think that only people who are racially biased find it difficult to identify people of other races? Tell me how you formed that opinion.
- Do you think that if a White person has a family member or a close friend who is Black, then that White person will have no difficulty in identifying a Black person? Tell me about that opinion.

Voir dire allows defenders to explore whether any of the potential jurors appear overly confident about the accuracy of cross-racial identifications. In general, whenever cross-racial misidentification forms part of the defense theory, attorneys should use voir dire to determine whether potential jurors believe that witnesses can be honest and confident, but nevertheless wrong in their identification of a perpetrator; whether they understand the concept of cross-racial impairment; and whether they believe that cross-racial impairment may affect even non-prejudiced witnesses. *See* Kathryn M. Kase, *Eyewitness Identification: Tools for Litigating the Identification Case* in the Race Materials Bank at www.ncids.org (select "Training & Resources").

You may also consider petitioning the court for use of a questionnaire in cases involving eyewitness identifications issues in general and cross-racial identification issues in particular. Jeff Robinson & Jodie English, *Confronting the Race Issue During Jury Selection*, THE ADVOCATE, May 2008, at 57, 61. Potential jurors "may be more likely to reflect honestly and independently when answers are given in writing . . . versus in the public and intimidating environs of a criminal court." *Id.* For examples of questionnaire questions, see Kathryn M. Kase, *Eyewitness Identification: Tools for Litigating the Identification Case* in the Race Materials Bank at www.ncids.org (select "Training & Resources").

On potentially sensitive issues such as the impact of race on eyewitness identifications, attorneys may want to request permission to voir dire prospective jurors individually. There is little North Carolina law addressing individual voir dire in non-capital cases, but the trial judge's discretion over the conducting of voir dire implies the authority to order individual voir dire concerning sensitive matters. *See* 2 NORTH CAROLINA DEFENDER MANUAL Ch. 25 (Selection of Jury) (2d ed. 2012).

Avoiding "stake out" questions while exploring cross-racial impairment. Lawyers are prohibited from asking questions that attempt to indoctrinate potential jurors as to their theory of the case. *See State v. Parks*, 324 N.C. 420, 423 (1989). For this reason, lawyers may not "stake out" jurors by asking questions that attempt to commit prospective jurors to a specific course of action in the case. *See State v. Chapman*, 359 N.C. 328, 345–46 (2005). It is possible, however, to determine whether jurors will be open to expert testimony on eyewitness identification without running afoul of the prohibition on staking out jurors. For example, the North Carolina Supreme Court found that the following question did not constitute an attempt to stake out jurors: "If someone is offered as an expert in a particular field such as psychiatry, could you accept him as an expert, his testimony as an expert in that particular field." *State v Smith*, 328 N.C. 99, 131 (1991). These types of questions may allow you to determine whether potential jurors will bring an open mind to testimony from an expert witness on subjects such as cross-racial impairment.

In conducting voir dire in a cross-racial identification case, the following points should be kept in mind:

- Language matters. During voir dire, and throughout the case, eyewitness testimony should "be referred to as the eyewitness's 'belief' or 'opinion.'" EYEWITNESS TESTIMONY at § 9-7[b].
- Jurors in eyewitness identification cases should be willing to form conclusions that are independent of an eyewitness's opinion when presented with evidence or information that calls reliability into doubt.
- Lawyers should build trust with potential jurors before diving into issues of race. Addressing less sensitive issues first will help you maintain a comfortable and honest conversation when the subject turns to race.

- Recommended approaches for discussing race include discussions of historical racial prejudice and clarification that cross-racial impairment phenomenon is not indicative of racial prejudice or animus.
- When panelists describe incidents in which they or others were involved, inquire into possible cross-racial issues. For example, "What was the race of the perpetrator?" And, if the perpetrator was of a different race, "Did you have difficulty describing him or her?" Overly confident answers may suggest that the juror would not be receptive to evidence about the cross-racial impairment phenomenon.

Seek racially diverse and representative juries. Research suggests that racial diversity alters jury deliberations. Samuel R. Sommers, *On Racial Diversity and Group Decision Making: Identifying Multiple Effects of Racial Composition on Jury Deliberations*, 90 J. PERSONALITY & SOC. PSYCHOL. 597 (2006). A study by Samuel R. Sommers concluded that racially diverse juries "had longer deliberations, greater focus on the actual evidence, greater discussion of missing evidence, fewer inaccurate statements . . . and greater discussion of race-related topics." Jerry Kang et al., *Implicit Bias in the Courtroom*, 59 UCLA L. REV. 1124, 1180–81 (2012) (summarizing findings of Sommers' study). Sommers' study also revealed pre-deliberation effects: "Simply by knowing that they would be serving on diverse juries (as compared to all-White ones), White jurors were less likely to believe, at the conclusion of evidence but before deliberations, that the Black defendant was guilty." *Id.* at 1181. For further discussion of the value of diverse juries, see *infra* Ch. 8, Addressing Race at Trial.

C. Cross-Examination

Do not suggest an eyewitness is racially prejudiced where not supported by evidence. In a criminal case where the defense theory is mistaken cross-racial identification, the defense attorney's cross-examination of an eyewitness can be a delicate matter. Eyewitnesses often arouse jury sympathy, and villainizing an eyewitness may alienate jurors. When there is no evidence suggesting that an eyewitness harbors explicit racial biases, an aggressive cross-examination designed to demonstrate that an eyewitness is unable to recognize and identify members of other races may be seen as offensive and runs the risk of alienating the jury. "Counsel opposing an eyewitness wants to communicate the impression that he or she is confident that the eyewitness is wrong and that he or she does not ask the jurors to blame the witness for it." EYEWITNESS TESTIMONY at § 10-12.

However, when there is evidence that the eyewitness is racially biased, eliciting such testimony may lead jurors to distance themselves emotionally from the eyewitness and may bolster the defendant's theory of the case. *See Simmons v. Collins,* 655 So. 2d 330 (La. 1995) (evidence of eyewitness's use of racial epithets to demonstrate eyewitness's bias against Black people ruled admissible by Louisiana Supreme Court). In the O.J. Simpson murder trial, for example, commentators viewed evidence of racist remarks by Detective Mark Fuhrman as a key factor that caused the jury to be critical of his testimony and ultimately return a not-guilty verdict. *See, e.g.,* Leonard M. Baynes,

A Time to Kill, the O.J. Simpson Trials, and Storytelling to Juries, 17 LOY. L.A. ENT. L.J. 549, 563 (1997) ("The clincher for the jury was the Mark Fuhrman tapes.").

Where an expert witness will testify for the defense on the subject of eyewitness identification, and where the defense attorney knows that the eyewitness has had limited exposure to members of the defendant's race, it may be useful to cross-examine the eyewitness in a non-accusatory manner concerning the nature and extent of his or her interactions with members of the defendant's race. *See* June E. Chance & Alvin G. Goldstein, *The Other-Race Effect and Eyewitness Identification, in* PSYCHOLOGICAL ISSUES IN EYEWITNESS IDENTIFICATION 153, 170–72 (1996).

Eyewitness confidence should not be the focus of the cross-examination. Historically, cross-examination of eyewitnesses tended to focus on witness confidence, but research shows that confidence is an unreliable indicator of accuracy. Steven Penrod & Brian Cutler, *Witness Confidence and Witness Accuracy: Assessing Their Forensic Relation*, 1 PSYCH. PUB. POL. & L. 817 (1995). Defense attorneys should avoid a line of questioning that focuses too heavily on witness confidence so as not to suggest that jurors should associate confidence with accuracy, and may want to file a motion in limine prohibiting the prosecutor from implying that confidence is correlated with accuracy. *See* Lisa Steele, *Trying Identification Cases: An Outline For Raising Eyewitness Id Issues*, THE CHAMPION, Nov. 2004, at 8.

Lay the foundation for expert testimony during cross-examination. Cross-examination can help lay the foundation for expert testimony (when admitted) by establishing facts such as poor lighting, the presence of a weapon, the witness's experience with members of the defendant's race, or the difference between the race of the perpetrator and the race of the witness. *See supra* § 3.2B, Factors Affecting Eyewitness Identifications. Even where expert testimony will not be offered or has not been admitted, cross-examination presents an opportunity to elicit the factors that make eyewitness opinions less reliable. *See id.*

Cross-examination of officers. When cross-examining police officers, attorneys should be familiar with department policies and procedures, and the requirements of the Eyewitness Identification Reform Act. A key goal in cross-examining officers involved in pretrial identification procedures is to point out any differences between the procedures used and the legislatively mandated procedures and departmental policies. In a case involving a pretrial lineup constructed by an officer of a different race than the suspect, counsel may want to question the officer about department policies or practices concerning cross-racial lineup construction. *See supra* § 3.6A, Motions to Suppress Pretrial Identifications and Prevent In-Court Identifications.

Cross-examination alone may not convince jurors of eyewitness unreliability. Some research suggests that cross-examination alone may not drive home for jurors the distinction between accurate and inaccurate eyewitness identification. R. C. L. Lindsay et al., *Mock-juror Belief of Accurate and Inaccurate Eyewitnesses: A Replication and Extension,* 13 LAW & HUM. BEHAVIOR 333 (1989). In eyewitness identification cases, defense attorneys should consider the cross-examination of an eyewitness as one piece of a multi-pronged strategy to address unreliable identifications. Suppression of eyewitness identifications, expert witnesses on eyewitness identification, and jury instructions on eyewitness identifications should also be pursued in order to prevent jurors from unduly relying on eyewitness identification evidence.

D. Expert Testimony

Purpose. One goal of introducing expert testimony on the hazards of eyewitness identification is to dispel potential misconceptions about the reliability of eyewitness identification testimony. One study found that jurors who heard expert psychological testimony in eyewitness identification cases "rated the defense's case to be significantly stronger than did jurors who heard no expert testimony." MISTAKEN IDENTIFICATION at 227. Another study found that such testimony assists jurors in grasping the complex factors that influence eyewitness identification accuracy. *Id.* at 240–41.

General standard. The North Carolina Supreme Court has held that "expert testimony is properly admissible when such testimony can assist the jury to draw certain inferences from facts because the expert is better qualified." *State v. Locklear*, 349 N.C. 118, 147 (1998) (quotation omitted). Expert testimony will be admitted when it is helpful to the jury, and "North Carolina case law requires only that the expert be better qualified than the jury as to the subject at hand." *State v. Martin*, __ N.C. App. __, 729 S.E.2d 717, 720 (2012) (quoting *State v. Davis*, 106 N.C. App. 596, 601 (1992)). "The trial judge is afforded wide latitude of discretion when making a determination about the admissibility of expert testimony." *State v. Bullard*, 312 N.C. 129, 140 (1984).

Rule 702. In addition to meeting the general standard of helpfulness, expert testimony concerning eyewitness identification generally, and cross-racial eyewitness identification in particular, must satisfy the requirements of North Carolina Rule of Evidence 702, Testimony by experts. That rule provides that

> (a) If scientific, technical or other specialized knowledge will assist the trier of fact to understand the evidence or to determine a fact in issue, a witness qualified as an expert by knowledge, skill, experience, training, or education, may testify thereto in the form of an opinion, or otherwise, if all of the following apply:
>
> (1) The testimony is based upon sufficient facts or data.
> (2) The testimony is the product of reliable principles and methods.
> (3) The witness has applied the principles and methods reliably to the facts of the case.

Rule 702(a) was amended in 2011 to require that the expert's testimony be "based upon sufficient facts or data" and the expert have "applied the principles and methods reliably to the facts of the case." These amendments essentially codified the principles in *Daubert v. Merrell Dow Pharmaceuticals, Inc.*, 509 U.S. 579 (1993). *State v. McGrady*, ___ N.C. App. ___, 753 S.E.2d 361 (2014) (so holding). In essence, Rule 702(a) requires the judge to serve a gatekeeping function, ensuring that expert testimony is relevant and reliable. *See also* Alyson Grine, Legislative Change Regarding Expert Testimony, IDS FORENSIC RESOURCES BLOG (Aug. 17, 2011). Scientific research supports that the study of eyewitness identification is a valid and empirically based area of expertise beyond the understanding of most jurors, and defenders should be prepared with studies to this effect when offering expert testimony about eyewitness identification. *See supra* § 3.2, Overview of Risks of Misidentification; § 3.3, Cross-Racial Impairment.

Rule 403. Expert testimony on eyewitness identification also must satisfy North Carolina Rule of Evidence 403, Exclusion of relevant evidence on grounds of prejudice, confusion, or waste of time. In North Carolina, "the admission of expert testimony regarding memory factors is within the trial court's discretion, and the appellate court will not intervene where the trial court properly appraises probative and prejudicial value of the evidence under Rule 403 and the Rules of Evidence." *State v. Cole*, 147 N.C. App. 637, 642–43 (2001) (quoting *State v. Cotton*, 99 N.C. App. 615, 621 (1990), *aff'd*, 329 N.C. 764 (1991)) (holding that the trial court did not abuse its discretion by refusing to admit expert testimony from a psychology professor on factors complicating eyewitness identifications where the probative value of the proposed testimony "was outweighed by the risk of confusing the jury").

Rejection of expert testimony on eyewitness identification may constitute abuse of discretion. In states that review the exclusion of expert testimony on eyewitness memory for abuse of discretion, the rejection of such testimony has been held reversible error in some cases. *See, e.g., State v. Chapple,* 660 P.2d 1208 (Ariz. 1983); *People v. McDonald*, 690 P.2d 709 (Cal. 1984) (holding that exclusion of such testimony will ordinarily constitute an abuse of discretion where eyewitness identification is a key element of the prosecution's case, not corroborated by evidence of independent reliability, and defendant offers a qualified expert on eyewitness issues not likely to be fully known or understood by jury), *overruled on other grounds by* People v. Mendoza, 4 P.3d 265 (Cal. 2000). *See also United States v. Brownlee*, 454 F.3d 131 (3d Cir. 2006) (reversal for failure to allow expert to testify about effect of showup identifications, the lack of correlation between confidence and accuracy, confirming feedback, and time delay, even where trial court had allowed testimony on cross-racial impairment and other identification variables); *People v. Legrand,* 867 N.E.2d 374 (N.Y. 2007) (where there is little or no corroborating evidence supporting an eyewitness identification, it is an abuse of discretion to exclude expert testimony).

Failure to offer expert witness testimony on eyewitness identification may amount to ineffective assistance of counsel. In a federal habeas petition, a U.S. District Judge ruled that a North Carolina defense attorney rendered ineffective assistance of counsel by failing to consult with and call as a witness an expert on the reliability of eyewitness testimony generally and on cross-racial identifications specifically. *Moore v. Keller*, 917 F. Supp. 2d 471 (E.D.N.C. 2012), *rev'd sub nom, Moore v. Hardee*, 723 F.3d 488 (4th Cir. 2013). This ruling was reversed on appeal because the Fourth Circuit determined that counsel was not so ineffective as to meet the "doubly deferential" standard mandated by *Strickland v. Washington,* 466 U.S. 668 (1984) (holding that ineffective assistance of counsel requires a demonstration that counsel's representation fell below an objective standard of reasonableness and, but for counsel's unreasonable errors, the case outcome probably would have been different), and the Antiterrorism and Effective Death Penalty Act of 1996 (providing that, when state petitioners raise ineffective assistance of counsel claims in federal habeas actions, the reviewing court must determine whether the state court's interpretation of *Strickland* was reasonable). Despite its reversal, the district court's ruling underscores the need for defense attorneys to consider challenging the reliability of eyewitness identification in appropriate cases. *See also People v. Kindle*, 2002 WL 1554118 (Cal. Ct. App. 2002) (unpublished) (failure to consult with an eyewitness identification expert constituted ineffective assistance of counsel given the weakness of the evidence against defendant, lack of explanation for the failure to consult an expert, and reasonable probability of a different result had defense counsel presented expert testimony).

Expert testimony on cross-racial identification. Some courts have excluded expert testimony on cross-racial identification, reasoning that such testimony was within the common knowledge of the jury. *See, e.g.*, *United States v. Hudson*, 884 F.2d 1016, 1024 (7th Cir. 1989) (expert testimony regarding, among other things, the difficulty of cross-racial identification would "not aid the jury because it addresses an issue of which the jury already generally is aware, and it will not contribute to their understanding of the particular dispute"). Defenders should be prepared to counter the argument that cross-racial impairment is common sense by presenting the judge with cross-racial impairment studies and research showing that many jurors do not understand the phenomenon. *See State v. Henderson*, 27 A.3d 872 (N.J. 2011) (referencing the Report of the Special Master, *available at* www.eyeID.org, and noting that while 90% of experts recognize the problem of cross-racial impairment, only 47% of jurors do). Without expert witness testimony (and instruction from a judge on cross-racial impairment), deliberations may be inhibited because jurors may "not want to appear to harbor racist views" by suggesting that White people have difficulty distinguishing Black people. *Id.*

Practice note: If the court denies your motion to present expert testimony on eyewitness identification on the basis that the testimony is within the "common knowledge" of the jury, you may ask the judge to: take judicial notice of scientific findings about eyewitness identification generally and cross-racial identification in particular; inform the jury that it has taken judicial notice of the findings; and allow you to publish them to the jury. You may then incorporate the findings into your closing argument and request an appropriate jury instruction. *See* Lisa Steele, *Trying Identification Cases: An Outline For Raising Eyewitness Id Issues*, THE CHAMPION, Nov. 2004, at 8; Lisa Steele, *Public Knowledge, Popular Wisdom and Urban Legend: Educating the Jury About Memory on Closing Argument*, 36 CRIM. L. BULL. 316 (2000).

Judges' views on this subject may be shifting. In some cases, courts have recognized that expert testimony on eyewitness identification unreliability may be necessary, observing that "other means of attacking eyewitness identifications do not effectively substitute for expert testimony on their inherent unreliability." *Ferensic v. Birkett*, 501 F.3d 469, 481 (6th Cir. 2007). It is hard to estimate how frequently trial judges are admitting expert testimony on eyewitness identification since "when expert testimony is admitted, there is no appeal on the admissibility issue, and no opinion is issued. Similarly, when the defendant is acquitted there is no appeal of a decision to exclude expert testimony." MISTAKEN IDENTIFICATION at 20.

The Fourth Circuit has recognized that cross-racial impairment falls into a narrow category of circumstances in which expert testimony on the reliability of eyewitness identifications may be appropriate in order to complement effective cross-examination of eyewitnesses. *United States v. Harris*, 995 F.2d 532, 535 (4th Cir. 1993). A number of courts have acknowledged that experts have found that cross-racial identifications are "particularly unreliable." *Gonzales v. Thaler*, 643 F.3d 425, 432 (5th Cir. 2011); *see also United States v. Jernigan*, 492 F.3d 1050, 1054 (9th Cir. 2007) ("Cross-racial identifications . . . are particularly suspect.").

It does not appear that North Carolina appellate courts have specifically addressed the admissibility of expert testimony on cross-racial impairment. In 2002, the North Carolina Court of Appeals recognized that "expert testimony concerning eyewitness identification may be appropriate in some cases," while reaffirming that the admissibility of expert testimony on eyewitness identification is generally a matter for the trial court's discretion. *State v. Lee*, 154 N.C. App. 410, 417 (2002). In an earlier case, the North Carolina Court of Appeals, in upholding the rejection of expert testimony on eyewitness identification, cautioned against interpreting the ruling as prohibiting such testimony across the board: "Criminal defendants have increasingly presented expert testimony on the reliability of eyewitness identification, and some courts have held its exclusion reversible error." *State v. Knox*, 78 N.C. App. 493, 496–97 (1985). The door is therefore open in North Carolina to arguments that expert testimony on cross-racial impairment is necessary and appropriate in a given case.

Practice note: In seeking the admission of expert testimony on cross-racial eyewitness identification, defendants should highlight consequences that may result from exclusion. For example, two North Carolina defendants who were denied the opportunity to present expert testimony on the unreliability of cross-racial identification, were convicted, served time in prison, and have since been exonerated.

The first was Ronald Junior Cotton. *See State v. Cotton,* 99 N.C. App. 615, 621–22 (1990) (affirming exclusion of expert witness on ground that the effects of stress, cross-racial factors, priming of memory, and confidence malleability were commonly known to jurors), *aff'd*, 329 N.C. 764 (1991); *DNA Test Frees Innocent Man*, NEWS & RECORD (Greensboro), July 1, 1995, at A1. *See supra* "Illustration" in § 3.2B, Factors Affecting Eyewitness Identifications.

The second was Terence Levonne Garner. *See State v. Garner,* 136 N.C. App. 1, 7–10 (1999); *FRONTLINE: An Ordinary Crime* (PBS television broadcast, Jan. 10, 2002); *Garner's Conviction Thrown Out*, NEWS AND OBSERVER (Raleigh), February 6, 2002, at A1. *See supra* "Case study: *State v. Terence Garner*" in § 3.3B, Impact of Cross-Racial Impairment.

Role of the expert in eyewitness identification cases. Eyewitness experts typically provide background information about factors influencing eyewitness accuracy. *See, e.g.*, MISTAKEN IDENTIFICATION at 19. An expert witness may not offer testimony as to the credibility of a witness. *See generally State v. Ryan*, __ N.C. App. __, 734 S.E.2d 598, 603 (2012) (in the absence of a proper foundation, an expert may not testify as to whether sexual abuse in fact occurred, as such testimony amounts to opinion on credibility of victim); *see also State v. Stancil*, 355 N.C. 266 (2002) (same). In the context of cross-racial identifications, experts cannot testify as to the accuracy of a particular cross-racial identification, since "the evidence . . . suggests that once a suspect has been selected from a lineup by an eyewitness, there is no known way to make a useful judgment about the likelihood that the eyewitness is correct." Steven M. Smith et al., *Postdictors of Eyewitness Errors: Can False Identifications be Diagnosed in the Cross-Race Situation?*, 7 PSYCHOL. PUB. POL'Y & L. 153, 166 (2001). Nevertheless, the context provided by an expert would assist jurors in evaluating the accuracy of the eyewitness's identification.

Case specific expert testimony. North Carolina courts may be more receptive to expert testimony on eyewitness identification when it is "case specific." In three cases, the North Carolina Court of Appeals upheld the exclusion of expert testimony on eyewitness identification where the trial court found that the proffered testimony was insufficiently tied to the facts of the case. *See State v. Lee*, 154 N.C. App. 410, 417 (2002); *State v. Suddreth,* 105 N.C. App. 122, 134 (1992); *State v. Knox*, 78 N.C. App. 493, 495–96 (1985). Thus, the court in *Lee* observed that although expert testimony "may be appropriate in some cases," it was not warranted in this case where the expert had "not interviewed the victims, did not visit the crime scene, and did not observe any of the eyewitnesses' testimony at trial." *Lee*, 154 N.C. App. 410, 417 (also discussing other factors that supported trial judge's ruling). Similarly, when reviewing the admissibility of expert testimony on eyewitness identification, courts in other jurisdictions have examined the "fit" between the testimony offered and the facts of the case. *See, e.g.*, *United States v. Dowling*, 855 F.2d 114, 118 (1988), *aff'd*, 493 U.S. 342 (1990); *United States v. Harris*, 995 F.2d 532, 535 (4th Cir. 1993). For example, testimony regarding weapon focus may properly be excluded where it is not linked to evidence about the presence of weapons at the time the eyewitness observed the perpetrator and, therefore, would not assist the jury. *Dowling,* 855 F.2d 114, 119. Defenders should ensure that the proposed expert testimony bears a close relationship to the facts of the case and that the expert has familiarized him or herself with the facts of the case before testifying. Although the defense does not have a right to have an expert interview the victim, our expanded discovery statutes ensure that the defense will be able to obtain, and an expert will be able to review, any statements of the victim or notes or other materials reflecting the victim's observations.

Indigent defendants entitled to appointment of experts. Indigent defendants are entitled to the assistance of counsel and other necessary expenses, including expert assistance. G.S. 7A-450(b); G.S. 7A-454; *State v. Tatum*, 291 N.C. 73 (1976). Defenders in cases involving cross-racial identifications may file motions for funds for an expert witness in the field of eyewitness identification, as such experts may be necessary to guarantee the defendant's fundamental right to a fair trial and to effective assistance of counsel, including the effective cross-examination of the State's witnesses. In certain circumstances, the refusal to grant funds for an expert witness on issues concerning eyewitness identification may deprive the defendant of an opportunity to present a defense of mistaken identity and violate the defendant's constitutional right to due process under the North Carolina Constitution and United States Constitution. *See generally Tatum*, 291 N.C. 73; *State v. Ballard*, 333 N.C. 515 (1993); *Ake v. Oklahoma*, 470 U.S. 68 (1985).

For a discussion of obtaining funds for an expert witness, including applying ex parte for funds, see 1 NORTH CAROLINA DEFENDER MANUAL Ch. 5 (Experts and Other Assistance) (2d ed. 2013). *See also* Motion for Funds for Defense Expert in Eyewitness Identification and for Ex Parte Hearing in the Race Materials Bank at www.ncids.org (select "Training & Resources").

Further resources. A sample motion for appropriate relief and petition for habeas corpus challenging the rejection of expert testimony on cross-racial identification may be found in the Race Materials Bank at www.ncids.org (select "Training & Resources"). A list of local experts in the field of eyewitness identification can be accessed on the North Carolina Indigent Defense Services Forensic Resources website. Additional resources, including a sample direct examination of an expert on cross-racial identification by Innocence Project Attorney Barry C. Scheck, can be accessed at www.eyeID.org.

E. Jury Instructions

Another way of addressing cross-racial impairment is to educate jurors about the problem through the use of jury instructions. "The purpose of a specific jury instruction on cross-racial identification is to permit juries to consider the increased possibility of misidentification in determining whether or not there is sufficient evidence of guilt." American Bar Association, *American Bar Association Policy 104D: Cross-Racial Identification*, 37 SW. U. L. REV. 917, 925 (2008).

General instructions. Jury instructions relevant to eyewitness identification cases include N.C.P.I. 101.15, credibility, including opportunity to see and hear; N.C.P.I. 104.90, identification of defendant as perpetrator of a crime; and N.C.P.I. 104.94, testimony of expert witness. In North Carolina, there is not a pattern jury instruction on cross-racial impairment. Proposed instructions are discussed below in this section.

EIRA Instruction. EIRA provides that the Court shall instruct the jurors that they may consider credible evidence of non-compliance with EIRA in evaluating the reliability of eyewitness identification. In any case in which compliance with EIRA is at issue, the defendant should tender in writing a jury instruction as governed by the statute and reflected in pattern jury instruction N.C.P.I. 105.70, live lineup requirements, and/or N.C.P.I. 105.65, photo lineup requirements.

Cross-racial impairment jury instructions in other jurisdictions. Some courts have granted jury instructions advising jurors of the empirical findings about cross-racial impairment. In *State v. Cromedy*, 727 A.2d 457, 467 (N.J. 1999), the New Jersey Supreme Court considered forty years of empirical studies concerning the psychological factors affecting eyewitness identifications in holding that a cross-racial identification "requires a special jury instruction in an appropriate case." The court noted that most, although not all, experts agreed that people experience more difficulty identifying people of other races. The court found that, "notwithstanding those differences [in expert opinions], there is an impressive consistency in results showing that problems exist with cross-racial eyewitness identification." *Cromedy*, 727 A.2d 457, 467.

Thereafter, in *State v. Henderson*, 27 A.3d 872 (N.J. 2011), the New Jersey Supreme Court revisited and updated the state's jury instructions concerning cross-racial impairment on the basis of research conducted after *Cromedy*. The court noted that one "meta-analysis conducted after *Cromedy*, involving thirty-nine studies and nearly 5,000 identifications, confirmed the Court's prior finding" that witnesses may have more difficulty making a cross-racial identification. *Henderson*, 27 A.3d 872, 907 (citing Christian A. Meissner & John C. Brigham, *Thirty Years of Investigating the Own-Race Bias in Memory for Faces: A Meta-Analytic Review*, 7 PSYCHOL. PUB. POL'Y & L. 3, 21 (2001)). That meta-analysis concluded that a mistaken identification is 1.56 times more likely in cross-race conditions; in other words, an innocent Black suspect has a 56% greater chance of being misidentified by a White eyewitness than by a Black eyewitness. Christian A. Meissner & John C. Brigham, *Thirty Years of Investigating the Own-Race Bias in Memory for Faces: A Meta-Analytic Review*, 7 PSYCHOL. PUB. POL'Y & L. 3, 15 (2001). The court recognized that most potential jurors were not aware of this issue: a 2006 study found that while 90% of experts recognize the problem of own-race bias, only 47% of jurors do. *Henderson*, 27 A.3d 872, 910 (referencing the Report of the Special Master, *available at* www.eyeID.org). As a result of these findings, the Court expanded its holding in *Cromedy* and concluded that an instruction cautioning jurors about the problems of cross-racial identification should be given whenever cross-racial identification is an issue at trial. *Henderson*, 27 A.3d 872, 926.

Other states in which cross-racial identification jury instructions must be given in these circumstances include Utah, *see State v. Long*, 721 P.2d 483, 494 n.8 (Utah 1986) (instruction that would satisfy the court's concerns instructs jurors to "consider whether the witness is of a different race than the criminal actor. Identification by a person of a different race may be less reliable than identification by a person of the same race."); *State v. Brink*, 173 P.3d 183, 185 n.1 (Utah 2007) (discussing with approval an instruction providing in part that "a witness identification of a person of a different race may be less reliable"); and California, *see People v. Palmer*, 203 Cal. Rptr. 474, 475 n.2 (Cal. Ct. App. 1984) (reversible error to reject defendant's proposed jury instruction that would have instructed jurors to "consider whether or not the witness is the same race as the individual he is attempting to identify. If they are not, you should consider the effect this would have on an accurate identification.").

Cross-racial jury instructions in North Carolina. The rejection of proposed jury instructions on cross-racial impairment was upheld by the North Carolina Supreme Court in 1980 and by the North Carolina Court of Appeals in 1984. *State v. Allen,* 301 N.C. 489

(1980); *State v. Miller*, 69 N.C. App. 392 (1984). Since that time, scientific evidence of cross-racial impairment has grown.

In *Allen,* the Court upheld the rejection of jury instructions on cross-racial identification because there was "no indication that race in any way affected the identification of defendant by the witnesses." *Allen*, 301 N.C. 489, 495. When requesting an instruction on cross-racial identification, counsel should argue that the reasoning of *Allen* does not account for later scientific findings concerning cross-racial impairment. *See, e.g.*, Christian A. Meissner & John C. Brigham, *Thirty Years of Investigating the Own-Race Bias in Memory for Faces: A Meta-Analytic Review*, 7 PSYCHOL. PUB. POL'Y & L. 3, 21 (2001); *see supra* § 3.3A, Empirical Evidence of Cross-Racial Impairment. Further, defense attorneys should argue that *Allen* does not require that the defendant show that the cross-racial identification was erroneous, only that a reasonable jury could find that the identification was affected by cross-racial factors. As appropriate, defense attorneys should also distinguish the facts of their client's case from those in *Allen*, which involved an eyewitness identification occurring during the daytime in close quarters.

Recently, in *State v. Watlington,* ___ N.C. App. ___, 759 S.E.2d 116, 127 (2014), the North Carolina Court of Appeals upheld the rejection of proposed jury instructions concerning eyewitness identification that "bore a strong resemblance to the New Jersey instruction developed as a result of the *Henderson* decision." Among other things, the defendant requested that the court instruct the jury that, "since research has shown that people may have greater difficulty in accurately identifying members of a different race, [the jurors should consider] whether the witness and the alleged perpetrator are of the same or different races." *Id.* (internal quotations omitted). The court concluded that the defendant failed to offer evidentiary support for the facts embedded in the proposed instructions and that it would be improper for an appellate court to make the factual findings necessary to reverse the trial court's failure to deliver the proposed instructions. *Id.* at 129–30. The *Watlington* opinion indicates that, when proposing jury instructions concerning eyewitness identification generally and cross-racial impairment specifically, defendants should support the proposed instructions with empirical research supporting the factual assertions contained in the proposed instructions. *See supra* § 3.3A, Empirical Evidence of Cross-Racial Impairment.

Content of cross-racial impairment jury instructions. Chief Judge Bazelon of the D.C. Circuit Court of Appeals proposed a jury instruction on the issue of cross-racial identification in his concurring opinion in *United States v. Telfaire,* which has served as a model in many jurisdictions. *United States v. Telfaire*, 469 F.2d 552 (D.C. Cir. 1972) (Bazelon, C.J., concurring). *But see State v. Allen,* 301 N.C. 489 (1980) (citing majority opinion in *Telfaire* as support for its conclusion that a cross-racial jury instruction was not mandated). This instruction, though still widely cited, contains a potentially misleading suggestion that, despite possible risks of cross-racial misidentification, jurors may "conclude that the witness has had sufficient contacts with members of the defendant's race that he would not have greater difficulty in making a reliable identification." *Telfaire*, 469 F.2d 552, 561 (Bazelon, C.J., concurring). Scientific research indicates that exposure to members of the defendant's racial group alone does not necessarily improve the accuracy of cross-racial identifications. *See supra* "Practice note" in § 3.3C, Causes of Cross-Racial Impairment. For this reason, defense attorneys should not include this language in proposed jury instructions on cross-racial impairment.

An alternative instruction that incorporates both everyday experience and evidence from psychological studies was proposed by Professor Sherri Lynn Johnson:

> In this case the identifying witness is of a different race than the defendant. In the experience of many it is more difficult to identify members of a different race than members of one's own. Psychological studies support this impression. In addition, laboratory studies reveal that even people with no prejudice against other races and substantial contact with persons of other races still experience difficulty in accurately identifying members of a different race. Quite often people do not recognize this difficulty in themselves. You should consider these facts in evaluating the witness's testimony, but you must also consider whether there are other factors present in this case that overcome any such difficulty of identification.

Sherri Lynn Johnson, *Cross-Racial Identification Errors In Criminal Cases*. 69 CORNELL L. REV. 934, 976 (1984).

You may want to be prepared to propose alternative wording if the court refuses the above instruction, such as:

> Research has shown that people may have greater difficulty in accurately identifying members of a different race. You should consider whether the fact that the witness and the defendant are not of the same race may have influenced the accuracy of the witness's identification.

New Jersey Identification Instruction: In-Court and Out-of-Court Identifications at 5, New Jersey Criminal Model Jury Charges, revised February 2014.

Further resources. For a discussion of strategies for seeking a jury instruction on cross-racial impairment and examples of jury instructions considered in other jurisdictions, see *A New Legal Architecture: Litigating Eyewitness ID Cases in the 21st Century* 323–66, PowerPoint presentation, NYU School of Law (March 14, 2008). *available at* www.eyeID.org.

Chapter 4
Pretrial Release

4.1 Scope of Chapter

"The bail determination is crucial to the legitimacy of the criminal process." THE ABELL FOUNDATION, THE PRETRIAL RELEASE PROJECT: A STUDY OF MARYLAND'S PRETRIAL RELEASE AND BAIL SYSTEM vi (2001). Pretrial detention not only results in loss of liberty pending resolution of a case, it also may increase the chances of conviction and further incarceration. Pretrial release determinations thus have a huge impact on defendants' cases and lives.

There are two primary ways in which racial minorities may be at a disadvantage in the context of pretrial release. First, pretrial release decisions may be affected by implicit or explicit racial biases of court actors. Second, Black and Latino defendants are more likely to live in poverty and therefore less able to satisfy financial conditions of release. Thus, non-White defendants may be more likely to remain in pretrial confinement than their White counterparts in cases in which a secured bond is imposed. The strategies discussed in this chapter are aimed at addressing these two ways in which pretrial release determinations may produce racially disparate outcomes.

State and federal constitutional provisions guarantee equal protection and due process and prohibit excessive bail. North Carolina statutes state generally that pretrial release is favored and make money bail a last resort. Lawyers can rely on these protections in at least three contexts: (1) arguing for more favorable pretrial release conditions at bond reduction hearings; (2) seeking relief in some cases following an unlawful pretrial release decision; or (3) working with other court actors in implementing systemic changes to address any disparities in pretrial detention. The legal bases for these claims and strategies for raising them are discussed *infra* in § 4.3, Legal Restrictions, and § 4.4, Pretrial Advocacy Strategies.

4.2 Overview

A. Increased Reliance on Pretrial Detention

On an average day, there are approximately 440,000 unconvicted accused people in American jails awaiting action on criminal charges, accounting for approximately 60% of all jail inmates. Todd D. Minton & Daniela Golinelli, Bureau of Justice Statistics, *Jail Inmates at Midyear 2013—Statistical Tables*, 2014, at 1. Nationally, the number of people who remain in jail pretrial rather than obtain pretrial release is increasing, the number of people released on their own recognizance is decreasing, and the percentage of defendants with financial conditions attached to their conditions of pretrial release is on the rise. THOMAS H. COHEN & BRIAN A. REAVES, BUREAU OF JUSTICE STATISTICS, STATE COURT PROCESSING STATISTICS, 1990–2004: PRETRIAL RELEASE OF FELONY DEFENDANTS IN STATE COURTS 3 (2007). Defenders therefore need to be prepared to advocate for pretrial release on behalf of their clients. *See generally* Shima Baradaran & Frank McIntyre, *Predicting Violence*, 90 TEX. L. REV. 497, 558 (2012) (concluding that 25% more pretrial detainees could be released than are currently being released).

B. Race and Pretrial Detention

Historically, studies examining the relationship between race and pretrial decisions and outcomes showed differing results. *See, e.g.,* Marvin D. Free, Jr., *Race and Presentencing Decisions: The Cost of Being African American, in* RACIAL ISSUES IN CRIMINAL JUSTICE: THE CASE OF AFRICAN AMERICANS 137, 140–41 (Marvin D. Free Jr. ed., 2003) (of 25 studies on the role of race in bail determinations, 17 concluded that race influenced bail determinations and/or pretrial release decisions, but eight did not find evidence for the hypothesis that race influences such decisions). However, recent studies (discussed below), employing a variety of methodologies, have found that race plays a role in both pretrial release decisions and pretrial release outcomes. *See DeWolfe v. Richmond*, 76 A.3d 1019, 1023 (Md. 2013) (recognizing that "studies show that the bail amounts are often improperly affected by race"); *see also* Marvin D. Free, Jr., *Race and Presentencing Decisions: The Cost of Being African American*, *in* RACIAL ISSUES IN CRIMINAL JUSTICE: THE CASE OF AFRICAN AMERICANS 137, 139 (Marvin D. Free Jr. ed., 2003) ("Studies using more recent data were more likely than those using older data to reflect racial disparities [in bail and pretrial release decision-making].").

A 2003 analysis of administrative data collected by the State Courts Processing Statistics (SCPS) program of the Bureau of Justice Statistics considered bail determinations in more than 30,000 cases and found that: (1) Black and Hispanic defendants were over 20% more likely to be denied bail—that is, to be subjected to preventive detention—than White defendants; (2) Hispanic defendants were 39% more likely than White or Black defendants to have financial requirements attached to the conditions of their release; (3) Black defendants were 66% more likely than White defendants to be detained pretrial; and (4) Hispanic defendants were 91% more likely than White defendants to be detained pretrial. Stephen Demuth, *Racial and Ethnic Differences in Pretrial Release Decisions and Outcomes: A Comparison of Hispanic, Black, and White Felony Arrestees*, 41 CRIMINOLOGY 873, 894–96 (2003). This study concluded that Hispanic defendants suffer a "triple disadvantage at the pretrial release stage, [as] they are the group most likely to have to pay bail, the group with the highest bail amounts, and the group least able to pay bail." *Id.* at 899–900 (internal quotation omitted).

Another study using SCPS data from 1990 to 2000 also found racial and ethnic disparities in decisions to deny bail and impose secured bonds. Traci Schlesinger, *Racial and Ethnic Disparity in Pretrial Criminal Processing*, 22 JUST. Q. 170 (2005). This study concluded that, "when there is disparity in the treatment of Black and Latino defendants with similar legal characteristics, Latinos always receive the less beneficial decisions." *Id.* at 186. Still another examination of SCPS data concluded that Latinos are placed on monetary bail at a higher rate than White and Black defendants. DAVID LEVIN, PRETRIAL JUSTICE INSTITUTE, PRETRIAL RELEASE OF LATINO DEFENDANTS (2008).

In a study of five large metropolitan counties, two researchers found "evidence of substantial judicial bias" against Black people in bail setting in two of the counties examined. SHAWN D. BUSHWAY & JONAH B. GELBACH, TESTING FOR RACIAL DISCRIMINATION IN BAIL SETTING USING NONPARAMETRIC ESTIMATION OF A PARAMETRIC MODEL 37 (Nat'l Sci. Found., Working Paper No. SES0718955, 2011). Researchers studying the bail bond market in New Haven, Connecticut concluded that courts routinely "overdeter" Black and male Hispanic defendants from fleeing after release on bail by setting bail at higher levels and that commercial bail bondsmen recognize this difference and charge lower rates for Black and male Hispanic defendants. Ian Ayers & Joel Waldfogel, *A Market Test for Race Discrimination in Bail Setting*, 46 STAN. L. REV. 987 (1994).

Race also may play a role in a defendant's ability to access pretrial diversion programs. Generally, when an offender completes a pretrial diversion program, his or her charges are dropped. Traci Schlesinger, *Racial Disparities in Pretrial Diversion: An Analysis of Outcomes Among Men Charged with Felonies and Processed in State Courts*, 3 RACE & JUST. 210, 211 (2013). Approximately 8% of the people arrested and charged with felonies each year are selected by prosecutors for pretrial diversion programs. *Id.* (citing Bureau of Justice Statistics data). A recent analysis of SPCS data uncovered racial disparities in pretrial diversions granted to men charged with felonies in metropolitan counties. According to the study, "[o]verall, prosecutors are more likely to grant pretrial diversions to White defendants than they are to grant these diversions to Black, Latino, or Asian and Native American defendants with similar legal characteristics." *Id.* at 228.

Studies such as these led one scholar to conclude: "[M]any of the problems in bail determinations that create dysfunction and arbitrariness in bail determinations—the lack of relevant background information on the defendant and the over-reliance on money bonds—also contribute to racial disparities in bail outcomes among African American and white defendants." Cynthia E. Jones, *"Give Us Free": Addressing Racial Disparities in Bail Determinations*, 16 N.Y.U. J. LEGIS. & PUB. POL'Y 919, 955 (2013).

C. The Relationship between Race and Other Factors (Socioeconomic Status, Age, Gender, Employment, and Homelessness) in Pretrial Release Decisions

Various factors may contribute to racial disparities in pretrial release decisions and outcomes. One factor identified by researchers is the use of secured bonds or other financial conditions of release. *See* JUSTICE POLICY INSTITUTE, BAIL FAIL: WHY THE U.S. SHOULD END THE PRACTICE OF USING MONEY FOR BAIL 15 (2012). Studies have found that secured bonds affect racial and ethnic minorities in particular because such defendants are more likely to be low-income.

> Among defendants required to pay bail, the odds of detention for black and Hispanic defendants are more than twice those for white defendants. That is, controlling for the amount of bail (and other legal and contextual factors), black and Hispanic defendants are significantly less able to post bail. These results suggest that bail is particularly prohibitive for minority defendants.

Stephen Demuth, *Racial and Ethnic Differences in Pretrial Release Decisions and Outcomes: A Comparison of Hispanic, Black and White Felony Arrestees*, 41 CRIMINOLOGY 873, 897 (2003). *See also* Jonathan Zweig, Note, *Extraordinary Conditions of Release Under The Bail Reform Act*, 47 HARV. J. ON LEGIS. 555, 556 (2010) (noting that some wealthy defendants may avoid pretrial detention by paying for special conditions of release, while "defendants who pose equivalent risks, but who cannot afford to pay for extraordinary terms of in-home detention, are detained in conditions that are often worse than those in which convicted criminals are held").

In addition, where a bond is initially too high for a person to satisfy, a defendant with financial means is more likely to be able to retain private counsel to seek a bond modification and may even be able to secure release on the day of arrest. In contrast, a low-income person charged with the same offense may remain in jail because he or she cannot hire counsel to seek a modification right away. When a judge appoints counsel for an indigent defendant at the first appearance, the bond is typically not addressed until a subsequent court date. The defendant may wait in jail, for example, while the Office of the Public Defender assigns his case to a particular assistant public defender, the attorney has time to visit the jail to conduct an intake interview, and the attorney then moves for a bond modification. *See infra* § 4.4A, Enter the Case at the Earliest Possible Opportunity.

Other non-statutory factors, such as age, also may have an influence on racial disparities in pretrial release. For example, in Minnesota, one of the factors judicial officials once considered in determining whether a defendant was a flight risk was whether the defendant was under age 21 at the time of his arrest. Research revealed that this factor was not a significant predictor of pretrial offending or flight risk but *was* strongly correlated with race. In other words, judicial officials considering the age of defendants in setting pretrial release conditions were unknowingly contributing to racial disparities. ASHLEY NELLIS ET AL., THE SENTENCING PROJECT, REDUCING RACIAL DISPARITY IN THE CRIMINAL JUSTICE SYSTEM: A MANUAL FOR PRACTITIONERS AND POLICYMAKERS 31 (2d ed. 2008).

Certain other factors considered in pretrial release decisions, such as a defendant's employment status, may be correlated with race. *See* G.S. 15A-534(c) (listing employment as factor for judicial officials to consider in determining conditions of release). For example, since African Americans generally have higher rates of unemployment than Whites, African American defendants may be at a disadvantage when employment status is a factor in a judicial official's pretrial release decision. At the end of 2012, the African American unemployment rate in North Carolina was 17.3 percent compared to 6.7 percent for Whites. MARY GABLE & DOUGLAS HALL, ECONOMIC POLICY INSTITUTE, ONGOING JOBLESSNESS IN NORTH CAROLINA: UNEMPLOYMENT RATE FOR AFRICAN AMERICANS FOURTH IN NATION, MORE THAN DOUBLE THE STATE'S WHITE RATE 1 (2013); *see also* United States Dep't of Labor, *Bureau of Labor Statistics Economic News Release*, Table A-2: Employment Status of the Civilian Population by Race, Sex, and Age, BLS.GOV (showing higher rates of unemployment among African Americans). Defenders therefore need to be prepared to present other indicia comparable to employment, such as community ties, ongoing responsibilities (such as caring for a child), and other factors.

Similarly, if homelessness is considered in making pretrial release decisions, minorities are at a disadvantage because of their higher representation in the homeless population. *See, e.g.,* Ralph De Costa Nunez, *Homelessness: It's About Race, Not Just Poverty*, CITY LIMITS, March 2012 (nationally, members of Black families are over seven times more likely to seek refuge in a homeless shelter than members of White families). Anecdotal evidence suggests that some judicial officials may be reluctant to release homeless defendants, perhaps in reliance on an assumed correlation between homelessness and flight risk.

Some studies have considered the ways in which race interacts with multiple factors in the pretrial release setting, such as age, gender, and socioeconomic status. One study found a correlation between race and pretrial release decisions when the interaction between race and such factors was considered. The study concluded that African Americans were at a disadvantage relative to White defendants in terms of bail amounts and likelihood of release on their own recognizance (the equivalent of a written promise to appear in North Carolina); and that African Americans males aged 18–29 received the highest bail amounts of all defendants. John Wooldredge, *Distinguishing Race Effects on Pre-Trial Release and Sentencing Decisions*, 29 JUST. Q. 41 (2012).

Other studies have considered the relationship between gender and race. In one study, researchers concluded that White women were more likely than White men to receive bail below the amounts recommended in a bail schedule, but Black women were not treated any differently than Black men. E. Britt Patterson & Michael J. Lynch, *Biases in Formalized Bail Procedures, in* RACE AND CRIMINAL JUSTICE 365 (Michael J. Lynch & E. Britt Patterson eds., 1991). Another study concluded that White mothers benefited from having children for pretrial release determinations, while Black mothers who had children did not obtain any advantage. Gayle S. Bickle & Ruth D. Peterson, *The Impact of Gender-Based Family Roles on Criminal Sentencing*, 38 SOC. PROBS. 372 (1991). A later study found that White female defendants received more advantageous pretrial release decisions than male, minority defendants and were the most likely to be released pretrial. Stephen Demuth & Darrell Steffensmeier, *The Impact of Gender and Race-Ethnicity in the Pretrial Release Process*, 51 SOC. PROBS. 222 (2004). Another study concluded that the odds of release for White women "were not significantly different than [those] of White and Black males," but that Black Women were the least likely group to be detained pretrial. Tina L. Freiburger & Carly M. Hilinski, *The Impact of Race, Gender, and Age on the Pretrial Decision*, 35 CRIM. JUST. REV. 318, 330 (2010) (suggesting that judicial consideration of family obligations might be responsible for the increased likelihood of release for Black women).

D. Defendants Detained Pretrial Achieve Worse Outcomes

The United States Supreme Court has described the pretrial process as "perhaps the most critical period of the [criminal] proceedings." *Powell v. Alabama*, 287 U.S. 45, 57 (1932). Defendants detained pretrial are at a number of disadvantages in comparison to those who are released pretrial.

> The time spent in jail awaiting trial has a detrimental impact on the individual. It often means loss of a job; it disrupts family life; and it enforces idleness. Most jails offer little or no recreational or rehabilitative programs. The time spent in jail is simply dead time. Moreover, if a defendant is locked up, he is hindered in his ability to gather evidence, contact witnesses, or otherwise prepare his defense.

> Imposing those consequences on anyone who has not yet been convicted is serious. It is especially unfortunate to impose them on those persons who are ultimately found to be innocent.

Barker v. Wingo, 407 U.S. 514, 532–33 (1972) (addressing speedy trial rights).

Studies have found a link between pretrial detention and case outcomes. 78% of defendants detained pretrial—contrasted with 60% of defendants released pretrial—are ultimately convicted. THOMAS H. COHEN & BRIAN A. REAVES, BUREAU OF JUSTICE STATISTICS, STATE COURT PROCESSING STATISTICS, 1990–2004: PRETRIAL RELEASE OF FELONY DEFENDANTS IN STATE COURTS 7 (2008). Studies have also found that pretrial detainees are more likely to plead guilty, be convicted of a felony, receive a sentence of incarceration, and receive longer sentences compared with people who are released pretrial. *See* GERARD RAINVILLE & BRIAN A. REAVES, BUREAU OF JUSTICE STATISTICS, FELONY DEFENDANTS IN LARGE URBAN COUNTIES, 2000 24 & Table 24 (2003) ("Seventy-seven percent of the defendants who were detained until case disposition were eventually convicted of some offense, compared to 55% of those released pending disposition"); *Campbell v. McGruder*, 580 F.2d 521, 531 (D.C. Cir. 1978) (noting that a defendant who is not incarcerated pending trial "stands a better chance of not being convicted or, if convicted, not receiving a prison sentence") (quotation omitted); *United States v. Gallo*, 653 F. Supp. 320, 337–38 (E.D.N.Y. 1986) (citing studies indicating that detention likely increases the chances of conviction at trial); Cassia Spohn & Dawn Beichner, *Is Preferential Treatment of Female Offenders a Thing of the Past? A Multisite Study of Gender, Race, and Imprisonment*, 11 CRIM. JUST. POL'Y REV. 149 (2000).

Defendants who are detained pretrial may feel pressure to accept a plea bargain because of the adverse consequences of remaining in jail. *See* JUSTICE POLICY INSTITUTE, BAIL FAIL: WHY THE U.S. SHOULD END THE PRACTICE OF USING MONEY FOR BAIL 13 (2012). Jailed defendants who ultimately receive a non-custodial sentence or prevail at trial also experience the adverse consequences faced by defendants incarcerated following a conviction: difficulty keeping or finding a job, lower wages, greater likelihood of recidivism, and even lower likelihood of marriage. Traci Schlesinger, *Racial and Ethnic Disparity in Pretrial Criminal Processing*, 22 JUST. Q. 170 (2005). One scholar has suggested that there may be a link in some cases between pretrial detention and wrongful convictions. Andrew D. Leipold, *How the Pretrial Process Contributes to Wrongful Convictions*, 42 AM. CRIM. L. REV. 1123, 1130 (2005) (positing "a positive correlation between the falsity of the accusation and the suspect's need to assist in the defense. It might be precisely when the wrong person has been charged that factual development, alibis, and hard-to-find evidence are the most vital to the case.").

Given the influence of pretrial detention on ultimate case outcomes, the pretrial release determination may be one of the most important stages of a criminal case for addressing racial disparities. *See* Traci Schlesinger, *The Cumulative Effects of Racial Disparities in Criminal Processing*, 7 J. INST. JUST. & INT'L STUD. 261, 262 (2007) ("Focusing on sentencing decisions may obscure this important moment of disparate punishment.").

E. Other Factors that May Contribute to Racial Disparities in Bail Determinations

Delayed representation. The U.S. Supreme Court has recognized that counsel plays a vital role at bail hearings. *See Coleman v. Alabama*, 399 U.S. 1, 9 (1970) ("[C]ounsel can also be influential at the preliminary hearing in making effective arguments for the accused on such matters as . . . bail."); *see also* Douglas L. Colbert, *Thirty-Five Years After Gideon: The Illusory Right To Counsel At Bail Proceedings*, 1998 U. ILL. L. REV. 1, 6 (1998) (observing that lawyers representing defendants in bail proceedings play a crucial role in "protecting [a client's] due process right against an unreasonable denial of liberty during pretrial detention"). Empirical studies have also demonstrated the importance of legal representation at this stage in a criminal case. In a comparison of indigent defendants accused of nonviolent offenses, the 4,000 people who were represented by counsel at bail hearings were over two and a half times more likely to be released on their own recognizance and over four times more likely to have their bail reduced than were unrepresented defendants. Douglas L. Colbert et al., *Do Attorneys Really Matter? The Empirical and Legal Case for The Right Of Counsel at Bail*, 23 CARDOZO L. REV. 1719, 1752–53 (2002). A previous study found that early representation of defendants resulted in earlier pretrial release, less time spent in jail pretrial, and an increased likelihood of release on personal recognizance. ERNEST J. FAZIO ET AL., U.S. DEP'T OF JUSTICE, NATIONAL INSTITUTE OF JUSTICE, EARLY REPRESENTATION BY DEFENSE COUNSEL FIELD TEST: FINAL EVALUATION REPORT (1985).

The Maryland Court of Appeals recently observed that, even when an attorney represents a defendant at a first appearance held just a day or two after the defendant's initial appearance, the decision made when the defendant appeared pro se at his or her initial appearance often sets the course for subsequent pretrial decisions. *DeWolfe v. Richmond*, 76 A.3d 1019, 1031 (Md. 2013) (holding that the state constitution guarantees an indigent defendant's right to state-furnished counsel at an initial hearing before a District Court Commissioner). In an earlier proceeding in the same case, the Maryland Court of Appeals considered a study finding that, in roughly 50% of all cases in the analyzed sample, judges presiding over bail review hearings maintained bail conditions set at initial appearances. *DeWolfe v. Richmond*, 76 A.3d 962, 977 (Md. 2012).

Since defendants frequently are not represented by counsel at initial appearances, the judicial official (usually a magistrate in North Carolina) may not have all the facts relevant to the bail determination. The Maryland court observed about the process in that state:

> As numerous briefs to this Court pointed out, the failure of a Commissioner to consider all the facts relevant to a bail determination can have devastating effects on the arrested individuals. Not only do the arrested individuals face health and safety risks posed by prison stays, but the arrested individuals may be functionally illiterate and unable to read materials related to the charges. Additionally, they may be employed in low wage jobs which could be easily lost because of

> incarceration. Moreover, studies show that the bail amounts are often improperly affected by race.

DeWolfe v. Richmond, 76 A.3d 1019, 1023 (Md. 2013); *see also* John Wooldredge, *Distinguishing Race Effects on Pre-Trial Release and Sentencing Decisions*, 29 JUST. Q. 41, 67 (2012) (observing that biases may influence "initial court appearances if judges attempt to assess an offender's risk for flight and dangerousness to the community with little available information at hand, leading to considerations of criminal stereotypes"). Since people of color are more likely to be represented by appointed counsel, they are more likely to be unrepresented at the initial appearance before a magistrate and first appearance before a judge. *See* CHRISTOPHER HARTNEY & LINH VUONG, NATIONAL COUNCIL ON CRIME AND DELINQUENCY, CREATED EQUAL: RACIAL AND ETHNIC DISPARITIES IN THE U.S. CRIMINAL JUSTICE SYSTEM 14 (2009) (reporting that African Americans are nearly five times as likely as Whites to rely on appointed counsel). G.S. 7A-453 states that for defendants who have been in custody for 48 hours without appointment of counsel, the authority having custody of the defendant must notify the designee of the Office of Indigent Defense Services (IDS) in counties designated by IDS (the public defender in districts that have public defender offices) and the clerk of court in all other counties, who must then take steps to ensure appointment of counsel. This statutory provision may not be followed consistently, however. For a discussion of possible strategies for counteracting these circumstances, see *infra* § 4.4, Pretrial Advocacy Strategies.

Wide discretion and limited information. Criminologists reviewing evidence of disparities in pretrial release have identified several factors that contribute to the phenomenon. In addition to those discussed in subsection D., above, scholars have considered the interaction of discretion, limited information, and implicit bias on such decisions. One scholar observed:

> Legal decision making is complex, repetitive, and often constrained by information, time, and resources in ways that may produce considerable ambiguity or uncertainty for arriving at a "satisfactory" decision. As an adaptation to these constraints, a "perceptual shorthand" for decision making emerges that allows for more simple and efficient processing of cases by court actors. . . . [L]egal agents may rely not only on the defendant's current offense and criminal history, but also on stereotypes linked to the defendant's race, ethnicity, gender, or social class. On the basis of these stereotypes, judges may project behavioral expectations about such things as the offender's risk of recidivism or danger to the community. Once in place and continuously reinforced, such patterned thinking and acting are resistant to change and may result in the inclusion of racial and ethnic biases in criminal case processing.

Stephen Demuth, *Racial and Ethnic Differences in Pretrial Release Decisions and Outcomes: A Comparison of Hispanic, Black and White Felony Arrestees*, 41

CRIMINOLOGY 873, 880–81 (2003) (internal citation omitted).

These concerns, applicable to many decision-making stages of the criminal justice process, may be especially acute in the context of bail determinations, where officials making bail determinations may not be lawyers, defendants may not be represented by counsel, the decision-maker may have little information about the defendant, and the decision-maker generally does not have to record the reasoning for his or her pretrial release determination. Judges making pretrial release determinations at first appearances may be disinclined to modify bail conditions imposed by a magistrate because they also may have limited information. For example, if there is a high secured bond, a judge may assume the magistrate knew something worrisome about the case or the defendant and may not want to disturb the decision. One scholar opined:

> The lack of background information on the arrestee, the scant legal restrictions placed on bail determinations, and the overall lack of formality and accountability of the bail determination process create the "perfect storm" for arbitrary bail determinations and offer very little protection against the consideration of race or any other impermissible factor when making bail determinations.

Cynthia E. Jones, *"Give Us Free": Addressing Racial Disparities in Bail Determinations*, 16 N.Y.U. J. LEGIS. & PUB. POL'Y 919, 934 (2013).

4.3 Legal Restrictions

A. Protections against Excessive Bail

The North Carolina Constitution and the United States Constitution prohibit the imposition of excessive bail. N.C. CONST. art. I, § 27; U.S. CONST. amend. VIII. The United States Supreme Court has held that "[b]ail set at a figure higher than an amount reasonably calculated to fulfill th[e] purpose [of assuring the presence of defendant at trial] is 'excessive' under the Eighth Amendment." *Stack v. Boyle*, 342 U.S. 1, 5 (1951); *see also State v. Jones*, 295 N.C. 345, 355 (1978) (relying in part on *Stack*, court notes that primary purpose of appearance bond is to assure defendant's presence at trial). While bail will not be held unconstitutionally excessive "merely because the defendant is unable to pay it," *Hodgdon v. United States*, 365 F.2d 679, 687 (8th Cir. 1966), "[i]t would be unconstitutional to fix excessive bail to assure that a defendant will not gain his freedom," and "in the case of an indigent defendant, the fixing of bail in even a modest amount may have the practical effect of denying him release." *Bandy v. United States*, 81 S. Ct. 197, 198 (1960) (application for bail pending certiorari denied by Justice Douglas, sitting in capacity as Circuit Justice, without prejudice to hearing on application in federal district court or court of appeals).

The constitutional prohibitions against excessive bail do not guarantee a right to bail in all cases, but instead require that, if monetary bail is set, it shall not be excessive. *See, e.g.*, *United States v. Salerno*, 481 U.S. 739 (1987); *State v. Hocutt*, 177 N.C. App. 341 (2006) (constitutional and statutory right to reasonable bail does not prohibit courts from denying bail altogether in some instances; pursuant to G.S. 15A-533(c), the trial court had discretion to deny bail to defendant charged with first degree murder). Although North Carolina statutes deny pretrial release in some cases, the general rule is that a defendant is entitled to conditions of pretrial release. 1 NORTH CAROLINA DEFENDER MANUAL Ch. 1 (Pretrial Release) (2d ed. 2013). If your client remains in jail because of an inability to post bond, you may wish to consider raising a claim of excessive bail in reliance on article I, section 27 of the N.C. Constitution and the Eighth Amendment of the U.S. Constitution. This is a race-neutral claim, but it is a potential tool for obtaining bail relief. Claims of excessive bail may be raised in a bond reduction hearing, appeal of a pretrial release order, motion to dismiss, or post-conviction challenge.

Attorneys may not be given a great deal of time to argue constitutional claims in bond reduction hearings. One strategy for getting the court to consider such claims is to prepare a template memorandum of law, which can be particularized and submitted to the judge in a bond reduction hearing. In raising a claim of unconstitutionally excessive bail in a bond reduction hearing or on an appeal of a pretrial release order, attorneys should be prepared to demonstrate that:

- bail was not set in accordance with the requirements in G.S. 15A-534, *see infra* § 4.3D, Protections Created by State Law;
- bail was set in an amount substantially higher than is generally required for the charge or charges at issue in the case, without evidence justifying such a departure from general practices;
- factors relevant to defendant's risk of flight weigh in favor of a bond reduction or unsecured bond;
- bail was set at an amount intended to assure that the defendant would not gain his freedom.

See Stack v. Boyle, 342 U.S. 1 (1951) (bail was excessive in violation of the Eighth Amendment where: (1) it was not fixed by proper methods; (2) it was set far in excess of that usually set for defendants charged with similar offenses, without justification for such a departure; and (3) defendants submitted substantial evidence concerning financial resources, family relationships, health, prior criminal records, and other matters weighing in favor of lower bail); *Murphy v. State*, 807 So. 2d 603 (Ala. Crim. App. 2001) (bond set far in excess of amount recommended for offenses charged, without justification, constituted excessive bail in violation of the U.S. and Alabama Constitution).

In the post-conviction context, claims of unconstitutionally excessive bail must demonstrate prejudice, must be particularized, and may not be sustained by unsupported allegations. *State v. Jones*, 295 N.C. 345, 356 (1978); *State v. O'Neal*, 108 N.C. App. 661, 666 (1993). The defendant must present evidence demonstrating how the excessive bail interfered with his right to present a defense. *Jones*, 295 N.C. 345, 356; *see also McCabe v. North Carolina*, 314 F. Supp. 917 (M.D.N.C. 1970). To support a motion to dismiss, a defendant may need to show irreparable or irretrievable prejudice to his rights.

See generally 1 NORTH CAROLINA DEFENDER MANUAL § 1.11 (Dismissal as Remedy for Violations) (2d ed. 2013). This is an undeveloped area of case law in North Carolina and nationwide. Claims of unconstitutionally excessive bail may not succeed at the trial level but, over time, they may lead to development of useful case law. To preserve post-conviction claims of excessive bail, as well as to support such claims at the trial level, it is important for trial attorneys to develop a record showing the ways in which the client's pretrial detention, caused by excessive bail, impeded his ability to assist in the preparation of his defense. *See infra* "State law creates right to pretrial release conditions" in § 4.3D, Protections Created by State Law. A claim of excessive bail will be strengthened by evidence that:

- The defendant has not been able to take counsel to places relevant to the investigation of charges, and counsel has not been able to find these places on his or her own.
- The defendant was unable to assist counsel in locating witnesses, who became less available and/or less willing to speak during the time the defendant was confined.
- Potential defense witnesses refused to speak to counsel outside of the presence of the defendant, because the attorney was unfamiliar to them or belonged to a different race or socioeconomic background.
- Witnesses sought by the defendant could only be identified by sight and not by name and, therefore, could not be located while the defendant was detained.
- The defendant's relationships suffered as a result of pretrial detention, which had a negative impact on his ability to procure witnesses.
- The defendant was unable to assist counsel in investigation of other possible suspects.
- The defendant was placed in a jail located a considerable distance from counsel, resulting in fewer visits with counsel.
- The defendant had limited phone use, limited ability to communicate privately over the phone while in jail, and therefore limited ability to contact potential witnesses.
- Limited jail visitation hours interfered with the defendant's ability to plan a defense with counsel.

B. Equal Protection

Race-based equal protection challenges to pretrial decisions. The Equal Protection Clause of the Fourteenth Amendment to the U.S. Constitution and article I, section 19 of the N.C. Constitution recognize the right to equal protection under the law. Under the intent doctrine, a defendant raising an equal protection claim must show that the challenged state action was motivated by a discriminatory purpose and had a discriminatory effect on a specific racial group. *See supra* § 2.3, Equal Protection Challenges to Police Action. While this doctrine poses a significant hurdle for defendants seeking relief on equal protection grounds, it is not insurmountable.

Where such evidence exists, an equal protection claim may be based on direct evidence that a defendant's race or ethnicity played a role in an unfavorable pretrial release decision—for example, where a magistrate's notes justifying a bond determination reveal assumptions about gang membership or immigration status. In cases without direct evidence of discriminatory purpose, counsel should consider framing equal protection challenges to the use of race in pretrial release decisions in accordance with *Castaneda v. Partida*, 430 U.S. 482 (1977) (finding that evidence of discriminatory impact was sufficient to sustain a prima facie claim of intentional discrimination in grand jury selection). Under *Castaneda*, a defendant makes out a prima facie equal protection claim in a challenge to grand jury selection if he demonstrates that: (1) he belongs to a "recognizable, distinct class, singled out for different treatment under the laws, as written or as applied"; (2) the group is underrepresented in the grand jury process, as established by "comparing the proportion of the group in the total population to the proportion called to serve as grand jurors, over a significant period of time"; and (3) "a selection procedure that is susceptible of abuse . . . supports the presumption of discrimination raised by the statistical showing." *Id.* at 494.

Defendants raising equal protection challenges to racial discrimination in the setting of pretrial release conditions should distinguish their claims from those rejected in *McCleskey v. Kemp*, 481 U.S. 279 (1987). In that case, the defendant's claim that capital sentencing decisions were unconstitutionally influenced by race was rejected in part because of the difficulty of attributing intent to the diffuse group of decision-makers, namely, jurors in capital trials over a period of several years. In contrast, pretrial decisions are made by repeat players (judicial officials) applying statutory factors and therefore can be measured against one another more easily. Additionally, the wide discretion afforded judicial officials in setting pretrial release conditions may result in a "procedure that is susceptible of abuse" within the meaning of *Castaneda*. These characteristics provide support for arguing that evidence of disparities in the setting of pretrial conditions should be sufficient to demonstrate a prima facie case of discriminatory intent when the defendant is "a member of a historically disadvantaged class that has been overrepresented in the population of [pretrial jail detainees] . . . over a significant period of time." Perry L. Moriearty, *Combating The Color-Coded Confinement Of Kids: An Equal Protection Remedy*, 32 N.Y.U. REV. L. & SOC. CHANGE 285, 332 (2008) (suggesting this approach for equal protection claims challenging racial disparities in the pretrial detention of juveniles).

Attorneys concerned that race may be playing an unlawful role in the setting of pretrial release conditions should consider partnering with social scientists, academics, or other court actors to perform statistical analyses, described *infra* in § 4.4C (Present Findings about Race at Bond Hearings). If an analysis reveals racial disparities in the setting of pretrial release conditions, counsel may introduce it in support of an equal protection challenge.

Equal protection challenges to pretrial release decisions may be raised in a bond reduction hearing, appeal of a pretrial release order, motion to dismiss, or post-conviction challenge. In a bond reduction hearing, an attorney raising an equal protection challenge to an unfavorable pretrial release condition should present evidence in support of the claim and submit a supporting memorandum of law. *See infra* § 4.4, Pretrial Advocacy Strategies.

The following questions should be considered when investigating equal protection claims relating to pretrial release decisions:

- Did the factors considered by the judicial official setting pretrial conditions—factors mandated by statute, judicial district policy, or neither—have an adverse impact on racial and ethnic minorities?
- Is there anecdotal evidence suggesting that racial or ethnic minorities receive less advantageous pretrial release decisions than similarly situated White defendants? Such evidence may serve as an indication that further investigation is necessary. *See supra* "Case study: A judge reflects on implicit bias" in § 1.3D, Implicit Bias.
- Is there statistical evidence suggesting that minority defendants fare worse in the setting of pretrial release conditions? *See infra* § 4.4C, Present Findings about Race at Bond Hearings.
- Are diversion programs, alternatives to detention, and pretrial services programs available for all defendants, regardless of race or ethnicity? Are there any programs that are restricted to English speakers? Are all court actors aware of those programs, and are they administered equitably?
- Are interpreters available at first appearances, bond reduction hearings, and pretrial services interviews, not only for Spanish-speaking defendants but for all defendants with limited English language skills?
- Are representatives from minority communities and grassroots organizations encouraged to participate in identifying and developing pretrial diversion programs that could be used as an alternative to pretrial detention in appropriate cases? *See supra* § 4.2B, Race and Pretrial Detention (discussing pretrial diversion programs).
- Does the discussion of pretrial release conditions in bond hearings focus on flight risk and the risk of pretrial offending, or do other reasons predominate?
- Are there substance abuse programs in jail that are only available to English language speakers? Is participation in these programs viewed positively at bail reduction hearings, so that defendants who do not have the opportunity to participate in such programs are: (1) less likely to have a claim of changed circumstances justifying reconsideration of pretrial release conditions; and (2) less likely to obtain release on a bond reduction motion?
- Are forms used in the pretrial process accessible and available in your client's language?
- Is there a delay in the appointment of counsel for indigent defendants? G.S. 7A-453 states that for defendants who have been in custody for 48 hours without appointment of counsel, the authority having custody of the defendant must notify the designee of the Office of Indigent Defense Services (IDS) in counties designated by IDS (the public defender in districts that have public defender offices) and the clerk of court in all other counties, who must then take steps to ensure appointment of counsel. This statutory provision may not be followed consistently, however. Delays in appointment of counsel for indigent defendants may have a disproportionate impact on minority defendants, who are more likely to rely on appointed counsel.

If counsel determines that there is insufficient evidence to raise an equal protection challenge based on race, the above questions still may be useful in identifying grounds for modifying pretrial release for minority clients.

Poverty-based equal protection challenges to pretrial decisions. In a study of felony defendants in state courts in the 75 largest counties in the United States, the Bureau of Justice Statistics concluded that 5 of 6 defendants detained until case disposition between 1990 and 2004 remained in jail because they did not satisfy the financial conditions attached to their release, not because they were denied bail. THOMAS H. COHEN & BRIAN A. REAVES, BUREAU OF JUSTICE STATISTICS, STATE COURT PROCESSING STATISTICS, 1990–2004: PRETRIAL RELEASE OF FELONY DEFENDANTS IN STATE COURTS 1 (2007). Nationwide in 2012, the Black poverty rate was 35% and the Latino poverty rate was 33%, while the White poverty rate was 13%. The Henry J. Kaiser Family Foundation, *Poverty Rate by Race/Ethnicity*, KFF.ORG (2012). Poverty-based equal protection challenges, while not directly about racial disparities, may provide relief to minority clients unable to satisfy monetary release conditions.

North Carolina judicial officials are also required by statute to take into account the defendant's financial resources when determining which conditions of release to impose. G.S. 15A-534(c). This statutory provision provides defendants with some protection against pretrial detention resulting from the inability to afford secured bond.

Defendants raising poverty-based equal protection challenges to pretrial release decisions have argued that the Equal Protection Clause prohibits setting bail in an amount that an indigent defendant cannot meet. *See, e.g.*, 4 WAYNE R. LAFAVE ET AL., CRIMINAL PROCEDURE § 12.2(a), (b) (3d ed. 2007) (discussing equal protection challenges by indigent defendants to unaffordable bail amounts). Courts generally have not been sympathetic to broad claims that unaffordable bail violates the equal protection rights of indigent defendants. *See id.* Some authority exists in support of such an argument, however. Justice Douglas, in reliance on the U.S. Supreme Court's holding that "an indigent defendant is denied equal protection of the law if he is denied an appeal on equal terms with other defendants, solely because of his indigence," observed that it "raises considerable problems for the equal administration of the law" when "an indigent [is] denied freedom where a wealthy man [is] not, because he does not happen to have enough money to pledge for his freedom." *Bandy v. United States*, 81 S. Ct. 197, 197–98 (1960) (acting on bail application in his capacity as Circuit Justice), (quoting *Griffin v. Illinois*, 351 U.S. 12 (1956)); *see also* Jonathan Zweig, Note, *Extraordinary Conditions of Release Under the Bail Reform Act*, 47 HARV. J. ON LEGIS. 555, 557 (2010) (arguing that "taking into account an arrestee's access to funds to pay for bail conditions violates the Equal Protection Clause because it conditions access to a fundamental right—pretrial release—on the basis of wealth"). Additional authority is discussed below where applicable.

Poverty-based equal protection challenges to bail may be raised in bond reduction hearings, appeals of pretrial release determinations, motions to dismiss, or post-conviction challenges. *See supra* § 4.3A, Protections Against Excessive Bail. The following factors may support a challenge to unaffordable bail:

- Is there evidence that the judicial official required a secured bond in violation of G.S. 15A-534(b)? In other words, did the judicial official fail to give priority to nonfinancial release conditions, in violation of statutory and constitutional requirements? In some judicial districts, the pretrial release policy will require the judicial official to record the reasons for finding that less restrictive pretrial release conditions were not appropriate. If the judicial official's written findings or statements suggest that less restrictive pretrial release conditions should have been imposed, you may raise a claim that the secured bond was set in violation of North Carolina statutes and the U.S. and N.C. Constitutions. *See Pugh v. Rainwater*, 572 F.2d 1053, 1058 (5th Cir. 1978) (en banc) ("in the case of an indigent, whose appearance at trial could reasonably be assured by one of the alternative forms of release, pretrial confinement for inability to post money bail would constitute imposition of an excessive restraint"); *Lee v. Lawson*, 375 So. 2d 1019 (Miss. 1979) (poverty-based equal protection challenge to bail prompted court to examine availability of non-financial release; case remanded to trial court with instructions to consider alternative forms of release).
- Is there evidence that your client's bail was set according to a bond schedule, without regard to the statutory considerations that must be taken into account when setting pretrial release conditions pursuant to G.S. 15A-534(c)? If so, the automatic application of a bond schedule may violate both the statutory requirement of individual consideration of the defendant's circumstances as well as equal protection. *See Ackies v. Purdy*, 322 F. Supp. 38, 41–42 (S.D. Fla. 1970) ("not only is there no compelling interest in incarcerating the poor man because he cannot make the master bond bail, but the classification fails to meet the traditional test for equal protection"; court finds that master bond schedule creates two categories of defendants: those able to afford bond and secure release and those unable afford bond and therefore detained "for extended periods of time").
- Is there evidence that secured bonds are generally set in excess of any schedule of secured bond amounts in your judicial district's pretrial release policy? *See, e.g.*, Johanna Hawfield Foster, *Striving for Equity in Criminal Justice: An Analysis of Variability of Bail Bonds in the Tenth Judicial District of North Carolina* (finding that, in the Tenth Judicial District, mean bail exceeded the upper limit of the bond's suggested policy guidelines by at least 30 percent) in the Race Materials Bank at www.ncids.org (select "Training & Resources"). This information could be submitted as evidence supporting a bond reduction motion, appeal of a pretrial release determination, motion to dismiss, or post-conviction challenge. In addition, consider alerting supervising judicial officials in your district about this departure from suggested bond amounts and the consequences for low-income, minority defendants.
- Has the court delayed a bond hearing at the prosecutor's request or granted the prosecutor's request for some period of notice before a hearing? If so, the defendant may have an equal protection claim because, as observed by one court about such a procedure in that state, a "defendant with financial means who is charged with a noncapital violent felony . . . can obtain immediate release simply by posting bail,"

but "an indigent defendant charged with a relatively minor misdemeanor who cannot obtain release by cash bail, a bail bond, or property bail, must remain incarcerated for a minimum of three days, and perhaps longer, before being able to obtain judicial public bail." *State v. Blake*, 642 So. 2d 959, 968 (Ala. 1994) (72-hour notice to prosecutor before judicial bail hearing violated equal protection). Under these circumstances, the relief sought would be an immediate opportunity to be heard on a bond modification motion.

- Is there evidence that your client was denied house arrest and release from pretrial custody because of an inability to pay for electronic monitoring? If so, your client may have a claim of a statutory and equal protection violation. *See* G.S. 7A-313.1 (county may not collect an electronic house arrest fee from a defendant who is indigent and entitled to court-appointed counsel); *see generally* Jonathan Zweig, Note, *Extraordinary Conditions of Release Under the Bail Reform Act*, 47 HARV. J. ON LEGIS. 555, 556 (2010). In this instance, the defendant should file a bond reduction motion seeking either a more favorable pretrial release order or a waiver of the fee for electronic monitoring. Similarly, an equal protection claim may arise if your client was denied pretrial release because of an inability to pay for continuous alcohol monitoring (CAM), for which no state funding exists. *See* G.S. 15A-534(a) (authorizing abstinence from alcohol verified by CAM as a condition of pretrial release for any criminal offense committed on or after December 1, 2012).
- Did the court require the posting of cash because the judicial official employed a variant of the term cash, such as "U.S. currency," "cash money," or "green money," and your client remained in jail because he was not able to come up with cash? This practice may violate equal protection because it places indigent defendants at a substantial disadvantage vis-à-vis more affluent defendants who are able to pay the full bail amount, and violates statutory provisions allowing the posting of bond by a surety bondsman in lieu of cash. *See* G.S. 15A-531(4) (bail bond signed by a surety is considered the same as a cash deposit in all cases except those involving child support contempt).
- Did the court set the bond in an amount intended to result in detention, as it is too low for bail bondsmen to service and too high for the defendant to pay?
- Was your client in pretrial custody as a result of an inability to post bond for an offense for which the maximum penalty was a fine? If so, his detention may violate his right to equal protection of the law. *See Robertson v. Goldman*, 369 S.E.2d 888 (W. Va. 1988). In these circumstances, a detained defendant should seek release on a written promise to appear or unsecured bond. Some judicial districts have adopted bond policies providing that if a defendant is arrested for a Class 3 misdemeanor, the judicial official should generally set an unsecured bond to avoid detaining defendants for an offense that may carry no jail time. *See* John Rubin, *Appointment of Counsel for Class 3 Misdemeanors*, SOG.UNC.EDU (November 2013); *see also Robertson v. Goldman*, 369 S.E.2d 888, 892 (W. Va. 1988) (ordering lower court officials to cease "practice of jailing indigents facing charges which do not carry a potential jail term solely because they are unable to post bond").

C. Due Process

Federal and state due process protections guarantee criminal defendants a fundamental right to freedom before trial, which may be restricted only when the government has a compelling interest. *See United States v. Salerno*, 481 U.S. 739, 747 (1987); *see also Ackies v. Purdy*, 322 F. Supp. 38, 41 (S.D. Fla. 1970) ("The right to pretrial release under reasonable conditions is a fundamental right."). For example, the government's compelling interest in public safety defeated a due process challenge to preventive detention provisions of the federal Bail Reform Act. *Salerno*, 481 U.S. 739, 749 (holding that "[t]he government's interest in preventing crime by arrestees is both legitimate and compelling").

The case of *Kinney v. Lenon,* 425 F.2d 209 (9th Cir. 1970), is an example of a successful due process challenge to a pretrial release decision. In that case, a juvenile who was detained pretrial for charges arising out of a fight at school claimed that "there were many potential witnesses to the fight, that he cannot identify them by name but would recognize them by sight, that [his] attorneys are white though he and the potential witnesses are black, that his attorneys would consequently have great practical difficulty in interviewing and lining up the witnesses, and that [the juvenile] is the sole person who can do so." *Id.* at 210. In a candid assessment of the role of race in the juvenile's due process claim, the court observed that "[i]t would require blindness to social reality not to understand that these difficulties [in convincing wary potential witnesses to testify] may be exacerbated by the barriers of age and race. Yet the alternative to some sort of release for appellant is to cast the entire burden of assembling witnesses onto his attorneys, with almost certain prejudice to appellant's case." *Id.* The court held that his pretrial confinement interfered with his constitutional right to compulsory process to obtain witnesses on his own behalf and that release of the juvenile was necessary to ensure "his due-process right to a fair trial." *Id.* This case illustrates the type of evidence that lawyers may present when claiming that a client's pretrial detention violates due process.

Practice note: A due process claim along the above lines can be raised in a bond reduction motion or an appeal of a pretrial release determination. In both instances, the defendant would seek more favorable pretrial release conditions that would allow her to participate fully in the preparation of her defense. If the claim is raised in a post-conviction challenge, the defendant would need to demonstrate prejudice resulting from her inability to assist in the preparation of her defense. The trial attorney should preserve the record for a potential post-conviction claim by presenting factual evidence demonstrating the hurdles faced by the attorney in collecting evidence and interviewing witnesses without the assistance of the defendant. *See supra* § 4.3A, Protections Against Excessive Bail (also discussing potential basis for motion to dismiss).

D. Protections Created by State Law

State law creates right to pretrial release conditions. G.S. 15A-531 through 15A-547.1 contain the basic provisions on pretrial (and posttrial) release for criminal charges. *See also* G.S. 15A-1345(b), (b1) (release conditions in probation cases); 1 NORTH CAROLINA

DEFENDER MANUAL Ch. 1 (Pretrial Release) (2d ed. 2013). These provisions reflect a preference for release on conditions other than a secured bond. Conditions other than a secured bond or house arrest—including release on a written promise to appear, unsecured bond, and custodial release—must be imposed unless none of these conditions will reasonably assure the appearance of the defendant or the judicial official finds a risk of injury to any person, destruction of evidence, subornation of perjury, or intimidation of potential witnesses. G.S. 15A-534(b). Generally, North Carolina defendants charged with a noncapital offense must be accorded their right to pretrial release conditions. G.S. 15A-533(b). A judicial official cannot deny a bond to such a defendant for preventive detention except as otherwise expressly provided by law. *See* John Rubin, Exceptions to Pretrial Release Procedures: A Guide for Magistrates, SOG.UNC.EDU (Aug. 2011).

These statutory provisions should be relied on when seeking favorable pretrial release determinations in first appearances and bond reduction hearings. When making a motion to dismiss or raising a post-conviction challenge to a pretrial release determination in violation of G.S. 15A-534, attorneys will need to demonstrate prejudice resulting from a violation. *See State v. Labinski*, 188 N.C. App. 120 (2008) (finding substantial statutory violation by setting of secured bond where there was no evidence that defendant would pose injury to another person without a secured bond, but upholding denial of motion to dismiss charges because defendant was not prejudiced in preparation of her defense); *see also infra* § 4.4A, Enter the Case at the Earliest Possible Opportunity (including list of circumstances to consider in supporting claim of interference with a right to present a defense).

Pursuant to G.S. 15A-535(a), the senior resident superior court judge, in consultation with the chief district court judge or all district court judges in the district, must issue pretrial release policies. Attorneys should obtain a copy of the pretrial release policy for their judicial district and review it to determine what additional guidance it provides to judicial officials in making pretrial decisions, whether it contains a suggested bond schedule, and whether it requires magistrates to document in writing the reasons for imposing secured bonds or other restrictive pretrial release conditions. *See* G.S. 15A-534(b) (when ordering house arrest or secured bond, the judicial official "must record the reasons for so doing in writing to the extent provided in the policies or requirements issued by the senior resident superior court judge"); *see also, e.g.,* Administrative Order Setting 10th Judicial District Pretrial Release Policies (requiring magistrates to record reasons supporting any secured release imposed outside of the recommended guidelines for the offense class) in the Race Materials Bank at www.ncids.org (select "Training & Resources"). If the district's policy requires written reasons to support a secured bond or house arrest, attorneys should obtain copies of the magistrate's justification in preparation for a bond reduction motion.

Statutory preference for summons over arrest warrant. G.S. 15A-303 sets forth the procedures for a criminal summons, and G.S. 15A-304 sets forth the procedures for a warrant for arrest. The latter statute authorizes a warrant if a judicial official concludes that the person at issue should be taken into custody in light of such factors as "failure to appear when previously summoned, facts making it apparent that a person summoned will fail to appear, danger that the person accused will escape, danger that there may be injury to person or property, or the seriousness of the offense." G.S. 15A-304(b). Likewise, the Official Commentary to G.S. 15A-303 states:

> The appropriate use of the criminal summons is in any case in which it appears that it is not necessary to arrest the defendant and take him into custody in order to ensure his appearance in court. This should be true in many misdemeanors and a number of felonies. If the defendant simply is directed to appear in court on the appropriate date, the entire machinery of arrest, processing, and bail can be avoided with resultant savings to the system of criminal justice. This section is separated from the warrant provisions (unlike the present statute), and placed first, in order to call it to the attention of readers of the statutes and encourage its use.

These provisions express a preference for a summons over an arrest warrant in appropriate cases and the avoidance of pretrial custody, among other things.

Judicial pretrial release determinations should not be based on a defendant's actual or perceived immigration status. A defendant's perceived immigration status may play a role in Latinos generally receiving the worst outcomes at the pretrial release stage. *See* Traci Schlesinger, *Racial and Ethnic Disparity in Pretrial Criminal Processing*, 22 JUST. Q. 170 (2005); Stephen Demuth, *Racial and Ethnic Differences in Pretrial Release Decisions and Outcomes: A Comparison of Hispanic, Black and White Felony Arrestees*, 41 CRIMINOLOGY 873, 895 (2003). Judicial officials generally have no role in addressing citizenship matters. A defendant's immigration status is not a factor listed in G.S. 15A-534(c) as relevant to the determination of conditions of pretrial release, and a defendant's immigration status typically is not included in the information provided to judicial officials during an initial appearance or a first appearance. However, anecdotal evidence suggests that judicial officials may at times delay or deny pretrial release in cases in which they believe the defendant is in the United States unlawfully. In cases in which a client may be perceived as undocumented, it is especially important to stress family and community ties when advocating for favorable conditions of release, so as to counter any stereotypes that may be associated with noncitizens who are undocumented.

Future legislation may require judicial officials to take a defendant's immigration status into consideration in making pretrial release determinations. Pursuant to the Reclaim NC Act, S.L. 2013-418, the Department of Public Safety recently reported to the Chairs of the Joint Legislative Oversight Committee on Justice and Public Safety regarding, among other things, establishing a rebuttable presumption against the pretrial release of individuals without documentation who are charged with serious crimes and/or requiring a secured appearance bond as a condition of pretrial release. *See* Memorandum from Frank L. Perry, Secretary of the Department of Public Safety, *Study and Recommendation Regarding Immigration Measures* (Mar. 2014) (assessing potential changes). No such requirements are currently part of North Carolina law.

Relevance of immigration status to defendants in pretrial detention facilities. Under G.S. 162-62, when a person charged with a felony or impaired driving offense is confined to a jail or other detention facility, the person in charge of the facility must attempt to determine whether the inmate is a legal resident and, where possible, make inquiry to Immigration and Customs Enforcement (ICE) if the inmate's status cannot be determined. However, the statute provides that "[n]othing in this section shall be construed to deny bond to a prisoner or to prevent a prisoner from being released from confinement when that prisoner is otherwise eligible for release." G.S. 162-62(c). *See* John Rubin, *2007 Legislation Affecting Criminal Law and Procedure*, ADMINISTRATION OF JUSTICE BULLETIN No. 2008/01 at 33–34 (UNC School of Government, Jan. 2008) (describing implications of this law, including Fifth Amendment right not to answer possibly incriminating questions that could lead to criminal prosecution).

A defendant's conditions of pretrial release may be complicated by the involvement of ICE, which may choose to issue a "detainer" or "hold" on the individual. Such a detainer is a request to the jail to notify ICE that the individual is to be released and to hold the individual for up to 48 hours (excluding weekends and holidays) beyond the time the detainee would ordinarily be released in order for ICE to take custody of the person. 8 C.F.R. § 287.7. Thus, ICE may take custody of the defendant as soon as a state bond is paid or a defendant is released on a written promise to appear. The jail, not the magistrate, is responsible for implementing the 48-hour detainer, and neither the jail nor a magistrate may delay or deny release to give ICE more time to file a detainer or assume custody of the defendant. *See* 1 NORTH CAROLINA DEFENDER MANUAL § 1.4G (Circumstances Not Justifying Delay or Denial of Pretrial Release) (2d ed. 2013). It should be noted that a detainer is simply a request and is not mandatory or binding.

Anecdotal evidence suggests that, in practice, ICE may not always pick up an individual subject to a detainer within the 48-hour period, and some individuals may be held unlawfully past the expiration of the 48-hour detainer. *See, e.g.*, *Case Description: Quezada v. Mink*, ACLU.ORG (last visited Aug. 7, 2014); *Quezada v. Mink Complaint*, ACLU.ORG (last visited Aug. 7, 2014). Failure to release a detainee after the expiration of the 48-hour detainer is unlawful and could expose the detention facility to liability for false imprisonment and constitutional violations. *See id.*; *see also* SEJAL ZOTA & JOHN RUBIN, IMMIGRATION CONSEQUENCES OF A CRIMINAL CONVICTION IN NORTH CAROLINA § 7.3 (Immigration Detainer) (2008). If a defendant is detained beyond the 48-hour detainer period, counsel should consult with the defendant to determine whether or not the defendant wants to seek release, either by contacting counsel for the sheriff or jail and pressing for release or by filing a writ of habeas corpus seeking release. There may be circumstances in which a client does not wish to do so. A sample petition for writ of habeas corpus, with supporting documents, is available on the non-capital motions bank on the IDS website, www.ncids.org. *See also* 1 NORTH CAROLINA DEFENDER MANUAL § 1.4G (Circumstances Not Justifying Delay or Denial of Pretrial Release) (2d ed. 2013).

Defense attorneys should be aware of the many ways in which a defendant may be affected by an ICE detainer:

- The detainee may be adversely affected when seeking bond on the state charges.
- After ICE takes custody of the defendant, he or she may be moved out of state and consequently unable to participate adequately in the defense of his or her state criminal charges, as it is difficult for defense counsel to communicate with a detainee in an ICE detention center.
- Any time spent in an ICE detention center will not count as jail credit toward any eventual sentence of imprisonment in the defendant's criminal case.
- The defendant may be deported before resolution of his or her criminal case.
- A defendant who posts bond or family members who post bond may end up forfeiting the bond if the defendant is transferred into ICE custody.

To protect the rights of clients who are under ICE detainers and facing removal proceedings, you will need to determine whether they want to contest the criminal charges, whether they want to contest the immigration deportation, and whether they want to be released from custody before deportation proceedings. If they want to do any of these three things, you should advise them not to post their state bond until they have either consulted with an immigration attorney or you are prepared to seek an immigration bond on their behalf since, as soon as they post their state bond, they may be transferred to ICE custody and also moved to an out-of-state detention facility. *See generally* SEJAL ZOTA & JOHN RUBIN, IMMIGRATION CONSEQUENCES OF A CRIMINAL CONVICTION IN NORTH CAROLINA Ch. 7 (2008) (explaining eligibility for immigration bond).

Defendants without identification. A magistrate may not insist on official U.S. or North Carolina identification as a condition of release; any reasonable form of identification should be sufficient, even if not in writing (for example, a member of the community might vouch for the defendant's identity). *See* JESSICA SMITH, CRIMINAL PROCEEDINGS BEFORE NORTH CAROLINA MAGISTRATES 17-18 (UNC School of Government, 2014). Insistence on official U.S. or N.C. identification may work a particular hardship on noncitizen clients. If a noncitizen client is still in custody because of such a condition when you enter the case, make a motion to the court to determine whether the client has produced sufficient identification for release.

4.4 Pretrial Advocacy Strategies

A. Enter the Case at the Earliest Possible Opportunity

Defendants achieve better pretrial release outcomes when they are represented by an attorney at the earliest possible opportunity. *See supra* § 4.2E, Other Factors that May Contribute to Racial Disparities in Bail Determinations. In North Carolina, while defendants with retained counsel are typically represented at their first appearance before a judge (and potentially at their initial appearance before a magistrate), the point at which appointed counsel enters a defendant's case varies around the state. Indigent defendants usually are not represented by counsel at initial appearances or first appearances. Some districts have experimented with assigning a "bond attorney" from the Public Defender's office to represent defendants at first appearances, but this practice appears to be relatively uncommon. Even when appointed counsel is present for a defendant's first appearance, counsel may have had little opportunity to obtain information in support of a motion to modify bond. If the appearance is conducted via audio-video feed between the courtroom and jail, counsel's ability to obtain needed information may also be limited (although counsel must be given an opportunity to communicate with the client in confidence). *See* G.S. 15A-532 (during the video transmission, "[i]f the defendant has counsel, the defendant shall be allowed to communicate fully and confidentially with his attorney during the proceeding"). If release is not obtained at the first appearance, counsel should try to set the matter for the first possible court date for a bond hearing or ask the judge to leave the matter open until an afternoon session of court so that counsel (or an intern or investigator) can learn more about the client and confirm information such as place of residence and ties to the community. Where appointed counsel does not represent defendants at first appearances, it is especially important to return to court for a bond reduction hearing as soon as possible after entering the case.

When client is detained pretrial, consider moving for a speedy trial. When counsel is unable to secure a client's pretrial release, it may be advantageous to move for a speedy trial. The United States Supreme Court has held that a defendant's incarceration before trial is a relevant consideration in determining whether a defendant has been afforded his constitutional right to a speedy trial. *Barker v. Wingo*, 407 U.S. 514 (1972). Violation of the constitutional right to a speedy trial results in the dismissal of all charges. Although North Carolina no longer has a speedy trial statute, there is an older statute prohibiting lengthy pretrial incarceration. *See* G.S. 15-10. If a defendant is incarcerated in jail on a felony warrant and demands a speedy trial in open court, the defendant must either be indicted during the next term of court or released from custody, unless the State's witnesses are not available. *Id.* Similarly, if an incarcerated person accused of a felony demands a speedy trial and is not tried within a statutorily set period (two terms of court, provided the two terms are more than four months apart), the person is entitled to release from incarceration. *See id.*; *State v. Wilburn*, 21 N.C. App. 140 (1974). *See also generally* 1 NORTH CAROLINA DEFENDER MANUAL §7.1F (Pretrial Release) (2d ed. 2013).

Practice note: Pretrial diversion provides an opportunity for defendants to avoid both conviction and the "broad array of social and economic outcomes associated with felony convictions, including [negative] employment, income, family stability, and mental health [consequences]." Traci Schlesinger, *Racial Disparities in Pretrial Diversion: An Analysis of Outcomes Among Men Charged with Felonies and Processed in State Courts*, 3 RACE & JUST. 210, 211 (2013). Counsel should investigate the availability of local pretrial diversion programs and, where available, coordinate with any pretrial services program in the district as early as possible both to explore the possibilities of pretrial diversion and to increase the likelihood of an early, favorable decision on pretrial release. *See* North Carolina Dep't of Public Safety, *County Resource Guide*, NCDPS.GOV (last modified June 3, 2014). A pretrial services program may interview the defendant before the first appearance and may provide the defender with a copy of the report and recommendations, which will furnish some basic information at first appearance.

B. Counter Potential Racial Stereotypes in Pretrial Release Arguments

Studies have found that, where discretion is greatest and information limited, implicit and explicit biases are most likely to have an impact on decision-making. *See supra* § 1.3E, Discretionary Decision-Making and the Cumulative Nature of Disparities. Judicial officers enjoy wide discretion in setting pretrial release conditions and often must make decisions with limited information about the evidence and the defendant. In recent years, researchers have found that negative stereotypes about Black and Latino defendants can play a role in pretrial release decisions. *See, e.g.,* Traci Schlesinger, *Racial and Ethnic Disparity in Pretrial Criminal Processing*, 22 JUST. Q. 170 (2005). In North Carolina, pretrial decisions can be based on such subjective considerations as "character" and a catch-all for "any other evidence relevant to issue of pretrial release." G.S. 15A-534(c). Judicial district policies may include other subjective factors, such as "negative attitude or lack of cooperation by the defendant." *See* Administrative Order Setting 10th Judicial District Pretrial Release Policies in the Race Materials Bank at www.ncids.org (select "Training & Resources").

The argument on pretrial release is counsel's first opportunity to distinguish the client from possible stereotypes that may influence a judge in his or her exercise of discretion. Accordingly, you should be aware of stereotypes that may be in operation and be prepared to present information countering potential preconceptions about your client. *See generally* 1 NORTH CAROLINA DEFENDER MANUAL Ch. 1 Appendix 1-1 (Interview Checklist for Bond Hearing) (2d ed. 2013); *see also* NORTH CAROLINA COMMISSION ON INDIGENT DEFENSE SERVICES, PERFORMANCE GUIDELINES FOR INDIGENT DEFENSE REPRESENTATION IN NON-CAPITAL CRIMINAL CASES AT THE TRIAL LEVEL 2–6 (2004). In your first interview with your client, ask questions aimed at discovering the realities of her life. For example, if you ask your client whether she is employed, she may say no, but, on further questioning, may reveal that she takes care of her niece after school or cares for her elderly grandmother. Such information allows you to present a picture of your client's life beyond impersonal statements about, for example, her county of residence and how long she has lived there. Information gathered by any pretrial services program in your district may also be useful in this regard; counsel should make an effort to review any materials prepared by pretrial services in preparing a request to modify pretrial conditions.

While defense counsel usually presents the information rather than offering testimony, counsel can tender relatives, employers, teachers, clergy members, or friends to the court and prosecutor for questioning. The presence of supportive family or community members can have a powerful influence even if they do not intend to speak. Counsel also can present documentary evidence to help the court see the client as a complex individual. For example, counsel may tender report cards, performance reviews, or reference letters from community leaders. (The rules of evidence do not apply at pretrial release hearings. *See* G.S. 15A-534(g).) When possible, have the client dress in his or her own neat, clean clothing for the bond hearing rather than appear in a jail jumpsuit, which will aid the judge in seeing the client as a fully dimensional individual. *See* Jenny

Montgomery, Dressing Defendants, THE INDIANA LAWYER (May 23, 2012) (quoting former president of the National Association of Criminal Defense Lawyers who indicated that "the bottom line is we know people judge a book by its cover," and these judgments influence "the fundamental fairness [of the] process").

C. Present Findings about Race at Bond Hearings

Evidence of racial disparities in pretrial decisions or outcomes, even when insufficient to meet the legal standard of an equal protection claim, may be persuasive when representing a client at a first appearance or on a bond reduction motion. Counsel can make the court aware of the growing body of scholarship finding that African American and Latino defendants receive less favorable treatment at the pretrial release stage than their White counterparts. *See supra* § 4.2, Overview. Counsel should inform the court of any disparity applicable to the case—for example, a codefendant who received more favorable conditions, was similarly situated to the defendant, and was White. *See supra* "Case study: A judge reflects on implicit bias" in § 1.3D, Implicit Bias.

Either independently or in partnership with other attorneys or researchers, you may be able to conduct research into pretrial release decisions in your geographic area broken down by race. *See infra* § 4.5A, Policies, Forms, Practices, and Criteria Influencing Pretrial Decisions. This may involve information obtained from databases, or simply an observational study of first appearances and bond modification hearings, whereby observers note the outcomes of such hearings and then pull the files associated with each of the cases observed to compile a record of pretrial release decisions. If such a study has been conducted in your district, or if you have the ability to conduct one, the data may persuade the court of the importance of guarding against bias in pretrial release decisions.

4.5 Policy Considerations

A. Policies, Forms, Practices, and Criteria Influencing Pretrial Decisions

Generally. Indigent defenders should coordinate with other court actors, including prosecutors, pretrial services programs, court officials, and police, to determine whether any practices, guidelines, forms, or policies employed in the pretrial release process may contribute to racial disparities in pretrial outcomes. A helpful starting point in determining whether pretrial practices in your county conform with best practices is to consult the protocols for pretrial decisions developed by the National Association of Pretrial Services Agencies (NAPSA), which aim to reduce the potential for disparities. NATIONAL ASSOCIATION OF PRETRIAL SERVICES AGENCIES, STANDARDS ON PRETRIAL RELEASE (3d ed. 2004).

Risk assessment tool in Minnesota's Fourth Judicial District. In Minnesota's Fourth Judicial District (covering Hennepin County and the City of Minneapolis), researchers recently evaluated the pretrial risk assessment tool utilized by the Community Corrections Pretrial Unit. This tool used certain factors to evaluate pretrial risk.

Researchers considered whether reliance on these factors resulted in racial disparities in pretrial detention. They concluded that three of the nine factors employed in evaluating risk—whether a weapon was used during the commission of the crime, whether the defendant lived alone, and whether the defendant was under age 21 when booked—bore little relation to flight risk or reoffending, but were strongly correlated with race. The court adopted a recommendation to eliminate these three factors correlating with race but not with risk, and put a new risk assessment tool in place. ASHLEY NELLIS ET AL., THE SENTENCING PROJECT, REDUCING RACIAL DISPARITY IN THE CRIMINAL JUSTICE SYSTEM: A MANUAL FOR PRACTITIONERS AND POLICYMAKERS 11 (2d ed. 2008) (summarizing FOURTH JUDICIAL DISTRICT OF MINNESOTA RESEARCH DIVISION, FOURTH JUDICIAL DISTRICT PRETRIAL EVALUATION: SCALE VALIDATION STUDY (2006)). North Carolina statutes require magistrates to defer setting pretrial release conditions if they find that a person is charged with a felony or Class A1 misdemeanor involving a firearm and the person is currently on pretrial release for or has been convicted of another such offense. G.S. 15A-533(f). The statute does not preclude a judge from setting pretrial release conditions in these circumstances, however. G.S. 15A-533(g).

Bail reform by Duluth Racial Justice Task Force. In Saint Louis County (which includes the City of Duluth), Minnesota, a racial justice task force supported by the Criminal Justice Section of the American Bar Association's Racial Justice Improvement Project, spent two years evaluating and addressing racial disparities in bail and pretrial detention/release. *See* Cynthia E. Jones, *"Give Us Free": Addressing Racial Disparities in Bail Determinations*, 16 N.Y.U. J. LEGIS. & PUB. POL'Y 919, 946–55 (2013); ROBERT R. WEIDNER, RACIAL JUSTICE IMPROVEMENT PROJECT: PRETRIAL DETENTION & RELEASE DECISIONS IN ST. LOUIS COUNTY, MN, IN 2009 & 2010: INTERIM FINDINGS (2011). The task force consisted of the County Attorney (the county's chief prosecutor), the Chief Public Defender, the Deputy Chief of Police, a trial judge, a representative of the American Indian Commission, the head of probation/pretrial services, a representative from the local jail, and an administrative coordinator. The project was divided into three stages: investigation, education, and implementation. In the investigation stage, the task force:

- collected data from the court on bail determinations;
- retained a criminologist from a local university to analyze the data (he concluded that White defendants were twice as likely as defendants of other races to be released on their own recognizance, racial minorities were more likely to have money bond imposed, and the median bond imposed on African American defendants was twice that of the bond amounts set for White defendants);
- formed a subcommittee that met with each arraignment court judge in the county and asked them how they weighed the statutory factors governing bail determinations; and
- interviewed the probation office, which in Saint Louis County supervises defendants placed on supervised pretrial release, regarding their practices in arraignment court.

Based on its investigation, the task force concluded that: (1) judges typically make bail determinations without critical information relevant to the determination; (2) money bonds are overused, and this practice has a disparate impact on African Americans and Native Americans; and (3) probation officers were imposing strict standards on defendants on supervised release that were more appropriate for post-conviction defendants on probation. The task force also concluded that certain logistical factors may contribute to disparities in bail determinations. For example, judges reported that probation officers, when advising the court regarding pretrial decisions, would tell the court when they would prefer not to supervise defendants who lived far from probation offices. Because of the distance between the probation office and the Native American reservation in the county, this recommendation resulted in the disproportionate pretrial confinement of Native Americans.

In the next stage of the project (education), task force members attended trainings on best practices in bail determinations and pretrial services, including conferences by the ABA Racial Justice Improvement Project and by the National Association of Pretrial Services (NAPSA). As a result of the NAPSA conference, the Duluth trial judge who attended concluded he had been overusing money bonds and changed his bail determination practices. Cynthia E. Jones, *"Give Us Free": Addressing Racial Disparities in Bail Determinations*, 16 N.Y.U. J. LEGIS. & PUB. POL'Y 919, 953 (2013). This stage of the project also included a day-long training by the task force for all judges and probation officers, including training on laws, pretrial release standards, best practices for imposing supervised release, and discussion of the task force's findings regarding racial disparities in local bail determinations.

The last stage of the task force project (implementation) involved the following initiatives:

- ensuring that judges have bail reports (reports prepared by the probation office including background information on each arrestee) in all felony cases before making bail determinations;
- improving risk assessment tools to reduce the risk of subjective biases;
- preparing a chart for judges to use when making pretrial release determinations that sets forth the range of available non-financial release options;
- expanding community release options;
- collecting data regularly to monitor racial disparities.

Owing in large part to the commitment and involvement of all local court actors, as well as support from national organizations and experts involved in pretrial release issues, the task force's work may serve as a model for other communities seeking to revise their bail determination practices. "Other jurisdictions faced with similar bail practices, and similar patterns of racial disparities, will likely find the formula successfully executed in Duluth to be [a] useful model for pretrial reform." *Id.* at 955.

North Carolina Commission on Racial and Ethnic Disparities in the Criminal Justice System Pretrial Subcommittee. The North Carolina Commission on Racial and Ethnic Disparities in the Criminal Justice System (NCCRED), comprised of prosecutors, defense attorneys, police chiefs, judges, and community advocates, is an organization aimed at reaching a consensus on the presence and causes of racial disparities in particular areas of the criminal justice system and making recommendations for reform that have the support of representatives of a broad range of criminal justice stakeholders. *See* North Carolina Advocates for Justice, *North Carolina Commission on Racial and Ethnic Disparities in the Criminal Justice System*, NCAJ.COM (last visited July 23, 2014). The Commission's Pretrial Subcommittee (PTSC), funded in part by the American Bar Association's Racial Justice Improvement Project, is currently collecting data in an urban area, Guilford County, and a rural area, Halifax County, to examine whether there are disparate outcomes for minority defendants at the pretrial stage of the criminal process. *See* North Carolina Advocates for Justice, *NCCRED Pretrial Subcommittee*, NCAJ.COM (last visited July 23, 2014). The data collected includes bond amounts and conditions for defendants charged with Class H felonies. This effort involves data collection and analysis by race and ethnicity across a range of variables, including age, sex, economic status, employment, mental and physical health, case disposition, length of time in custody, bond amount, method of posting bond, criminal history, and failure to appear history. The PTSC currently expects that the collected data will be presented to the Commission as a whole in 2014. After that presentation, the Commission intends to explore the factors contributing to any racial disparities and try to identify an approach to eliminate or minimize them.

UNC MPA Student's Examination of Wake County Bail Determinations. A study undertaken by UNC School of Government Master of Public Administration (MPA) graduate student Johanna Hawfield Foster examined arrest data and jail admissions records in Wake County to determine whether race was playing a role in pretrial release determinations. She concluded that African American defendants pay 16 percent more in bail than White defendants. *See* Johanna Hawfield Foster, *Striving for Equity in Criminal Justice: An Analysis of Variability of Bail Bonds in the Tenth Judicial District of North Carolina* (also finding that, in the Tenth Judicial District, mean bail exceeded the upper limit of the bond's suggested policy guidelines by at least 30 percent) in the Race Materials Bank at www.ncids.org (select "Training & Resources"). Subsequently, the Tenth Judicial District adopted a policy of requiring magistrates to record reasons supporting any secured release imposed outside of the recommended guidelines for the offense class. *See* Administrative Order Setting 10th Judicial District Pretrial Release Policies in the Race Materials Bank at www.ncids.org (select "Training & Resources"). Lawyers seeking information on the racial and ethnic demographics of arrestees and pretrial jail detainees may consult the databases utilized in this study: a City County Bureau of Identification (CCBI) database with information regarding race, ethnicity, sex, place of resident, country of origin, employment, information on prior arrests, and court appearance history; and the County Sheriff's Office's database with bail bond amounts and charge descriptions. For assistance interpreting the data, you may wish to seek help from graduate students in public administration or political science who are capable of performing regression analysis to control for variables affecting pretrial release decisions.

Pretrial Release Project in Baltimore, Maryland. Another study of bail practices in a single locale was conducted by the Abell Foundation's Pretrial Release Project (PRP).

The study, which compared bail practices in the City of Baltimore to statewide averages, was authorized by the Maryland Court of Appeals following a request by the Maryland State Bar Association. Like the Duluth task force study discussed above, the PRP concluded that judicial officers were making bail determinations with insufficient information and relied too heavily on financial release; and that African American men were detained pretrial due to their inability to satisfy financial conditions of release at a "strikingly higher rate" than their representation in the overall population. THE ABELL FOUNDATION, THE PRETRIAL RELEASE PROJECT: A STUDY OF MARYLAND'S PRETRIAL RELEASE AND BAIL SYSTEM 28 (2001).

B. Collaborative Partnerships with Other Stakeholders in the Justice System

Defense attorneys and other stakeholders in the justice system may share overlapping interests in pretrial release procedures. For example, former Mecklenburg County Chief District Judge Lisa Bell, when interviewed about the county's new bail policy in 2010, observed that, because of better access to information under the new policy, "your incarceration isn't tied to your ability to pay money. People without means don't necessarily have a higher risk associated with them." Jeff Atkinson, *Mecklenburg Courts – New Bail Policy*, WBTV 3 NEWS (July 6, 2010) (reviewing new policy and finding that dangerous offenders, who present a greater risk to the community, will have higher bonds while defendants who pose little risk will have the opportunity to get out of jail). Additionally, many counties have a concern about the cost of pretrial detention. This concern presents opportunities for partnerships to reduce reliance on pretrial detention. Partnerships with stakeholders in the criminal justice system—including prosecutors, pretrial services officers, diversion programs, social service programs, faith-based organizations, local and state bar associations, and representatives from minority communities—may result in:

- development of training programs on issues of race in pretrial decision-making for all actors involved in the pretrial release process, including magistrates, judges, prosecutors, and defense attorneys;
- development of community education programs that help people understand how to navigate the pretrial process;
- public education campaigns regarding the importance of pretrial release;
- examination of the pretrial process to determine if racial disparities are present in pretrial release decisions, including release on a written promise to appear, setting of bail amounts, or consideration for diversion programs resulting in deferred prosecution;
- assignment of a bond prosecutor to the county jail to facilitate early risk assessments and the release of unnecessarily detained arrestees, as is currently done in Durham County;
- examination of the jail population to determine the percentage of the population detained pretrial because of an inability to post bond;
- development of additional community-based programs and resources that may be used as an alternative to pretrial detention when appropriate;

- funding for indigent people ordered to participate in fee-based pretrial programs such as continuous alcohol monitoring pursuant to S.L. 2012-146, as amended by S.L. 2012-194 (expanding authorization for the use of continuous alcohol monitoring (CAM));
- understanding of the importance of early release and the early involvement of defense counsel in the pretrial process, including consistent representation of defendants in bail hearings;
- development of standardized, evidence-based, validated risk assessments to determine who may safely be released into the community;
- development of increased oversight and accountability measures in the bail determination process, including the adoption of policies requiring magistrates to make written findings supporting bail and pretrial release determinations.

Chapter 5
Selective Prosecution: Plea Negotiations and Charging Decisions by Prosecutors

---

5.1 Scope of Chapter

Prosecutors have wide discretion in deciding what charges to pursue and plea bargains to offer. For example, they can charge a person as a habitual felon if he or she has a certain number of prior felony convictions and commits a new felony, which significantly enhances the potential punishment, while charging a similarly situated person with the new felony without "habitualizing" the person. Guarantees of equal protection in the Fourteenth Amendment to the U.S. Constitution and article I, section 19 of the N.C. Constitution prohibit the State from making charging or plea bargaining decisions based on improper grounds such as race or ethnicity. However, demonstrating that a prosecutor's decision was unconstitutionally selective may be challenging. Attorneys must present evidence of both discriminatory intent and discriminatory effect to prevail on a claim of selective prosecution. This chapter reviews the legal requirements for selective prosecution claims, including the showing an attorney must make up front to require the State to turn over information about its charging practices as well as the statistical showing needed to establish a violation.

5.2 Overview

A. The Scope and Consequences of Prosecutorial Discretion

The first and most consequential discretionary decision a prosecutor makes is the charging decision. Determining whether to charge a suspect, and with what charge, has been described as "the broadest discretionary power in criminal administration." James Vorenberg, *Narrowing the Discretion of Criminal Justice Officials*, 1976 DUKE L. J. 651, 678. "[S]o long as the prosecutor has probable cause to believe that the accused committed an offense defined by statute, the decision whether or not to prosecute, and what charge to file or bring before a grand jury, generally rests entirely in his discretion." *Bordenkircher v. Hayes*, 434 U.S. 357, 364 (1978); *see also* Josh Bowers, *Legal Guilt, Normative Innocence, and the Equitable Decision Not to Prosecute*, 110 COLUM. L. REV. 1655, 1659–60 (2010) ("Laws are shells, and prosecutors retain almost unfettered discretion to decide how to fill the void within."). As laws proscribing criminal conduct and sentencing enhancements expand, so too does the prosecutor's discretionary charging and plea bargaining power. *See, e.g.*, William J. Stuntz, *The Pathological Politics of Criminal Law*, 100 MICH. L. REV. 505, 509 (2001) ("As criminal law expands, both lawmaking and adjudication pass into the hands of police and prosecutors . . . [resulting in] criminal codes that . . . delegate power to district attorneys' offices and police departments"); Jeff Welty, *Growth of Chapter 14*, N.C. CRIM. L., UNC SCH. OF GOV'T BLOG (Oct. 30, 2013) (discussing growth of criminal code in North Carolina).

The prosecutor's choice of charges affects defendants in obvious ways and also in ways that may not be immediately apparent. Of course, the charges prescribe the range of available criminal penalties. Additionally, criminal charges may result in innumerable collateral consequences for those ultimately convicted, including include loss of professional licenses; ineligibility for government benefits, public housing, or student loans; loss of voting rights and ineligibility for jury duty; and deportation for immigrants. Charges also can influence pretrial release determinations. *See* G.S. 15A-534(c) (judicial official must take into account nature and circumstances of the offense charged, among other factors, in setting conditions of pretrial release). This determination in turn may influence case outcomes, as defendants released pretrial generally achieve better case outcomes. *See supra* § 4.2D, Defendants Detained Pretrial Achieve Worse Outcomes.

The charging decision also bears on plea negotiations. For example, by offering not to pursue a habitual felon charge if the defendant pleads guilty, a prosecutor provides a strong incentive to a defendant to accept a plea of guilty to the underlying felony offense rather than proceed to trial. H. Mitchell Caldwell, *Coercive Plea Bargaining: The Unrecognized Scourge of the Justice System*, 61 CATHOLIC U. L. REV. 63, 84 (2013). Reflecting on prosecutorial discretion, Professor Angela Davis concluded that, "[i]n conjunction with the plea bargaining process, the charging decision almost predetermines the outcome of a criminal case, because the vast majority of criminal cases result in guilty pleas or guilty verdicts." Angela J. Davis, *Prosecution and Race: The Power and Privilege of Discretion*, 67 FORDHAM L. REV. 13, 23 (1998).

B. Studies of Prosecutorial Decision-Making and Racial Disparities

As mentioned elsewhere in this manual, studies have concluded that, where discretion is greatest, implicit and explicit biases exert the greatest influence. *See supra* § 1.3E, Discretionary Decision-Making and the Cumulative Nature of Disparities. The broad discretionary power afforded to prosecutors—in bringing criminal charges, enabling access to diversion programs, dismissing charges, reducing charges, approving deferred prosecutions, negotiating guilty pleas, evaluating defendants' cooperation with the government, and recommending sentences—creates the potential for bias to enter in and generate disparate outcomes for defendants of different races.

Some scholars have concluded that the exercise of prosecutorial discretion is a key point at which racial disparities may be introduced into the criminal proceeding. "Understanding the impact of [prosecutors'] decisions on the higher incarceration rates of blacks and Latinos is crucial to determining whether, or how, race and ethnicity influence outcomes in the criminal justice system." BESIKI KUTATELADZE ET AL., VERA INSTITUTE OF JUSTICE, DO RACE AND ETHNICITY MATTER IN PROSECUTION? A REVIEW OF EMPIRICAL STUDIES 1 (2012). In considering the possible influence of implicit biases on prosecutorial discretion, it is worth noting that 95% of North Carolina prosecutors are White. DR. MATTHEW ROBINSON, THE DEATH PENALTY IN NORTH CAROLINA: A SUMMARY OF THE DATA AND SCIENTIFIC STUDIES 40 (2011). This figure, on its own, does not compel any particular conclusion concerning the influence of race on prosecutorial decision-making. However, since "the social category you belong to can influence what sorts of biases you are likely to have," the figure is not without relevance. *See* JERRY KANG, IMPLICIT BIAS: A PRIMER FOR COURTS 3–5 (National Center for State Courts 2009) (noting that "most Whites (and Asians, Latinos, and American Indians) show an implicit attitude in favor of Whites over Blacks").

Researchers have found that the plea bargaining process can result in racially disparate outcomes for similarly situated individuals. An examination of the pretrial negotiations in nearly 700,000 criminal cases in California concluded that "'[a]t virtually every stage of pretrial negotiation, whites are more successful than non-whites.' Of 71,000 adults charged with felonies and with no prior record in [a study conducted by the *San Jose Mercury News*], one third of whites had charges reduced to misdemeanors or infractions, while only one quarter of blacks and Hispanics received these outcomes." Marc

Mauer, *Racial Impact Statements as a Means of Reducing Unwarranted Sentencing Disparities*, 5 OHIO ST. J. CRIM. L. 19, 26 (2007) (quoting Christopher H. Schmitt, *Plea Bargaining Favors Whites as Blacks, Hispanics Pay Price*, SAN JOSE MERCURY NEWS, Dec. 8, 1991, at 1A). In one example highlighted in this report, two defendants, one black and one white, both began serving prison terms for similar crimes the same year:

> Both offenders initially were charged with four counts: three burglary charges and one charge of receiving stolen property. Both had one, non-violent prior offense. Neither had been to prison before. Both had been on probation previously. Neither had used a weapon in the offense. Drugs were not involved. Both plea-bargained their outcomes. The black man was convicted on the four original charges and drew an eight-year prison term. The white man got three charges dismissed, was convicted on a single burglary charge and got 16 months.

Christopher H. Schmitt, *Plea Bargaining Favors Whites as Blacks, Hispanics Pay Price*, SAN JOSE MERCURY NEWS, Dec. 8, 1991, at 1A. The impact of prosecutorial discretion in plea bargaining is magnified by the fact that the vast majority of criminal cases are resolved by plea agreements, which are rarely reviewed on appeal.

Researchers have found that prosecutorial discretion is one possible factor contributing to racial disparities in criminal justice outcomes. *See A Conversation with Cassie Spohn*, VERA INSTITUTE OF JUSTICE BLOG (June 4, 2012) (professor and director of the School of Criminology and Criminal Justice, Arizona State University). Nevertheless, "[r]elative to the attention that police and the courts have received from researchers analyzing disproportionate minority contact with the criminal justice system, there has been little study of prosecution." BESIKI KUTATELADZE ET AL., VERA INSTITUTE OF JUSTICE, DO RACE AND ETHNICITY MATTER IN PROSECUTION? A REVIEW OF EMPIRICAL STUDIES 1 (2012). One group examining race and prosecutorial decision-making concluded that "[p]rosecutors' exercise of discretion operates with minimal external oversight, yet has more impact on case outcomes than the decisions made by any other actor in the criminal justice process." ASHLEY NELLIS ET AL., THE SENTENCING PROJECT, REDUCING RACIAL DISPARITY IN THE CRIMINAL JUSTICE SYSTEM: A MANUAL FOR PRACTITIONERS AND POLICYMAKERS 35 (2d ed. 2008) (describing work of Vera Institute of Justice).

Research into the intersection of race and prosecutorial decision-making faces inherent challenges; for example, many aspects of the plea bargaining process are "not documented in any formal way." *See A Conversation with Cassie Spohn*, VERA INSTITUTE OF JUSTICE BLOG (June 4, 2012). It is difficult to find records of plea bargains offered to and rejected by defendants, which would be needed to study the role of race in discretionary determinations regarding plea bargains. Additionally, factors including "the strength of [a] case, the prosecution's general deterrence value, the Government's enforcement priorities, and the case's relationship to the Government's overall enforcement plan" are difficult to quantify in empirical analyses; the presence of such race-neutral factors makes it difficult for researchers to isolate the influence of race. *Wayte v. United States*, 470 U.S. 598, 607–08 (1985). Without access to the internal policies regarding plea bargains or habitual felon determinations of a given district attorney's office, it is hard to assess whether a racially disparate prosecution record reflects the improper influence of racial factors or legitimate policy choices. *See, e.g., State v. Parks*, 146 N.C. App. 568 (2001), *discussed infra* "Illustrative cases: insufficient evidence of discriminatory effect" in § 5.3E, First Prong of a Selective Prosecution Claim: Discriminatory Effect.

Recently, however, studies have emerged that analyze the possible impact of prosecutorial decision-making on racial disparities in the criminal justice system. Researchers studying North Carolina capital charging decisions concluded that, between 1990 and 2009, prosecutors brought 17.21% of death eligible cases to capital trial where the case included at least one white victim, and 8.86% of such cases to capital trial where the case did not include at least one white victim. *Affidavit of Catherine Grosso and Barbara O'Brien* (exhibit to motion to prohibit death penalty under the Racial Justice Act) at 5 in the Race Materials Bank at www.ncids.org (select "Training and Resources"). Controlling for non-racial statutory aggravating and mitigating factors, cases including at least one white victim were 1.53 times more likely to advance to a capital trial. *Id.* In the federal context, researchers have concluded that Black and Latino people, men, older defendants, noncitizens, and high school dropouts receive fewer and smaller substantial-assistance sentencing discounts than White people, women, young people, citizens, and high school graduates. LINDA DRAZGA MAXFIELD & JOHN H. KRAMER, U.S. SENTENCING COMM'N, SUBSTANTIAL ASSISTANCE: AN EMPIRICAL YARDSTICK GAUGING EQUITY IN CURRENT FEDERAL POLICY AND PRACTICE 31, 34 (1998). Researchers who conducted a two year study of cases handled by the District Attorney of New York City concluded that, "compared to similarly situated white defendants, black and Latino defendants were more likely to be detained at arraignment (remanded or have bail set, but not met), to receive a custodial sentence offer as a result of the plea bargaining process, and to be incarcerated, but they were also more likely to have their cases dismissed." *See* BESIKI KUTATELADZE ET AL., VERA INSTITUTE OF JUSTICE, RACE AND PROSECUTION IN MANHATTAN 3 (2014). A 2012 review of 34 empirical studies considering prosecutorial decision-making and race reported that, while the influence of race and ethnicity on prosecutorial decision-making was inconsistent across the studies, they generally demonstrated overall that race and/or ethnicity do influence "case outcomes, even when a host of other legal and extra-legal factors are taken into account." BESIKI KUTATELADZE ET AL., VERA INSTITUTE OF JUSTICE, DO RACE AND ETHNICITY MATTER IN PROSECUTION? A REVIEW OF EMPIRICAL STUDIES 17 (2012).

5.3 Equal Protection Limits on Selective Prosecution

A. Identifying Selective Prosecution

The following list is not exhaustive, but may be helpful in considering whether your client may have been subjected to unconstitutional selective prosecution:

- Have you noticed that only (or primarily) defendants of a certain race or races are prosecuted for a specific crime or category of crimes within your judicial district?
- Does your client face more severe charges than equally or more culpable co-defendants of a different race, with comparable prior record levels?
- Is there evidence that your client is facing more severe charges than similarly situated offenders because of the race of the victim in your client's case? Similarly, have you noticed that only offenders charged with victimizing members of a certain race face certain charges or penalty enhancements? Does the race of the victim play a role in which defendants are offered favorable outcomes, such as a PJC or a deferred prosecution agreement?
- Do your Black or Latino clients tend to receive less favorable plea offers than your similarly situated White clients?
- Have you noticed racial disparities in the deferral of defendants to diversionary courts, such as drug treatment courts, in which defendants may earn dismissals or reduction of charges?
- Are racial minorities in your district more frequently prosecuted as habitual felons than similarly situated White defendants?
- Was your Black client referred for federal prosecution while similarly situated White defendants were tried in state court? *See United States v. Jones*, 36 F. Supp. 2d 304, 311–13 (E.D. Va. 1999) (the challenged program "would be vulnerable on selective prosecution grounds if African-American defendants were routinely diverted from state to federal prosecution while prosecutors allowed similarly situated Caucasian defendants to remain in state court"). In such a case, it may be the federal defender who will need to investigate a claim of selective enforcement, but the state defender may provide useful context about the number and type of cases that are "federalized." In order to spot possible patterns of disparate transfers to federal court, state defenders could keep records of such transfers, collaborate with federal defenders to investigate potential violations, and/or discuss any concerning patterns with the district attorney for that district.
- Was your Black client, following an acquittal in federal court, arrested on state charges stemming from the same event, while defendants of other races are not prosecuted in state court following an acquittal on similar charges in federal court? *See* Gail Robinson, *Selective Prosecution*, THE ADVOCATE, May 2008, at 5, 5. *Cf.* G.S. 90-97 (prohibiting prosecution under North Carolina's Controlled Substances Act of acts forming the basis of a conviction or acquittal in federal court).
- Has the prosecutor, or any member of the district attorney's office involved in your client's case, said anything to you, the media, or others indicating that race may have played a role in a prosecutorial decision in your client's case? *See, e.g.*, *Wake D.A. Rejected Plea Deal in Taft Murder Case*, WRAL.COM (July 25, 2012) (reporting defense attorney's recollection of comments by district attorney, based on which he believed that race was a factor in the prosecutor's decision to pursue the death penalty).

Addressing charges of particular concern. Racial disparities may be greater in some types of prosecutions than in others. For example, a recent study found that, in North Carolina in 2011, Black people represent 21.5% of the state's total population, 69.6% of the habitual felon prison population, and 53.2% of the prison population incarcerated for drug offenses. *See* NCAJ Racial Justice Task Force, NC Habitual Felon Prison Population Data – June 2011, NCAJ.COM (last visited Aug. 4, 2014); NCAJ Racial Justice Task Force, *NC Drug Prison Population Data – June 2011*, NCAJ.COM (last visited Aug. 4, 2014). Many of the well-known selective prosecution claims have been raised in response to drug prosecutions. *See, e.g., United States v. Armstrong*, 517 U.S. 456 (1996); *United States v. Jones*, 159 F.3d 969 (6th Cir. 1998); *see also supra* § 1.3G, Legislation (explaining how crack-cocaine penalties resulted in racial disparities in punishment). Attorneys have also raised claims that the exercise of prosecutorial discretion has contributed to racial disparities in habitual felon prosecutions. *See* Habitual Felon Motion and Affidavit in the Race Materials Bank at www.ncids.org (select "Training & Resources").

B. Potential Benefits of Raising Selective Prosecution Claims

Reasons for raising claim. There are several reasons for raising good faith claims of selective prosecution, even though they may be difficult to win:

- In some instances, you may prevail on the merits. *See, In re Register*, 84 N.C. App. 336, 346 (1987) (dismissing juvenile petitions against several co-defendants after finding that a prosecutor engaged in selective prosecution in violation of the Equal Protection Clause by making the ability of a juvenile to pay compensation to a victim the "determinative factor in the decision of whether to file a complaint as a juvenile petition").
- Where the evidence suggests that your client may have been subjected to selective prosecution, investigating and raising a claim of selective prosecution is consistent with your ethical obligation of zealous advocacy. *See* North Carolina Rules of Professional Conduct 0.1[2] ("As advocate, a lawyer zealously asserts the client's position under the rules of the adversary system.").
- If a client appears to have been the subject of selective prosecution, you are, in all likelihood, the only person who can effectively inquire into the possibility of inequitable treatment.
- Selective prosecution claims, even if unsuccessful in district or superior court, may lay the groundwork for a successful appeal. The failure to object to selective prosecution usually waives the issue for appellate review or federal review.
- Data collected as part of a selective prosecution investigation may be useful in subsequent cases involving similar issues, charges, or state actors.
- Even when unsuccessful, litigating selective prosecution may reduce disparities by drawing the attention of court actors to the possibility that race may be playing a role in case decisions, which may cause those concerned to consider the possible influence of implicit racial bias. *See supra* § 1.3D, Implicit Bias.

- While reported cases of success on selective prosecutions claims are rare, this scarcity may not be an accurate reflection of the potential for positive results. On occasion, when a defendant's selective prosecution claim is strong, an attractive plea offer or a dismissal in the interests of justice may lead to a favorable result for the client not reflected in any judicial opinion. *See, e.g.*, Racial Disparity Project Website, *Summary of Selective Enforcement Litigation*, RDP.DEFENDER.ORG (last visited Aug. 4, 2014).
- Prosecutorial responses to discovery requests in selective prosecution claims, whether voluntary or compelled, can reveal instructive information about the prosecutorial charging processes and may lead to greater dialogue between defense attorneys and prosecutors about ways to reduce racial disparities in prosecutions.
- Litigating selective prosecution claims may lead to the development of selective prosecution jurisprudence that accounts for the potential influence of implicit bias. *See supra* § 1.3D, Implicit Bias.

Case study: Raising a claim of selective prosecution. Below are the reflections of Assistant Federal Defender Gregory Davis on raising a claim of selective prosecution in a federal case:

I raised a claim of racially selective prosecution in a federal case when I believed that there was strong evidence supporting the claim and I knew that raising the claim was in my client's best interest.

My client and his juvenile co-defendant, both young African American males, were charged with killing a former UNC student body president, a young White woman. From the outset, I could not identify any aspects of the charged offense that justified seeking the death penalty in federal court, other than the identity of the victim. My suspicion that the victim's race and identity as a widely admired student leader played a role in the prosecution of my client was supported by statistical data I discovered on the SBI website concerning similar cases. In the history of the Middle District of North Carolina, there was only one other case in which the death penalty was sought in federal court. The facts of that case were more egregious than the facts of my client's case and, in that case, I represented one of the two co-defendants and was able to persuade the prosecutors not to seek the death penalty at an early stage of the case. I also discovered other cases with multiple victims and more heinous crimes that were not tried capitally in the Middle District. Because it appeared to me that the decision to try my client capitally in federal court was based on the race and identity of the victim, I filed a motion to bar the death penalty based on selective prosecution and/or for discovery of information pertaining to the government's decision to charge the defendant and pursue the case capitally.

After filing the selective prosecution motion, I was able to negotiate a plea to a life sentence. The judge did not rule on the motion because it never advanced to a hearing. However, the filing of the motion may have played a role in the prosecutor's eventual willingness to accept a plea to a life sentence.

While I don't believe that the decision to prosecute my client capitally in federal court was motivated by conscious racism, I do believe that race influences all of our decisions, consciously and unconsciously. I have known the prosecutor in the case for a long time and consider him a friend. I feel certain that he was upset when the motion was filed, but the case has now been resolved, and we are still friends. It hasn't had a negative impact on our ability to work well together in other cases. In any event, I cannot let concerns about a prosecutor's reaction dissuade me from filing a meritorious motion on my client's behalf. One has to be selective in determining when to raise the issue of race. However, when the evidence suggests that race has played a role in my client's prosecution, it is my duty to raise the issue.

C. Selective Prosecution Distinguished from Selective Enforcement

Selective prosecution and selective enforcement claims may both arise in a given case. For this reason, this chapter should be considered in conjunction with the principles on selective enforcement discussed in Chapter 2. *See supra* § 2.3, Equal Protection Challenges to Police Action. Both claims involve a defendant's allegation that he has received harsher treatment than similarly situated individuals in the criminal justice system on account of his race in violation of his right to equal protection of the law. In some cases, the evidence may suggest that a defendant's criminal prosecution was influenced by race, but it may be unclear whether law enforcement officers, prosecutors, or both were responsible for the exercise of discretion. In such cases, it may be important to raise claims of both selective enforcement and selective prosecution.

While the case law often blurs the distinction between selective enforcement and selective prosecution, these two practices are distinct. *See supra* "Selective enforcement distinguished from selective prosecution" in § 2.3E, Burden of Proof and Burden Shifting. Racially selective enforcement of the law occurs when police or other law enforcement officers make enforcement decisions based on race, and racially selective prosecution occurs when a prosecutor treats one accused person less favorably than another based on race. The elements of the selective prosecution and selective enforcement claims are identical, but courts may accord more deference to prosecutorial decision-making in light of concerns that are unique to the district attorney's office:

> This broad discretion [afforded prosecutors] rests largely on the recognition that the decision to prosecute is particularly ill-suited to judicial review. Such factors as the strength of the case, the prosecution's general deterrence value, the Government's enforcement priorities, and the case's relationship to the Government's overall enforcement plan are not readily susceptible to the kind of analysis the courts are competent to undertake. Judicial supervision in this area, moreover, entails systemic costs of particular concern. Examining the basis of a prosecution delays the criminal proceeding, threatens to chill law enforcement by subjecting the prosecutor's motives and decisionmaking to outside inquiry, and may undermine prosecutorial effectiveness by revealing the Government's enforcement policy. All of these are substantial concerns that make the courts properly hesitant to examine the decision whether to prosecute.

Wayte v. United States, 470 U.S. 598, 607–08 (1985).

D. Elements of a Selective Prosecution Claim

Racially discriminatory selective prosecution violates the right to equal protection guaranteed by both the United States Constitution and the North Carolina Constitution. *United States v. Armstrong*, 517 U.S. 456 (1996); *State v. Rogers*, 68 N.C. App. 358, 368 (1984); *see generally supra* § 2.3, Equal Protection Challenges to Police Action. The exercise of selectivity in enforcing criminal statutes is inherent in the prosecutorial function and, standing alone, is not a denial of equal protection. *Bordenkircher v. Hayes*, 434 U.S. 357 (1978); *Oyler v. Boles*, 368 U.S. 448, 456 (1962) ("[T]he conscious exercise of some selectivity in enforcement is not in itself a federal constitutional violation."). To sustain a claim of selective prosecution, a defendant must show "that in the exercise of . . . discretion there has been intentional or deliberate discrimination by design." *In re Register*, 84 N.C. App. 336, 341, 346 (1987) (prosecutor engaged in selective prosecution in violation of the Equal Protection Clause by making the ability of a juvenile to pay compensation the "determinative factor in the decision of whether to file a complaint as a juvenile petition"). As with all equal protection claims, a claim of selective prosecution will succeed where the defendant demonstrates that the prosecution of the case had a discriminatory effect and was motivated by a discriminatory purpose. *Wayte v. United States*, 470 U.S. 598, 608 (1985) ("It is appropriate to judge selective prosecution claims according to ordinary equal protection standards."). The two prongs of an equal protection claim of selective prosecution are discussed in more detail in the succeeding sections.

Significance of "some evidence" of discriminatory effect and discriminatory intent. In interpreting federal discovery rules, the United States Supreme Court has held that discovery related to selective prosecution allegations will be granted only if defendants first demonstrate "some evidence" of discriminatory effect and discriminatory intent. *See United States v. Armstrong*, 517 U.S. 456, 463 (1996); *see infra* § 5.4A, Obtaining Discovery Relevant to a Selective Prosecution Claim (discussing significance of this ruling in North Carolina courts). For this reason, when analyzing the two elements of a selective prosecution claim, many of the federal rulings discussed below focus on whether the defendant has presented "some evidence" sufficient to obtain discovery.

E. First Prong of a Selective Prosecution Claim: Discriminatory Effect

"Similarly situated" defined. To establish that a particular prosecution or prosecutorial policy had a discriminatory effect, a defendant must demonstrate that similarly situated individuals belonging to a different racial group were not prosecuted or received more favorable treatment. *United States v. Armstrong*, 517 U.S. 456, 465 (threshold for discovery is "a credible showing of different treatment of similarly situated persons"); *Ah Sin v. Wittman*, 198 U.S. 500 (1905); *State v. Pope*, 213 N.C. App. 413 (2011) (defendant raising selective prosecution claim must show "that he has been singled out for prosecution while others similarly situated and committing the same acts have not" (quotation omitted)); *United States v. Tuitt*, 68 F. Supp. 2d 4 (D. Mass. 1999) (similarly situated White defendants receiving more favorable treatment constituted evidence of discriminatory effect). A claim of selective prosecution will also lie where the charging decision is influenced by the race of the victim. *See State v. Garner*, 340 N.C. 573, 587 (1995) (affirming trial court's rejection of selective prosecution claim based in part on the finding that "[t]here is no evidence before the Court that the District Attorney in making these decisions is in any way influenced by the race, sex or national origin of the defendant or the victim").

The defendant's ability to demonstrate discriminatory effect will often turn on the court's understanding of the term "similarly situated." *See, e.g.*, *State v. Johnson,* 125 Wash. App. 1040 (Wash. Ct. App. 2005) (unpublished) (analyzing definition of "similarly situated" individuals that trial court used to define scope of discovery in selective enforcement case). The leading case on selective prosecution, *United States v. Armstrong*, 517 U.S. 456, 458 (1996)—in which the Supreme Court overturned an order requiring the Government to provide discovery related to allegedly racially selective prosecution of crack cocaine offenses because the defendants "failed to show that the Government declined to prosecute similarly situated suspects of other races"—left this term largely undefined. The United States Supreme Court has not defined this critical term in other cases. *See* Giovanna Shay, *Similarly Situated*, 18 GEO. MASON L. REV. 581, 586 (2011) ("[m]any important equal protection opinions contain no substantive 'similarly situated' analysis").

"Similarly situated" in North Carolina courts. Defendants raising claims of selective prosecution should always raise parallel claims under article I, section 19 of the North Carolina Constitution. While some North Carolina appellate decisions examining constitutional claims of selective prosecution cite the leading U.S. Supreme Court cases on the topic, there has not been a North Carolina appellate decision expressly adopting federal standards when reviewing claims of selective prosecution based on the N.C. Constitution. *See, e.g.*, *State v. Spicer*, 299 N.C. 309, 314 (1980); *State v. Howard*, 78 N.C. App. 262 (1985). North Carolina cases concerning selective prosecution have held that selectivity in prosecution is permissible when based on assessments of "the likelihood of successful prosecution, the social value of obtaining a conviction as against the time and expense to the State, and [the prosecutor's] own sense of justice in the particular case." *State v. Spicer*, 299 N.C. 309, 311 (1980) (internal quotations omitted); *S.S. Kresge Co. v. Davis*, 277 N.C. 654, 662 (1971); *State v. Blyther*, 175 N.C. App. 226, 228 (2005). As the North Carolina Supreme Court confirmed in *McNeill v. Harnett County*, 327 N.C. 552 (1990), interpretations of federal constitutional protections, while persuasive, do not control the North Carolina Supreme Court's construction of rights guaranteed by the North Carolina Constitution.

"Similarly situated" in federal courts. The Fourth Circuit has adopted a narrow interpretation of "similarly situated" for federal claims of selective prosecution. In *United States v. Olvis*, 97 F.3d 739, 744 (4th Cir. 1996), the Court held that defendants are similarly situated only "when their circumstances present no distinguishable legitimate prosecutorial factors that might justify making different prosecutorial decisions with respect to them." The *Olvis* court provided this list of possible legitimate prosecutorial factors justifying differential treatment of different offenders:

- the strength of the evidence against a particular defendant;
- the defendant's role in the crime;
- the defendant's candor and willingness to plead guilty;
- the amount of resources required to convict a defendant;
- the extent of prosecutorial resources;
- the potential impact of a prosecution on related investigations and prosecutions; and
- prosecutorial priorities for addressing specific types of illegal conduct.

Id.; *see also United States v. Khan*, 461 F.3d 477, 498 (4th Cir. 2006) (upholding denial of discovery motion on selective prosecution claim in reliance on the *Olvis* court's definition of "similarly situated"). According to the Fourth Circuit's formulation, if the individuals of another race who were treated more favorably than your client can be distinguished on any of the above-listed bases, they are not "similarly situated."

North Carolina courts are not bound by the narrow interpretation of "similarly situated" in *Olvis.* Some observers have posited that the definition announced in *Olvis* misconstrues the *Armstrong* holding, as the court appears to have replaced "similarly situated" with "identically situated." *See, e.g.*, Thomas P. McCarty, Note, United States v. Khan, *461 F.3d 477 (4th Cir. 2006): Discovering Whether "Similarly Situated" Individuals and the Selective Prosecution Defense Still Exist*, 87 NEB. L. REV. 538, 562 (2008) (arguing that *Olvis* elevated the similarly situated requirement announced in *Armstrong* by requiring that defendant and those receiving more favorable treatment be "virtually identical").

Other jurisdictions have adopted a more flexible approach to "similarly situated" in selective prosecution cases. A typical formulation, used by the Second Circuit, is that when identifying similarly situated individuals for comparison to the defendant, "exact correlation is neither likely nor necessary; the test is whether a prudent person would think them roughly equivalent." *Holmes v. Gaynor,* 313 F. Supp. 2d 345, 355 (S.D.N.Y. 2004) (quotation omitted); *see also Chavez v. Illinois State Police*, 251 F.3d 612, 636 (7th Cir. 2001) (in selective enforcement case court found no "magic formula" for determining who is similarly situated; the inquiry is a common sense one); *United States v. Lewis*, 517 F.3d 20, 27 (1st Cir. 2008) ("A similarly situated offender is one outside the protected class who has committed roughly the same crime under roughly the same circumstances but against whom the law has not been enforced.").

Illustrative cases: sufficient evidence of discriminatory effect. Whether similarly situated individuals must be virtually identical in all respects other than race, or merely similar, the defendant will need to present evidence substantiating his or her allegation that similarly situated individuals of another race received more favorable treatment. In the following cases, the court held or suggested that the evidence was sufficient to show that a defendant was treated less favorably than similarly situated suspects of a different race or races:

United States v. Jones, 159 F.3d 969 (6th Cir. 1998). The Sixth Circuit Court of Appeals held that, where the police department in Murfreesboro, Tennessee, over a five year span of time, referred only the Black defendant and his White co-defendant "for a federal prosecution that involved crack cocaine, and failed to refer for federal prosecution eight [non-Black defendants] who were arrested and prosecuted for crack cocaine," the defendant presented sufficient evidence to warrant discovery on a selective prosecution claim. While the number of defendants compared for purposes of alleging selective prosecution was small, the evidence of discriminatory intent in this case was fairly stark and may have been the deciding factor in the Court's ruling that the district court abused its discretion by denying the defendant's motion to compel discovery.

United States v. Greene, 697 F.2d 1229 (5th Cir. 1983). In a case that did not involve race, evidence that 300 people committed the same crime of participating in a strike while employed by the federal government, but only six (including three union leaders) were prosecuted, satisfied the first prong of the selective prosecution test. *Id.* at 1234 (cited with approval in *State v. Rogers*, 68 N.C. App. 358, 373 (1984)). In this case, the court was ruling on the merits of the defendants' claims, not on a discovery motion.

United States v. Wilson, 639 F.2d 500, 504 (9th Cir. 1981). In a case involving a claim of selective prosecution in response to the exercise of a constitutional right, the court assessed the merits of the defendants' claim, and found that evidence that hundreds of people committed the same tax-related offense as the defendant but an IRS investigator only recalled prosecuting tax protesters for the offense constituted some evidence of discriminatory effect. However, since defendants did not meet their burden of demonstrating that similarly situated offenders who did not exercise their constitutional right were treated differently, their selective prosecution claims did not succeed.

United States v. Tuitt, 68 F. Supp. 2d 4 (D. Mass. 1999). The federal district court found evidence of a significant racial disparity between federal and state defendants charged with similar crimes in the same geographic area sufficient to warrant discovery on a selective prosecution claim. In *Tuitt,* a Black defendant charged with a crack-cocaine offense in federal court presented evidence that Whites comprised 0% of defendants charged with crack-cocaine offenses in federal court in his region while they comprised at least 10% of defendants charged with crack-cocaine offenses in state court in his region. The court concluded that, by undertaking "a comprehensive survey of the local state courts in order to provide an appropriate comparison," the defendant had succeeded in demonstrating some evidence of similarly situated White defendants receiving more favorable treatment, and was therefore entitled to discovery on his claims. *See supra* "Significance of 'some evidence' of discriminatory effect and discriminatory intent" in § 5.3D, Elements of a Selective Prosecution Claim.

Illustrative cases: insufficient evidence of discriminatory effect. Courts have found the following evidence insufficient to meet the "similarly situated" test:

United States v. Bass, 536 U.S. 862 (2002). The United States Supreme Court held that a nationwide study showing that the federal government seeks the death penalty against

Black death-eligible defendants twice as often as White death-eligible defendants was insufficient to show some evidence of discriminatory effect. *See supra* "Significance of 'some evidence' of discriminatory effect and discriminatory intent" in § 5.3D, Elements of a Selective Prosecution Claim. The Court concluded that, "[e]ven assuming that the *Armstrong* requirement can be satisfied by a nationwide showing (as opposed to a showing regarding the record of the decision-makers in respondent's case), raw statistics regarding overall charges say nothing about charges brought against *similarly situated defendants*. And the statistics regarding plea bargains are even less relevant, since respondent was offered a plea bargain but declined it."

United States v. Armstrong, 517 U.S. 456 (1996). The United States Supreme Court reversed a discovery order related to a defendant's selective prosecution claim where the defendant's evidence consisted of (1) an affidavit of a paralegal from a federal public defender's office stating that all 24 crack-cocaine cases resolved by the office over the course of a year involved Black defendants; (2) a newspaper article reporting that federal defendants charged with crack offenses are punished more severely than those charged with powder cocaine offenses and that almost all federal crack defendants are Black; (3) an affidavit recounting an attorney's conversation with a drug treatment center employee who stated that there are an equal number of White and non-White drug users and dealers; and (4) an affidavit from a criminal defense attorney who stated that non-Black crack offenders are typically prosecuted in state court. This evidence did not constitute "some evidence" of discriminatory effect because (1) the paralegal's affidavit did not identify that similarly situated offenders of other races were not prosecuted; (2) the newspaper article pertained to disparities produced by federal sentencing laws, not the decision to prosecute; and (3) the attorneys' affidavits consisted of hearsay, anecdotes, and personal conclusions.

In re United States, 397 F.3d 274 (5th Cir. 2005). The Fifth Circuit Court of Appeals has held that "sharing a charge alone," i.e., being charged with the same offense, is not enough to establish that two offenders are similarly situated. "A much stronger showing, and more deliberative analysis, is required before a district judge may permit open-ended discovery into a matter that goes to the core of a prosecutor's function." In this case, the Latino co-conspirators were not similarly situated to the Black defendant because, during the commission of the crime, the defendant had a greater opportunity than the co-conspirators to mitigate the harm caused by the crime.

Johnson v. Outlaw, 659 F. Supp. 2d 732, 736 (M.D.N.C. 2009). Vague claims that similarly situated persons of other races and/or from other counties were not indicted as habitual felons are insufficient to demonstrate discriminatory effect. The defendant's "failure to indicate the[] criminal histories [of those he alleged were similarly situated] is a critical omission where the issue is status as an habitual felon." *Id.* at 736–37.

State v. Parks, 146 N.C. App. 568 (2001). The North Carolina Court of Appeals ruled that, although prosecutors in one judicial district may have a policy of charging all eligible defendants as habitual felons while prosecutors in a neighboring district do not, this is not evidence of discriminatory effect, as it does not show that the defendant was treated differently than similarly situated individuals of a different race, religion, or other arbitrary classification.

State v. Rogers, 68 N.C. App. 358, 373 (1984). The North Carolina Court of Appeals concluded that a similarly situated "class of two members is too statistically small a sampling to accurately measure a claim of selective prosecution."

Evidence of discriminatory effect may be unnecessary in certain cases. When defense counsel has evidence of a direct admission of discriminatory intent by a prosecutor, it may not be necessary to present evidence of similarly situated members of another race receiving more favorable treatment. In *United States v. Armstrong*, the Supreme Court "reserve[d] the question whether a defendant must satisfy the similarly situated requirement in a case involving direct admissions by prosecutors of discriminatory purpose." 517 U.S. 456, 469 n.3 (1996) (internal quotation omitted). In *United States v. Al Jibori*, 90 F.3d 22, 25–27 (2d. Cir. 1996), the Government introduced into evidence an affidavit of an Assistant U.S. Attorney explaining that the defendant was prosecuted for presenting a false passport at least in part because of his Iraqi national origin. Even in the absence of some evidence of discriminatory effect, this affidavit was enough to cause the U.S. Court of Appeals for the Second Circuit to remand the defendant's case for further inquiry into his selective prosecution claim. *See supra* "Significance of 'some evidence' of discriminatory effect and discriminatory intent" in § 5.3D, Elements of a Selective Prosecution Claim.

F. Second Prong of a Selective Prosecution Claim: Discriminatory Intent

The second element of a selective prosecution claim is discriminatory intent. To demonstrate that differential treatment was "motivated by a discriminatory purpose," *Armstrong*, 517 U.S. 456, 465, the defendant must show that the prosecutor's action was "deliberately based upon an unjustifiable standard such as race, religion, or other arbitrary classification." *Oyler v. Boles*, 368 U.S. 448, 456 (1962). As with claims of selective enforcement, discriminatory intent in a selective prosecution claim may be proven with direct or circumstantial evidence. *See supra* § 2.3C, Elements of a Selective Enforcement Claim.

There is some uncertainty about what sort of evidence would satisfy the defendant's burden to demonstrate discriminatory intent in a case of selective prosecution. In the leading case of *United States v. Armstrong*, 517 U.S. 456 (1996), the court ruled that the defendants had not presented sufficient evidence of discriminatory effect to warrant discovery, and the court therefore declined to consider the defendant's evidence of discriminatory intent. *See United States v. Thorpe*, 471 F.3d 652, 659 (6th Cir. 2006) ("For the purpose of satisfying the discriminatory-intent prong, what 'some evidence' means is not entirely clear."); *United States v. Tuitt*, 68 F. Supp. 2d 4, 10 (D. Mass. 1999) (concluding that since the *Armstrong* Court "claims to address the discriminatory *effect* element only . . . it is hard to tell what evidence of *intent* a defendant must produce in order to obtain discovery," and noting that the Court "in some ways appears to conflate the elements of effect and intent"); *see also supra* "Significance of 'some evidence' of discriminatory effect and discriminatory intent" in § 5.3D, Elements of a Selective Prosecution Claim. No United States Supreme Court case decided since *Armstrong* has addressed the proof necessary to show discriminatory intent.

Intent may be inferred where evidence of discriminatory effect is stark. In cases where the discriminatory effect is extreme, the discriminatory effect itself may satisfy the discriminatory intent prong. *See Gomillion v. Lightfoot*, 364 U.S. 339 (1960); *Yick Wo v. Hopkins*, 118 U.S. 356 (1886). "If the Supreme Court [in *Armstrong*] meant to hold defendants to actual knowledge of a discriminatory choice on the part of a prosecutor . . . the discovery standard [the standard at issue in the case] would be impossible to meet. It is exceedingly rare for a prosecutor to admit that the decision to prosecute was based on ethnicity or nationality." *United States v. Tuitt*, 68 F. Supp. 2d 4, 10 (D. Mass. 1999) (concluding that "[t]he evidence offered by Defendant suggests not only a discriminatory effect but—given the fact that no whites were prosecuted federally, although whites were prosecuted in the state courts—an inference of discriminatory intent"). *See also Washington v. Davis*, 426 U.S. 229, 254 (1976) (Stevens J., concurring) ("the line between discriminatory purpose and discriminatory impact is not . . . bright"); *United States v. Thorpe*, 471 F.3d 652, 661 (6th Cir. 2006) (recognizing that, if severe enough, statistical evidence of discriminatory effect can raise an inference of discriminatory intent); *United States v. Alameh*, 341 F.3d 167, 173 (2d Cir. 2003) (discriminatory purpose "may . . . be demonstrated through circumstantial or statistical evidence").

For purposes of obtaining discovery, evidence of discriminatory impact, alone or in combination with other evidence, may constitute "some evidence" of discriminatory intent for purposes of obtaining additional discovery. *See supra* "Significance of 'some evidence' of discriminatory effect and discriminatory intent" in § 5.3D, Elements of a Selective Prosecution Claim; *see also infra* § 5.4A, Obtaining Discovery Relevant to a Selective Prosecution Claim. The Supreme Court has held that discriminatory "impact alone is [rarely] determinative and the Court must look to other evidence" to find discriminatory intent. *Arlington Heights v. Metro Hous. Dev. Corp.*, 429 U.S. 252, 266 (1977). This formulation suggests that, while discriminatory impact "alone" will not sustain a prima facie case, it may constitute "some evidence" of discriminatory intent, and "some evidence" is all that a defendant pursuing a selective prosecution claim needs at the discovery stage. *See United States v. Armstrong*, 517 U.S. 456, 468–69 (1996) (holding that, before defendant will be granted discovery on a claim of selective prosecution, he must show some evidence supporting such a claim); *Roberts v. United States*, 741 F.3d 152, 161 (D.C. Cir. 2014) (in a ruling on the merits, evidence of disparate impact was not irrelevant to equal protection claim but could not sustain it without evidence of discriminatory intent). *But cf. United States v. Thorpe*, 471 F.3d 652, 661 (6th Cir. 2006) (rejecting defendant's argument that "the government's pursuit of a program despite knowledge of that program's discriminatory effect is by itself 'some evidence' of discriminatory intent").

Practice note: In proving discriminatory intent, defendants should distinguish their claims from those in *McCleskey v. Kemp*, 481 U.S. 279 (1987), a capital case in which the Court ruled that discriminatory purpose could not be proven by system-wide statistical findings suggesting disparate impact. The *McCleskey* court acknowledged that it had "accepted statistics as proof of intent to discriminate in other contexts," but concluded that such evidence was not sufficient in the capital sentencing context, because the nature of that decision and the "relationship of the statistics to that decision are fundamentally different." *Id.* at 294–95.

In a non-capital case, a pretrial claim of selective prosecution will generally differ from the claim raised in *McCleskey* because it will focus on a single prosecutor or group of prosecutors instead of countless jurors and prosecutors, and because it will typically be filed shortly after the initiation of prosecution rather than "years after" the defendant has been convicted. *Id.* at 296 (quotation omitted); *see also Belmontes v. Brown*, 414 F.3d 1094, 1127 (9th Cir. 2005) ("statistics relating to the charging entity . . . are materially more probative of discrimination in capital charging than those considered by the Supreme Court in *McCleskey* . . . [and consequently] may support a prima facie showing of unlawful charging discrimination"), *rev'd on other grounds sub nom Ayers v. Belmontes*, 549 U.S. 7 (2006). Also, in cases in which defendants are seeking discovery, they can point out that the *McCleskey* ruling concerned the standard of proof necessary for proving discriminatory intent, not for seeking discovery.

G. Gathering Evidence to Support Selective Prosecution Claims

Gathering evidence of discriminatory effect. To develop a claim of selective prosecution on the basis of race, a defendant generally will need to examine statistical data from his or her judicial district. In some cases, extensive data collection may not be necessary, as when the defendant argues that he or she has been treated less favorably than similarly situated co-defendants in the case on account of race. *See, e.g., United States v. Jones*, 159 F.3d 969 (6th Cir. 1998) (police officers' custom-made t-shirts celebrating arrest of two Black defendants—but not their White co-defendant—along with postcard sent by police officer to Black defendant awaiting trial featuring Black woman with bananas on her head constituted evidence of discriminatory intent). In such cases, evidence from the defendant's case may be sufficient to demonstrate racially disparate impact. However, in most cases, the defendants' claims will be broader in scope and will require data beyond that produced in his or her case.

Statistics sufficient to demonstrate the discriminatory effect prong of a selective prosecution claim (discussed *supra* in § 5.3E, First Prong of a Selective Prosecution Claim: Discriminatory Effect) will compare the group to which a selective prosecution claimant belongs with similarly situated individuals of other races. For example, a Black man in Durham County indicted as a habitual felon with an underlying offense of armed robbery and a prior record level of IV might gather data on the percentage of cases in which prosecutors have sought habitual felon indictments for other men in the geographic area with the same charge and record level, and examine whether the rates differ for offenders based on race.

Attorneys may obtain data from a variety of sources, including the ACIS computer system maintained by the Administrative Office of the Courts, which includes race of defendants, and the superior court docket sheets maintained by the Clerk of Court. *See* Habitual Felon Motion and Affidavit (using such sources in a motion to dismiss based on selective enforcement and selective prosecution) in the Race Materials Bank at www.ncids.org (select "Training & Resources"). For a list of sources of statistics relevant to selective prosecution claims, see *infra* Chapter 10, Sources of Information about Matters of Race.

For those working in public defender offices, information contained in the records of their own offices may prove a good starting point. For example, internal data reflecting the racial and ethnic makeup of clients facing drug charges or habitual felon sentencing enhancements and the outcome in those cases, including plea arrangements, may prove useful in litigating selective prosecution claims. Additionally, data on prosecutions for similar crimes in federal court, broken down by race, may provide evidence of differential treatment by state prosecutors of similarly situated offenders. *See United States v. Armstrong*, 517 U.S. 456, 470 (1996) (suggesting that one strategy for collecting evidence of selective prosecution in federal prosecution is to compare whether similarly situated persons of other races were prosecuted in state court but not in federal court); *United States v. Tuitt*, 68 F. Supp. 2d 4 (D. Mass. 1999). Coordination with regional federal defender offices may facilitate gathering and analysis of such data. *See also* Bureau of Justice Statistics, *Federal Criminal Case Processing Statistics*, BJS.GOV (last visited Aug. 7, 2014) (a searchable database maintained by the U.S. Department of Justice).

Additionally, public health records may contain information about the estimated percentage of Black drug users in a given region over a certain time period, which can be compared with the percentage of Black defendants charged with drug possession in that region during the same time period. *See, e.g.*, KATHERINE BECKETT, RACE AND DRUG LAW ENFORCEMENT IN SEATTLE 28–34 (2008); *see also* Substance Abuse and Mental Health Services Administration, *Data, Outcomes, and Quality*, SAMHSA.GOV (last visited Aug. 8, 2014). A report analyzing the racial and ethnic ethnographic composition of participants in the illegal drug market in Seattle, Washington contains examples of the types of data sources that may prove useful in conducting such comparisons, including drug use surveys of city residents, drug use surveys of public school students, mortality data collected by the Medical Examiner's office, a survey conducted at a public health needle exchange agency, drug treatment admission data collected by the State, and an observational study of two of the city's open air drug markets. KATHERINE BECKETT, RACE AND DRUG LAW ENFORCEMENT IN SEATTLE (2008).

Some district attorney's offices may be willing to collect data regarding prosecutorial decisions to learn whether race is playing a role in them. Professor Angela Davis suggests that prosecutors employ Racial Impact Statements to examine the influence of race or ethnicity in prosecutions in their region and make the results of such analyses publicly available. Angela Davis, *Prosecution and Race: The Power and Privilege of Discretion*, 67 FORDHAM L. REV. 13, 54 (1998). One resource available to interested prosecutors is the Vera Institute of Justice's Prosecution and Racial Justice Program, which partners with district attorneys' offices to analyze the racial impact of their discretionary decisions and to promote transparency regarding the results of their analysis and the programs instituted to address any discriminatory practices. *See infra* § 5.5, Beyond Litigation.

To meet the standards facing selective prosecution claimants, defendants will often need to partner with social scientists, public health researchers, or other interested academics to collect and analyze data relevant to an appropriate pool of similarly situated offenders. The data collected should be extensive enough to reflect any possible patterns of selective prosecution. For example, if you are investigating prosecution patterns for a common charge such as marijuana possession, data reflecting a one-year time period including your client's charge may be sufficient to indicate any possible pattern of selective prosecution. Graduate students in political science, statistics, mathematics, or public administration at local universities may be interested in conducting some of the necessary analysis. *See* Habitual Felon Motion and Affidavit (explaining analysis of the habitual felon data submitted in support of defendant's selective prosecution and selective enforcement claim) in the Race Materials Bank at www.ncids.org (select "Training & Resources"). In light of the statistical showing that is generally required to demonstrate selective prosecution, a defendant may have grounds to request funds to hire a statistician. *Compare State v Moore*, 100 N.C. App. 217 (1990) (initial motion for statistical expert to analyze race discrimination in grand and petit juries granted; motion for funds for additional study denied), *rev'd on other grounds*, 329 N.C. 245 (1991), *with State v. Massey*, 316 N.C. 558 (1986) (finding defendant did not make adequate showing to warrant funds for a statistician). For a further discussion of requesting funds for expert assistance, see 1 NORTH CAROLINA DEFENDER MANUAL Ch. 5 (Experts and Other Assistance) (2d ed. 2013).

Gathering evidence of discriminatory intent. While *Armstrong* is not instructive on the subject of proving discriminatory intent, a broader survey of case law provides some guidance for lawyers about potential evidence of discriminatory intent:

- Evidence of the actions, statements, or practices of prosecutors will be most persuasive when it reflects the behavior of a narrow group of prosecutors in a specific county or even of a specific prosecutor. The Supreme Court in *Bass* suggested that a study revealing practices in a more discrete region would be more powerful than the broader showing of "nationwide statistics" presented by the defendant in that case. *United States v. Bass*, 536 U.S. 862, 863–64 (2002).
- Circumstantial evidence of factors other than disparate impact may constitute "some evidence" of discriminatory intent. *Johnson v. Outlaw*, 659 F. Supp. 2d 732, 737 (M.D.N.C. 2009) ("intent may be proved by circumstantial as well as direct evidence"). *See supra* "Significance of 'some evidence' of discriminatory effect and discriminatory intent" in § 5.3D, Elements of a Selective Prosecution Claim. For example, the "specific sequence of events leading up to the challenged decision also may shed some light on the decisionmaker's purposes." *Arlington Heights v. Metro Hous. Dev. Corp.*, 429 U.S. 252, 267 (1977); *see also United States v. Heatley*, 1999 WL 61816, at *16 (S.D.N.Y. Jan. 29, 1999) (unpublished) (in ruling on defendant's discovery motion in support of his selective prosecution claim, then-District Judge Sotomayor noted that intent may be established by "circumstantial evidence of

disproportionate impact"). In the selective prosecution context, that might include deviations from standard prosecutorial practices, such as a failure to offer a deferred prosecution in circumstances in which such an offer is generally made.

- Evidence that the prosecutor declined to prosecute one offender or group of offenders while proceeding against a comparable offender or group of offenders based on the ability or willingness of the non-charged group to pay restitution to a victim may demonstrate discriminatory intent. *In re Register*, 84 N.C. App. 336, 341, 352 (1987) (citations omitted) (prosecutor engaged in selective prosecution in violation of the Equal Protection Clause by making the ability of a juvenile to pay compensation the "determinative factor in the decision of whether to file a complaint as a juvenile petition"). This is an example of a race-neutral selective prosecution claim that, given the correlation between race and poverty, might serve as a useful tool in addressing potential racial disparities.
- Evidence that prosecutors "followed unusual discretionary procedures in deciding to prosecute" or failed to follow an office policy not to prosecute a certain crime may demonstrate discriminatory intent. *United States v. Greene*, 697 F.2d 1229, 1236 (5th Cir. 1983); *see also United States v. Falk*, 479 F.2d 616 (7th Cir. 1973) (defendant's evidence of unusual procedures, including an agreement between the military and the Department of Justice that they would not prosecute registrants who turned in their draft cards rather than burning them, succeeded in shifting burden to prove nondiscriminatory intent to government); *United States v. Steele*, 461 F.2d 1148 (9th Cir. 1972) (same).
- The U.S. Supreme Court "has accepted statistics as proof of intent to discriminate in certain limited contexts." *McCleskey v. Kemp*, 481 U.S. 279, 293 (1987) (explaining that "statistical proof normally must present a 'stark' pattern to be accepted as the sole proof of discriminatory intent under the Constitution"). Statistical evidence alone may be sufficient to show discriminatory intent if it involves extensive data collection, rigorous statistical analysis, and findings of gross disparities. In extreme cases, raw data has been stark enough on its own to demonstrate discriminatory intent. For example, in *Yick Wo v. Hopkins*, 118 U.S. 356 (1886), where a race-neutral ordinance was applied against all Chinese laundry-shop operators but not against other similarly situated laundry-shop operators and sophisticated multiple regression studies were not available, "the raw statistics were still accepted by the Supreme Court as proof of discriminatory intent." Kristen E. Kruse, Comment, *Proving Discriminatory Intent in Selective Prosecution Challenges - An Alternative Approach to United States v. Armstrong*, 58 SMU L. REV. 1523, 1542 (2005); *see also McCleskey v. Kemp*, 481 U.S. 279, 293 n.12 (recognizing *Yick Wo* as a case in which raw data alone was sufficient to demonstrate both the discriminatory effect and discriminatory intent prongs of a selective prosecution claim); *United States v. Armstrong*, 517 U.S. 456, 466 (1996) (same). Even if insufficient alone to show discriminatory intent, statistical analysis may be used to bolster other evidence of discriminatory intent. *See supra* "Intent may be inferred where evidence of discriminatory effect is stark" in § 5.3F, Second Prong of a Selective Prosecution Claim: Discriminatory Intent.

- Discriminatory intent may be demonstrated by "direct admissions by [prosecutors] of discriminatory purpose." *United States v. Al Jibori*, 90 F.3d 22, 25 (2d. Cir. 1996). In *Al Jibori*, the Government submitted an affidavit from an Assistant U.S. Attorney explaining that one of the reasons the defendant was prosecuted for presenting a false passport was his Iraqi national origin. *Id.* This apparently discriminatory purpose was confirmed by another Assistant U.S. Attorney on questioning from the district judge at a hearing on the matter. This evidence was enough to cause the U.S. Court of Appeals for the Second Circuit to remand the defendant's case for further inquiry into his selective prosecution claim. *Id.* at 26–27.
- Demonstrating the prosecutor's awareness of similarly situated offenders receiving preferable treatment may help establish discriminatory intent. *See, e.g.*, *State v. Rogers*, 68 N.C. App. 358, 373 (1984) (defendant failed to show that "he was deliberately prosecuted on the basis of any impermissible ground" in part because he "presented no evidence to show that the [similarly situated offender] was called to the attention of a prosecutor"). In *Armstrong*, the U.S. Supreme Court suggested that the defendants may have been able to meet the discovery standard if they had investigated whether similarly situated defendants of other races were "known to . . . law enforcement officers, but . . . not prosecuted." *United States v. Armstrong*, 517 U.S. 456, 470 (1996). Attorneys can create a record that prosecutors were aware of similarly situated offenders by putting them on notice in writing and filing it with the court.

5.4 Making Out a Claim of Selective Prosecution

A. Obtaining Discovery Relevant to a Selective Prosecution Claim

Importance of discovery to selective prosecution claims. Discovery is important in a selective prosecution claim, as the decisions made by prosecutors generally are not publicly available. Therefore, evidence of discriminatory practices is difficult to uncover without discovery. *See Wayte*, 470 U.S. 598, 624 (Marshall J., dissenting) ("[M]ost of the relevant proof in selective prosecution cases will normally be in the Government's hands."). Where the State fails to comply with a discovery order pertaining to a selective prosecution claim, the court may impose sanctions, including potentially dismissal. *See People v. Ochoa*, 212 Cal. Rptr. 4 (Cal. Ct. App. 1985) (where the State refused to comply with a discovery order related to defendants' claim of selective prosecution based on race and the discovery materials would have allowed defendants to compare the population of offenders to the population of defendants prosecuted, the trial court properly dismissed the charges against the defendants).

Discovery standard announced in *United States v. Armstrong*. In interpreting federal rules, the United States Supreme Court held that, because a selective prosecution claim is not a defense to the merits of a criminal charge but instead is an independent claim of prosecutorial misconduct, discovery related to selective prosecution allegations will be granted only if defendants first demonstrate "some evidence" of discriminatory effect and discriminatory intent. *See United States v. Armstrong*, 517 U.S. 456, 463 (1996); *see also United States v. Bass*, 536 U.S. 862, 863 (2002) (per curiam). The *Armstrong* court stated that the "showing necessary to obtain discovery should itself be a significant barrier to the litigation of insubstantial claims." 517 U.S. 456, 464. This creates what some have described as a Catch 22: selective prosecution claimants "cannot even get discovery without evidence, and one can rarely get evidence which will satisfy a court without discovery." Gabriel J. Chin, *Race, the War on Drugs, and the Collateral Consequences of Criminal Conviction,* 6 J. GENDER RACE & JUST. 253, 267 (2002); Kristen E. Kruse, Comment, *Proving Discriminatory Intent in Selective Prosecution Challenges - An Alternative Approach to United States v. Armstrong*, 58 SMU L. REV. 1523, 1534 (2005). While the discovery standard applicable to selective prosecution claims in federal court is rigorous, it is "less stringent" than that required to prove a selective prosecution claim on the merits. *United States v. James*, 257 F.3d 1173, 1178 (10th Cir. 2001). As one court observed, "defendants need not establish a prima facie case of selective prosecution to obtain discovery on these issues." *Id.*

In some federal criminal cases decided after *Armstrong*, courts have found that defendants presented the requisite "some evidence" of discriminatory effect and intent to satisfy the discovery standard. *See United States v. Jones*, 159 F.3d 969 (6th Cir. 1998) (police officers' custom-made t-shirts celebrating arrest of two Black defendants—but not their White co-defendant—along with postcard sent by police officer to Black defendant awaiting trial featuring Black woman with bananas on her head constituted prima facie evidence of discriminatory intent; referral of Black defendant for federal prosecution of crack cocaine charges combined with failure to refer for federal prosecution eight non-Black defendants who were arrested and prosecuted for crack cocaine charges constituted "some evidence" of discriminatory effect); *United States v. Tuitt*, 68 F. Supp. 2d 4 (D. Mass. 1999) (where Black defendant was federally prosecuted for crack cocaine charges, evidence that no Whites were prosecuted for crack cocaine charges in four federal courts during a time period in which some Whites were prosecuted for crack cocaine charges in state courts in the same area constituted sufficient evidence of discriminatory effect and discriminatory intent for purpose of obtaining discovery).

Discovery related to selective prosecution claims in North Carolina courts. Since few North Carolina appellate cases have addressed selective prosecution claims in any detail, it is unclear whether North Carolina has adopted the discovery standard announced in *Armstrong*. In a case interpreting a previous version of North Carolina's discovery statute, the court denied discovery in a selective prosecution claim. *See State v. Rudolph*, 39 N.C. App. 293 (1979) (where defendant challenged prosecutor's "career criminal" program as a non-legislative enactment of a criminal law, defendant was not entitled to discovery of materials related to the program because, under previous version of discovery statute, they were not material to the preparation of the defense, intended for use by the State as evidence, or obtained from the defendant). However, now that North Carolina's discovery statute is broader, it may be easier for defendants to obtain such materials. *See* G.S. 15A-903; 1 NORTH CAROLINA DEFENDER MANUAL § 4.3 (Discovery Rights under G.S. 15A-903) (2d ed. 2013). Further, whether or not the discovery statute specifically authorizes discovery related to claims of selective prosecution, the trial court has inherent authority to order disclosure if the discovery statutes do not specifically restrict disclosure. *See State v. Hardy*, 293 N.C. 105 (1977).

Type of discovery relevant to selective prosecution claims. When seeking discovery on a selective prosecution claim, the defendant should request information that will allow him to analyze whether race played a role in the prosecutorial decisions made in his case. The following example, from a selective prosecution claim in a federal cocaine prosecution, illustrates the type of information commonly sought by defendants raising claims of selective prosecution:

> 1. A list of all federal cases in which the defendant has been charged with a cocaine offense, specifying whether the charge involved cocaine base or cocaine powder.
>
> 2. The racial or ethnic identity of each defendant in the listed case.
>
> 3. A statement identifying (a) each of the law enforcement agencies, including joint federal-state-local task forces or other inter-Governmental organizations, involved in the selection of targets for investigation of cocaine powder or cocaine base criminal offenses, and (b) the policies followed in making that determination.
>
> 4. Statements identifying (a) the agencies involved and (b) the policies followed in determining which particular persons will be prosecuted in state or federal court.
>
> 5. A statement of the practices followed in implementing each policy articulated in response to requests 3(b) and 4(b) including articulable criteria employed in actual practice.
>
> 6. An explanation of how the decisions to investigate and prosecute Defendant [] in the present case were made and how they were compliant with the policy and practices articulated in responses to requests 3 through 5.

United States v. Tuitt, 68 F. Supp. 2d 4, 17 (D. Mass. 1999).

Additionally, defendants may want to request any standards, policies, practices, or criteria employed by the district attorney's office to guard against the influence of racial, political, or other arbitrary or invidious factors in the selection of cases and defendants for prosecution. *See* Selective Prosecution Motion in the Race Materials Bank at www.ncids.org (select "Training & Resources"). The absence of such policies, in conjunction with other evidence, may lend support to a selective prosecution claim.

In some cases, the type of information described above may be voluntarily disclosed by the prosecution without the need for court-ordered discovery. *See, e.g., United States v.*

Olvis, 97 F.3d 739, 743 (4th Cir. 1996); *United States v. Turner* 104 F.3d 1180 (9th Cir. 1997); *United States v. Graham*, 146 F.3d 6, 9 (1st Cir. 1998).

B. Selective Prosecution Motion

Form of the motion. Claims of selective prosecution should be raised in motions to dismiss all charges. The grounds for the motion to dismiss in a selective prosecution case are the Equal Protection Clause of the Fourteenth Amendment to the U.S. Constitution and article I, section 19 of the N.C. Constitution.

Motions to dismiss the indictment might be filed along with a motion in the alternative for discovery. The motions should include a description of all direct, circumstantial, and statistical evidence tending to show discriminatory effect and discriminatory intent in a defendant's prosecution, and should be accompanied by supporting exhibits. *See* Habitual Felon Motion and Selective Prosecution Motion in the Race Materials Bank at www.ncids.org (select "Training & Resources"). If the court does not find the evidence sufficient to dismiss the indictment, it may find a sufficient basis for granting the motion for additional discovery.

Timing of the motion. A selective prosecution claim should be raised pretrial or it may be deemed waived. *See, e.g.*, *People v. Carter*, 450 N.Y.S.2d 203 (N.Y. App. Div. 1982).

C. Burden of Proof and Relief

"To prevail on a selective prosecution challenge, a defendant must first make a prima facie showing that he has been singled out for prosecution while others similarly situated and committing the same acts have not." *State v. Rogers*, 68 N.C. App. 358, 367 (1984) (quotation omitted). A defendant alleging "that he has been selectively prosecuted . . . must establish discrimination by a clear preponderance of proof." *State v. Pope*, 213 N.C. App. 413, 415–16 (2011) (internal quotation omitted). The burden shifting that occurs after a defendant sustains a prima facie case of selective prosecution is explained in Chapter 2. *See supra* § 2.3E, Burden of Proof and Burden Shifting.

When a criminal defendant prevails on a selective prosecution claim, the proper remedy is dismissal. *State v. Howard*, 78 N.C. App. 262, 266 (1985) (discussing this right in the context of selective enforcement); *see also supra* "Dismissal" in § 2.3F, Remedy for an Equal Protection Violation. It follows that if the selective prosecution concerns an enhancement, such as habitualization, the remedy would be dismissal of the enhancement. Any lesser remedy would be inadequate. *But see United States v. Armstrong*, 517 U.S. 456, 461 n.2 (1996) ("We have never determined whether dismissal of the indictment, or some other sanction, is the proper remedy if a court determines that a defendant has been the victim of prosecution on the basis of his race.").

Dismissal may also be a sanction for discovery violations. *See generally* G.S. 15A-910 (listing permissible discovery sanctions). Where the trial court orders the State to produce discovery relevant to the defendant's selective prosecution claim and the State refuses to comply with the discovery order, the court may dismiss the indictment. *See People v. Ochoa*, 212 Cal. Rptr. 4 (Cal. Ct. App. 1985).

D. Evidentiary Hearing

The North Carolina Supreme Court has held that defendants are entitled to an evidentiary hearing on a selective prosecution claim if they present "substantial evidence" of discrimination. *State v. Spicer*, 299 N.C. 309, 314 (1980); *see also State v. Rogers*, 68 N.C. App. 358, 367 (1984). Where a defendant presents "no evidence that he was subjected to any intentional or deliberate discrimination upon any unjustifiable standard," he will not be granted an evidentiary hearing on his selective prosecution claim. *Spicer*, 299 N.C. 309, 312. In considering the defendant's selective prosecution claim in *State v. Rogers*, 68 N.C. App. 358, 371 (1984), the North Carolina Court of Appeals observed that, while "the trial court did not conduct a full evidentiary hearing and take the testimony of witnesses, the court did consider defendant's proffer of proof and statements made by the attorneys which, without objection, were received as evidence. Based on these, the court made extensive findings of fact and conclusions of law that the prosecution did not result from impermissible considerations." In these circumstances, the court ruled that the "hearing afforded the defendant in this case met the requirements of due process." *Id.* at 371 n.4.

Spicer does not specify whether "substantial evidence" constitutes something less than a prima facie showing, but the court's use of that term suggests that less is required. Federal courts have reached different conclusions about whether a defendant must establish a prima facie showing of selective prosecution before an evidentiary hearing will be granted. *See, e.g., United States v. Peterson*, 652 F.3d 979, 982 (8th Cir. 2011) (suggesting that the applicable standard is "some evidence"); *United States v. Parham*, 16 F.3d 844, 848 n.1 (8th Cir. 1994) (Heaney, J., dissenting) (noting split); *United States v. Bourgeois*, 964 F.2d 935, 938 (9th Cir. 1992) (requiring prima facie case); *United States v. Silien*, 825 F.2d 320, 322 (11th Cir. 1987) ("An evidentiary hearing is not automatically required; instead, the defendant must present facts 'sufficient to create a reasonable doubt about the constitutionality of a prosecution. . . .'" (citation omitted)).

E. Success on the Merits

Defendants appealing a trial court's denial of a selective prosecution claim have achieved success on the merits in North Carolina appellate courts on at least one occasion, although it did not involve race discrimination. In *In re Register*, 84 N.C. App. 336, 347 (1987), the North Carolina Court of Appeals dismissed juvenile petitions against several co-defendants after finding that a prosecutor engaged in selective prosecution in violation of the Equal Protection Clause by making the ability of a juvenile to pay compensation to a victim the "determinative factor in the decision of whether to file a complaint as a juvenile petition."

5.5 Beyond Litigation

Partnerships. The high bar set by the United States Supreme Court in *United States v. Armstrong*, 517 U.S. 456 (1996) "establishes the need for creative non-judicial remedies" in addressing potential issues of race in prosecutorial decisions. Angela Davis, *Prosecution and Race: The Power and Privilege of Discretion*, 67 FORDHAM L. REV. 13, 42 (1998). For example, external organizations have worked with prosecutors to analyze their record of decision-making and exercise of discretion. The Vera Institute's Prosecution and Racial Justice Program (PRJ) partners with prosecutors "to enhance fairness, efficiency, and accountability and to address unwarranted racial disparity in the exercise of discretion[;] . . . serve[s] as a resource for research, technical assistance, innovation, and policy development; and . . . seek[s] to engage communities in improving prosecutorial accountability[.]" Alice Chasan, *Q & A with Whitney Tymas, Director of the Prosecution and Racial Justice Program*, JUST 'CAUSE, Summer/Fall 2012, at 4, 4–5. The first step taken by the PRJ when working with a prosecutors' office is to "present them with an accurate picture of what is actually happening in their offices" by "analyz[ing] voluminous data to see whether they are exercising discretion in a racially neutral way." This analysis consists of multivariate statistical calculations controlling for a number of factors to isolate the influence of race at various decision points. *Id.* Prosecutor's offices in Milwaukee, Wisconsin; Mecklenburg County, North Carolina; San Diego, California; Lancaster County, Nebraska; and Manhattan, New York have worked with the PRJ to collect and analyze data reflecting the exercise of prosecutorial discretion.

The PRJ attributes its success in finding prosecutors' offices to partner with to the "great benefits associated with getting in front of the toxic issue of race and addressing it head on." *Id.* Among other things, such efforts may help ease "[t]ensions . . . between prosecutors and . . . the general public." As Whitney Tymas explains:

> Prosecutors are often frustrated by weak participation among communities, particularly in the context of violent crime. They complain that witnesses won't come forward, victims won't testify, and therefore even cases most needing attention can't be prosecuted successfully—meaning less justice and safety for everyone. We help potential partners recognize that working with PRJ will increase their accountability to the communities that trust them least, leading to better public safety outcomes.

Id.; *see also* BESIKI KUTATELADZE ET AL., VERA INSTITUTE OF JUSTICE, RACE AND PROSECUTION IN MANHATTAN 3 (2014) (quoting Manhattan District Attorney Cyrus R. Vance, Jr. as stating: "The shame is not in finding that we have unconscious biases or that our current policies have a disproportionate racial impact—the shame lies in refusing to ask the questions and correct the problems.").

Case study: Partnership between the Vera Institute's Prosecution and Racial Justice Program and the Mecklenburg County District Attorney's office. One of the first partnerships formed by the PRJ was with the Mecklenburg County District Attorney's Office (MCDA) in 2005. That partnership is the subject of the reflections of Peter S. Gilchrist III, Mecklenburg County District Attorney (Ret.) 1974–2010, below.

Around 2003, Nick Turner and Dan Wilhelm of the Vera Institute of Justice (Vera) told me that they were interested in studying how prosecutors make discretionary decisions. I stated that I was interested in related topics: early screening of cases, allocation of limited resources, identification of active and repeat offenders, and consistency in treatment of like offenders.

Our conversations continued intermittently and in 2005 when their Prosecution and Racial Justice Program (PRJ) was launched, the Mecklenburg County District Attorney's Office (MCDA) was invited to join as a partner. The goal of this partnership was to develop data collection systems that would allow our office to identify and address racial disparities in the exercise of prosecutorial discretion. The vision of the PRJ—to enhance fairness and efficiency in prosecutions and reduce unwarranted racial and ethnic disparities by collecting empirical data about the exercise of prosecutorial discretion—is one that I wholeheartedly endorse. Data collection is important because it allows district attorneys to better understand what's going on in their own offices. Also, the release of such information to the public increases transparency, accountability, and trust between prosecutors and the communities they serve.

When I informed my staff that I had invited Vera's researchers into our office, I joked that I felt like I had invited a bunch of termites into my house. I knew that they might uncover troubling data, but was committed to the project of examining and addressing any possible problems they discovered. Before starting the project I informed Vera that our existing, paper-based data collection system was completely inadequate. Very little of the data that Vera needed to conduct their analyses was available in our files. Vera made an independent review of our local and state court data as well as police department data and decided that we could still proceed.

After trying to work with our data systems Vera determined that it was too problematic. This led to a joint effort by Vera and our staff to develop a more robust, electronic data collection system called MeckStat that allowed us to conduct a more informed examination of our discretionary decisions. However, the limits of both available software and staff time led to the decision that the project could only examine drug cases. MeckStat represented a vast improvement over our paper-based data systems and ultimately became a model for a new, statewide data collection system implemented by the Administrative Office of the Courts. However, because certain data was not entered into the MeckStat system, it still wasn't robust enough to answer all the questions posed by the Vera researchers.

I was disappointed that our research partnership was inconclusive, but I was proud of and grateful for the unexpected benefits that resulted from this project. These benefits included the development of a better data collection system, both in our office and statewide; enhanced quality control in the handling of our drug cases; the reinforcement of polices—and the development of new policies—regarding the exercise of discretion; and engagement in a number of productive discussions regarding cases that Vera researchers flagged as outliers. I have absolutely no regrets about embarking upon this partnership. If North Carolina data collection systems continue to improve, I expect that even more meaningful conclusions could be drawn from these types of studies.

Guidelines. Another non-judicial remedy to address questions of race is the development of "race-sensitive guidelines for charging, discovery, bail/release recommendations, plea bargaining and prosecutorial diversion." *See* ASHLEY NELLIS ET AL., THE SENTENCING PROJECT, REDUCING RACIAL DISPARITY IN THE CRIMINAL JUSTICE SYSTEM: A MANUAL FOR PRACTITIONERS AND POLICYMAKERS 34 (2008). The American Bar Association and National District Attorneys Association standards may be useful in developing such guidelines. *Id.*; *see also* American Bar Association Criminal Justice Section Standards: Prosecution Function, Standard 3-3.1(b), Investigative Function of the Prosecutor ("A prosecutor should not invidiously discriminate against or in favor of any person on the basis of race, religion, sex, sexual preference, or ethnicity in exercising discretion to investigate or to prosecute. A prosecutor should not use other improper considerations in exercising such discretion."); National District Attorneys Association, National Prosecution Standards, Third Edition, Standard 3-1.2, Fairness in Investigations (criminal investigation may not be motivated by victim's or offender's race, ethnicity, religion, sexual orientation, or political affiliation), Standard 4-1.4, Factors Not to Consider (screening decision should be made without regard to characteristics of the accused that have been recognized as the basis for invidious discrimination), Standard 5-1.4, Uniform Plea Opportunities (plea agreement opportunities should be made without regard to the defendant's race, religion, sex, sexual orientation, national origin, or political association or belief), In addition to providing guidance to individual prosecutors, such guidelines may be useful in explaining to defense attorneys and the public how the office makes discretionary decisions, such as how to determine whether to seek the full punishment of the law or reduce or dismiss charges.

On a less formal level, prosecutors can create "meaningful liaisons with local community representatives to enhance their understanding of the community's concerns and ways in which the prosecution office can address them, and to enhance the public understanding of how their offices operate." ASHLEY NELLIS ET AL., THE SENTENCING PROJECT, REDUCING RACIAL DISPARITY IN THE CRIMINAL JUSTICE SYSTEM: A MANUAL FOR PRACTITIONERS AND POLICYMAKERS 37 (2008). Regular meetings with public defenders, law enforcement, judges, victims, and community representatives can provide a forum to explore racially sensitive issues. Criminal defense attorneys can play a role in such discussions, as their work has familiarized them with the impact of prosecutorial decisions in individual cases and on communities generally.

Chapter 6
Composition of the Grand Jury and Trial Jury

6.1 Scope of Chapter

This chapter discusses the mix of constitutional and statutory requirements governing the composition of the jury pool from which grand jurors and trial (petit) jurors are ultimately selected. (Jury selection is addressed in Chapter 7 of this manual.) The fair cross-section requirement—grounded in the Sixth Amendment and article I, sections 24 and 26 of the North Carolina Constitution—requires that juries reflect the demographic composition of the surrounding communities. State and federal constitutional guarantees of equal protection protect against the race-based exclusion of people from jury service and selection as grand jury forepersons. This chapter describes the evidence required to establish those claims, reviews studies analyzing jury composition issues, and discusses the role of expert assistance in analyzing data. The chapter also discusses statutory requirements for the creation of a jury pool. Section 6.7 includes a glossary of terms used in North Carolina jury formation, as well as a flowchart illustrating the stages of the jury formation process.

Whatever the basis of a jury composition challenge, the starting place for exploring the viability of a potential claim is a request for discovery and a factual investigation of the policies, practices, and outcomes of the jury composition process in your county and judicial district. Because of the evidence necessary to litigate and sustain a fair cross-section, equal protection, or statutory challenge in the jury composition context, your factual investigation must begin well before the potential jurors enter the courtroom on your client's trial date. The types of information that you will need to support the claims discussed in this chapter include, among other things, procedures used to assemble the master jury list and to summon jurors; standards used to rule on hardship excusals; and the demographics of previous jury panels in your county. *See infra* § 6.5B, Mechanics of Challenging Jury Formation.

6.2 Overview

> When any large and identifiable segment of the community is excluded from jury service, the effect is to remove from the jury room

> qualities of human nature and varieties of human experience, the range of which is unknown and perhaps unknowable. It is not necessary to assume that the excluded group will consistently vote as a class in order to conclude, as we do, that its exclusion deprives the jury of a perspective on human events that may have unsuspected importance in any case that may be presented.

Peters v. Kiff, 407 U.S. 493, 503–04 (1972).

Although the right to be judged by a fair and impartial jury of one's peers is a bedrock principle of the American criminal justice system, jury pools from which jurors are selected do not necessarily reflect the racial and ethnic composition of the communities from which they are drawn. Courts "throughout the country have found minority underrepresentation in jury composition, most notably in the makeup of the jury pool from which the jury ultimately is selected." *See* NEBRASKA MINORITY AND JUSTICE TASK FORCE, FINAL REPORT 17 (2003) (noting that "many researchers have found that this is 'the rule' rather than the exception"); FLORIDA SUPREME COURT RACIAL & ETHNIC BIAS COMM'N, "WHERE THE INJURED FLY FOR JUSTICE": REFORMING PRACTICES WHICH IMPEDE THE DISPENSATION OF JUSTICE TO MINORITIES IN FLORIDA 13 (Deborah Hardin Wagner ed., 1991) ("The present system of selecting jurors . . . does not result in juries which are racial and ethnic composites of the community."); *see also* MINNESOTA SUPREME COURT TASK FORCE ON RACIAL BIAS IN THE JUDICIAL SYSTEM, FINAL REPORT 32 (1993) ("[J]ury pools rarely, if ever, are representative of the racial composition of our communities.").

A. Benefits of Representative Juries

Legitimacy of the criminal justice system. The right to trial by jury is protected by both the federal and North Carolina constitutions, and North Carolina citizens have a corresponding right to serve as jurors. Criminal defendants and potential jurors share an interest in a non-discriminatory jury formation process; the courts have therefore held that it is "necessary and appropriate for the defendant to raise the rights of the juror[s]" prevented from participating in jury service on account of their race. *Powers v. Ohio*, 499 U.S. 400, 414 (1991).

Juries play an important role in upholding democratic values by vesting decision-making authority in ordinary citizens. *See id.* at 406 ("The opportunity for ordinary citizens to participate in the administration of justice has long been recognized as one of the principal justifications for retaining the jury system."); *Balzac v. Porto Rico*, 258 U.S. 298, 310 (1922) ("The jury system postulates a conscious duty of participation in the machinery of justice. . . . One of its greatest benefits is in the security it gives the people that they, as jurors actual or possible, being part of the judicial system of the country can prevent its arbitrary use or abuse."). Reliance on juries "validates the justice system through community participation, provides a check against governmental abuses of power, educates citizens and promotes civic engagement, and promotes integration and mutual understanding across social groups." *State v. Saintcalle*, 309 P.3d 326, 368 (Wash. 2013) (Gonzalez, J., concurring). Exclusion or underrepresentation of racial minorities on juries undermines these democratizing effects. *See* EQUAL JUSTICE INITIATIVE, ILLEGAL RACIAL DISCRIMINATION IN JURY SELECTION: A CONTINUING LEGACY 38 (2010).

Juries and jury pools that underrepresent racial minorities also may create a perception of unfairness, a problem that is distinct from the actual fairness of decisions rendered by such juries. *Id.* (noting that "[c]ommunities of color across the country have rejected and continue to reject criminal verdicts handed down by all- or predominantly-white juries"). Juries are often faced with difficult, complicated questions, and the right answers may not always be popular. In such cases, the absence of diversity may make a questionable jury verdict difficult to accept. Leslie Ellis & Shari Seidman Diamond, *Race, Diversity, and Jury Composition: Battering and Bolstering Legitimacy*, 78 CHI.-KENT L. REV. 1033, 1048 (2003) (observers may be less likely to conclude that a trial is fair when an all-White jury finds a defendant guilty).

Jury deliberations. The racial composition of juries may affect jury deliberations. Some studies have concluded that racial diversity improves the deliberative processes of the jury. *See, e.g.*, NEIL VIDMAR & VALERIE P. HANS, AMERICAN JURIES: THE VERDICT 74 (2007) (concluding that research on heterogeneous decision-making groups supports claim that diversity on juries improves fact-finding); Kim Taylor-Thompson, *Empty Votes in Jury Deliberations*, 113 HARV. L. REV. 1261, 1285–95 (2000) (considering the influence of race on jury deliberations and observing that jurors of color may be more likely to raise the subject of race, thereby broadening the jury's discussion of relevant issues). In one study, researchers observed that mock juries that were racially diverse deliberated longer, considered a wider range of information, perceived evidence more accurately, were more likely to correct factual errors, and perceived themselves as more legitimate than all-White, homogeneous mock juror groups. Samuel R. Sommers, *On Racial Diversity and Group Decision Making: Identifying Multiple Effects of Racial Composition in Jury Deliberation*, 90 J. PERSONALITY & SOC. PSYCHOL. 597 (2006). Researchers conducting the study concluded that "diverse groups were also more open-minded in that they were less resistant to discussions of controversial race-related topics." *Id.* at 608.

Some researchers have found that the risk of racial bias is higher when issues of race are not "salient"—in other words, when they are present but not discussed. *See supra* § 1.3, Potential Factors Relevant to Racial Disparities in the Criminal Justice System; *see also* Sammuel R. Sommers & Phoebe C. Ellsworth, *Race in the Courtroom: Perceptions of Guilt and Dispositional Attributions*, 26 PERSONALITY & SOC. PSYCHOL. BULL. 1367 (2001). Diverse juries may be more likely to make the subject of race salient by openly discussing race. One researcher concluded that jurors on racially diverse juries are more likely to acknowledge the influence of race on their own perceptions and the perceptions of other jurors. William J. Bowers et al., *Crossing Racial Boundaries: A Closer Look at the Roots of Racial Bias in Capital Sentencing When the Defendant is Black and the Victim is White*, 53 DEPAUL L. REV. 1497, 1532 (2004). Another study suggests that diverse juries may be more likely to discuss sensitive issues of race, including racial profiling. Samuel R. Sommers, *Determinants and Consequences of Jury Racial*

Diversity: Empirical Findings, Implications and Directions for Future Research, 2 SOC. ISSUES & POL'Y REV. 65, 86 (2008); *see also* Ellen S. Cohn et al., *Reducing White Juror Bias: The Role of Race Salience and Racial Attitudes*, 39 J. APPLIED SOC. PSYCHOL. 1953 (2009).

Case outcomes. Some researchers have concluded that the racial composition of jury pools may influence case outcomes. For example, one recent study conducted by Duke University researchers found that when there are no potential Black jurors in the pool, Black defendants are more likely than Whites to be convicted of at least one crime (81% chance for Black defendants versus 66% chance for White defendants). *See* Shamena Anwar et al., *The Impact of Jury Race in Criminal Trials*, 127 Q. J. ECON. 1017, 1021, 1032 (2012) (concluding that "defendants of each race do relatively better when the jury pool contains more members of their own race"). The authors found this effect regardless of whether potential Black jurors are actually seated on a trial jury. This study found, for example, that juries formed from all-White jury pools convict Black defendants of drug crimes at a 25% higher rate than they convict White defendants. *Id.* at 1038. When at least one Black potential juror is added to the pool, conviction rates of White defendants rise and Black defendants fall. *Id.*

Other studies have concluded that the race of seated jurors influences case outcomes. *See, e.g.*, Nancy J. King, *Postconviction Review of Jury Discrimination: Measuring the Effects of Juror Race on Jury Decisions*, 92 MICH. L. REV. 63, 82–99 (1993); Tara L. Mitchell et al., *Racial Bias in Mock Juror Decision-Making: A Meta-Analytic Review of Defendant Treatment*, 29 LAW & HUM. BEHAV. 621, 633 (2005) (finding small but statistically significant influence of juror race on verdicts).

Sentencing. The racial composition of the seated jury also may make a difference in jury sentencing. In one study, researchers found that the racial composition of the jury affected sentencing in non-capital felony cases. *See* Howard C. Daudistel et al., *Effects of Defendant Ethnicity on Juries' Dispositions of Felony Cases*, 29 J. APPLIED SOC. PSYCHOL., 317 (1999). The study found that the higher the composition of Latinos in the jury, the longer the sentences received by white defendants. *Id.* Although North Carolina jurors in non-capital cases play a limited role in sentencing determinations, they make certain consequential determinations, such as assessing disputed aggravating factors and determining habitual felon status. G.S. 15A-1340.16(a3); G.S. 14-7.5.

B. Possible Causes of Unrepresentative Jury Pools

Underrepresentation on jury pools may result from a variety of practices and methods used to identify, qualify, and excuse potential jurors. Section 6.5 of this chapter explains in greater detail the methods used to form juries in North Carolina, along with strategies for addressing racial disparities that may arise at various stages of the jury formation process. Some examples of jury composition methods that may result in underrepresentation include:

- Exclusive reliance on voter registration lists. Voter registration lists are the most common source of juror names, and these lists tend to underrepresent Black and Latino citizens who are eligible to serve as jurors. *See* Nancy J. King, *Racial Jurymandering: Cancer or Cure? A Contemporary Review of Affirmative Action in Jury Selection*, 68 N.Y.U. L. REV. 707 (1993); *see also United States v. Weaver*, 267 F.3d 231, 244–45 (3d Cir. 2001) ("[I]f the use of voter registration lists over time did have the effect of sizably underrepresenting a particular class or group on the jury venire, then under some circumstances, this could [violate the Sixth Amendment]." (quotation omitted)).
- Reliance on a limited number of source lists that do not reflect the diversity of the jury-eligible community. *See* Paula Hannaford-Agor, *Systematic Negligence In Jury Operations: Why The Definition Of Systematic Exclusion In Fair Cross Section Claims Must Be Expanded*, 59 DRAKE L. REV. 761, 779–82 (2011). Even in jurisdictions where voter lists are supplemented with driver lists, as is the case in North Carolina, some studies have shown that exclusive reliance on these two lists underrepresents racial minorities. *See* ELIZABETH M. NEELEY, NEBRASKA MINORITY JUSTICE COMMITTEE, REPRESENTATIVE JURIES: EXAMINING THE INITIAL AND ELIGIBLE POOLS OF JURORS (2008).
- Insufficient renewal of master jury lists. Paula Hannaford-Agor, *Systematic Negligence In Jury Operations: Why The Definition Of Systematic Exclusion In Fair Cross Section Claims Must Be Expanded*, 59 DRAKE L. REV. 761, 782–83 (2011). When lists are "not updated frequently . . . people who move often, such as renters, are often omitted." Samuel R. Sommers, On the Obstacles to Jury Diversity, THE JURY EXPERT (American Society of Trial Consultants), Jan. 2009, at 1 (last visited Aug. 28, 2014).
- Jury composition methods that rely on the return of jury questionnaires and do not provide for subsequent steps to follow up on undelivered jury summonses. Paula Hannaford-Agor, *Systematic Negligence In Jury Operations: Why The Definition Of Systematic Exclusion In Fair Cross Section Claims Must Be Expanded*, 59 DRAKE L. REV. 761, 783–85 (2011). "[U]ndeliverable, disqualification, excusal and failure-to-appear rates tend to disproportionately decrease minority representation due to socio-economic factors such as mobility rates, criminal records, and financial hardship for lower-income individuals." National Center for State Courts, *Jury Managers Toolbox: A Primer on Fair Cross Section Jurisprudence*, NCSC CENTER FOR JURY STUDIES (2010); *see also* NEW YORK STATE UNIFIED COURT SYSTEM OFFICE OF COURT RESEARCH, JURY REPRESENTATIVENESS: A DEMOGRAPHIC STUDY OF JUROR QUALIFICATION AND SUMMONING IN MONROE COUNTY, NEW YORK (2011) (finding higher undeliverable rates, rates of non-response to qualification questionnaires, and excusals for service among Black people in Monroe County, New York).
- Glitches in automated jury composition systems. In some cases, computing errors have resulted in the unintended underrepresentation of racial minorities. For example, during a routine upgrade to the computerized voter system in Kent County, Michigan, the software was accidentally programmed to choose names from the first 125,000 names entered on the master jury list instead of from the entire list of 500,000 names. Since the list was sorted alphabetically by zip code and the greatest proportion of

Black people in Kent County lived in sequentially higher zip codes, the error suppressed Black representation on Kent County jury panels. Paula Hannaford-Agor, *Systematic Negligence In Jury Operations: Why The Definition Of Systematic Exclusion In Fair Cross Section Claims Must Be Expanded*, 59 DRAKE L. REV. 761, 770 (2011)

- Qualification methods that erroneously exclude racial minorities from jury service. For example, in North Carolina, persons convicted of a felony are eligible to serve as jurors once their citizenship rights have been restored. G.S. 9-3. However, unless this point is explained clearly in the juror summons, potential jurors may erroneously conclude that they are permanently disqualified as a result of a felony conviction.
- Jury composition systems that permanently remove names upon disqualification where the disqualification should have been categorized as temporary. For example, if a juror is disqualified because he or she does not speak English, is not a citizen, or has a felony conviction, his or her disqualification is temporary, and procedures should ensure that the juror's name is not permanently excluded from future juror lists. *See* NORTH CAROLINA ADMINISTRATIVE OFFICE OF THE COURTS, A MANUAL FOR NORTH CAROLINA JURY COMMISSIONERS AND CLERKS OF SUPERIOR COURT 10 (5th ed. 2013) (instructing that "if any persons were disqualified for reasons that are not permanent, then the commission must be sure that the reason for the disqualification remains if they are to be removed," and that "the jury commission should review the computer's list of persons previously found to be ineligible to be jurors regardless of the reason before any . . . names are deleted from the new jury list").
- Jury composition practices that do not address barriers to jury service for low-income individuals. These barriers include lengthy terms of jury service, low compensation, risk of job loss, and hardships related to transportation, homelessness or insecure housing, or childcare costs. Paula Hannaford-Agor, *Systematic Negligence In Jury Operations: Why The Definition Of Systematic Exclusion In Fair Cross Section Claims Must Be Expanded*, 59 DRAKE L. REV. 761, 785–88 (2011). Such barriers may produce racially disparate rates of hardship excusals, which may be granted before the potential juror enters the courthouse.

6.3 Fair Cross-Section Challenges

The Sixth Amendment guarantees criminal defendants an impartial jury, and "an essential component" of that guarantee is "the selection of a petit [trial] jury from a representative cross section of the community." *Taylor v. Louisiana*, 419 U.S. 522, 528 (1975). This right also may apply to grand juries. *See infra* "Application to grand jury" in subsection A., below.

Fair cross-section challenges to the composition of the grand and trial jury may be the most promising avenues of relief for defendants challenging racial disparities in jury formation. This is because, in contrast to equal protection claims, defendants raising fair cross-section challenges do not have to prove discrimination. *See* Nina W. Chernoff & Joseph B. Kadane, *The 16 Things Every Defense Attorney Should Know About Fair Cross-Section Challenges*, THE CHAMPION, Dec. 2013, at 14, 15 ("The Sixth Amendment fair cross-section claim is not concerned with discrimination; it is only concerned with whether the system has *produced* a representative jury pool, whether by accident or design."). As one court explained,

> An Equal Protection challenge concerns the *process* of selecting jurors, or the allegation that selection decisions were made with discriminatory intent. The Sixth Amendment, on the other hand, is concerned with *impact,* or the systematic exclusion of a co gnizable group regardless of how benevolent the reasons. It looks to discriminatory *effects,* while the Equal Protection clause looks to discriminatory *purposes.* Even practices that are race-neutral but have a disparate impact on the representation of a cognizable class in the jury venire fit within the Sixth Amendment's protections, while they would not be cognizable under the Equal Protection clause.

United States v. Green, 389 F. Supp. 2d 29, 51 (D. Mass. 2005) (emphasis in original) (internal citations omitted), *rev'd on other grounds,* 426 F.3d 1 (1st Cir. 2005); *see also United States v. Gelb*, 881 F.2d 1155, 1161 (2d Cir. 1989) (observing that the Sixth Amendment is stricter than the Equal Protection Clause because it is unconcerned with motive).

A. Applicability and Standing

Application to trial jury. The Sixth Amendment to the United States Constitution provides that a jury must be drawn from a "representative cross-section" of the community and that no identifiable group may be systematically excluded from jury service. *See Duren v. Missouri*, 439 U.S. 357 (1979); *Taylor v. Louisiana*, 419 U.S. 522 (1975). The Supreme Court has explained that "[t]rial by jury presupposes a jury drawn from a pool broadly representative of the community as well as impartial in a specific case. . . . [T]he broad representative character of the jury should be maintained, partly as assurance of a diffused impartiality and partly because sharing in the administration of justice is a phase of civic responsibility." *Taylor*, 419 U.S. 522, 530–31 (quotation omitted). The North Carolina Supreme Court has held that this right to a jury representing a fair cross section of the community derives not only from the Sixth Amendment to the U.S. Constitution, but also from article I, sections 24 and 26 of the North Carolina Constitution. *See State v. Bowman*, 349 N.C. 459, 467 (1998). North Carolina courts apply the same standards when evaluating claims raised under the state and federal constitutions. *Id.* at 467–68.

Application to grand jury. The United States Supreme Court has not determined whether the Sixth Amendment "fair cross-section" right applies to the selection of grand juries in state court. *See Campbell v. Louisiana*, 523 U.S. 392 (1998) (declining to reach issue). However, a strong argument can be made that where a state chooses to use a grand jury to formally charge defendants, then the grand jury it uses must be fair and representative. *See, e.g., Morgan v. Illinois*, 504 U.S. 719 (1992) (where a state chooses to rely on jury sentencing, the sentencing jury must be fair and impartial). Courts in some jurisdictions have held that the Sixth Amendment's fair cross-section requirement applies to grand juries. *See, e.g.*, *Murphy v. Johnson*, 205 F.3d 809, 818 (5th Cir. 2000) (noting court's precedent on the issue); *O'Neal v. Delo,* 44 F.3d 655, 662 (8th Cir.1995); *United States v. Osorio*, 801 F. Supp. 966, 974 (D. Conn. 1992); *State v. Porro*, 385 A.2d 1258, 1260 (N.J. Super. Ct. App. Div. 1978). *But see Henley v. Bell*, 487 F.3d 379, 387 (6th Cir. 2007) (application of Sixth Amendment to grand jury not a "clearly established" right).

Standing. A defendant does not have to be a member of the excluded group to have standing to raise a Sixth Amendment fair cross-section challenge. *Taylor v. Louisiana*, 419 U.S. 522 (1975) (male defendant could challenge systematic exclusion of female jurors); *Holland v. Illinois,* 493 U.S. 474 (1990) (White defendant had standing to challenge exclusion of Black jurors).

B. Overview of the Elements of a Fair Cross-Section Claim

To make out a prima facie fair cross-section challenge, a defendant must show "[1] that the group alleged to be excluded is a 'distinctive' group in the community; [2] that the representation of this group in venires from which juries are selected is not fair and reasonable in relation to the number of such persons in the community; and [3] that this underrepresentation is due to the systematic exclusion of the group in the jury-selection process." *State v. Williams,* 355 N.C. 501 (2002) (quoting *Duren v. Missouri*, 439 U.S. 357 (1979)). The three prongs of this prima facie showing are discussed in the following sections.

C. Burden Shifting

The burden is on the defendant raising a fair cross-section claim to make out a prima facie case of "an infringement of his constitutional right to a jury drawn from a fair cross section of the community." *Duren,* 439 U.S. 357, 368. If a defendant succeeds in making out a prima facie fair cross-section violation, the burden shifts to the State to prove "that a significant state interest [is] manifestly and primarily advanced by those aspects of the jury-selection process . . . that result in the disproportionate exclusion of a distinctive group." *Id.* at 367–68. On its face, this burden would appear to be difficult for the State to meet. Few cases have addressed it.

D. First Prong of a Fair Cross-Section Claim: Distinctive Group

The first prong of the *Duren* test is satisfied if the defendant alleges that Black jurors, Latino jurors, or female jurors are underrepresented in the jury formation process. *Taylor v. Louisiana*, 419 U.S. 522, 538 (1975); *see State v. Golphin,* 352 N.C. 364, 393 (2000) (noting that "[t]here is no question . . . that defendants satisfied the first prong . . . because African-Americans are unquestionably a 'distinct' group for purposes of [this] analysis"); *see also* Paula Hannaford-Agor, *Systematic Negligence In Jury Operations: Why The Definition Of Systematic Exclusion In Fair Cross Section Claims Must Be Expanded*, 59 DRAKE L. REV. 761, 763 (2011) ("It is fairly well-settled that the first prong of *Duren* refers to gender, race, and ethnicity, or in rare circumstances, religious affiliation and national origin." (footnotes omitted)). The North Carolina Supreme Court has rejected a defendant's claim that young people between the ages of 18 and 29 constitute a distinctive group for purposes of fair cross-section claims. *See State v. Price*, 301 N.C. 437, 446 (1980).

Courts have varied somewhat in their treatment of other groups. *See* Nina W. Chernoff & Joseph B. Kadane, *The 16 Things Every Defense Attorney Should Know About Fair Cross-Section Challenges*, THE CHAMPION , Dec. 2013, at 14, 17 (noting that some courts have recognized Native Americans, Jews, Asians, and gay people as distinctive groups, and collecting cases); *see also Thiel v. Southern Pacific Co*., 328 U.S. 217, 222 (1946) (treating daily wage earners as a distinctive group). The North Carolina Supreme Court has explained that:

> In determining whether a group is distinctive or cognizable for the purposes of a challenge to a jury selection plan, three factors must be weighed as being pertinent to the decision. First, there must be some quality or attribute in existence which defines or limits the membership of the alleged group; second, there must be a cohesiveness of attitudes, ideas, or experiences which serves to distinguish the purported group from the general social milieu; and third, a community of interest must be present within the alleged group which may not be represented by other segments of the populace.

Price, 301 N.C. 437, 445–46.

E. Second Prong of a Fair Cross-Section Claim: Underrepresentation

Generally. The second prong of a fair cross-section claim requires that a claimant show that a distinctive group is not fairly represented in the pool of individuals from which jurors are selected. "[T]he jury wheels, pools of names, panels, or venires from which juries are drawn must not systematically exclude distinctive groups within the community *and thereby fail to be reasonably representative thereof*." *Taylor v. Louisiana*, 419 U.S. 522, 538 (1975) (emphasis added). In analyzing the second prong of a fair cross-section claim, courts focus on the representativeness of the sources from which grand and trial juries are selected. *See Berghuis v. Smith*, 559 U.S. 314, 319 (2010) (fair cross-section right involves guarantee of a "jury drawn from *sources* reflecting a cross section of the community" (emphasis added)).

While fair cross-section claims often involve challenges to the representativeness of the groups of potential jurors summoned or arriving at the courthouse for jury service, "the right to a jury selected from a fair cross-section of the community . . . extends to all aspects of the jury selection process . . . *up until the point* that an individual petit jury is selected." Nina W. Chernoff & Joseph B. Kadane, *The 16 Things Every Defense Attorney Should Know About Fair Cross-Section Challenges*, THE CHAMPION, Dec. 2013, at 14, 15; *see, e.g.*, *Duren*, 439 U.S. 357, 367 (violation of fair cross-section guarantee demonstrated with evidence of "disproportionate and consistent exclusion of women from the [Jackson County] jury wheel and at the venire stage"). In other words, underrepresentation may be shown by demonstrating that the master jury list from which potential jurors' names are selected for summoning purposes underrepresents a distinctive group, that the potential jurors sent into a courtroom for voir dire examination underrepresent a distinctive group, or that any stage between these two steps introduces the underrepresentation of a distinctive group into the jury formation process. Nina W. Chernoff & Joseph B. Kadane, *The 16 Things Every Defense Attorney Should Know About Fair Cross-Section Challenges*, THE CHAMPION , Dec. 2013, at 14, (the number of the distinctive group members in the community can be compared to "the number on the master list of all jurors, or . . . the number who showed up to court for jury service and thereby became members of jury venires, or . . . the number at any other stage of the jury process" before the selection of the jury"); *see also infra* § 6.5, Challenges to North Carolina Procedures for Jury Formation. Determining the representation of the distinctive group in one or more of those stages of the jury pool formation process will require some combination of discovery, factual investigation, and expert analysis. *See infra* "Discovery" and "Type of information to seek in discovery" *in* § 6.5B, Mechanics of Challenging Jury Formation.

North Carolina courts typically evaluate the second prong of a fair-cross section claim by reviewing evidence from the defendant's case. Courts disagree as to whether underrepresentation must occur over a period of time to satisfy the second prong, or whether evidence of underrepresentation from the defendant's individual case is sufficient. *See, e.g.*, *People v. Bryant*, 822 N.W.2d 124, 156 (Mich. 2012) (Marilyn Kelly, J., dissenting) (arguing that majority erred in concluding that *Duren* demands evidence of underrepresentation over time to satisfy second prong of a fair cross-section claim).

North Carolina appellate courts generally have indicated that evidence of underrepresentation from the jury pool or venire in a defendant's individual case may be sufficient to satisfy the second prong of a fair cross-section claim. In North Carolina, the obligation to demonstrate underrepresentation extending beyond the venire in the defendant's individual case appears to be treated as a component of the third, rather than the second, prong of the defendant's prima facie case. For example, in *State v. McNeill*, 326 N.C. 712, 717 (1990), the N.C. Supreme Court reviewed a fair cross-section claim in which the alleged disparity between African Americans in Harnett County and African Americans on the defendant's jury pool was 18%. The State conceded that the disparity in the defendant's jury pool constituted sufficient evidence of underrepresentation to meet the second prong of the *Duren* test. Focusing on the third prong of the *Duren* test, however, the court found that a disparity in the composition of a single jury pool did not establish the systematic exclusion required to satisfy the third prong of the *Duren* test. *Id.* at 718. *See also State v. Blakeney*, 352 N.C. 287, 297 (2000) ("The second prong of the *Duren* test requires us to determine whether the representation of African–Americans in the [defendant's] venire was fair and reasonable."); *State v. Bowman*, 349 N.C. 459, 469 (1998) ("statistics concerning one jury pool, standing alone, are insufficient to meet the *third prong* of *Duren*" (emphasis added)); *State v. Jackson,* 215 N.C. App. 339, 343–44

(2011) (noting that the *Duren* court considered composition of venires over time in analysis of third prong). *See also infra* § 6.3F, Third Prong of a Fair Cross-Section Claim: Systematic Exclusion.

Elsewhere, courts have held that the second prong of the prima facie case will not be satisfied by showing that a distinctive group is underrepresented among the jury venire in the defendant's individual case. As the Sixth Circuit explained, a "petitioner raising [a fair cross-section] claim is challenging the pool from which the jury is drawn, and not necessarily the venire panel directly before him. Accordingly, the composition of one panel does not indicate whether a fair cross-section claim exists." *Ambrose v. Booker*, 684 F.3d 638, 645 (6th Cir. 2012). "The irrelevance of the composition of a single venire panel is underscored by the fact that a petitioner may bring a claim even if minorities are included in his panel." *Ambrose,* 684 F.3d 638, 645.

Underrepresentation claims must be supported by evidence. It is not sufficient for the defendant merely to assert that the percentage of the distinctive group is larger in the county than in the jury pool or venire without providing supporting evidence. *See State v. Hardy*, 293 N.C. 105, 114 (1977) (where defendant offered no evidence of the percentage of women in Burke county in support of Equal Protection claim, court could not take judicial notice "of the fact that women make up at least 50% of our population"); *State v. Jackson*, 215 N.C. App. 399, 342 (2011) (evidence that only three out of sixty potential Orange County jurors were African Americans was insufficient alone to support second and third prongs of *Duren* test; defense counsel's statement that the African American population in the county was "certainly greater than . . . five percent" was insufficient where no demographic data was presented to show racial composition of county); *State v. Durant*, 154 N.C. App. 521 (2002) (unpublished) (rejecting claim unsupported by statistical evidence where defendant alleged that eight members of jury pool were African American and Columbus County's population was forty percent African American).

Determining the representation of the distinctive group in the community. To satisfy the second prong, the defendant will need to present evidence comparing the number of distinctive group members in the community and the number of distinctive group members at some stage of the jury formation process. *See* Nina W. Chernoff & Joseph B. Kadane, *The 16 Things Every Defense Attorney Should Know About Fair Cross-Section Challenges*, THE CHAMPION, Dec. 2013, at 14, 17–18.

The number of distinctive group members in the community usually may be demonstrated with census data reflecting the total population and need not identify the jury-eligible population. *Teague v. Lane*, 489 U.S. 288, 301 n.1 (1989); *Duren*, 439 U.S. 357, 365; *Castaneda v. Partida*, 430 U.S. 482, 495–96 (1977) (equal protection case in which the Supreme Court relied on total population figures in reviewing a challenge to grand jury composition); *U.S. v. Rodriguez-Lara*, 421 F.3d 932, 942 (9th Cir. 2005) ("the Supreme Court's acceptance of comparisons using total population figures clearly indicates that a defendant is not required to gather data reflecting the age-eligible population of the distinctive group in question"), *overruled on other grounds, United States v. Hernandez-Estrada*, 749 F.3d 1154 (9th Cir. 2014); *Azania v. State*, 778

N.E.2d 1253, 1259 (Ind. 2002) (noting that courts generally uphold the use of census figures in challenges to jury procedures). If voting-age population data is available courts may consider it, but courts generally do not require such precision. *See Rodriguez-Lara*, 421 F.3d 932, 942, 943 n.9 (9th Cir. 2005) ("where the record contains population data broken down by age, the representativeness of the jury pool is to be compared to this refined set of data for the purpose of the defendant's prima facie case under *Duren*"); *United States v. Butera*, 420 F.2d 564, 569 n.13 (1st Cir. 1970) ("It may be so difficult to obtain full and accurate figures for 'jury eligibles' that to require such figures would—at least in some cases—place an insuperable burden on defendant."), *overruled on other grounds*, *Barber v. Ponte*, 772 F.2d 982 (1st Cir. 1985); *U.S. v. Osorio*, 801 F. Supp. 966, 979 (D. Conn. 1992) ("Data as to the population eligible for jury service are rarely available, however, and federal courts typically rely on voting-age population, a figure readily available in census data, as a proxy."). *But see Smith v. State*, 571 S.E.2d 740, 746–47 (Ga. 2002) (general population is not always an adequate proxy for jury eligible population).

When presenting courts with census data, defense attorneys may also consider presenting evidence that the census generally undercounts racial and ethnic minorities. *See State v. Price*, 301 N.C. 437, 444, (1980) (accepting expert demographer's analysis of underrepresention in the Wayne County jury pool, including expert's adjustment of census data "for an undercount of 2 percent for whites and 8 percent for blacks"); *see also* Nina W. Chernoff & Joseph B. Kadane, *The 16 Things Every Defense Attorney Should Know About Fair Cross-Section Challenges*, THE CHAMPION, Dec. 2013, at 14, 17 n.73 (citing *Dep't of Comm. v. U.S. House of Representatives*, 525 U.S. 316 (1999), as an example of the Supreme Court recognizing the failure of the Census Bureau to capture a portion of the population); *United States v. Duran De Amesquita*, 582 F. Supp. 1326, 1330 n.5 (S.D. Fla. 1984) (adjusting population figures based on "generally recognized population undercount").

Defining underrepresentation. There is no set percentage of underrepresentation required to satisfy the second prong of the *Duren* test, nor is there a clear methodology for measuring underrepresentation. *See infra* "Practice note: calculating underrepresentation" in this subsection E (noting that, recently, the U.S. Supreme Court declined to adopt a 10% absolute disparity threshold for calculating underrepresentation in fair cross-section claims; also discussing the difference between the concepts of absolute and comparative disparities). The question of unfair and unreasonable representation is answered on a case-by-case basis. Since, unlike in equal protection claims, the disparity calculation in a fair cross-section claim is "not being used as evidence of discrimination, it does not need to be substantial enough to indicate discrimination—it simply has to fail to be 'fairly representative of the local population otherwise eligible for jury service.'" Nina W. Chernoff, *Wrong About the Right: How Courts Undermine the Fair Cross-Section Guarantee by Confusing It with Equal Protection*, 64 HASTINGS L.J. 141, 159 (2012) (quoting *Taylor v. Louisiana*, 419 U.S. 522, 537 (1975)).

To the extent that courts have focused on a particular disparity threshold in fair cross-section claims, such a focus may have resulted from a blurring of the elements of equal protection and fair cross-section claims. *See id.* at 160 n.90 (arguing that it is not appropriate to apply a 10% absolute disparity threshold developed in equal protection jurisprudence to fair cross-section claims; citing as support *Waller v. Butkovich*, 593 F. Supp. 942, 954 (M.D.N.C. 1984) where the court declined to adopt the 10% rule because "[w]hether a fair cross section exists is entirely different from whether intentional discrimination occurred"); *see also* Nina W. Chernoff & Joseph B. Kadane, The 16 Things Every Defense Attorney Should Know About Fair Cross-Section Challenges, THE CHAMPION, Dec. 2013, at 14, 19 (noting that defense attorneys should resist adoption of a 10% absolute disparity threshold because (1) the U.S. Supreme Court declined to adopt it; (2) it would leave groups comprising less than 10% of the community without a remedy for underrepresentation; and (3) it has been mistakenly imported from the equal protection context).

Generally, North Carolina courts considering fair cross-section claims have evaluated evidence of the difference between the distinctive group's representation in the total population and the group's representation in the jury pool (the "absolute disparity"). For example, if Black people comprised 50% of the total population and 30% of the jury pool, the absolute disparity would be 20%. However, North Carolina courts may consider other measurements of underrepresentation in future cases since, in *Berghuis v. Smith*, 559 U.S. 314, 329 (2010), the U.S. Supreme Court stated that there is no perfect test for underrepresentation, and quoted with approval the Michigan Supreme Court's holding that, "[p]rovided . . . the parties proffer sufficient evidence . . . the results of all of the tests [of underrepresentation, including absolute disparity, comparative disparity, and standard deviation,] should be considered." *Id.* (internal quotations omitted). *See also* Paula Hannaford-Agor, *The fair cross section requirement in the wake of Berghuis v. Smith*, THE COURT MANAGER, Summer 2010, at 66, 68 ("Certainly the law has changed [after *Berghuis v. Smith*] for courts located in states . . . that previously adopted absolute disparity as the only valid measure of representational disparity.").

Of the fair cross-section cases that relied on absolute disparity evidence in North Carolina, decisions have found that defendants did not meet the second part of the *Duren* test with absolute disparities of between 6.3% (*State v. Taylor*, 304 N.C. 249 (1981)) and 16.17% (*State v. Bowman*, 349 N.C. 459 (1998)). *See State v. Williams*, 355 N.C. 501 (2002); *State v. Blakeney,* 352 N.C. 287 (2000); *State v. Golphin*, 352 N.C. 364 (2000). In some of the cases in which absolute disparities did not satisfy the *Duren* test, North Carolina appellate courts rejected the fair cross-section claim at least in part because the defendant failed to present evidence of disparities beyond the jury pool in the defendant's own case and therefore failed to satisfy the third prong of the *Duren* test. *See, e.g.*, *Bowman*, 349 N.C. 459, 469 ("[d]efendant's only evidence in the instant case consisted of the statistical makeup of this particular jury venire"; court found that evidence failed to show systemic exclusion under third prong of *Duren* test). If the defendants had presented evidence of such disparities beyond their individual cases, the outcomes may have been different.

Successful fair cross-section challenges include *Duren* in which women made up 54% of the jury-eligible population but accounted for less than 15% of jury venires, and *U.S. v. Osorio*, 801 F. Supp. 966, 979 (D. Conn. 1992), in which the "exclusion of approximately two-thirds of blacks and Hispanics in the Division as a source of names for jury selection," despite the fact that the absolute disparities were only 3.26% and 4.3%, respectively, was sufficient evidence of underrepresentation. In that case, the court found the comparative disparity more significant than the absolute disparity, given the low numbers of Blacks and Latinos in the total population. *See infra* "Practice note: calculating underrepresentation," in this subsection E. Additionally, defendants in two U.S. Supreme Court cases decided before *Duren* succeeded with evidence of a 23% absolute disparity (*see Turner v. Fouche*, 396 U.S. 346 (1970)) and a 15% absolute disparity (*see Jones v. Georgia*, 389 U.S. 24 (1967)). *See also Azania v. State*, 778 N.E.2d 1253 (Ind. 2002) (vacating death sentence on the basis of the defendant's fair cross-section claim where absolute disparity between African American population and presence in jury pools was 4.1%, and comparative disparity was 48.2%). In reviewing fair cross-section cases analyzing the significance of underrepresentation data, the Georgia Supreme Court observed that

> Generally speaking . . . an absolute disparity between the percentage of a group in the population and its percentage in the jury pool of less than 5% is almost always constitutional; an absolute disparity between 5% and 10% is usually constitutional; and an absolute disparity of over 10% is probably unconstitutional.

Smith v. State, 571 S.E.2d 740, 745 (Ga. 2002) (quotation omitted).

Practice note: Calculating underrepresentation. As noted above, North Carolina appellate courts generally have required defendants to substantiate claims of underrepresentation with evidence of absolute disparities. An absolute disparity reflects the difference between the representation of the distinctive group in the total population and the representation of the group in the jury pool. Another way to measure underrepresentation is by calculating the comparative disparity, which measures "the percentage by which the number of distinctive group members in the jury pool falls short of their number in the community." Paula Hannaford-Agor, *Systematic Negligence In Jury Operations: Why The Definition Of Systematic Exclusion In Fair Cross Section Claims Must Be Expanded*, 59 DRAKE L. REV. 761, 768 (2011). Measuring comparative disparity involves dividing the absolute disparity by the percentage of the distinctive group in the community. "The comparative disparity in *Duren* was 73%, indicating the percentage of women in the jury pool was 73% less than would ordinarily be expected for the female population of Jackson County, Missouri, in 1976." *Id.* (footnote omitted). Two final methods for calculating disparity are standard deviation analysis and probability analysis. *See* Nina W. Chernoff & Joseph B. Kadane, *The 16 Things Every Defense Attorney Should Know About Fair Cross-Section Challenges*, THE CHAMPION, Dec. 2013, at 14, 18 (explaining these methods).

Some scholars, practitioners, and judges have observed that comparative disparity can be a useful tool for highlighting underrepresentation of groups that comprise a fairly small portion of the community. *See United States v. Rogers*, 73 F.3d 774, 776 (8th Cir. 1996) ("Although utilizing the absolute disparity calculation may seem intuitive, its result understates the systematic representative deficiencies . . . ."); *United States v. Levasseur*, 704 F. Supp. 1158, 1162–63 (D. Mass. 1989) (holding that "only a comparative disparity analysis will afford sufficient protection to defendants' right to be tried by a fair cross-section of the community"); *see also* Brief for Social Scientists, Statisticians, and Law Professors, Jeffrey Fagan, et al., as Amici Curiae Supporting Respondent, *Berghuis v. Smith*, 559 U.S. 314 (2010) (No. 08-1402). For example, since absolute disparities measuring less than 10% generally have not been found sufficient to demonstrate underrepresentation, a distinctive group comprising 9% of the total population probably would not be able to demonstrate underrepresentation using absolute disparity figures, even if the group's representation in the jury pool was 0%. When the U.S. Supreme Court declined to rule on the government's argument for a 10% absolute disparity requirement, the Court observed that acceptance of the argument would result in no remedy for a group's complete exclusion if it comprised less than 10% of the community. *Berghuis v. Smith,* 559 U.S. 314, 330 n.4 (2010). In such cases, a calculation of comparative disparity may highlight the underrepresentation:

> [I]f African-Americans represented 10% of a jury-eligible community, but only 4% of the jury pool, the absolute disparity would be 6% and the comparative disparity would be 60%. . . . Like absolute disparity, few courts have articulated the degree of underrepresentation that reflects a constitutional violation using this measure. Most courts that have discussed this issue cite values of 50% comparative disparity or higher to establish a fair cross section claim."

Paula Hannaford-Agor, *Systematic Negligence In Jury Operations: Why The Definition of Systematic Exclusion In Fair Cross Section Claims Must Be Expanded*, 59 DRAKE L. REV. 761, 768–69 (2011). For these reasons, defense attorneys should consider presenting evidence of comparative disparities in fair cross-section cases.

F. Third Prong of a Fair Cross-Section Claim: Systematic Exclusion

To meet the third prong of a fair cross-section claim, defendants must show that the jury formation method produces the systematic exclusion of the distinctive group. Underrepresentation is "systematic" if it was an "inherent" product of the jury selection mechanism that was used or if it resulted from a rule or practice over which the state actor had control. *Duren v. Missouri*, 439 U.S. 357, 366 (1979).

Examples of systematic exclusion. Examples of systematic exclusion have involved automated computer processes that inadvertently generate underrepresentative jury pools, *see, e.g., State v. Long*, 499 A.2d 264 (N.J. Super. Ct. Law. Div. 1985); a summoning process reliant on telephonic communication with potential jurors, *see, e.g., State v. LaMere*, 2 P.3d 204, 221 (Mont. 2000); and initiatives intended to lessen the burden of jury service by assigning jurors to courthouses close to their homes, *see, e.g.*, *Spencer v. State*, 545 So.2d 1352, 1353–54 (Fla. 1989). For example, in *United States v. Osorio*, 801 F. Supp. 966, 972–73 (D. Conn. 1992), registered voters from the cities of Hartford and New Britain, Connecticut were accidentally left out of a computer-generated master jury list. These two cities included the largest concentration of Black and Latino residents in the state of Connecticut. *See also* Paula Hannaford-Agor, *Systematic Negligence In Jury Operations: Why The Definition Of Systematic Exclusion In Fair Cross Section Claims Must Be Expanded*, 59 DRAKE L. REV. 761, 769–71 (2011) (listing additional examples of systematic exclusion related to jury formation).

Underrepresentation over time constitutes evidence of systematic exclusion. North Carolina courts generally consider evidence of underrepresentation over time as a component of the third prong of a fair cross-section claim. *Compare supra* "North Carolina courts typically evaluate the second prong of a fair cross-section claim by reviewing evidence from the defendant's case" in § 6.3E, Second Prong of a Fair Cross-Section Claim: Underrepresentation. There is no clear answer as to how extensive the evidence of underrepresentation must be, but the period of review must be long enough to show that the jury selection process produces disparities. North Carolina courts have cited with approval the *Duren* court's consideration of disparities between the representation of women in the community and in the venire that "occurred not just occasionally, but in every weekly venire for a period of nearly a year." *State v. Jackson,* 215 N.C. App. 339, 344 (2011) (quoting *Duren*). The U.S. Supreme Court recently reviewed a case in which the underrepresentation alleged by the defendant was based on the representation of African Americans in the jury pool in the six months leading up to the defendant's trial. *Berghuis v. Smith*, 559 U.S. 314, 323 (2010) (defendant also submitted evidence that the comparative disparity dropped in the 11 months after the policy allegedly responsible for the underrepresentation was modified). Shorter periods may be sufficient if they show a pattern of underrepresentation.

Does persistent underrepresentation alone constitute systematic exclusion? *Duren* suggests that evidence of consistent underrepresentation of a distinctive group may constitute sufficient evidence of systematic exclusion, regardless of whether the defendant can pinpoint the cause of the underrepresentation. *Duren*, 439 U.S. 357, 366 (defendant's demonstration that "a large discrepancy occurred not just occasionally but in every weekly venire for a period of nearly a year manifestly indicates that the cause of the underrepresentation was systematic"). In *Duren*, the Court noted that, while the defendant had not proven which of two identified policies was responsible for the underrepresentation of women, the underrepresentation of women "was quite obviously due to the *system* by which juries were selected. . . . Women were therefore systematically underrepresented . . . ." *Duren*, 439 U.S. 357, 367 (emphasis in original); *see* Nina W. Chernoff, *Wrong About the Right: How Courts Undermine the Fair Cross-Section Guarantee by Confusing It with Equal Protection*, 64 HASTINGS L.J. 141, 163 (2012).

In applying *Duren*, North Carolina courts have suggested that a showing of underrepresentation in jury pools over a sufficient time period would be sufficient to satisfy the systematic exclusion prong of the defendant's prima facie case. *See, e.g., State v. Bowman*, 349 N.C. 459 (1998) (holding that statistics concerning one jury pool, standing alone, were insufficient to show a systematic exclusion of a distinctive group, and implying that statistics concerning multiple jury pools may be sufficient to show systematic exclusion); *State v. McNeill*, 326 N.C. 712, 718 (1990) (underrepresentation was not systematic for purposes of third prong because the defendant failed to show either a flaw in the system producing the racial disparities *"or that there is a history of relatively few blacks serving on Harnett County juries"* (emphasis added)); *State v. Jackson,* 215 N.C. App. 339, 344 (2011) (rejecting fair cross-section claim based on composition of a single jury panel and noting in *Duren*, the "large discrepancy [between the number of women in the jury venire and the number of women in the community] occurred not just occasionally, but in every weekly venire for a period of nearly a year," and explaining that such evidence "manifestly indicate[d] that the cause of the underrepresentation was systematic" (quoting *Duren*)).

Courts in other jurisdictions have interpreted *Duren* in this manner as well. "Under *Duren*, 'systematic exclusion' can be shown by a large discrepancy repeated over time such that the system must be said to bring about the underrepresentation." *United States v. Weaver*, 267 F.3d 231, 244 (3d Cir. 2001); *see also United States v. Biaggi*, 680 F. Supp. 641, 653 (S.D.N.Y. 1988) ("*Duren* permits the defendant to focus solely on the composition of the venires over time, not on the intent of the registrars, in endeavoring to assemble that proof."), *aff'd in part, rev'd in part on other grounds*, 909 F.2d 662 (2d Cir. 1990). *But cf. United States v. Rioux*, 97 F.3d 648, 658 (2d Cir. 1996) (court observed that it was "unclear whether statistics alone can prove systematic exclusion," but held that defendant had not demonstrated systematic exclusion where the evidence revealed "statistically insignificant" absolute disparities of 1.58% and 2.14%).

The U.S. Supreme Court's opinion in *Berghuis v. Smith* affirmed the *Duren* standard and clarified that, while it is not necessary to identify the degree to which various systematic factors produced the underrepresentation, defendants must show that systematic factors were the cause of the underrepresentation. *Berghuis*, 559 U.S. 314, 332 (2010) ("No 'clearly established' precedent of this Court supports Smith's claim that he can make out a prima facie case merely by pointing to a host of factors that, individually or in combination, *might* contribute to a group's underrepresentation." (emphasis in original)). In *Duren,* the Court held that a nearly year-long pattern of underrepresentation of women "manifestly indicate[d] that the cause of the representation was systematic." *Duren*, 439 U.S. 357, 366., The *Berghuis* Court explained that the finding of systematic exclusion in *Duren* was based on the defendant's showing that the underrepresentation was: (1) persistent, occurring in every weekly venire for almost a year; (2) produced at two stages of the jury formation process, each of which exacerbated the underrepresentation; and (3) stark in comparison to federal district court jury pools (women comprised 14.5% of the jury venires in defendant's courthouse vs. 40% of the jury venires in federal district court serving the same area). *Berghuis*, 559 U.S. 314, 328. According to the *Berghuis* court, it was the combined significance of this evidence in *Duren* that demonstrated that the underrepresentation "was quite obviously due to the *system* by which juries were selected," rather than some other reason. *Id.* (quoting *Duren*, 439 U.S. 357, 367) (emphasis in original). The Court held that the defendant in *Berghuis* failed to satisfy the systematic exclusion prong because he failed to show that the underrepresentation was a result of the juror assignment system complained of, rather than other, non-systemic factors. *Berghuis*, 559 U.S. 314, 330–31. The Court suggested that the defendant may have been able to demonstrate systematic exclusion by comparing the alleged underrepresentation in his circuit to the representation of African Americans in local district court venires or federal district court venires for the same region, or offering evidence that ruled out alternative, non-systematic explanations for the underrepresentation. *Id.* at 331.

Even though *Duren* and *Berghuis* require a showing that the jury formation system caused the underrepresentation, they do not appear to require the defendant to identify the exact stage of the process responsible for the underrepresentation. Thus, in *Duren* itself, cited with approval in *Berghuis*, the defendant did not demonstrate with specificity where in the process the underrepresentation was produced. *See* Nina W. Chernoff and Joseph B. Kadane, *The 16 Things Every Defense Attorney Should Know About Fair Cross-Section Challenges*, THE CHAMPION, Dec. 2013, at 14, 20 n.112 (*Duren* Court recognized that the defendant had merely "narrowed the possibilities down to two stages of the selection process" without proving which of the two was responsible for the underrepresentation).

In order to identify systematic factors affecting one or more stages of the jury formation process, "defense attorneys should request discovery about each stage of the jury selection system, and not just demographic data about the venires." Nina W. Chernoff & Joseph B. Kadane, *The 16 Things Every Defense Attorney Should Know About Fair Cross-Section Challenges*, THE CHAMPION, Dec. 2013, at 14, 20; *see also infra* "Discovery" and "Type of information to seek in discovery" in § 6.5B, Mechanics of Challenging Jury Formation. Additionally, attorneys may want to gather data from federal courts covering the same area for comparative purposes, as suggested in *Berghuis*, 559 U.S. 314, 331.

Unanswered questions about socioeconomic factors and systemic exclusion following *Berghuis v. Smith*. Courts have reached divergent conclusions about whether underrepresentation caused by socioeconomic factors, such as racially disparate non-response or excusal rates related to poverty and mobility or disparate rates of voter registration, may satisfy the "systematic exclusion" prong of a fair cross-section claim. Most courts that have considered such questions have held that, because these factors are not caused by the court's jury procedures, they cannot. *See, e.g.*, Paula Hannaford-Agor, *Systematic Negligence In Jury Operations: Why The Definition Of Systematic Exclusion In Fair Cross Section Claims Must Be Expanded*, 59 DRAKE L. REV. 761, 772–77 (2011) (explaining that courts generally rule that underrepresentation due to socioeconomic factors does not constitute systematic exclusion); *United States v. Bates*, 2009 WL 5033928, at *19 (E.D. Mich. Dec. 15, 2009) (unpublished) ("The consensus among courts is that, like nonresponses, [socioeconomic] factors are usually not inherent to the jury-selection plans. Therefore, [even if they] substantially reduce the presence of minorities in jury pools, this does not amount to systematic exclusion."), *aff'd*, 473 Fed. Appx. 446 (6th Cir. 2012) (unpublished).

However, in *Smith v. Berghuis*, 543 F.3d 326, 341–42 (6th Cir. 2008), *rev'd,* 559 U.S. 314 (2010), where the defendant presented evidence that the underrepresentation of Black jurors was partially caused by a juror excusal policy that routinely granted requests for hardships relating to lost income and difficulties arranging for transportation or childcare, the Sixth Circuit Court of Appeals held that because the "particular jury selection process employed . . . made social or economic factors relevant to whether a[] . . . juror would be excused from service; and because . . . [such] factors disproportionately impact African Americans," the process employed constituted systematic exclusion sufficient to satisfy the third prong of the fair cross-section test. The court explained that "the Sixth Amendment is concerned with social or economic factors when the particular *system* of selecting jurors makes such factors relevant to who is placed on the qualifying list and who is ultimately called to or excused from service." *Id.* at 341 (emphasis in original). When the U.S. Supreme Court reversed the Sixth Circuit's ruling, holding that the defendant's fair cross-section claim did not constitute a violation of clearly established federal law, the Court declined to decide whether socioeconomic factors could constitute systematic exclusion.

In arguing that underrepresentation produced by socioeconomic factors should be considered systematic exclusion for purposes of fair cross-section claims, the following sources may be of use:

- Paula Hannaford-Agor, *Systematic Negligence In Jury Operations: Why The Definition Of Systematic Exclusion In Fair Cross Section Claims Must Be Expanded*, 59 DRAKE L. REV. 761 (2011);
- *People v. Harris*, 679 P.2d 433, 446 (Cal. 1984) (exclusive reliance on voter registration lists underrepresenting African Americans and Latinos constituted systematic exclusion that was no longer justifiable, given the relative ease of merging different source lists);
- *United States v. Green*, 389 F. Supp. 2d 29, 40, 75–76 (D. Mass. 2005) (court expressed "grave concerns" about data reflecting underrepresentation of black people on death-qualified juries), *overruled*, 426 F.3d 1 (1st Cir. 2005).

Practice note: The North Carolina courts have sometimes conflated the third prong of the fair cross-section test with the third prong of the equal protection test. In *State v. Avery*, 299 N.C. 126 (1980), in analyzing the defendant's equal protection claim, the court relied on the holding in *Washington v. Davis,* 426 U.S. 229 (1976), that "[t]he fact that a particular jury or series of juries does not statistically reflect the racial composition of the community does not in itself make out an invidious discrimination forbidden by the [Equal Protection] clause." However, in subsequent North Carolina appellate cases, courts have relied on this language when reviewing fair cross-section claims and implied that a showing of intentional discrimination is required to prevail on such a claim. *See, e.g., State v. Golphin,* 353 N.C. 364, 394–95 (2000) (quoting *Avery* and suggesting that fair cross-section claim requires showing of discrimination); *State v. Bowman,* 349 N.C.

459, 469 (1998) (same); *State v. Johnson*, 317 N.C. 343, 381 (1986) (rejecting third prong of the defendant's fair cross-section claim because "[t]here [was] no evidence that . . . the Commission *intended* systematically to exclude blacks from the jury list") (emphasis added). As discussed above, the *Duren* test does not require defendants to demonstrate discrimination. For more information about courts confusing equal protection and fair cross-section standards, see Nina W. Chernoff, *Wrong About the Right: How Courts Undermine the Fair Cross-Section Guarantee by Confusing It with Equal Protection*, 64 HASTINGS L.J. 141 (2012).

Case study: Litigating fair cross-section claims. Below are the reflections of Russ Hollers, appointed defense counsel from Orange County, on litigating a fair cross-section claim:

The week before my client's armed robbery trial, I checked the list of prospective jurors in the clerk's office to see if I knew anyone. I noticed that many members of the panel had been excused or deferred by the clerk due to their advanced age or prior plans. The list did not contain any demographic information, such as race.

The next week, in came the panel. Based on my visual observation, of the sixty prospective jurors, there were three African American women and zero African American men. It definitely did not look like Orange County.

My client and his fraternal twin, who was also on trial, were African American, and the prosecuting witness was White. Counsel for the co-defendant made an oral motion to strike the panel as not being representative of the county's population. I joined in the motion and said to the judge that the African American proportion of the population of Orange County was greater than 5%, and that the proportion of African American men in our county's population was certainly greater than 0%. I also gave the judge a copy of the clerk's marked-up panel roster to demonstrate that there was no way to tell from the list the race of the excused jurors. The motions were denied. We moved for mistrials based on the flawed panel, but those motions were also denied.

I didn't make a written motion before trial because I wasn't aware of any way to learn the demographics of the panel until I laid eyes on them. I have since learned that it is possible to discover the race of registered voters, so counsel may be able to learn the race of at least some members of the panel in advance by comparing the names on the list in the clerk's office to voter registration data. In smaller counties, counsel might recognize more names on the list.

Also, if I had known the law better, I would have asked for some time to gather demographic information on Orange County's African American population using census data that is easily accessed online, and submitted that as evidence. I also would have sought information from the court on the demographics of the master jury pool and the jury formation process. Although I think the judge could have taken judicial notice that Orange County contained African American men who had driver's licenses and were registered to vote, I would have been in a far stronger position if I had specific data to present.

In making my motion, I was basically reacting to what struck me as a single bad panel. My motion would have been much stronger if I had been able to put on evidence that Orange County panels showed a pattern of minority underrepresentation over time. I could have moved for discovery to try to learn about the racial makeup of past panels, but I don't think there has been a culture of attorneys asking for that information to be made part of the record, so the State may not have been able to provide it. With a little foresight that this issue may crop up, defense attorneys can request that judges have all panel members report their race in every case, and that would generate some data that everyone practicing in the area could use to support fair cross-section motions going forward. I may have been able to learn about how my particular panel ended up looking so White by asking for things through discovery like the master list, a list of every person who was taken off the list and the reason why, and information about the summonses that went out. Even if statutes on jury pool formation have been followed to the letter, I could still prevail on constitutional grounds by showing that, over time, the procedures have nevertheless resulted in pools that don't look like Orange County.

6.4 Equal Protection Challenges

A. Overview

The Equal Protection Clause of the Fourteenth Amendment to the United States Constitution guarantees a defendant the right to have the charges against him considered by a jury selected free of race-based inclusions or exclusions. *See Cassel v. Texas,* 339 U.S. 282, 286 (1950) (Constitution requires a "fair jury selected without regard to race"). The Supreme Court has held that for both grand and trial juries, "[a] person's race 'simply is unrelated to his fitness as a juror.'" *See Batson v. Kentucky,* 476 U.S. 79, 84 n.3, 87 (1986) (citation omitted). Equal protection challenges based on the Fourteenth Amendment may be raised in response to discrimination in the composition of the grand jury, trial jury pool, and selection of the grand jury foreperson (as well as in the selection of the jury, discussed in Chapter 7). Generally, the standard for demonstrating an equal protection violation in the jury formation context is more demanding than the standard applicable to fair cross-section claims, because defendants must show both intentional discrimination and substantial underrepresentation as opposed to showing "underrepresentation" in fair cross-section cases. *Compare Castaneda v. Partida*, 430 U.S. 482 (1977), *with Duren v. Missouri*, 439 U.S. 357 (1979). However, in light of North Carolina's adoption of and emphasis on constitutional protection against race-based exclusions from jury service, defendants' equal protection rights in this context should not be ignored.

Article I, sections 19 and 26 of the North Carolina Constitution prohibit jury procedures that deny equal protection, discriminate, or exclude people from jury service on account of race, sex, color, religion, or national origin. The North Carolina Supreme Court has long held that racial discrimination in the grand jury, grand jury foreperson, and trial jury selection processes "violates not only the federal constitution, but the equal protection guarantees of our state constitution as well." *State v. Cofield*, 320 N.C. 297 (1987) (citing *State v. Covington*, 258 N.C. 495 (1963)); *State v. Perry*, 248 N.C. 334 (1958). The importance of this right was emphasized in 1970, when North Carolina voters amended the North Carolina Constitution to provide that "[n]o person shall be excluded from jury service on account of sex, race, color, religion, or national origin." Our Supreme Court underscored the significance of the vote to add article I, section 26 to our State's constitution:

> The people of North Carolina have declared in this provision that they will not tolerate the corruption of their juries by racism, sexism and similar forms of irrational prejudice. They have recognized that the judicial system of a democratic society must operate evenhandedly if it is to command the respect and support of those subject to its jurisdiction.

Cofield, 320 N.C. 297, 302. In adopting N.C. Constitution article I, section 26, "[t]he people of North Carolina . . . guaranteed *unto themselves* a judicial system free of both the appearance and reality of racism." *Id.* at 311 (Mitchell, J., concurring) (emphasis in original).

B. Standing

The defendant does not have to be a member of the distinctive group that is discriminated against to raise an equal protection claim. The U.S. Supreme Court has permitted non-members of the excluded group to raise equal protection challenges to race-based peremptory strikes. *See Powers v. Ohio*, 499 U.S. 400 (1991). Likewise, the U.S. Supreme Court has held that a non-member of the group has standing to challenge the composition of the grand jury on equal protection grounds. *See Campbell v. Louisiana*, 523 U.S. 392 (1998). The Court explained that, regardless of his or her race, the accused suffers when the composition of the grand jury is tainted by racial discrimination, as such exclusion "strikes at the fundamental values of [the] judicial system." *Id.* at 398 (quotation omitted).

C. Required Showing

The Supreme Court set out the showing necessary to sustain an equal protection challenge to the composition of the jury in *Castaneda v. Partida*, 430 U.S. 482 (1977). To establish a prima facie equal protection violation, the defendant must first show that a recognizable, distinct class or group has been discriminated against and singled out for different treatment under the laws as written or applied. The defendant must then show that the procedures employed for the selection of jurors has resulted in substantial underrepresentation of the race or identifiable group for a significant period of time. Last, the defendant must show that the selection procedure is susceptible of abuse or is not racially neutral. *Id.* Once the defendant has established a prima facie case, the burden shifts to the State to rebut the prima facie case by showing a race-neutral reason for the disparity. *Id.* The North Carolina Supreme Court has held that the guarantee of equal protection in the Fourteenth Amendment is "coextensive with" the equal protection guarantee in article I, sections 19 and 26 of the North Carolina Constitution. *State v. Cofield*, 320 N.C. 297, 308 (1987). In other words, state and federal equal protection claims require the same showing.

D. First Prong of an Equal Protection Claim: Recognizable and Distinct Group

To satisfy the first prong of the *Castaneda* equal protection test, the defendant must show that the jury exclusion operates on a "recognizable, distinct class or group which has been purposely discriminated against and singled out for different treatment under the laws, as written or as applied." *State v. Hough*, 299 N.C. 245, 250 (1980) (citing *Castaneda,* 430 U.S. 482). African Americans and Latinos have been considered recognizable groups for purposes of equal protection challenges to jury formation. *See Washington v. Davis*, 426 U.S. 229, 241 (1976); *Hernandez v. Texas*, 347 U.S. 475 (1954); *State v. Hough*, 299 N.C. 245 (1980).

E. Second Prong of an Equal Protection Claim: Substantial Underrepresentation

To satisfy the second prong of the *Castaneda* test, the defendant must demonstrate that the procedures employed for the selection of jurors resulted in a substantial underrepresentation of the identifiable group over a significant period of time. *See State v. Hardy*, 293 N.C. 105 (1977). The substantial underrepresentation must be proven by comparing the proportion of the group in the total population to the proportion of the group at some stage of the jury formation process over a significant period of time. *Id.* In *Castaneda v. Partida*, 430 U.S. 482 (1977), evidence reflecting eleven years of jury pools was sufficient, and in *Cofield*, 320 N.C. 297, 309 (1987), data from an 18-year period constituted evidence over a significant period of time. However, it is not necessary to present evidence of substantial underrepresentation over several years to establish the second prong of the *Castaneda* test. In *Alexander v. Louisiana*, 405 U.S. 625, 629–32 (1972), evidence that pertained only to the grand jury formation process in the defendant's individual case constituted sufficient evidence to make out a prima facie equal protection claim.

When evaluating claims of underrepresentation, North Carolina appellate courts have examined absolute disparity figures, which have been considered on a case-by-case basis. This means that the courts have compared the percentage of the group in the jury pool to the percentage of eligible members of the group in the county. *See State v. Hough,* 299 N.C. 245, 252 (1980). For example, if African Americans comprise 40% of the population but only 10% of the jury pool, the absolute disparity would be 30%. For a further discussion of various measures of disparities, see *supra* "Practice note: calculating underrepresentation" in § 6.3E, Second Prong of a Fair Cross-Section Claim: Underrepresentation. North Carolina courts have not found violations with absolute disparities of:

- 9.6 percent, *see State v. Avery*, 315 N.C. 1 (1985)
- 6.4 percent, *see State v. Hough*, 299 N.C. 245 (1980)
- 9 percent, *see State v. Avery*, 299 N.C. 126 (1980)
- 11 percent, *see State v. Brower*, 289 N.C. 644 (1976)
- 10 percent, *see State v. Cornell*, 281 N.C. 20 (1972)

Equal protection claims of exclusion from jury service generally will not succeed where the defendant does not present statistical analysis in support of his or her claim of underrepresentation. *See State v. King*, 299 N.C. 707, 710 (1980) (holding there was "no constitutional violation since defendant has not shown any significant underrepresentation of his race on the jury list or jury venire from which to infer there was intentional discrimination"); *State v. Hardy*, 293 N.C. 105, 114 (1977) (claim defeated where defendants presented evidence that 22% of grand jurors were women, but failed to present evidence substantiating the percentage of women in the total county population, and therefore "failed to show any under-representation of women on grand juries in Burke County"). Cases in which defendants have demonstrated substantial underrepresentation and achieved success on the merits of equal protection challenges to jury composition include:

- *State v. Cofield*, 320 N.C. 297 (1987) (defendants made out a prima facie case of discrimination where the evidence showed that, while 61% of the county's population was Black, only one of 33 grand jury forepersons appointed over an 18-year period was Black).
- *Castaneda v. Partida*, 430 U.S. 482 (1977) (40% disparity between Mexican-Americans in the county versus Mexican-Americans summoned for grand jury service over an eleven-year period found constitutionally impermissible).
- *Turner v. Fouche*, 396 U.S. 346 (1970) (23% absolute disparity between total population of Black citizens and number of Black people on a single jury list violated Equal Protection Clause).
- *Whitus v. Georgia*, 385 U.S. 545 (1967) (18% absolute disparity between Black people on the annual tax lists (used as a source of names in jury formation) and Black people on defendant's grand jury and 19.3% absolute disparity between Black people on the annual tax lists and Black people on defendant's trial jury venire held impermissible).
- *Jones v. Georgia,* 389 U.S. 24 (1967) (14.7% absolute disparity between Black people listed on annual tax lists and Black people selected for a jury list used in assembling the grand jury list deemed impermissible).
- *Hernandez v. Texas*, 347 U.S. 475 (1954) (14% absolute disparity between people of Mexican descent in the county and such people on a jury commission, grand jury, or petit jury over a period of 25 years deemed impermissible; no one with a Mexican surname had served on any of these bodies in 25 years).

As in the fair cross-section context, courts have refrained from adopting a bright line rule concerning how great the disparity must be before it violates equal protection. However, absolute disparities over 10%, and especially those over 15%, are generally considered constitutionally significant. The Supreme Court of Louisiana found constitutionally significant disparities with an absolute disparity between 15.5% and 15.9% for African Americans and 25.4% women in grand jury foreperson selection. *See State v. Langley,* 813 So. 2d. 356 (La. 2002). The court held that those absolute disparities were "sufficient statistically to establish the degree of underrepresentation from which the district court could find that the defendant had established a prima facie case of intentional discrimination." *Id.* at 371. Similarly, the Appellate Court of Illinois held that a 20% disparity in conjunction with discriminatory selection of White jurors was constitutionally significant. *See People v. Hollins*, 852 N.E.2d 414 (Ill. App. Ct. 2006); *see also Stephens v. Cox*, 449 F 2d 657, 659–60 (4th Cir. 1971) (prima facie case shown by 15% disparity); *Rideu v. Whitley*, 237 F.3d 472 (5th Cir. 2000) (prima facie case satisfied with showing of 14.5% disparity). *Cf. Woodfox v. Cain*, 926 F. Supp. 2d 841 (M.D. La. 2013) (22.3% disparity found significant for grand jury forepersons).

The only case in which a North Carolina appellate court found a sufficient absolute disparity to constitute prima facie evidence of an equal protection violation was *State v. Cofield*, 320 N.C. 297 (1987), where there was a nearly 60 percent disparity between the percentage of Black people serving as grand jury forepersons over an 18-year period and the percentage of Black people in the county. In other cases, North Carolina appellate courts have noted that the absolute disparity demonstrated by the defendant did not rise to the level of those found constitutionally significant in other cases. *See, e.g.*, *State v. Avery*, 299 N.C. 126 (1980) (nine percent disparity between Black population in Mecklenburg County and Black people represented on county jury pool insignificant in comparison to cases in which disparities of between 18% and 40% were demonstrated, especially since the evidence did not support a finding that the jury pool composition process was susceptible of abuse).

For information on gathering statistical evidence to support a claim of underrepresentation, see "Expert assistance in substantiating claims of underrepresentation" in § 6.5B, Mechanics of Challenging Jury Formation. As with fair cross-section claims, courts generally have considered absolute disparities when reviewing equal protection challenges to jury formation, though in many cases, other measurements of disparity may better reflect underrepresentation. *See supra* "Practice note: calculating underrepresentation" in § 6.3E, Second Prong of a Fair Cross-Section Claim: Underrepresentation. As the U.S. Supreme Court recently recognized in the related context of a fair cross-section challenge, no method of measuring disparity is perfect, and defenders should therefore consider calculating disparities according to the methods that best illustrate the underrepresentation at issue. *See id.*

F. Third Prong of an Equal Protection Claim: Procedures that Are not Racially Neutral or Are Susceptible of Abuse

Last, a successful equal protection claim requires evidence that the jury selection procedure is susceptible of abuse or not racially neutral. A presumption of purposeful discrimination arises from "the combined force of the statistical showing and the highly subjective method of selection." *See Castaneda v. Partida,* 430 U.S. 482, 495 n.14 (1977). Such evidence supports an inference of invidious and purposeful discrimination. *Id.* Without this proof, the statistical evidence will not raise an inference of discrimination sufficient to establish a prima facie case. This prong is related to the second prong of the test, since "a borderline disparity figure looks more troubling if the system uses subjective selection policies, and less worrisome if the polices are objective and race-neutral." Nina W. Chernoff, *Wrong About the Right: How Courts Undermine the Fair Cross-Section Guarantee by Confusing It with Equal Protection*, 64 HASTINGS L.J. 141, 159 (2012); *see also infra* "Gathering evidence of underrepresentation" in § 6.5B, Mechanics of Challenging Jury Formation.

G. Burden Shifting

Once the defendant has made out a prima facie equal protection claim, the burden of proof shifts to the State to "dispel the inference of intentional discrimination." *Castaneda v. Partida*, 430 U.S. 482, 497–98 (1977). *See also Alexander v. Louisiana*, 405 U.S. 625, 631–32 (1972) ("Once a prima facie case of invidious discrimination is established, the burden of proof shifts to the State to rebut the presumption of unconstitutional action by showing that permissible racially neutral selection criteria and procedures have produced the monochromatic result.").

H. Raising Due Process Claims Alongside Equal Protection Claims

Before the adoption of article I, sec. 24 and 26 of the North Carolina Constitution and the development of fair cross-section jurisprudence, some challenges to the exclusion of racial minorities from jury service were raised and analyzed as due process violations under the law of the land clause now found in art. 1, sec. 19 of the state constitution. In *State v. Lowry*, 263 N.C. 536, 545–46 (1965), the North Carolina Supreme Court declared that "[t]his Court has held in a long and unbroken line of cases beginning with *State v. Peoples*, 131 N.C. 784, 42 S.E. 814 (1902), that arbitrary exclusion of citizens from service on grand juries on account of race is a denial of due process to members of the excluded race charged with indictable offenses." *See also State v. Yoes*, 271 N.C. 616 (1967); *State v. Covington*, 258 N.C. 501, 504 (1963). For example, in *State v. Speller,* 229 N.C. 67 (1948), the North Carolina Supreme Court relied on the right to due process in rejecting the practice in Union County by which "the names of Negroes in the jury box were printed in red, while those of whites were printed in black. When the name of a Negro was drawn from the box it was discarded and the juror was not summoned. This Court ruled that these practices are discriminatory and arbitrary, and declared . . . that the law knows no distinction among those whose names are rightly in the jury box, and none should be recognized by the administrative officials." *State v. Lowry*, 263 N.C. 536, 545–46 (1965) (quotation omitted).

In recent years, North Carolina appellate courts have confined their consideration of constitutional challenges to jury composition to fair cross-section and equal protection claims. Thus, there is no recent North Carolina case discussing the elements necessary to make out a due process challenge to exclusion of racial minorities from the jury system. However, given the historical reliance on the due process right when considering cases of racial discrimination in jury composition, defenders should consider raising due process claims alongside equal protection claims if the evidence suggests that racial discrimination may have played a role in the jury formation process.

6.5 Challenges to North Carolina Procedures for Jury Formation

A. North Carolina Procedures for Jury Formation

G.S. 9-1 through 9-7 describe the statutory requirements for compiling the lists of people for jury service. The provisions are as follows:

- G.S. 9-1 details the composition and funding mechanisms of the jury commission.
- G.S. 9-2 sets out the requirements for the preparation of the master jury list. It describes the timing of preparation; the acceptable sources from which the lists may be drawn, including the mandatory use of driver and voter lists; the mandatory size of the jury list; the random method that must be used to select jury panels; and the mandate that the procedures for preparing the master list be in writing and available for public inspection with the clerk of the court.
- G.S. 9-3 outlines the qualifications of prospective jurors. It provides that citizens of the state and residents of the county are qualified to serve as jurors if they have not served as jurors during the preceding two years, are over the age of 18, are physically and mentally competent, can understand the English language, and if they have been convicted of a felony, have had their citizenship rights restored.
- G.S. 9-4 describes how and where the jury list should be kept. It requires that the public be able to examine the alphabetized list of names of each juror, but provides that juror addresses are confidential and may not be discovered without an order of the court.
- G.S. 9-5 describes the procedure for drawing panels of jurors from the master jury list.
- G.S. 9-6 sets forth the reasons why a juror may be excused from jury duty. It mandates that chief district court judges publish procedures by which they or the court administrator will entertain and rule on applications to be excused from jury service. This section does not affect the discretionary authority judges have to excuse jurors at the beginning or during a session of court.
- G.S. 9-7 requires that the names of people summoned and their dates of service be noted on the master jury list and sets out a two-year period where those individuals cannot be called again for jury service. It also allows the clerk of court to assign duties to the court administrator.

See NORTH CAROLINA ADMINISTRATIVE OFFICE OF THE COURTS, A MANUAL FOR NORTH CAROLINA JURY COMMISSIONERS AND CLERKS OF SUPERIOR COURT 13 (5th ed. 2013).

In a case decided before the U.S. Supreme Court clarified the standards applicable to jury formation equal protection challenges in *Castaneda v. Partida*, 430 U.S. 482 (1977), the North Carolina Supreme Court held that North Carolina's statutory procedure for selecting and drawing jurors for service is non-discriminatory. *State v. Cornell*, 281 N.C. 20, 37 (1972). The court determined that the jury formation statutes leave little room for exercising discretion, and thus serve as a system of jury selection that is not susceptible to abuse if followed. *Id.*; *see also Folston v. Allsbrook,* 691 F.2d 184, 186 (4th Cir. 1982) (impartiality of North Carolina jury selection procedures dispelled any inference of discrimination arising from statistical disparity). In *State v. Hardy*, 293 N.C. 105, 116 (1977), the court concluded that, by following the statute and utilizing a race neutral selection procedure for selecting names from the list, the State was not in violation of a defendant's right to equal protection. *See also State v. Blakeney*, 352 N.C. 287 (2000) (observing that G.S. 9-2, which governs the selection of the jury pool, "has been expressly recognized as providing a system for objective selection of veniremen" (quotation omitted)).

These cases do not preclude the possibility that constitutional or statutory violations may occur in North Carolina's jury formation process, however. First, they only address the right to equal protection, not the right to a fair cross section of the community, which does not require a showing of discriminatory intent. *See, e.g.*, *State v. Price*, 301 N.C. 437, 445 (1980) (even if "the procedure followed by the . . . Jury Commission comport[s] with the statutory requirements for constituting a jury pool . . . that observation does not [end the inquiry]"). Second, a statutory or equal protection challenge might lie where the statutory process is not followed. Third, the leading North Carolina cases are over thirty years old, and North Carolina courts may find that the statutory plan should be reconsidered if it is consistently producing disparities. The following section describes violations that may arise at various stages of the jury formation process and how to raise them.

B. Mechanics of Challenging Jury Formation

Time to investigate claims. The North Carolina Supreme Court has held that a defendant must be allowed a reasonable time and opportunity to inquire into and present evidence regarding the alleged exclusion of a racial group from the jury pool. *State v. Spencer,* 276 N.C. 535 (1970). Whether a defendant has been given a reasonable time and opportunity to investigate and produce evidence of racial discrimination in the drawing and selection of jurors depends on the facts of each case. *State v. Perry,* 248 N.C. 334 (1958). In rejecting a claim that a defendant's due process rights were violated when he was denied a continuance to investigate possible underrepresentation in the jury pool, the North Carolina Supreme Court provided the following guidance on what might constitute a reasonable time to investigate such claims:

> It places no undue burden on defense counsel to require them to make investigations into jury composition and selection procedures prior to the time of trial, so long as the time between retention or appointment of counsel, the date the jury panel is drawn, and the date of trial is not so brief as to make such investigation impractical. The jury list from which petit jurors are selected is prepared biennially, G.S. 9-2, is a public record, G.S. 9-4, and the jury commissioners who possess knowledge of the sources from which the master jury list is compiled are local residents. G.S. 9-1. Persons who wish to be excused from jury duty must apply to the chief district judge, or another district judge designated by him, at a publicly announced time and place.

> 9-6(b). The record here shows that the names of the sixty jurors were publicly known for fifty-five days prior to the time the case was called for trial. This afforded defense counsel reasonable time and opportunity to inquire into the race of each juror, the composition of the jury box, the procedures for drawing the jury, the race and number of jurors not summoned by the sheriff and the reason therefor, the race and number of jurors excused, and the practices and procedures employed by the chief district judge when passing upon excuses. Failure to make such inquiry creates no c onstitutional right, in the name of Due Process, to additional time for such investigation simply because all jurors who reported for jury duty on the day defendant's case was called for trial were white. An automatic continuance for such inquiries, upon motion lodged for the first time when the case is called for trial, would fatally disrupt every session of court.
>
> Under the facts of this case defendant has not been deprived of a reasonable opportunity to investigate the "possibility" of systematic exclusion of blacks from the petit jury.

State v. Harbison, 293 N.C. 474, 481–82 (1977) (internal citation omitted). In light of this holding as well as the requirements for showing a violation in the jury formation process, defense attorneys should conduct factual investigations and seek discovery, discussed further below, well before their client's case is scheduled for trial.

Discovery. Because of the showing required to establish underrepresentation in the jury formation process, commentators and courts have recognized that a defendant's right to question whether a jury reflects a fair cross section of the community is "meaningless without an entitlement to discovery." *See* Nina W. Chernoff & Joseph B. Kadane, *The 16 Things Every Defense Attorney Should Know About Fair Cross-Section Challenges*, THE CHAMPION, Dec. 2013, at 14, 16. The same can be said of equal protection guarantees.

Courts interpreting the fair cross-section guarantees of the Sixth Amendment have generally held that there is no threshold showing required to obtain discovery about the jury formation process when preparing a fair cross-section claim. *See, e.g.*, *Mobley v. United States*, 379 F.2d 768, 772 (5th Cir. 1967) (trial court erred by denying defendant's motion for discovery on claim of racial discrimination in formation of grand and petit jury); *State v. Ciba-Geigy Corp.*, 573 A.2d 944, 950 (N.J. Super. Ct. App. Div. 1990) ("It would be virtually impossible for defendants who are endeavoring to ascertain if a successful attack on the grand jury selection process can be advanced if the facts necessary to prove a defect in the selection process are withheld."). *But see People v. Jackson*, 920 P.2d 1254, 1268 (Cal. 1996) (defendant entitled to discovery concerning jury formation process "upon a particularized showing supporting a reasonable belief that underrepresentation in the jury pool or the venire exists as the result of practices of systematic exclusion"). The Jury Selection and Service Act of 1968 (JSSA), 28 U.S.C. §§ 1861–1878, a federal statute that guarantees grand and trial juries composed of a randomly selected fair cross section of the community, includes a right to discovery. The

U.S. Supreme Court has interpreted the JSSA as providing "essentially an unqualified right to inspect" jury selection materials, and has held that this right is based not only on the statutory language, but also on the law's "overall purpose of insuring 'grand and petit juries selected at random from a fair cross section of the community,'" a purpose inherent in the Sixth Amendment fair cross-section guarantee as well. *Test v. United States*, 420 U.S. 28, 30 (1975) (quoting 28 U.S.C. § 1861); *see* Nina W. Chernoff & Joseph B. Kadane, *The 16 Things Every Defense Attorney Should Know About Fair Cross-Section Challenges*, THE CHAMPION, Dec. 2013, at 14, 16.

The Missouri Supreme Court, although finding that a fair cross-section claimant's discovery rights were not guaranteed by either the federal JSSA or Missouri state statutes, recognized that a state court defendant's Sixth Amendment fair cross-section right "would be without meaning if a defendant were denied all means of discovery in an effort to assert that right." *State ex rel. Garrett v. Saitz*, 594 S.W.2d 606, 608 (Mo. 1980) (upholding defendant's request for jury list data on constitutional grounds); *see also Commonwealth v. Arriaga*, 781 N.E.2d 1253, 1268 (Mass. 2003) ("The right to a trial before a jury representing a fair cross section of the community is a critical constitutional protection and should be scrupulously honored by providing defendants with reasonable access to accurate information concerning the race and ethnicity of prospective jurors."). *See* Discovery Motion – Fair Cross Section Claim in the Race Materials Bank at www.ncids.org (select "Training and Resources").

Type of information to seek in discovery. Discovery requests should be tied to the specific showing necessary to support the claims you intend to raise. For example, in the case of a fair cross-section claim, a defendant may want to seek:

- demographic information concerning the groups allegedly underrepresented, at each stage of the jury formation process;
- where such information is unavailable or not collected, information from which demographic data can be obtained, such as jury questionnaires and, in some cases, opportunities to send additional questionnaires to past jurors to collect demographic data; *see* Nina W. Chernoff & Joseph B. Kadane, *The 16 Things Every Defense Attorney Should Know About Fair Cross-Section Challenges*, THE CHAMPION Dec. 2013, at 14, 20 (noting that "when a jury selection system has failed to collect the relevant demographic data, courts typically order the disclosure of information from which racial, ethnic, and gender data can be gleaned" and collecting cases in which courts issued such orders);
- master jury lists;
- data reflecting excusals, deferrals, or disqualifications occurring at any stage in the jury formation process;
- data reflecting the process by which jury commissioners determine whether a person's name should be removed from the master jury list because he or she does not speak English, is not a citizen, or is a felon whose rights have not been restored;
- data concerning the summoning process;
- data reflecting the procedures for responding to undeliverable summonses;

- depositions of jury commissioners or others involved in the jury formation process. *See* Nina W. Chernoff & Joseph B. Kadane, *The 16 Things Every Defense Attorney Should Know About Fair Cross-Section Challenges*, THE CHAMPION Dec. 2013, at 14, 20 (noting that courts have ordered "jury system administrators to participate in depositions designed to improve the defendant's understanding of the jury selection system" and collecting cases).

For more information on seeking discovery in fair cross-section cases, see Nina W. Chernoff & Joseph B. Kadane, *The 16 Things Every Defense Attorney Should Know About Fair Cross-Section Challenges*, THE CHAMPION Dec. 2013, at 14, 20.

Gathering evidence of underrepresentation. Defendants cannot wait until the potential jurors enter the courtroom to begin collecting evidence relevant to an underrepresentation claim. A viable fair cross-section claim may exist, for example, where a master jury list has been assembled using a process that systematically underrepresents a distinctive group regardless of whether the particular venire for a given case is representative. Additionally, evidence of a historical pattern of underrepresentation typically must be produced by defendants raising fair cross section claims. Defendants often will not have time to conduct such research immediately before trial, as North Carolina courts have denied continuances for the purposes of investigating claims of underrepresentation where there was a reasonable opportunity to do so before trial. *See, e.g.*, *Harbison,* 293 N.C. 474, 481–82. Thus, in addition to seeking discovery, it is important, alone or in partnership with other defenders, to investigate the racial composition of jury panels in your county over an extended period of time to lay the groundwork for a successful claim. In some cases, counsel may be able to obtain records from the clerk of superior court regarding the demographic information of past jurors and juror panelists. *See, e.g.*, *State v. Cofield*, 320 N.C. 297 (1987) (defendant "introduced a report prepared by Mr. R.J. White, Northampton County's Clerk of Superior Court, listing all who had served as grand jury foreman since 1960 by name, race, and sex"). To prepare for jury selection, attorneys can check the list of jurors on a defendant's jury panel in the clerk's office approximately one week before trial. Attorneys can review that list to ensure that there are no obvious violations of the randomness requirement (e.g., not all people have last names beginning with the same letters), and may try to discover the race of the people listed on the jury panel by searching on the Board of Election's website or on LexisNexis peoplefinder.

Where it appears that either (1) proper jury formation procedures have not been followed, or (2) racial minorities are consistently underrepresented on the jury panels in the county, attorneys should be prepared to document the problems observed and put that documentation in the record. For example, if you rarely observe Black jurors on jury panels in a county with a sizable Black population, you may consider working with an investigator or other defense attorneys to take notes of the number of jurors reporting for service along with their gender, ethnicity, and race (to the extent that such information can be gathered from observation). If the evidence collected through informal observation over a sustained period of time (for example, six months) suggests that a distinctive racial group or groups is not represented fairly in comparison to county census data, this evidence may provide support for a challenge to the composition of the jury pool. Informal data collection methods may be particularly useful in this context since "[t]ypically only the court and the jury selection system have access to information about . . . preliminary stages of the selection process." *See* Nina W. Chernoff & Joseph B. Kadane, *The 16 Things Every Defense Attorney Should Know About Fair Cross-Section Challenges*, THE CHAMPION, Dec. 2013, at 14, 15. The observed disparities may indicate the need to seek discovery in an individual case and/or constitute evidence supporting a constitutional or statutory challenge. *See supra* § 6.5A, North Carolina Procedures for Jury Formation; *see also infra* § 6.6, Beyond Litigation: Efforts to Ensure Representative Juries (discussing analysis of jury formation in North Carolina judicial district 15B). Trial attorneys should develop a practice of asking the trial court to have panel members state their race on the record to ensure the reliability of the evidence. *See State v. Mitchell*, 321 N.C. 650, 656 (1988) (inappropriate for court reporter to note the race of the jurors based on his or her perception; "if there is any question as to the prospective juror's race, this issue should be resolved by the trial court based upon questioning of the juror or other proper evidence"); *see* Motion for Court Reporter to Note Race of All Jurors Examined for Selection in the Race Materials Bank at www.ncids.org (select "Training and Resources").

Expert assistance in substantiating claims of underrepresentation. A statistical showing is generally required to demonstrate underrepresentation. When you believe that data available through discovery or investigation may support a claim of underrepresentation, consider seeking funds to hire an expert in statistics to analyze data relevant to your anticipated claims. An expert qualified to perform such an analysis will usually be a university statistics professor, or a PhD candidate with at least a Master's level knowledge of statistics. *See, e.g.,* Website of Professor Joseph B. Kadane, STAT.CMU.EDU (last visited Sept. 2, 2014) (expert witness in at least two successful fair cross-section cases).

North Carolina courts have granted requests for funds for a statistician to analyze jury data where adequately supported. *Compare State v Moore*, 100 N.C. App. 217 (1990) (initial motion for statistical expert to analyze race discrimination in grand and petit juries granted; motion for funds for additional study denied), *rev'd on other grounds*, 329 N.C. 245 (1991), *with State v. Massey*, 316 N.C. 558 (1986) (finding defendant did not make adequate showing to warrant funds for statistician). *See also Isaacs v. State*, 386 S.E.2d 316, 324 (Ga. 1989) ("in an appropriate case, based upon a sufficient showing of need, the denial of funds for expert assistance might violate due process"). For a further discussion of requesting funds for expert assistance, see 1 NORTH CAROLINA DEFENDER MANUAL § 5.3 (Applying for Funding) (2d ed. 2013).

Defense attorneys should work with their experts to identify the information needed to assess whether the underrepresentation occurred by chance. The expert can start by accessing the county's master jury list, which is available to the public in the clerk of superior court's office, along with the procedures used to assemble it. This list does not include the race or ethnic background of potential jurors. For this reason, the expert may have to independently research the race of those listed on the master jury list, for example, by searching public databases containing voter registration data. North Carolina records the race and ethnicity of all registered voters, and voter registration information is available in electronic databases such as Lexis. *See* G.S. 163-82.4. Additionally, the defendant may file a discovery motion to obtain background information from the clerk of court. *See* "Type of information to seek in discovery," above, in this subsection B.

Once the expert has gathered information about the racial composition of the jury pool, the procedures used to gather jurors, and the racial composition of the county (using census data reflecting the voting age population), the expert should attempt to determine the stages of the jury selection process at which underrepresentation may be occurring. *See supra* "Does persistent underrepresentation alone constitute systematic exclusion?" in § 6.3F, Third Prong of a Fair Cross-Section Claim: Systematic Exclusion (discussing possible requirement to identify systematic cause of underrepresentation).

Timing and procedure for challenges to grand jury. In the grand jury context, challenges to the propriety of a grand jury indictment, based either on discrimination in the selection of grand jurors or discrimination in the selection of the grand jury foreperson, must be made at or before arraignment in the form of a motion to dismiss. *See* G.S. 15A-952(b)(4); G.S. 15A-955; *State v. Cofield,* 320 N.C. 297 (1987); *State v. Miller*, 339 N.C. 663 (1995) (motion challenging selection of grand jury foreperson is waived if not made by arraignment). If the defendant pleads guilty, he waives the right to challenge discrimination in grand jury composition. *State v. Newkirk*, 14 N.C. App. 53 (1972) (objections to composition of grand jury waived if not raised before plea entered); *see also State v. Green*, 329 N.C. 686 (1991) (plea of guilty constitutes waiver of challenge to selection of grand jury foreperson).

The defendant waives arraignment unless he or she files a timely written request for arraignment with the clerk of court. If arraignment is waived, certain pretrial motions, including challenges to grand jury proceedings, must be filed with 21 days of the return of the indictment. *See* G.S. 15A-941(d), 15A-952(c). Where the motion is not filed within the statutory deadlines, courts have discretion to grant relief from waiver. *See* G.S. 15A-952(e). *See State v. Wilson,* 57 N.C. App 444 (1982).

Remedy for constitutional violation in grand jury. "[D]iscrimination in the grand jury undermines the structural integrity of the criminal tribunal itself, and is not amenable to harmless-error review." *Vasquez v. Hillery*, 474 U.S. 254, 263–64 (1986); *see also State v. Moore,* 329 N.C. 245, 246–48 (1991) (noting that when art. I, sec. 26 is violated, "[t]he integrity of the judicial system is at issue, and a harmless error analysis under these circumstances is inapposite"). The Supreme Court has reasoned that, because discrimination on the basis of race in the selection of grand jurors strikes at the fundamental values of our judicial system and society as a whole, reversal is the only appropriate remedy at the appellate level. *Vasquez*, 474 U.S. 254, 261–62. If the motion to dismiss succeeds at the trial level and the indictment is dismissed, the State is free to reindict. *See State v. Pigott*, 331 N.C. 199 (1992).

Timing and procedure for challenges to jury panel. A challenge to the jury panel (the group of potential jurors from which jurors for a particular trial may be drawn) must be made in accordance with G.S. 15A-1211(c). The challenge must be made on the ground that the panel members were not selected or drawn according to law, and should take the form of a written motion to discharge the trial panel. *Id.* Be sure the record reveals the race of each panel member. *State v. Mitchell*, 321 N.C. 650, 656 (1988) (inappropriate for court reporter to note the race of the jurors based on his or her perception; "if there is any question as to the prospective juror's race, this issue should be resolved by the trial court based upon questioning of the juror or other proper evidence"); *see* Motion for Court Reporter to Note Race of All Jurors Examined for Selection in the Race Materials Bank at www.ncids.org (select "Training and Resources"). If the challenge to the panel is sustained, the judge must discharge the panel. G.S. 15A-1211(c).

The motion to discharge the panel must specify the facts constituting the ground of challenge, and it must be made and decided before any juror is examined. *Id.* Failure to follow these steps may constitute a waiver of the claim. *See State v. Smith*, 359 N.C. 199 (2005) (defendant failed to preserve his challenge to the randomness of the jury where he did not comply with G.S. 15A-1211(c)); *State v. Johnson*, 161 N.C. App. 68, 75 (2003) (although a trial judge's failure to follow a statutory mandate usually preserves an error without an objection, the defendant waived appellate review because he failed to follow the procedures outlined in G.S. 15A-1211(c) for challenging a jury panel). The requirements of G.S. 15A-1211(c) may apply to statutory violations only, but to minimize the risk of waiver, counsel should follow them when raising constitutional challenges as well. *See generally* Nina W. Chernoff & Joseph B. Kadane, *The 16 Things Every Defense Attorney Should Know About Fair Cross-Section Challenges*, THE CHAMPION, Dec. 2013, at 14, 15 ("Constitutional fair cross-section claims, however, are not required to meet the . . . timeliness requirements of state statutes. Instead, courts generally require constitutional challenges to the selection of the petit jury to be raised *before trial*, pursuant to Federal Rule of Criminal Procedure 12(b) or the state equivalent." (emphasis in original) (footnote omitted)).

Preserving denial of challenges to the trial jury panel. If a challenge to the trial jury panel is denied, the issue must be properly preserved or the appellate court may find waiver. To obtain relief on appeal for some violations, the defendant also may need to show prejudice by exhausting all of his or her peremptory challenges. The cases do not always distinguish clearly between the requirements for preserving error and for showing prejudice.

To preserve a challenge to the jury panel based on the right to a fair and impartial jury under the state and federal constitutions, you must object and state the constitutional basis for the objection. Failure to challenge the jury panel on constitutional grounds at the trial level will waive review of the constitutional issue on appeal. *See State v. Tirado*, 358 N.C. 551, 571 (2004); *State v. Wiley*, 355 N.C. 592, 606 (2005).

To preserve a statutory challenge to a jury panel for appellate review, counsel must follow the mandates of G.S. 15A-1211(c). *See State v. Johnson*, 161 N.C. App. 68

(2003). This statute requires that challenges to the panel:

1. be made on the ground that the jurors were not lawfully selected or drawn;
2. be in writing;
3. specify the facts supporting the ground for the challenge; and
4. be made and decided before the examination of any juror.

G.S. 15A-1211(c).

If you consent to the jury procedures used by the trial judge, appellate review of the issue will be waived. *See, e.g.*, *State v. Meyer*, 353 N.C. 92 (2000) (not only did defendant never object to the jury selection process or follow the statutory procedures for challenging the jury panel, he expressly approved of the reassignment of a prospective juror; court concluded that defendant failed to preserve the issue for appellate review).

Counsel also should be wary of expressing satisfaction with the jury once jury selection has concluded. *See State v. Bell*, 359 N.C. 1 (2004) (denying appellate review where defendant failed to follow the procedures set out in G.S. 15A-1211(c) and noting that defendant answered in the affirmative when asked if he approved of the panel).

For a detailed discussion of how to preserve jury challenges, see "Recommended approach" in 2 NORTH CAROLINA DEFENDER MANUAL § 25.1G (Preserving Denial of Challenges to the Panel) (2d ed. 2012).

C. Statutory Claims

In addition to constitutional challenges, defendants may raise claims that the jury formation process did not comply with North Carolina statutes. G.S. 9-1 through 9-7 describe the statutory requirements for juror selection and outline the procedures for preparing juror lists for grand and trial juries. *See supra* § 6.5A, North Carolina Procedures for Jury Formation. North Carolina appellate courts have held that evidence of a statutory violation alone is not a sufficient basis to sustain a challenge to the jury composition; the defendant must demonstrate "corrupt intent, discrimination, or irregularities which affect the actions of the jurors actually drawn and summoned." *State v. Vaughn*, 296 N.C. 167, 175 (1978) (internal citations omitted). The North Carolina Court of Appeals has suggested that a defendant must also demonstrate that a statutory irregularity affected the defendant. *See State v. Riggs,* 79 N.C. App 398 (1986). Statutory claims should always be raised alongside appropriate constitutional claims.

D. Challenges to Source Lists

Source lists defined. The earliest stage in the jury formation process at which disparities may arise is in the use of source lists. A source list is a list of names that county jury commissions use to compile the master jury list, which is a list compiled each odd-numbered year of all prospective jurors qualified to serve in the two years starting January 1 of the following year. *See* G.S. 9-2(a). (Each county has a jury commission composed of three members who serve two-year terms; one member is appointed by the board of county commissioners, the second by the senior resident superior court judge, and the third by the clerk of superior court. *See* G.S. 9-1.) Since the source lists "define[] the total population from which prospective jurors may be qualified and summonsed . . . the choice of source lists is an important policy decision for state courts insofar that it establishes the inclusiveness and the initial demographic characteristics of the potential jury pool." GREGORY E. MIZE ET AL., NATIONAL CENTER FOR STATE COURTS, THE STATE-OF-THE-STATES SURVEY OF JURY IMPROVEMENT EFFORTS: A COMPENDIUM REPORT 13 (2007).

Source lists in North Carolina. G.S. 9-2(b) identifies the source lists that may be used to compile a master jury list:

> In preparing the master list, the jury commission shall use the list of registered voters and persons with drivers license records supplied to the county by the Commissioner of Motor Vehicles pursuant to G.S. 20-43.4. The commission may use fewer than all the names from the list if it uses a random method of selection. The commission may use other sources of names deemed by it to be reliable.

North Carolina follows the trend of many other states that have begun mandating the use of drivers' lists as a supplement or replacement for voter registration lists because drivers' lists may be more representative of racial minorities than voter registration lists alone. Empirical research into this presumption has resulted in mixed conclusions. *See, e.g.*, Ronald Randall et al., *Racial Representativeness of Juries: An Analysis of Source List and Administrative Effects on the Jury Pool*, 29 JUST. SYS. J. 71 (2008) (study of source lists in one Ohio county revealed that moving from voter registration lists to lists of licensed drivers decreased the representativeness of Black jurors but increased the representativeness of Hispanic jurors); GREGORY E. MIZE ET AL., NATIONAL CENTER FOR STATE COURTS, THE STATE-OF-THE-STATES SURVEY OF JURY IMPROVEMENT EFFORTS: A COMPENDIUM REPORT (2007).

Most of the constitutional challenges to the source lists used to assemble jury pools in North Carolina were raised before the state legislature mandated the use of driver and voter lists in assembling the master jury list. While there were sound reasons to assume that the use of these two lists would draw from a wider cross-section of the community than the previous methods used to assemble juror lists (including property tax lists and the key-man system where "prominent" community members recommended jurors), there is little data available to verify whether this expectation has been borne out. In Nebraska, where juror names are also drawn from a combination of driver and voter lists, a committee examining the representativeness of the jury composition process concluded in 2008 that racial and ethnic minorities were still significantly underrepresented in the initial and eligible pools of jurors. *See* ELIZABETH M. NEELEY, NEBRASKA MINORITY JUSTICE COMMITTEE, REPRESENTATIVE JURIES: EXAMINING THE INITIAL AND ELIGIBLE POOLS OF JURORS (2008). In response to these disparities, the Committee explored whether additional source lists could improve the racial and ethnic diversity of the jury lists. Ultimately, the committee recommended, and the State enacted, legislation mandating the addition of names of residents with state issued identification. Elizabeth Neeley, *Addressing Nonsystematic Factors Contributing to the Underrepresentation of Minorities as Jurors*, 47 CT. REV. 96, 98 (2011) (noting that racial minorities "comprise a much greater percentage of state-identification-card holders than of registered drivers"). North Carolina counties do not include "[i]ndividuals with state issued identification cards from the DMV . . . on the jury list unless they were a licensed, cancelled or suspended driver in the previous eight years." NORTH CAROLINA ADMINISTRATIVE OFFICE OF THE COURTS, A MANUAL FOR NORTH CAROLINA JURY COMMISSIONERS AND CLERKS OF SUPERIOR COURT 5 (5th ed. 2013).

The process of creating the list must be random. The State Board of Elections and the Division of Motor Vehicles create a merged "raw" list of registered voters and licensed drivers, with duplicates removed by the Commissioner of Motor Vehicles, and provide it to the jury commission of each county. *See* G.S. 20-43.4; G.S. 163-82.11. The jury commission may supplement the list using any other reliable source, but this practice happens rarely, if at all. *See* NORTH CAROLINA ADMINISTRATIVE OFFICE OF THE COURTS, A MANUAL FOR NORTH CAROLINA JURY COMMISSIONERS AND CLERKS OF SUPERIOR COURT 5 (5th ed. 2013) ("In recent practice, no counties have elected to supplement the two required lists."). From this raw list, the jury commission creates the master jury list by removing deceased or disqualified people (*see* 1 NORTH CAROLINA DEFENDER MANUAL § 9.1B (Qualifications of Individual Grand Jurors) (2d ed. 2013)) and then randomly selecting the number of names needed. *See* G.S. 9-2(e). "Random" is defined in G.S. 9-2(h) as a method of selection that results in each name on a list having an equal opportunity to be selected.

Source lists in your county. You can discover the source lists used by the jury commission in your county by reviewing the procedure for preparing the master list. Pursuant to G.S. 9-2(j), the jury commission's procedure must be in writing, adopted by the jury commission, and kept available for public inspection in the office of the clerk of court.

Supplementing driver and voter lists with other sources of reliable names. Although it occurs infrequently, G.S. 9-2 allows the jury commission to use other sources of names that it deems to be reliable. North Carolina is among the minority of states that allows jury commissions to supplement mandated source lists with additional lists. *See* GREGORY E. MIZE ET AL., NATIONAL CENTER FOR STATE COURTS, THE STATE-OF-THE-STATES SURVEY OF JURY IMPROVEMENT EFFORTS: A COMPENDIUM REPORT 13 (2007), ("15 states and the District of Columbia permit local courts to supplement the required lists with additional lists").

If the jury commission is using a list other than the drivers' license or voter registration list, there may be grounds for objection. For example, North Carolina previously utilized tax lists to select jurors, but these lists have fallen out of favor as they may exclude low-income, minority, and female residents from jury service. *See* Kurt M. Sanders, *Balancing the Jury Pool*, 69 PA. B.A. Q. 133, 136 (1998) ("Reliance on . . . tax lists [has] a disproportionate impact on economically disadvantaged groups who . . . do not pay taxes."). *But see State v. Cornell*, 281 N.C. 20, 31 (1972) (in a case decided before the fair cross-section right was closely considered by the U.S. Supreme Court, court noted that "a jury list is not discriminatory or unlawful because it is drawn from the tax list of the county").

Process for raising challenge to source list. Since the same source lists underlie the formation of the grand jury and the trial jury, unlawful source lists may taint both juries. For this reason, a defendant challenging the source lists relied on by the jury commission should always challenge the composition of both the grand jury and the trial jury.

To challenge the composition of the jury based on the use of improper source lists, a defendant should file written motions to dismiss the grand jury indictment and quash the trial jury panel. *See supra* § 6.5B, Mechanics of Challenging Jury Formation. The motion to dismiss the grand jury's indictment must be made at or before arraignment. *See* G.S. 15A-952(b)(4); G.S. 15A-955. The motion to quash the trial jury panel must be made and decided before any juror is examined. *See* G.S. 15A-1211(c)(4). Both motions should be made in writing, setting forth the facts constituting the grounds of challenge.

Required showing to challenge source list. Generally speaking, a single unrepresentative panel is not sufficient to show a violation of statutory or constitutional rights; however, a flaw in a single source list that produces underrepresentation may support a statutory or constitutional claim. Defendants challenging source lists should present any evidence that:

- the source list procedures laid out in G.S. 9-2(b) were not followed, resulting in either a statutory violation or fair cross-section violation for underrepresentation; or
- the jury commission relied on an unreliable or unrepresentative source of names in addition to the lists of drivers and registered voters mandated by statute (equal protection and/or fair cross-section violation).

If the county jury commission is relying on an additional source list beyond the voter and driver lists, defense attorneys should determine whether that source list is representative of the demographic composition of the community. This may require assistance from an expert in statistics. *See supra* "Expert assistance in substantiating claims of underrepresentation" in § 6.5B, Mechanics of Challenging Jury Formation.

Defense attorneys should compare the demographic composition of the source list to census data reflecting the population in the county as a whole to determine whether there is underrepresentation. While the jury commission's alphabetized master list is public record (*see* G.S. 9-4), the source lists are not (*see* G.S. 20-43.1; G.S. 20-43.4). However, the source lists may be discoverable by order of the court. *See* G.S. 20-43.1(a) (requiring Division to disclose personal information from motor vehicle records in accordance with 18 U.S.C. § 2721(b)(4)); 18 U.S.C. § 2721(b)(4) (stating that personal information collected by a state Department of Motor Vehicles may be disclosed "in connection with any civil, criminal, administrative, or arbitral proceeding in any Federal, State, or local court or agency or before any self-regulatory body, including the service of process, investigation in anticipation of litigation, and the execution or enforcement of judgments and orders, or pursuant to an order of a Federal, State, or local court").

Equal protection challenge to source lists. Given our Supreme Court's holding that the statutory procedures governing jury formation are facially non-discriminatory (*see State v. Cornell*, 281 N.C. 20 (1972)), the most viable equal protection claim based on source lists in North Carolina would be one against the use of additional lists. *See also supra* § 6.5A, North Carolina Procedures for Jury Formation (discussing possible limitations of the *Cornell* court's holding). If the jury commission relies on additional source lists, the defendant can argue that the procedure in G.S. 9-2(b) allowing jury commissions to supplement driver and voter lists with additional lists deemed reliable is susceptible to abuse as it allows individual jury commissioners to exercise discretion in determining what additional source lists are reliable or representative. This evidence would support the third prong of the test laid out in *Castaneda v. Partida*, 430 U.S. 482 (1977), a procedure susceptible of abuse. The second prong of the test—underrepresentation of a distinctive group—would have to be shown with statistical evidence.

Source lists of drivers and voters are not public record (*see* G.S. 20-43.4), but if research suggests that the additional source lists are being used and do not fairly represent a distinctive group, the defendant should seek discovery of information about the additional source lists, including names and any demographic information. The defense attorney and the expert retained to challenge the additional source list should compare the rate at which the distinctive group appears in the voting age community from U.S. census data with the rate at which the group appears in the additional source list. Evidence that the distinctive group is underrepresented in the source list, especially where the absolute disparity is over 10%, would support the first two prongs of an equal protection claim. *See supra* § 6.4, Equal Protection Challenges.

Fair cross-section challenge to source lists. To support a fair-cross section challenge to source lists, the defendant must show that the representation of a distinctive group (such as African Americans or Latinos) in the source lists was not fair and reasonable in relation to the number of jury-eligible members of that group in the community. In a challenge to source lists, this can be done by comparing county census data to an analysis of the representation of the distinctive group in the additional challenged source lists.

In addition, the defendant must show that the underrepresentation was due to a systematic exclusion of the group. *See Duren v. Missouri*, 439 U.S. 357 (1979). In a challenge to source lists, systemic exclusion could be demonstrated by showing that the jury commission relied on a source list that itself inherently underrepresents the distinctive group. For example, a jury commission that uses membership lists from groups primarily consisting of a particular race, gender, or economic status would result in a systemic exclusion of other classes of people. *See, e.g.*, *People v. White*, 278 P.2d 9 (Cal. 1954) (holding that the jury commissioner's use of membership lists from clubs such as the Rotary Club, the Lion's Club, and certain women's groups tended to produce venires that were not representative of a cross-section of the community).

Defendants also may challenge source lists for grand juries. *See supra* "Application to grand jury" in § 6.3A, Applicability and Standing (discussing argument for applying fair cross-section guarantee to grand juries).

Defendants alleging that the source lists used to form the grand or trial jury did not reflect a fair cross section of the community should also raise claims based on article I, sections 24 and 26 of the North Carolina Constitution. *See supra* § 6.3A, Applicability and Standing (North Carolina courts use the same standards when reviewing fair cross-section claims raised pursuant to federal and state constitutional guarantees).

E. Challenges to the Master Jury List

After the sources are identified, the jury commission takes the names from the source lists, removes the names of deceased and disqualified people, and randomly selects the number of names needed to form the master jury list from which individual jury panels are drawn for specific trial proceedings. This procedure is governed by G.S. 9-2.

Challenges to master jury list based on North Carolina statutes. At least one court has recognized that "if [the master jury] list is not representative of a cross-section of the community, the process is constitutionally defective *ab initio*." *People v. Wheeler*, 583 P.2d 748 (Cal. 1978). As with other statutorily-based challenges to jury formation procedures, the defendant must demonstrate a statutory violation along with evidence of corrupt intent, systemic discrimination, or irregularities affecting the jurors. *State v. Vaughn*, 296 N.C. 167, 175 (1978) (internal citations omitted); *see also State v. Johnson*, 317 N.C. 343, 379 (1986).

"Irregularities" might result from a failure to use the required random selection method in assembling the master jury list. A random selection method is one "that results in each name on a list having an equal opportunity to be selected." G.S. 9-2(h). When raising a statutory violation, a defendant should raise constitutional claims as well, as the court may view statutory irregularities as circumstantial evidence of discriminatory intent supporting an equal protection claim or systemic exclusion supporting a fair cross-section claim.

Equal protection or fair cross-section challenge to the master jury list. Where disparities in jury panels exist and suggest possible constitutional violations in the construction of the master jury list, the defense attorney should work with an expert to examine the composition of the list. *See supra* "Expert assistance in substantiating claims of underrepresentation" in § 6.5B, Mechanics of Challenging Jury Formation. The expert can start by accessing the county's master jury list, which is available to the public in the Clerk of Court's office, along with the procedures used to assemble it. However, this list does not include the race or ethnic background of potential jurors. For this reason, the expert will either have to independently research the race of those listed on the master jury list, by searching voter registration data or other public databases, or the defendant will have to file a discovery motion seeking background information sufficient to support the defendant's constitutional claim. *See supra* "Expert assistance in substantiating claims of underrepresentation" in § 6.5B, Mechanics of Challenging Jury Formation; *see also* Nina W. Chernoff & Joseph B. Kadane, *The 16 Things Every Defense Attorney Should Know About Fair Cross-Section Challenges*, THE CHAMPION, Dec. 2013, at 14, 20. ("[W]hen a jury selection system has failed to collect the relevant demographic data, courts typically order the disclosure of information from which racial, ethnic, and gender data can be gleaned."); Discovery Motion – Fair Cross Section Claim in the Race Materials Bank at www.ncids.org (select "Training and Resources"). The North Carolina Supreme Court has held that, even if juror commissioners can guess the race of potential jurors from their home addresses, that alone is not enough to raise an inference of intentional discrimination. *State v. Cornell*, 281 N.C. 20, 34–35 (1972).

Required showing and procedure. The master jury list is used for both grand and trial juries. For this reason, if there is a flaw in the compilation of the master jury list, the defendant should raise challenges to both the grand and the trial jury. To challenge the use of an improper master jury list, a defendant should file written motions to dismiss the grand jury's indictment and quash the trial jury panel. *See supra* § 6.5B, Mechanics of Challenging Jury Formation. The motion to dismiss the grand jury's indictment must be made at or before arraignment. *See* G.S. 15A-952(b)(4). The motion to quash the trial jury panel should be made before any juror is examined. *See* G.S. 15A-1211(c)(4). Both motions should be made in writing, setting forth the facts constituting the grounds of challenge.

F. Challenges to the Exclusion of Qualified Jurors from the Jury List

A defendant may object to the master jury list if he or she can show that the list excludes qualified jurors who should appear on the list. Under G.S. 9-3, qualified jurors include residents of the county who have not served as a juror during the past two years (six years for grand jury service) and are eighteen or older, mentally and physically competent, citizens of the State, able to understand English, and, if ever convicted of a felony, have had their citizenship rights restored. When a person convicted of a felony completes his or her sentence, including any period of probation or parole or other required actions such as community service or restitution payments, his or her citizenship rights are automatically restored pursuant to statute. *See* G.S. 13-1; G.S. 13-2. However, jury commissioners may face practical challenges in ensuring that felons whose citizenship rights have been restored are not excluded from the master jury list. *See, e.g.*, NORTH CAROLINA ADMINISTRATIVE OFFICE OF THE COURTS, A MANUAL FOR NORTH CAROLINA JURY COMMISSIONERS AND CLERKS OF SUPERIOR COURT 8 n.11 (5th ed. 2013) (noting that jury commissioners may request a list of convicted felons from the Administrative Office of the Courts, but warning that "extreme caution" should be exercised in using such lists to remove names from the master jury list since neither the clerks nor the Administrative Office of the Courts are notified when a felon's rights are restored).

English language requirement. The requirement that jurors be able to "hear and understand the English language" has been challenged as a violation of article I, section 26 of the North Carolina Constitution, which prohibits exclusion from jury service based on national origin, and as a violation of the equal protection guarantee found in article I, section 19 of the North Carolina Constitution. *State v. Smith*, 352 N.C. 531 (2000). The North Carolina Supreme Court has rejected this argument, holding that differences in ethnicity or national origin do not preclude English comprehension and concluding that the provision does not violate due process or equal protection guarantees. *Id.* Other courts that have considered this challenge have also rejected it. *See People v. Eubanks*, 266 P.3d 301 (Cal. 2011).

However, jury commissioners must apply the English language requirement properly. If you observe, for example, underrepresentation of native Spanish-speakers on jury panels in your judicial district, check the jury commissioners' procedures to find out how they are determining whether potential jurors listed on the merged lists speak and understand English, and whether potential jurors have been improperly disqualified because they have Hispanic-sounding names. *See* NORTH CAROLINA ADMINISTRATIVE OFFICE OF THE COURTS, A MANUAL FOR NORTH CAROLINA JURY COMMISSIONERS AND CLERKS OF SUPERIOR COURT 7–8 (5th ed. 2013) (noting that jury commissioners shall remove non-English speakers from the jury list, but manual does not provide standards by which this determination is to be made).

Administrative practices that may remove qualified jurors from jury lists. Certain methods to remove unqualified or inaccurate names from the master jury list or jury panels could present constitutional concerns. For example, in Santa Barbara County, California, the court routinely removed from the master jury list individuals who had failed to appear for jury service in the past, with the intention of following up with these individuals in the future. When a defendant raised a challenge claiming that Latinos were underrepresented in the jury pool, the court discovered that a disproportionate number of individuals whose names were removed from the master jury list for this reason had Latino last names. National Center for State Courts, *Jury Managers Toolbox: Characteristics of an Effective Master Jury List*, NCSC CENTER FOR JURY STUDIES (2009).

In Wayne County, Michigan, potential jurors who had not responded to a questionnaire were removed from the master jury list indefinitely. As it turned out, the vast majority of those removed from the jury list for this reason were residents of Detroit, a city whose residents are 80% African American. *Id.* at 4–5.

In Washington, D.C., individuals convicted of felonies have the right to serve on a jury ten years after the completion of their sentence. The administrative method used to ensure that these individuals were returned to the juror lists was flawed and kept felons off the jury list longer than the statute allowed, resulting in the improper removal of qualified jurors. *Id.* at 5.

Uncovering evidence of the exclusion of qualified jurors. The examples listed above illustrate the importance of obtaining your county jury commission's procedures for removing unqualified jurors from the master juror list and ensuring that names previously removed from the juror list are not permanently removed. Such policies may then be analyzed for any potentially disparate effect on distinctive groups. For example, how do jury commissioners determine whether a person should be removed from the master jury list because the person doesn't speak English, is not a citizen, or is a felon whose rights have not been restored? These procedures should be available in the Clerk or Court's office or through discovery.

If, in reviewing the jury commission's procedures, you uncover evidence suggesting that a technique used to remove unqualified jurors from the master jury list results in the underrepresentation of a distinctive group from jury service, you may challenge that technique as a violation of the defendant's fair cross-section and equal protection rights. *See supra* § 6.3, Fair Cross-Section Challenges; § 6.4, Equal Protection Challenges.

G. Challenges to the Selection of the Grand Jury

Raising challenges to the composition of the grand jury presents unique challenges because the grand jury operates in secret and sometimes issues an indictment before counsel is appointed. The information below is designed to help assemble evidence about the selection of the grand jury and determine whether any challenges are warranted.

Discrimination in the selection of the grand jury. To establish a claim of discrimination in violation of the state and federal guarantees of equal protection in the selection of grand jurors, defendants must show that a recognizable, distinct class or group has been discriminated against; that the procedures employed for the selection of jurors has resulted in substantial underrepresentation of the race or identifiable group for a significant period of time; and that the selection procedure is susceptible of abuse or is not racially neutral. *Castaneda v. Partida,* 430 U.S. 482 (1977); *see also State v. Foddrell*, 291 N.C. 546, 554, (1977) ("defendants are generally required to produce not only statistical evidence establishing that blacks were underrepresented on the jury but also evidence that the selection procedure itself was not racially neutral, or that for a substantial period in the past relatively few [Black people] have served on the juries of the county notwithstanding a substantial [Black] population therein, or both"; cited with approval in *State v. Cofield*, 320 N.C. 297 (1987)). The same type of evidence may be used to support a fair cross-section claim based on the selection of grand jurors.

Improper grand jury selection procedures. A defendant is entitled to learn the identity of the grand jurors who issued the indictment. *See generally* G.S. 15A-955 (court may dismiss indictment if it finds there is ground to challenge the array); *State v. Kirkland*, 119 N.C. App. 185 (1995) (defendant moved to compel disclosure of jury records in support of motion to quash indictment on ground that grand jury, grand jury foreman, and petit jury were unlawfully selected on basis of race; trial court did not err in denying defendant's motions where motion to quash was untimely), *aff'd per curiam,* 342 N.C. 891 (1996); *see also* G.S. 132-1 (public records law). A defendant may move to dismiss an indictment if the grand jury as a whole was illegally constituted or individual grand jurors were unqualified. 1 NORTH CAROLINA DEFENDER MANUAL Ch. 9 (Grand Jury Proceedings) (2d ed. 2013).

H. Challenges to the Selection of the Grand Jury Foreperson

The courts may quash an indictment if there was discrimination in the selection of the grand jury foreperson. In North Carolina, the presiding judge selects the grand jury foreperson. G.S. 15A-622(e); *see also State v. Cofield*, 320 N.C. 297, 301 (1987). The North Carolina Supreme Court has stated that racial discrimination in the selection of grand jury foremen violates article I, section 26 of the North Carolina Constitution, irrespective of whether there was discrimination in selection of the grand jury itself. *See State v. Cofield,* 320 N.C. 297, 303 (1987); *see also State v. Miller,* 339 N.C. 663 (1995); *State v. Pigott*, 331 N.C. 199 (1992); *State v. Robinson*, 327 N.C. 346 (1990). Discrimination in the selection of a grand jury foreperson also violates the Equal Protection Clause of the Fourteenth Amendment. *Cofield*, 320 N.C. 297, 306 (identifying and agreeing with federal courts reaching this conclusion). Therefore, if the defendant can make a sufficient showing of racial discrimination in the foreman selection process, the conviction must be overturned. *Id.* at 308.

The defendant is entitled to discover the identities of the members of his or her grand jury, including the identity of the foreperson. *See* G.S. 15A-955, G.S. 132-1; *see also supra* § 6.5G, Challenges to the Selection of the Grand Jury. To make out a prima facie case of an equal protection violation, the defendant must show either that:

- the selection process was not racially neutral, or
- that for a substantial period in the past, relatively few members of the distinctive class have served as forepersons on grand juries, although a substantial number have served on grand juries.

Cofield, 320 N.C. 297, 308; *see also State v. Jefferies*, 333 N.C. 501, 506; *State v. Phillips*, 328 N.C. 1, 11. If this showing is made, the indictment must be dismissed unless the State can rebut the prima facie case by showing that the foreperson in this particular case was chosen in a racially neutral manner. *Cofield*, 320 N.C. 297, 308. *See also Chin v. Runnels*, 343 F. Supp. 2d 891 (N.D. Cal. 2004) (petitioner made out prima facie case of race discrimination in selection of grand jury foreperson based on exclusion of Chinese-Americans from such positions, but state court's finding that the State had rebutted the prima facie case was not an unreasonable application of clearly established federal law).

Racially neutral selection method. To meet the racially neutral standard, the method of selecting a grand jury foreperson must ensure that all grand jurors were considered by the presiding judge and that the selection was made on a racially neutral basis. *See State v. Cofield,* 324 N.C. 452, 461 (1989) (*Cofield II*). The focus is on whether the process used to select the foreperson was influenced by race; neither the race of the foreperson nor the race of the defendant determines the viability of the claim. *See State v. Moore,* 329 N.C. 245, 246–48 (1991) (applying article I, section 26 of the North Carolina Constitution and rejecting the State's argument that a Black defendant had no standing to object to the replacement of a White foreperson with a Black one). Where a district court judge, on the suggestion of the prosecutor, removed a White foreperson and replaced him with a Black foreperson in order to correct for the "historical custom in Rutherford County of failing to appoint black persons as foremen," the North Carolina Supreme Court found that selecting a particular foreman on the basis of his race was unconstitutional even if intended to remedy past discrimination. *Id.*

What constitutes consideration of race by the judge may sometimes be at issue. For example, former North Carolina Supreme Court Justice Mitchell repeatedly questioned whether the consideration of each member equally is racially neutral, and he suggested a random selection method to eliminate the potential for racial bias. *Cofield*, 324 N.C. 452, 465–66 (Mitchell, J., concurring) (*Cofield II*), *State v. Jefferies,* 333 N.C. 501, 513 (1993) (Mitchell, J., dissenting).

If the defendant makes out a prima facie case that the selection method was not racially neutral, the burden shifts to the State to explain the discrepancy. The court then determines whether the practice was race neutral. For example, the N.C. Supreme Court held that the State had rebutted a prima facie case when the foreperson chosen was the first person to volunteer for the position. *See Jefferies*, 333 N.C. 501.

Evidence of past discrimination. In *State v. Cofield*, 320 N.C. 297 (1987), the defendant made out a prima facie case of racial discrimination with historical evidence showing that the racial composition of the county was approximately 61% Black and 39% White, and that the racial composition of the county's grand juries, on average, reflected the county as a whole. In an 18 year-period, only one Black person had been appointed grand jury foreperson, although 50 appointments had been made and 33 different people had been appointed.

I. Challenges to Jury Panel Selection Procedures

Assembling the Jury Panel. Once the appropriate lists are merged into the master jury list, G.S. 9-5 outlines the process for preparing the list of jurors necessary for the jury panels for a particular session of court. The process requires a clerk to prepare or obtain a computer generated, randomized list of names of individuals who will be prospective grand jurors or petit jurors for a particular session.

Defendants may challenge panel selections that are not conducted randomly. For example, if only jurors with a name starting with the same letter were chosen, this may result in underrepresentation of certain racial groups. Defense counsel should be able to check the list of jurors on a defendant's jury panel in the clerk's office approximately one week before the case goes to trial. While demographic information will not be included on the list, defense counsel can look at voting registration records to determine the race of the potential jurors. *See also supra* "Expert assistance in substantiating claims of underrepresentation" in § 6.5B, Mechanics of Challenging Jury Formation. Additionally, defense attorneys should be alert to lists that do not look random. For example, in a small town, if a large number of the last names on the jury panel begin with the same letter, that may be evidence that the selection was not random.

Attorneys also should be aware of possible glitches in computer-generated lists. Courts in other jurisdictions have overturned convictions based on glitches in computer operated jury systems. For example, problems in the application of a computer system resulted in the exclusion of 4,364 people from jury service and caused the Indiana Supreme Court to reverse a death sentence and mandate a new penalty phase of a murder trial. *See Azania v. State,* 778 N.E.2d 1253 (Ind. 2002). The computer error in *Azania* produced racial disparities as it excluded a portion of the jury pool that contained three-fourths of the African American population in the county. Counsel discovered the glitch after noticing the racial disparity between the jury venire and the surrounding community.

Last, defense attorneys should be alert to disparities that may result from policies and practices used to evaluate applications for excusal from jury service. For example, if excusals are routinely granted for low-wage workers or stay-at-home moms, a distinctive group may be underrepresented on jury panels as a result. Attorneys investigating such claims should obtain records of the procedures promulgated by the chief district court judge for reviewing applications for excuses from jury service pursuant to G.S. 9-6(b), as well as the list of all people excused by the judge pursuant to G.S. 9-6. *See* G.S. 9-6(e) ("[T]he clerk shall keep a record of excuses separate from the master jury list.").

Prejudice. The procedure for calling jurors to the jury box from the jury panel is governed by G.S. 15A-1214(a). The N.C. Supreme Court has held that a defendant must show prejudice from a randomness violation resulting from a deviation from the procedures set out in G.S. 15A-1214(a). *State v. Thompson*, 359 N.C. 77 (2004). It is not clear what evidence would suffice to demonstrate prejudice. In *State v. Golphin*, 352 N.C. 364 (2000), the N.C. Supreme Court found that even if a violation of the statutory requirement of randomness occurred, the defendants failed to show prejudice because they did not exhaust their peremptory challenges, which the court considered to be evidence of the defendants' satisfaction with the seated jury. *See also State v. Tirado*, 358 N.C. 551 (2004) (even assuming that G.S. 15A-1214(a) was violated by the placing of a hearing-impaired prospective juror into the last panel, defendants could show no prejudice where they did not show that they were forced to accept an undesirable juror and, in fact, consented to her excusal). In light of these cases, trial counsel should exhaust peremptories to show prejudice and object to the last seated juror (which should be done outside the presence of the jury). Counsel should also state on the record how the violation will affect the jury and prejudice the defendant.

For a detailed discussion of how to preserve challenges to jury panel selection errors, see "Recommended approach" in 2 NORTH CAROLINA DEFENDER MANUAL § 25.1G (Preserving Denial of Challenges to the Panel) (2d ed. 2012).

J. Challenges to Supplemental Juror Selection Procedures

At times, the court may order the sheriff to summon additional jurors beyond those included on the master jury list. *See* G.S. 9-11. This type of juror is "selected infrequently and only to provide a source from which to fill the unexpected needs of the court." *See State v. White*, 6 N.C. App. 425, 428 (1969). These practices have the potential to result in discrimination. There is no set method proscribed by statute or case law for the selection of supplemental jurors. *Id.* Instead, the sheriff may use his or her discretion in determining the method of selection of supplemental jurors, limited only by the mandate that he or she "must act with entire impartiality." *Id.* (citation omitted); *see also State v. Nolen*, 144 N.C. App. 172, 180 (2001) (finding that G.S. 9-11, on its face, did not violate the right to an impartial jury, and finding no error where sheriff selected supplemental jurors by contacting people in the county that he and his senior staff members "knew that [jury duty] wouldn't cause a financial hardship for"). However, as noted by the court in *White*, it obviously "would be possible for a sheriff, sent out to execute . . . an order of the court [to summon supplemental jurors], to discriminate in the selection of persons to be summoned." *White*, 6 N.C. App. 425, 427 (quotation omitted); *see also Russell v. Wyrick*, 736 F.2d 462 (8th Cir. 1984) (noting dangers of allowing sheriffs to select jurors, e.g., a sheriff might choose jurors favorable to the prosecution or jurors with whom the sheriff is acquainted).

Challenges to the selection of the supplemental jurors are sustainable if "there is partiality or misconduct in the Sheriff, or some irregularity in making out the list." *State v. Dixon*, 215 N.C. 438, 440 (1939) (quotation omitted); *see also Bass v. State*, 368 So.2d 447, 449 (Fla. Dist. Ct. App. 1979) (reversing defendant's conviction and holding that "[t]he choice of a special venire from an all-Caucasian church body, or from one's Caucasian friends, is a systematic, if unintended, exclusion of blacks"; the selection of supplemental jurors "must be administered in such a way as not to exclude identifiable segments of the populace systematically"). The North Carolina Court of Appeals has rejected a facial constitutional challenge to G.S. 9-11; counsel should therefore challenge the statute as applied. *See State v. Nolen*, 144 N.C. App 172 (2001).

Practice note: If the supplemental jurors selected by the sheriff do not represent a fair cross section of the community, consider moving to discharge the jurors. You may need a continuance to obtain statistical information to support your claim of a fair cross-section violation. If your motion to discharge the jurors is denied, you need to exhaust your peremptory challenges to preserve the issue for appellate review. *See* 2 NORTH CAROLINA DEFENDER MANUAL § 25.1G (Preserving Denial of Challenges to the Panel) (2d ed. 2012); *see also State v. Wilson*, 313 N.C. 516 (1985) (defendant could not complain about judge's order requiring sheriff to recruit supplemental jurors where defendant failed to exhaust his last peremptory challenge to remove twelfth juror, who was one of the supplemental jurors); *State v. Shaw*, 284 N.C. 366, 369 (1973) (no error in trial judge's denial of defendant's motion to allow defense counsel or his representative to be present during the summoning of the jury by the sheriff; defendant failed to challenge array or "offer any proof that the Sheriff violated the trust placed in him as an elected official"), *overruled on other grounds*, *Batson v. Kentucky*, 476 U.S. 79 (1986).

Constitutional challenges to supplemental jurors. Counsel may raise a constitutional challenge if the use of supplemental jurors results in underrepresentation of a distinctive group in the community. For purposes of an equal protection violation, defense attorneys should argue that the discretion afforded sheriffs in selecting supplemental jurors constitutes "a selection procedure that is susceptible of abuse." *Castaneda v. Partida*, 430

U.S. 482, 494 (1977). For purposes of a fair cross-section claim, defense attorneys should present evidence that the supplemental jurors resulted in a panel that was not fair or reasonable in relation to the demographic composition of the community, and that the State did not have a "significant interest" that could only be achieved by the sheriff's selection of supplemental jurors. This showing should not be difficult, since the State could have summoned supplemental jurors from the master jury list. *See* G.S. 9-11(b).

For a further discussion of supplemental jurors, see 2 NORTH CAROLINA DEFENDER MANUAL Ch. 25.1E (Supplemental Jurors) (2d ed. 2012).

6.6 Beyond Litigation: Efforts to Ensure Representative Juries

Fair and representative jury pools protect not only the rights of criminal defendants, but also the entitlement of all North Carolinians to participate in the jury system. Because of their shared interests, defense attorneys may find many partners—including community members, civil attorneys, and other court actors such as prosecutors and judges—when seeking to ensure the representativeness of North Carolina jury pools.

Policy changes that have been suggested to improve jury representativeness include: increasing the number of reliable, representative source lists; increasing the renewal frequency of the master list; addressing non-responsive jurors through effective enforcement; minimizing the length of time jurors serve; and increasing compensation. *See* Paula Hannaford-Agor, *Systematic Negligence In Jury Operations: Why The Definition Of Systematic Exclusion In Fair Cross Section Claims Must Be Expanded*, 59 DRAKE L. REV. 761, 779–87 (2011). New York, for example, has adopted what has been referred to as "the gold standard for achieving representativeness, including use of five source lists, multiple follow-up mailings to reduce non-response, higher jury pay than that of other states, a one-day one-trial policy, and allowing summoned jurors an automatic postponement to a convenient date." NEW YORK STATE UNIFIED COURT SYSTEM OFFICE OF COURT RESEARCH, JURY REPRESENTATIVENESS: A DEMOGRAPHIC STUDY OF JUROR QUALIFICATION AND SUMMONING IN MONROE COUNTY, NEW YORK (2011).

Raising underrepresentation challenges may spur initiatives to address systemic problems in the jury formation process. For example, in 2008, defense attorneys in a capital case tried in downtown San Diego presented evidence that Latinos were underrepresented by 50% in the jury pool for the city's downtown courts. Evidence suggested that a flaw in the juror summons process was responsible for producing this disparity. Specifically, under the existing procedures, fewer juror summons were sent to judicial districts with large populations of jury-eligible Latino residents. The San Diego District Attorney wrote to the court to request immediate action to cure the defect in the juror summons process. Although the defendant's constitutional challenge was denied, the issue prompted procedural changes and drew attention to the underrepresentation of Latinos on juries. *See* ASHLEY NELLIS ET AL., THE SENTENCING PROJECT, REDUCING RACIAL DISPARITY IN

THE CRIMINAL JUSTICE SYSTEM: A MANUAL FOR PRACTITIONERS AND POLICYMAKERS 36 (2008).

Similarly, evidence presented by defendants in Colorado in support of a fair cross-section claim prompted corrective action by the court. While the claim in the individual case was ultimately unsuccessful, the court nevertheless recommended changes to practices used to assemble juries:

> [T]he underrepresentation of African–Americans and Hispanics on jury panels in Arapahoe County at the time of the defendants' trials was statistically significant. For this reason, we disapprove of the practice of giving double credit to prospective jurors for service in Aurora municipal court, and we direct that this practice be stopped immediately.
>
> However, our review of all the statistical evidence presented by Washington leads us to conclude that the underrepresentation of African–Americans and Hispanics on jury panels in Arapahoe County was not unfair or unreasonable.

Washington v. People, 186 P.3d 594, 605–06 (Colo. 2008).

In Massachusetts, a federal court found that the higher undeliverable and failure-to-appear rates from potential jurors living in predominantly minority neighborhoods produced unrepresentative juries, and ordered the court to re-mail undeliverable summons to different addresses within the same zip code as a possible remedy. While this order was overturned as beyond the scope of the court's authority, the United States District Court for the District of Massachusetts eventually changed its jury plan to respond to undeliverable summonses in the manner proposed by the district court. *See* Paula Hannaford-Agor, *Systematic Negligence In Jury Operations: Why The Definition Of Systematic Exclusion In Fair Cross Section Claims Must Be Expanded*, 59 DRAKE L. REV. 761, 778 n.99 (2011) (discussing *United States v. Green*, 389 F. Supp. 2d 29, 38 (D. Mass. 2005)).

Any irregularities in the jury composition process, as well as disparities in the jury pool, should be brought to the attention of the court. *See* AMERICAN BAR ASSOCIATION, AMERICAN JURY PROJECT, PRINCIPLES FOR JURIES AND JURY TRIALS (2005) ("It is the duty of the courts to enforce and protect the rights to jury trial and jury service[.]"). Any concerns also can be presented to standing committees examining diversity issues in criminal justice system administration. Attorneys should determine whether their judicial district has such a committee and, if not, consider (1) starting such a committee; (2) bringing concerns to the attention of the county's jury commission; (3) contacting the North Carolina Advocates for Justice Racial and Ethnic Bias in the Criminal Justice System Task Force; and/or; (4) contacting the North Carolina Commission on Racial Disparities in the Criminal Justice System. Information about both the Task Force and the Commission can be found at http://www.ncaj.com/index.cfm?pg=NC_Racial_Justice.

One reform that could be explored is the adoption of a local rule that all panel members report their race on the record as a standard procedure.

Case study: Jury Formation Process in Judicial District 15B. In North Carolina Judicial District 15B, comprised of Orange and Chatham counties, court actors have expressed concerned about the possible underrepresentation of racial minorities in jury pools. *See, e.g.*, James Williams Letter to Representative Hackney in the Race Materials Bank at www.ncids.org (select "Training and Resources"). Recently, the Judicial District Executive Council, which includes local leaders such as the resident Superior Court judge, the Chief District Court judge, the Chief Public Defender, the elected District Attorney, and the elected Clerk of Court, decided to undertake a study to determine whether anecdotal observations about underrepresentation are correct and, if so, to try to identify where in the process the racial disparities are produced. With the support of faculty and students in the UNC School of Government's Masters in Public Administration program, a process of gathering and analyzing data regarding jury pools and examining jury formation procedures in Orange and Chatham Counties is underway. Below, Allen Baddour, Resident Superior Court Judge for North Carolina Judicial District 15B, reflects on this process.

Over the years, questions have arisen as to whether the jury pool adequately represents a fair cross section of the community. No one has ever claimed actual bias, or discrimination, to my knowledge. But regularly, the question has arisen: does the jury pool reflect too few persons of color? This is an incredibly difficult question to deal with as a trial judge. We are used to accepting at face value that those brought before us as the jury pool came there randomly, and are as diverse as the county they come from, based on geography, race, ethnicity, gender, and age. And even more difficult to handle as a part of any given case: if there was some sort of discrepancy, what is the solution? Do we dismiss the pool, and call another? Do we throw out the master list (from which this week's names were pulled)?

It finally occurred to me that the best way to resolve these questions, and plenty of others, was to systematically collect data. I have never seen anyone act in a discriminatory way in jury selection, or in the creation of the jury pool. I have traveled the state and seen pools in dozens of counties. Inevitably, some jury pools contain a greater percentage of minorities than others. Do differences in the jury pool track the population of a county as a whole? It is hard to say. I also know that I cannot "tell" someone's race just by looking at them.

Another difficulty in sorting out whether a disparity exists is in the difference between who we ask to join us (by summons) as compared to who actually shows up. Some counties approach a 100% response rate (meaning that all jurors summonsed actually appear), and others are much closer to 50%. Orange County's population is notoriously transient, as many students make it onto the jury list, only to be long gone once they are actually summoned. I have always felt that many people who didn't show up for jury duty were doing the best they could with a very real dilemma: the choice of an hourly wage earner or one who stays home with children giving up that pay or risking putting the children in an unsafe or unstable situation, as compared to risking ignoring a court order. I have tried issuing show cause orders to have those who fail to show for jury duty, but that involves deputy time (to serve the orders), court time (to hear the case), and ultimately, the sanction ($50 fine) really isn't worth it.

I have some concern and empathy for those who don't show up for jury duty when their reasons are economic. I am not sure if there is any correlation between those most affected economically in Orange and Chatham and race.

But I am getting a little bit ahead of myself. Before we can take measures to ensure we consistently have the most representative jury pools possible, before we can decide how representative is "enough," and before we can balance - if at all- the rights of defendants accused of crimes with the circumstances of jurors (and is the defendant most helped by a willing juror or a recalcitrant, distracted, or hostile juror?) . . . before all that, we must understand the data.

And so, District 15B, with great assistance from the School of Government, is undertaking an examination of our jury system. We are analyzing everything: how does the master jury list get created? Who shows up for jury service? Who gets deferred? Who fails to show up? Along the way, we'll examine the decision points - what decisions are made by court officials that may have unintended consequences for who stays in the jury pool? What can we do to improve the response rate for jury summonses? What should we do?

I approach this process with an open mind. I do not have any preconceived notions about what the numbers suggest, other than to believe that no one is intentionally behaving in a discriminatory fashion. It is my hope that with good, reliable data, we can first make a determination about whether anything is to be done, and then, if so, what we should do. This process is just beginning, and it may be awhile before we can meaningfully assess the situation. But the effort must begin somewhere, and so . . . onward!

Defense attorneys interested in reading more about best practices in jury composition should consult the following resources:

- GREGORY E. MIZE ET AL., NATIONAL CENTER FOR STATE COURTS, THE STATE-OF-THE-STATES SURVEY OF JURY IMPROVEMENT EFFORTS: A COMPENDIUM REPORT 13 (2007).
- National Center for State Courts, *Jury Managers Toolbox: Characteristics of an Effective Master Jury List*, NCSC CENTER FOR JURY STUDIES (2009).
- AMERICAN BAR ASSOCIATION, AMERICAN JURY PROJECT, PRINCIPLES FOR JURIES AND JURY TRIALS (2005).

6.7 Glossary of Jury Terms and Jury Formation Flowchart

Jury commission. Each county has a jury commission composed of three members who serve two-year terms; one member is appointed by the board of county commissioners, the second by the senior resident superior court judge, and the third by the clerk of superior court. *See* G.S. 9-1.

Jury panel. The prospective jurors randomly drawn from the master jury list and summoned for jury service for a particular session or sessions of court. *See* G.S. 9-2(f); G.S. 9-2(i); G.S. 9-2(j); G.S. 9-5; G.S. 9-10(a).

Jury pool. In North Carolina, "jury pool" appears to be used synonymously with "jury panel" and "jury venire." *See, e.g.*, NORTH CAROLINA ADMINISTRATIVE OFFICE OF THE COURTS, A MANUAL FOR NORTH CAROLINA JURY COMMISSIONERS AND CLERKS OF SUPERIOR COURT (5th ed. 2013). In cases from other jurisdictions, the term "pool" may be used to refer to a broader group. *See, e.g., Ambrose v. Booker*, 684 F.3d 638, 645 (6th Cir. 2012). ("[P]etitioner raising [a fair cross-section] claim is challenging the pool from which the jury is drawn, and not necessarily the venire panel directly before him. Accordingly, the composition of one panel does not indicate whether a fair cross-section claim exists.").

Jury summons. A written order to appear for jury service, issued by either the clerk or the sheriff, and served on prospective jurors at least 15 days before the session of court for which the juror is summoned. *See* G.S. 9-5; G.S. 9-10.

Jury venire. In North Carolina, "jury venire" appears to be used synonymously with "jury panel" and "jury pool."

Master jury list. The list compiled by the jury commission each odd-numbered year of all prospective jurors qualified to serve in the two years starting January 1 of the following year. *See* G.S. 9-2(a).

Source lists. Lists of names used to compile the master jury list. In North Carolina, jury commissions use the list of registered voters and persons with drivers license records supplied to the county by the Commissioner of Motor Vehicles. Jury commissions may use other sources of names if they deem them reliable.

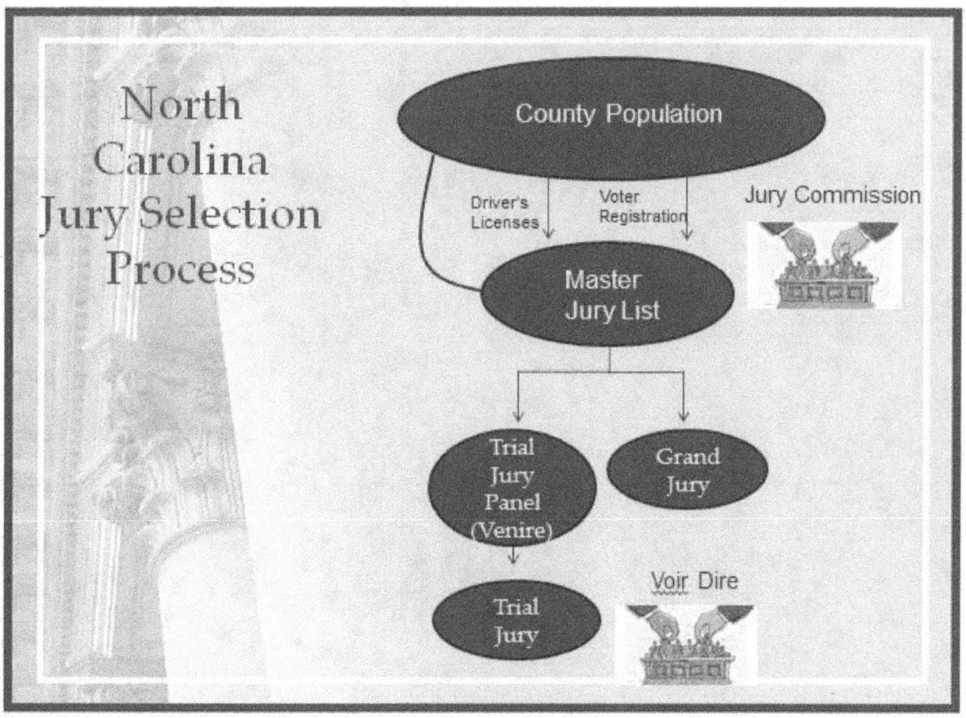

Chapter 7
Selection of the Trial Jury: Peremptory Challenges

7.1 Scope of Chapter

In criminal cases, parties may challenge jurors for cause during jury selection (for example, when a juror expresses an inability to be fair and impartial) or may use a certain number of peremptory challenges to remove jurors without cause. Peremptory challenges, or strikes, influenced by race violate the constitutional rights of both defendants and improperly struck jurors, and impair the reputation and democratic function of the justice system as a whole. *See infra* § 7.2A, Consequences of Discrimination in Jury Selection.

This chapter reviews the federal and state constitutional limits on the use of peremptory challenges. Most significantly, in the landmark U.S. Supreme Court decision *Batson v.*

Kentucky, 476 U.S. 79 (1986), the U.S. Supreme Court established a three-step approach for assessing whether a party used a peremptory challenge for a discriminatory reason. Under this approach, an attorney may establish a violation by showing that the prosecutor failed to offer a sufficient race-neutral reason for exercising a peremptory challenge. Statistical evidence is not required to establish a violation; however, such data may be used to support an alleged violation. This chapter therefore reviews studies that have been conducted in North Carolina (and can be replicated) about disparities in the use of peremptory challenges. The chapter describes the procedures for raising a *Batson* claim, including raising the issue properly during jury selection, conducting a hearing on the issue, remedies, and preserving the record for appeal.

7.2 Overview

A. Consequences of Discrimination in Jury Selection

Recent publications have raised concerns about the potential influence of race on peremptory challenges, both nationally and in North Carolina. *See, e.g.,* Catherine M. Grosso & Barbara O'Brien, *A Stubborn Legacy: The Overwhelming Importance of Race in Jury Selection in 173 Post-*Batson *North Carolina Capital Trials*, 97 IOWA L. REV. 1531 (2012) (concluding that in the cases of inmates on North Carolina's death row as of July 1, 2010, the strike rate of eligible Black jurors was about 2.5 times that of eligible non-Black jurors); EQUAL JUSTICE INITIATIVE, ILLEGAL RACIAL DISCRIMINATION IN JURY SELECTION: A CONTINUING LEGACY 14 (2010) (reporting that "[f]rom 2005 to 2009, in cases where the death penalty has been imposed, prosecutors in Houston County, Alabama, have used peremptory strikes to remove 80% of the African Americans qualified for jury service").

The consequences of discrimination in jury selection extend beyond the violation of an individual defendant's constitutional rights. Courts have recognized that racial minorities suffer harm from discrimination in jury selection, "for prosecutors drawing racial lines in picking juries establish state-sponsored group stereotypes rooted in, and reflective of, historical prejudice." *Miller-El v. Dretke*, 545 U.S. 231, 237–38 (1995) (internal quotations omitted); *see also State v. Saintcalle*, 309 P.3d 326, 337 (Wash. 2013) (observing that when the judicial system "allow[s] the systematic removal of minority jurors, we create a badge of inferiority, cheapening the value of the jury verdict"). The U.S. Supreme Court has observed: "The harm from discriminatory jury selection extends beyond that inflicted on the defendant and the excluded juror to touch the entire community." *Batson*, 476 U.S. 79, 87. When the jury selection procedure is "tainted with racial bias, that overt wrong casts doubt over the obligation of the parties, the jury, and indeed the court to adhere to the law throughout the trial. That is, the very integrity of the courts is jeopardized when a prosecutor's discrimination invites cynicism respecting the jury's neutrality, and undermines public confidence in adjudication." *Miller-El*, 545 U.S. 231, 238 (internal citations and quotations omitted).

B. Development of Law

Racial discrimination in the selection of trial jurors has long been recognized as unconstitutional. *See Strauder v. West Virginia*, 100 U.S. 303 (1880). "For more than a century, [the U.S. Supreme] Court consistently and repeatedly has reaffirmed that racial discrimination by the State in jury selection offends the Equal Protection Clause." *Georgia v. McCollum*, 505 U.S. 42, 44 (1992); *see also Batson*, 476 U.S. 79, 85 (describing the Court's "unceasing efforts to eradicate racial discrimination" in jury selection).

In the era before Reconstruction, jury service was generally restricted to White men. EQUAL JUSTICE INITIATIVE, ILLEGAL RACIAL DISCRIMINATION IN JURY SELECTION: A CONTINUING LEGACY 9 (2010). The Civil Rights Act of 1875 outlawed racial discrimination in jury service and, in 1880, the U.S. Supreme Court overturned a West Virginia statute restricting jury service to Whites. *Strauder*, 100 U.S. 303, 308 (holding that racial discrimination in jury selection compromises the right of trial by jury and violates the Equal Protection Clause); *see also Batson*, 476 U.S. 79, 89 ("The principles announced in *Strauder* never have been questioned in any subsequent decision of this Court."). In practice, however, the Civil Rights Act of 1875 was rarely enforced, and the *Strauder* holding was circumvented by the replacement of statutes restricting jury service to Whites with statutes that, while race-neutral on their face, had the effect of excluding African Americans from jury service. For example, laws restricting jury service to eligible voters resulted in all-white juries when voting was restricted to those who could pass a literacy test and pay a poll tax. *See Williams v. Mississippi*, 170 U.S. 213 (1898). In addition, local officials excluded African Americans from jury service based on vague jury service requirements such as intelligence or good character. *See, e.g.*, *State v. Speller*, 229 N.C. 67, 69 (1948) ("The Chairman of the Board of [Bertie] County Commissioners testified that there had been 'no discrimination at all' in the selection of persons to serve on juries; that he had never 'known a Negro's name to be on the list of persons chosen for [service] on a grand or petit jury', but that all rejections were for want of good moral character and sufficient intelligence."); *see also* EQUAL JUSTICE INITIATIVE, ILLEGAL RACIAL DISCRIMINATION IN JURY SELECTION: A CONTINUING LEGACY 10–11 (2010).

In the 1960's, there was an increase in the number of minorities on jury venires as a result of the civil rights movement and the U.S. Supreme Court's fair cross-section jurisprudence. However, some scholars have concluded that these gains were undercut by the advent of racial discrimination in the exercise of peremptory challenges. *See, e.g.*, EQUAL JUSTICE INITIATIVE, ILLEGAL RACIAL DISCRIMINATION IN JURY SELECTION: A CONTINUING LEGACY 12 (2010); Seth Kotch & Robert P. Mosteller, *The Racial Justice Act and the Long Struggle with Race and the Death Penalty in North Carolina*, 88 N.C. L. REV. 2031, 2072–76, 2106–2110 (2010).

In *Swain v. Alabama*, 380 U.S. 202 (1965), the U.S. Supreme Court held that the use of race in the exercise of peremptory strikes violates the Equal Protection Clause, but required defendants raising challenges to show a pattern or practice of discrimination over a number of cases; evidence of discrimination from the defendant's individual case was not sufficient to establish an equal protection violation. The Court later recognized that the *Swain* standard was difficult to meet: it imposed a "crippling burden of proof [leaving] prosecutors' peremptory challenges . . . largely immune from constitutional scrutiny." *Batson*, 476 U.S. 79, 92–93; JEFFREY ABRAMSON, WE, THE JURY: THE JURY SYSTEM AND THE IDEAL OF DEMOCRACY 134 (1994) (noting that the *Swain* standard was not satisfied in federal court over a twenty year period).

In 1986, the U.S. Supreme Court altered the evidentiary burden for proving discrimination in the exercise of peremptory challenges by holding that Equal Protection Clause violations could be demonstrated with evidence from a defendant's case alone; historical evidence of discriminatory patterns was no longer required. *Batson*, 476 U.S. 79, 95–96; *see also infra* § 7.3, Legal Restrictions on Peremptory Challenges. The *Batson* framework continues to govern challenges to discrimination in jury selection, but subsequent U.S. Supreme Court cases, including *Miller El v. Dretke* and *Snyder v. Louisiana*, have refined the standards necessary to sustain a *Batson* challenge.

Despite the Court's condemnation of racial discrimination in jury selection, "[t]he rub has been the practical difficulty of ferreting out discrimination in selections discretionary by nature." *Miller El v. Dretke*, 545 U.S. 231, 238 (2005). Just as the *Batson* Court concluded that *Swain* had not succeeded in ending the practice of race-based peremptory challenges, in recent years the Supreme Court has recognized that *Batson's* three-step test for detecting racial motivations behind peremptory strikes has also had a "weakness of its own owing to its very emphasis on the particular [race-neutral] reasons [for a strike that] a prosecutor might give." *Miller-El*, 545 U.S. 231, 239–40; *see also Miller-El*, 545 U.S. 231, 270 (Breyer, J., concurring) ("the use of race- and gender-based stereotypes in the jury-selection process seems better organized and more systematized than ever before").

In 1970, North Carolina amended its state constitution to explicitly prohibit discrimination in jury selection. Article I, section 26 of the North Carolina Constitution provides that "[n]o person shall be excluded from jury service on account of sex, race, color, religion, or national origin." Additionally, North Carolina courts have held that the *Batson* framework is applicable under North Carolina constitutional law. *See State v. Maness*, 363 N.C. 261, 271–72 (2009). Nonetheless, a number of researchers, attorneys, and other observers have noted that legal prohibitions have not succeeded in eliminating race discrimination from jury selection in our state. *See infra* § 7.2D, Studies of Peremptory Challenges in North Carolina.

In recent years, legislators, judges, and researchers have examined the role that race may play in peremptory challenges in North Carolina capital cases. In 2009, the North Carolina General Assembly enacted the Racial Justice Act (RJA), which prohibited the sentencing or execution of any person "pursuant to any judgment that was sought or obtained on the basis of race." S.L. 2009-464. The law provided relief for defendants who could demonstrate that race "was a significant factor in decisions to exercise peremptory challenges during jury selection" in "the county, the prosecutorial district, the judicial division, or the State" at the time the defendant's death sentence was sought or imposed. *Id.* The law was amended in 2012 and repealed in 2013. Before its repeal, statistical information concerning racial disparities in jury selection in North Carolina capital cases was compiled in connection with RJA claims. *See infra* § 7.2D, Studies of Peremptory Challenges in North Carolina.

Four defendants' RJA claims advanced to trial court hearings. *See* *State v. Marcus Reymond Robinson*, Order Granting Motion for Appropriate Relief, ACLU.ORG (last visited Aug. 12, 2014) [Robinson Order]; *State v. Tilmon Golphin, Christina Walters, and Quintel Augustine*, Order Granting Motions for Appropriate Relief, ACLU.ORG (last visited Aug. 12, 2014) [Golphin Order]. In all four cases, the trial court found violations of the RJA relating to patterns of discrimination in peremptory strikes, among other things. These cases are now under review by the North Carolina Supreme Court. Regardless of the ultimate outcome in those cases, the evidence collected by the trial court, and the lengthy, detailed analysis of jury selection issues in North Carolina contained within the Golphin and Robinson Orders may serve as useful information for attorneys raising challenges to peremptory strikes. *See* Cassandra Stubbs, *Strengthening* Batson *Challenges with the MSU Study* in the Race Materials Bank at www.ncids.org (select "Training and Resources").

C. How Race May Influence the Exercise of Peremptory Challenges

Discretion. Because of the broad discretion afforded their exercise, the U.S. Supreme Court has recognized that "peremptory challenges constitute a jury selection practice that permits those to discriminate who are of a mind to discriminate." *Batson v. Kentucky*, 476 U.S. 79, 96 (1986) (internal quotations omitted); *see also Rice v. Collins*, 546 U.S. 333, 344 (2006) (Breyer, J., concurring) (it has been difficult to harmonize, "on the one hand, what Blackstone called an inherently 'arbitrary and capricious' peremptory challenge system, and, on the other hand, the Constitution's nondiscrimination command" (internal quotations and citations omitted)). In his concurring opinion in *State v. Saintcalle,* 309 P.3d 326, 347–71 (2013) (Gonzalez, J., concurring), Washington State Supreme Court Justice Gonzalez identified several ways in which race may unlawfully influence the exercise of peremptory challenges:

- A peremptory challenge may be based on an overt racial stereotype. *Id.* at 355–56; *see also Howard v. Senkowski*, 986 F.2d 24, 25 (2d Cir. 1993) (prosecutor believed Black jurors were more likely to sympathize with the defendant).
- A peremptory challenge may be based on a juror profile that treats race as an indicator of how a juror may view a given type of case. *Saintcalle*, 309 P.3d 326, 356 (Gonzalez, J., concurring) (discussing TED A. DONNER & RICHARD K. GABRIEL, JURY SELECTION: STRATEGY AND SCIENCE 6–23 (3d ed. 2007)).
- A peremptory challenge may be part of an effort to achieve some particular racial balance on the jury as a whole. *Saintcalle*, 309 P.3d 326, 356 (Gonzalez, J., concurring); *see also Miesner v. State*, 665 So. 2d 978, 980–81 (Ala. Crim. App.

1995) (prosecutor stated that he was looking for White jurors in order to achieve a racially balanced jury).

- A peremptory challenge may be based on unconscious bias. *Saintcalle*, 309 P.3d 326, 356 (Gonzalez, J., concurring); *see also* Samuel R. Sommers & Michael I. Norton, *Race-Based Judgments, Race-Neutral Justifications: Experimental Examination of Peremptory Use and the Batson Challenge Procedure*, 31 LAW & HUM. BEHAV. 261, 269 (2007) (studying influence of implicit bias in simulated peremptory challenges and finding "clear empirical evidence that a prospective juror's race can influence peremptory challenge use and that self-report justifications are unlikely to be useful for identifying this influence"); *infra* "Implicit bias" in this subsection C.

Time pressure. Researchers have concluded that time pressure may exacerbate the influence of biases on decision-making:

> [S]ituations that involve time pressure [or] that force a decision maker to form complex judgments relatively quickly . . . limit the ability to fully process case information. Decision makers who are rushed, stressed, distracted, or pressured are more likely to apply stereotypes—recalling facts in ways biased by stereotypes and making more stereotypic judgments—than decision makers whose cognitive abilities are not similarly constrained.

NATIONAL CENTER FOR STATE COURTS, HELPING COURTS ADDRESS IMPLICIT BIAS: STRATEGIES TO REDUCE THE INFLUENCE OF IMPLICIT BIAS 4. Evaluating this phenomenon in the *Golphin* case, the trial court observed: "When prosecutors evaluate potential jurors, they must quickly decide—often on the basis of the prosecutor's gut feel—whether a particular venire member will be a 'good' juror for the State. This is precisely the type of decision and environment likely to be most susceptible to implicit bias." Golphin Order at 92.

Implicit bias. Even before contemporary implicit bias studies improved our understanding of unconscious stereotypes, Justice Marshall recognized the difficulty of uncovering the role that both conscious and unconscious bias may play in the exercise of peremptory strikes:

> A prosecutor's own conscious or unconscious racism may lead him easily to the conclusion that a prospective black juror is "sullen," or "distant," a characterization that would not have come to his mind if a white juror had acted identically. A judge's own conscious or unconscious racism may lead him to accept such an explanation as well supported. As Justice Rehnquist concedes, prosecutors' peremptories are based on their "seat-of-the-pants instincts" as to how particular jurors will vote. Yet "seat-of-the-pants instincts" may often be just another term for racial prejudice. Even if all parties approach the Court's mandate with the best of conscious intentions, that

> mandate requires them to confront and overcome their own racism on all levels—a challenge I doubt all of them can meet.

Batson v. Kentucky, 476 U.S. 79, 106 (Marshall, J., concurring).

Researchers have concluded that race influences peremptory strikes and that, as a result of implicit biases, "good people often discriminate, and they often discriminate without being aware of it." Antony Page, *Batson's Blind-Spot: Unconscious Stereotyping and the Peremptory Challenge*, 85 B.U. L. REV. 155, 160–61 (2005). By requiring prosecutors to provide a race-neutral explanation for challenged peremptory strikes, the *Batson* framework presumes that individuals generally are aware of the factors motivating their own behavior. However, "[e]ven presuming that lawyers are always entirely honest and open about their motivations for striking jurors, there are powerful reasons to believe that much discrimination occurs at the subconscious level." Russell D. Covey, *The Unbearable Lightness of Batson: Mixed Motives and Discrimination in Jury Selection*, 66 MD. LAW. REV. 279, 326 (2012) (noting that a lawyer facing a *Batson* challenge may "even lie to herself and identify some other nominally neutral trait or character on which to pin her unease"). In the *Golphin* case, the trial court found "unrebutted, credible expert testimony . . . indicating that individuals are not reliable reporters of the extent to which their decisions are influenced by race." Golphin Order at 28; *see also* Judge Mark W. Bennett, *Unraveling the Gordian Knot of Implicit Bias in Jury Selection: The Problems of Judge-Dominated Voir Dire, the Failed Promise of Batson, and Proposed Solutions*, 4 HARV. L. & POL'Y REV. 149 (2010).

Ease of identifying race-neutral reasons for peremptory strikes. Many have observed that even if a prosecutor's peremptory strike has been consciously or unconsciously influenced by race, it is easy to justify the strike on race-neutral grounds. *See* Michael J. Raphael & Edward J. Ungvarsky, *Excuses, Excuses: Neutral Explanations Under* Batson v. Kentucky, 27 U. MICH. J. L. REFORM 229, 236 (1993) (concluding that "in almost any situation a prosecutor can readily craft an acceptable neutral explanation to justify striking black jurors because of their race"). The ease of identifying a race-neutral strike justification raises concerns, since "people will act on unconscious bias far more often if reasons exist giving plausible deniability (e.g. an opportunity to present a race-neutral reason)." *State v. Saintcalle*, 309 P.3d 326, 336 (Wash. 2013).

Researchers have found that individuals "are remarkably facile at recruiting race-neutral characteristics to justify jury selection judgments." Samuel R. Sommers & Michael I. Norton, *Race-Based Judgments, Race-Neutral Justifications: Experimental Examination of Peremptory Use and the Batson Challenge Procedure*, 31 LAW & HUM. BEHAV. 261 (2007). Some prosecutors' trainings have included "cheat sheets" listing race-neutral strike justifications, such as crossed arms. *See Top Gun II Batson Training: Articulating Juror Negatives* in the Race Materials Bank at www.ncids.org (select "Training and Resources"); *see also* Robinson Order at 156–57 (reviewing the training materials from the *Top Gun II* CLE and finding that the "training [was not] intended to teach prosecutors how to avoid discrimination in jury selection, but that the training was focused on how to avoid a finding of a *Batson* violation in case of an objection by opposing counsel").

Unless defense counsel effectively raises concerns about the reasons offered for a peremptory strike, a judge may have difficulty discerning the prosecutor's motivations and therefore may accept the race-neutral reason for the strike at face value.

D. Studies of Peremptory Challenges in North Carolina

North Carolina appellate courts have been deferential to trial court rejections of *Batson* claims. Only one reported decision has reversed a trial court's rejection of a defendant's *Batson* claim, and in that case the prosecutor did not offer any race-neutral justifications for striking at least one, and possibly two, Black venire members. *State v. Wright*, 189 N.C. App. 346 (2008). It is difficult to quantify the extent to which race may influence the exercise of peremptory strikes in North Carolina, however. The affirmance of trial court decisions overruling *Batson* objections does not necessarily resolve the question. Appellate decisions may not reflect whether defendants are prevailing on *Batson* claims at trial, which generally would not be the subject of appellate review. To the extent the appellate decisions show a pattern, some may argue that they show that prosecutors generally exercise peremptory strikes in a race-neutral fashion, while others may view them as evidence of the need for closer scrutiny of peremptory challenges to effectuate the rights sought to be guaranteed. *See* Amanda S. Hitchcock, Recent Development, *"Deference Does Not By Definition Preclude Relief": The Impact of* Miller-El v. Dretke *on* Batson *Review in North Carolina Capital* Appeals, 84 N.C. L. REV. 1328 (2006) (reviewing North Carolina capital cases involving *Batson* claims between 1986 and 2005, arguing that the process has been unduly deferential to race-neutral justifications, and suggesting that, following the U.S. Supreme Court's opinion in *Miller-El v. Dretke*, 545 U.S. 231 (2005), North Carolina appellate courts reviewing *Batson* claims should grant greater weight to statistical evidence, complaints regarding disparate questioning, and comparative juror analysis); Mary R. Rose, *The Peremptory Challenge Accused of Race or Gender Discrimination? Some Data from One County*, 23 LAW & HUM. BEHAV. 695 (1999) (studying jury selection in Durham, North Carolina felony trials and concluding that race appeared to play a role in peremptory strikes by both prosecutors and defense attorneys); Paul H. Schwartz, Comment, *Equal Protection in Jury Selection? The Implementation of* Batson v. Kentucky *in North Carolina*, 69 N.C. LAW REV. 1533, 1577 (1991) (reviewing North Carolina decisions in the five years following *Batson* and finding no decisions in the appellate courts finding a *Batson* error on merits).

Most recently, two Michigan State University (MSU) researchers found that, in the trials of the 173 prisoners on death row in North Carolina at the time of the study, prosecutors used peremptory challenges to strike 52.6% of Black strike-eligible jurors and 25.7% of all other strike-eligible venire members. *See* Catherine M. Grosso & Barbara O'Brien, *A Stubborn Legacy: The Overwhelming Importance of Race in Jury Selection in 173 Post-*Batson *North Carolina Capital Trials*, 97 IOWA L. REV. 1531, 1548 (2012). The strike rate of Black venire members was higher in cases involving Black defendants: in those cases, prosecutors struck 60% of Black venire members and 23.1% of other venire members. *Id.* at 1549; *see also* Golphin Order at 138 (finding MSU study "highly reliable"). Where relevant, this chapter describes how this study's findings may support challenges to discriminatory peremptory strikes in noncapital cases, and how defense attorneys may conduct their own studies of peremptory strike patterns. *See infra* § 7.4A, Pretrial Preparation for a *Batson* Challenge; *see also* Cassandra Stubbs, *Strengthening* Batson *Challenges with the MSU Study* in the Race Materials Bank at www.ncids.org (select "Training and Resources").

E. Potential Benefits of Raising *Batson* Challenges

There are a number of reasons why defenders should raise *Batson* challenges to peremptory strikes that appear motivated by race or ethnicity. These include:

- Raising meritorious *Batson* challenges may result in more racially diverse juries. Diverse juries are consistent with the guarantee of a jury of one's peers; and empirical studies have concluded that diverse juries may be more likely to deliberate longer and conduct a more rigorous analysis of the issues presented. *See* Samuel R. Sommers, *On Racial Diversity and Group Decision Making: Identifying Multiple Effects of Racial Composition in Jury Deliberation*, 90 J. PERSONALITY AND SOC. PSYCHOL. 597, 608 (2006) ("By every deliberation measure . . . heterogeneous groups outperformed homogeneous groups.").
- You must raise a *Batson* challenge to a potentially discriminatory peremptory strike to preserve the issue for appellate review.
- Making the issue of race salient in this manner may reduce the influence of implicit bias on prosecutors, defenders, jurors, and judges. *See* Samuel R. Sommers & Phoebe C. Ellsworth, *"Race Salience" in Juror Decision-Making: Misconceptions, Clarifications, and Unanswered Questions*, 27 BEHAV. SCI. & L. 599 (2009).
- The ABA Guidelines counsel that attorneys should raise "appropriate issues" regarding jury panel selection and the exercise of challenges for cause and peremptory challenges. ABA Defense Standard 4-7.2.
- Raising such a challenge may strengthen your relationship with your client by demonstrating that you are willing to tackle difficult issues.
- By raising meritorious *Batson* challenges to questionable strikes, you help develop a record of prosecutorial *Batson* justifications for use in future *Batson* challenges. *See supra* § 7.4A, Pretrial Preparation for a *Batson* Challenge.

7.3 Legal Restrictions on Peremptory Challenges

A. Statutory Right to Peremptory Challenges in North Carolina

There is no constitutional right to peremptory challenges; they are a statutory creation. *See Rivera v. Illinois*, 556 U.S. 148, 157 (2009). In North Carolina, the State and each defendant in a non-capital case are entitled to six peremptory challenges. *See* G.S. 15A-1217. If there are co-defendants, the State gets six additional peremptory challenges per co-defendant. G.S. 15A-1217(b). Generally, trial judges do not have authority to grant additional peremptory challenges. *State v. Hunt*, 325 N.C. 187, 198 (1989). The court has found no error, however, where the trial judge granted each defendant an additional peremptory challenge because one juror who had been accepted by all parties was dismissed because of a family emergency. *State v. Barnes*, 345 N.C. 184, 208 (1997). Trial judges may take away peremptory challenges as a sanction. *State v. Banks*, 125 N.C. App. 681 (trial judge stripped State of two peremptory challenges for failure to preserve evidence), *aff'd per curiam*, 347 N.C. 390 (1997).

For further discussion of the laws governing peremptory challenges in North Carolina, see 2 NORTH CAROLINA DEFENDER MANUAL § 25.5B (Statutory Right to Peremptory Challenges) (2d ed. 2012).

B. Overview of *Batson* Challenges

Generally. The U.S. Supreme Court has held that racial and ethnic discrimination in the exercise of peremptory challenges violates the Equal Protection Clause of the Fourteenth Amendment. *Batson v. Kentucky*, 476 U.S. 79 (1986); *Hernandez v. New York*, 500 U.S. 352 (1991). Discrimination in jury selection also violates article I, section 26 of the N.C. Constitution, which provides that no person may be "excluded from jury service on account of sex, race, color, religion, or national origin." *See State v. White*, 349 N.C. 535 (1998) (racial discrimination in jury selection violates both state and federal constitutions). The North Carolina Supreme Court has held that the test for proving a violation of article I, section 26 of the N.C. Constitution is identical to the three-part test in *Batson*. *State v. Augustine*, 359 N.C. 709, 715 (2005).

Standing. There is no standing requirement for *Batson* claims. In *Powers v. Ohio*, 499 U.S. 400 (1991), the U.S. Supreme Court held that the defendant does not have to be of the same race as improperly excluded jurors to raise a *Batson* challenge. Any defendant has standing to assert the equal protection rights of jurors. *See also State v. Locklear*, 349 N.C. 118 (1998) (explaining *Powers*); *State v. Williams*, 343 N.C. 345 (1996) (same).

All racial groups protected under *Batson*. *Batson* challenges can be raised in response to the use of discriminatory peremptory strikes against venire members of all races. For example, Native Americans are recognized as "a racial group cognizable for *Batson* purposes." *State v. Locklear*, 349 N.C. 118, 136 (1998) (quoting *State v. Porter*, 326 N.C. 489, 499 (1990)); *see also United States v. Iron Moccasin*, 878 F.2d 226 (8th Cir. 1989); *United States v. Chalan*, 812 F.2d 1302 (10th Cir. 1987).

Strikes based on gender prohibited. The Equal Protection Clause also prohibits peremptory strikes based on gender. *J.E.B. v. Alabama ex rel. T.B.*, 511 U.S. 127 (1994); *see also State v. Maness*, 363 N.C. 261, 272, (2009) ("A party alleging either a race-based or gender-based discriminatory peremptory challenge of a prospective juror must make a prima facie showing of intentional discrimination before the party exercising the challenge is required to explain the basis for the strike." (quotations omitted)).

Subgroups. The U.S. Supreme Court has not decided whether subgroups, such as African American women, are a cognizable group under *Batson.* If the only African

Americans accepted without peremptory challenge by the State are men, arguably there is a *Batson/J.E.B.* violation. In *State v. Best*, 342 N.C. 502 (1996), the defendant argued that the prosecutor had discriminated against African American women, but the court found the claim had not been preserved and did not address it.

C. *Batson* Step One: The Prima Facie Case

Batson v. Kentucky, 476 U.S. 79 (1986), held that the party raising an equal protection challenge to a peremptory strike must first establish a prima facie case of discrimination. *See, e.g.*, *State v. Golphin*, 352 N.C. 364 (2000) (citing *Hernandez v. New York*, 500 U.S. 352, 358–59 (1991)). In considering whether the party has established a prima facie case, the trial judge must consider all circumstances relevant to a claim of discrimination. *See Miller-El v. Dretke*, 545 U.S. 231, 239 (2005) (prima facie claim will be evaluated based on "the totality of the relevant facts" (quotations omitted)); *Snyder v. Louisiana*, 552 U.S. 472 (2008) ("[I]n considering a *Batson* objection . . . all of the circumstances that bear upon the issue of racial animosity must be consulted."); *Golphin*, 352 N.C. 364, 426; *State v. White*, 349 N.C. 535, 548. Some of the circumstances relevant to establishing a prima facie case include the percentage of minorities challenged peremptorily; disparate questioning of minority and non-minority potential jurors; the race of the defendant, victim, and witnesses; and historical data, such as sustained *Batson* challenges against the prosecutor in prior cases. For an illustrative list of evidence, see *infra* "Evidence supporting defendant's prima facie case at step one" in § 7.4B, Presenting an Effective *Batson* Challenge.

"Step one of the *Batson* analysis, a prima facie showing of racial discrimination, is not intended to be a high hurdle for defendants to cross." *State v. Hoffman*, 348 N.C. 548, 553 (1998). *Hoffman* ruled that the trial judge erred in failing to find that the defendant had made out a prima facie case with respect to the prosecutor's peremptory challenge of certain Black jurors where the defendant was Black, the victim was White, and the prosecutor had filled eleven seats with White jurors and struck every other Black prospective juror not excused for cause. The case was remanded so that the prosecutor could place his or her reasons for the strikes on the record. *See also State v. McCord*, 140 N.C. App. 634 (2000) (remanding for *Batson* hearing after trial judge erroneously failed to find prima facie case).

Improper strike of one juror sufficient. If even one juror is struck for racial reasons, there is constitutional error in the jury selection. *State v. Robbins*, 319 N.C. 465, 491 (1987) ("Even a single act of invidious discrimination may form the basis for an equal protection violation."); *see also United States v. Vasquez–Lopez*, 22 F.3d 900, 902 (9th Cir. 1994) ("the Constitution forbids striking even a single prospective juror for a discriminatory purpose"; quoted with approval in *Snyder v. Louisiana*, 552 U.S. 472, 478 (2008)); *United States v. Joe*, 928 F.2d 99, 103 (4th Cir. 1991) (striking a single black prospective juror for a discriminatory reason violates equal protection guarantees, even where prosecutor accepts other black jurors). *See also infra* "Comparative juror analysis at step one" in § 7.4B, Presenting an Effective *Batson* Challenge.

Significance of minority acceptance rate. North Carolina appellate courts have often considered the "minority acceptance rate" or "Black juror acceptance rate" when evaluating the defendant's prima facie *Batson* claim on appeal. *See, e.g.*, *State v. Smith*, 328 N.C. 99, 121 (1991) (observing that an important consideration bearing on whether a prima facie case is established is whether the prosecutor uses a disproportionate number of peremptory challenges to strike Black jurors). This number reflects the percentage of eligible minorities accepted, rather than peremptorily stricken, by the prosecutor. For example, if a prosecutor used peremptory strikes to remove three of five Black venire members, the acceptance rate of Black jurors would be 40%. *See, e.g.*, Excerpt from Motion for Appropriate Relief - *Batson* Claim in the Race Materials Bank at 6 in the Race Materials Bank at www.ncids.org (select "Training and Resources") (calculating acceptance rate of Black potential jurors). The N.C. Supreme Court has found that the defendant failed to establish a prima facie case at step one where the minority acceptance rate was 66%, *State v. Ross*, 338 N.C. 280 (1994); 50%, *State v. Nicholson*, 355 N.C. 1, 24 (2002); 40%, *State v. Fletcher*, 348 N.C. 292, 320 (1998), and 37.5%, *State v. Gregory*, 340 N.C. 365, 398 (1995). The N.C. Supreme Court reversed a finding that a defendant failed to make out a prima facie case of discrimination when the prosecutor's acceptance rate of Black jurors was 28.6%, and the overall minority acceptance rate was even lower. *State v. Barden*, 356 N.C. 316, 344–45 (2002). In that case, the court stressed that "numerical analysis of the type employed here is not necessarily dispositive." *Id.* at 344.

In order to make arguments regarding strike rates during voir dire, the defense team will need to take careful notes of strikes and continually calculate acceptance rates as voir dire progresses. *See* Scott Holmes's Spreadsheet for Calculating Juror Strike Ratios and Cassandra Stubbs's Strike Data Spreadsheet in the Race Materials Bank at www.ncids.org (select "Training and Resources"). Where a prosecutor's "acceptance rate" of minority jurors is low, defense attorneys should make note of this fact in support of a *Batson* challenge.

However, defense attorneys should not refrain from challenging strikes that appear to be race-based simply because the minority acceptance rate is not one that North Carolina appellate courts have found to be evidence supporting a prima facie claim of discrimination. The U.S. Supreme Court has observed that disparate strike rates are not a necessary element of a defendant's prima facie *Batson* claim: "More powerful than … bare statistics . . . are side-by-side comparisons of some Black venire panelists who were struck and white panelists who were allowed to serve." *Miller-El*, 545 U.S. 231, 241. Additionally, defense attorneys should carefully consider the circumstances surrounding the prosecutor's strikes. For example, a minority acceptance rate of 60% reflecting the acceptance of three of five Black jurors may mask the fact that, when the three Black jurors were accepted by the prosecutor, he or she was running low on peremptory strikes. Under these circumstances, the prosecutor's acceptance of three Black jurors does not necessarily constitute evidence supporting a race-neutral justification for striking the other two Black jurors. *See Miller El*, 545 U.S. 231, 249 (fact that the State grew more "sparing with peremptory challenges as the jury selection wore on . . . weaken[s] any suggestions that the State's acceptance of . . . the one Black juror [towards the end of the jury selection] shows that race was not in play"). As the Supreme Court has recognized, strike rates in a given case may not accurately represent the degree to which race played a role in peremptory challenges.

D. *Batson* Step Two: The Prosecutor's Race-Neutral Justification

If the defendant establishes a prima facie showing of discrimination, the burden of production shifts to the State to provide a race-neutral reason for the strike. *Purkett v. Elem*, 514 U.S. 765 (1995); *Hernandez v. New York*, 500 U.S. 352 (1991). A bare denial of discrimination will not suffice. "The [State's] explanation must be clear and reasonably specific, but need not rise to the level justifying exercise of a challenge for cause." *State v. Bonnett*, 348 N.C. 417, 433 (1998) (quotation omitted). In *Purkett*, the U.S. Supreme Court held that, at step two, the proffered race-neutral explanation does not have to be persuasive or even plausible as long as it is facially non-discriminatory; however, the Court recognized that an implausible reason will probably fail at step three, when the court determines whether the reason offered is pretextual. 514 U.S. 765, 768; *see also State v. Fletcher*, 348 N.C. 292 (1998) (following *Purkett*); *Bonnett*, 348 N.C. 417, 433 ("unless a discriminatory intent is inherent in the prosecutor's explanation, the reason offered will be deemed race neutral" (quotation omitted)). For a discussion of identifying and challenging justifications that are not race-neutral, see *infra* "Challenging justifications that are not race-neutral at step two" in § 7.4B, Presenting an Effective *Batson* Challenge.

E. *Batson* Step Three: The Pretext Determination

In the third step of a *Batson* challenge, the trial judge assesses the State's proffered reason and determines whether the defendant has met the burden of proving purposeful discrimination. Before the trial judge makes this determination, the defendant is entitled to an opportunity to rebut the proffered race-neutral reasons for excusing the juror. *See, e.g.*, *State v. Gaines*, 345 N.C. 647, 668 (1997); *State v. Peterson*, 344 N.C. 172 (1996). If the judge finds that the prosecutor's proffered reasons are pretextual and the real reason for the strike is discriminatory, the judge must find an equal protection violation. *Hernandez*, 500 U.S. 352, 359; *Gaines*, 345 N.C. 647, 668. "At [this] stage, implausible or fantastic justifications may (and probably will) be found to be pretexts for purposeful discrimination." *Purkett*, 514 U.S. 765, 768 (1995).

Because it is relatively easy for the State to proffer a race-neutral reason for a strike, defense counsel should be prepared to show that the State's proffered explanations for strikes are not credible. Implausible reasons unrelated to the juror's fitness to serve, such as demeanor or a remote connection to a relatively minor State witness, may be pretextual. Also, if a prosecutor accepts a White juror with certain characteristics, and then challenges a Black juror based on those same characteristics, defense counsel has grounds to argue that the stated reasons for the challenge are pretextual. For example, if the prosecutor claims he struck a Black juror because she was young, list for the judge the young White jurors accepted by the prosecutor. For an illustrative list of evidence that may support a finding of pretext, see *infra* "Evidence supporting a determination of pretext at step three" in § 7.4B, Presenting an Effective *Batson* Challenge.

Practice note: At step three, you must renew your objection to the challenged strikes. The North Carolina Supreme Court has held that a defendant's failure to attempt to demonstrate that the prosecutor's strike justifications were pretextual amounts to an expression of satisfaction with the explanations offered. *State v. Porter*, 326 N.C. 489, 501 (1990). Thus, silence following a prosecutor's proffer of race-neutral reasons supporting a challenged peremptory strike can be fatal to your *Batson* claim.

Suspect strike justifications. North Carolina appellate courts have been deferential to trial court decisions on *Batson* challenges. Some appellate decisions have remanded the defendant's *Batson* claims for further hearing (*see, e.g.*, *State v. Barden*, 356 N.C. 316, 344–45 (2002) (remanded for *Batson* hearing when judge improperly rejected the defendant's prima facie case); *State v. Barden*, 362 N.C. 277 (2008) (remanded for additional *Batson* hearing in light of U.S. Supreme Court cases clarifying *Batson* standards)), but only one North Carolina appellate decision has found a *Batson* violation. In that case, the prosecutor did not offer any race-neutral reason for striking at least one, and possibly two, Black jurors. *State v. Wright*, 189 N.C. App. 346 (2008).

Courts from other jurisdictions have more often found certain types of reasons for strikes insufficient. Reasons that have been viewed as indicative of pretextual discrimination include juror age, neighborhood, hairstyle, membership in predominantly African American organizations, demeanor, intelligence, and clothing. These decisions provide guidance in assessing the reasons offered by the State for peremptory challenges. *See infra* "Challenging justifications that are not race-neutral at step two" in § 7.4B, Presenting an Effective *Batson* Challenge.

Practice note: If the prosecutor explains that a challenged strike of a panelist was motivated by an objectionable demeanor that you did not observe, you should ask the court to require the prosecutor to describe the demeanor with particularity, contest the prosecutor's allegations when appropriate, and offer your own characterization of the juror's demeanor for both the trial judge and the record for possible appellate review. *See, e.g.*, *Davis v. Fisk Elec. Co.*, 268 S.W.3d 508, 518 (Tex. 2008) ("Peremptory strikes may legitimately be based on nonverbal conduct, but permitting strikes based on an assertion that nefarious conduct 'happened,' without identifying its nature and without any additional record support, would strip *Batson* of meaning.").

For example, if the prosecutor states that a potential juror appeared nervous, and the panelist appeared calm and comfortable to you, you should make the judge aware of your disagreement with the prosecutor's characterization. You may do so by, when possible, presenting testimonial evidence of a courtroom witness such as an investigator or paralegal. Otherwise, you may note your disagreement and ask the judge to make findings based on the judge's observations. Unless you have created a record, deference will be given on appeal to a trial judge's rulings on demeanor. *Snyder*, 552 U.S. 472, 477 ("determinations of credibility and demeanor lie peculiarly within a trial judge's province" (quotation omitted)); *see also Thaler v. Haynes*, 559 U.S. 43 (2010) (per curiam) (holding that although a judge must take into account, among other things, his or her observations of a juror's demeanor when a challenge is based thereon, neither *Batson* nor *Snyder* require that a "demeanor-based explanation must be rejected if the judge did not observe or cannot recall the juror's demeanor"). Additionally, if the allegedly objectionable demeanor was exhibited by an accepted panelist of a different race, be sure to note this on the record.

No right to cross-examine prosecutor on race-neutral explanation. The North Carolina Supreme Court has held that a defendant does not have the right to call the prosecutor as a witness to show that his or her proffered explanations are pretextual. *State v. Porter*, 326 N.C. 489, 497 (1990); *State v. Jackson*, 322 N.C. 251 (1988). Courts in other jurisdictions have allowed defendants to cross-examine prosecutors regarding their reasons for peremptory strikes (*see, e.g.*, *Keeton v. State*, 749 S.W.2d 861 (Tex. Crim. App. 1988); *Ex Parte Lynne*, 543 So. 2d 709, 712 (Ala. 1988)); and divergent judicial approaches to this question were recently the subject of a petition for certiorari to the U.S. Supreme Court. Petition for Writ of Certiorari, *Drake v. Louisiana*, No. 09-998, 2010 WL 638483 (Feb. 18, 2010). Although the petition was denied (560 U.S. 925 (2010)), the issue is potentially subject to reconsideration, particularly in light of U.S. Supreme Court holdings stressing that *Batson* claims turn on prosecutorial credibility. *See, e.g.*, *Purkett*, 514 U.S. 765, 769 (court's determination of racial motivation "turn[s] primarily on an assessment of [the prosecutor's] credibility").

Defendant does not have to show race was the "sole factor" motivating the peremptory strike. At times, a peremptory strike may be motivated by both constitutional race-neutral factors and unconstitutional race-based factors. A *Batson* challenge will succeed when, during the third step, the court determines that "race was *significant* in determining who was challenged and who was not." *State v. Waring*, 364 N.C. 443, 480 (2010) (quoting *Miller-El*, 545 U.S. 231, 252 (emphasis added in *Waring*)). The defendant does not have "to establish that race was the sole reason" for the prosecutor's use of a peremptory strike. *Waring*, 364 N.C. 443, 480–81 (holding that "sole basis" is not the correct standard and observing that the significant or motivating factor standard is "less stringent" than the "sole basis" standard; remanded for further hearing).

The U.S. Supreme Court has not determined whether the "significant factor" standard permits a peremptory strike when the "party defending the action [can] show that [the unconstitutional] factor was not determinative." *Snyder v. United States*, 552 U.S. 472, 485 (2008) (declining to reach the question). The N.C. Supreme Court's treatment of the question in *Waring* indicates that, in North Carolina, the party raising the *Batson* challenge must demonstrate only that race was a significant factor, and not a determinative one, behind the peremptory strike. The N.C. Supreme Court has not adopted a "but for" test, which would require a showing that, but for the venire person's race, the State would not have used a peremptory strike. Justice Marshall has explained that such a test "is inappropriate in the *Batson* inquiry . . . because of the special difficulties of proof that a court applying that standard to a prosecutor's peremptory-challenge decisions necessarily would encounter." *Wilkerson v. Texas*, 493 U.S. 924, 926 (1989) (Marshall, J., dissenting from denial of cert.); *see also Cook v. Lamargue*, 593 F.3d 810, 815 (9th Cir. 2010) (summarizing circuit split on treatment of strikes in which race plays some role but is not necessarily a determinative factor and holding that a *Batson* challenge should succeed whenever race was a substantial motivating factor).

There is some support for arguing that a standard less stringent than the "substantial motivating factor" one should apply in cases of mixed prosecutorial motives for peremptory strikes. *Batson* announced an "unqualified requirement that the State offer a *neutral* explanation for its peremptory challenge. To be neutral, the explanation must be based *wholly* on nonracial criteria." *Wilkerson v. Texas*, 493 U.S. 924, 926 (1989) (Marshall, J., dissenting from denial of cert.) (emphasis in original) (internal citation omitted); Russell D. Covey, *The Unbearable Lightness of Batson: Mixed Motives and Discrimination in Jury Selection*, 66 MD. LAW. REV. 279, 311 (2012) (observing that mixed-motive explanations are not neutral). Defense attorneys can argue that the "significant factor" standard should be interpreted to mean that a strike motivated in part by race is unconstitutional. "A judicial inquiry designed to safeguard a criminal defendant's basic constitutional rights should not rest on the unverifiable assertions of a prosecutor who, having admitted to racial bias, subsequently attempts to reconstruct what his thought process would have been had he not entertained such bias." *Wilkerson*, 493 U.S. 924, 927–28 (Marshall, J., dissenting from denial of cert.). This reasoning also would apply to instances in which racial motivations were not admitted but were detected by the judge at step three of the *Batson* test. Such a standard would be consistent with research recognizing the difficulty of assigning different weights to multiple motivations. *See, e.g.*, Russell D. Covey, *The Unbearable Lightness of Batson: Mixed Motives and Discrimination in Jury Selection*, 66 MD. LAW. REV. 279 (2012).

Comparative juror analysis at step three. *Miller-El v. Dretke*, 545 U.S. 231, 241–46 (2005), identified side-by-side comparisons between Black and White panelists as an important type of evidence at step three of the *Batson* test. If a prosecutor accepts a White juror with certain characteristics, and then uses those characteristics to strike a Black juror, discrimination can be inferred. For example, in *Miller-El*, the prosecutor claimed that he struck a Black venireman because the venireman purportedly expressed the opinion that he would vote against the death penalty if he believed the defendant could be rehabilitated. This was not a race-neutral reason, the Court found, where the prosecutor accepted White jurors with comparable views. Further, the Court noted that the prosecutor's justification for the strike was a mischaracterization of the venireman's stated position regarding rehabilitation and the death penalty. Defense counsel's challenge to this mischaracterization at voir dire prompted the prosecutor to offer the additional explanation that the strike was based on the venireman's indication that his brother had prior criminal convictions. The Court found this explanation for the strike to be pretextual based on its timing and lack of inquiry by the prosecutor into the venireman's relationship with his brother or whether the prior convictions had any influence on the venireman.

In 2008, the U.S. Supreme Court reemphasized the importance of comparative juror analysis in *Snyder v. Louisiana*, 552 U.S. 472 (2008). In *Snyder*, the Court found that the trial judge erred in overruling the defendant's *Batson* objection to the State's use of a peremptory challenge to remove a prospective Black juror. The State had offered two race-neutral explanations for striking the juror: (1) the juror looked very nervous during the questioning; and (2) the juror was a student teacher and was concerned about missing class. As a result of the juror's concerns, the prosecutor asserted that he felt that the juror might agree to a lesser verdict in order to bypass the penalty phase and finish quickly. The Court did not rule on the first proffered explanation because the record did not show that the trial judge made a determination about the juror's demeanor. However, the Court found the prosecutor's second explanation implausible and highly speculative because the prospective juror had not seemed overly concerned about the student-teaching situation once his dean was contacted and gave assurances that the class time could be made up. The Court compared the testimony of the juror who was struck with that of two White jurors who also were concerned about conflicting obligations. Although one of those jurors had asked to be excused based on a hardship and related obligations that seemed "substantially more pressing" than the struck juror's concerns, the prosecutor did not strike him. *Snyder*, 552 U.S. 472, 484. A second White prospective juror also expressed concern about serving, stating that he would "'have to cancel too many things,' including an urgent appointment at which his presence was essential." *Id.* Despite these concerns, the prosecutor did not strike this juror. Based on these circumstances, the Court held that discriminatory intent was a substantial or motivating factor in the actions taken by the prosecutor and reversed the lower court's decision upholding the validity of the peremptory strike. *Miller-El* and *Snyder* both stand for the principle that side-by-side comparisons of jurors can be powerful evidence of discriminatory intent. *See also infra* "Comparative juror analysis at step one" in § 7.4B, Presenting an Effective *Batson* Challenge.

Practice note: It is improper for the judge to substitute a better reason than the prosecutor offers. *See, e.g.*, *Galarza v. Keane*, 252 F.3d 630, 639 (2d Cir. 2001) (where trial court judge did not evaluate prosecutor's race neutral justifications for three challenged peremptory strikes and stated that "either side could have struck [one of the stricken jurors] for cause," failure to consider prosecutor's own justifications constituted reversible error). If you find that the trial judge is "saving" the prosecutor's explanations, you should object and make a record of the difference between the reason advanced by the prosecutor and the reason found by the judge.

Disparate questioning. In *Miller-El*, the Court held that intentional discrimination can be shown by patterns of questioning or other conduct—for example, if a prosecutor asks questions of Black jurors that he or she does not ask of White jurors, such as whether they think the criminal justice system is fair. In *Miller-El*, the Court found discrimination where the prosecutor described the death penalty vividly and explicitly to Black jurors but blandly to White jurors. The following types of disparate questioning practices may constitute evidence of discrimination:

- Asking repetitive, scrutinizing questions only of Black jurors. *See, e.g.*, Golphin Order at 114 (describing this practice); *Miller-El v. Dretke*, 545 U.S. 231, 249 (2005) (prosecutor "repeatedly questioned [a Black juror] on his capacity and willingness to impose a sentence of death" while failing to do so of a White juror who expressed concern that the death penalty was too easy on a convict).
- Asking follow-up questions only of Black jurors when White jurors make the same or similar statements. *See, e.g.*, *Miller-El*, 545 U.S. 231, 245 (observing that "nonblack jurors whose remarks on rehabilitation could well have signaled a limit on their willingness to impose a death sentence were not questioned further and drew no objection, but the prosecution expressed apprehension about a black juror's belief in the possibility of reformation even though he repeatedly stated his approval of the death penalty and testified that he could impose it according to [the law]").
- Providing prefatory information before asking questions of Black jurors that differs from the prefatory information provided before asking questions of other jurors, which may reflect an attempt to elicit different answers from Black jurors to support challenges for cause or peremptory strikes. *See, e.g.*, *Miller-El*, 545 U.S. 231, 256 (6% of White potential jurors, but 53% of Black potential jurors, were provided a graphic description of capital punishment before questioning on their views concerning the death penalty).
- Asking race-related questions of Black jurors that are not asked of non-Black jurors. *See, e.g.*, Golphin Order at 114 (describing case in which a prosecutor asked a black juror if her "black friends" would criticize her if she voted to convict the defendants).

Practice note: Texas, where *Miller-El* originates, allowed any party to "shuffle" the venire cards during jury selection. The U.S. Supreme Court criticized the prosecutor's practice of shuffling the cards when there were several Black jurors in the next group of jurors to be called into the box. The effect of the shuffling was to move those jurors back in line. A North Carolina equivalent might occur where jurors are divided into panels—for example, if at the end of a panel there are two Black venire members left and no Whites, and the prosecutor asks to merge the remaining members of the panel with the next panel. *See* 2 NORTH CAROLINA DEFENDER MANUAL § 25.1C (Random Selection Requirement) (2d ed. 2012).

F. Remedy for *Batson* Violations at Trial

Batson does not specify the proper remedy for a violation that is found at trial. *Batson,* 476 U.S. 79, 99 n.24 (declining to determine whether it is "more appropriate in a particular case . . . to discharge the venire . . . or to disallow the discriminatory challenges and resume selection with the improperly challenged jurors reinstated on the venire"). In *State v. McCollum*, 334 N.C. 208 (1993), the N.C. Supreme Court held that if the trial judge finds that the State has violated *Batson,* the better practice is to dismiss the venire and begin jury selection again. The *McCollum* court did not preclude the court from exercising its discretion to seat improperly struck jurors, but noted that reseating a juror improperly struck by the State may not be appropriate where the juror knows that he or she was struck and may have difficulty being impartial.

Practice note: Concerns regarding the impartiality of an improperly struck juror might be addressed two different ways, both of which may increase confidence that an improperly struck juror could be seated and remain impartial. The favored method is to conduct all peremptory strikes at the bench, out of hearing of the jurors. If this approach is taken, counsel should make sure that the bench hearing is on the record. Alternately, if the peremptory strikes are made within earshot of the potential jurors, judicial questioning of an improperly struck juror may be able to resolve questions about the juror's impartiality.

North Carolina trial courts have not always dismissed the venire in response to a *Batson* claim. In *State v. Fletcher*, 348 N.C. 292 (1998), the prosecutor initially struck a juror because the juror was a member of the NAACP. When the trial judge found the prosecutor's reason to be discriminatory, the prosecutor withdrew his strike and accepted the juror. The trial judge then found no *Batson* violation, and the N.C. Supreme Court affirmed. Chief Justice Mitchell, dissenting in *Fletcher*, would have ordered a new trial, emphasizing that dismissing the venire is the better practice where the prosecutor makes an invalid strike. In *State v. Parker*, a capital trial reviewed by a superior court judge ruling on an RJA claim, the trial court judge seated the improperly struck juror after sustaining the defendant's *Batson* challenge. Golphin Order at 71.

Trial courts in other jurisdictions have fashioned different remedies for *Batson* violations. In *Foster v. State*, 111 P.3d 1083 (Nev. 2005), the Nevada Supreme Court observed:

> In implementing *Batson*, the states have generally followed one of three different approaches. Some jurisdictions require the trial courts to disallow a peremptory strike made in violation of *Batson* or to reseat the improperly stricken juror. Other jurisdictions require the trial courts to discharge the venire and commence jury selection anew from an entirely new venire. The majority of courts, however, have delegated to the discretion of the trial judge the determination of the appropriate remedy for a *Batson* violation.

Id. at 1089 (internal quotation omitted); *see also McCrory v. Henderson*, 82 F.3d 1243, 1247 (2d Cir. 1996) ("If the objection is raised during jury selection, the error is remediable in any one of a number of ways. Challenges found to be abusive might be disallowed; if this is not feasible because the challenged jurors have already been released, additional jurors might be called to the venire and additional challenges granted to the defendant; or in cases where those remedies are insufficient, the jury selection might begin anew with a fresh panel.")

Practice note: Judges may ask the parties for suggestions regarding the proper remedy. *See, e.g.*, *State v. McCollum*, 334 N.C. 208, 235 (1993) (after sustaining defendant's *Batson* objection, "[t]he trial court then inquired as to how the defendant and the State desired to proceed to correct the *Batson* violation"). Defense attorneys should consider one or more of the following remedies depending on the circumstances of the case:

- reseating of the improperly struck juror, especially if the strike and *Batson* challenge were conducted out of the hearing of the struck juror; *see* Jeffrey Bellin & Junichi P. Semitsu, *Widening Batson's Net to Ensnare More than the Unapologetically Bigoted or Painfully Unimaginative Attorney*, 96 CORNELL L. REV. 1075, 1110–12 (2011) (explaining that the benefits of this remedial procedure include the voiding of the unconstitutional act, vindication of improperly struck juror's right to equal protection, the procedure's express contemplation by the *Batson* Court, and relative administrative efficiency);
- mistrial;
- discharging the entire venire and reseating a new venire from which juror panels are drawn;
- discharging the jury panel and assembling a new panel;
- denying the prosecutor peremptory strikes;
- returning individuals struck by the prosecutor to the panel.

Discharging an entire venire may not be a desirable outcome because it essentially upholds the improper strike, wastes judicial time and resources, does not vindicate the improperly struck juror's equal protection rights, and may not deter racially motivated peremptory strikes. *See generally Powers v. Ohio*, 499 U.S. 400 (1991) (prospective juror's right not to be excluded from jury service because of race is protected by the Equal Protection Clause).

The N.C. Superior Court Judges' Benchbook, an online compilation from the School of Government, states that if a judge finds a discriminatory use of a peremptory challenge, the judge "must get rid of the whole jury panel and start over" and may not reseat the wrongly excused juror. Jury Selection (Criminal) at 2–3 ("*Batson* challenges in a nutshell"), *in* N.C. SUPERIOR COURT JUDGES' BENCHBOOK (Jessica Smith ed.). The discussion does not address the authorities or alternatives discussed in this section.

G. *Batson* Challenges to a Defendant's Strikes

The *Batson* rule applies to defendants as well as to the State. The Equal Protection Clause prohibits criminal defendants from exercising peremptory strikes in a manner that discriminates on the basis of race, gender, or other suspect characteristic. *Georgia v. McCollum*, 505 U.S. 42 (1992); *accord State v. Locklear*, 349 N.C. 118 (1998) (citing *McCollum*); *State v. Cofield*, 129 N.C. App. 268 (1998) (same).

A challenge to a defendant's exercise of peremptory challenges, referred to as a "reverse *Batson* claim," is made in the same way as a *Batson* claim. First, the State must show a prima facie case of discrimination. The burden then shifts to the defendant to explain his or her strikes in a race-neutral manner. The judge then assesses whether the reason offered by the defense attorney is pretextual, and determines whether the State has met its burden of proving purposeful discrimination.

Practice note: In defending against a *Batson* challenge, note for the record how many African American or other minority jurors were passed to you for questioning. It may be that you exercised 90% of your strikes against White jurors, but that 95% of the jurors passed to you were White, either because the panel was not racially diverse, or because Black or other minority jurors had already been excused for cause or struck by the State.

Reverse *Batson* claims have rarely been made in North Carolina, possibly as a result of a fear by prosecutors that if the trial judge is deemed to have erred in disallowing a defendant's peremptory challenge, the appellate court will grant the defendant a new trial. *See, e.g.*, *State v. Scott*, 749 S.E.2d 160, 165 (S.C. Ct. App. 2013) (where the State's *Batson* claim was erroneously granted, the court vacated the defendant's conviction and remanded for a new trial); *see also* Jeff Welty, *Rivera v. Illinois* and "Reverse Batson," N.C. CRIM. L., UNC SCH. OF GOV'T BLOG (Apr. 7, 2009).

Although the question of the remedy for improperly denied challenges has not been directly answered, the U.S. Supreme Court discussed it in *Rivera v. Illinois*, 556 U.S. 148 (2009). In *Rivera*, the judge, based on his own concerns about discrimination, required the defendant to explain his peremptory challenge of a Black female juror. After hearing the explanation, the judge denied the defendant's peremptory challenge and required that the juror be seated on the jury. That juror later became the jury foreperson. On appeal, the defendant argued that the trial judge's error in denying his peremptory challenge violated his rights under the Due Process Clause and amounted to structural error—that is, the defendant was entitled to a new trial without having to show prejudice. The Illinois Supreme Court found that the defendant was deprived of his state right to exercise his peremptory challenges but determined that the error was harmless beyond a reasonable doubt in light of the overwhelming evidence against him. The U.S. Supreme Court affirmed the decision of the lower court, holding that "the loss of a peremptory challenge due to a state court's good-faith error is not a matter of federal constitutional concern. Rather, it is a matter for the State to address under its own laws." *Id.* at 157. The Court noted that structural errors requiring automatic reversal are typically reserved for the type of error that "necessarily renders a criminal trial fundamentally unfair or an unreliable vehicle for determining guilt or innocence." *Id.* at 160 (quotation omitted). The Court held that "the mistaken denial of a state-provided peremptory challenge," under the circumstances presented in *Rivera*, did not constitute an error of that magnitude. *Id.* at 161.

No North Carolina decision has addressed the remedy available on appeal where the trial court improperly denies the defendant's peremptory challenge.

H. Implicit Bias and the *Batson* Framework

In *State v. Saintcalle*, 309 P.3d 326 (Wash. 2013), the Washington Supreme Court considered the place of implicit bias in the *Batson* framework. Justice Wiggins' lead opinion in the case called for explicit recognition of implicit bias in the analysis. He reasoned that the prevalence of implicit biases "upends the *Batson* framework," and he called for the replacement of the state's *Batson* test with a more robust one that "necessarily accounts for and alerts trial courts to the problem of unconscious bias, without ambiguity or confusion." *Id.* at 336, 339. Justice Wiggins noted that "trial courts may often interpret [the requirement of purposeful discrimination] to require conscious discrimination." *Id.* at 338. If the "purposeful discrimination" standard excludes acts motivated by implicit bias, sustaining a *Batson* challenge requires a trial judge to "look a member of the bar in the eye and level an accusation of deceit or racism. And if the judge chooses not to do so despite misgivings about possible race bias, the problem is compounded by the fact that we defer heavily to the judge's findings on appeal." *Id.* Explicit recognition of implicit bias in the *Batson* framework, according to Justice Wiggins, "would take the focus off of the credibility and integrity of the attorneys and ease the accusatory strain of sustaining a Batson challenge . . . [and thus] simplify the task of reducing racial bias in our criminal justice system, both conscious and unconscious." *Id.* at 339.

The recognition of implicit bias by judges and attorneys involved in litigation of *Batson* challenges may engender a more accurate and complete consideration of the possible role of race in the exercise of peremptory strikes. Additionally, if court actors accept that a prosecutor's race-neutral justification for a strike may be sincerely held but the strike nevertheless may be motivated by unconscious racial motivations, the defense attorney challenging an apparently discriminatory strike does not have to level a charge of overt racism and intentional discrimination; the prosecutor defending the strike does not face the potential stigma attached to a finding of a violation; and the judge ruling on the strike does not have to conclude that the prosecutor lied to conceal an intentional violation of the constitution. Jeffrey Bellin & Junichi P. Semitsu, *Widening Batson*'s *Net to Ensnare More than the Unapologetically Bigoted or Painfully Unimaginative Attorney*, 96 CORNELL L. REV. 1075, 1121–23 (2011). In light of the fact that defense attorneys, prosecutors, and judges are repeat actors who interact with each other both in and out of the courtroom on a regular basis, the alleviation of these disincentives to raising and sustaining *Batson* claims could improve the effectiveness of the *Batson* framework.

Some argue that under current equal protection jurisprudence, race-based peremptory strikes motivated by implicit biases are already captured within the *Batson* framework. *See State v. Saintcalle*, 309 P.3d 326, 338 n.8 (Wash. 2013) (observing that the argument that strikes motivated by implicit bias violate *Batson* under existing jurisprudence "makes sense," but declining to consider it as it was not raised by the parties). Professors Ralph Richard Banks and Richard Thompson Ford argue that the line of cases requiring proof of "discriminatory purpose" to sustain an equal protection claim does not distinguish between conscious and unconscious bias. Ralph Richard Banks & Richard Thompson Ford, *(How) Does Unconscious Bias Matter?: Law, Politics, and Racial Inequality*, 58 EMORY L. J. 1053 (2009). In their view, peremptory challenges based on race violate the Equal Protection Clause whether the reliance was conscious or unconscious: "[t]here is no exemption for strikes that are discriminatory, but not intentionally so." *Id.* at 1099 (but cautioning about the evidentiary difficulty in succeeding on a claim of covert bias); *see also* Sheila Foster, *Intent and Incoherence*, 72 TUL. L. REV. 1065, 1094–97 (1998) (explaining why peremptory challenges motivated by race may be successfully challenged without proof of conscious intent to discriminate).

Practice note: In recent years, judicial recognition of the influence of implicit bias on decision-making has increased. *See* Equal Justice Society, *Packet on Scholarship and Jurisprudence Related to Implicit Bias and the Intent Doctrine*, EQUALJUSTICESOCIETY.ORG (last visited Aug. 13, 2014). In cases without evidence of overt racial discrimination on the part of the prosecutor, incorporating implicit bias research into your *Batson* challenge may strengthen your claim. Consider arguing that whether motivated by unconscious or conscious bias, a strike influenced by race contravenes the guarantee of equal protection. Raising this issue may lead to the adoption of a broader understanding of the "purposeful discrimination" standard in *Batson* claims, and allow court actors to move away from allegations of overt discrimination.

7.4 Litigating a *Batson* Challenge

A. Pretrial Preparation for a *Batson* Challenge

Come prepared. Before trial, it is impossible to know whether peremptory strikes will be exercised in a discriminatory manner. For this reason, defense attorneys should prepare in advance by gathering data and preparing potential motions and a note-taking system.

Assemble historical data. You should make a habit of arriving at every trial with records that, under appropriate circumstances, may be submitted as evidence in support of a *Batson* claim. While *Batson* challenges to peremptory strikes can be based solely on evidence of discrimination in the defendant's individual case, patterns suggestive of discrimination in jury selection also constitute evidence of discrimination at steps one and three of the *Batson* analysis. *See Miller-El v. Dretke*, 545 U.S. 231, 239 (2005) (*Batson* evidence includes "totality of the relevant facts" (quotation omitted)); *see also supra* § 7.3C, *Batson* Step One: The Prima Facie Case, § 7.3E, *Batson* Step Three: The Pretext Determination. Because evidence of past strikes may be relevant in meeting the defendant's burden of showing discrimination, defenders should keep track of patterns of strikes in particular prosecutor's offices and with respect to particular prosecutors, including:

- copies of voir dire from previous trials, including past *Batson* challenges and prosecutors' stated reasons for strikes;
- manuals or training materials regarding responding to *Batson* challenges, *see, e.g., Top Gun II Batson Training: Articulating Juror Negatives* in the Race Materials Bank at www.ncids.org (select "Training and Resources"); *see also Miller-El v. Dretke*, 545 U.S. 231 (2005) (discriminatory training manual on exclusion of Black people from juries constituted evidence supporting finding of Batson violation);
- any available strike rate data, including strike rates in capital cases in your county and judicial district from the MSU study, *see* Affidavit Regarding MSU Study in the Race Materials Bank at www.ncids.org (select "Training and Resources"); challenges by county and prosecutor in capital cases can also be found in the Golphin Order or

Robinson Order by referencing charts sorted by county and defendant on the IDS website;

- any other patterns, practices, or evidence relating to the influence of race on prosecutorial decision-making, *see, e.g.*, Affidavit Regarding Peremptory Strikes Exercised in Capital Cases in a Single North Carolina County in the Race Materials Bank at www.ncids.org (select "Training and Resources").

Defenders should be prepared to integrate any relevant information into upcoming trials. For example, if a particular prosecutor usually responds to *Batson* challenges by explaining that the struck African American venire person appears nervous, you should make the judge aware of this pattern when a prosecutor defends a peremptory strike on this basis. "A prosecutor who repeats the same race-neutral reasons at every trial loses credibility, but only when you point it out, and back it up." Susan Jackson Balliet and Bruce P. Hackett, *Litigating Race in Voir Dire*, THE ADVOCATE, May 2008, at 42, 46.

Practice note: Past *Batson* justifications by particular prosecutors can point to additional evidence to assemble before trial. For example, if the prosecutor in your client's case has previously justified challenged strikes by noting that the panelist lives in an objectionable neighborhood, you can pull census data about the demographic composition of neighborhoods identified in past strikes in preparation for a possible argument that such a justification serves as a proxy for race and is not race-neutral. Similarly, attorneys can pull data about the demographic composition of the neighborhoods of Black venire members in the present case. This information can be found on the website of the U.S. Census Bureau.

Calculating strike data. The methodology employed by the MSU researchers is described in a law review article about the study's procedure and findings, and can be replicated by defense attorneys for other types of cases (for example, all felony cases in a certain judicial district over an eight-month period; all felony cases handled by a particular prosecutor; or all cases involving a Black defendant and a White victim in a certain county during a certain year). *See* Catherine M. Grosso & Barbara O'Brien*, A Stubborn Legacy: The Overwhelming Importance of Race in Jury Selection in 173 Post-*Batson *North Carolina Capital Trials*, 97 IOWA L. REV. 1531 (2012). A modified approach based on the study's methodology would involve creating a file for each type of proceeding examined that includes:

- The names of every "strike-eligible" venire member. This population includes venire members who were questioned on voir dire, not excluded for cause, and whom the prosecutor had the opportunity to strike.
- The race of every venire member included on the list. This may be obtained from juror questionnaires, the juror's statement of his or her race on the record in the voir dire transcript, or electronic databases such as the State Board of Elections website, or LexisNexis "Locate a Person (Nationwide) Search Non-regulated". *See* Examples of Juror Questionnaires in the Race Materials Bank at www.ncids.org (select "Training and Resources"). Summons lists with addresses may be available in court files. The

addresses listed on juror summons may be compared to the addresses found in web-based sources identifying racial information to confirm that the two sources refer to the same person. Because of the potential for error, attorney observation is a disfavored method of identifying the race of venire members.

- Other demographic characteristics of strike-eligible jurors, including gender, marital status, employment, and educational background, to the extent revealed in juror questionnaires or during voir dire.
- Prior experiences with the legal system of strike-eligible jurors.
- Expressed views by strike-eligible jurors concerning law enforcement officers, prosecutors, or the criminal justice system.
- The number of questions asked of each prospective juror.
- Whether the prospective juror was struck. This information can be obtained by reviewing clerk charts or transcripts.
- If a *Batson* challenge was raised, the prosecutor's explanation for the challenge and the judge's ruling on the challenge.

Once this information has been collected, attorneys should be able to calculate basic statistical data, such as the relative strike rates of Black venire members versus other venire members. Attorneys should also be able to compile data regarding the number of questions asked of venire members of various races, and the race-neutral justifications offered in response to *Batson* challenges by prosecutors. Additional analysis of strike patterns to control for personal characteristics of venire members may require assistance from a statistician or an attorney trained in statistical methods. *See* Catherine M. Grosso & Barbara O'Brien, *A Stubborn Legacy: The Overwhelming Importance of Race in Jury Selection in 173 Post-*Batson *North Carolina Capital Trials*, 97 IOWA L. REV. 1531 (2012).

Learn the trial judge's approach to *Batson*. Trial judges have discretion in conducting voir dire and establishing procedures for resolving *Batson* claims. Before trial, ascertain the *Batson* procedures followed by the judge and his or her past *Batson* rulings if available. In particular, you will want to learn:

- whether the judge allows *Batson* challenges to be raised and resolved out of hearing of the potential juror at issue;
- whether *Batson* hearings are routinely held;
- the procedures generally followed by the judge in *Batson* hearings;
- how often the judge has granted *Batson* challenges; and
- what remedy the judge has ordered in response to any violations.

Prepare note-taking method. To effectively identify and challenge equal protection violations, you should develop a thorough and efficient system for recording all aspects of the voir dire process. One effective practice is to use a spreadsheet to record each venire member's race, gender, physical appearance, and other notable attributes; the number of questions asked of the juror; the type of questions asked of the juror; and all statements made by that juror. *See* Scott Holmes's Spreadsheet for Calculating Juror Strike Ratios and Cassandra Stubbs's Strike Data Spreadsheet, both in the Race Materials Bank at www.ncids.org (select "Training and Resources"). Ideally, these notes should be compiled by a separate member of the defense team who can focus on preparing them, such as an attorney, paralegal, administrative assistant, intern, or investigator who is familiar with the note-taking method. Precise, accurate records are essential for identifying similarities between venire members struck and accepted, discerning historical patterns, and calculating strike rates. Susan Jackson Balliet & Bruce P. Hackett, *Litigating Race in Voir Dire*, THE ADVOCATE, May 2008 at 42, 46.

B. Presenting an Effective *Batson* Challenge

Raising a *Batson* challenge. *Batson* claims are raised orally during voir dire. The attorney should state that the defendant objects to the State's peremptory challenge and would like to be heard at the bench. It is preferable to state the legal grounds for the challenge at the bench and out of earshot of the jurors, to prevent affecting the impartiality of potential jurors who are the subjects of *Batson* challenges. Counsel should make sure that the bench hearing is on the record.

***Batson* hearing.** A *Batson* challenge triggers an automatic right to a hearing. "[I]t is not the prima facie case that triggers the right to a hearing." Susan Jackson Balliet & Bruce P. Hackett, *Litigating Race in Voir Dire*, THE ADVOCATE, May 2008 at 49. As one court explained, "*Batson v. Kentucky* requires that upon *timely* objection to peremptory challenges for alleged discrimination, the court shall hold a hearing to determine if a prima facie case of discrimination can be made." *Simmons v. Com.*, 746 S.W.2d 393, 397 (Ky. 1988) (emphasis in original). If you are denied a hearing, be sure to make a proffer of the evidence that would support a prima facie *Batson* claim.

Practice note: It is important to raise a *Batson* claim whenever you suspect that race may have been a motivating factor in a prosecutor's exercise of a peremptory strike. At times, the basis for your challenge may grow stronger as voir dire progresses. If, for example, a Black juror is struck early in voir dire and your *Batson* challenge to the strike is denied, and later a White juror is questioned or treated differently, you should renew your objection based on the additional evidence. If you did not object when the juror was initially struck, your *Batson* claim may be deemed waived.

Ensure inclusion of jurors' race on record. To preserve a *Batson* challenge for appellate review, the record must be clear as to the race of the jurors peremptorily challenged by the State as well as the race of the other members of the jury panel (prospective and selected); otherwise, the appellate court will find insufficient evidence in the record to support the defendant's claim. *See State v. Brogden*, 329 N.C. 534, 546 (1991) (defendant "failed to carry his burden of establishing an adequate record for appellate review"; defense counsel's subjective impressions regarding race and notations by the court reporter of her subjective impressions regarding race were not sufficient); *State v. Payne*, 327 N.C. 194, 198–201 (1990) (affidavit containing defense counsel's perceptions of the race of potential jurors was not adequate to support defendant's claim of improper use of peremptory challenges under *Batson* and defendant's request to have "courtroom clerk record the race and sex of the 'prospective' jurors who had already been seated or excused" was properly rejected; the trial court noted "that had the defendant made his motion prior to jury selection, the court would have had each prospective juror state his or her race during the court's initial questioning"); *State v. Mitchell*, 321 N.C. 650, 654–56 (1988) (inappropriate for court reporter to note the race of the jurors based on his or her perception; "if there is any question as to the prospective juror's race, this issue should be resolved by the trial court based upon questioning of the juror or other proper evidence").

Practice note: Before jury selection begins, counsel should request that the trial judge have each prospective juror state his or her race for the record during the judge's initial questioning. *See* Motion for Court to Note the Race of all Potential Jurors Examined for Selection and Trial Brief and Pretrial Motions in the Race Materials Bank at www.ncids.org (select "Training and Resources").

Case study: In the following anecdote, Durham attorney Scott Holmes reflects on his experience raising *Batson* challenges in state and federal court:

Before jury selection begins, I think it is best practice to file a trial brief summarizing the most basic facts and raising the most routine pretrial motions in limine. See Trial Brief and Pretrial Motions in the Race Materials Bank at www.ncids.org (select "Training and Resources"). I think it is good to include in the trial brief/pretrial motions a request to record the race of the potential jurors. I think including it with the other pretrial motions takes some of the edge off. At the pretrial stage I ask the Court to include the self-identification of race with each juror's name and where they are from. It is easier for the court to ask for it than the parties. If the Court denies my request and refuses to ask about their race, I think it is best to ask for the Court's permission to get them to put their race on the record before they are stricken by either side. If that is denied, then I put it on the record myself based on my own observations, pointing out that I asked the Court to make the record and was refused. This is important because North Carolina courts have found observations by counsel or the court reporter about jurors' race insufficient to create a record. In state court, I've never had a prosecutor contest my motion or a judge deny it. The North Carolina Supreme Court has held that where there is any question about juror race, the trial court should resolve the question by questioning the juror or reviewing other proper evidence establishing juror race. *State v. Mitchell*, 321 N.C. 650, 654–56 (1988).

When I'm in trial, I use an excel spreadsheet to capture and synthesize data on the prosecutor's exercise of juror strikes. *See* Scott Holmes's Spreadsheet for Calculating Juror Strike Ratios in the Race Materials Bank at www.ncids.org (select "Training and Resources"). Every time the prosecutor accepts or peremptorily strikes a juror, I record the juror's race in the spreadsheet. The spreadsheet formula automatically calculates the prosecutor's strike ratio for White jurors, Black jurors, and other minority jurors, allowing me to see, in real time, any developing pattern.

One time, when using this tool during a trial in federal court, a very disparate strike ratio developed. The prosecutor struck 6 of 7 eligible Black jurors for a strike ratio of .857, and only 1 of 6 eligible White jurors for a strike ratio of .166. That case was unusual because, to my surprise, the federal judge denied my motion to record the race of all potential jurors. When I raised a *Batson* challenge objecting to the prosecutor's disparate pattern of striking Black jurors, the judge questioned how I was able to determine the race of the struck jurors. It was a Catch-22: I had to rely on my own observations in determining juror race because the judge had denied my motion to record juror race, and the judge rejected my *Batson* claim at least in part based on a finding that my observations of juror race were unreliable.

While I did not prevail on my *Batson* claim in that case, simply raising it had an effect on the prosecutor. The prosecutor stopped using strikes to remove minority jurors, and we ended up with a very diverse jury. This case was an example of the powerful impact of raising *Batson* challenges, even when they do not succeed. I believe that I may have prevailed on the *Batson* challenge in state court and would encourage North Carolina defenders to raise the challenge even with less dramatic strike ratios. Although it may feel awkward to raise the issue because discussing race in general is hard, and specifically accusing a fellow attorney of racial bias is difficult, I believe that it is important to raise the issue. Even raising the issue sets a tone for everyone involved that I am planning on protecting all of my client's rights to the best of my ability. Litigating *Batson* challenges helps to safeguard a client's right to equal protection in the jury selection process and uphold the integrity of the jury system as a whole.

Consider filing a pretrial motion for *Batson*-related discovery. Before voir dire begins, consider seeking discovery on any *Batson*-related trainings or policies for prosecutors in your county. Such information may prove relevant in evaluating the totality of the circumstances surrounding an allegedly discriminatory strike. You also may be able to obtain the information by filing a public records request.

Ensure transcription of voir dire. In North Carolina, the party "alleg[ing] impropriety in the jury selection process must provide the reviewing court with the relevant portions of the transcript of the jury voir dire" or documents capable of reconstructing the relevant details of jury selection. *State v. Shelman*, 159 N.C. App. 300, 311 (2003) (quotation omitted) (rejecting defendant's *Batson* challenge where there was neither a transcript of voir dire nor any other document that could reconstruct the factual details of jury selection). The *Shelman* court held that relevant details of jury selection include:

- the number of jurors questioned by the prosecutor;
- the race and gender of jurors questioned by the prosecutor;
- the number and/or percentage of jurors accepted, by race and gender;
- whether similarly situated venire members received disparate treatment correlated with race and/or gender; and
- whether remarks to jurors made by prosecutors evinced racial bias.

Shelman, 159 N.C. App. 300, 310.

The best way to preserve this information is to ensure that voir dire is transcribed in accordance with G.S. 15A-1241. *See State v. Holloway*, __ N.C. App. __, 734 S.E.2d 139, *5 (2012) (unpublished) ("transcript of the trial court's discussion with defense counsel regarding defendant's *Batson* challenge is not an adequate substitute for these factual details"). Defense attorneys should file a pretrial motion to transcribe voir dire in every case. *See* Motion to Transcribe Voir Dire in the Race Materials Bank at www.ncids.org (select "Training and Resources"). To ensure meaningful appellate review, the motion should ask the court to direct the court reporter to indicate in the transcript the name of the venire member each time he or she speaks. In addition, before the trial begins, counsel should file any jury questionnaires, jury lists, and strike sheets in the record for appellate purposes. Susan Jackson Balliet & Bruce P. Hackett, *Litigating Race in Voir Dire*, THE ADVOCATE, May 2008, at 42, 46; *see also* 2 NORTH CAROLINA DEFENDER MANUAL § 28.7C (Complete Recordation) (2d ed. 2012).

Evidence supporting defendant's prima facie case at step one. A wide range of evidence may be submitted in support of a prima facie *Batson* claim. Illustrative examples include:

- The race of the defendant, victim, and key witnesses. *See State v. Quick*, 341 N.C. 141, 146 (1995) (the fact that victims were White and defendant was Black arguably constituted a circumstance tending to establish discriminatory intent). *Cf. State v. Taylor*, 362 N.C. 514 (2008) (evidence that defendant was Black and victim was White "does not, standing alone, establish a prima facie case of discrimination"). To preserve your challenge for appellate review, be sure that all facts relevant to your *Batson* challenge—such as the race of the defendant, victim, and witnesses—are included in the record.
- Disparate questioning of minority and non-minority panelists. *See supra* "Disparate questioning" in § 7.3E, *Batson* Step Three: The Pretext Determination.
- Numerical use of strikes of minority panelists (for example, 3 of 4 African American panelists struck). As voir dire progresses, the defense team should tabulate the percentage of minorities and African Americans challenged peremptorily, the percentage of the prosecutor's peremptory strikes used on minorities and African Americans, and the minority and African American acceptance rates. *See supra* "Significance of minority acceptance rate" in § 7.3C, *Batson* Step One: The Prima Facie Case.
- Any pattern of seeking to strike minority panelists for cause, taking care to ensure that your voir dire notes include detailed information about challenges for cause.
- Any possible racial disparities in other aspects of the case (e.g., uncharged White co-defendants).
- Race issues present in the facts of the case, e.g., the case involves a cross-racial identification.
- Disparate treatment of minority and non-minority panelists. For example, does the prosecutor refer to non-minority panelists formally, but minority panelists by their first names?
- The prosecutor's record in other cases. How many *Batson* claims have been raised against strikes by that prosecutor? What are his or her acceptance rates in other cases?
- Race-neutral justifications in training materials regarding defending against *Batson* claims that match those offered by prosecutor. *See Top Gun II Batson Training: Articulating Juror Negatives* in the Race Materials Bank at www.ncids.org (select "Training and Resources"); *see also Miller-El v. Dretke*, 545 U.S. 231 (2005)

(discriminatory training manual on exclusion of Black people from juries constituted evidence supporting finding of *Batson* violation).

- Historical data demonstrating a pattern of discrimination. *See supra* § 7.4A, Pretrial Preparation for a *Batson* Challenge.
- Side-by-side comparisons of struck minority jurors and accepted non-minority jurors. *See infra* "Comparative juror analysis at step one," in this subsection B.
- The State's peremptory strike of one Black juror, which may constitute relevant evidence when considering the propriety of its strike of another Black juror. *See*. *Snyder v. Louisiana*, 552 U.S. 472, 478 (2008).

Comparative juror analysis at step one. Recent U.S. Supreme Court opinions have stressed that comparisons of similarly situated jurors constitute perhaps the strongest evidence relevant to *Batson* claims, and a recent study of *Batson* claims in federal court revealed that comparative juror analysis "is the circumstance most likely to convince a court to grant a *Batson* challenge on appeal." Jeffrey Bellin & Junichi P. Semitsu, *Widening Batson's Net to Ensnare More than the Unapologetically Bigoted or Painfully Unimaginative Attorney*, 96 CORNELL L. REV.1075, 1099 (2011). It is important to present these comparisons at trial when making your objections, as the "retrospective comparison of jurors based on a cold appellate record may be very misleading when alleged similarities were not raised at trial." *Snyder*, 552 U.S. 472, 475 (holding that, since the similarity at issue was "thoroughly explored by the trial court when the relevant jurors asked to be excused for cause," the Court was able to rule on the basis of the comparative juror analysis). At step one, when you do not yet have the prosecutor's race-neutral justification to consider, comparative juror analysis consists of pointing out disparate treatment of similarly situated jurors. For example, you may compare the number of questions asked of a minority panelist regarding family members involved in the criminal justice system to the number of similar questions asked of a non-minority panelist.

The U.S. Supreme Court has held that the comparative juror analysis need not involve jurors who are "identical in all respects." *Miller-El v. Dretke*, 545 U.S. 231, 247 n.6 (2005) ("A *per se* rule that a defendant cannot win a *Batson* claim unless there is an exactly identical white juror would leave *Batson* inoperable; potential jurors are not products of a set of cookie cutters"); *see also Reed v. Quarterman*, 555 F.3d 364, 376 (5th Cir. 2009) ("If the State asserts that it struck a black juror with a particular characteristic, and it also accepted nonblack jurors with that same characteristic, this is evidence that the asserted justification was a pretext for discrimination, even if the two jurors are dissimilar in other respects.").

Importance of strong prima facie case at step one. Defense attorneys should present all relevant, available evidence and analysis when making a prima facie *Batson* claim. While step one is not meant to be a particularly high threshold, the strength of the prima facie cases will be relevant at step three, when the judge rules on the ultimate question of discrimination.

Challenging justifications that are not race-neutral at step two. At step two, you should object to the prosecutor's justification for the challenged strike if any of the asserted reasons do not constitute "permissible racially neutral selection criteria." *Batson*, 476 U.S. 79, 94 (quotation omitted); *see also Purkett v. Elem*, 514 U.S. 765, 769 (1995) (at step two, prosecutor is not required to identify a reason for the strike that makes sense, "but [must provide] a reason that does not deny equal protection"). Examples of *Batson* justifications that may be challenged as not being race-neutral include:

- An admission that the strike was based, in whole or in part, on race. In the *Golphin* litigation, the judge found that in a case from Davie County, a prosecutor explained a peremptory strike on the following basis: "The victim is a black female. That juror is a black female. I left one black person on the jury already." *See* Golphin Order at 113. *See also infra* "Defendant does not have to show race was the "sole factor" motivating the peremptory strike" in § 7.3E, *Batson* Step Three: The Pretext Determination.
- Residence in a predominantly minority neighborhood. "When potential jurors are excluded because they live in an all-black or nearly all-black community, 'neighborhood' as a justification for the strike cannot be disentangled from race." Golphin Order at 54. *See also infra* "Practice note" in § 7.4A, Pretrial Preparation for a *Batson* Challenge.
- Hairstyles and/or styles of dress associated with African Americans, such as cornrows or other hairstyles worn almost exclusively by African Americans.
- Association with African American institutions such as historically Black colleges and universities, Black churches, or the NAACP. *See* Golphin Order at 113 (citing four North Carolina cases in which prosecutors explained that jurors were struck because of their affiliation with African American institutions).
- Failure to present a race-neutral justification. *See State v. Wright*, 189 N.C. App. 346 (2008) (finding that prosecutor failed to offer any race-neutral justification for striking at least one, and possibly two, Black venire members); Golphin order at 119 (finding that, in ten North Carolina capital cases, prosecutors provided no race-neutral justification for striking a total of seventeen eligible African-American panelists).

If you are able to demonstrate that the prosecutor has not articulated a race-neutral justification for the challenged strike, you should prevail on your *Batson* challenge at step two without proceeding to step three.

Practice note: Be sure the prosecutor's race-neutral explanations for challenged peremptory strikes are on the record for potential appellate review. Once the prosecutor has provided a race-neutral explanation for the strike and "the trial court has ruled on the ultimate question of discrimination," the prima facie case becomes moot for purposes of appellate review. *Hernandez v. New York*, 500 U.S. 352, 359 (1991); *see also State v. Bell*, 359 N.C. 1 (2004); *State v. Headen*, 206 N.C. App. 109, 115 (2010). If the State offers an explanation of a challenged strike before the trial court rules on the defendant's prima facie case, the appellate court cannot dispose of the case by finding that the defendant failed to make out a prima facie case, but instead must analyze the prosecutor's justifications and your response to those justifications, resulting in a fuller consideration of your *Batson* claim. *But cf. State v. Smith,* 347 N.C. 453, 463 (1998) (holding that prima facie case is not moot for purposes of appellate review in cases where the prosecutor puts a race-neutral justification on the record after the trial court has already rejected the defendant's prima facie case).

Justifications suggestive of pretext at step three. The following strike justifications may be suggestive of pretext, as illustrated by the cases cited:

- Age. *See, e.g., Richmond v. State*, 590 So. 2d 384, 385 (Ala. Crim. App. 1991) (age as reason for peremptory strikes is "'highly suspect because of its inherent susceptibility to abuse'" (citation omitted)); *Washington v. Commonwealth*, 34 S.W.3d 376, 379 (Ky. 2000) ("[c]ertainly age was not a sufficient reason to strike a 43-year-old man"). *But see State v. Caporasso*, 128 N.C. App. 236, 244 (1998) (no error where trial judge allowed prosecutor to peremptorily challenge a Black juror based on prosecutor's explanation that the juror was excused based on his "young age and lack of maturity"; the prosecution is allowed to "seek jurors who are stable and mature").
- Facial expressions or other non-verbal behavior. *Bernard v. State*, 659 So. 2d 1346 (Fla. Dist. Ct. App. 1995) (fact that juror made facial expression during another juror's comment insufficient reason for strike where expression not observed by trial judge and not confirmed by judge in record); *Somerville v. State*, 792 S.W.2d 265 (Tex. Ct. App. 1990) (reversing conviction where State improperly struck juror who prosecutor thought had muttered under his breath, purportedly showing disrespect for judge, and who was member of NAACP); *Avery v. State*, 545 So. 2d 123, 127 (Ala. Crim. App. 1988) (reasons such as looks, body language, and negative attitude are susceptible to abuse and must be "closely scrutinized" by courts); *Harris v. Hardy*, 680 F.3d 942, 965 (7th Cir. 2012) ("Demeanor-based explanations for a strike are particularly susceptible to serving as pretexts for discrimination.").
- Clothing or jewelry. *See Rector v. State*, 444 S.E.2d 862 (Ga. Ct. App. 1994) (case reversed where prosecutor struck juror because she had gold tooth); *People v. Bennett*, 614 N.Y.S.2d 430 (N.Y. App. Div. 1994) (prosecutor struck an African American juror who was wearing a headscarf because it showed "a certain disrespect for the proceedings"; pretextual basis found and conviction reversed); *Roundtree v. State*, 546 So. 2d 1042, 1044–45 (Fla. 1989) (prosecutor's reasons for striking two African American jurors were an "obvious pretext" where prosecutor asserted that he struck the jurors based on their clothing, "specifically commenting that the first juror was wearing maroon socks and 'pointy New York shoes'").
- Intelligence. *See* Golphin Order at 115–16 (noting that in several cases, prosecutors justified strikes of Black jurors by stating that they were not articulate, smart, or educated enough to serve as jurors, and concluding that "[t]hese explanations evoke the troubling stereotype of African-American inferiority").
- Lack of community connection. *See* Golphin Order at 117–18 (observing that this justification is "evocative of a time when African Americans were not citizens and full members of the communities in which they lived").

Evidence supporting a determination of pretext at step three. Several different factors may support a finding that the stated race-neutral justification was a pretext for discrimination. Once the prosecutor identifies the reason for the challenged strike, the defense attorney should renew the objection to the challenged strike, reemphasize the prima facie case, and present any evidence or arguments beyond the prima facie case at step one. For example, if a prosecutor states that he struck a juror because she looked nervous, the first opportunity the defense attorney will have to challenge this assertion is at step three. Evidence that may show that the proffered explanation is a pretext for discrimination may include:

- The race-neutral justification offered by the prosecutor is not true. For example, if a prosecutor argues that a struck juror fell asleep during voir dire, but you watched the juror carefully and did not see her fall asleep, you can challenge the justification as inaccurate and suggestive of a discriminatory motive. You may be able to offer the testimony of an investigator or paralegal to substantiate your challenge to the prosecutor's characterization of the juror's behavior.
- The facts identified by the prosecutor, while true, are not disadvantageous to the prosecution and therefore do not explain the strike. This type of showing can be made, for example, by demonstrating that the identified justification is not credible because it is a factor typically viewed favorably by prosecutors, such as a close connection to law enforcement. *See, e.g.*, *State v. Porter*, 326 N.C. 489, 498 (1990) (State may lawfully seek jurors who are government oriented and sympathetic to the pressures of law enforcement); Golphin Order at 123 (listing examples of cases in which Black jurors ostensibly were struck because of their connections to law enforcement officers).
- The reasons given for a challenged strike apply equally to an accepted juror of a different race. *See supra* "Comparative juror analysis at step three" in § 7.3E, *Batson* Step Three: The Pretext Determination.
- The State's justification is irrelevant to serving as a juror on the case (for example, the juror had a hyphenated last name, *see* Golphin Order at 124).
- The prosecutor has mischaracterized the struck juror's responses to voir dire questions.
- The strike rate of Black or minority panelists is higher than that of non-minority panelists.
- The prosecutor has used the same justifications, or vague justifications (such as demeanor or dress), when defending peremptory strikes against minorities in the present case or past cases. *See supra* § 7.4A, Pretrial Preparation for a *Batson* Challenge; *State v. Porter*, 326 N.C. 489, 498–99 (1990) (prosecutor's explanation should be evaluated "in light of the explanations offered for the prosecutor's other peremptory strikes" (quotation omitted)).
- There are similarities between the prosecutor's stated justifications and training materials designed to help prosecutors defeat *Batson* claims. *See Top Gun II Batson Training: Articulating Juror Negatives* in the Race Materials Bank at www.ncids.org (select "Training and Resources"); *Miller-El v. Dretke*, 545 U.S. 231 (2005)

(discriminatory training manual on exclusion of Black people from juries constituted evidence supporting finding of *Batson* violation).

- The prosecutor has expressed animus toward having one or more racial minority groups serving on juries. *See, e.g.,* Jeffrey Bellin & Junichi P. Semitsu, *Widening Batson's Net to Ensnare More than the Unapologetically Bigoted or Painfully Unimaginative Attorney*, 96 CORNELL L. REV. 1075, 1079 (2011) (describing a training video in which a prosecutor explained, "Let's face it . . . there's the blacks from the low-income areas . . . you don't want those people on your jury").
- The prosecutor engaged in disparate questioning of minority and non-minority jurors. *See supra* "Disparate questioning" in § 7.3E, *Batson* Step Three: The Pretext Determination.
- The prosecutor's office, or the particular prosecutor in the case, has engaged in a pattern of discrimination in jury selection. *See, e.g., Miller-El v. Cockrell*, 537 U.S. 322, 334 (2003) ("Dallas County district judge and former assistant district attorney from 1976 to 1978 testified that he believed the office had a systematic policy of excluding African-Americans from juries"); *see supra* § 7.4A, Pretrial Preparation for a *Batson* Challenge.
- The reasons supporting defendant's prima facie case at step one have not been adequately explained or overcome by the State's explanation. At step three, counsel should reemphasize the reasons offered at step one as well as offer any additional evidence and arguments. *State v. Porter*, 326 N.C. 489, 498–99 (1990) (prosecutor's justification for the strikes will be evaluated in light of "the strength of the prima facie case") (quotation omitted).

Preserving your *Batson* challenges at the conclusion of the trial. Be sure that all relevant materials are made part of the record in the event your *Batson* claim is denied and the defendant is convicted, including jury questionnaires, information about denied discovery requests, and other pertinent materials.

Improving the success rate of *Batson* claims in North Carolina. Despite the limited success of *Batson* challenges in the North Carolina appellate courts, *Batson* claims are not unwinnable. The success of *Batson* challenges at trial in North Carolina is largely unknown. When the defendant is "initially successful in a *Batson* challenge, a judicial opinion will almost never reflect it" because regardless of the ultimate outcome of the trial, prosecutors ordinarily have no ability to appeal. Jeffrey Bellin & Junichi P. Semitsu, *Widening Batson's Net to Ensnare More than the Unapologetically Bigoted or Painfully Unimaginative Attorney*, 96 CORNELL L. REV. 1075, 1092 (2011).

One possible explanation for the low success rate of *Batson* claims on appeal is that defense attorneys may not be raising challenges whenever there are grounds to do so. Also, *Batson* challenges may have sparse records on appeal; results may improve if attorneys build fuller records that include both historical and contemporaneous evidence of possible racial motivations for peremptory strikes. Further, recent years have seen significant developments in the law governing *Batson* challenges and potential data that may support *Batson* claims in North Carolina. *See, e.g., State v. Barden*, 362 N.C. 277,

279 (2008) (remanding for additional *Batson* hearing in light of recent U.S. Supreme Court cases). Appellate rulings in North Carolina before 2008 did not reflect the holding in *Snyder v. Louisiana*, 552 U.S. 472 (2008), clarifying that a single unconstitutional strike constitutes a *Batson* violation; and, as the trial court recognized in the *Golphin* case, "none of the previous courts that denied *Batson* challenges had the opportunity to consider data from the MSU study" finding that Black jurors in North Carolina capital cases were over twice as likely as White jurors to be peremptorily struck by prosecutors. Golphin Order at 27.

7.5 Beyond Litigation

Criticism of the *Batson* framework has been widespread. *See, e.g.*, *Rice v. Collins*, 546 U.S. 333, 343 (Breyer, J., concurring); Leonard L. Cavise, *The* Batson *Doctrine: The Supreme Court's Utter Failure to Meet the Challenge of Discrimination in Jury Selection*, 199 WIS. L. REV. 501 (1999); Antony Page, Batson's *Blind-Spot: Unconscious Stereotyping and The Peremptory Challenge*, 85 B.U. L. REV. 155, 161 (2005); Catherine M. Grosso & Barbara O'Brien, *A Stubborn Legacy: The Overwhelming Importance of Race in Jury Selection in 173 Post-*Batson *North Carolina Capital Trials*, 97 IOWA L. REV. 1531, 1533 (2012) (noting widespread disappointment).

Some jurists have expressed concern about detecting discrimination in jury selection because it commonly occurs at an unconscious level and is therefore difficult to identify. *See, e.g.*, *Rice v. Collins*, 546 U.S. 333, 343 (2006) (Breyer, J., concurring) (observing that "sometimes, no one, not even the lawyer herself, can be certain whether a decision to exercise a peremptory challenge rests upon an impermissible racial, religious, gender-based, or ethnic stereotype," and wondering, under such circumstances, "[h]ow can trial judges second-guess an instinctive judgment the underlying basis for which may be a form of stereotyping invisible even to the prosecutor?"). For this reason, some have proposed eliminating peremptory strikes altogether. *See, e.g.*, *Batson v. Kentucky,* 476 U.S. 79 at 108 (Marshall, J., concurring) (proposing eliminating peremptory strikes altogether); *Rice v. Collins*, 546 U.S. 333 at 343–44 (Breyer, J., concurring) (joining in Justice Marshall's call to abolish the peremptory strike); *State v. Saintcalle*, 309 P.3d 326, 350 (Wash. 2013) (Gonzalez, J., concurring) (identifying several shortcomings of the *Batson* framework, including the difficulty facing trial judges in determining whether a strike is discriminatory, and calling for the elimination of the peremptory strike in Washington state). The proposal to eliminate peremptory challenges suffers from problems of its own, including the disadvantage to defendants of losing the opportunity to strike jurors who cannot be struck for cause but who may have difficulty accepting the defendant's theory of the case. Eliminating peremptory challenges also may have little support among prosecutors or defense attorneys, making it unlikely to occur.

In addition to vigorously enforcing the rights afforded by *Batson*, other measures have been suggested as ways to reduce the potential for racial bias in jury selection and to strengthen the judiciary's ability to respond to bias, including:

- Videotaping of voir dire, so that demeanor-based explanations for peremptory strikes can be assessed meaningfully.
- Trainings for court actors on the influence of implicit bias on decision-making.
- Explicit recognition that peremptory strikes motivated by implicit biases violate equal protection within the meaning of *Batson*.
- Disciplinary action by the State Bar or court against attorneys who engage in racial discrimination in jury selection. EQUAL JUSTICE INITIATIVE, ILLEGAL RACIAL DISCRIMINATION IN JURY SELECTION: A CONTINUING LEGACY 7 (2010).
- Engagement with civil attorneys who share concerns about racial discrimination in jury selection, as *Batson* challenges can be raised in civil as well as criminal cases.
- State legislation providing "remedies to people called for jury service who are illegally excluded on the basis of race." *Id.*
- Examination of the role implicit biases play in one's own decision-making. *See, e.g.*, Andrea D. Lyon, *Race Bias and the Importance of Consciousness for Criminal Defense Attorneys*, 35 SEATTLE U. L. REV. 755, 765 (2012) (because defense attorneys mostly represent non-White clients, there is a tendency to "falsely assume that we are less likely to have racial bias").
- Investigation of patterns of discrimination by the Justice Department under 18 U.S.C. § 243, which prohibits racial discrimination in jury selection and imposes civil penalties for violations.
- Supplemental state law procedures to strengthen *Batson*. For example, in Florida, prosecutors must provide a race-neutral justification for a challenged strike any time a defendant makes a timely challenge to the strike of a potential juror belonging to a distinct racial group; the defendant does not need to establish a prima facie case of discrimination at step one. *Melbourne v. State*, 679 So. 2d 759, 764 n.5 (Fla. 1996) (explaining that a prior case "eliminated the requirement that the opponent of the strike make a prima facie showing of racial discrimination"). Also, some Florida decisions have held that a prosecutor's race neutral justification will be accepted only where supported by the record. *See, e.g., State v. Slappy*, 522 So. 2d 18 (Fla. 1988) ("when the state engages in a pattern of excluding a minority without apparent reason, the state must be prepared to support its explanations with neutral reasons based on answers provided at voir dire or otherwise disclosed on the record itself"); *Reeves v. State,* 632 So. 2d 702 (Fla. Dist. Ct. App. 1994) (where the State defended its peremptory strikes of two Black employees of the Department of Health and Rehabilitative Services by stating that the employees would be hostile to the prosecution, but the potential jurors were not questioned about their feelings toward the prosecutor's office, the strike justification was not supported by the record and the strikes were therefore impermissible); *see also* EQUAL JUSTICE INITIATIVE, ILLEGAL RACIAL DISCRIMINATION IN JURY SELECTION: A CONTINUING LEGACY 23 (2010) (citing *Cobb v. State*, 825 So. 2d 1080 (Fla. Dist. Ct. App. 2002)).

Chapter 8
Addressing Race at Trial

8.1 Scope of Chapter

This chapter offers guidance on issues of race that may arise at trial, and the extent to which defense attorneys can and should address racial dynamics at trial. For example, the chapter addresses voir dire, and how counsel may raise relevant issues of race in order to evaluate bias on the part of potential jurors. The chapter also addresses evidentiary matters such as impeaching a witness with evidence of bias and the admissibility of lay and expert witness opinion testimony on matters such as gang activities or the racial makeup of neighborhoods. Other topics include the legality of making references to race in opening statements and in closing arguments, and jury instructions that counsel may propose to mitigate potential racial bias.

8.2 Raising Race During Jury Selection and at Trial

A. Importance of Addressing Race

The United States Supreme Court has recognized "some risk of racial prejudice influencing a jury's decision in a criminal case. . . . The question is at what point that risk becomes constitutionally unacceptable." *McCleskey v. Kemp*, 481 U.S. 279, 308–09 (1987) (internal quotation omitted). In recent decades, scholars have reflected on how race affects various stages of a criminal trial. "Because race is such a salient characteristic in our society, a juror will notice the race of the defendant, the witnesses, the attorneys, the judge, and other jurors." Sheri Lynn Johnson, *Racial Imagery in Criminal Cases*, 67 TUL. L. REV. 1739, 1743 (1993) (footnote omitted). Jurors' perceptions of what is "happening in the courtroom will be affected by [their] prior exposure to racial imagery." *Id.* Whether or not defense attorneys address the racial dynamics at play in a trial, jurors notice them. John M. Conley et al., *The Racial Ecology of the Courtroom: An Experimental Study Of Juror Response To The Race Of Criminal Defendants*, 2000 WIS. L. REV. 1185, 1213–14 (2000).

While a "colorblind" approach—in which counsel acts as if race does not exist—may seem like a safer course of action than raising the subject of racial bias, such an approach may create a greater risk to clients:

> The problem with colorblindness is that it ignores reality. Even if we believe that race should not matter, the fact is that it does matter. . . . Pretending that race does not matter . . . only exacerbates the problem of implicit bias. When individuals are not cognizant of their implicit biases, those biases can automatically trigger stereotypes and prejudice. It is conscious awareness of racial bias, not blindness to race, that encourages one to correct assumptions that one might otherwise make about others because of their race. If we really want to counter racial bias, we should be race-conscious, not colorblind.

Cynthia Lee, *Making Race Salient: Trayvon Martin and Implicit Bias in a Not Yet Post-*

Racial Society, 91 N.C. L. REV. 1555, 1610 (2013) (footnotes omitted). Studies have shown that raising the subject of race may cause implicit racial biases to recede, while avoiding it may leave racial biases in place. *See* john powell & Rachel Godsil, *Implicit Bias Insights as Preconditions to Structural Change*, 20 POVERTY & RACE, no. 3 (Poverty & Race Research Action Council), 2011, at 3, 6. By failing to confront the issue of race at trial, criminal defense attorneys risk allowing "unconscious racial bias [to] act[] as an invisible witness against the African American defendant, buttressing the prosecution's claims concerning his incorrigibility and undermining his case." Pamela A. Wilkins, *Confronting the Invisible Witness: The Use of Narrative to Neutralize Capital Jurors' Implicit Racial Biases*, 115 W. VA. L. REV. 305, 305 (2012).

Addressing race at trial involves (1) neutralizing any stereotypes that may prejudice the jury's observations, deliberations, and verdict; and (2) challenging any racially inflammatory argument or evidence. The task of addressing race at trial poses a challenge for criminal defense attorneys: How can you address the racial dynamics in your client's case without exacerbating biases or inviting the charge that you are "playing the race card"? *See, e.g.*, *In re Marshall*, 191 N.C. App. 53, 56 (2008) (reviewing a case in a which a judge told a defense attorney, "I'm not going to let you play that [race] card in the courtroom in front of a jury," and vacating the judgment of criminal contempt against the defense attorney since, after several contentious exchanges between the attorney and the judge, the judge's objectivity may reasonably have been questioned); Robin Walker Sterling, *Raising Race*, THE CHAMPION, Apr. 2011, at 24. Counsel must be prepared to counter such concerns and demonstrate that the issue is relevant and bears on the client's ability to receive a fair outcome at trial based on legal authority, social science research, and data.

B. Strategies for Addressing Race

Analyze possible stereotypes and devise a plan for interrupting them. When representing a person of color, you should consider the following questions in determining how to neutralize potential stereotypes and biases throughout trial:

- What stereotypes may be attached to your client? For example, could he or she be cast as a "trafficker," "alcoholic," or "gang banger" because of his or her race? *See, e.g.*, *Soap v. Carter*, 632 F.2d 872, 878 (10th Cir. 1980) (Seymour, J., dissenting) (prosecutor argued in closing that "when you see an Indian that drinks liquor, you see a man that can't handle it").
- What do social scientists know about the implicit biases that may be triggered by people resembling your client? *See, e.g.*, Pamela A. Wilkins, *Confronting the Invisible Witness: The Use Of Narrative To Neutralize Capital Jurors' Implicit Racial Biases*, 115 W. VA. L. REV. 305, 330–32 (2012) (describing techniques for neutralizing biases that may be triggered by defendants). For example, research has found that Asians may be stereotyped as passive and unassertive (*see Chin v. Runnels*, 343 F. Supp. 2d 891, 907 (N.D. Cal. 2004) (recognizing that such implicit biases are widespread)); and that defendants with more Afrocentric facial features receive more severe criminal punishment in some contexts. *See* Irene V. Blair et al.,

The Influence of Afrocentric Facial Features in Criminal Sentencing, 15 PSYCHOL. SCI. 674, 674 n.1 (2004) (defining Afrocentric features as "those physical features that are perceived as typical of African Americans"); R. Richard Banks et al., *Discrimination and Implicit Racial Bias in a Racially Unequal Society*, 94 CALIF. L. REV. 1169 (2006).

- What evidence could you introduce to interrupt the stereotypes that might otherwise be attached to your client? For example, evidence of your client's care of an elderly grandparent or other responsibilities could serve to distinguish him from stereotypes associated with criminality. Or, if you are representing a defendant who might be stereotyped as an "illegal alien" based on his nationality, you may want to present evidence of his lawful status.

By anticipating and contesting the assumptions that might otherwise be made about your client, you may be able to counteract the operation of biases and stereotypes in jurors' judgments about the case. *See, e.g.,* Jerry Kang, *Trojan Horses of Race*, 118 HARV. L. REV. 1489, 1503 n.63 (2005) (explaining that "role schemas"—associations based on a person's occupation or other role—may trump race or gender schemas). Analyze the causes of possible stereotypes that may be at play, and obtain information about your client to effectively differentiate him or her from the negative stereotype. One study concluded that exposure to people who do not conform to stereotypes can reduce biases by more than half. *Id.* at 1558.

Reinforce norms of fairness and equality. Just as certain images, behavior, and references can trigger stereotypes, discussions of fairness and equality may trigger open-mindedness. "[T]here is reason to believe one can prime persons with ideals of fairness and equality that might suppress, to a degree, racial and other stereotypes." Pamela A. Wilkins, *Confronting the Invisible Witness: The Use Of Narrative To Neutralize Capital Jurors' Implicit Racial Biases*, 115 W. VA. L. REV. 305, 332 (2012). Addressing fairness and equality during voir dire, your opening statement, or your summation might stimulate thought processes that counteract the influence of stereotypes on decision-making. Gary Blasi, *Advocacy Against the Stereotype: Lessons from Cognitive Social Psychology*, 49 UCLA L. REV. 1241, 1249–50 (2002). These findings suggest that reminding jurors of their obligation to apply the law fairly and without prejudice may reduce the impact of biases on their decision-making processes.

Consider the issue of race in cases without obvious racial content. Defenders may be under the impression that it is only necessary to formulate a plan for addressing race or racial bias in cases where race is obviously at issue. However, racial biases may influence a jury's decision-making process in a run-of-the-mill case in which race does not appear to be a central issue and has not been highlighted:

> When race is an obvious issue at trial, White jurors may be on guard against racial bias. However, in trials without salient racial issues, White jurors may be less likely to monitor their behavior for signs of prejudice, and therefore more likely to render judgments tainted by racial bias.

Samuel R. Sommers & Phoebe C. Ellsworth, *White Juror Bias: An Investigation of Prejudice Against Black Defendants in the American Courtroom*, 7 PSYCHOL. PUB. POL'Y & L. 201, 210 (2001). For this reason, defenders should devise a plan for addressing issues of race in all cases in which race may potentially be a factor, not only those in which race appears to have played a role in the commission, investigation, or prosecution of the offense. *See, e.g.*, James McComas & Cynthia Strout, *Combating the Effects of Racial Stereotyping in Criminal Cases*, THE CHAMPION, Aug. 1999, at 22, 23 (describing the development of a five-part plan for addressing race in a self-defense trial).

Recognize the potential impact of your behavior. The way you relate to your client at trial—your body language and facial expressions when interacting with him, whether you display interest in his responses to the evidence, and whether you consult with him as you try the case—may communicate as much to the jury about your regard for your client as what you argue to the jury. One strategy to interrupt negative stereotypes about your client is to attempt to transfer some of the positive associations the jurors have of you, as an attorney, to your client.

For example, when representing Black clients, Seattle defense attorney Jeff Robinson asks himself:

> "How do I get jurors not to look at my client as an 'other,' as just another thug?" One of the things I do is I try to put myself out there in a way that connects the client to me, the educated black attorney. I try to change the dynamic of how they view us. . . . If they like me or respect me when they go back to deliberate and think about whether to convict, I want them to feel a bit like they have to convict both of us—the client and me.
>
> My basic strategy is I treat my clients with respect. Jurors see me engage with them as equals. I always put a paper and pad in front of my client, just like I have. When I finish questioning or cross-examining a witness, I walk over and speak with my client. I actually want to know what the client thinks and whether the client feels I should do anything more. However, it is rare that the client will ask me to continue a cross-examination when I think the cross should stop. It may be that all I say is "I think we're done with this guy." What is as important as the client's opinion is the appearance of conversing with the client, looking at his note pad for information, including him in decisions as an equal during the trial. If they see me as a legitimate, intelligent, and good person, that rubs off on my client.

Anthony V. Alfieri & Angela Onwuachi-Willig, *Next Generation Civil Rights Lawyers: Race and Representation in the Age of Identity Performance*, 122 YALE L.J. 1484, 1525–26 (2013) (quoting from telephone interview with Jeff Robinson).

Failing to object to appeals to racial bias effectively precludes review. Many North Carolina appellate opinions addressing challenges to improper statements about race by prosecutors involve trials in which defense attorneys failed to object to the statements at trial. Staples Hughes, Curbing Prosecutorial Misconduct and Preserving the Record in Closing Argument (Nov. 6, 2008) (training material presented at public defender conference). Since these challenges are reviewed for plain error, they are far less likely to succeed. *Id.* Defenders should be prepared to object to any unconstitutional or otherwise improper race-based argument to ensure that the objection will receive proper consideration, both at trial and on appeal. The manuscript cited above includes general categories of objectionable arguments. *See also* 2 NORTH CAROLINA DEFENDER MANUAL § 33.7C (Limitations on the Prosecution's Argument) (2d ed. 2012).

Consider the influence of your own race and possible stereotypes surrounding it on juror perceptions. An attorney's race may play a role in juror perceptions of the case. *See generally* Anthony V. Alfieri & Angela Onwuachi-Willig, *Next Generation Civil Rights Lawyers: Race and Representation in the Age of Identity Performance*, 122 YALE L.J. 1484, 1548 (2013). For example, Black criminal defense attorney Jeff Robinson concluded that, by zealously questioning a potential juror for 45 minutes about racial bias in order to get the potential juror struck for cause, he may have evoked the "angry Black man" stereotype and alienated some of the other jurors. *Id.* He speculates that some of the remaining jurors may have felt defensive and attacked, and that these reactions may have rendered them less receptive to the defendant's theory of the case. *See id.*

Some attorneys who are aware of the stereotypes that may be triggered by their own race may attempt to connect with jurors to neutralize potential stereotypes. *See* Pamela A. Wilkins, *Confronting The Invisible Witness: The Use Of Narrative To Neutralize Capital Jurors' Implicit Racial Biases*, 115 W. VA. L. REV. 305, 331 (2012). Another strategy is to explore stereotypes that jurors may hold about the attorney by addressing them explicitly during voir dire. *See generally infra* § 8.3, Jury Selection. Other attorneys may not believe it is effective or appropriate to alter their natural lawyering style or personality. Whatever approach you take, it is worthwhile to consider the impact that your own race may have on juror perceptions so that you can make considered choices. *See, e.g.*, Anthony V. Alfieri & Angela Onwuachi-Willig, *Next Generation Civil Rights Lawyers: Race and Representation in the Age of Identity Performance*, 122 YALE L.J. 1484, 1540 (2013) (noting that civil rights lawyers need to "think carefully about how they define their own roles and language in the courtroom, both individually and as a group"). Since racial or ethnic stereotypes can be triggered by people of all races, these considerations may be applicable to all attorneys. *See, e.g., United States v. Richardson*, 161 F.3d 728, 735 (D.C. Cir. 1998) (agreeing with defendant's argument that "the prosecutor's closing argument was improper and prejudicial because it interposed the issue of race into the case with the intent of disparaging [White] defense counsel [on the basis of race] and of fostering an identification of the prosecutor with the jury at the expense of defense counsel").

Be prepared to present statistics on racial disparities. Another way to address race at trial is to gather evidence of any racial disparities related to the charges your client faces.

For example, in a cross-racial identification case, you may want to introduce expert testimony about the increased likelihood of misidentification in that context. *See, e.g., supra* Ch. 3, Eyewitness Identifications.

8.3 Jury Selection

A. Importance of Diverse Juries

Researcher Samuel R. Sommers has examined the differences between racially diverse and all-White juries, and has concluded that "racial diversity in the jury alters deliberations . . . in a way that most judges and lawyers would consider desirable." Jerry Kang et al., *Implicit Bias in the Courtroom*, 59 UCLA L. REV. 1124, 1180 (2012) (discussing Samuel R. Sommers, *On Diversity and Group Decision Making: Identifying Multiple Effects of Racial Composition on Jury Deliberation*, 90 J. PERSONALITY & SOC. PSYCHOL. 597 (2006)).

One study concluded that more diverse juries:

- deliberate longer;
- focus more on the evidence;
- make fewer inaccurate statements;
- make fewer uncorrected statements; and
- discuss race-related topics at greater length.

Id. Additionally, "[s]imply by knowing that they would be serving on diverse juries . . . White jurors were less likely to believe, at the conclusion of evidence but before deliberations, that the Black defendant was guilty." *Id.* The Sommers study suggests that selecting a diverse jury may be the most effective way to minimize the impact of racial bias in jury deliberations.

There may be a greater risk of explicit biases in jury deliberations when juries are not diverse, as illustrated by the following letter from a White juror to the judge who presided over a trial involving a civil rights complaint filed by Black plaintiffs:

> During deliberations, matter-of-fact expressions of bigotry and broad-brush platitudes about "those people" rolled off the tongues of a vocal majority as naturally and unabashedly as if they were discussing the weather. Shocked and sickened, I sat silently, rationalizing to myself that since I did agree with the product, there was nothing to be gained by speaking out against the process (I now regret my inaction). Had just one African-American been sitting in that room, the content of discussion would have been quite different. And had the case been more balanced—one that hinged on fine distinction or subtle nuances

> —a more diverse jury might have made a material difference in the outcome.
>
> I pass these thoughts onto you in the hope that the jury system can some day be improved.

Janet Bond Arterton, *Unconscious Bias and the Impartial Jury*, 40 CONN. L. REV. 1023, 1033 (2008) (quoting letter from anonymous juror).

B. Orientation Sessions before Jury Service

Because juror bias jeopardizes a defendant's constitutional right to a fair trial, many scholars and practitioners have considered possible steps before jury service to address potential juror bias. One proposal is to conduct orientation sessions for potential jurors to educate them about implicit bias and the importance of rendering verdicts free from bias. *See* Anna Roberts, *(Re)forming the Jury: Detection and Disinfection of Implicit Juror Bias*, 44 CONN. L. REV. 827 (2012). *See also* JERRY KANG, IMPLICIT BIAS: A PRIMER FOR COURTS, NATIONAL CENTER FOR STATE COURTS 4–5 (National Center for State Courts 2009) (collecting evidence that "implicit biases are malleable and can be changed"); Jerry Kang et al., *Implicit Bias in the Courtroom*, 59 UCLA L. REV. 1124, 1180 (2012). Attorneys may suggest incorporating implicit bias training into juror orientation sessions to the county's Jury Commission, Judicial Committee, or Chief Resident Superior Court Judge.

C. Why Ask Questions about Race during Voir Dire

People generally avoid discussing the subject of race with strangers. Reasons for this may include general discomfort with the subject; fear of being labeled biased; fear of offending others; concern that expression of one's views may provoke hostility, defensiveness, or anger; perception that race is a historical phenomenon that is not relevant to today's society; or a belief that "color-blindness" is a preferred approach and requires avoiding discussions of race. *See, e.g.*, Jeff Robinson & Jodie English, *Confronting the Race Issue During Jury Selection*, THE ADVOCATE, May 2008, at 57.

Despite these challenges, there are a number of reasons why it is important for defense attorneys to address the subject of race during voir dire:

- Discussing the subject allows attorneys to "discover [jurors' views on race], and how strongly they are held, and how they may impact [the] verdict." *Id.*
- Forthright exchanges about race during voir dire enhance the defense attorney's ability "to intelligently exercise preemptory challenges and challenges for cause." *Id.*
- Attorneys who do not engage in a frank discussion of racial attitudes may be more likely to rely on their own "generalized stereotypes" of the jurors and "make assumptions based on jurors' race." Andrea D. Lyon, *Race Bias and the Importance of Consciousness for Criminal Defense Attorneys*, 35 SEATTLE U. L. REV. 755 (2012)

(also observing that if criminal defense attorneys use a "process of elimination based on stereotypes, jurors will know it").

- A growing body of evidence indicates that when issues of race are brought to the forefront of a discussion or "made salient," individuals tend to think more critically about the issues, and the influence of stereotypes and implicit biases on decision-making recedes. For this reason, having an open and honest conversation about race during voir dire may enable jurors to avoid reliance on stereotypes during trial and in deliberations. NATIONAL CENTER FOR STATE COURTS, HELPING COURTS ADDRESS IMPLICIT BIAS: STRATEGIES TO REDUCE THE INFLUENCE OF IMPLICIT BIAS; *see also* Regina A. Schuller et al., *The Impact of Prejudice Screening Procedures on Racial Bias in the Courtroom*, 33 LAW & HUM. BEHAV. 320 (2009) (voir dire regarding racial bias appeared to diminish racial bias from assessments of guilt).
- Discussing race during voir dire allows defenders to explore whether individuals are comfortable discussing issues of race and to consider striking "jurors who ignored the issue or who asserted that race did not matter." Anthony V. Alfieri & Angela Onwuachi-Willig, *Next Generation Civil Rights Lawyers: Race and Representation in the Age of Identity Performance*, 122 YALE L.J. 1484, 1526 (2013) (quoting L. Song Richardson, Professor of Law, Univ. of Iowa Coll. Of Law); *see also* Jonathan Rapping, *The Role of the Defender in a Racially Disparate System*, THE CHAMPION, July 2013, at 46, 50 (suggesting that "[d]uring voir dire defense counsel should work to make jurors aware of the problem of race bias and identify those jurors who appreciate its influence").

Case study: Discussing race during voir dire. In the case study below, an Assistant Public Defender in North Carolina reflects on the experience of discussing race with jurors during voir dire:

In 2013, I represented a client charged with Driving While Impaired and Possession of a Stolen Firearm. After I received discovery in the case, I reviewed the DRE (drug recognition expert) paperwork. In that paperwork I noticed that under the section for the race of the suspect, the DRE expert wrote "mulatto," a dated and derogatory term for a person of mixed Black and White ancestry. At that moment, I realized that I would need to explore the officer's use of this term on cross to impeach his credibility.

I also realized that because I would be exploring race issues as a part of my impeachment of the DRE expert, I would also need to talk about race during jury selection. My goal was two-fold: first, to learn if any of the prospective jurors were racially biased, and second, to educate the jurors why I was raising this issue during my cross-examination. Although I was apprehensive about talking about race during jury selection, I knew that if I did not talk about it then my client would be even more detrimentally impacted.

When it was time to begin talking about race during jury selection, I introduced the topic in terms of how we see or hear about race issues in society. I kept a very calm, affirming, and open demeanor in order to project that it was okay to share their views in this very public forum and no one would judge them for doing so. I started by saying something akin to "Sometimes in our society we've seen circumstances where someone might have been treated badly or just differently because of their race." Then, I asked an open-ended question, such as, "Tell me about the most serious time you saw, or just knew about, someone being treated differently or badly because of their race." To my surprise, one juror raised her hand and volunteered a response about how society treats people differently because their race. I noted which other jurors were listening and responding with their body language about what this juror was sharing. I followed up by asking those jurors questions like "Juror B, what do you think about what Juror A just shared?" "Do you agree that people can be treated differently because of their race?" "How do you feel about that?" I kept my questions as open as possible to keep the jurors talking. Also, I followed their lead in talking about race in terms of societal expectations because I felt that I was able to learn their views that way without making them too uncomfortable. I sensed that they were a little nervous at first but the more naturally and comfortably I spoke about race, the easier it became for them to discuss the issues they encountered in the media and even in their own neighborhoods.

To my relief, I didn't have anyone say that race issues don't exist, or that we live in a post-racism society. Thus, I did not end up using the responses I heard to make a challenge for cause or a peremptory strike. But the discussion we had during jury selection was important. It made the jurors start thinking about race and disparate treatment, which prepared them for when I cross-examined the DRE expert.

As for the cross-examination, I ended up addressing the mulatto issue last to make the most of its impact. In the end, the officer admitted that he was not trained or instructed to use that term by his office. Although my client was convicted of the Possession of a Stolen Firearm, he was acquitted of the DWI.

D. Purpose of Voir Dire

North Carolina appellate courts recognize that jury voir dire serves two basic purposes: 1) helping counsel determine whether a basis for a challenge for cause exists, and 2) assisting counsel in intelligently exercising peremptory challenges. *State v. Wiley*, 355 N.C. 592 (2002); *State v. Anderson*, 350 N.C. 152 (1999); *State v. Brown*, 39 N.C. App. 548 (1979); *see also Mu'Min v. Virginia*, 500 U.S. 415, 431 (1991) ("Voir dire examination serves the dual purposes of enabling the court to select an impartial jury and assisting counsel in exercising peremptory challenges."). The N.C. Supreme Court has stated that the purpose of voir dire examination and the exercise of challenges, both peremptory and for cause, "is to eliminate extremes of partiality and to assure both the defendant and the State that the persons chosen to decide the guilt or innocence of the accused will reach that decision solely upon the evidence produced at trial." *State v. Conner*, 335 N.C. 618, 629 (1994).

Practice note: A proposed voir dire question is legitimate if the question is necessary to determine whether a juror is excludable for cause or to assist you in intelligently exercising your peremptory challenges. If the State objects to a particular line of questioning, defend your proposed questions by linking them to one or both of the purposes of voir dire.

E. Law Governing Voir Dire Questions about Race

Generally. Criminal defendants have a constitutional right under the Sixth and Fourteenth Amendments to voir dire jurors adequately. "[P]art of the guarantee of a defendant's right to an impartial jury is an adequate voir dire to identify unqualified jurors." *Morgan v. Illinois*, 504 U.S. 719, 729–30 (1992) (holding that capital defendant constitutionally entitled to ask specific "life qualifying" questions to the jury); *see also Rosales-Lopez v. United States*, 451 U.S. 182, 188 (1981) (plurality opinion) ("Without an adequate voir dire the trial judge's responsibility to remove prospective jurors who will not be able impartially to follow the court's instructions and evaluate the evidence cannot be fulfilled."). *But cf. Mu'Min v. Virginia*, 500 U.S. 415, 425 (1991) (emphasizing extent of trial judge's discretion in controlling voir dire and holding that voir dire questions about the content of pretrial publicity to which jurors might have been exposed are not constitutionally required).

North Carolina statutes likewise give the parties the right to "personally question prospective jurors individually concerning their fitness and competency to serve as jurors in the case to determine whether there is a basis for a challenge for cause or whether to exercise a peremptory challenge." G.S. 15A-1214(c); *see also* G.S. 15A-1212(9) recognizing right to challenge for cause an individual juror who is unable to render a fair and impartial verdict). For a further discussion of voir dire, see 2 NORTH CAROLINA DEFENDER MANUAL § 25.3 (Voir Dire) (2d ed. 2012).

Voir dire about race. A defendant has a constitutional right to ask questions about race on voir dire in certain circumstances. In *Ham v. South Carolina*, 409 U.S. 524 (1973), the U.S. Supreme Court held that a Black defendant, who was a civil rights activist and whose defense was that he was selectively prosecuted for marijuana possession because of his civil rights activity, was entitled to voir dire jurors about racial bias. In *Ristaino v. Ross*, 424 U.S. 589, 597 (1976), the Court held that the Due Process Clause does not create a general right in non-capital cases to voir dire jurors about racial prejudice, but such questions are constitutionally protected when cases involve "special factors," such as those presented in *Ham*. In *Rosales-Lopez v. United States*, 451 U.S. 182, 192 (1981), the Court held that trial courts must allow voir dire questions concerning possible racial prejudice against a defendant when the defendant is charged with a violent crime and the defendant and victim are of different racial or ethnic groups. *See also Turner v. Murray*, 476 U.S. 28 (1986) (plurality opinion) (defendants in capital cases involving interracial crime have a right under the Eighth Amendment to voir dire jurors about racial biases).

In other cases, courts have held that whether to allow questions about racial and ethnic attitudes and biases is within the discretion of the trial judge. *See State v. Robinson,* 330 N.C. 1, 12–13 (1991) (trial judge allowed defendant to question prospective jurors about whether racial prejudice would affect their ability to be fair and impartial and allowed the defendant to ask questions of prospective White jurors about their associations with Black people; trial judge did not err in sustaining prosecutor's objection to other questions, such as "Do you belong to any social club or political organization or church in which there are no black members?" and "Do you feel like the presence of blacks in your neighborhood has lowered the value of your property . . . ?"). Undue restriction of the right to voir dire is error. *See State v. Conner*, 335 N.C. 618, 629 (1994) (holding that pretrial order limiting right to voir dire to questions not asked by court was error).

The N.C. Supreme Court has recognized that voir dire questions aimed at ensuring that "racially biased jurors [will] not be seated on the jury" are proper. *State v. Williams*, 339 N.C. 1, 18 (1994). In *Williams*, a capital case involving a Black defendant and a White victim, the court found no error when, during jury selection, the prosecutor asked whether the jurors could "put the issue of race completely out of [their minds]." The court's conclusion that "[t]he mere mention of race in a trial such as this is not evidence of racial animus" may provide support for a defendant's effort to explore the question of racial bias during jury selection. *Id.*

Defenders should be prepared to show how questions concerning racial attitudes are relevant to the case, the defendant's theory of defense, and the purposes of voir dire, by raising considerations such as the following:

- Is your client charged with an interracial crime of violence? If so, you have a constitutionally protected right to inquire into racial bias. *Rosales-Lopez v. United States*, 451 U.S. 182, 192 (1981).
- Do you intend to demonstrate that your client was subjected to unconstitutional selective enforcement or selective prosecution on account of his or her race or ethnicity? If so, you have a constitutionally protected right to inquire into racial bias. *Ristaino v. Ross*, 424 U.S. 589, 597 (1976); *Ham v. South Carolina*, 409 U.S. 524 (1973).
- Does your theory of defense involve consideration of racial issues, such as cross-racial misidentification, racial epithets, or racial biases held by a witness for the prosecution? If so, you may have a constitutionally protected right to inquire into racial bias. *See Ristaino*, 424 U.S. 589, 597.
- If the case does not involve one of the above grounds specifically giving a defendant the right to inquire into racial bias, argue that your inquiry is nevertheless necessary given the constitutional and statutory purposes of voir dire.

When your case is not one with unique racial dimensions, you may want to highlight empirical findings suggesting that "juror racial bias is most likely to occur in run-of-the-mill trials without blatantly racial issues." Samuel R. Sommers, *On Racial Diversity and Group Decision Making: Identifying Multiple Effects of Racial Composition on Jury Deliberations*, 90 J. PERSONALITY & SOC. PSYCHOL. 597, 601 (2006).

Practice note: If the inquiry is particularly sensitive, counsel may request individual voir dire. A sample motion can be found on the Office of Indigent Defense Services website, http://www.ncids.org. *See* Motion for Individual Voir Dire on Sensitive Subjects in the Motions Bank, Non Capital (select "Training and Resources").

F. Voir Dire Preparation, Techniques, and Sample Questions

Know your judge. Before voir dire begins, determine the practices of the judge presiding over the trial. Does he or she typically allow for questions about racial attitudes and racial bias when not constitutionally required? Generally, how extensive is the questioning the judge allows about race? How has the judge responded to motions for individual voir dire on sensitive topics in previous cases? *See supra* § 7.4A, Pretrial Preparation for a *Batson* Challenge.

Recognize the role that bias may play in a juror's evaluation of the case. One experienced attorney summarized the body of research on juror prejudice in the following manner:

- People who come to jury duty bring with them prejudices, biases, and preconceived notions about crime, trials, and criminal justice.
- Jurors are individuals. There is little correlation between the stereotypical aspects of a juror's makeup (race, gender, age, ethnicity, education, class, hobbies, reading material) and whether a particular juror may have biases or preconceived notions in an individual case.
- The prejudices and ideas jurors bring to court affect the way they decide cases even if they honestly believe they will be fair and can set preconceived notions aside.
- Jurors may decide cases based on their biases and preconceived notions regardless of what the judge may instruct them.
- Rehabilitation and curative instructions are not necessarily effective.
- Jurors may have made up their minds about the defendant's guilt before they hear any evidence.

Ira Mickenberg, Voir Dire and Jury Selection 2 (training material presented at 2011 North Carolina Defender Trial School).

Formulate voir dire questions ahead of time. Exploring racial attitudes often requires moving outside of your comfort zone. Andrea D. Lyon, *Naming the Dragon: Litigating Race Issues During a Death Penalty Trial*, 53 DEPAUL L. REV. 1647 (2004). If you intend to ask questions regarding racial attitudes, develop your questions ahead of time and consider practicing them with others to ensure that they are unlikely to evoke defensive responses, that you are comfortable asking them, and that you're prepared to respond to the answers you receive. You will not be able to use the same questions in every case; your voir dire should be "tailored to your factual theory of defense in each individual case." Ira Mickenberg, Voir Dire and Jury Selection 6 (training material presented at 2011 North Carolina Defender Trial School). Sample questions can be found below under "Sample Questions."

Create conditions for jurors to speak openly about race. Discussing the subject of race will not help you identify juror bias unless you are able to elicit open responses from potential jurors. Consider beginning the conversation by explaining why you need to address the subject and acknowledging that it can be a difficult or uncomfortable topic to discuss. It is generally not effective to jump into a conversation about race by asking potential jurors if they harbor racial prejudice. Cynthia Lee, *Making Race Salient: Trayvon Martin and Implicit Bias in a Not Yet Post-Racial Society*, 91 N.C. L. REV. 1555

(2013). This approach may provoke defensiveness, seem patronizing or insulting, and reveal little about the jurors' views.

One trial attorney suggests that a productive approach may be to inform jurors about the concept of implicit bias and then solicit their views on it. Jonathan A. Rapping, *Implicitly Unjust: How Defenders Can Affect Systemic Racist Assumptions*, 16 N.Y.U. J. LEGIS. & PUB. POL'Y 999, 1032–35. For example, the attorney might say, "Some researchers have found that people have implicit biases, which are stereotypes that people are not aware of that can influence their thoughts and behavior. For example, an employer might pass over a Black applicant for a job based on lack of relevant experience and consider a White applicant with a similar experience level, even though that employer does not consciously believe in discriminating against people based on their race. While research suggests that implicit biases arise from the brain's natural tendency to associate categories, the concern is that they may result in unequal treatment when they go unexamined." Then, the attorney can follow up to determine the jurors' reactions:

> You have just learned about the concept of [implicit racial bias]. Not everyone agrees on t he power of its influence or that they are personally susceptible to it. I'd like to get a sense of your reaction to the concept of subconscious racial bias and whether you are open to believing it may influence you in your day-to-day decision-making.

Id. at 1032.

Consider sharing an example about recognizing biases to jumpstart the discussion. One method for starting a conversation about race is to share a brief example about a judgment shaped by a racial stereotype. For example, some defense attorneys share and discuss the famous Jesse Jackson admission that "there is nothing more painful to me at this stage in my life than to walk down the street and hear footsteps and start thinking about robbery. Then look around and see somebody white and feel relieved." Bob Herbert, *In America; A Sea of Change on Crime*, N.Y.TIMES, Dec. 12, 1993 (quoting Jackson). Criminal defense attorney Jeff Robinson sometimes talks with potential jurors about his assuming that a "black kid with cornrows" blasting rap music and driving a new BMW must be a drug dealer before catching himself and recognizing that his assumption was based on a racial stereotype. Anthony V. Alfieri & Angela Onwuachi-Willig, *Next Generation Civil Rights Lawyers: Race and Representation in the Age of Identity Performance*, 122 YALE L.J. 1484, 1551 (2013); *see also* Cynthia Lee, *Making Race Salient: Trayvon Martin and Implicit Bias in a Not Yet Post-Racial Society*, 91 N.C. L. REV. 1555 (2013).

Such examples illustrate that people of all races and occupations possess implicit biases, "diffuse[] the emotional content of the race discussion," give prospective jurors "permission to admit their own [biased] thinking," and may help to begin a conversation in which potential jurors are comfortable discussing racial bias. James McComas & Cynthia Strout, *Combating the Effects of Racial Stereotyping in Criminal Cases*, THE CHAMPION, Aug. 1999, at 22, 23. Sharing an example about your own bias shows that you are not asking jurors to do anything that you are not willing to do yourself. Ira Mickenberg, Voir Dire and Jury Selection 10 (training material presented at 2011 North Carolina Defender Trial School). Of course, attorneys should avoid expressions of overt racism, which are inappropriate and may constitute ineffective assistance of counsel. *See State v. Davis*, 872 So. 2d 250 (Fla. 2004) (holding that defense attorney was ineffective when he made explicit expressions of racial prejudice in an effort to bring jurors' latent biases out into the open); *see infra* § 8.4C, Improper References to Race by the Defense.

Avoid expressing judgments. Generally speaking, if a juror reveals something personal or potentially embarrassing, a good strategy is to acknowledge how difficult it must have been to share that information and thank the juror for his or her honesty. Ira Mickenberg, Voir Dire and Jury Selection (training material presented at 2011 North Carolina Defender Trial School). This response may encourage other potential jurors to share their views openly. Defense counsel might follow up by saying, "I appreciate that Mrs. Jones was willing to share [sensitive topic or viewpoint]. Has anyone else had a similar experience/Does anyone else have an opinion on this topic?"

When a juror reveals information suggestive of racial bias, the attorney's instinct may be to change the subject, recharacterize the response to something more palatable, try to help the juror overcome his bias, or avoid the juror's statement altogether. These responses are typically aimed at putting everyone at ease and ensuring that the other panelists are not influenced by the biased statement. This intuitive response may be counterproductive. *Id.* A better strategy is to restate the juror's statement and ask an open-ended question to learn more about the juror's opinion. The additional exchange with the juror may provide a basis for a challenge for cause or, at least, additional information to evaluate the use of a peremptory challenge. *Id.* at 14–15 (discussing how to establish basis for challenge for cause).

Criminal defense attorney Jeff Robinson offers his insights into effective responses to admissions of racial bias:

> Now if someone makes a racist statement during jury selection, I say "Thank you very much for your comment! You have a First Amendment right to express your views openly! We all have those rights and should feel free to state what we think. And besides, I kind of think that view is not so unusual. Does anyone else have similar views?" Then, I see what other jury pool members have to say. It is strange, but by rewarding the worst possible answer you can imagine, I am trying to get other people in the pool to reveal themselves as people who hold like-minded racial views. My goal is to create an atmosphere where people can admit to their racially tinged thoughts. I want to create an environment where people feel free to say what they really are thinking.
>
> Even if I cannot get the person excluded, it is still good because they have now "outed" themselves to the rest of the jury. I can ask all the

> other jurors later, "What are you going to do if you notice that some of the arguments in the jury room are being influenced by racism?" That person has outed themselves, and their credibility with everyone may be compromised.

Anthony V. Alfieri & Angela Onwuachi-Willig, *Next Generation Civil Rights Lawyers: Race and Representation in the Age of Identity Performance*, 122 YALE L.J. 1484, 1549 (2013) (quoting from telephone interview with Jeff Robinson).

Focus questions on past, analogous behavior. Many attorneys have concluded that "the best predictor of what a person will do in the future is not what they say they will do, but what they have done in the past in analogous situations." *See, e.g.*, Ira Mickenberg, Voir Dire and Jury Selection 6 (training material presented at 2011 North Carolina Defender Trial School). When asked to share opinions on sensitive topics, "jurors will usually avoid the possibility of public humiliation by giving the socially acceptable answer—even if that answer is false." *Id.* at 3. When asked to predict how they will behave in hypothetical situations, "jurors will usually give an aspirational answer. This means they will give the answer they hope will be true, or the answer that best comports with their self-image. These jurors are not lying. Their answers simply reflect what they hope (or want to believe or want others to believe) is the truth, even if they may be wrong." *Id.* The influence of implicit bias may make it more difficult for individuals to predict their own future behavior.

Sample questions. Some questions that may be useful in eliciting views and reactions about past experiences involving race are identified below. For a further discussion of how to construct such questions, see Ira Mickenberg, Voir Dire and Jury Selection 10 (training material presented at 2011 North Carolina Defender Trial School).

- "Tell us about the most serious incident you [or someone close to you] ever saw where someone was treated badly because of their race." *Id.* at 11.
- "Tell us about the worst experience you or someone close to you ever had because someone stereotyped you because of your [race]." *Id.*
- "Tell us about the most significant interaction you have ever had with a person of a different race." *Id.*
- "Tell us about the most difficult situation where you, or someone you know, stereotyped someone, or jumped to a conclusion about them because of their [race] and turned out to be wrong." *Id.*
- Tell us about the most diverse environment you have ever worked in.
- Tell us about the most diverse neighborhood you have ever lived in.
- Tell us about the most memorable story you have heard, either in the news or from a friend or family member, of a White person experiencing discrimination on the basis of his or her race.
- Tell us about the last time you heard other people express racially prejudiced beliefs or opinions. How did you respond?

Another voir dire technique for encouraging potential jurors to express themselves is the "show of hands technique" recommended by jury selection expert Robert Hirschhorn. Jeff Robinson & Jodie English, Confronting the Race Issue During Jury Selection, THE ADVOCATE, May 2008, at 57, 60. This technique allows attorneys to identify jurors to follow up with on opinions expressed by raised or unraised hands. Some yes-or-no questions about race that may elicit useful responses with this technique include:

- Is racism against Black people a thing of the past?
- Do affirmative action programs discriminate against Whites?
- Do Black people commit more crimes per capita than Whites?
- Have any of you ever seen an example of racism?

Id. at 60–61. You will need to proceed slowly with this technique, ideally with the assistance of a fast note-taker, in order to capture responses.

Questionnaires. In cases involving particularly sensitive race issues, Robert Hirschhorn suggests petitioning the court for use of a questionnaire. Potential jurors may be more willing to provide honest but potentially embarrassing responses to questions about race in writing. *Id.* at 61. In one mock jury simulation, those who completed a questionnaire that prompted potential jurors to consider their own racial attitudes were less likely to find the defendant guilty than those who completed a pretrial juror questionnaire that did not address any issues of race. Samuel R. Sommers, *On Racial Diversity and Group Decision Making: Identifying Multiple Effects of Racial Composition on Jury Deliberations*, 90 J. PERSONALITY & SOC. PSYCHOL. 597, 601 (2006). Sample questions for such a questionnaire may be found on pages 61–62 of Jeff Robinson & Jodie English, Confronting the Race Issue During Jury Selection, THE ADVOCATE, May 2008, at 57.

G. Role of Client in Devising Voir Dire Strategy

Where the defendant and defense attorney reach an absolute impasse about how to conduct jury selection, the defendant's wishes control unless they are unlawful. *State v. Ali,* 329 N.C. 394, 404 (1991) (noting principal-agent nature of the attorney-client relationship). In *State v. Williams,* 191 N.C. App. 96, 104–05 (2008), the North Carolina Court of Appeals held that, even if there was an absolute impasse as to jury selection tactics, defense counsel could not defer to the defendant's wishes to engage in racially discriminatory jury selection where the defendant did not want White people on his jury.

Practice note: Before voir dire, make sure to discuss the purposes of voir dire with your client and incorporate the client's input into your voir dire strategy. Especially when you plan to address sensitive issues such as race or ethnicity during voir dire, it is important for the client to understand the subjects you plan to discuss with potential jurors and why you intend to discuss them. Pretrial discussions with your client allow you to respond to client concerns, devise a strategy that reflects your client's objectives, and avoid catching your client off guard if discussions during voir dire become challenging or sensitive. *See* *generally* John Pray & Byron Lichstein, *The Evolution Through Experience of Criminal Clinics: The Criminal Appeals Project at the University of Wisconsin Law School's Remington Center,* 75 MISS. L.J. 795, 815–16 (2006) (discussing "client-centered" approach to advocacy in which "communication with, and input from, the client are essential to achieve optimal results and client satisfaction"); Stephen Ellmann, *Lawyers and Clients*, 34 UCLA L. REV. 717, 720 (1987) (describing a "client-centered practice" as one which takes seriously client input and the principle of client decision-making).

8.4 References to Race at Trial

A. Is the Reference Relevant?

References to race in the presentation of evidence and argument at trial are not necessarily improper if relevant to the issues in the case. For example, race may be relevant to the question of intent when the crime was allegedly motivated by racial animus. "Although it is improper gratuitously to interject race into a jury argument where race is otherwise irrelevant to the case being tried, argument acknowledging race as a motive or factor in a crime may be entirely appropriate." *State v. Diehl*, 353 N.C. 433, 436 (2001); *see also State v. Williams*, 339 N.C. 1, 18 (1994) ("[t]he mere mention of race . . . is not evidence of racial animus").

> [When a] prosecutorial reference to race has its basis in other evidence, it may serve a valuable role in the criminal justice system. When it appeals to passion and prejudice rather than facts and law, it compromises the fundamental guarantees of equal protection and an impartial trial. The problem for courts lies not in recognizing this distinction, but in determining into which category a racial reference fits.

Elizabeth L. Earle, Note, *Banishing the Thirteenth Juror: An Approach to the Identification of Prosecutorial Racism*, 92 COLUM. L. REV. 1212, 1222; *see also* Stephen A. Saltzburg, *Race: Fair and Unfair Use*, CRIM. JUST., Summer 1999, at 36, 40 ("There are permissible and impermissible uses of race in the trial of a criminal case.").

B. Improper References to Race by the State

Generally. The United States Supreme Court has recognized that statements capable of inflaming jurors' racial or ethnic prejudices "degrade the administration of justice." *Battle v. United States*, 209 U.S. 36, 39 (1908). "Where such references are legally irrelevant, they violate a defendant's rights to due process and equal protection of the laws—whether the remarks occur during the prosecution's presentation of evidence or argumentation." *United States v. Runyon*, 707 F.3d 475, 494 (4th Cir. 2013); *see also United States v. Doe*, 903 F.2d 16, 24–25 (D.C. Cir.1990); *McCleskey v. Kemp*, 481 U.S. 279, 309 & n.30 (1987).

North Carolina appellate courts generally hold that "[n]onderogatory references to race are permissible . . . if material to issues in the trial and sufficiently justified to warrant 'the risks inevitably taken when racial matters are injected into any important decision-making.'" *State v. Williams*, 339 N.C. 1, 24 (1994) (citation omitted). However, attorneys may not make statements that appear "calculated to mislead or prejudice the jury." *State v. Jordan*, 149 N.C. App. 838, 843 (2002) (quotation omitted) (where prosecutor compared defense counsel to Joseph McCarthy throughout his closing argument, reversible error to deny defendant's motion for mistrial); *see also infra* § 8.6E, Closing Argument. The same rule prohibits defense attorneys from making derogatory references about race. *See infra* § 8.4C, Improper References to Race by the Defense.

Many North Carolina appellate opinions review challenges to racial references at trial without clearly identifying the source or sources of law governing the issue. *See, e.g.*, *State v. Williams*, 339 N.C. 1, 24 (1994) (observing that prosecutor may not make statements intended to inflame passion or prejudice, use racial slurs, or emphasize race gratuitously, but not identifying the constitutional, statutory, evidentiary, or ethical provisions such statements violate). As one court has observed, improper references to race by the prosecution mark "the point where the due process and equal protection clauses overlap or at least meet." *United States ex rel. Haynes v. McKendrick*, 481 F.2d 152, 159 (2d Cir. 1973) (holding that guarantees of equal protection and due process were violated when "prosecutor's remarks introduced race prejudice into the trial"); *see also* Elizabeth L. Earle, Note, *Banishing the Thirteenth Juror: An Approach to the Identification of Prosecutorial Racism*, 92 COLUM. L. REV. 1212, 1218 n.38, 1223 n.73 (1992) (concluding that Sixth and Fourteenth Amendments overlap in analyzing prosecutorial appeals to race). What is clear is that "[t]he Constitution prohibits racially biased prosecutorial arguments." *McCleskey v. Kemp*, 481 U.S. 279, 309, n.30 (1987). Defenders concerned that prosecutorial references to race are improper should raise all potential constitutional protections.

Constitutional guarantee of an impartial jury. The Sixth Amendment to the United States Constitution and article I, section 24 of the N.C. Constitution guarantee a defendant's right to a fair and impartial jury. *See State v. Garcell*, 363 N.C. 10 (2009). "Nothing is more fundamental to the provision of a fair trial than the right to an impartial jury." *Miller v. North Carolina*, 583 F.2d 701 (4th Cir. 1978). This guarantee mandates that the jury be "indifferent" to considerations of race and other immutable characteristics "regardless of the heinousness of the crime charged, the apparent guilt of the offender or the station in life which he occupies." *Irvin v. Dowd*, 366 U.S. 717, 722 (1961). Racially inflammatory statements, questions, or arguments, "by threatening to cultivate bias in the jury . . . offend[] the defendant's right to an impartial jury." *Calhoun v. United States*, 568 U.S. ___, 133 S. Ct. 1136, 1137 (2013) (Sotomayor, J., concurring in denial of cert.); *see also*, Elizabeth L. Earle, Note, *Banishing the Thirteenth Juror: An Approach to the Identification of Prosecutorial Racism*, 92 COLUM. L. REV. 1212, 1215–18 (1992).

Substantive and procedural due process. The North Carolina Supreme Court has recognized that "[t]he substantive and procedural due process requirements of the Fourteenth Amendment mandate that every person charged with a crime has an absolute right to a fair trial before an impartial judge and an unprejudiced jury." *State v. Miller*, 288 N.C. 582, 598 (1975), *rev'd sub nom. on other grounds*, *Miller v. North Carolina*, 583 F.2d 701 (1978). "It is the duty of both the court and the prosecuting attorney to see that this right is protected." *Id.* A conviction will be reversed where a prosecutor's improper appeal to racial prejudice "so infected the trial with unfairness as to make the resulting conviction a denial of due process." *Donnelly v. DeChristoforo*, 416 U.S. 637 (1974) (quoted in *Darden v. Wainwright*, 477 U.S. 168, 181 (1986)). Substantive and procedural due process challenges to a prosecutor's appeal to racial prejudice should also be raised under the law of the land clause in article I, section 19 of the North Carolina Constitution.

Equal protection guarantees. A prosecutor's appeal to racial prejudice also violates the guarantees of the Equal Protection Clause of the Fourteenth Amendment and article I, section 19 of the N.C. Constitution. *See, e.g.*, *Calhoun v. United States*, 568 U.S. ___, 133 S.Ct. 1136, 1137 (2013) (Sotomayor, J., concurring in denial of cert.) (racially biased prosecutorial argument "is an affront to the Constitution's guarantee of equal protection of the laws"). As the Fourth Circuit explained when condemning a prosecutor's argument that a White woman would never consent to sexual intercourse with a Black man, "an appeal to racial prejudice impugns the concept of equal protection of the laws. One of the animating purposes of the equal protection clause of the fourteenth amendment, and a continuing principle of its jurisprudence, is the eradication of racial considerations from criminal proceedings." *Miller v. North Carolina*, 583 F.2d 701, 707 (1978); *see also* Elizabeth L. Earle, Note, *Banishing the Thirteenth Juror: An Approach to the Identification of Prosecutorial Racism*, 92 COLUM. L. REV. 1212, 1218 (1992).

Evidentiary rules. Various rules of evidence may apply to exclude evidence about race. If evidence about race is irrelevant to a disputed issue, it is inadmissible under N.C. Rules of Evidence 401 and 402. If evidence is improperly offered to show the defendant's character to commit an offense, it is inadmissible under N.C. Rule of Evidence 404(a).

N.C. Rule of Evidence 403 provides that relevant, otherwise admissible evidence should be excluded where its probative value is outweighed by its prejudicial effect. "The meaning of 'unfair prejudice' in the context of Rule 403 is 'an undue tendency to suggest decision on an improper basis, commonly, though not necessarily, as an emotional one.'" *State v. Rainey*, 198 N.C. App. 427, 433 (2009) (quoting *State v. DeLeonardo*, 315 N.C. 762, 772 (1986)). Evidence regarding, for example, racial demographics of the area in which a crime occurred, elicited for the apparent purpose of demonstrating that a Black defendant went to a "White neighborhood" with the intention of committing a crime, may violate Rule 401 because it is irrelevant, Rule 404(a) because it suggests that the defendant was more likely to have committed the crime because of his race, and Rule 403 because the prejudicial effect of the evidence outweighs its probative value.

Professional ethics. In addition to the constitutional prohibitions on appeals to racial prejudice, which serve the purpose of ensuring a fair and impartial jury and the integrity of the criminal justice system, various professional standards prohibit prosecutors from exploiting race to a defendant's disadvantage. For example, the American Bar

Association Criminal Justice Standards provide that "[t]he prosecutor should not make arguments calculated to appeal to the prejudices of the jury." ABA Standards for Criminal Justice (1992) 3-5.8(c). Additionally, Comment 1 to N.C. Rule of Professional Conduct 3.8 provides that "[a] prosecutor has the responsibility of a minister of justice and not simply that of an advocate; the prosecutor's duty is to seek justice, not merely to convict. This responsibility carries with it specific obligations to see that the defendant is accorded procedural justice . . . . A systematic abuse of prosecutorial discretion could constitute a violation of Rule 8.4."

Removal of District Attorney from office. G.S. 7A-66 provides that "[c]onduct prejudicial to the administration of justice which brings the office into disrepute" may provide grounds for suspension or removal of a district attorney from office. In *In re Spivey*, 345 N.C. 404 (1997), the North Carolina Supreme Court upheld a district attorney's removal from office following his verbal attack on a Black man in bar, involving repeated use of the word "n*****." For a discussion of the procedures governing removal, see G.S. 7A-66.

C. Improper References to Race by the Defense

While defense counsel may raise the subject of raise when relevant, defense attorneys are prohibited from appealing to racial prejudice at trial. *See* ABA Standards for Criminal Justice (1992) 4-7.7C ("Defense counsel should not make arguments calculated to appeal to the prejudices of the jury"). "Neither the prosecution nor the defense is entitled to offer irrelevant evidence or to argue improperly to the jury about race." Stephen A. Saltzburg, *Race: Fair and Unfair Use*, CRIM. JUST., Summer 1999, at 36, 40 ("Both prosecutors and defendants have a right to complain about the misuse of race to prejudice a jury."). Since the State cannot appeal acquittals, reported accounts of prosecutorial objections to defense appeals to prejudice are rare. In one example, in the trial of former U.S. Secretary of Agriculture Mike Espy for receiving improper gifts, the prosecution filed a motion to preclude irrelevant evidence and a request for a corrective instruction. The prosecution argued that the defense planned to pursue a jury nullification strategy, arousing the sympathy of the predominantly Black jury by introducing testimony about the racially hostile nature of the defendant's workplace. *See id.* at 36–38.The court denied the State's motion, finding that the evidence was relevant to the defendant's theory of the case.

In extreme cases, a defense attorney's appeals to racial prejudice may violate a defendant's right to effective assistance of counsel, guaranteed by the Sixth Amendment to the U.S. Constitution. *See, e.g.*, *State v. Davis*, 872 So. 2d 250, 252 (Fla. 2004) (defense attorney who stated during voir dire "[s]ometimes black people make me mad just because they're black" rendered ineffective assistance of counsel). For example, when a defense attorney stated during his closing argument that he had previously told the defendants "Y'all n****** 40 or 50 years ago would be lynched for something like this," the Georgia Court of Appeals reversed the defendants' convictions on the ground that, "[r]acial prejudice being a highly volatile and incipient and cancerous factor, its deliberate introduction rendered counsel's performance deficient." *Kornegay v. State*, 329 S.E.2d 601, 603, 605 (Ga. Ct. App. 1985) (observing that "[a]ppeals to the prejudice engendered by belief in racial inferiority have no place in our system of criminal justice, even if the theory is that the prejudice would work in defendants' favor" (internal citation omitted)).

These cases should not discourage defense attorneys from addressing considerations of race in appropriate cases, including exploring potential biases during voir dire, but instead reinforce that neither side may make gratuitous, degrading, or inflammatory racial remarks. "The issue is not that [defendant's] trial counsel chose to question jurors on their feelings about race but rather what counsel stated about his own racial prejudices. The manner in which counsel approached the subject unnecessarily tended either to alienate jurors who did not share his animus against African Americans . . . or to legitimize racial prejudice without accomplishing counsel's stated objective of bringing latent bias out into the open." *State v. Davis*, 872 So. 2d 250, 256 (Fla. 2004); *see also infra* "Avoiding the invited response doctrine" in § 8.6E, Closing Argument.

Practice note: Because evidence and argument concerning race can be inflammatory, "counsel who rely upon it should be prepared to articulate clearly the theory that justifies the use of the evidence or the making of the argument." Stephen A. Saltzburg, *Race: Fair and Unfair Use*, CRIM. JUST., Summer 1999, at 36, 56. For example, in the Espy case described above, the prosecution's objection to the defendant's evidence was rejected because the defense attorney clearly articulated how evidence concerning the defendant's race—in particular his status as the first African American Secretary of Agriculture and the difficulties, pressures, and hostilities this entailed—was relevant to the question of intent. *Id.*

8.5 Examples of Improper Appeals to Racial Prejudice

"Appeals to racial passion can distort the search for truth and drastically affect a juror's impartiality." *United States v. Doe*, 903 F.2d 16, 25 (D.C. Cir. 1990). In order to challenge the improper exploitation of race at trial, defenders must be alert to racial imagery and appeals to racial prejudice, both subtle and overt. "Racial imagery can be conveyed in pictures, stories, examples, and generalizations." Sheri Lynn Johnson, *Racial Imagery in Criminal Cases*, 67 TUL. L. REV. 1739, 1743 (1993). The following non-exhaustive list identifies categories of evidence or argument that run the risk of inflaming jury prejudice and bias and may constitute grounds for a corrective jury instruction, mistrial, or other remedy.

A. Animal Imagery

Generally. Prosecutors may not degrade or compare criminal defendants to animals. *State v. Roache*, 358 N.C. 243, 297 (2004) (improper for prosecutors to characterize defendants as a pack of wild dogs "high on the taste of blood and power over their victims"); *State v. Jones*, 355 N.C. 117, 133 (2002) (court vacated death sentence for, among other reasons, prosecutor's prejudicial argument that defendant was "lower than the dirt on a snake's belly"); *State v. Richardson*, 342 N.C. 772, 792 (1996) (court does not condone comparisons between defendants and animals, but isolated reference to defendant as "animal" not prejudicial); *State v. Smith*, 279 N.C. 163, 165 (1971) (awarding new trial to defendant after prosecutor described him as "lower than the bone belly of a cur dog"); *State v. Ballard*, 191 N.C. 122, 124 (1926) (reference to "human hyena" improper, but cured by court's immediate intervention). Such imagery violates the defendant's right to a fair, impartial jury, as it "improperly [leads] the jury to base its decision not on the evidence relating to the issue submitted, but on misleading characterizations, crafted by counsel, that are intended to undermine reason in favor of visceral appeal." *Jones*, 355 N.C. 117, 134.

Animal imagery with racial content. Animal imagery may have subtle or overt racial overtones, both of which run the risk of inflaming jurors' biases. For example, researchers studying capital sentencing found that as the number of references to apes by prosecutors during closing arguments increased, "so too did the likelihood of that defendant being sentenced to death." CHERYL STAATS, ET AL., OHIO STATE KIRWAN INSTITUTE FOR THE STUDY OF RACE AND ETHNICITY, STATE OF THE SCIENCE: IMPLICIT BIAS REVIEW 2013 44–45 (2013) (citing Phillip A. Goff et al., *Not Yet Human: Implicit Knowledge, Historical Dehumanization, and Contemporary Consequences*, 94 J. PERSONALITY & SOC. PSYCHOL. 292 (2008)). In the following examples of overtly racialized animal imagery, North Carolina prosecutors compared Black defendants to predatory, violent African animals:

- In *State v. Sims*, 161 N.C. App. 183 (2003), the State devoted several paragraphs of its closing argument to explaining how the defendant and his coconspirators, all of whom were Black, were "[j]ust like the predators of the African plane [sic]," like a "pack of wild dogs or hyenas in a group attack[ing] a herd of wildebeests" on "Discovery Channel [or] Animal Planet." The prosecutor described how a wild African predator would grasp "its jaws about the throat of the wildebeest, ultimately, crushing the throat and taking the very life out of that animal." He stated that the defendant and his coconspirators "stalked their prey. They chased after their prey. They attacked their prey. Ultimately, they fell their prey." While the court found it permissible to use the phrase "he who hunts with the pack is responsible for the kill" to explain the theory of acting in concert, the court found that the prosecutor acted improperly by making such a close association between the defendant and the animal kingdom, especially where the prosecutor discussed hunting on the African plane at length and the defendant was Black. The court concluded, however, that, "although improper, the district attorney's comments did not deny defendant due process entitling him to a new trial."
- In *State v. McCail*, 150 N.C. App. 643 (2002), the prosecutor compared the Black defendant to Curious George, a monkey in a series of children's books. The judge intervened ex mero motu and instructed the jury to disregard the characterization of the defendant. The Court of Appeals held that the prosecutor's statement was improper but did not require reversal in light of the substantial evidence of the defendant's guilt and the curative instruction.

In another jurisdiction, a defendant's conviction was reversed based on the prosecutor's racially prejudicial analogy between the defendant's case and the story depicted in the movie "Gorillas in the Mist." *State v. Blanks*, 479 N.W.2d 601 (Iowa Ct. App. 1991). In that case, the Black male defendant faced charges of attacking and beating his White girlfriend at a party in the presence of his Black friends. The court found that the racially inflammatory comparison to "Gorillas in the Mist" constituted reversible error because (1) the movie tells the story of a White woman who is brutally murdered by a group of Black poachers; and (2) the prosecutor referred to the defendant and his friends as apes and animals. *See also* Sheri Lynn Johnson, *Racial Imagery in Criminal Cases*, 67 TUL. L. REV. 1739 1753 (1993) (noting that in the trial of the officers charged with beating Rodney King, one of the testifying officers had previously described an incident involving Black people as "right out of 'Gorillas in the Mist'"). In another case involving both indirect and direct appeals to racial prejudice in the prosecutor's closing argument to an all-White jury, references to the Black defendants as animals were so prejudicial that a mistrial should have been granted. *State v. Wilson*, 404 So. 2d 968 (La. 1981). *Cf. Allen v. State*, 871 P.2d 79 (Okla. Crim. App. 1994) (in the capital trial of Wanda Jean Allen, a Black lesbian whose intelligence was near the threshold of mental retardation, the court found no racial content where the prosecutor made references to a snake and a gorilla in his closing argument).

Historical reliance on animal imagery. Reliance on animal imagery plays into a long and brutal history of dehumanizing Black people. The "Black brute" caricature dates back at least to the era of Reconstruction, and "portrays black men as innately savage, animalistic, destructive, and criminal—deserving punishment, maybe death. This brute is a fiend, a sociopath, an anti-social menace. Black brutes are depicted as hideous, terrifying predators who target helpless victims, especially white women." David Pilgrim, *The Brute Caricature*, FERRIS.EDU (last visited Sept. 12, 2014). This caricature continues to appear in prominent trials of the post-civil rights era. *See* Andrea D. Lyon, *Setting the Record Straight: A Proposal for Handling Prosecutorial Appeals to Racial, Ethnic, or Gender Prejudice During Trial*, 6 MICH. J. RACE & L. 319, 336 n.96 (2001) (recounting officers' testimony that Rodney King "groaned like a wounded animal" and gave out a "bear-like yell").

Counsel should remain vigilant for references to such images. "[T]he stereotype of the Black brute [remains] current within American society, [and] in all its iterations, including those that serve to 'racially construct' Latino and other minority youth, it has been proven to be one of the most enduring and powerful stereotypes in the nation's history." Ryan Patrick Alford, *Appellate Review of Racist Summations: Redeeming the Promise of Searching Analysis*, 11 MICH. J. RACE & L. 325, 346 (2006). "Since [the Black brute] stereotype is associated with fear and loathing, it is likely to be a strong motivating force, motivating a fear response when activated by external stimuli, such as a racist summation during a criminal trial." *Id.* at 345.

Practice note: In support of a motion for a mistrial based on a prosecutor's use of animal imagery, emphasize the inherently prejudicial nature of such stereotypes. You may also consider presenting the research described above to demonstrate that, by drawing the jury's attention to a racial caricature, the prosecutor has dangerously "call[ed] forth the [stereotype] in the minds of the listeners." *Id.* at 347. Link the comment to any other racially inflammatory evidence or arguments in the case. *See infra* "When objecting to improper remarks, link all improper references to race" in § 8.6.E., Closing Argument. If your motion for a mistrial is denied, seek curative instructions that inform the jury of the historical caricature of Black people as subhuman, the continuing power of such stereotypes on both conscious and subconscious levels, and the jury's role in deciding the case fairly without regard to the inflammatory racial imagery. *See* Animal Imagery Curative Instruction in the Race Materials Bank at www.ncids.org (select "Training and Resources").

B. Racial Demographics of Geographic Areas

It is improper to suggest that the defendant, because of his race, had no business being in the area where the crime occurred. For example, in *State v. Russell*, 163 N.C. App. 785 (2004) (unpublished), the North Carolina Court of Appeals considered a defendant's objection to a detective's testimony concerning the racial demographics of south Smithfield. In that case, the court "recognize[d] the apparent inference that the prosecutor sought to convey in eliciting testimony that Defendant [and codefendants], who are African-American, were apprehended in an area 'predominantly occupied by white residents,'" but declined to consider whether this testimony was improper because it found that any error would be harmless in light of the evidence against the defendant. *Id.*

This type of improper appeal may take the form of evidence concerning neighborhood demographics, as in *Russell*, or argument that a defendant had "no reason . . . to be [at the scene of the crime] except to cause trouble." *People v. Johnson*, 581 N.E.2d 118, 126 (Ill. App. Ct. 1991) (prosecutor pointed out that the Black defendant lived on south side of Chicago and crime occurred in North Lincoln Park; defendant argued that the implication was that "a public park on the north side of Chicago is or should be off limits to a black man from the south side of Chicago"; court concluded that prosecutor's comment was not an improper appeal to racial prejudice but an attempt to counter defendant's theory that his presence at the scene of the crime was a coincidence). Courts have reversed convictions when a prosecutor argued that the Black-on-Black crime problem faced by Detroit should not be permitted to reach the neighboring town of Joliet, *People v. Lurry*, 395 N.E.2d 1234, 1237 (Ill. App. Ct. 1979), and when a prosecutor lambasted a defendant for committing a crime in "our streets" and not in "some ghetto." *People v. Nightengale*, 523 N.E.2d 136, 141 (Ill. App. Ct. 1988).

C. Associations Between Race and Criminality

A statement or suggestion that a defendant's actions, motivations, or beliefs can be inferred from the defendant's race or ethnicity violates the guarantees of equal protection and due process, deprives a defendant of a fair trial, and violates North Carolina Rules of Evidence 401, 402, 403, and 404(a). *See, e.g.*, *United States v. Doe*, 903 F.2d 16, 24–25 (D.C. Cir. 1990). For example, the First Circuit Court of Appeals held that the admission of an identification card showing the defendant's Columbian nationality in a case in which his alleged co-conspirators were Colombian was reversible error. *United States v. Rodriguez Cortes*, 949 F.2d 532, 540–43 (1st Cir. 1991). Similarly, in a case involving a Jamaican defendant, the D.C. Circuit held that the admission of expert testimony on the role of Jamaicans in the local market for illegal drugs constituted reversible error. *United States v. Doe*, 903 F.2d 16, 25 (D.C. Cir. 1990) (observing that "[r]acial fairness of the trial is an indispensable ingredient of due process and racial equality a hallmark of justice," and concluding that "[a]ppeals to racial passion can distort the search for truth and drastically affect a juror's impartiality" (footnotes omitted)).

Recently, a prosecutor's injection of race into the trial was condemned by United States Supreme Court Justice Sotomayor, joined by Justice Breyer, concurring in a denial of certiorari. *Calhoun v. United States*, 568 U.S. ___, 133 S. Ct. 1136 (2013). When cross-examining a Black defendant in a drug case, the prosecutor challenged the defendant's statement that he was unaware of the drug transaction going on in the hotel room in the following manner:

> You've got African-Americans, you've got Hispanics, you've got a bag full of money. Does that tell you—a light bulb doesn't go off in your head and say, This is a drug deal?

Id. at 1136. For procedural reasons, Justice Sotomayor concurred with the denial of certiorari. However, she stated that the prosecutor's question should never have been posed and constituted a violation of both the Equal Protection Clause and the Sixth Amendment right to an impartial jury.

> [The prosecutor] tapped a deep and sorry vein of racial prejudice that has run through the history of criminal justice in our Nation. . . Such conduct diminishes the dignity of our criminal justice system and undermines respect for the rule of law. We expect the Government to seek justice, not to fan the flames of fear and prejudice.

Id. at 1138.

D. Racial Slurs or Stereotypes

Reliance on racial slurs or stereotypes has been found to violate a defendant's constitutional right to a fair trial and equal protection of the laws. *United States v. Runyon*, 707 F.3d 475, 494 (4th Cir. 2013). For example, a prosecutor's reference to the defendant as a "chola punk" during closing argument was improper. *State v. Martinez*, 658 P.2d 428, 430 (N.M. 1983). In a federal death penalty trial, it was improper to allow the State to introduce an interrogation video into evidence containing the following exchange:

> Detective Rilee asked Runyon: "[Y]ou're Asian, right, Asian–American? You're an honorable Asian man, aren't you?" "Yes sir," he answered. Imploring Runyon to be honest, Rilee continued, "You

> know, if you're an honorable Asian man and your integrity is intact and you have any respect for anybody at all, then you'll do the right thing today, okay?" The officers proceeded to invoke Runyon's "honor" on multiple occasions during the interrogation.

United States v. Runyon, 707 F.3d 475, 494 (2013). The court found the exchange improper for four reasons:

> One, the references came directly from the mouths of law enforcement. Two, they directly alluded to the defendant himself. Three, they bore no relevance to the particular issues that the jury was being asked to resolve. And four, they conveyed what were, frankly, stereotyping and insulting notions about how "an honorable Asian man" is supposed to act.

Id.

The discussion above illustrates the importance of context in analyzing the admissibility and constitutionality of racial references. For example, in *State v. Moose*, 310 N.C. 482 (1984), a case in which the State's evidence was sufficient to raise an inference that a murder was racially motivated, the North Carolina Supreme Court found no error in the prosecutor's references to the victim as an "old black gentleman" and a "black man" and the admission into evidence of the defendant's reference to the victim as a "damn n******," to which the defendant did not object. However, in a Florida case in which irrelevant testimony that a defendant used a racial slur was introduced, the court found that failure to grant a mistrial was an abuse of discretion. *McBride v. State,* 338 So. 2d 567, 568–69 (Fla. Dist. Ct. App. 1976).

In two recent cases, courts found reversible error where the prosecutor argued that Black people do not "snitch" to police about crimes committed by other Black people. In Washington state, a prosecutor questioned Black witnesses, who had recanted their original testimony, about a "code" allegedly adhered to by Black people that prohibits "snitching" to police. *State v. Monday*, 257 P.3d 551 (Wash. 2011). The prosecutor then argued in his closing argument that "black folk don't testify against black folk. You don't snitch to the police." The Washington Supreme Court concluded that the conduct deprived the defendant of his right to a fair trial and reversed the conviction. In Illinois, a prosecutor spoke at length about the Black community's hostility toward the police: "[The] black community here in Marion . . . most of these people were raised to believe that the police and prosecutors are the enemy . . . In their mindset, the biggest sin that you could-that you can commit is to be a snitch in the community." *People v. Marshall*, 995 N.E.2d 1045, 1047–48 (Ill. App. Ct. 2013). The prosecutor argued to the all-White jury that this attitude was foreign to "our white world," but that the jury should "keep in the back of your mind how many people in [the Black] community feel about law enforcement." *Id.* The appellate court reversed the conviction, noting that the prosecutor improperly urged the jury to rely on these race-based generalizations when assessing witness credibility, and concluded that the "prosecutor improperly aligned himself with the jury [by] contrast[ing] the [distrust of police in the] 'black community' with [the respect for police in] 'our white world.'" *Id.* at 1050.

E. Improper Invocations of Race in Sex Offense Cases

While appeals to racial prejudice are unlawful in all cases, "[c]oncern about fairness should be especially acute where a prosecutor's argument appeals to race prejudice in the context of a sexual crime, for few forms of prejudice are so virulent." *Miller v. North Carolina*, 583 F.2d 701, 707 (4th Cir. 1978); *see also* David Pilgrim, *The Brute Caricature*, FERRIS.EDU (last visited Sept. 12, 2014) (explaining that the stereotype of the "Black brute" depicts Black men "as hideous, terrifying predators who target helpless victims, especially white women"); JOHN HOPE FRANKLIN, THE FREE NEGRO IN NORTH CAROLINA 1790–1860 at 98–99 (1943) (during the slave period, rape was a capital offense when committed by a Black man when the victim was White, but not when the victim was Black).

In one North Carolina case in which a Black defendant and two other Black men were charged with raping a White woman, the prosecutor argued that "[d]on't you know and I argue if that [i.e., consent] was the case she could not come in this courtroom and relate the story that she has from this stand to you good people, because I argue to you that the average white woman abhors anything of this type in nature that had to do with a black man. It is innate within us." *State v. Miller*, 288 N.C. 582, 597 (1975). The majority opinion for the North Carolina Supreme Court expressed disapproval of these remarks but found that they did not constitute prejudicial error requiring a new trial. *Id.* at 601. An opinion by three concurring justices found the majority's "mild disparagement" of the language insufficient, stating that it was "both improper and prejudicial" and "deserves censure"; however, the concurrence found the evidence of the defendant's guilt so decisive that "there was no way for the State to have lost this case." In a separate concurrence, one justice found no impropriety in the argument, finding the assertions a matter of common knowledge and criticizing the "tidal wave of civil rights fanaticism" that "has swept over this nation" and "washed into judicial opinions." *Id.* at 605.

The Fourth Circuit Court of Appeals overturned the conviction:

> Where the jury is exposed to highly prejudicial argument by the prosecutor's calculated resort to racial prejudice on an issue as sensitive as consent to sexual intercourse in a prosecution for rape, we think that the prejudice engendered is so great that automatic reversal is required. In such a case, the impartiality of the jury as a fact-finder is fatally compromised. Because that contamination may affect the jury's evaluation of all of the evidence before it, speculation about the effect of the error on the verdict is fruitless. Reversal must be automatic.

Id. at 708. *See also State v. Richmond*, 904 P.2d 974 (Kan. 1995) (improper for prosecutor to ask jury to "[t]hink about having to divulge to your husband that you were raped by a black male. . . . Both of the females are white."); *State v. Reynolds*, 580 So. 2d 254 (Fla. Dist. Ct. App. 1991) (in sexual battery case involving Black male defendant and White female victim, conviction reversed as a result of prosecutor's racialized language throughout case, including voir dire questions as to whether any potential White jurors had dated or married "a person of the black race," and a closing argument in which the prosecutor asked jurors "to think about how embarrassing it is for an 18-year-old white girl from Crestview to admit she was raped by a black man. It is humiliating").

Practice note: Inflammatory remarks or implications that lie at the volatile intersection of race and sex may take the form of:

- Suggestions that White people generally find Black people sexually undesirable. *See, e.g.*, *Miller v. North Carolina*, 583 F.2d 701 (4th Cir. 1978); *People v. Richardson*, 363 N.E.2d 924, 926, 927 (Ill. App. Ct. 1977) (prosecutor argued that a White male witness must be telling the truth because his story included admitting to sexual intercourse with a Black woman, and "[i]f he is going to lie about anything else, he wouldn't admit having intercourse with a black woman"; court found that prosecutor's statements "so prejudiced and inflamed the jury against Richardson's defense that he was deprived of a fair trial.").
- Attempts to inflame jurors' fear by suggesting that, while the victim of sexual assault in the present case is Black, the next victim could be a White person. *See, e.g.*, *Kelly v. Stone*, 514 F.2d 18, 19 (9th Cir. 1975) (comment that "maybe the next time it won't be a little Black girl from the other side of the tracks; maybe it will be somebody that you know" constituted appeal to prejudice over evidence, and in combination with other inflammatory remarks, denied defendant a fair trial).
- Derogatory references to interracial relationships. *See, e.g.*, *State v. Deas*, 25 N.C. App. 294 (1975) (prosecutor argued that interracial relationships "don't happen in Transylvania County"; however, court found no abuse of discretion and no prejudicial error).

F. Emphasis on Victim's Race

Emphasis on the race of the victim poses a risk to the impartiality of the jury. Recent studies in capital cases, for example, have found that the race of the victim is a significant factor in imposition of the death penalty in North Carolina. Michael L. Radelet & Glenn L. Pierce, *Race and Death Sentencing in North Carolina, 1980–2007*, 89 N.C. L. REV. 2119 (2011) (statewide from 1980 to 2007, homicides of White victims faced odds of resulting in a death sentence that were nearly 3.0 times higher than cases involving homicides of Black victims); Affidavit of Catherine M. Grosso & Barbara O'Brien Regarding MSU Study at 35 in the Race Materials Bank at www.ncids.org (select "Training and Resources") (statewide from 1990 through 2009, death eligible cases with at least one White victim were 2.59 times more likely to result in a death sentence than all other cases); *see also* Seth Kotch & Robert P. Mosteller, *The Racial Justice Act and the Long Struggle with Race and the Death Penalty in North Carolina*, 88 N.C. L. REV. 2031,

2097 (2010) (describing the "continuing heavy predominance of white victims in death sentences").

Defense counsel should be prepared to object to any irrelevant reference to the race of the victim and to move for mistrial in appropriate cases. *See, e.g., Wallace v. State*, 768 So. 2d 1247 (Fla. Dist. Ct. App. 2000) (prosecutor's repeated reference to the race of the Black male defendant and the White female café patron allegedly harassed by him was not harmless error where race of café patron was irrelevant to the question of guilt and all jurors hearing the case were White).

G. Derogatory References to Defense Witnesses Based on Race

Another category of appeals to racial prejudice involves racially inflammatory statements attacking the credibility of Black defense witnesses. For example, in the closing argument of a trial involving a Black defendant, a federal prosecutor emphasized that "not one White witness" had been produced in the case contradicting the victim's testimony, implying that the testimony of non-White witnesses was not credible. *Withers v. United States*, 602 F.2d 124 (6th Cir. 1979). Prosecutors have argued that the testimony of a racial or ethnic minority should be discredited when it reflects favorably on someone of the same race or ethnicity. *See State v. Monday*, 257 P.3d 551 (Wash. 2011) (reversing conviction where prosecutor suggested and then argued that Black people don't testify against Black people); *State v. Thompson*, 654 P.2d 453 (Kan. 1982); *People v. Richardson*, 363 N.E.2d 924, 926 (Ill. App. Ct. 1977) (prosecutor referred to Black defendant and Black defense witnesses as "street people" and said "they lie every day"); *People v. Kong*, 517 N.Y.S.2d 71, 72 (N.Y. App. Div. 1987); *State v. Kamel*, 466 N.E.2d 860, 866 (Ohio 1984) (reviewing case in which prosecutor argued that defense witnesses, natives of Syria, were biased because they were originally from the defendant's country of origin and "unreliable by reason of their foreign birth").

Referring to witnesses who are racial minorities by their first name may improperly diminish a witness's stature. In *Hamilton v. Alabama*, 376 U.S. 650 (1964) (per curiam), the Supreme Court reversed the judgment of contempt imposed on a Black witness who refused to answer when a lawyer insisted on calling her by her first name. *See also State v. Torres*, 554 P.2d 1069, 1071 (Wash. Ct. App. 1976) (noting that prosecutor repeatedly referred to defendants as Mexicans or Mexican Americans while referring to the complaining witness with title "Ms." or "Mrs."). Defenders should be alert to such efforts to undermine defense witnesses' credibility or standing, and raise challenges when appropriate.

H. Defendant's Racial Conduct or Remarks

Defense counsel may object where the State seeks to introduce evidence of a defendant's racist or racially inflammatory remarks on the grounds that they are irrelevant under N.C. Rules of Evidence 401 and 402, constitute inadmissible character evidence under Rule 404(a), violate the defendant's constitutional right to a fair trial, and are more prejudicial than probative under Rule 403. Courts may admit such evidence only if it is probative of a disputed issue and its probative value is not substantially outweighed by the danger of unfair prejudice. For example, a White defendant's reference to a Black victim as a "damn n*****," along with evidence that the Black victim was seen driving through a predominantly White area, was admissible and sufficient to support a jury argument that the crime by the White defendant was racially motivated. *State v. Moose*, 310 N.C. 482, 492 (1984).

Two unpublished decisions of the North Carolina Court of Appeals illustrate the importance of clear, immediate objections to the introduction of evidence concerning a defendant's racial comments when irrelevant to the issues in the case. In both cases, the defendants failed to convince the court that admission of racial slurs uttered by the defendants constituted reversible error. *See State v. Bell*, 164 N.C. App. 228 (2004) (unpublished) (reviewing case in which defendant uttered racial slurs to a police officer); *State v. Valentine*, 200 N.C. App. 436 (2009) (unpublished) (reviewing case in which defendant referred to a magistrate as a "f***ing white cracker"). Both arguments were rejected in large part because of defense counsel's failure to object clearly and consistently to the evidence at trial.

I. References to Race of Defense Counsel or Jurors

It is improper for a prosecutor to incorporate the race of the jurors or defense counsel into closing argument. "Indeed, it is difficult to envision a criminal trial in which the *jurors'* race would constitute a proper matter for argument." *State v. Diehl*, 353 N.C. 433, 439 (2001) (Martin, J., dissenting) (emphasis in original); *see also id.* at 437 (trial judge sustained defendant's objection to prosecutor's reference to "twelve white jurors in Randolph county"; however, denial of defendant's motion for a mistrial was not abuse of discretion). In *United States v. Richardson*, 161 F.3d 728 (D.C. Cir. 1998), the defendant's conviction was reversed on the basis of an improper prosecutorial argument suggesting that, because defense counsel was White, he was out of touch with the world inhabited by his Black client (and, by extension, the predominantly Black jury), and his characterization of his client's life should therefore be discounted.

J. Challenging Improper References to Race

Given the difficulty of measuring a jury's impartiality following exposure to appeals to racial prejudice, defendants should object and consider moving for a mistrial any time racially inflammatory rhetoric threatens the fairness of the defendant's trial. G.S. 15A-1061; *see also Vasquez v. Hillery*, 474 U.S. 254, 263 (1986) (observing in the grand jury context that "[w]hen constitutional error calls into question the objectivity of those charged with bringing a defendant to judgment, a reviewing court can neither indulge a presumption of regularity nor evaluate the resulting harm"); *State v. Warren,* 327 N.C. 364, 376 (1990) (mistrial warranted where the "improprieties in the trial [are] so serious that they substantially and irreparably prejudice the defendant's case and make it impossible for the defendant to receive a fair and impartial verdict" (quotation omitted)). If you fail to object, your client will have to show on appeal that the prosecutor "stray[ed] so far from the bounds of propriety" that the trial court should have intervened ex mero motu. *See State v. Smith*, 351 N.C. 251, 269 (2000). If your motion for a mistrial is not made in a timely manner, i.e., "at some time sufficiently close to the occurrence of the error to permit its correction," then denial of the motion may not be preserved for appellate review. *See* G.S. 15A-1446 Official Commentary, *see also State v. Smith*, 96 N.C. App. 352 (1989) (defendant waived appellate review where his motion for mistrial based on the prosecutor's alleged improper opening statement was not made until after the jury began deliberating); N.C. Rule of Appellate Procedure 10 (requiring a timely objection or motion to preserve the error for appellate review). Other remedies include proposing a curative jury instruction and moving to prohibit racially inflammatory language before it is used where circumstances suggest that it might be introduced. Consider proffering some of the empirical studies cited earlier to explain the impact of racially inflammatory language on the jury in support of your objection, motion for a mistrial, or motion in limine. *See supra* "Practice note" in § 8.5A, Animal Imagery; *infra* "Practice note" in § 8.6E, Closing Argument.

8.6 Considerations at Certain Stages of Trial

A. Motion for Change of Venue

A defendant may obtain a change of venue by filing a motion pursuant to G.S. 15A-957. This motion must allege that there exists such great prejudice against the defendant in the county where the prosecution was initiated that the defendant would be unable to receive a fair trial. Any motion under G.S. 15A-957 should allege that failure to change venue would deny the defendant his or her due process rights under the Fourteenth Amendment.

When a "pattern of deep and bitter prejudice [is] shown to be present throughout the community," the defendant is entitled to a change of venue. *Irvin v. Dowd*, 366 U.S. 717, 727 (1961); *see also McCleskey v. Kemp*, 481 U.S. 279, 309 n.30 (1987) ("[w]idespread bias in the community can make a change of venue constitutionally required"); *State v. Moore*, 319 N.C. 645 (1987) (defendant moved for a change of venue or for a special venire due to extensive inflammatory media coverage of the case, pervasive county-wide discussion of it, and the social prominence of the alleged victim and her family). Exposure of the jury to excessive and prejudicial news coverage may violate due process. *See Sheppard v. Maxwell*, 384 U.S. 333 (1966) (holding that extensive media coverage denied due process right to fair trial); *see also State v. Jerrett*, 309 N.C. 239 (1983) (due process requires that defendant be tried by jury free from outside influences).

Media accounts of crime shaped by the race of the victim and the perpetrator may support a motion for change of venue. Reports of crime often include the perpetrator's race when he or she is a person of color, and crimes committed by people of color against White victims may receive more coverage than other crimes. *See* Sheri Lynn Johnson, *Racial Imagery in Criminal Cases*, 67 TUL. L. REV. 1739, 1744 (1993). Researchers have found that the way in which an issue is framed in the media influences jurors' decisions. For example, an increase in articles critical of the death penalty has been linked to fewer death sentences, while publication of positive articles about the death penalty results in more death sentences. Susan Hardy, *Death Watch: Are Capital Punishment's Days*

Numbered?, ENDEAVORS.UNC.EDU (April 26, 2011) (discussing FRANK R. BAUMGARTNER ET AL., THE DECLINE OF THE DEATH PENALTY AND THE DISCOVERY OF INNOCENCE (2008)); *see also* Travis L. Dixon & Cristina L. Azocar, *Priming Crime and Activating Blackness: Understanding the Psychological Impact of the Overrepresentation of Blacks as Lawbreakers on Television News*, 57 J. COMM. 229, 229 (2007). Racially disparate coverage of crimes may inject bias into a trial before it begins. For a further discussion of practical and strategic considerations concerning motions for change of venue, see 1 NORTH CAROLINA DEFENDER MANUAL § 11.3 (Change of Venue) (2d ed. 2013).

Practice note: When moving for a change of venue, it is advisable to have a preferred venue in mind. (G.S. 15A-957 specifies the counties to which venue may be transferred.) Defense attorneys should consider researching the racial demographics and attitudes of people residing in possible alternative venues to ensure that the defendant will receive a fair trial in the alternative venue. *See, e.g.*, Sheri Lynn Johnson, *Racial Imagery in Criminal Cases*, 67 TUL. L. REV. 1739, 1768 (1993) (describing attorneys' investigation of racial attitudes in neighboring counties when considering moving for a change of venue in the Joan Little case).

Under the Sixth Amendment to the United States Constitution and article I, sections 24 and 26 of the North Carolina Constitution, a criminal defendant is entitled to a jury venire drawn from a fair cross-section of the community where the offense occurred. *See, e.g.*, *Duren v. Missouri*, 439 U.S. 357 (1979); *State v. Bowman*, 349 N.C. 459 (1998). The U.S. Supreme Court has yet to decide whether a change of venue to a county that is demographically dissimilar to the county where the offense occurred violates the fair cross-section requirement. *See Mallett v. Missouri*, 494 U.S. 1009 (1990) (Marshall, J., dissenting from denial of cert.) (two of the three justices dissenting from denial of certiorari would have reached this issue). Counsel should rely on the fair cross-section requirement in requesting a change of venue to a demographically similar county.

B. Opening Statement

Defendant's Opening Statement. Opening statements are a critical part of trial. *See* Richard Lempert, *Telling Tales in Court: Trial Procedure and the Story Model*, 13 CARDOZO L. REV. 559, 565 (1991) (arguing that "winning the battle of stories" in opening statements may influence how evidence is considered, interpreted, and remembered). Opening statement is counsel's first uninterrupted opportunity to communicate the defendant's theory of the case to the jury, and to counter any harmful stereotypes that jurors may harbor. Cynthia Lee, *Making Race Salient: Trayvon Martin and Implicit Bias in a Not Yet Post-Racial Society*, 91 N.C. L. REV. 1555 (2013) ("[I]f an attorney is concerned that implicit racial bias may adversely affect the verdict, he may wish to tell a story that makes race salient in his opening statement.").

The opening statement provides an opportunity for counsel to "consider (1) how to prime themes based on fairness and equality, (2) how to incorporate counter-stereotypical exemplars in the narrative, and (3) what kinds of schemas might 'fit' a client while supplanting jurors' unconscious racial schemas." Pamela A. Wilkins, *Confronting The*

Invisible Witness: The Use Of Narrative To Neutralize Capital Jurors' Implicit Racial Biases, 115 W. VA. L. REV. 305, 362 (2012). *See also supra* "Reinforce norms of fairness and equality" in § 8.2B, Strategies for Addressing Race. For example, some have suggested that, in the trial of George Zimmerman, the prosecution should have explored the possibility that Zimmerman perceived a threat where no real threat existed as a result of a racial stereotype he attached to Trayvon Martin. *See, e.g.*, Cynthia Lee, *Making Race Salient: Trayvon Martin and Implicit Bias in a Not Yet Post-Racial Society*, 91 N.C. L. Rev. 1555 (2013); *see also* James E. Coleman, Jr., *Ignoring Race a Mistake in Zimmerman Trial*, NEWS AND OBSERVER (Raleigh), July 20, 2013 (arguing that the State of Florida created conditions for verdict of acquittal by failing to address the role of race in Zimmerman's perception of Martin as a threat). In a case in which the victim mistakenly believed that the defendant was carrying a gun, counsel might forecast expert testimony regarding the common implicit association between Black males and guns.

> Various studies show many persons draw a strong association between black males and guns. For example, in one well-known study, persons were faster to recognize guns and frequently mistook tools for guns when primed with pictures of black male faces. This was true without regard to the conscious prejudice of the subject of the test. Scholars have opined that "the stereotype of African-Americans as violent and criminally inclined is one of the most pervasive, well-known, and persistent stereotypes in American culture. Where other negative cultural stereotypes about Blacks have significantly diminished, this one has remained strong and influential, particularly among Whites."

Pamela A. Wilkins, *Confronting The Invisible Witness: The Use Of Narrative To Neutralize Capital Jurors' Implicit Racial Biases*, 115 W. VA. L. REV. 305, 323 (2012) (footnotes omitted). It is proper to include a discussion of implicit or explicit biases in your opening statement where you have a reasonable expectation that you will be able to introduce expert or lay testimony about the influence of such biases on the victim's or other witness's perceptions.

Prosecutor's opening statement. While most challenges to racially inflammatory prosecutorial language occur during closing argument, defenders should also be alert to the possibility that such language may creep into opening statements as well. Sheri Lynn Johnson, *Racial Imagery in Criminal Cases*, 67 TUL. L. REV. 1739, 1746 (1993). If a prosecutor's opening statement includes racially inflammatory language, imagery, or stereotypes, counsel should object and consider moving for a mistrial.

C. Testimony

Defense use of lay witness testimony to make race salient. Defense attorneys may use lay witness testimony to present evidence that the defendant's race played a role in the case. For example, one study found that testimony from a defense witness about racial slurs shouted at a defendant by White victims had the effect of reducing racial bias in jurors. Ellen S. Cohn et al., *Reducing White Juror Bias: The Role of Race Salience and*

Racial Attitudes, 39 J. APPLIED SOC. PSYCHOL. 1953, 1966 (2009). In this study, testimony that White victims surrounded the defendant's car and shouted racial slurs at the defendant and his wife before the defendant got into his car and struck the victims with his car while driving away reduced racial bias even in jurors who scored highly on tests measuring racism. *Id.* at 1959–60. *See also* Cynthia Lee, *Making Race Salient: Trayvon Martin and Implicit Bias in a Not Yet Post-Racial Society*, 91 N.C. L. REV. 1555, 1595 (2013) (discussing the Cohn study).

Objections to racially inflammatory lay witness testimony. A defendant may object to the introduction of racially inflammatory lay witness testimony on various grounds. Courts have reversed convictions based on the improper admission of irrelevant, racially inflammatory evidence where a witness was asked about sexual relations between a black defendant and a white woman that were not germane to the case. *See, e.g.*, *Johnson v. Rose*, 546 F.2d 678, 678–79 (6th Cir. 1976). A defendant may object to the admission of racially inflammatory testimony on grounds that it is irrelevant under N.C. Evidence Rule 401, constitutes character evidence generally inadmissible under Rule 404(a), is more prejudicial than probative under Rule 403, and violates the defendant's constitutional rights. *See Calhoun v. United States*, 568 U.S. ___, 133 S. Ct. 1136 (2013) (Sotomayor, J., concurring in denial of cert.) (cross-examination of defendant suggesting connection between race and drug dealers violated equal protection and right to impartial jury; "[I]f government counsel . . . is allowed to inflame the jurors by irrelevantly arousing their deepest prejudices, the jury may become in his hands a lethal weapon directed against defendants who may be innocent." (quotation omitted)); *see also supra* § 8.4B, Improper References to Race by the State.

Impeachment with evidence of racial bias. A witness may be impeached with evidence that the witness is biased. Extrinsic evidence may be used to impeach regarding bias. ROBERT P. MOSTELLER ET AL., NORTH CAROLINA EVIDENTIARY FOUNDATIONS 6-35 (2d ed. 2006).

Evidence of immigration status. "The terms 'illegal alien,' 'illegal immigrant,' and 'undocumented worker' now more than ever create a great deal of fear and distress in our society." Benny Agosto, Jr. et al., *"But Your Honor, He's an Illegal!" Ruled Inadmissible and Prejudicial: Can the Undocumented Worker's Alien Status be Introduced at Trial?*, 17 TEX. HISP. J. L. & POL'Y 27 (2011). A defendant should object to any mention of his or her undocumented status and consider seeking a pretrial order preventing the State from introducing such evidence. As with all other evidence, evidence of a defendant's status as undocumented should be admitted only if it is relevant to a disputed fact and more probative than prejudicial. N.C. R. EVID. 401, 402, 403, 404; *see also, e.g., Guerra v. Collins*, 916 F. Supp. 620, 636 (S.D. Tex. 1995) (concluding, under parallel Federal Rules of Evidence, that prosecutor should not have mentioned defendant's status as undocumented to jurors because it was irrelevant and prejudicial).

Expert testimony introduced by the State. At times, expert testimony introduced by the State may be racially inflammatory. For example, a psychologist who was called as an expert in approximately 150 death penalty cases repeatedly testified at the penalty phase of capital trials that "Hispanic and black men were more likely to be dangerous in the future." Brandi Grissom, *Texas Ends Deal with Psychologist Over Race Testimony*, THE TEXAS TRIBUNE, Oct. 31, 2011. Defense counsel should object and move for a mistrial if the prosecution offers expert testimony linking race and criminality.

Cultural experts for the defense. Where community norms or cultural mores are relevant to the case, defense counsel may seek a "cultural expert." For example, the San Francisco Public Defender's Office has worked with cultural experts to provide information to the court about Asian youth and families, and to provide contextual information that may exculpate the client. *See* Robin Walker Sterling, *Raising Race*, THE CHAMPION, Apr. 2011, at 24. For example, if among Hmong immigrants in a particular community, it is a common practice to share cars among a large group of extended family and friends, a defendant's argument that he didn't know he was driving a stolen car may be more persuasive when placed in this cultural context.

The use of cultural experts raises some concerns. First, a defense expert's cultural testimony may open the door to race-based argument. In *State v. Robinson*, 336 N.C. 78, 129–30 (1994), a prosecutor argued to the jury:

> [The defendant] didn't have to put his culture down here with us. What this means is that anyone who is poor and black and lives in an inner city has a license to commit murder, because it's not their fault. That none of these folks can ever rise above where they start out. Because they are poor, they are black, and they come from an inner city, they have no right, they have no way, that's it.
>
> And they have a license to commit crime, because that's just what happens there, and there's nothing you can do about it. That's what their doctor says.

The N.C. Supreme Court found that the prosecutor's argument was not improper, as it was a response to the defense expert's testimony that the "defendant's inner-city upbringing was, in part, a cause of his criminal behavior." *Id.* One way to avoid this pitfall is to limit the scope of the expert testimony. If the testimony you present does not suggest that a defendant's race or culture reduces his or her culpability, but rather explains a fact in dispute (as in the example about Hmong immigrants in Fresno, above), you may avoid opening the door to this type of race-based argument. *See also infra* "Avoiding the invited response doctrine" in § 8.6E, Closing Argument.

Second, some judges may resist the introduction of cultural expert testimony because of uncertainty about how to qualify someone as an expert or how to establish a link between the defendant and the expert's testimony. *See* Robin Walker Sterling, *Raising Race*, THE CHAMPION, Apr. 2011, at 24, 29. "[When] arguing in favor of admission of the cultural expert's testimony, defense attorneys can offer that the expert's background and qualifications go to weight and not admissibility." *Id.* at 29. Even if the evidence does not influence the jury's determination of guilt or innocence, the judge may learn "about cultural differences of that individual client, may rely on it in the sentencing disposition, and may apply this knowledge to other cases." *Id.*

Experts on implicit bias. Defense counsel may seek to introduce expert testimony from a social scientist concerning empirical findings on implicit biases. Cynthia Lee, *Making Race Salient: Trayvon Martin and Implicit Bias in a Not Yet Post-Racial Society*, 91 N.C. L. REV. 1555, 1595–96 (2013). Examples include:

- in a case where a Black defendant claims that he was mistakenly identified as the offender, evidence of implicit associations between Black people and criminality;
- in a case in which a Black defendant claims he didn't have a weapon on him but the assault victim claims he did, evidence of shooter/weapon bias (discussed *supra* in § 8.6B, Opening Statement); or
- the tendency of jurors to "automatically and unintentionally evaluate ambiguous trial evidence in racially biased ways." Justin D. Levinson & Danielle Young, *Different Shades of Bias: Skin Tone, Implicit Racial Bias, and Judgments of Ambiguous Evidence*, 112 W.VA. L. REV. 307, 309 (2010).

In support of the admissibility of such evidence, defenders may explain that the proffered testimony "will provide the jury with helpful 'information about the social and psychological context in which contested . . . facts occurred and . . . the context will help the jury interpret the . . . facts.'" Cynthia Lee, *Making Race Salient: Trayvon Martin and Implicit Bias in a Not Yet Post-Racial Society*, 91 N.C. L. REV. 1555, 1595–96 (2013) (quoting Neil Vidmar & Regina A. Schuller, *Juries and Expert Evidence: Social Framework Testimony*, 52 LAW & CONTEMP. PROBS. 133, 133 (1989)). If the judge does not admit your expert testimony on implicit bias on the basis that it is within the common knowledge of the jury, you may consider asking the judge to take judicial notice of the influence of implicit bias on cognitive processes and decision-making.

D. Jury Instructions

Jury instructions present a key opportunity to inform the ultimate decision-makers in your client's case about issues related to race and bias. For example, California has a model jury instruction instructing jurors in criminal cases that they may "not let bias, sympathy, prejudice, or public opinion influence [their] decision." California Criminal Jury Instruction No. 101 (2014). In North Carolina, if a party requests a special instruction that is legally correct in itself and is pertinent to the evidence and the issues in the case, the judge "must give the instruction at least in substance." *State v Lamb,* 321 N.C. 633, 644 (1988) (quotation omitted); *State v Craig,* 167 N.C. App. 793 (2005). The judge need not give the instruction in the exact language of the request, but he or she may not change the sense of it or so qualify it "as to weaken its force." *State v Puckett,* 54 N.C. App. 576, 581 (1981).

Pre-voir dire jury instructions on bias. Some scholars have suggested that juror instructions on implicit bias may be given to jurors before the case begins in order to alert them to the possibility of biased judgments before they are exposed to evidence and argument. *See, e.g.*, Cynthia Lee, *Making Race Salient: Trayvon Martin and Implicit Bias in a Not Yet Post-Racial Society*, 91 N.C. L. REV. 1555, 1599 (2013). While jury instructions are typically given at the end of a trial, early delivery serves to focus jurors' attention on judging fairly and not allowing racial stereotypes to influence their decision-making. *Id.*

For example, Judge Mark Bennett, U.S. District Judge for the Northern District of Iowa, spends about twenty-five minutes during jury selection addressing implicit bias. Jerry Kang et al., *Implicit Bias in the Courtroom*, 59 UCLA L. REV. 1124, 1181–82 (2012). He starts by screening a clip from *What Would You Do?*, a show produced by ABC that catches bystanders' responses to staged events. The episode shows the reactions of bystanders to three different people—a casually dressed young White man, a similarly dressed young Black man, and an attractive young White woman—each of whom use a hammer, saw, and bolt cutter to try to break a chain securing a bicycle to a pole. No one says anything to the White man and several men attempt to assist the White woman. In contrast, a crowd starts shouting angrily at the Black man and some people call the police. *Id.* at 1182 n.250. Judge Bennett then gives the following juror instruction on implicit bias before attorneys present opening statements:

> Do not decide the case based on "implicit biases." As we discussed in jury selection, everyone, including me, has feelings, assumptions, perceptions, fears, and stereotypes, that is, "implicit biases," that we may not be aware of. These hidden thoughts can impact what we see and hear, how we remember what we see and hear, and how we make important decisions. Because you are making very important decisions in this case, I strongly encourage you to evaluate the evidence carefully and to resist jumping to conclusions based on personal likes or dislikes, generalizations, gut feelings, prejudices, sympathies, stereotypes, or biases. The law demands that you return a just verdict, based solely on the evidence, your individual evaluation of that evidence, your reason and common sense, and these instructions. Our system of justice is counting on you to render a fair decision based on the evidence, not on biases.

Id. at 1182–83. Defenders may inform local judges of this approach to educating jurors on implicit bias, and suggest using similar materials in juror orientation sessions or during jury selection to illustrate the ways in which bias can influence decision-making. *See* Cynthia Lee, *Making Race Salient: Trayvon Martin and Implicit Bias in a Not Yet Post-Racial Society*, 91 N.C. L. REV. 1555, 1598–99 (2013) (quoting instruction given by Judge Bennett).

Pre-voir dire pledge on bias. During jury selection in Judge Bennett's courtroom, all jurors are required to sign the following pledge:

> I will not decide this case based on biases. This includes gut feelings, prejudices, stereotypes, personal likes or dislikes, sympathies or generalizations.

Jerry Kang et al., *Implicit Bias in the Courtroom*, 59 UCLA L. REV. 1124, 1182 (2012). Defenders may consider requesting that jurors be required to sign such a pledge before serving. Even when such a request is denied, it brings concerns about the role that racial bias may play in jury decision-making to the judge's attention, and may cause the judge to allow counsel more latitude to explore biases during voir dire.

Race-switching instruction. In cases that run the risk of triggering implicit biases—such as an interracial sexual assault case, a self-defense case in which the defendant is Black and the victim White, or any case involving a defendant who is a racial minority—defenders should consider seeking a "race-switching" instruction. This instruction asks jurors to examine the possible influence of implicit bias on their decision-making by imagining how they would respond if the race of the defendant and/or victim were different. *See* Cynthia Kwei Yung Lee, *Race And Self-Defense: Toward A Normative Conception Of Reasonableness*, 81 MINN. L. REV. 367, 488 (1996). While defense attorneys themselves may be able to ask jurors to perform a race-switching exercise during voir dire or closing argument, a race-switching instruction is generally preferable, as jury instructions, "coming as [they do] from the court [rather than from the defense attorney], . . . [help] diffuse any reactions from the jury that the defense [i]s 'playing the race card.'" James McComas & Cynthia Strout, *Combating the Effects of Racial Stereotyping in Criminal Cases*, THE CHAMPION, Aug. 1999, at 22, 24. Law Professor Cynthia Lee suggests the following model race-switching instruction:

> It is natural to make assumptions about the parties and witnesses in any case based on stereotypes. Stereotypes constitute well-learned sets of associations or expectations correlating particular traits with members of a particular social group. You should try not to make assumptions about the parties and witnesses based on t heir membership in a particular racial group.
>
> If you are unsure about whether you have made any unfair assessments based on racial stereotypes, you may engage in a r ace-switching exercise to test whether stereotypes have colored your evaluation of the case before you. Race-switching involves imagining the same events, the same circumstances, the same people, but switching the races of the parties. For example, if the defendant is White and the victim is Latino, you could imagine a Latino defendant and a White victim. In intraracial cases in which both the defendant and the victim are persons of color, you may simply assign a different race to these actors. For example, if both the defendant and victim are Black, you may imagine that both are White. If your evaluation of the case before you is different after engaging in race-switching, this suggests a subconscious reliance on stereotypes. You may then wish to reevaluate the case from a neutral, unbiased perspective.

Cynthia Kwei Yung Lee, *Race And Self-Defense: Toward A Normative Conception Of Reasonableness*, 81 MINN. L. REV. 367, 482 (1996).

In at least one case, a trial judge agreed to give a race-switching instruction substantially similar to the above instruction, "noting that he personally engaged in a race-switching exercise whenever he was called upon to impose sentence on a member of a minority race, to insure that he was not being influenced by racial stereotypes." James McComas & Cynthia Strout, *Combating the Effects of Racial Stereotyping in Criminal Cases*, THE CHAMPION, Aug. 1999, at 22, 24. The case in which the instruction was given involved a 16 year-old Black male charged with assaulting an 18 year-old White male; the defendant claimed self-defense. The defense attorneys employed a "five-part plan for addressing the racial dynamics of the case," involving (1) testing the case in front of a mock jury; (2) proposing a written jury questionnaire addressing issues of race; (3) devising a strategy for dealing with race during voir dire; (4) preparation of an expert research psychologist to testify regarding the effect of racial stereotypes on memory and perception; and (5) a written jury instruction requiring the race-switching exercise. *Id.* at 22. The defendant was acquitted on all counts. *Id.* at 24.

Certification or pledge to render bias-free judgment. Following closing arguments, Judge Mark Bennett again instructs jurors to reach a verdict free from biases:

> Reach your verdict without discrimination. In reaching your verdict, you must not consider the defendant's race, color, religious beliefs, national origin, or sex. You are not to return a verdict for or against the defendant unless you would return the same verdict without regard to his race, color, religious beliefs, national origin, or sex. To emphasize the importance of this requirement, the verdict form contains a certification statement. Each of you should carefully read that statement, then sign your name in the appropriate place in the signature block, if the statement accurately reflects how you reached your verdict.

The certification statement is as follows:

> By signing below, each juror certifies that consideration of the race, color, religious beliefs, national origin, or sex of the defendant was not involved in reaching his or her individual decision, and that the individual juror would have returned the same verdict for or against the defendant on the charged offense regardless of the race, color, religious beliefs, national origin, or sex of the defendant.

Jerry Kang et al., *Implicit Bias in the Courtroom*, 59 UCLA L. REV. 1124, 1183 n.252 (2012). This certification is similar to the one shown to all potential jurors in jury selection, discussed in "Pre-voir dire pledge on bias," above. North Carolina defenders may want to ask judges to consider this innovative method of addressing juror bias. *See generally id.* at 1179–86.

E. Closing Argument

Challenge improper references to race in prosecutor's closing argument. Racially biased closing arguments are prohibited by the constitution. *See supra* § 8.4B, Improper References to Race by the State. "Closing argument may properly be based upon the evidence and the inferences drawn from that evidence" (*State v. Diehl*, 353 N.C. 433, 436 (2001)), and "[p]rosecutors are granted wide latitude in the scope of their [closing] argument." *State v. Zuniga*, 320 N.C. 233, 253 (1987). However, "our courts have consistently refused to tolerate . . . remarks calculated to . . . prejudice the jury." *State v. Jordan*, 149 N.C. App. 838, 842 (2002) (quoting *State v. Smith*, 352 N.C. 531, 560 (2000)); *see also State v Matthews*, 358 NC 102, 111 (2004) (closing argument, "no matter how effective, must . . . be premised on logical deductions, not on appeals to passion or prejudice" (quoting *State v. Jones*, 355 N.C. 117, 135 (2002))). For example, describing a Black defendant and his Black accomplices as "wild dogs or hyenas" hunting on the "African plain" has been found to constitute an improper closing argument. *State v. Sims*, 161 N.C. App. 183 (2003).

The risk of improper appeals to race may be greatest at closing argument. *See* Ryan Patrick Alford, *Appellate Review of Racist Summations: Redeeming the Promise of Searching Analysis*, 11 MICH. J. RACE & LAW 325, 329 (2006) (noting that closing argument "is relatively unencumbered by formal restraints"). Improper summations may activate implicit biases and influence trial outcomes. CHERYL STAATS, ET AL., OHIO STATE KIRWAN INSTITUTE FOR THE STUDY OF RACE AND ETHNICITY, STATE OF THE SCIENCE: IMPLICIT BIAS REVIEW 2013 45 (2013). For example, one study found that, as the number of references to apes by prosecutors during closing arguments increased, "so too did the likelihood of that defendant being sentenced to death." *Id.* at 44–45 (citing Phillip A. Goff et al., *Not Yet Human: Implicit Knowledge, Historical Dehumanization, and Contemporary Consequences,* 94 J. PERSONALITY & SOC. PSYCHOL. 292 (2008)).

Practice note: "It is not impolite to interrupt opposing counsel's summation—it is mandatory to preserve error and stop the prejudice." Ira Mickenberg, Preserving the Record and Making Objections at Trial: A Win-Win Proposition for Client and Lawyer 4 (training material presented at 2005 North Carolina Defender Trial School). Assert both statutory and constitutional grounds for the objection. State on the record that the improper appeal to racial prejudice violates the Sixth, Eighth, and Fourteenth Amendments to the U.S. Constitution, as well as article I, sections 19 and 24 of the N.C. Constitution. If your objection is sustained, immediately ask the judge to instruct the jury to disregard the improper statements. You should also consider whether further remedy is necessary or whether it would only draw further attention to the comments. If you decide that the prejudice resulting from a prosecutor's improper argument was severe and in need of further remedy, you may ask the judge to: admonish the prosecutor to refrain from that line of argument; require the prosecutor to retract the improper argument; repeat the curative instruction during the jury charge; or grant a mistrial. *See State v. Jones*, 355 N.C. 117, 129 (2002) (it is incumbent on trial judge to vigilantly monitor closing arguments, "to intervene as warranted, to entertain objections, and to impose any remedies pertaining to those objections"); *Wilcox v. Glover Motors, Inc.*, 269 N.C. 473

(1967) (listing several methods by which a trial judge, in his or her discretion, may correct an improper argument).

If the judge does not allow you to explain the grounds for your objection during the prosecutor's closing argument, make notes of the improper argument and ask for a hearing outside of the presence of the jury to "flesh out the basis of your objection" after argument and before jury instruction. Staples Hughes, Curbing Prosecutorial Misconduct and Preserving the Record in Closing Argument 5 (Nov. 6, 2008) (training material presented at public defender conference). Additionally, if you have concerns that the prosecutor may make improper arguments, consider filing a motion asking the judge to prohibit such arguments, tailored to the specific facts of the case (e.g., to prohibit the prosecutor from referencing animal imagery). Whether you win or lose the motion, to preserve the issue for appeal you must object during the argument to any improper references to race. *See id.*

Avoiding the invited response doctrine. The invited response doctrine comes into play when defense counsel presents an improper closing argument that is "out of bounds" of zealous advocacy. *U.S. v. Young*, 470 U.S. 1, 11, 13 (1985) (noting that the doctrine applies to cases involving "two improper arguments-two apparent wrongs"). Defenders should be prepared to respond to a prosecutor's assertion that, by raising race during closing argument, defense counsel opened the door to the prosecutor's otherwise improper discussion of race during closing argument. *See, e.g.*, *State v. Oliver*, 309 N.C. 326 (1983) (finding no reversible error where the prosecutor made biblical references during closing argument because defense counsel argued that the New Testament teaches forgiveness and mercy); *see generally* 2 NORTH CAROLINA DEFENDER MANUAL § 33.7D (Invited Response) (2d ed. 2012).

Defense counsel may argue that the invited response doctrine cannot excuse or justify the prosecutor's inappropriate discussion of race where the defendant's references to race were proper. *See, e.g.*, *United States v. Doe*, 903 F.2d 16, 22–23 (D.C. Cir. 1990) (holding that the "[defendant's] questions [about racial bias] on voir dire calculated to obtain a qualified and impartial jury [do not] open the door to introduction of evidence harboring a decided penchant for harm," and reasoning that "[a]n accused cannot be compelled to sacrifice this means to an impartial jury in order to assure the evidentiary fairness of the trial"); *United States ex rel. Haynes v. McKendrick*, 481 F.2d 152, 160–61 (2d Cir. 1973) (where prosecutor failed to identify alleged "blatant racial appeals" by defense counsel, prosecutor's appeals to racial prejudice "went beyond the bounds of propriety, passing those of due process"). *Cf. Darden v. Wainwright*, 477 U.S. 168 (1986) (improper references to defendant as an animal who "shouldn't be out of his cell unless he has a leash on him" did not deprive defendant of a fair trial in part because arguments were invited by defense attorney's argument that, among other things, referred to the alleged actual perpetrator as an "animal"). Any time you make explicit or implicit references to race, you should be prepared to explain the relevance of the evidence and the theory that justifies including it. *See* Stephen A. Saltzburg, *Race: Fair and Unfair Use*, CRIM. JUST., Summer 1999, at 36, 56. You are more likely to neutralize an invited response argument if your closing argument focuses on the evidence presented, warns against the operation of stereotypes and itself avoids stereotypes, and reinforces norms of fairness and equality.

Practice note: When you anticipate that you will raise an issue of race at trial, consider filing a motion in limine to prevent improper references to race in response. Forecast in the motion your proposed evidence and its purpose, and ask for a ruling that it does not open the door to the injection of a harmful or improper discussion of race.

When objecting to improper remarks, link all improper references to race. Convictions might be upheld despite improper appeals to racial prejudice if the references to race are viewed as isolated rather than thematic or widespread. *See, e.g.*, *People v. Ali*, 551 N.Y.S.2d 54, 55 (N.Y. App. Div. 1990) (defendant must show "thematic reference to . . . race" to warrant reversal (citation omitted)); *Thomas v. Gilmore*, 144 F.3d 513 (7th Cir. 1998) (prosecutor's isolated remark, in opening argument of capital trial, that detective would testify that one or both of defendant's prior sexual offenses involved young White women, did not deprive defendant of a fair trial); *Russell v. Collins*, 944 F.2d 202, 204 n.1 (5th Cir. 1991) (habeas petition rejected in part because prosecutor's improper argument concerning race was "isolated"); *see also* Andrea D. Lyon, *Setting the Record Straight: A Proposal for Handling Prosecutorial Appeals to Racial, Ethnic, or Gender Prejudice During Trial*, 6 MICH. J. RACE & L. 319, 326 (2001) (noting this approach by some courts).

Challenges to the improper use of race will be strengthened if you are able to link your objection to other incidents that occurred at trial. For example, if you object to the prosecutor's reference to what "twelve White jurors" should conclude (*see, e.g.*, *State v. Diehl*, 353 N.C. 433 (2001)), you might support your objection by linking it to other objectionable matters involving race, such as the use of peremptory strikes to eliminate eligible Black jurors, disrespectful treatment of a Black witness, or an argument that the Black defendant did not belong in the White neighborhood where the crime occurred. Linking your objection to other improper appeals to racial prejudice in this manner may make your objection more persuasive both at trial and on appeal. *See, e.g.*, *People v. Marshall*, 995 N.E.2d 1045, 1049–50 (Ill. App. Ct. 2013) (conviction reversed where "[t]he prosecutor's [racially inflammatory] remarks were not an isolated event in this case"; instead, "[t]he State's use of race was an egregious and consistent theme throughout the trial").

Address racial dynamics in defendant's closing argument. It is often said that a central task of a defender is to humanize his or her client. "In part this means conveying the multidimensional complexity of human beings who may otherwise be understood by reference to one label or group." Gary Blasi, *Advocacy Against the Stereotype: Lessons from Cognitive Social Psychology*, 49 UCLA L. REV. 1241, 1279 (2002); *see also* Jerry Kang et al., *Implicit Bias in the Courtroom*, 59 UCLA L. REV. 1124, 1185 (2012) (studies have shown that "actively contemplating others' psychological experiences weakens the automatic expression of racial biases" (citing Andrew R. Todd et al., *Perspective Taking Combats Automatic Expressions of Racial Bias*, 100 J. PERSONALITY & SOC. PSYCHOL. 1027 (2011))). Closing argument provides a powerful opportunity to humanize your client and reduce the influence of implicit bias by differentiating him or her from stereotypes and reinforcing antidiscrimination norms. *See supra* § 8.2B, Strategies for Addressing Race.

In addition to other arguments in closing, you may suggest that jurors engage in a race-switching exercise. *See, e.g.,* James McComas & Cynthia Strout, *Combating the Effects of Racial Stereotyping in Criminal Cases*, The CHAMPION, Aug. 1999 at 22, 23; Cynthia Lee, *Making Race Salient: Trayvon Martin and Implicit Bias in a Not Yet Post-Racial Society*, 91 N.C. L. REV. 1555, 1600–01 (2013). While a race-switching instruction from the court is generally preferable, *see supra* "Race-switching instruction" in § 8.6D, Jury Instructions, you may want to present the exercise to the jury whether or not the court has given such an instruction.

Chapter 9
Sentencing

9.1 Scope of Chapter

While North Carolina's sentencing laws regulate the range of sentences a judge may impose for a given offense, judges retain discretion within those ranges, such as the authority to choose, in many instances, between a probationary sentence and imprisonment, a decision with significant consequences for the defendant. The guarantees of equal protection and due process provide protection against arbitrary and discriminatory sentencing decisions. This chapter reviews the requirements for raising a constitutional challenge, recent studies in North Carolina on the question of race in sentencing, and other sources of statistical information that may be useful in addressing the potential influence of race in sentencing. Additionally, in light of the discretion that judges have at sentencing, the chapter provides guidance on sentencing advocacy to help attorneys inform the court about a client's background, identify services and resources to assist clients, and advocate for alternatives to incarceration. This chapter focuses on the sentence imposed based on the charge and conviction. For a discussion of charging and plea decisions, see *supra* Chapter 5, Selective Prosecution: Plea Negotiations and Charging Decisions by Prosecutors.

9.2 Sentencing Policies and Practices

A. History of Race in Sentencing

In the past, racially disparate criminal punishment was the law of the land. Harsher punishment of Black people supported the institution of slavery and, following the abolition of slavery, served to maintain their subjugation. For example, under slavery, rape was a capital offense when committed by a Black man when the victim was White, but not when the victim was Black. JOHN HOPE FRANKLIN, THE FREE NEGRO IN NORTH CAROLINA 1790–1860 98–99 (1943). North Carolina's Black Codes, adopted in 1866, imposed different punishments for people based on their race. ERIC FONER, RECONSTRUCTION: AMERICA'S UNFINISHED REVOLUTION, 1863–77 (1988). *See also McCleskey v. Kemp*, 481 U.S. 279, 330–33 (1987) (Brennan, J., dissenting) (discussing history of race-based criminal punishment in the United States, and arguing that the influence of that history should be considered in assessing modern evidence of racially disparate sentencing practices); Loic Wacquant, *Deadly Symbiosis: Rethinking Race and Imprisonment in Twenty-First-Century America*, BOSTON REV., Apr.–May 2002 (discussing history of slavery, Black codes, Jim Crow laws, urban ghettos, and mass incarceration).

Laws singling out Black people for greater punishment were often defended as necessary in light of perceived Black criminality. For example, when reviewing a statute criminalizing rebellious behavior by "negroes or other slaves," an early North Carolina Supreme Court decision stated that "the more debased or licentious a class of society is, the more rigorous must be the penal rules of restraint." *State v. Tom, a slave*, 13 N.C. 569 (1830); *see also Luke, a slave v. State*, 5 Fla. 185, 192 (1853) (considering racially disparate schemes and determining that "there is an obvious propriety in visiting the[] offences [of African Americans] with more degrading punishment than is inflicted on the white citizens").

Disparate criminal punishment also provided a source of cheap labor through involuntary servitude. Black people who were convicted of minor crimes could in essence be sold on the courthouse steps for inability to pay fines. "The act of 1831, directs that when a free negro or free persons of colour shall be convicted of an offence against the criminal law and sentenced to pay a fine, if it shall appear to the satisfaction of the Court that he is unable to pay the fine imposed, the Court shall direct the Sheriff of the County to hire out the free negro or free person of color so convicted to any person who will pay the fine for his services . . . . It further makes it the duty of the Sheriff . . . publicly, at the door of the Court-house to hire out the convict . . . ." *State v. Manuel*, 20 N.C. 144, 147–48 (1838).

B. Modern Sentencing Schemes and Studies of Potential Sentencing Disparities

Over the last 30 years, most states and the federal government have adopted sentencing guidelines aimed, at least in part, at reducing racial disparities. However, studies have concluded that race continues to influence criminal sentencing. For example, in February 2013, the United States Sentencing Commission released a report concluding that, between 2007 and 2011, federal prison sentences for Black men were nearly 20% longer than those imposed on White men for similar crimes. Mark Hansen, *Black Prisoners are Given Longer Sentences than Whites, Study Says*, ABAJOURNAL.COM (Feb. 15, 2013). This study was cited by U.S. Attorney General Eric Holder in a recent speech citing racial disparities in sentencing and announcing a plan to address them. *See* Eric Holder, United States Attorney General, Remarks at the Annual Meeting of the American Bar Association's House of Delegates (Aug. 12, 2013).

A review of thirty years of sentencing studies concluded that Black and Latino offenders, in both state and federal courts, face "significantly greater odds" of incarceration than similarly situated White offenders and, in some jurisdictions, longer sentences and fewer downward departures from sentencing guidelines. Cassia C. Spohn, *Thirty Years of Sentencing Reform: The Quest for a Racially Neutral Sentencing Process,* CRIM. JUST., July 2000, at 427, 458. Another analysis of data from seventy-one studies reached similar conclusions, finding that African Americans and Latinos are generally sentenced more harshly than Whites, and that these differences are most significant in the context of: (1) drug offenses, (2) the decision whether to imprison a defendant, and (3) other discretionary sentencing decisions. Ojmarrh Mitchell, *A Meta-Analysis of Race and Sentencing Research: Explaining the Inconsistencies*, 21 J. QUANTITATIVE CRIMINOLOGY 439 (2005).

In recent years, researchers examining the influence of race on criminal sentences have refined methods for examining the interaction between race and other factors, such as age, sex, offense type, and income, that may influence sentencing determinations. *See, e.g.,* Traci Schlesinger, *The Failure of Race Neutral Policies: How Mandatory Terms and Sentencing Enhancements Contribute to Mass Racialized Incarceration*, 57 CRIME & DELINQ. 56 (2011). For example, one study of federal sentencing concluded that sentencing disparities between Black and White offenders were most pronounced in the context of drug trafficking offenses; on average, controlling for relevant factors, Black defendants convicted of such offenses received sentences 10.5 months longer than White defendants. David B. Mustard, *Racial, Ethnic, and Gender Disparities in Sentencing: Evidence from the Federal Courts*, 44 J. L. & ECON. 285, 304 (2001). Another study of sentencing data in Pennsylvania found that nonwhite offenders are most likely to face harsher punishment when they are young, male, and unemployed. *See, e.g.*, Darrell Steffensmeier et al., *The Interaction of Race, Gender, and Age in Criminal Sentencing: The Punishment Cost of Being Young, Black, and Male*, 36 CRIMINOLOGY 763 (1998). Researchers have referred to this as "the punishment cost of being young, black, and male." *Id.*

Extensive research has been conducted about sentencing in capital cases. Studies have concluded that the race of the victim results in disparities in the imposition of capital punishment. In the Baldus study reviewed by the U.S. Supreme Court in *McCleskey v. Kemp*, 481 U.S. 279 (1987), for example, researchers found that people convicted in Georgia of murdering White victims were approximately four times as likely to receive a death sentence as those convicted of murdering Black people. In North Carolina, a recent study examining approximately 15,000 homicides committed in the state between 1980 and 2007 concluded that the odds of a death sentence for those accused of killing White victims are around three times higher than for those accused of killing Black victims. Michael L. Radelet & Glenn L. Pierce, *Race and Death Sentencing in North Carolina: 1980–2007*, 89 N.C. L. REV. 2119, 2120 (2011); *see also* Seth Kotch & Robert P. Mosteller, *The Racial Justice Act and the Long Struggle with Race and the Death Penalty in North Carolina*, 88 N.C. L. REV. 2031, 2097–2100 (2010) (discussing continuing predominance of White victims in North Carolina death sentences).

Few studies have examined whether racial disparities exist in sentencing in non-capital cases in North Carolina. A study conducted by the North Carolina Sentencing and Policy Advisory Commission in 2002 found that while extralegal factors such as age, type of defense, judicial division, mode of disposition, and sex influenced sentencing determinations, the offender's race did not have an identifiable effect on sentencing. NORTH CAROLINA SENTENCING AND POLICY ADVISORY COMMISSION, SENTENCING PRACTICES UNDER NORTH CAROLINA'S STRUCTURED SENTENCING LAWS (2002) (noting, however, that eligible White offenders were slightly less likely to be convicted as habitual felons than non-white offenders). The study did not examine the possible link between race and socioeconomic indicators considered by criminal justice decision-makers, including "family situation and community ties, education and income, ability to make restitution, and general attitude and demeanor." *Id.* at 70. For this reason, the authors concluded that the influence of socioeconomic factors, "their impact on justice and their possible link with race are worth further exploration." *Id.*

A later student project focused on sentences of imprisonment and found that nonwhite offenders were more likely than White offenders to be sentenced to terms of imprisonment for felony convictions in the years 2008–09. Michelle L. Hall, Disparity under Structured Sentencing in North Carolina: Do Similarly Situated Offenders Receive Different Outcomes Based on Legally Irrelevant Factors? (Spring 2011) (unpublished UNC School of Government MPA Thesis). Researchers studying sentencing outcomes in an administrative drug court in a large, urban North Carolina jurisdiction (not named in the study's published results) found racial disparities in the sentencing of felony drug offenders convicted in the year 2000. White offenders received less severe punishment than both Black and Hispanic offenders, with Hispanic offenders receiving the most severe punishments. Pauline K. Brennan & Cassia Spohn, *Race/Ethnicity and Sentencing Outcomes Among Drug Offenders in North Carolina*, 24 J. CONTEMP. CRIM. JUST. 371 (2008).

The North Carolina Sentencing and Policy Advisory Commission also publishes annual statistics regarding felony and misdemeanor convictions; however, only the conviction data is disaggregated by race, not the sentencing data. *See* North Carolina Sentencing and Policy Advisory Commission, *Structured Sentencing Statistical Report for Felonies and Misdemeanors-Fiscal Year 2011/12 (July 1, 2011 - June 30, 2012)*, 9 Fig. D (2013) (showing that, in FY 2011/2012, 50% of people convicted of felonies were Black, 44% were White, 3% were Hispanic, 2% were Native American, and 1% were Other/Unknown).

C. Causes of Potential Sentencing Disparities

Potential for racially disparate effects from race-neutral policies. Disparities in sentencing may occur from sentencing laws and policies that, while facially race-neutral, have disparate effects. *See, e.g.,* Traci Schlesinger, *The Failure of Race Neutral Policies: How Mandatory Terms and Sentencing Enhancements Contribute to Mass Racialized Incarceration*, 57 CRIME & DELINQ. 56 (2011). The most familiar example of this phenomenon is the 100:1 crack/cocaine drug quantity differential established by Congress in 1986. Before the ratio was modified to 18:1 in 2010, the sale of 5 grams of crack triggered a mandatory minimum prison term of five years, while a sale of 500 grams of powder cocaine triggered the same term. This law had a disproportionate impact on Black people, who were vastly overrepresented among those convicted of crack-cocaine violations. The U.S. Sentencing Commission reported that 88.3% of those convicted of crack offenses in federal courts in 1994 were Black. *See* U.S. SENTENCING COMMISSION, SPECIAL REPORT TO CONGRESS: COCAINE AND FEDERAL SENTENCING POLICY Ch. 7 (1995).

Laws that increase penalties for drug activity conducted within a school zone have also been found to produce racial disparities. The Sentencing Project's Marc Mauer posits that these effects are largely a result of housing patterns. "Since urban areas are much more densely populated than rural or suburban areas, it is more likely that any given drug offense will take place within a school zone district. And since persons of color disproportionately reside in urban areas, a drug offense committed by an African American or Latino person will be more likely to incur these enhanced penalties." Marc Mauer, *Addressing Racial Disparities in Incarceration*, 91 PRISON J. 87S, 95S (2011). A recent review of criminal sentencing in New Jersey discovered that 96% of offenders incarcerated for violations of school zone laws were African American or Latino. *Id.* As a result of this discovery, the New Jersey legislature eliminated the mandatory sentencing enhancement for school zone violations in 2010. *Id.*

Additionally, laws that increase penalties based on an offender's prior record may result in greater punishment for racial minorities, who are more likely to have prior convictions. In North Carolina, African Americans are 2.46 times more likely than Whites to be incarcerated as habitual felons. *See, e.g.*, *North Carolina Advocates for Justice: Task Force on Racial and Ethnic Bias Executive Summary*, NCAJ.COM (African Americans represent 21.5% of the population of North Carolina but 69.6% of those incarcerated as habitual felons) (last visited Sept. 18, 2014).

Potential for bias. Studies have shown that bias tends to arise when actors are making discretionary decisions. *See generally* TONY FABELO ET AL., BREAKING SCHOOLS' RULES, A STATEWIDE STUDY OF HOW SCHOOL DISCIPLINE RELATES TO STUDENTS' SUCCESS AND JUVENILE JUSTICE INVOLVEMENT (Council for State Gov'ts Justice Ctr. 2011) (finding that racial disparities in school discipline were most pronounced when disciplinary action was discretionary: African American students had a 31 percent higher likelihood of a school discretionary action as compared to otherwise identical White and Hispanic students); FRANK BAUMGARTNER & DEREK EPP, NORTH CAROLINA TRAFFIC STOP ANALYSIS (2012) (observing in an analysis of over 13 million North Carolina traffic stops that "disparities appear greatest when the level of officer discretion is highest—seat belts, vehicle equipment, and vehicle regulatory issues").

In evaluating jury sentencing in capital cases, the U.S. Supreme Court has observed that the discretion afforded jurors provides "a unique opportunity for racial prejudice to operate but remain undetected." *Turner v. Murray*, 476 U.S. 28, 35 (1986). More broadly, some researchers have concluded that biases may cause decision-makers unwittingly to ignore the positive aspects of a non-White person's employment record, while crediting the same attributes of a White person's employment record. *See* GEOFFREY BEATTIE, OUR RACIST HEART? AN EXPLORATION OF UNCONSCIOUS PREJUDICE IN EVERYDAY LIFE 241 (2013); *see also* Jennifer L. Eberhardt et al., *Seeing Black: Race, Crime, and Visual Processing,* 87 J. PERSONALITY & SOC. PSYCH. 876 (2004).

Researchers examining the influence of biases on sentencing decisions have found that facial features associated with Black people (sometimes referred to as "Afrocentric" features) activate negative associations and stereotypes that lead to longer sentences. One study found that defendants whose facial features were more Afrocentric received longer sentences than similarly situated offenders with less Afrocentric features. Irene V. Blair et al., *The Influence of Afrocentric Facial Features in Criminal Sentencing*, 15 PSYCH. SCI. 674 (2004). Researchers examining death-eligible cases from 1979–99 in Philadelphia concluded that, in capital cases involving Black defendants and White victims, defendants with more Afrocentric facial features were more likely to be sentenced to death than those with less Afrocentric ones. Jennifer L. Eberhardt et al., *Looking Deathworthy: Perceived Stereotypicality of Black Defendants Predicts Capital-Sentencing Outcomes*, 17 PSYCHOL. SCI. 383 (2006).

Poverty. Black and Latino people are more likely to live in poverty, which can negatively affect them at the sentencing phase in various ways. *See infra* § 9.4C, Pretrial Strategies. For example, under the impaired driving sentencing scheme, Level One and Level Two offenders can reduce or avoid otherwise mandatory periods of imprisonment if they can verify abstinence from alcohol using Continuous Alcohol Monitoring, a costly device for which there is not state funding. G.S. 20-179(g), (h).

D. Impact of Incarceration Rates

Nationwide, it is estimated that nearly one out of three Black men in their twenties is currently under correctional control, either in jail, prison, or under a community supervision program such as probation or parole. Equal Justice Initiative, *Our Work: Race and Poverty*, EJI.ORG (last visited Sept. 18, 2014). In North Carolina in 2012, Black inmates comprised 57% of the prison population, more than double their representation in the general population. North Carolina Department of Public Safety, *Prison Statistics Fact Card, 2012*, DOC.STATE.NC.US (last visited Sept. 18, 2014); The Henry J. Kaiser Family Foundation, *Population Distribution by Race/Ethnicity*, KFF.ORG (last visited Sept. 18, 2014) (reporting that in 2012 Black people comprised 21% of the general population of North Carolina). Disparities in sentencing may be a contributing factor. *See* Traci Schlesinger, *The Cumulative Effects of Racial Disparities in Criminal Processing*, THE ADVOCATE, May 2008, at 22 (racial disparities may influence various stages of a criminal proceeding and produce a cumulative effect on outcomes, making it difficult to isolate the influence of sentencing decisions); *see also U.S. v. Leviner*, 31 F. Supp. 2d 23 (D. Mass. 1998) (recognizing the possible influence of racially disparate policing practices on defendant's criminal history and ultimate sentence).

Incarceration often triggers consequences such as loss of employment, housing, or child custody. Black children are far more likely than other children to have an incarcerated parent: one in nine Black children has an incarcerated parent, compared to one in 28 Latino children and one in 57 White children. BRUCE WESTERN & BECKY PETTIT, THE PEW CHARITABLE TRUSTS, COLLATERAL COSTS: INCARCERATION'S EFFECT ON ECONOMIC MOBILITY 4 (2010); *see also* Rebecca Ballard DiLoreto, *Disparate Impact: Racial Bias in the Sentencing and Plea Bargaining Process*, THE ADVOCATE, May 2008, at 15 (discussing impact on children and non-incarcerated parent trying to raise children alone).

The psychological effects of higher imprisonment rates on communities of color are difficult to quantify. One scholar has observed that "[w]hole generations have already accepted prison as the norm. This is the destructive effect of mass incarceration on community consciousness and personal aspirations." TANYA E. COKE, CRIMINAL JUSTICE IN THE 21ST CENTURY: ELIMINATING RACIAL AND ETHNIC DISPARITIES IN THE CRIMINAL JUSTICE SYSTEM 22 (2012) (quoting Dr. Divine Pryor, Executive Director of the NuLeadership Center for Urban Solutions).

9.3 Constitutional Limits

The constitution forbids the consideration of race in the determination of criminal punishment, and Congress has prohibited explicit race-based punishment since the passage of the Civil Rights Act of 1866. Civil Rights Act of 1866, Ch. 31, § 1, 14 Stat. 27-30 (1866). As one court observed, differential punishment based on an improper factor such as race "obviously would be unconstitutional." *U.S. v. Gomez*, 797 F.2d 417, 419 (7th Cir. 1986). In considering challenges to sentences based on unlawful consideration of race, ethnicity, national origin, or immigration status, some courts have applied an equal protection framework, while others have focused on due process guarantees. A number of opinions do not specify the constitutional provision protecting defendants against race-based punishment, but nevertheless recognize that such punishment is constitutionally prohibited. As the following discussion suggests, any time a defendant's sentence appears to have been influenced by race, defendants should raise challenges to the sentence based on both equal protection and due process grounds.

A. Equal Protection

General principles. Criminal sentences based on a defendant's race violate state and federal guarantees of equal protection. U.S. CONST. amend. XIV; N.C. CONST. art. I., § 19; *U.S. v. Smart*, 518 F.3d 800, 804 n.1 (8th Cir. 2008) (a sentence based on race "would violate the Equal Protection Clause of the Fourteenth Amendment, which makes the specific characteristic of race an impermissible government consideration in the absence of compelling reasons to the contrary"); *see also U.S. v. Gomez*, 797 F.2d 417, 419 (7th Cir. 1986) (differential treatment at sentencing based on race, nationality, or immigration status would violate due process and equal protection guarantees). A sentencing decision will violate equal protection when similarly situated defendants are subjected to disparate treatment based on race; any proffered justification for such disparate treatment must meet strict scrutiny. *U.S. v. Roberts*, 915 F.2d 889 (4th Cir. 1990).

No North Carolina appellate decisions have addressed race-based equal protection challenges to criminal sentences, but the courts have provided a framework for such a challenge in opinions reviewing other types of equal protection challenges to criminal sentences. In an early ruling based on both former N.C. Constitution article I, section 7 (which is substantially similar to current article I, section 32) and the Fourteenth Amendment to the U.S. Constitution, the North Carolina Supreme Court declared that "every valid enactment of a general law applicable to the whole state shall operate uniformly upon persons and property, giving to all under like circumstances equal protection and security, and neither laying burdens nor conferring privileges upon any person that are not laid or conferred upon others under the same circumstances or conditions." *State v. Fowler*, 193 N.C. 290, 292 (1927) (statute immunizing residents of five counties from prison sentence applicable to residents in all other counties violated equal protection). In a case addressing an equal protection challenge to punishment without parole eligibility, the North Carolina Supreme Court explained that "equal protection of the laws is not denied by a statute prescribing the punishment to be inflicted on a person convicted of a crime, unless it prescribes different punishments for the same acts committed under the same circumstances by persons in like situations." *State v. Dunlap*, 298 N.C. 725, 735–36 (1979) (quoting *State v. Benton*, 276 N.C. 641, 660 (1970)).

More recently, the North Carolina Court of Appeals rejected an equal protection challenge by a defendant claiming that he was sentenced differently from other defendants who, like him, had no aggravating or mitigating factors present. *State v. Streeter*, 146 N.C. App. 594, 599 (2001). However, the defendant in *Streeter* did not claim that his sentence was based on an unconstitutional factor such as race. In an earlier case addressing an equal protection challenge to a criminal sentence, the North Carolina Supreme Court held that the mere fact that a statute grants the trial court wide discretion in determining a criminal sentence is not a violation of equal protection. *See State v.*

Jenkins, 292 N.C. 179, 191 (1977). As in *Streeter*, the defendant in *Jenkins* did not allege that the trial judge improperly considered race in determining his criminal sentence.

In other jurisdictions, constitutional claims based at least in part on the Equal Protection Clause have succeeded where:

- A judge, in sentencing a defendant from Guinea for heroin trafficking, explained that the sentence was designed in part to send a message to the people of the defendant's background that heroin trafficking isn't tolerated in the United States. The Court of Appeals for the Second Circuit concluded that, even if the judge was not biased, the appearance of a sentence based on race or national origin was unlawful. *U.S. v. Kaba*, 480 F.3d 152 (2d Cir. 2007).
- In sentencing a Chinese-born Canadian citizen, the judge asserted that "[w]e have enough home-grown criminals in the United States without importing them," and expressed hope that the defendant's sentence would send a message to the "Asiatic community . . . that we don't permit dealing in heroin . . . and if people want to come to the United States they had better abide by our laws." *U.S. v. Leung*, 40 F.3d 577, 585 (2d Cir. 1994). The appellate court observed that "[a] defendant's race or nationality may play no adverse role in the administration of justice, including at sentencing," and held that, while it did not believe that the judge was biased against the defendant because of her ethnic origin, "even the appearance that the sentence reflects a defendant's race or nationality will ordinarily require a remand for resentencing." *Id.* at 586.
- A judge based his sentence of a drug trafficker, at least in part, on the defendant's country of origin, Columbia. His statements during two different sentencing hearings reflected his belief that the defendant deserved greater punishment because of his country of origin, which he described as "the total scourge of this country right now, and I am not going to tolerate it, and I want the message to go to Colombia that we are not going to accept this kind of thing." The defense attorney objected at sentencing, noting that the judge had sentenced an "Anglo" codefendant to seven years imprisonment while her Columbian client was sentenced to twelve years imprisonment, to which the judge replied in part, "importantly, he was not from a source country, and I want people in Colombia to know it is not going to be tolerated." *U.S. v. Borrero-Isaza*, 887 F.2d 1349 (9th Cir. 1989).
- A judge stated, in reference to the Columbian defendants before him for sentencing, "[t]hey don't have too much regard for Judges [in Columbia]" and "they should have stayed where they were. Nobody told them to come here." *U.S. v. Edwardo-Franco*, 885 F.2d 1002, 1005 (2d Cir. 1989). In vacating the sentence, the appellate court concluded that the defendant's "plaintive request that she be sentenced 'as for my person, not for my nationality' mirrors what would be the objective reaction of anyone familiar with the above-quoted comments of the district court, namely that ethnic prejudice somehow had infected the judicial process in the instant case." *Id.*
- A judge, "who is Caucasian, use[d] words such as 'ghetto,' 'jungle,' 'animals,' and 'people like Mr. Jackson' who come 'from the city' in describing an African-American defendant," and thereby "called into question, whether his comments might

also have constituted racial bias, or the appearance of racial bias." *Jackson v. State*, 772 A.2d 273, 278 (Md. 2001). Maryland's highest court vacated the defendant's sentence and remanded the case for resentencing, concluding that "matters of race and matters of a defendant's place of residence or origins are inappropriate sentencing considerations." *Id.* at 279.

These cases suggest the following bases for equal protection challenges to sentences:

Defendant received more punitive sentence than co-defendant based on race. An equal protection challenge may lie when a non-white defendant receives a harsher sentence than a White codefendant, especially where the defendants are similarly situated in terms of culpability, prior record level, and other factors. *See, e.g., U.S. v. Borrero-Isaza*, 887 F.2d 1349 (9th Cir. 1989).

Before the sentencing hearing, defense counsel may present a memorandum detailing any disparate treatment the defendant experienced at an earlier stage in the case or in past cases. *See, e.g., U.S. v. Leviner*, 31 F. Supp. 2d 23 (D. Mass. 1998) (judge granted downward departure to sentencing range based on the possible impact of racial profiling on defendant's criminal history). For example, if you are representing a Black defendant detained pretrial, and a similarly situated White codefendant was released pretrial and consequently had the opportunity to find and secure employment, thereby improving his position at sentencing, you may wish to bring this disparate treatment to the court's attention and request that the sentencing judge correct for it to avoid violating equal protection guarantees. Due process grounds should also be raised. *See infra* § 9.3B, Due Process.

Defendant punished pursuant to statute that produces racial disparities. Courts have generally rejected facial challenges to race-neutral statutes that produce racially disparate sentences. *See, e.g., U.S. v. Rogers*, 409 Fed. Appx. 607, 612 (4th Cir. 2010) (unpublished) ("We have repeatedly rejected claims that the crack-to-powder ratio violates either the Equal Protection Clause or a defendant's due process rights."). However, the U.S. Supreme Court has held that the unwarranted disparities produced by the crack-cocaine ratio constitute a proper consideration at sentencing and a justifiable basis for a downward departure from federal sentencing guidelines. *See Spears v. United States*, 555 U.S. 261 (2009) (per curiam); *Kimbrough v. United States*, 552 U.S. 85 (2007). In a sentencing memorandum, or orally during a sentencing hearing, a defendant may argue that, as applied, statutory schemes that produce racially disparate outcomes violate state and federal guarantees of equal protection. Counsel may ask, in the alternative, that the court correct for disparities caused by the statutes by imposing a sentence in the mitigated range. *See also* G.S. 15A-1340.13(g) (authorizing extraordinary mitigation in some circumstances).

Judge states or implies that race was a factor at sentencing. If the trial judge refers to the race of the defendant, the race of the victim, or makes other statements suggesting that race played a role in the sentencing determination, the defendant should raise an equal protection claim challenging the sentencing process and the sentence imposed. *See,* *e.g.*, *People v. Wardell,* 595 N.E.2d 1148, 1155 (Ill. App. Ct. 1992) (remanding for new sentencing hearing where trial judge implied that the cross-racial nature of the sexual offense played a role in his sentencing determination). This circumstance should also be challenged on due process grounds. *See infra* § 9.3B, Due Process.

Defendant denied equal protection based on inequitable availability of alternatives to incarceration. An equal protection claim may arise if, for example, English-speaking defendants can be sentenced to a residential treatment facility but there is no such facility available for Spanish-speaking defendants. *See, e.g.,* Jamie Markham, New Substance Abuse Treatment Center for Female Probationers, N.C. CRIM. L., UNC SCH. OF GOV'T BLOG (March 11, 2010) (noting that, before the establishment of Black Mountain Residential Substance Abuse Treatment Center for Women, some wondered if the availability of a residential treatment facility for men but not for women violated equal protection).

B. Due Process

The substantive and procedural due process requirements of the Fourteenth Amendment, along with the parallel provisions of the North Carolina Constitution, require that all defendants have an "'absolute right to a fair trial before an *impartial judge* and unprejudiced jury.'" *State v. Wright*, 172 N.C. App. 464, 468–71 (2005) (emphasis in original) (quoting *State v. Miller,* 288 N.C. 582, 598 (1975)), *aff'd per curiam*, 360 N.C. 80 (2005); *In re Murchison*, 349 U.S. 133, 136 (1955). This includes the right to criminal proceedings untainted by racial bias. *See Batson v. Kentucky*, 476 U.S. 79 (1986) (Marshall, J., concurring).

Due process guarantees have specifically been held applicable to sentencing proceedings. *U.S. v Onwuemene*, 933 F.2d 650 (8th Cir. 1991) (sentence based on race, national origin, or alienage violates due process); *People v. Wardell,* 595 N.E.2d 1148, 1155 (Ill. App. Ct. 1992) (in cross-racial rape case, appellate court vacated defendant's sentence on due process grounds where "defendants' race was considered by the judge when he imposed these long, consecutive sentences[;] [i]f it is on his tongue, it most assuredly must be on his mind").

Even if a judge's statements regarding a defendant's race, ethnicity, or national origin do not establish that the defendant's sentence was based on one of these impermissible factors, due process may be violated on the ground that such statements do not satisfy "the appearance of justice." *Martinez v. State*, 961 P.2d 143, 145 (Nev. 1998) (vacating and remanding for resentencing where trial judge observed at sentencing, "[t]here's something that heightens the nature of an offense when people come from foreign lands to do offenses in another land"). Defendants should raise a due process challenge when there are indications that the judge is considering the defendant's race, ethnicity, immigration status, or national origin in making the sentencing determination. *See also supra* § 9.3A, Equal Protection.

C. Prohibitions Against Cruel and/or Unusual Punishment

The Eighth Amendment to the United States Constitution provides that "[e]xcessive bail shall not be required, nor excessive fines imposed, nor cruel and unusual punishments inflicted." Similarly, article I, section 27 of the North Carolina Constitution prohibits cruel or unusual punishment. North Carolina courts have "analyzed cruel and/or unusual punishment claims by criminal defendants the same under both the federal and state Constitutions." *State v. Green*, 348 N.C. 588, 603 (1998).

Both state and federal constitutional provisions guarantee proportionality in sentencing. The U.S. Supreme Court has held that the right to proportionality in sentencing is violated only when a comparison between the offense gravity and the sentence severity reveals "gross disproportionality." In cases where a court finds gross disproportionality, the court must review both sentences received within the state for more and less serious crimes, and sentences received in other states for the same crime. *Solem v. Helm*, 463 U.S. 277 (1983); *State v. Hensley*, 156 N.C. App. 634, 639 (2003). "Only in exceedingly unusual non-capital cases will the sentences imposed be so grossly disproportionate as to violate the Eighth Amendment's proscription of cruel and unusual punishment." *State v. Ysaguire*, 309 N.C. 780, 786 (1983); *State v. LaPlanche*, 349 N.C. 279, 284 (1998).

Drug trafficking penalties and those based on an offender's status as a habitual felon have been the subject of Eighth Amendment proportionality challenges in North Carolina. To date, neither of these challenges has succeeded on appeal. *See, e.g., State v. Ford*, 71 N.C. App. 748 (1984) (punishment of 35 years imprisonment and $200,000 fine not disproportionate to the crime of possessing more than 10,000 pounds of marijuana); *State v. Smith*, 112 N.C. App. 512, 514–15 (1993) (sentence enhancement based on habitual felon status does not constitute cruel and unusual punishment under the Eighth Amendment); *accord State v. Todd,* 313 N.C. 110, 117–19 (1985); *State v. McDonald,* 165 N.C. App. 237, 241–42 (2004); *State v. Clifton,* 158 N.C. App. 88, 95–96 (2003); *State v. Hensley,* 156 N.C. App. 634, 638–39 (2003).

While not a race-based challenge, a proportionality challenge may be a viable option for challenging a "grossly disproportionate" sentence in an extreme case, and may have a greater chance of success when raised alongside an equal protection or due process claim. For example, in two superior court cases involving Black defendants charged with drug possession as habitual felons, trial court judges have found that the prohibition against cruel and unusual punishment as well as the guarantees of due process and equal protection prohibited the imposition of the sentence mandated by the habitual felon statute. *See State v. Griffin*, 215 N.C. App. 391 (2011) (unpublished) (finding appellate court had no jurisdiction to hear State's appeal of granting of motion for appropriate relief in defendant's favor); *State v. Starkey*, 177 N.C. App. 264 (2006) (same). In both cases, the trial court imposed the sentence mandated by the habitual felon statute before, sua sponte, entering an order granting its own motion for appropriate relief. In the *Starkey* case, the judge explained that sentencing a defendant with no prior crimes involving drugs or violence to 70 to 93 months for possession of a tenth a gram of cocaine, the smallest quantity measurable by the State's lab, shocked the conscience: "It's unfair. It's inequitable, and it's wrong." *See* Order and Excerpt of Sentencing Transcript in the Race Materials Bank at www.ncids.org (select "Training and Resources") (trial judge noted that defendant's punishment was as harsh as it would have been had his substantive offense been trafficking in 399 grams of cocaine, terrorism by contaminating a public water supply, armed robbery, assault with a deadly weapon with intent to kill inflicting serious injury, malicious castration, second degree rape, voluntary manslaughter, or first degree kidnapping).

D. Raising Constitutional Challenges

The defendant may raise constitutional challenges in a sentencing memorandum or during a sentencing hearing. Constitutional challenges to a sentence that has been imposed also may be raised in a motion for appropriate relief or on appeal. *State v. Curmon,* 171 N.C. App. 697 (2005).

Generally, "constitutional matters that are not raised and passed upon at trial will not be reviewed for the first time on appeal." *State v. Garcia,* 358 N.C. 382, 410 (2004) (quotation omitted). However, a defendant does not appear to waive his right to object to the constitutionality of his sentence if the constitutional challenge is not raised at the trial level. The North Carolina Court of Appeals stated in *State v. Curmon* that "[a]n error at sentencing is not considered an error at trial for the purpose of Rule 10(b)(1) [of the N.C. Rules of Appellate Procedure]." 171 N.C. App. 697, 703 (citing *State v. Hargett,* 157 N.C. App. 90, 93 (2003)). This approach reflects the practical difficulties that may be involved in objecting to the conduct of the judge at the time of sentencing. *See U.S. v. Kaba*, 480 F.3d 152, 158 (2d Cir. 2007) (concluding that defendant did not waive her argument on appeal because she was "understandably reluctant to suggest to a judge that an ambiguous remark reveals bias just as the judge is about to select a sentence" (quotation omitted)).

Nevertheless, it is important that the defense attorney object if race appears to influence a sentencing determination, both to allow the judge an opportunity to take the objection into consideration and to ensure the issue is preserved for appeal. Defense attorneys may feel reluctant to raise challenges to the improper influence of race at sentencing to avoid appearing to level a charge of racism against the judge. By couching objections in constitutional form, however, counsel may alert the judge to objectionable considerations without jeopardizing the client's interests. For example, where a judge makes a racial comment in sentencing, defense counsel may object that the statement introduced an unconstitutional factor into the sentencing hearing and determination.

9.4 Effective Sentencing Advocacy

The rules of evidence do not apply to sentencing hearings—any evidence that a court deems to have probative value may be received, including evidence of racial disparities. N.C. R. EVID. 1101(b)(3). Relevant information may include the client's cultural background; his or her experience with prejudice, racial profiling, or other forms of disadvantage; statistics reflecting racial disparities in the justice system; and social science evidence on the influence of implicit bias. In short, the door is open at sentencing in a way that it may not be at trial for defenders to place the full context of a client's life experience before the court and advocate for a just result. This section is not a comprehensive treatment of sentencing advocacy, but instead an outline of possibilities.

A. Early Advocacy

Sentencing advocacy begins at the outset of representation and lasts until the conclusion of your client's case. Rebecca Ballard DiLoreto, *Disparate Impact: Racial Bias in the Sentencing and Plea Bargaining Process*, THE ADVOCATE, May 2008, at 15. In the initial client interview, counsel should begin to seek information not only about the charged offense, but also about the client's life, including his or her immigration status, children, public benefits, experiences with the police, cultural background, family obligations, mental health, substance abuse history, employment, housing, and educational background. Robin Steinberg, *Addressing Racial Disparity in the Criminal Justice System Through Holistic Defense*, THE CHAMPION, July 2013, at 51, 52; *see also* The Bronx Defenders Arraignment Checklist, BRONXDEFENDERS.ORG (last visited Sept. 19, 2014). Such a "holistic" approach to advocacy may help to reduce potential racial disparities at sentencing and other stages of the case, and may have additional benefits, including:

1. An understanding of your client's life will strengthen your relationship with your client, particularly if he or she differs from you in terms of racial, ethnic, cultural, or socioeconomic background.

2. An early understanding of your client's background, community, and individual challenges and opportunities will strengthen your argument for pretrial release. Pretrial release may decrease the chances that your client will receive a sentence of incarceration. *See supra* Chapter 4, Pretrial Release.

3. Early understanding of your client's struggles, needs, and assets provides an opportunity to help the client get engaged in beneficial activities, employment, or programs that may serve as mitigating factors in plea negotiations and at the sentencing hearing. *See* James Tibensky, *What a Sentencing Advocate Can Do in a Non-Capital Case*, CORNERSTONE, Fall 2004, at 9.

4. Implicit bias research indicates that bias is most pronounced when individuals are unwilling to consider the possibility that they may be influenced by bias. In contrast, humility about the possible influence of bias causes people to think more carefully and deliberately and may minimize the influence of bias. *See generally* Emily Pronin, *Perception and Misperception of Bias in Human Judgment*, 11 TRENDS COGNITIVE SCI. 37 (2007). In the context of indigent representation, this research suggests that listening carefully and making an effort to avoid prejudgments about the conditions of your client's life will minimize the risk that you will make race-based assumptions about his or her circumstances.

B. Data and Record Collection

Data collection. Defense attorneys can benefit from gathering data concerning the individuals and communities they serve. Defender offices may rely on interns, volunteers, paralegals, or investigators to collect the following information.

1. **Sentencing patterns in your district.** The biographical data collected on intake forms, including the client's charges, prior record level, and racial and ethnic identity, may be entered into a database with the client's identity removed, so that defense counsel can track outcomes received by various categories of clients. For example, during plea negotiations, defense counsel may present the prosecutor with any data showing that Black defendants disproportionately received active sentences for the charge in question over the previous year in comparison with White defendants at the same prior record level. Sentences may be influenced by decisions that occur at earlier stages of the criminal justice process; therefore, it is important to record relevant data from all stages of a case, including the original charges, plea offers, plea entered, and sentences as well as any presentencing report or sentencing plan prepared before sentencing. *See infra* "Presentence reports and sentencing plans" in § 9.4E, Sentencing Hearing Advocacy.

2. **Favorable outcomes.** The office may maintain a file containing favorable plea offers and sentences that clients have received, including departures from presumptive ranges, deferred prosecutions, opportunities to receive substantial assistance departures pursuant to G.S. 90-95(h)(5), and charge dismissals, to use in plea negotiations and sentencing hearings. This data should include the race and ethnic background of the clients and the identity of the prosecutors and judges involved. The paralegal, administrative assistant, intern, or investigator tasked with collecting such information should make note of cases in which prosecutors declined to habitualize clients or declined to pursue trafficking charges.

3. **Sentencing patterns of judges.** Defenders may collect data on the sentencing patterns of judges, including which judges have found extraordinary mitigation pursuant to G.S. 15A-1340.13(g), which judges have a record of granting community-based sentences, and which judges have been receptive to arguments about implicit biases or sentencing disparities.

4. **Statewide averages.** In addition to collecting data, defenders may make use of available data sources reflecting the racial composition of those convicted of various offenses and the average sentences received for the charges your client faces. The North Carolina Sentencing and Policy Advisory Commission prepares annual reports reflecting the type of and length of sentences imposed for all convictions. *See* North Carolina Sentencing and Policy Advisory Commission, *Structured Sentencing Statistical Report for Felonies and Misdemeanors*, NCCOURTS.ORG (last visited Sept. 19, 2014); *see also* Jamie Markham, *Sentencing Commission Annual Statistical Report*, N.C. CRIM. L., UNC SCHOOL OF GOV'T BLOG (Sept. 19, 2013) (discussing the content and utility of the Commission's annual reports). Another useful compilation

of North Carolina criminal justice data disaggregated by race can be found at the North Carolina Advocates for Justice Racial Justice Task Force page. For example, if your client is facing marijuana charges in Durham County, you may consider obtaining statistics of overall enforcement of marijuana laws in Durham County. *See, e.g.*, Ian Mance, Southern Coalition for Social Justice, *Durham Police Department Stop-and-Search Data* (on file with authors) (reporting that, in Durham, "African-Americans . . . are approximately four times as likely as whites to be arrested on a misdemeanor marijuana possession charge, despite strong evidence that both whites and blacks use the drug at roughly the same rate (11.7% v. 12.7%)"). While some of the data sources listed above reflect arrest and/or conviction rates rather than sentencing patterns, the information may be useful to reference in plea negotiations and at sentencing hearings.

5. **"School-to-prison pipeline."** You may consider collecting information about whether Black students are more likely to have school disciplinary problems referred to court, which leads to the development of criminal records at a young age. ASHLEY M. NELLIS, JUVENILE JUSTICE EVALUATION CENTER, SEVEN STEPS TO DEVELOP AND EVALUATE STRATEGIES TO REDUCE DISPROPORTIONATE MINORITY CONTACT (DMC) 16 (2005). If your client's criminal history was a result of a "school to prison pipeline" phenomenon, counsel can share the client's experience with the prosecutor along with data reflecting such disparities. *See, e.g.*, Matt Cregor & Damon Hewitt, *Dismantling the School-to-Prison Pipeline: A Survey from the Field*, POVERTY AND RACE (Poverty & Race Research Action Council, Washington D.C.), Jan.–Feb. 2011, at 5; SUSAN MCCARTER & JASON BARNETT, THE SCHOOL-TO-PRISON PIPELINE: IMPLICATIONS FOR NORTH CAROLINA SCHOOLS AND STUDENTS 15 (2013) (according to the N.C. Department of Public Safety, Division of Juvenile Justice, for students aged 15 and younger, "there were a total of 16,000 school-based delinquency complaints filed in 2011 and of this total, 46.2% of the complaints were filed against African-American students," who made up 26.8% of the student population).

The recently formed North Carolina Public Defender Committee on Racial Equity (NC PDCORE) may be able to assist in creating a standardized collection process for aggregating and analyzing this data for public defender offices. *See* NC PDCORE Website, NCIDS.COM (last visited Sept. 19, 2014).

Record collection. It is critical to gather records relevant to potential mitigating factors, any alleged aggravating factors, and the sentence proposed. When a defense attorney fails to present evidence reflecting factors that may improve a defendant's prospects at sentencing, she leaves an opening for assumptions about the defendant, potentially based on racial or ethnic stereotypes, that may influence the discretionary process of sentencing. The following is a non-exclusive list of the type of records that may be useful:

- Employment history: paychecks, attendance history, W-2 forms, letter from employer
- Proof of education: transcript, class schedule, letter from registrar
- Medical/mental health records
- Any certifications and licenses

- Any evaluation and treatment documents
- Military documents
- Client's financial documents

See Robert C. Kemp, III, Art of Sentencing (Feb. 15, 2013) (training material presented at New Felony Defender Training, 2013).

C. Pretrial Strategies

Poverty can negatively affect defendants at multiple stages of the case, including the sentencing phase. Poor defendants, the majority of whom are racial or ethnic minorities, are less likely to be released pretrial, more likely to be convicted, more likely to be sentenced to a term of incarceration, and more likely to receive lengthier sentences than similarly situated offenders with greater financial resources. *See, e.g.*, Stephen Demuth, *Racial and Ethnic Differences in Pretrial Release Decisions and Outcomes: A Comparison of Hispanic, Black, and White Felony Arrestees*, 41 CRIMINOLOGY 873, 897 (2003) (finding that Black and Latino defendants are "significantly less able to post bail"); GERARD RAINVILLE & BRIAN A. REAVES, BUREAU OF JUSTICE STATISTICS, FELONY DEFENDANTS IN LARGE URBAN COUNTIES, 2000 24 & Table 24 (2003) (concluding that defendants detained pretrial achieve worse outcomes).

Defenders can play an important role in connecting indigent clients to services that address their extralegal needs and may lead to mitigating evidence for sentencing. Assessing clients' needs and helping to identify appropriate community-based programs, activities, and services is an important aspect of client advocacy. *See* Robin Steinberg, *Addressing Racial Disparity in the Criminal Justice System Through Holistic Defense*, THE CHAMPION, JULY 2013, at 51, 52 (observing that "[s]eamless access to legal and nonlegal services . . . is crucial for clients from historically disenfranchised Black and Latino communities" and that lack of access to needed services has contributed to "instability, poverty, and criminal justice involvement"); *see also* ASHLEY NELLIS ET AL., THE SENTENCING PROJECT, REDUCING RACIAL DISPARITY IN THE CRIMINAL JUSTICE SYSTEM: A MANUAL FOR PRACTITIONERS AND POLICYMAKERS 15 (2d ed. 2008) (noting that, in assessing how racial minorities may be disadvantaged at the sentencing stage of a case, court actors should consider whether a "range of community-based alternatives to detention [are] available in the lower and superior courts [and whether] this range [is] offered at the same rate to minorities and nonminorities with similar offenses and offense histories"). Pretrial efforts by defenders may include:

1. Staying informed of available community-based programs, including those that may be particularly effective at serving racial or ethnic minorities, such as programs offered in multiple languages. To the extent possible, determine the record of success of the programs under consideration, and your client's history, if any, with similar programs. One useful compilation of such programs is the Community Treatment and Resource Provider Directory an online directory maintained by the Office of Indigent Defense Services. *See also* Jamie Markham, *County Resource Guide*, N.C. CRIM. L., UNC SCHOOL OF GOV'T BLOG (September 26, 2013).

2. Ensuring that the programs under consideration are culturally appropriate for your client. For example, if your client is Spanish-speaking, ensure that the drug treatment program under consideration provides programs in Spanish.

3. Developing a specialized sentencing advocate or advocates in your office to investigate and develop mitigation evidence and address extralegal needs of clients.

4. Considering whether to seek funding for a mitigation specialist. In serious cases—including Class A, B1, and B2 felonies—defense attorneys should consider seeking funding to hire a mitigation specialist. Though these specialists typically work on capital cases, because of the stiff penalties attached to serious, non-capital felonies, you may be able to persuade a judge to approve funding for a mitigation specialist. Mitigation specialists are trained and experienced in obtaining evidence that may be difficult or time-consuming for a lawyer to obtain, including school records, and affidavits from teachers, neighbors, church officials, or others who can reflect on the struggles faced by your client.

5. Considering whether it is in your client's interest to seek a presentence report or sentencing plan. *See infra* § 9.5E, Sentencing Hearing Advocacy.

D. Sentence Negotiation Strategies

Nationwide, approximately 95% of all felony convictions in state courts result from guilty pleas. MATTHEW R. DUROSE & PATRICK A. LANGAN, BUREAU OF JUSTICE STATISTICS, U.S. DEPARTMENT OF JUSTICE, FELONY SENTENCES IN STATE COURTS, 2004 1 (2004). For this reason, few stages of the criminal process are more crucial than plea negotiations. Since plea agreements in North Carolina may include a specific negotiated sentence, negotiations with prosecutors require the same knowledge, skills, and preparation required to handle a sentencing hearing. The following techniques may be helpful in addressing considerations of race during plea negotiations:

1. By addressing the subject of race with the prosecutor when pertinent, you may be able to reduce the likelihood that either of you will allow implicit biases to affect decision-making in the sentence negotiation process. *See* Cynthia Lee, *Making Race Salient: Trayvon Martin and Implicit Bias in a Not Yet Post-Racial Society*, 91 N.C. L. REV. 1555 (2013) (summarizing research findings indicating that open discussions of race can reduce the operation of implicit biases).

2. In negotiating a sentence, it may be useful to describe to the prosecutor what you have learned about the client's circumstances and the pressures he or she confronts, e.g., the influence of poverty, racial profiling, mental illness, or family circumstances. *See* James Tibensky, *What a Sentencing Advocate Can Do in a Non-Capital Case*, CORNERSTONE, Fall 2004, at 9; *see also* Rebecca Ballard DiLoreto, *Disparate Impact: Racial Bias in the Sentencing and Plea Bargaining Process*, THE ADVOCATE, May 2008, at 15, 20 (describing plea negotiations as a time when the prosecutor may be persuaded to "see helping your client as part of a larger systemic effort to do

justice"). If defense counsel has a mitigation video about the client (*see infra* "Practice note" in § 9.4E, Sentencing Hearing Advocacy (discussing mitigation videos)), counsel may consider sharing the video with the prosecutor during plea negotiations.

3. Present the prosecutor with any statistics, disaggregated by race and ethnicity, of disparate sentencing and/or enforcement associated with the charges your client faces. *See supra* § 9.4B, Data and Record Collection. Even where such evidence may be insufficient to support a successful equal protection claim, prosecutors may be persuaded to reduce charges in light of such information. *See supra* "Case study: Pretextual traffic stops" in § 2.6B, The Fourth Amendment and Pretextual Traffic Stops (describing case in which public defender presented evidence of disparate enforcement to a prosecutor, who thereafter agreed to drop charges against her client).

4. Alert the prosecutor where there is evidence or data to suggest that your client's prior criminal history may have been influenced by improper racial considerations. *See supra* § 9.4B, Data and Record Collection.

5. Ensure that the opportunity to provide substantial assistance does not differ depending on the race of the defendant. For example, in cases involving drug trafficking charges, research from the federal criminal justice system indicates that Black and Latino offenders were significantly less likely to be recommended for substantial assistance departures, even when offense severity, criminal history, and the tendencies of the sentencing judge were taken into consideration. David Mustard, *Racial, Ethnic, and Gender Disparities in Sentencing: Evidence from the Federal Courts*, 44 J.L. & ECON. 285, 308–09 Table 10 (2001). It has been suggested that these disparities result from the tendency to assign qualities such as "sympathetic" or "salvageable" disproportionately to White offenders. Ilene H. Nagel & Stephen J. Schulhofer, *A Tale of Three Cities: An Empirical Study of Charging and Bargaining Practices Under the Federal Sentencing Guidelines*, 66 S. CAL. L. REV. 501 (1992) (introducing the concept of a "salvageable" or "sympathetic" defendant into the analysis of substantial assistance departures). The discretionary decision regarding a substantial assistance departure is a crucial one in North Carolina, as it is essentially the only way that people convicted under drug trafficking statutes in North Carolina (carrying mandatory minimum terms of imprisonment and fines) can receive a mitigated sentence. Jamie Markham, *Options to Mitigate Sentences for Drug Trafficking*, N.C. CRIM. L., UNC SCHOOL OF GOV'T BLOG (August 15, 2013).

6. Be prepared with any data showing that White defendants facing similar charges have received more lenient sentences than faced by your minority client. *See supra* § 9.4B, Data and Record Collection.

7. Know your client well enough before plea negotiations to distinguish him or her from potential racial or ethnic stereotypes. For example, counter possible stereotypes of your client as a gang member because he is a young, Latino male who lives in an area where the Latin Kings gang is active. Evidence such as school attendance records,

work records, or a letter from a local leader such as a pastor may assist in individualizing the client. Testimony from such character witnesses could also be included in a mitigation video. *See infra* "Practice note" in § 9.4E, Sentencing Hearing Advocacy.

8. If you present evidence of racial disparities to the prosecutor in negotiating a suggested plea and sentence, avoid stating or implying that the prosecutor is responsible for the disparities; doing so misstates the possible causes of disparities and may provoke defensiveness. Instead, frame the sentence you seek as an opportunity to offset factors that may have contributed to racial disparities (*see supra* § 1.3, Potential Factors Relevant to Racial Disparities in the Criminal Justice System), stressing that the sentencing stage provides the court system with a unique opportunity to achieve a just result for all involved.

E. Sentencing Hearing Advocacy

Effective sentencing advocacy involves the development of a sentencing theory that counsel can present to the judge in a sentencing hearing and/or sentencing memorandum. A sentencing theory serves to convince the court that the sentence you are asking the court to impose serves the interests of all relevant stakeholders, including the victim, the community, and the defendant. For example, if your theory is that your client suffers from drug addiction and the sentence you seek is an intermediate sentence at a drug treatment facility, be prepared to explain to the court how this result is in the best interests of all relevant stakeholders. *See* THE SENTENCING PROJECT, TEN PRINCIPLES OF SENTENCING ADVOCACY (2003) (listing, among other principles, that sentencing advocacy is "an exercise in problem-solving" and "opposes racial disparity and cultural bias"); *see also* James Tibensky, *What a Sentencing Advocate Can Do in a Non-Capital Case*, CORNERSTONE, Fall 2004, at 9 (problem-solving advocacy views the offense as "a problem for society, for the community, for the victim, for the court and for the defendant," and attempts to craft a sentencing recommendation that benefits as many of those parties as possible).

Practice note: In recent years, some defense attorneys have created mitigation or sentencing videos to show during sentencing hearings and plea negotiations. *See* Joe Palazzolo, *Leniency Videos Make a Showing at Criminal Sentencings: Some Lawyers Supplement Letters of Support with Mini-Documentaries, Effectiveness is Debated*, WALL STREET JOURNAL, May 29, 2014 (quoting assistant federal defender Doug Passon as stating that, when sentencing videos are introduced, "[t]he sentences are almost always better than they would otherwise be"). Mitigation video pioneer and assistant federal public defender Doug Passon, who made his first sentencing video in 1995, observes that such videos can be effective at bridging cultural gaps between defendants and court actors. *See* Doug Passon, *Using Mitigation Videos to Bridge the Cultural Gap at Sentencing*, *in* CULTURAL ISSUES IN CRIMINAL DEFENSE 979, 981 (Linda Friedman Ramirez ed., 3d ed. 2010) (stating that criminal defense attorneys should make empathy the focus of sentencing presentations to "bridge the chasm of the cultural divide" and effectively convey the client's circumstances to the judge, which may include poverty, abuse, mental illness, addiction, and other suffering;); *see also* Regina Austin, "Not Just a Common Criminal": The Case for Sentencing Mitigation Videos (April 15, 2014) (University of Pennsylvania Law School Faculty Scholarship Paper). These videos may be particularly useful at illustrating circumstances such as the impoverished conditions of a defendant's home or neighborhood, and may be a good way of introducing the voices of character witnesses who face difficulties coming to court or preparing a written statement on behalf of the defendant. While some film-makers charge between $5,000 and $20,000 for producing such videos, it is possible for defenders or investigators to produce modest videos on their own. *See* Doug Passon, *Using Mitigation Videos to Bridge the Cultural Gap at Sentencing*, *in* CULTURAL ISSUES IN CRIMINAL DEFENSE 979, 996 (Linda Friedman Ramirez, ed., 3d ed. 2010). Examples of sentencing videos may be viewed online. *See, e.g.*, Don Ayala Sentencing Documentary, NEW ORLEANS TIMES-PICAYUNE, Sept. 1, 2010 (sentencing video shown to a federal judge who ultimately imposed a term of probation on a defendant facing eight years in prison under federal sentencing guidelines for voluntary manslaughter).

Presenting evidence aimed at obtaining a favorable sentence. Defendants are entitled to sentencing hearings, during which the formal rules of evidence do not apply. G.S. 15A-1334. In a sentencing hearing, any evidence that a court deems to have probative value may be received. N.C. R. EVID. 1101(b)(3); *see also State v. Brown*, 320 N.C. 179, 203 (1987) ("the touchstone for propriety in sentencing arguments is whether the argument relates to the character of the [defendant] or the nature [or circumstances of the crime"). The court must consider any evidence presented by the defendant of mitigating factors. Mitigating factors must be proven to the court by a preponderance of the evidence. G.S. 15A-1340.16(a); *see State v. Knott*, 164 N.C. App. 212 (2004) (refusal to allow defense counsel an opportunity to present evidence of mitigating factors constitutes plain error). Twenty specific mitigating factors are set forth in G.S. 15A-1340.16(e), and the statute also allows judges to find "[a]ny other mitigating factor reasonably related to the purposes of sentences." G.S. 15A-1340.16(e)(21); *see also* G.S. 15A-1340.12 (describing the purposes of sentencing). This "catch-all" provision gives defense attorneys creative freedom to raise concerns about race that may be related to sentencing, including the potential impact of structural racialization and implicit bias (discussed *supra* in Chapter 1) and any disparity that may have affected an earlier stage of the case (for example, the inability of the client to obtain pretrial release). The following are possible strategies for addressing at sentencing the cumulative effects of any racial disparities:

1. Explain how any hardships associated with the defendant's racial, ethnic, or cultural background may support a reduced punishment. Some of the statutory mitigating factors, including successful completion of a drug treatment program, a positive employment history, or a defendant's support of his or her family, may carry more weight when presented alongside the defendant's struggles against racial barriers, poverty, or disadvantage. For example, in *United States v. Decora*, 177 F.3d 676 (8th Cir. 1999) and *United States v. One Star*, 9 F.3d 60 (8th Cir. 1993), the extreme difficulties of life on an Indian reservation, viewed alongside the defendants' records,

which included attributes such as community support, limited criminal history, and educational accomplishment, supported reduced sentences.

2. In cases in which you are concerned that racial stereotypes may influence the sentence under consideration, incorporate a race-switching exercise into your argument at the sentencing hearing or invite the court to engage in a race-switching exercise. A race-switching exercise is a mental exercise that involves switching the race of the parties to determine whether race may have played a role in assessing the evidence. *See supra* § 8.6D, Jury Instructions; Cynthia Kwei Yung Lee, *Race and Self-Defense: Toward a Normative Conception of Reasonableness*, 81 MINN. L. REV. 367, 482 (1996) (proposing race-switching jury instruction); James McComas & Cynthia Strout, *Combating the Effects of Racial Stereotyping in Criminal Cases*, THE CHAMPION, Aug. 1999, at 22, 24 (describing a case in which a judge noted "that he personally engaged in a race-switching exercise whenever he was called upon to impose sentence on a member of a minority race, to insure that he was not being influenced by racial stereotypes"). To avoid suggesting that the judge alone may be affected by implicit bias, counsel may wish to present this as an exercise for the entire courtroom. For example, counsel may posit: "All of us who work in the court system, the prosecutor and myself included, need to ask ourselves whether we would be doing or thinking anything different today if the defendant were White and/or the victim were Black; as members of the bar sworn to uphold the Constitution, we can't allow race to play a role at sentencing."

3. Inform the judge of any cultural factors that may be relevant to an evaluation of defendant's blameworthiness. For example, in one case, a Korean man argued for a downward departure from the federal sentencing guidelines on the basis that his upbringing in Korea caused him to believe that the money he provided to an Internal Revenue Service agent in the form of a bribe was legally and socially obligatory. *United States v. Yu*, 954 F.2d 951, 953 (3d Cir. 1992).

4. Explain to the court how race may have affected earlier stages of the process in your client's case, and that sentencing provides an opportunity to redress any taint. *See, e.g.,* Placido G. Gomez, *The Dilemma of Difference: Race as a Sentencing Factor*, 24 GOLDEN GATE U. L. REV. 357, 380 (1994) (arguing that race should be considered as a mitigating factor where it is likely that racial discrimination occurred at an earlier stage of the case); *see also* Traci Schlesinger, *The Cumulative Effects of Racial Disparities in Criminal Processing*, THE ADVOCATE, May 2008, at 22. For example, if you are able to show that a similarly situated White co-defendant was released pretrial, completed drug treatment, and based on that treatment, received a reduced sentence, while your Black client was detained pretrial with no such opportunity to engage in productive activities, the judge may consider this as mitigating evidence. *See also* Charles J. Ogletree, Jr., *The Death of Discretion? Reflections on the Federal Sentencing Guidelines*, 101 HARV. L. REV. 1938, 1960 (1988) (arguing that "to help remedy the pervasive racial discrimination in our criminal justice system, judges should be given discretion to take into account an offender's race as a mitigating factor").

5. Explain to the court whether your client's prior criminal history may have been influenced by race. For example, in *U.S. v. Leviner*, 31 F. Supp. 2d 23 (D. Mass. 1998), a federal judge imposed a reduced sentence on a Black defendant based on a finding that most of the defendant's prior convictions arose out of traffic stops conducted by the Boston police, and that the unlawful practice of racial profiling may have contributed to his prior record. *See supra* § 2.2, Overview of Racial Profiling Concerns (discussing recent studies regarding racial disparities in traffic stops in North Carolina).

6. Forecast for the judge—based on available statistics, your client's history, and familiar anecdotes—the likely future your client faces if he or she receives the non-incarcerative, community-based, or reduced sentence you seek, and contrast it with decreased life chances he or she faces if sentenced to lengthy incarceration. *See* Robert C. Kemp, III, Art of Sentencing (Feb. 15, 2013) (training material presented at New Felony Defender Training, 2013). For example, you could explain to the judge that a prison sentence will result in the loss of your client's job, while a community or intermediate sentence will allow him to continue working and providing for his family. Additionally, you could present the court with evidence showing that recidivism rates are generally lower for probationers than for prisoners in North Carolina. NORTH CAROLINA SENTENCING AND POLICY ADVISORY COMMISSION, CORRECTIONAL PROGRAM EVALUATION: OFFENDERS PLACED ON PROBATION OR RELEASED FROM PRISON IN FISCAL YEAR 2008/09 27 (2012) (finding that probationers in FY 2008/2009 were less likely than people released from prison to be rearrested during both one-year and two-year follow up periods). Explain to the judge any concerns about any contemplated sentences that are in conflict with your client's cultural values and individual characteristics. For example, a devout Muslim client may not succeed in a drug treatment facility that includes mixed gender treatment groups.

7. Inform the judge of community-based alternative sentences that meet the needs of your client and address the problems underlying the crime of conviction. *See* North Carolina Office of Indigent Defense Services, Community Treatment and Resource Provider Directory, NCIDS.COM (last visited Sept. 22, 2014). Some judges may be reluctant to impose probationary sentences because they do not know of local programs for which the defendant is eligible. *See* Jamie Markham, *County Resource Guide*, N.C. CRIM. L., UNC SCHOOL OF GOV'T BLOG (September 26, 2013). You can preliminarily evaluate your client's eligibility for programs and services and provide information to the judge regarding such matters as the proximity of the proposed community-based program to the client's home, available modes of transportation, and available spots for new participants. Knowledge of available, appropriate programs for which your client is eligible may, "in a close case, inform the judge's decision between an active and probationary sentence." *Id.*

8. Stress to the judge the importance of taking into account the defendant's resources to avoid penalizing defendants who are poor, the majority of whom are racial minorities. For example, you may want to inform the judge of cases in which similarly situated

defendants with private counsel have been able to craft desirable sentences funded by their own financial assets and argue that your client's sentence should not depend on his or her resources. Additionally, if your case is one in which your client may be ordered to pay restitution, present records regarding financial hardship, e.g. foreclosure records, a spreadsheet reflecting income vs. expenses, bankruptcy documents, etc., since the judge must take the defendant's ability to pay into consideration in ordering restitution. G.S. 15A-1340.36.

9. Explain to the judge the particular concerns about disparities in certain contexts, such as marijuana charges, drug trafficking charges, habitual felon charges, and substantial assistance departures. Sources for such data include your own collected reports of offender data as well as statistics collected by the NCAJ's Racial Justice Task Force, the Governor's Crime Commission, and the Department of Public Safety. This type of information has been referred to as "social framework evidence," and has been recognized as an important tool in mitigating the effects of race on criminal justice outcomes. THE SENTENCING PROJECT, REPORT OF THE SENTENCING PROJECT TO THE UNITED NATIONS HUMAN RIGHTS COMMITTEE REGARDING RACIAL DISPARITIES IN THE UNITED STATES CRIMINAL JUSTICE SYSTEM (2013). Argue that evidence of disparities provides support for a reduced sentence, as recognized by the U.S. Supreme Court in *Kimbrough v. United States*, 552 U.S. 85 (2007) (upholding district court's consideration of sentencing disparities as a basis for imposing a reduced sentence in a crack-cocaine case).

10. Make a formal presentation of mitigating evidence—which may include testimony from the client and witnesses, school or employment records, and a defense sentencing memorandum—aimed at constructing an individualized narrative supporting your sentencing recommendation. This approach may counter the potential effects of implicit bias by distinguishing your client from potential stereotypes, promoting a closer examination of your client's circumstances, and averting automatic or "snap" judgments. Jerry Kang et al., *Implicit Bias in the Courtroom*, 59 UCLA L. REV. 1124, 1177 (2012).

11. Provide the sentencing judge with evidence about implicit racial bias. Jonathan Rapping, *Implicitly Unjust: How Defenders Can Affect Systemic Racist Assumptions* 1040 (Working Paper, January 16, 2014). Because of the wide range of permissible considerations at sentencing, defense attorneys should use the opportunity to point out "how subconscious bias can affect how judges sentence." *Id.* This can be done by directing judges to social science research on implicit biases and their potential influence on judges. *Id.; see, e.g.*, Jeffrey J. Rachlinski et al., *Does Unconscious Racial Bias Affect Trial Judges?*, 84 NOTRE DAME L. REV. 1195, 1221 (2009) (study that involved administering the Implicit Association Test to trial judges concluded that judges do, in fact, harbor implicit racial bias).

12. Inform the judge about the connection between discretion and the operation of biases, including in evaluation of mitigating and aggravating factors. In the context of capital sentencing by juries, the U.S. Supreme Court recognized how the discretion involved

in determining a criminal sentence provides "a unique opportunity for racial prejudice to operate but remain undetected." *Turner v. Murray*, 476 U.S. 28, 35 (1986). For example, the Court explained that someone "who believes that blacks are violence prone or morally inferior might well be influenced by that belief in deciding whether petitioner's crime involved . . . aggravating factors . . . [and] . . . might also be less favorably inclined toward petitioner's evidence of mental disturbance as a mitigating circumstance. More subtle, less consciously held racial attitudes could also influence a juror's decision in this case." *Id.* Risks of implicit biases may be present when a defendant is subject to a discretionary sentencing determination by a judge. *See, e.g.*, David S. Abrams et al., *Do Judges Vary in Their Treatment of Race?*, 41 J. LEGAL STUD. 347 (2012) (finding that judges differ in the degree to which race influences their decisions regarding whether to incarcerate a defendant); *see also People v. Wardell,* 595 N.E.2d 1148, 1155 (Ill. App. Ct. 1992) (just as the trial judge must "shield the jury from considering racially prejudicial remarks by the participants during trial, so also must the judge at sentencing safeguard against racial considerations").

13. Learn the prosecutor's sentencing position before the sentencing hearing and devise a plan for responding to the aspects with which you disagree. If the prosecutor offers improper evidence during a sentencing hearing, object to the evidence as irrelevant to the purposes of sentencing. *See* G.S. 15A-1340.12; *see also People v. Riley*, 33 N.E.2d 872, 875 (Ill. 1941) (sentencing judge "owes the same duty to the defendant to protect his own mind from the possible prejudicial effect of incompetent evidence that he would owe in protecting a jury from the same contaminating influence").

Presentence reports and sentencing plans. Where the preparation of a presentence report by a probation officer or a sentencing plan by a sentencing specialist is an option, defense attorneys should consider whether one of these options may benefit the client. *See* Jamie Markham, *Presentence Reports and Sentencing Plans*, N.C. CRIM. L., UNC SCHOOL OF GOV'T BLOG (August 27, 2010).

When a probation officer prepares a presentence report, defense attorneys should be involved in the preparation of the report to the extent possible. Defendants and defense attorneys have a right to view any presentence report prepared by probation. G.S. 15A-1333(b). Defendants should request to see any report before it is presented to a judge, and to have an opportunity to advocate to the preparer of the report for changes to any irrelevant or inaccurate content. While the preparation of presentence reports by probation is permitted by statute, in practice, it rarely happens. NORTH CAROLINA ADMINISTRATIVE OFFICE OF THE COURTS, PRESENTENCE INVESTIGATIONS FEASIBILITY STUDY REPORT: SESSION LAW 2009-451, SECTION 19.14 (2010) (reporting that probation officers are rarely asked to prepare presentence reports, and that some superior and district court judges were unaware that existing law allowed for their preparation).

When reviewing a presentence report, be alert to any depictions of your client in an unflattering or racially stereotypical manner. For example, in a qualitative study performed in a northwestern city, researchers found that probation officers' assessments of motivations for offending differed by race in presentence reports in juvenile cases. In particular, the delinquency of Black youth was typically explained "as stemming from negative attitudinal and personality traits," while delinquent behavior of White youth "stressed the influence of the social environment." ASHLEY NELLIS ET AL., THE SENTENCING PROJECT, REDUCING RACIAL DISPARITY IN THE CRIMINAL JUSTICE SYSTEM: A MANUAL FOR PRACTITIONERS AND POLICYMAKERS 14 (2d ed. 2008). "Black youth were judged to be more dangerous, which translated into harsher sentences than for comparable white youth." *Id.*

As a result of the elimination of the statewide Sentencing Services program, which evaluated defendants for possible non-incarcerative sentences at the request of the defendant or the court, independent sentencing specialists are available to produce sentencing plans only in certain counties. Where such specialists are available, counsel must cite specific grounds for preparation of a plan and a judge must determine whether one is warranted, at a cost of $500 (paid by the Office of Indigent Defense Services). To find out if there is a sentencing specialist in or near your area who is available to be appointed by the court to prepare a sentencing plan, consult the Community Treatment and Resource Provider Directory, an online directory maintained by the Office of Indigent Defense Services. Regardless of whether a sentencing specialist is available in your area, you may apply to the court for funds to hire a mitigation specialist and offer information obtained by such a specialist to the court during sentencing. *See* Ex Parte Motion to Hire Mitigation Investigator, available at www.ncids.org (select "Training and Resources," then "Motions Bank, Non-Capital").

Anecdotal evidence suggests that, in counties where sentencing specialists are available, defense attorneys tend to seek their services when the sentencing grid calls for an active or intermediate sentence, for assistance in structuring an appropriate intermediate sentence. The sentencing specialist's plan generally will include detailed background information about the client, a risk assessment, and available treatment options. In some cases, the most useful function a sentencing specialist can serve is getting the client into a treatment program, which may be difficult for the defense attorney to arrange. Consult with the sentencing specialist for further details about the process and requirements for obtaining a sentencing plan.

Chapter 10
Sources of Information about Matters of Race

10.1 Police Investigation

Multiple sources of data are available to assist attorneys investigating claims of selective enforcement in violation of the state and federal guarantees of equal protection, or of unlawful search or seizure in violation of the Fourth Amendment and the parallel state constitutional provision, N.C. CONST. art. I, § 20. This section identifies the type of data available to support claims relating to unconstitutional law enforcement practices, and explains how such data can be located and analyzed.

A. Online Court Records

Information about charging patterns can be obtained from online resources maintained by the North Carolina Administrative Office of the Courts (AOC). Attorneys can conduct a search of criminal cases through the AOC's Criminal Information System (terminals are available in each courthouse). *See* AOC Computer Instructions in the Race Materials Bank at www.ncids.org (select "Training and Resources"). They may also query the AOC's online criminal calendar, by officer or agency, to produce a list of cases for a particular officer or agency. Once they obtain case numbers and other identifying information, they can access additional court records. *See* Statewide Officer Court Appearance Query, NCCOURTS.ORG (last visited Sept. 25, 2014).

For example, in the case of *State v. Villeda*, 165 N.C. App. 431 (2004), after a conversation with a trooper in which he mentioned that he believed most Hispanic males drive drunk over the weekend, attorney Leonor Childers searched an AOC criminal computer for cases in which the trooper at issue was identified as the "complainant." This search provided her with a list of the trooper's citations, which allowed her to pull the corresponding court "shucks" described below.

B. Court "Shucks"

Using records maintained in the courthouse by the clerk of court, and without employing expert assistance, attorneys have been able to determine stopping patterns of particular law enforcement officers. They have done so by pulling the "shuck" in each case (the envelope or folder containing the court records in each case) and looking at all of the citations that a particular officer has issued over a given time period. With these records, attorneys have been able to gather information about the race or ethnicity of drivers stopped by a particular officer, the specific geographic area where the stops occurred, and even the age and model of the vehicles stopped, which they then can compare with census data to determine whether the evidence suggests that the officer may be targeting minorities. An example of such an analysis appears in *State v. Villeda*:

> [Defense attorney] Childers further testified that, following her discussion with Trooper Carroll, she began looking into his citation history. She pulled up all of Trooper Carroll's citations from 1 January 2001 to 24 March 2002, a total of 716 citations, and found that 71% of DWI citations issued by Trooper Carroll involved Hispanic individuals. Only 16% of DWI stops were of Caucasians, 9% of African-Americans, and 2% of other racial backgrounds. After Trooper Carroll came under investigation by Internal Affairs in the spring of 2002 for racial profiling, no Hispanics were cited by him for DWI violations.
>
> In plotting the DWI stops on a map, Childers noted "two fairly concentrated areas": Area 1—the U.S. 70–Hillsborough Road–Main Street area in Durham (within a two-to-three-mile radius of La Maraca), and Area 2—encompassing Miami Boulevard, East Durham, Geer Street, and Holloway Street (including Circle K). According to the 2000 census data Childers reviewed, the Hispanic population in Durham County amounts to approximately 7% of the general population. However, the census data for LaSalle Street in the city of Durham, which is located in Area 1 and a quarter mile from La Maraca, reveals a population of 32% Hispanics and 36% African-Americans.

165 N.C. App. 431, 433–34 (2004).

C. Division of Criminal Statistics

The North Carolina Attorney General, through its Division of Criminal Statistics in the North Carolina Department of Justice, is required to collect information about criminal law administration, including crimes committed, arrests made, convictions, acquittals, and punishment, including the race of offenders. *See* G.S. 114-10(1). G.S. 114-10.01 mandates the collection of traffic stop data, including "[i]dentifying characteristics of the drivers stopped, including the race or ethnicity" and "the race or ethnicity . . . of each person searched." Pursuant to this law, the Division of Criminal Information of the North Carolina Department of Justice must collect statistics on traffic stops by state troopers and other state law enforcement officers. *Id.* This statute also requires the Division to collect statistics on many local law enforcement agencies. *Id.* A law enforcement officer subject to the provisions of G.S. 114-10.01 must record traffic stop data on State Bureau of Investigation Form SBI-122, which he or she must file with his or her local agency. The officer's agency must then electronically forward the information collected on the SBI-122 forms to the SBI Traffic Stops Unit.

Traffic stop reports reflecting traffic stop data collected pursuant to G.S. 114-10, including reports identifying the race and ethnicity of drivers or passengers stopped and/or searched, may be accessed on the North Carolina Traffic Stop Statistics section of the Division's website. This web-based tool allows users to create reports reflecting stops, searches, and enforcement actions taken by various law enforcement agencies during time periods designated by the user.

Attorneys may also request data collected on SBI-122 forms from the SBI Traffic Stops Unit. A subpoena or court order should not be necessary to obtain these records. Unless a specific statutory exception exists, records maintained by state and local government agencies are public records. *See generally News and Observer Publishing Co. v. Poole,* 330 N.C. 465 (1992). Counsel may tailor the request by asking for data for all stops made by the law enforcement agency in question during the time period and in the geographic location in which the client was stopped. Alternatively, counsel may submit a public records request to the relevant law enforcement agency for the traffic stop data sought. *See* Request for Public Records and Affidavit in Support of Motion to Suppress Illegal Stop and Illegal Search (noting that the contents of the affidavit were based in part on materials provided by the sheriff's department in response to a public records request) in the Race Materials Bank at www.ncids.org (select "Training and Resources").

In recent years, officers have begun to use additional numeric codes when entering the required data on the SBI-122 forms. For example, a motorist's race may be recorded as "3" and sex may be identified as "1". Therefore, attorneys must use a glossary of codes to decipher the recent forms. A glossary may be found in the Race Materials Bank at www.ncids.org (select "Training & Resources").

The officer's name is not included on the SBI-122 forms. In place of a name, the officer enters a number that is assigned by the officer's employing agency. G.S. 114-10.01(d) provides that the "correlation between the identification numbers and the names of the officers shall not be a public record." Although this information is not available to the public generally, the statute allows the officer's employing agency to disclose this information when required by a court order to resolve a claim or defense before the court. Motions for disclosure of an officer's identification number may be made before or alongside motions to suppress evidence arising out of a stop or search. *See* Motion to Suppress Illegal Stop and Search and Motion to Disclose Officer's ID Number in the Race Materials Bank at www.ncids.org (select "Training & Resources"). In addition to seeking disclosure of such information through a court order, some North Carolina attorneys have determined the identity of individual stopping officers associated with the SBI-122 numbers by comparing public court files with the data collected on SBI-122 forms. For example, Durham attorney Kerstin Walker Sutton has compared data from SBI forms, ACIS, and court files to determine an officer's SBI-122 number and analyze whether the evidence supported a claim of selective enforcement. Her approach to analyzing available sources of traffic stop data, along with materials from two cases in which she employed this approach, may be found in the Race Materials Bank at www.ncids.org (select "Training & Resources"). In these cases, identifying the officer listed on the SBI-122 forms allowed her to examine possible patterns by the officer, not just those that resulted in the filing of formal charges. *See id.*

D. Traffic Stop Data Search Tool under Development by the Southern Coalition for Social Justice

An additional resource for lawyers seeking North Carolina traffic stop data is currently under development by the Southern Coalition for Social Justice ("SCSJ"). SCSJ is developing a website to help users analyze possible racial disparities in traffic stops, searches, and arrests conducted by North Carolina law enforcement officers. The website will allow users to:

- generate statistical reports, drawn from the aggregate data reported to the SBI pursuant to G.S. 114-10.01, detailing the relative probability of Black, White, and Latino motorists being searched when stopped by a particular department for a given offense;
- access statewide averages for comparative purposes;
- generate reports on contraband discovery rates, broken down by race, age, and gender;
- identify any departments in North Carolina that are not in compliance with the requirements imposed by the data collection statute; and
- use the website as a management tool within law enforcement agencies to identify officers generating the largest racial disparities.

The website, which will be available beginning in late 2014 or early 2015 and updated regularly, will include all reported traffic stops that have occurred in the state of North Carolina since January 1, 2000—currently an estimated 14 million. Questions about the website may be directed to SCSJ attorney and Soros Justice Fellow Ian A. Mance at ianmance@southerncoalition.org, who, at the time of publication of this manual, was available to assist attorneys in analyzing traffic stop data as necessary. SCSJ also periodically releases reports analyzing North Carolina traffic stop data. *See, e.g.*, PowerPoint Slides of Ian A. Mance, *Racial Profiling in Durham*, NCIDS.COM (last visited Sept. 22, 2014).

E. U.S Bureau of Justice Statistics

The Bureau of Justice Statistics (BJS), a part of the of Office of Justice Programs in the U.S. Department of Justice, provides a tool for accessing and analyzing arrest data, including the race, age, and sex of arrestees. This tool allows the user to generate tables and graphs of arrests for various offenses. The data, which is reported by law enforcement agencies themselves, can be broken down by agency or state. For example, the user can generate the number of Black adults arrested by the Durham Police Department in 2008 for the offense of breaking or entering, and compare that to the number of White adults arrested for the same offense. *See* Bureau of Justice Statistics, Arrest Data Analysis Tool, BJS.GOV (last visited Sept. 22, 2014).

Additionally, the BJS conducts traffic stop surveys, collects data on state traffic stop data collection practices, and publishes reports concerning police behavior during traffic stops. The Bureau's traffic stop materials are available online. *See* Bureau of Justice Statistics, *Traffic Stops*, BJS.GOV (last visited Sept. 22, 2014).

F. The North Carolina Commission on Racial and Ethnic Disparities in the Criminal Justice System (NC-CRED)

NC-CRED is a collaborative, research-based organization whose mission is to identify, document, and alleviate racial and ethnic disparities in the criminal justice system. The Commission grew out of the North Carolina Advocates for Justice's Racial and Ethnic Bias in the Criminal Justice System Task Force (Task Force), a group of attorneys, policy makers, community leaders, and scholars who examined traffic stop data, drug and habitual felon convictions, and prison populations. The members of the subsequently-formed Commission include judges, police chiefs, public defenders, private defense attorneys, prosecutors, and professors. The history of the Commission and the Task Force is described on its website. *See* North Carolina Advocates for Justice, *Task Force History*, NCAJ.COM (last visited Sept. 22, 2014). Data collected and analyzed by NC-CRED and the Task Force may prove useful to attorneys litigating claims of racial profiling. For example, the Task Force has published reports on the prison population, the habitual felon prison population, and the drug prison population. Task Force and Commission publications are available online. *See* North Carolina Advocates for Justice, *NC-CRED Publications*, NCAJ.COM (last visited Sept. 22, 2014).

Baumgartner study. In 2012, the Task Force partnered with UNC professor Frank Baumgartner to publish a report analyzing state-wide traffic stop data, including approximately eleven years of traffic stop data. *See* FRANK R. BAUMGARTNER & DEREK EPP, NORTH CAROLINA TRAFFIC STOP STATISTICS ANALYSIS: FINAL REPORT TO THE NORTH CAROLINA ADVOCATES FOR JUSTICE TASK FORCE ON RACIAL AND ETHNIC BIAS 5 (2012) [hereinafter "Baumgartner Study"]. The study's authors concluded that, compared to White motorists, Black and Latino motorists and passengers in North Carolina are almost twice as likely to be searched and twice as likely to be arrested following a traffic stop. Using the data collected on SBI-122 forms, attorneys may be able to conduct their own small scale studies of patterns within a particular agency or of a particular officer. *See supra* § 10.1C, Division of Criminal Statistics. Traffic stop data study author Frank Baumgartner may be able to either assist attorneys in analyzing traffic stop data or direct attorneys to someone else who can do so.

G. Lippard and Page Study of Traffic Stop Data

In 2011, researchers conducted a study of available traffic stop data from 32 randomly selected North Carolina law enforcement agencies and concluded that minorities had higher stop rates than whites in over 50% of the sampled agencies. *See* Cameron D. Lippard & Amy Dellinger Page, *Driving While Non-White: Exploring Traffic Stops and Post-Stop Activities in North Carolina*, 2005–2009, 9 SOCIATION TODAY (Fall/Winter

2011) (Sociation Today is a peer-reviewed web-based publication of the North Carolina Sociological Association).

H. Expert Witnesses on the Subject of Racial Profiling

In some cases, attorneys may be able to enlist academics, researchers, consultants, or graduate students to assist with statistical analyses. The following is a brief list of researchers who have provided expert assistance in analyzing claims of racial profiling:

- Dr. Katherine Beckett, Professor, Law, Society & Justice Program and Department of Sociology, University of Washington
- Dr. Jeffrey Fagan, Isidor and Seville Sulzbacher Professor of Law, Columbia University
- Dr. John Lamberth, CEO of Lamberth Consulting
- Dr. Ralph B. Taylor, Professor of Criminal Justice, Temple University
- Dr. Frank Baumgartner, Richard J. Richardson Distinguished Professor of Political Science, University of North Carolina at Chapel Hill

I. North Carolina Public Defender Committee on Racial Equity (NC PDCORE)

The mission of NC PDCORE, a committee of the North Carolina Public Defender Association, is to reduce and ultimately eliminate racial and ethnic disparities in the criminal justice system through education, collaboration, and litigation. The NC PDCORE website contains a collection of litigation materials, data, publications, reports, books, links, and other tools regarding racial disparities in the criminal justice system, along with regular updates distributed to NC PDCORE members and posted on the committee's website. *See* NC PDCORE, NCIDS.COM/PD-CORE/ (last visited Sept. 22, 2014) (select "Resources").

J. Other Tools Related to Racial Profiling Data

If your client believes that she may have been subjected to racial profiling at a vehicle checkpoint, she may want to report this concern to the ACLU of North Carolina by completing a racial profiling checkpoint form. Such reports may facilitate data collection on this subject. The ACLU of North Carolina has recently published a report detailing the traffic stop data collection procedures in North Carolina and elsewhere, analyzing possible limitations of the collection procedures, and suggesting avenues for reform. *See* ACLU OF NORTH CAROLINA, ROAD WORK AHEAD (2014). The report may be useful in understanding the scope and limitations of the available data. In addition, some law enforcement agencies may have police civilian review boards, which may provide an avenue for filing complaints or providing feedback about policing practices. *See supra* § 2.8, Beyond Litigation.

10.2 Pretrial Release

A. Local Databases

Local databases are a source of data for claims of disparate treatment in the pretrial stage of a criminal prosecution. Some counties maintain their own repositories of data. For example, the City County Bureau of Identification (CCBI) for Wake County contains data on arrestees' race, ethnicity, sex, place of residence, country of origin, employment, prior arrests, and court appearance history. The Wake County Sheriff's Office also maintains a database on pretrial release conditions and offenses charged. In 2008, a student in the UNC School of Government's Masters of Public Administration program used these databases to conduct a study of variability in pretrial release conditions based on race, ethnicity, and sex for arrestees. *See Striving for Equity in Criminal Justice - An Analysis of Variability of Bail Bonds in the Tenth Judicial District of North Carolina* in the Race Materials Bank at www.ncids.org (select "Training and Resources"). Another example of a local database is the Bureau of ID of Buncombe County, which creates and maintains electronic records of warrants, citations, arrests, detention, and criminal history records, including mug shots.

B. NC-CRED's Pretrial Release Subcommittee

NC-CRED's Pre-Trial Release Subcommittee is currently analyzing pretrial release data in Halifax and Guilford counties for the purpose of determining whether racial disparities may be present in the counties' respective pretrial release processes. The data collected by the Subcommittee includes bond amounts and conditions of release imposed on defendants charged with Class H felonies. This effort involves data collection and analysis by race and ethnicity across a range of variables, including age, sex, economic status, employment, mental and physical health, case disposition, length of time in custody, bond amount, method of posting bond, criminal history, and failure to appear history. The project is supported in part by the American Bar Association's Racial Justice Improvement Project, which has supported similar efforts elsewhere in the country. A report documenting NC-CRED's findings concerning pretrial release in Guilford and Halifax counties will be posted on the Commission's website when it becomes available.

10.3 Plea Negotiations

In 2002, the North Carolina Sentencing and Policy Advisory Commission (Sentencing Commission) conducted a statewide study of sentencing practices under North Carolina's sentencing laws, focusing on two areas of discretion: plea negotiations and sentencing. NORTH CAROLINA SENTENCING AND POLICY ADVISORY COMMISSION, SENTENCING PRACTICES UNDER NORTH CAROLINA'S STRUCTURED SENTENCING LAWS (2002). The Sentencing Commission examined both legal and extralegal factors, such as race, affecting outcomes for defendants at those two stages. In the context of plea negotiations, the Commission examined whether similarly situated offenders received certain "breaks," such as a reduction from a felony charge to a misdemeanor, or imposition of a suspended sentence of imprisonment instead of an active one. The study did not conclude that race was a factor in sentence outcomes in North Carolina. In the spring of 2011, a candidate for the Masters of Public Administration degree at the UNC School of Government undertook a similar study, using more recent data to determine the extent to which legal and extralegal factors influenced sentencing outcomes, and concluded that race was a significant factor in discretionary decisions to impose an active sentence of imprisonment. *See* Michelle L. Hall, Disparity under Structured Sentencing in North Carolina: Do Similarly Situated Offenders Receive Different Outcomes Based on Legally Irrelevant Factors? (Spring 2011) (unpublished UNC School of Government MPA Thesis). Additional information on sentencing is discussed below.

10.4 Charging Decisions

Conducting a broad study of prosecutors' exercise of charging discretion is a complex and potentially costly undertaking. More targeted analyses of charging decisions can be conducted, however. An attorney representing an indigent client may apply to the court for expert funds to hire a law clerk or statistician to perform a targeted analysis. Attorneys also have enlisted the assistance of doctoral students at no charge to conduct data analyses.

A. Court Records

Attorneys may obtain data from a variety of sources, including the ACIS computer system maintained by the Administrative Office of the Courts, which includes the race of defendants; and the superior court docket sheets maintained by the Clerk of Court. *See* Habitual Felon Motion and Affidavit (using such sources in a motion to dismiss based on selective enforcement and selective prosecution) in the Race Materials Bank at www.ncids.org (select "Training & Resources").

In one case, an attorney enlisted the help of a law student as well as a doctoral student in statistics to examine court records on local prosecutors' exercise of discretion to charge people as habitual felons, and to determine whether the decision to "habitualize" was based on extralegal factors such as race. *See id.* The law student examined every superior court docket sheet in the relevant Superior Court Clerk's office and recorded every pending habitual felon indictment shown on those docket sheets. These were then compared to a District Attorney's Screening List, which listed the defendants' names, charges, and prosecutors assigned to the cases, and to computer records generated from ACIS. Based on the study, the attorney moved to dismiss and for further discovery. *See id.*

B. Defense Attorney Records

When analyzing charging patterns, information contained in client records may provide a good starting point. Internal data reflecting (1) the racial and ethnic makeup of clients facing drug charges or habitual felon sentencing enhancements, and (2) which clients receive favorable and unfavorable pleas, may be useful in litigating selective prosecution claims. *See supra* § 5.3G, Gathering Evidence to Support Selective Prosecution Claims. For example, one public defender's office maintained a "too good to be true" file of favorable plea arrangements that could be consulted by attorneys engaged in plea negotiations to ensure full awareness of the range of plea arrangements that might be possible in a certain type of case. This sort of information could be collected by an administrative assistant, or included within the case management system (CMS) used by public defender offices. The version of CMS currently under development will capture data reflecting the race of defendants but will not collect (1) data reflecting defendants' ethnicity; or (2) witness/victim race or ethnicity. Nevertheless, individual public defender offices could choose to populate a field in CMS with this data. Additionally, existing data on prosecutions for similar crimes in state and federal court, broken down by race, may provide evidence of differential treatment by state or federal prosecutors of similarly situated offenders. *See* Bureau of Justice Statistics, *Federal Criminal Case Processing Statistics*, BJS.GOV (last visited Sept. 22, 2014) (a searchable database maintained by the U.S. Department of Justice); *United States v. Tuitt*, 68 F. Supp. 2d 4 (D. Mass. 1999). Coordination with regional federal defender offices may facilitate gathering and analysis of such data.

C. Task Force Reports

The North Carolina Advocates for Justice's Racial and Ethnic Bias in the Criminal Justice System Task Force (Task Force) conducted a comparison of habitual felons and drug offenders incarcerated within North Carolina prisons to determine whether racial disparities were reflected in such populations. Their findings are broken down by county and available online. *See* North Carolina Advocates for Justice, *NC-CRED Publications*, NCAJ.COM (last visited Sept. 22, 2014). The data collected for these reports was obtained from the North Carolina Department of Correction Office of Research and Planning, which is now the North Carolina Department of Public Safety Office of Rehabilitative Programs and Services.

10.5 Jury Composition

A. Census Data

When challenging the jury pool or "venire," the defendant may present census figures that the representation of Black people in the pool does not reflect the number of such people in the community. Census data is available online. *See* United States Census Bureau website, CENSUS.GOV (last visited Sept. 22, 2014). Certified copies of census data available online can be obtained from the U.S. Census Bureau.

B. Records Maintained by the Court or Jury Commission

In raising fair cross-section or equal protection challenges to the jury pool, attorneys will generally compare census data to current and former records reflecting the names and demographic information of those included on master jury lists and on jury venires. Most of the time, defense counsel will need to seek such information through discovery. In some cases, counsel may be able to obtain records from the clerk of superior court regarding the demographic information of past jurors and juror panelists. *See, e.g.*, *State v. Cofield*, 320 N.C. 297, 299 (1987) (defendant "introduced a report prepared by Mr. R.J. White, Northampton County's Clerk of Superior Court, listing all who had served as grand jury foreman since 1960 by name, race, and sex"). To determine the identity of potential jurors before jury selection in a particular case, attorneys can check the list of jurors on a defendant's jury panel in the clerk's office approximately one week before trial. Attorneys can review that list to ensure that there are no obvious violations of the randomness requirement (e.g., not all people have last names beginning with the same letters), and may try to discover the race of the people listed on the jury panel by searching on the North Carolina Board of Election's website or on LexisNexis peoplefinder. The master jury list is available to the public in the clerk of superior court's office. Attorneys need to create a record of juror race by asking the judge to instruct potential jurors to self-report their race and ethnicity at the outset of questioning. *See infra* § 10.6C, Data Collection During Trial.

10.6 Jury Selection: Peremptory Challenges

A. Recent North Carolina Studies Regarding Peremptory Strikes

Recent analyses conducted in the wake of the North Carolina Racial Justice Act (RJA) of 2009 may serve as sources of data for non-capital cases and also as models for smaller scale analyses. Two in-depth statistical studies (Radelet-Pierce study and Michigan State University study) were conducted to examine the imposition of the death penalty in North Carolina and specifically the role of race in those cases. The authors of these reports relied on multiple sources of data, including Supplemental Homicide Reports from the FBI and records from the North Carolina Department of Adult Corrections and the State Office of the Chief Medical Examiner. The data, analyzed at the state, judicial division, prosecutorial district, and county levels, could be pertinent in non-capital cases to show historic disparities in the exercise of peremptory strikes during jury selection. While data is not required to support a claim of racial discrimination in the exercise of peremptory challenges, it may bolster a claim.

B. Data Collection Before Trial

Attorneys may want to review data from the Michigan State University (MSU) study before trial. For example, attorneys may review the statewide, county, and district strike ratios, and determine whether any individual strike rate ratios for the prosecutors involved in your case are included in the study.

Attorneys also may consider calculating the strike rate for serious felony cases within a given jurisdiction. This can be done by collecting transcripts, jury questionnaires, clerk records, and summons lists for prior cases. Cassandra Stubbs, Senior Staff Attorney for the ACLU Capital Punishment Project, has laid out a step-by-step guide for calculating strike ratios. *See* Cassandra Stubbs, *Strengthening* Batson *Challenges with the MSU Study* in the Race Materials Bank at www.ncids.org (select "Training and Resources"). Once obtained, strike data can be recorded and strike rates calculated by using a spreadsheet such as the following:

	A	B	C	D	E	F	G	H	I	J	K	L	M
1	Trial Date	Prosecutors	Defendant Name	Case No.	Presiding Judge	Defense Counsel	Total No. Jurors Questioned by State	Total No. Jurors Struck by State	Black Jurors Struck by State	White Jurors Struck by State	Latino Jurors Sturck by State	Asian Jurors Struck by State	Women Struck by State
2													
3													

Id.

Other relevant information that may be collected before trial in anticipation of *Batson* challenges includes RJA motions filed in your client's county; census data about race in the county or district; and evidence of past discrimination in jury selection. Attorneys may also consider making public records requests or discovery motions for information about the District Attorney's Office's jury selection policies and trainings.

C. Data Collection During Trial

In order to identify and raise equal protection violations, counsel should develop a system for recording the prosecutor's conduct and exercise of strikes during voir dire. One effective practice is to use a spreadsheet to record each venire member's race, gender, physical appearance, marital status, employment, and other notable attributes; the number of questions asked of the juror; the type of questions asked of the juror; and all statements made by that juror. If possible, it may be advantageous to develop ahead of time a chart of basic information about every venire member. This will assist with comparative juror analysis. Durham attorney Scott Holmes has created a spreadsheet that automatically calculates strike rates, which can be used during jury selection at trial. *See* Scott Holmes's Spreadsheet for Calculating Juror Strike Ratios and Cassandra Stubbs's Strike Data Spreadsheet, both in the Race Materials Bank at www.ncids.org (select "Training and Resources"). Ideally, these notes should be compiled by a member of the defense team who can focus on creating them, such as an attorney, paralegal, administrative assistant, intern, or investigator who has been trained ahead of time in how to quickly and accurately record all relevant data. Precise, accurate records are essential for noting similarities between venire members struck and passed on, for comparing any patterns with historical data, and for making quick strike rate calculations. Susan Jackson Balliet & Bruce P. Hackett, *Litigating Race in Voir Dire*, THE ADVOCATE, May 2008, at 42, 46. Additionally, during jury selection, counsel should ensure that the race and gender of every venire member struck is preserved on the record.

North Carolina attorneys have also been able to present statistical evidence of disparities in the jury selection process without an extensive study. One attorney handling a post-conviction case enlisted a doctoral student, who examined the "strike" ratio by prosecutors in the case and determined that they excused 77% of the eligible Black prospective jurors and 21% of eligible White prospective jurors. The student then examined the probability of the disproportionate strike ratio occurring by chance. The same attorney also obtained funds from the court to retain an expert to do a broader statistical study of the pattern of strikes by prosecutors in that county over a 20-year period. *See* Affidavits Regarding Peremptory Strike Patterns in Capital Cases in a Single North Carolina County and Examples of Juror Questionnaires in the Race Materials Bank at www.ncids.org (select "Training and Resources").

10.7 Sentencing

A. North Carolina Sentencing Commission

The North Carolina Sentencing Commission is a source of data on sentencing outcomes. Each year, the Sentencing Commission publishes its "Structured Sentencing Statistical Report for Felonies and Misdemeanors," which includes figures on the characteristics of offenders, broken down by race. *See, e.g.,* North Carolina Sentencing and Policy Advisory Commission, *Structured Sentencing Statistical Report for Felonies and Misdemeanors-Fiscal Year 2009/10 (July 1, 2009 - June 30, 2010)*, 9–10 (2011).

B. Reports Prepared by the North Carolina Advocates for Justice's Racial and Ethnic Bias in the Criminal Justice System Task Force

The North Carolina Advocates for Justice's Racial and Ethnic Bias in the Criminal Justice System Task Force is also a source of data analysis on imprisonment in North Carolina. For example, the Task Force collected and analyzed data from the North Carolina Department of Justice and Department of Correction, sorted by race and compared to county populations, on: (1) the overall North Carolina prison population; (2) drug convictions in North Carolina; and (3) habitual felon convictions in North Carolina. *See* North Carolina Advocates for Justice, *NC-CRED & Task Force Publications*, NCAJ.COM (last visited Oct. 8, 2014).

C. North Carolina Office of Indigent Defense Services

The North Carolina Office of Indigent Defense Services (IDS) intends to study sentencing outcomes by analyzing sentences and sentence lengths for given offenses, broken down by race. IDS projects that they are a number of years away from completing an analysis, however.

10.8 Miscellaneous

A. Additional Sources of State Data

Many North Carolina institutions are gathering data that may be useful in addressing possible racial disparities in criminal cases in North Carolina. For example, CJ LEADS "integrates data found within the State's [various criminal justice applications] and provides up-to-date criminal information about offenders in a centralized location via a secure connection for use by state and local government criminal justice professionals." CJ LEADS is managed by the North Carolina Office of the State Controller. At the present time, defense attorneys do not have access to CJ LEADS.

The Governor's Crime Commission and the Department of Juvenile Justice and Prevention also compile and analyze data on disproportionate minority contact with the juvenile justice system. Up until October 31, 2013, the Criminal Justice Analysis Center, housed within the Governor's Crime Commission, collected, analyzed, and disseminated criminal justice data. While the Center no longer exists, its publications may still be found online. *See* North Carolina Department of Public Safety, *Publications*, NCCRIMECONTROL.ORG (last visited Sept. 23, 2014). Additionally, in 2011, the North Carolina Office of the Juvenile Defender compiled a guidebook entitled Addressing Disproportionate Minority Contact (DMC) in Juvenile Delinquency Court, which contains practical tips for defense attorneys on addressing racial bias and racial disparities.

B. Additional Sources of National Data

On the national level, the Justice Mapping Center recently launched the National Justice Atlas of Sentencing and Corrections, "an online, interactive, mapping utility that gives policy makers, the media, researchers, and the public a neighborhood-level view of where prison inmates and offenders on probation and parole are from and where corrections spending is highest." Justice Mapping Center, *Justice Mapping Center Launches First National Atlas of Criminal Justice Data*, JUSTICEMAPPING.ORG (Oct. 5, 2010). For example, the atlas allows users to access data by state, county, zip code, or census area, reflecting prison admissions and release rates, demographic data, parolee and probationer rates, and costs of corrections.

Several national organizations have launched projects addressing race in the criminal justice system:

- The American Bar Association (ABA) launched a Racial Justice Improvement Project in 2010 to "identify and reform policies and practices that produce racial disparities in local criminal justice systems across the country." *See* American Bar Association Criminal Justice Section, *Racial Justice Improvement Project*, RACIALJUSTICEPROJECT.WEEBLY.COM (last visited Sept. 23, 2014).
- The ABA's Litigation Section created a Task Force on Implicit Bias and launched an Implicit Bias Initiative to educate lawyers, judges, and others about the "implications and effects of implicit bias." *See* American Bar Association Litigation Section Task Force on Implicit Bias, *Implicit Bias Initiative*, AMERICANBAR.ORG (last visited Sept. 23, 2014). The same section developed a "toolbox" of research and resources on implicit bias and strategies for "debiasing."
- The ABA's Judicial Division formed a Task Force on Perceptions of Justice in 2013, which has assembled resources and conducted training on racial bias and disparities

in the courts. *See* American Bar Association Judicial Division, *Task Force on Perceptions of Justice*, AMERICANBAR.ORG (last visited Sept. 23, 2014).

- The National Center for State Courts has developed a Gender and Racial Fairness Resource Guide, undertaken a project on implicit bias and judicial education, and developed resources such as a "Frequently Asked Questions" sheet to help court actors understand and address implicit bias. *See* National Center for State Courts, *Gender and Racial Fairness Resource Guide*, NCSC.ORG (last visited Sept. 23, 2014); National Center for State Courts, *Helping Courts Address Implicit Bias: Frequently Asked Questions*, NCSC.ORG (last visited Sept. 23, 2014).
- The National Consortium on Racial and Ethnic Fairness in the Courts encourages the highest courts of each state "to create commissions to examine the treatment accorded minorities in their courts[,]" and educates "the legal profession, the law enforcement community, and the general public concerning racial and ethnic fairness in the courts." *See* National Consortium on Racial and Ethnic Fairness in the Courts, *Mission*, NATIONAL-CONSORTIUM.ORG (last visited Sept. 23, 2014).

Other potentially useful sources of national data include the Institute on Race and Justice at Northeastern University; the National Institute of Justice's collection of materials on Race, Trust, and Police Legitimacy; and the Kirwan Institute for the Study of Race and Ethnicity, which publishes annual reports collecting empirical data concerning the operation of implicit biases.

www.ingramcontent.com/pod-product-compliance
Lightning Source LLC
LaVergne TN
LVHW080019210926
848481LV00011B/3059